CONQUERING PEACE

CONQUERING
PEACE

from THE ENLIGHTENMENT
to the EUROPEAN UNION

STELLA GHERVAS

 Harvard University Press

CAMBRIDGE, MASSACHUSETTS & LONDON, ENGLAND   2021

Library of Congress Cataloging-in-Publication Data

Names: Ghervas, Stella, author.
Title: Conquering peace : from the Enlightenment to the European Union / Stella Ghervas.
Description: Cambridge, Massachusetts : Harvard University Press, 2021. |
    Includes bibliographical references and index.
Identifiers: LCCN 2020032841 | ISBN 9780674975262 (hardcover)
Subjects: LCSH: Peace-building, European—History. | Political science—Europe—
    Philosophy. | Europe—Politics and government.
Classification: LCC JZ5538 .G53 2021 | DDC 327.1/72094—dc23
LC record available at https://lccn.loc.gov/2020032841

In memory of my father, Petru Ghervas (1944–2017),
luminary in times of darkness

Contents

CONQUERING PEACE

A peace is of the nature of a conquest;

for then both parties nobly are subdued,

and neither party loser.

—WILLIAM SHAKESPEARE, *HENRY IV PART 2,* BEFORE 1600

FIG. 1.1 Giovanni Battista Tiepolo, Allegory of the Planets and Continents, 1752.
Metropolitan Museum of Art, NY.

Introduction

EUROPE AND PEACE

*I*n the middle of the eighteenth century, Italian artist Giovanni Battista Tiepolo painted a splendid fresco titled *Allegory of the Planets and Continents* on the ceiling of the palatial residence of the prince-bishop in Würzburg, Bavaria. The work, towering above the monumental staircase, was breathtaking in its size and grandeur, as well as the richness of its details. One of its most fascinating figures is Europe as *Europa Regina,* a richly dressed queen, lying down, and representing the prosperity of peace.[1] Even though she is not the main character—Apollo, god of peace, intelligence, and beauty, holds the center of the painting—she is placed just over the stair's landing, so that visitors would face her when reaching the upper floor.

At first glance, this fresco portrays Europe's glory and its triumph over the other continents. There is, however, a subtly subversive note: a tamed bull lying beside the queen. What is that doing there? Through the bull's placement, Tiepolo merges the stately depiction of Europa-the-queen with that of another mythical character of the same name: a young Phoenician princess whom Zeus, disguised as a bull, abducted and raped.[2] Though both figures were symbolically connected to Europe, their representations were usually distinct: the *Rape of Europa* was conventionally depicted as a young woman sitting on a bull in a bucolic setting, blissfully ignorant of the crime about to occur.[3] In *Allegory of the Planets and Continents* Tiepolo twists this conventional motif to politicize its meaning: the bull is "mild enough to be an honorary cow," while Europa is no longer the hapless and innocent girl but a mature woman, a mother to her people, surrounded by artists, learned men, soldiers, and a host of other characters, as if to underscore that the

I

woman once enslaved has had her revenge on the brute. Indeed, Europa's bull is presumably a disguised representation of the mighty Habsburg emperors of the Holy Roman Empire, who had recently been defeated and forced to abandon their ambitions to rule the German lands, Spain, Europe, and indeed the world.[4]

Nevertheless, a tame bull is unnatural and therefore disquieting: Could it go on a rampage again? Indeed, the Old Continent was never as happily peaceful as Tiepolo portrayed it, nor were its rulers always as benevolent to conquered peoples, especially non-Europeans. The continent's history has been one of almost continuous internecine conflicts since the Middle Ages. At the time Tiepolo painted his monumental fresco, the War of Austrian Succession (1740–1748) had barely ended, and another major conflict, the Seven Years' War, was about to begin. Evidently, the Italian artist had not painted the Old Continent as it was, but an idealized version. Most large wars that had already occurred could be reduced to rulers' desire to aggrandize their lands, from Habsburg emperor Charles V to Bourbon king Louis XIV; the rest could be attributed to legal disputes between states that had to be settled through ritual duels between two armies.

With its unsettling collision between *Europa Regina* and the *Rape of Europa,* Tiepolo's fresco became a forerunner of a long tradition of anti-imperial or antiwar allegories (including Pablo Picasso's *Guernica*) that consciously exploited the tormented relationship between a woman and a bull. The aggressive animal, in all its forms and attitudes, started to symbolize the political plight of the European continent, torn between the Spirit of Peace and the Spirit of War, between law and force of arms, freedom and tyranny, civilization and barbarism.[5] Few artworks express this tension as vividly as Max Ernst's *Europe after the Rain,* painted two centuries after Tiepolo's fresco during World War II. Having emigrated to the United States to escape Nazi persecution, Ernst represents his native continent as a surrealist wasteland after the Deluge, with the ruins of buildings, rotten vegetation, and decayed corpses all fused into a shapeless mass. At the bottom, Jupiter the bull, still covered in armor, lies emaciated with vacant eyes. Europa, the Phoenician princess, stares forlornly into the distance, as if contemplating the downfall of her tormenter. On her right, an ominous warrior with a falcon's head looks down on her with contempt. Is it Horus (symbol of the

FIG. 1.2 Max Ernst, Europe after the Rain II, 1940–1942. Photo by Allen Phillips.
Wadsworth Atheneum Museum of Art, Hartford, CT.

Egyptian pharaohs) representing the chaos of war's madness?[6] How far this
apocalyptic desolation was from the glory of Tiepolo's fresco!

In truth, it was not far at all: it took only twenty minutes for a British air
raid to obliterate Würzburg Palace together with 80 percent of the sur-
rounding city, leaving five thousand dead civilians among the rubble. And
yet, as if to symbolize the resilience of peace ideals, the staircase and Tiepolo's
fresco survived intact the dreadful night of March 16, 1945, thanks to the
exceptional sturdiness of their architectural frame. From that miraculous
survivor, the rest of Würzburg's historical center was painstakingly recon-
structed after the war. The unusual personification in art of Europe as Europa serves, of course, to convey the concepts of beauty, fecundity, and the
restrained power of a mother. It is, nevertheless, a stark reminder that the
inner strength of that woman had grown in response to her inherent vulner-
ability to aggression and that what happened to her could conceivably
happen again. Europa's mythical tension with the bull thus conveys a
powerful message that forms the central theme of this book: Europe was
able to find lasting peace and prosperity only after it refused to bow down
to the arrogance of continental empires that attempted to seize territories and riches by force. Although *Conquering Peace* is a history book, it can
be viewed as a theatrical dialogue in five acts that portrays Europe's resistance to empires while trying to keep free of armed conflicts, which is indeed the most elementary definition of peace. This allegory of Europa has
the advantage of highlighting the two main political scourges of Europe—
continental empires and internecine wars—which did not prevent, alas,

several of its nations from exporting those two commodities overseas in the form of colonial empires.

But could there ever be a feasible solution to these two evils? What would be the point of a state to pursuing a peaceful foreign policy if it were only then to be conquered and subdued by some aggressive empire? Do not the Napoleonic wars, two world wars, and the Cold War conclusively prove that international trust and cooperation have been but utopias?[7] Knowing that empires constantly operated on the policy that "might makes right," only one answer seems possible: *si vis pacem, para bellum*—"if you want peace, prepare for war." So went the Latin maxim, attributed to the Roman author of Late Antiquity known as Vegetius. His work, *A Summary of Military Science*, enjoyed extraordinary success in the late Middle Ages, and his premises are still relevant today.[8]

All this would seem to lead to an obvious conclusion, which later underpinned the great shift in US foreign policy in 1945 after the death of Franklin D. Roosevelt: in the face of constant threats, the fundamental prerequisite of the freedoms and peace of citizens is to maintain forever a standing army, ready to fight. In 1985, when the Cold War was not yet over, Ronald Reagan pointedly referred to this deep-rooted belief when he declared in front of Congress, "You know, we only have a military-industrial complex until a time of danger, and then it becomes the arsenal of democracy. Spending for defense is investing in things that are priceless—peace and freedom."[9] It is important to note, however, that US foreign policy between 1917 and April 1945 pursued an entirely different doctrine: despite the Senate's conspicuous refusal to ratify the Covenant of the League of Nations after the World War I, the United States still aimed to bring peace to the world by replacing military confrontation with international treaties and a "machinery of peace" that would make war either illegal or unnecessary.

This book traces the history—from the early eighteenth century to our own days—of a profound and troubling question: How is it possible to prevent future wars while guaranteeing the liberties of all states? Stating the question in those terms also implies accepting that war has always been part of life and that one might be forced to accept it again in the future. It does not mean, however, that it is a desirable condition. European states progressively elaborated a doctrine that not only rejected the assumption that war was inexorable but also came to consider the belief in war's unavoidability as a self-fulfilling prophecy. This doctrine stated that an international configuration in which all great powers were convinced that strong standing armies were the condition for peace and liberty would never be in a state of true peace but would always be, at best, in a state of armed truce—and the risk would always be present that they would restart the vicious cycle of an arms race, which might then degenerate into another conflict, destruction, and general impoverishment. This bold theory, born at the turn of the eighteenth century, had as its original name *pax perpetua,* or *perpetual peace* (taking this "perpetual" label on faith, for now, because peace obviously never was eternal).

The hope of achieving peace through achieving political solidarity in Europe continued as a humble stream, flowing undeterred across the centuries, or as a mother "empty yet inexhaustible, giving birth to infinite worlds."[10] That is not to say this theory was immediately or generally supported; on the contrary, promoters of perpetual peace were quite often derided, denigrated, and defeated. The modern colonial empires of Europe thoroughly imposed their martial doctrines overseas, often with frightening "success." We thus have to deal with the evident paradox that the continent that originated a gentle conception of peace and came to reject *any* empire *in* Europe was at the same time the heart of colonial empires that ruthlessly conquered the world for 500 years. Nevertheless, this history of peace covering the past three centuries reveals the long process toward the realization that peace and freedom were achievable in Europe; indeed they were achieved in large parts of the continent, at least for a time. In addition, the means by which many Europeans resisted imperial oppression during the first half of the twentieth century fostered the widespread realization that acts of conquest against and suppression of non-Europeans also qualified as crimes against humankind—at which point the public withdrew its support for anti-independence wars and left national governments with little choice but to cut the last meager budgets assigned to colonial ventures.

This book examines five moments, each with its own spirit, that occurred soon after major geopolitical upheavals of European history and were marked by the impending threat of a pan-European empire: the bid of

Louis XIV for European hegemony (1701–1714); Napoleon and the French Empire (1799–1815); the German Empires in World War I (1914–1918) and World War II (1939–1945); and the Soviet dominance over half of Europe during the Cold War in the decades before 1991. This periodization illustrates how the aim of peace fostered the political idea of Europe (and its corollary of unification) over the *longue durée,* long before a European bloc came into existence and even before the age of nation-states. It also shows how the evolution of Europe—culturally, economically, and institutionally—shaped the concept of peace. Seen in this long-range perspective, the contemporary European Union is merely the latest—and perhaps not even the last—of several attempts to achieve the "Idea of Europe" as an arena of political peace.

In the course of her quest for peace, Europa had to question what she knew about herself and even—given the effects of colonialism—the sincerity of her own motives. Yet Europa was never just the Holy Alliance, the League of Nations, or the European Economic Community; neither is she, today, only the European Union. These institutions were mere avatars of an abstract ideal of peace; like Europa's feminine form, they are mundane political shapes through which she has been commonly perceived, and sometimes worshipped, by official propaganda and the press. Those political incarnations survived inasmuch as they were in harmony with her and faithful to her; as soon as they lost this connection, they withered away and died. The various attempts by political leaders and political opinions to commune metaphorically with that ideal of perpetual peace are what I call *spirits,* from the French *esprit,* as in *esprit de corps.* I use this word in its collective meaning as in "Spirit of the Enlightenment" for a group of individuals; it is a social phenomenon that brings forward a certain idea or ideal.

The reader should, however, refrain from putting on a pedestal the individuals who cultivated those spirits. Although these people made major intellectual contributions and their deeds often had grandeur, some also were flawed morally. Enlightenment philosopher Jean-Jacques Rousseau was socially insufferable, and his follower Immanuel Kant was a self-professed misogynist; nineteenth-century tsar Alexander I was nicknamed "will-o'-the-wisp" and ultimately embraced the cause of political Reaction; US president Woodrow Wilson blotted his liberal record by advancing the cause of racial segregation.[11] Several sincere partisans of the European tradition of peace under freedom did not believe in racial equality, and several thought colonialism advanced the cause of peace.

If we want to achieve an imaginative sympathy for these historical characters and get "inside their heads" (as well as in those of their critics), despite their inevitable errors, it is necessary to appreciate their complicated and fallible natures in the context of their time and place. To understand better how their minds worked, it will also be necessary for us—and especially profitable for diplomats—to dispel a few well-established myths that convey antipathy, scorn, or resentment; notably, that the "Holy Alliance" of 1815 was a reactionary conspiracy against liberals according to one version or the airy-fairy dream of a mystic baroness according to another; and that the "harsh" treatment of Germany or Hungary at the Treaties of Versailles and Trianon was entirely intentional. Among a few other common narratives are the following: the League of Nations was an unqualified failure in securing European peace, and conversely the United Nations was a success; American liberalism inspired the European Common Market, and Ronald Reagan was the one who convinced the USSR to withdraw the Red Army from Eastern Europe with the famous call, "Mr. Gorbachev, tear down this wall." Each good story must also have its villains: they are the imperialist characters of pan-European ambitions who prompted continental alliances to defeat them. So, each "Spirit of Peace" has its own villain: Louis XIV, who threatened to unite the Spanish and French Empires into a formidable world power; Napoleon Bonaparte, who conquered most of Europe; the Kaiser's hawks who championed total war in World War I; and, of course, the two absolute tyrants of the twentieth century, Hitler and Stalin.

"Success is not final, failure is not fatal; it is the courage to continue that counts." This maxim attributed to Churchill, which he arguably never uttered, is indicative of the persistent European pursuit of peace.[12] It was not the product of "nonviolent" dreamers who recoiled from a good fight, but of individuals who experienced more than their fair share of fighting during their lifetime. Indeed, each Spirit shows how experiments in what I call the "engineering of peace" were conducted at the end of great continental wars. At each moment when a mighty empire such as the Third Reich or the Soviet Union crumbled and fell, leaving oppressed peoples with a sense of relief, freedom, and empowerment, political leaders and their entourages envisioned a future made of peace and tranquility. The term "engineering" implies that the successive peace spirits built on previous experience to achieve a shared goal: perpetual peace. When I use the word "advances," it is thus toward that end. As we will see, this engineering was not limited to building "machineries of peace," to use a phrase in vogue during the interwar period; in the mid-twentieth century, the founders of the European Communities saw themselves as the caretakers of a living organism.

Like engineers, the promoters of perpetual peace attempted—with varying success—to channel chaotic events of history according to their will. This through-line of engineering does not necessarily help us make sense of the complicated twists and turns of European history, but it certainly sheds light on the general direction in which the five Spirits of Peace were headed. Leo Tolstoy's novel *War and Peace* expressed the dialectic between the "great sea of events" and the human will of a few historical figures:

> The turbulent sea of European history had settled within its shores. It seemed to have calmed down. . . . The historical figures that had led armies and reflected the movement of the masses by waging war, marching men about and going into battle now reflected that same seething movement in political and diplomatic stratagems, statutes and treaties.[13]

We may have an advantage over Tolstoy in that we have a broader horizon of experience. In addition, our notion of engineering is less fatalistic, because it presupposes that human beings are more than mere corks tossed about by the sea; they can still steer their way to a destination, at least up to a certain point. This quest for perpetual peace has thus been (to use Shakespeare's phrase) "in the nature of a conquest": it has been a struggle, not between two parties but against the odds.

To measure these practical advances of European states toward lasting peace I use an ad hoc scale that summarizes the steps that need to be traversed to achieve this purpose. Starting from a *state of war,* it goes upward through seven steps: *ceasefire* (armistice or capitulation), peace and settlement *treaties* that formally end the war, the establishment of a peace *system,* the foundation of peace *institutions,* the *reconciliation* of historical differences so as to avoid recurring disputes, the fostering of *solidarity* between states to create a permanent dynamic of amicable relations, and finally the (ideal and perhaps unreachable) state of *lasting, in fact true, peace.* This scale is a consolidated description of the method evolved so far in Europe to achieve lasting peace after war. It says nothing about all the thinking and experimentation that were required, over three centuries, to arrive at this straightforward formulation.

Indeed, as we see, the peaceful unification of Europe has been (and might always be) a journey, never a final destination. Looking back to 1713, 1815, 1919, 1945, and 1989, it is evident that the belief in the "end of history"—the start of a happy new world forevermore in peace—was at each moment a misguided idea; peace was a volatile and fragile commodity, and new threats were bound to emerge at some point. Nevertheless, the end of each great continental war was marked by a privileged moment when some new spirit of peace arose in Europe—after all the hatred and infighting, these were moments when such a spirit was most needed.

*I*t is important to note that the Spirits of Peace did not suddenly materialize fully formed, ready to shape innovation. During the last three centuries, states changed their practices of coexistence according to the necessities of the moment, as the concepts that went along with peace evolved and expanded. Some words changed meaning in different times or even in the same period; some terms, in particular "balance of power," did not mean exactly the same across different languages. It is thus important to start our historical journey from war to peace with a fresh mind, without assuming that any concepts we consider familiar today—international organizations, sovereignty, law, human rights, constitutions, including the idea of peace itself—had always been known or would even have been relevant in periods of past. Even though the European engineering of peace became a foundation for the global language of "international law," we should not forget that it was originally only the shared dialect of political leaders and diplomats on a relatively small continent; it does not automatically follow that it is the only possible language. This book is thus an account of the efforts to make peace durable within the confines of Europe, within its political culture, and amid its specific historical context. Yet, one point that can be made about the diplomatic practices of European states is that they gradually became more effective at preventing new continental wars, even though they are still far from foolproof.

On that continent, periods of peace and war long alternated according to a syntax defined by the *ius gentium* (law of nations), a substantial set of conventions and agreements that dominated relations between states—that is, until the term *international law,* coined by English author Jeremy Bentham in the 1780s, started to gain wide currency in the wake of the Congress of Vienna of 1814–1815. There is, however, a difference between the two concepts: the law of nations was more in the nature of a moral code or an etiquette of peace and war, essentially conceived as natural law applied to nations.[14] From this understanding to our current elaborate conception of the relations between states as regulated by international law (embodied in multilateral treaties and court decisions), there has clearly been quite an evolution. Yet, *diplomacy*—the art of negotiating with others and persuading them to go along with one's wishes—was already the tool of choice of those who thought it convenient to use peacetime means to achieve their aims. Or it was the last recourse of those who could not afford a military confrontation.[15]

The syntax of peace and war depended on a highly codified vocabulary: to understand it, it is necessary to recover the definition of a key word such as peace. In early modern French, the common language of diplomats, the meaning of "peace" was straightforward: it was "rest, the state of a people who is not at war."[16] Peace was associated with the moral notion of tranquility, in the sense of "calmness and lack of emotion," as in the collocation "peace and tranquility" (in this it followed the use of the Latin word *pax*). Such was the primary definition of peace from the first edition of the dictionary of the French Academy in 1694 to the fifth one produced after the French Revolution.[17] In a political sense, peace was literally a nonentity: a point of no movement, a void, or at best a subject for an allegory. Its secondary, more practical definition was that peace "also describes some particularly famous peace treaties," citing the peace of Westphalia.[18] *Amicitia* (friendship) was a distinct notion.

At the beginning of our story, treaties after a war ordinarily opened with precisely this language of peace: *Pax sit Christiana, universalis, et perpetua veraque et sincera amicitia inter . . .* ("There shall be a Christian, universal and perpetual peace, as well as sincere amity between . . .").[19] In fact, the expression "perpetual peace" was shorthand for a *treaty* of perpetual peace. But why should a peace treaty be *perpetual* while wars were a recurrent feature of this continent? The eighteenth-century Swiss jurist Emer de Vattel gave a surprisingly simple answer:

> In such treaties, the contracting parties reciprocally engage to preserve *perpetual peace:* which is not to be understood as if they promised never to make war on each other for any cause whatever. The peace in question relates to the war which it terminates: and it is in reality perpetual, inasmuch as it does not allow them to revive the same war by taking up arms again for the same subject which had originally given birth to it.[20]

In other words, Vattel emphasized that the peace treaty at hand must put a final end to the specific dispute of a specific war, not prevent future disputes. This subtle, but essential, distinction faded away at times: for example, the founders of the League of Nations in 1919 actually entertained the ambition to make future war impossible. Even though they achieved a few notable results in averting or solving border wars between European states, that part of their goal was inordinately ambitious, and—as we all know—was miserably defeated by the rise of totalitarianisms and the desertion, in rapid succession, of all the great powers that had promised to support the League. Franklin D. Roosevelt held the similar hope that the United Nations would mark the end of wars and political oppression.[21]

The basic purpose of the political tradition of "perpetual peace"—which included the creation of actual institutions—has thus been to ensure peace among the European states and generally in the world, not absolutely and forever but for as long as reasonably or humanly possible. It was certainly not to eradicate all wars within a generation. For simplicity, let us consider that "perpetual peace" was hyperbole for "lasting peace."

As a side note, the term *peace,* which is also a euphemism for death and the afterlife in most European languages, has always lent itself to puns, misinterpretations, and cynical corruptions. In 1795 Immanuel Kant quoted a tavern shingle that represented perpetual peace as a graveyard (as if to imply that the eradication of all humankind would certainly solve the problem of future wars, but that the radical kind of "peace" it would afford would hardly be called a remedy).[22] In the nineteenth century, troops fired on protesters to "restore the peace," and in a colonial context, bloody punitive operations against extra-European peoples who revolted were routinely called "pacification."[23] "Appeasement," the attempt to "grant concessions to angry opponents to maintain peace," went down unfavorably in history with the famous 1938 Munich agreement with Nazi Germany that compromised Czechoslovakia's territorial integrity.[24] This word potentially contains a contradiction in terms: if foes had already decided that peace was dead even though they had not yet formally declared war, then a diplomatic compromise with them would be equivalent to a capitulation without fighting.

And because a peace treaty could only exist to end a war and its content would be entirely determined by the outcome of that war, peace and war cannot be disassociated, as if "day" could be defined without also understanding "night." It is thus essential to understand the parts of the grammar that govern war. It is notable that, despite all the impressive evolution in the art of war, its basic principles have not much changed in the last four centuries. The Dutch philosopher and lawyer Hugo Grotius in the early seventeenth century defined war (*bellum*) as "the condition of those contending by force."[25] This made sense: in the highly fragmented continent of Europe, disputes were likely to arise between states; when goodwill, diplomacy, and mediation had all failed, the only recourse left was to address grievances with the force of arms. According to the 1694 French dictionary, war was defined as "a quarrel between two states, pursued with armed force."[26]

It is essential to note that war was never considered a breakdown of intercourse between two states, but rather a change in the form of this interaction: the two parts, leaving intellectual argumentation aside, continue their contest by exchanging blows until the strongest party prevails. As Vattel aptly put it (using Grotius's definition), "War is *that state in which we prosecute our right by force.*"[27] It is indeed a duel between states, where both opponents are entitled to kill legitimately each other's soldiers and to destroy each other's property. Drawing from a pre-Christian tradition that seems to parallel Germanic judicial duels between individuals (also called trials by combat), the prime function of war in European history was thus to serve as kind of trial procedure, albeit one more primitive and straightforward than in a court of law; the fundamental axiom was that "might makes right," that the party victorious in battle is considered to have won the case.[28] This was rationalized by an ancient religious tenet that the Heavens favor the arms of the virtuous. This belief was carried over in early Christianized societies, reformulated during the Reformation, and further developed during the Industrial Revolution to account for the superiority of European armament over the rest of the world. Although it has lost currency in most European nation-states after the military defeats of World War II, it remains an ideological foundation of political providentialism both in the United States and in Russia.[29]

A declaration of war was the all-important formal and unilateral act by which one state ended the *state of peace,* where laws of civil behavior and trade apply, to start a *state of war.* Obviously, unless a state that received such a declaration wanted to sue for peace, it could not reject it, on the penalty of being promptly defeated. Because a state unilaterally declaring war also threw its opponent into the state of war, it dispensed the latter from the obligation of declaring war in its turn, even though it would often do so ("either out of dignity or for the guidance of its subjects").[30] There is, however, a proviso: by the very act of declaring war, a state was naturally giving the same license to its opponent. As can be seen, a proper war of the Ancien Régime was a highly formal affair, strictly reserved to states (not to be waged by private persons) and obeying rigid protocols. That is in theory, because *warfare* (a specifically English word referring to "the practical waging of a war") is noisy, chaotic, and unpredictable, with the corollary that it is cruel; "war[fare] and pity do not go along," says a French proverb.[31] The winner of a conflict had the legal right to keep the spoils and conquered land if it so chose, a fact that presumably can be traced back to a time when early humans hunted in groups and sometimes fought each other for the same prey.

The European procedure for ending a war and returning to a state of peace was equally formal and elaborate: it required plenipotentiaries crossing the lines under a banner of truce, followed by a ceasefire; then an armistice or capitulation was signed by the military leaders of both camps. Then the diplomats took over and, after suitable negotiations, signed the peace treaty that, once and for all, was supposed to put an end to the specific dispute between the two states, while settling the ownership of territories and aspects such as populations, prisoners, war reparations, and other related issues. The interruption of a war was never an idle statement but materialized as an instantaneous and profound change in behavior and attitudes: a sudden return to calm and order, a point from which human life became sacred again and taking it away would be once again a crime. When peace was finally underwritten, the state of war was officially closed, and civil intercourse between the former belligerents was allowed to resume as before.

Although the expression "history is written by the victors" is commonplace, it is often overlooked that the chief way the winners do so is through the settlement treaties they impose on the defeated states. How they do so is, of course, shaped by a more psychological aspect, the deep-rooted need of human beings for self-justification. European historical literature shows how victorious powers tended to rationalize their own victory (and the harm inflicted on the other party) by elaborating a narrative in which their own party endorsed a noble cause, whereas the losers were standing in the path of the common good. That self-justifying factor no doubt helps explain the military mystique around the foundation of past European empires and nations. The point here is that the victors' prerogative to write history is yet another practical consequence of "might makes right": the winner's discretion to lay out the verdict of the judicial duel was always embedded in the very definition and modus operandi of war.[32] The new Europe of peacetime was defined, after each peace treaty, by the prerogative of the winning party to explain how its claims were justified and how the defeated party was in error. The task of lawyers was to provide a rationalization of the new state of affairs that would henceforth be supported by both parties and would serve as the foundation for moralists of future generations. In cases, however, where a great war ended without a clear winner and loser (such as the

War of Spanish Succession in 1713), the peace treaty bequeathed to posterity a more balanced interpretation of the dispute. In summary, the victorious allies in the various great wars found confirmation that they had been "in the right" in the fact of winning the war.

Given that the fate of arms thus defined the legal "right" and "wrong" in a final way and without appeal, an ex-post distinction between legally "just" and "unjust" war was moot: the peace treaty that concluded each war was just by the fact itself—providing, of course, the treaty was not overturned in the near future. By contrast, the question remained whether starting a war was morally right. For example, Irish writer Jonathan Swift listed, in 1711, five just motives for starting a war: to check the overgrown power of some ambitious neighbor, to recover what has been unjustly taken, to avenge some injury, to assist some ally in a just quarrel, and lastly to defend themselves when invaded. Implicitly, the chief unjustifiable war motives for war were conquest, taking another power's property by force, and inflicting injury.[33]

Unacceptable behavior after a declaration of war included killing prisoners, harming innocent civilians, engaging in torture, assassinating enemies, and inflicting disproportionate destruction of property—it took time, however, before the practice of sacking cities after a siege became broadly unacceptable and even more before it was effectively punished.[34] Needless to say, despite the theory, every European power happily disregarded those prescriptions at some point or other. It follows from the very nature of a peace treaty that a victorious belligerent was often able to commit these violations scot-free: in 1919, defeated Germany accepted full liability for starting the war; judges in the Stalinist regime in 1946 condemned Nazi dignitaries for crimes against humankind, while no international tribunal ever held Soviet leaders accountable for the war crimes committed under Stalin. In an attempt to remedy this logical flaw of judges being also parties, the Prussian-born American lawyer Francis Lieber wrote the so-called Lieber Code (*General Orders No. 100*), issued in 1862 by the United States in the context of the American Civil War, one of the first legal codes of martial law enacted by a belligerent.[35] Provisions relating to the consequences of war for civilians and their protection in occupied territories only appeared as appendixes to the Hague Conventions of 1899 and 1907.

The Fourth Geneva Convention relative to the Protection of Civilian Persons in Time of War dates only from 1949.[36]

If war was so destructive and its practices were so slow to change, this raised another question for the great powers that this book follows: Was it worth risking an arms race to preserve peace in times of crisis (in the broad collective interest of Europe, and humanity in general), or could peace somehow be preserved by some other means, without the danger of starting a new war? In each of the five great wars since 1700 when a continental coalition had to be assembled against a real threat of pan-European empire, the answer evidently depended on the circumstances and alternatives available. The first act, the War of Spanish Succession, opened with a political system that offered little alternative to war. In the second act, the Napoleonic wars, the great powers had no choice but to coalesce against the expansionism of a French Empire that would not let them alone. The third act, World War I, started in 1914 in the most ill-considered manner, despite the fact that the great powers had invested considerable effort in finding judicial alternatives to international disputes.[37] The collapse of the interwar order and the outbreak of World War II were among the darkest hours of the continent; once the Third Reich contemplated an invasion of Czechoslovakia in September 1938, it was presumably already too late for anything other than a pan-European military alliance to counter this threat. After the catastrophe of World War II, however, the question had to be raised as to what France and Britain could have done to prevent the rise of the Third Reich to the point where it threatened the liberties of Europe—or worse, did their blindness unintentionally facilitate the rise of tyranny, and what should be done if such a threat presented itself again? The fifth act, the Cold War, was largely caused by the transformation of an initially peace-seeking Soviet Union into a brutally aggressive empire that eventually occupied half of Europe. Similarly, the historian might retrospectively ask what the other powers (particularly the victorious United States and Britain) could have done in 1945 to avert a fifty-year Cold War with the Soviet Union that caused considerable human and economic suffering.

The purpose in asking such questions is, of course, not to assign blame in a futile effort to change the past. On the contrary, it is an exercise for the future, in the spirit of the engineering of peace. Is it possible to extract, from past experiments, some commonsense practices that could achieve the aims of a safe international community while at the same time reducing the necessity of waging war? The intellectual tradition of perpetual peace has traditionally claimed—against the realists—that a more efficient alternative than brute force should be sought. Its proponents argued that, in 1939 and 1945, the point of no return had been passed: all that was left was a deceptive quandary between a delusional "peace," that was really suppressed war, or open war and its immediate consequences. And, furthermore, the tradition claimed that such a solution should indeed exist, providing it is taken early enough and the opportunity has not been lost by error, moral compromise, or inaction.

Conquering Peace seeks to explore the hypothesis that perpetual peace might be a more effective alternative to force, and the corollary that striving for peace can itself be a means to avoid war. It is true that those who sought this alternative were often met with scorn by those who called themselves "practical men" (the past version of "realists"), who accused them of dreaming of utopias. The supporters of peace argued in turn that the certainties of the realists owed more to posture than fact. Kant wrote, in his essay on perpetual peace, that "those men have no practical science, they have only practices."[38] Suffice it to note that the partisans of perpetual peace had—in addition to all their failures—some arguments solidly confirmed by experience, such as a European construction that has survived now for some seventy years; by contrast, three "realist" continental empires were proved conclusively wrong in 1815, 1918, and 1945 by the very argument they valued most: force of arms. The notion that "might makes right"—regardless of whether it is used for self-aggrandizement or the good of humankind—would have to be considered successful if and only if its "rightness" were conducive to survival for a meaningful amount of time. The fact is that, in many blatant cases in European history, "political realism" led to defeat and humiliation—so much so, in fact, that it shares a fine border with short-termism.

Most empires collapsed not because they were defeated, but indirectly because the endless effort of repeated wars exhausted them financially: the tsar was ousted by a revolution in 1917; Austria-Hungary exploded in the last days of World War I; the Ottoman Empire of the nineteenth century was aptly named the "sick man of Europe" and was overthrown by a coup in 1922. The French and British Empires collapsed after 1945 once the metropoles were bankrupted, whereas the Soviet Union, incapable of refitting its industry in the 1980s and left behind by the computer revolution, crumbled at the end of the Cold War when it ran out of financial resources.[39] It is thus that the twentieth century can be seen as the age of mass extinctions for European empires, the culmination of a process that had started much earlier. Empires had undoubtedly been a successful genus in modern European history, only too well adjusted to their time and place. When conditions started changing, they were doomed.

*I*f this is a study of the demise of "European" empires and of the corresponding rise of new ways of establishing lasting peace, then how should we delimit this historical setting called "Europe"? This is a crucial question, because even though a few European experiences may undoubtedly have value for the rest of the world, it does not follow that observations or conclusions made in that locale can and should be translated to studies conducted in Africa, Asia, or the Americas.

It is fortunate that Europe, despite being a richly diverse environment, can still be defined by a few invariants. In the first place, and long before it took on a political meaning, Europe has been a geographical term. It is, of course, not a continent in any meaningful sense, but a mere peninsula of the Eurasian continent delimited by water on three sides: the Atlantic Ocean on the west, the Arctic Ocean in the north, and the Mediterranean Sea in the south. This raises the question, of course, of where is the region's eastern border. Today, the conventional limit is the Urals, though this has minimal value either from a geological viewpoint (those old mountains have played no role in plate tectonics for eons) or from a cultural viewpoint (the Russians who lived on both sides since the sixteenth century belonged to the same state and spoke the same language). The closest thing to a workable definition is really atmospheric: since the nineteenth century, Europe has been defined as the landmass on the Eurasian continent placed in the "westerly wind belt"; that is, where the westerly winds of the Atlantic Ocean can still make their influence felt year-round, together with their precipitation.[40] Beyond that belt are the comparatively drier plains and plateaus of Asia, chilled by Siberian air masses. If Europe should be defined by the Atlantic color and patterns of its skies, then setting an extreme eastern limit at the Urals makes some sense, and definitely more so at the Caucasus mountains, which cleanly separate the humid "European" basin of the Black Sea from the noticeably drier "Asian" basin of the Caspian Sea. One could see how the course of rain clouds influenced eastern populations in search of new pastures and why European farmers would make a cultural habit of looking westward, where the rain would be coming from.

Yet such a definition would also locate most of "Asia Minor" (today known as Anatolia or Asian Turkey) in Europe. It might make sense from a human perspective, because the populations that inhabited it have indeed been part and parcel of general European history. That would, however, require a significant shift from the original definition, since the terms "Europe" and "Asia" were coined by archaic Greeks who lived on both sides of the Aegean Sea: the denizens of the western shore were "Europeans," the easterners "Asians." Considering Europe as a continent—surrounded by water—was a plausible perspective initially, because on the north stood the straits leading to a vast, unexplored sea then thought to be infinite. When, however, Greek sailors and cartographers realized that the Black Sea was only an inland body, the geographical puzzle of Europe was born: supposing that mainland Greece was "Europe," that Anatolia was "Asia," and considering that one was able to travel by land from one to the other without interruption by walking around the Black Sea, it begged one question: North of that sea, where did Europe end and Asia start? Greek historian Herodotus proposed two makeshift solutions: a northern one that placed the border at the Don, a river that originates in central Russia and flows into the Azov Sea, or a more eastern one, at the River Phasis (the modern Rioni), currently in Georgia, which separates the northern Caucasus from its southern counterpart.[41] Herodotus was, of course, aware that there was no topologically correct solution to the puzzle, at least one following the proper definition of a continent: making quite a stretch of the imagination, he stated without conviction that, because rivers were made of water like the sea, perhaps one of them could be used as a partition line.

During Roman times, the question rested there; in any case, the one significant political frontier—that between the western and eastern parts of the empire—ran farther west through the western Balkans.[42] What mattered was that the empire brought *Pax Romana* to a significant portion of Europe. Yet, with the chaos of the barbarian invasions of Late Antiquity, the collapse of the Western Roman Empire, and the advent of the Middle Ages, the question of the eastern limits of Europe proposed itself afresh. The myriad small kingdoms and republics that succeeded Rome survived in an ever-shifting multicultural world (predominantly Latin, Germanic, and Slavic) in which they often engaged in petty wars, their existence never assured and often transient. Out of necessity, Europe developed not only its own specific type of warfare but also its own tradition of diplomacy.

In all of Christendom—of which Europe was only a region—the quest for peace relied on reviving the Roman Empire. People from England all the way to Constantinople and, even beyond to Muscovy, shared a common sentimental yearning for a past golden age of peace: the time when benevolent Roman emperors enforced peace over vast areas of the continent, allowing the free and abundant flow of people, goods, and ideas.[43] As one historian aptly wrote, "Antiquity had bequeathed to the Middle Ages the idea of an ecumenical civil entity, and that of a permanent peace achievable down here on Earth, the second being equated with the first."[44] The hope was still strong that a benevolent and powerful emperor like Constantine the Great would return to bring about the reign of Christ on Earth. On that day the *oikoumenê* (the human community) would live in peace under a "universal monarchy."[45] Unfortunately, the Frankish empire of Charlemagne, which briefly rekindled that hope in the west at the turn of the ninth century, rose and fell within a few decades. What remained was a loose and unstable German confederation of states, saddled with the impossible task of posing as a "Holy Roman Empire" bearing the standard of a *Pax Romana* that had no means to impose Christianity.

It is only after Christendom lost its last foothold in Anatolia after the Ottoman conquest and the fall of Constantinople in 1453 that the geographical term "Europe" took on a new political meaning as a collectivity of states that defined themselves as different from the rest of the world, particularly (but not only) the Ottoman Empire. Yet it is in the writings of the Italian writer Niccolò Machiavelli that Federico Chabod, the founding historian of the idea of Europe, saw the first formulation of Europe as "a community having its own characteristics outside of the realm of geography, characteristics that are 'of this lowly world,' 'secular' and non-religious."[46] Part of Machiavelli's positive definition of Europe was founded on the multiplicity of its states, which he opposed to the "sloth" (*ozio*) of large empires in Asia. Around 1520, he wrote that the opposition of each state against each other was, in his eyes, an explanation for why Europeans were so vigorous and adept at war.[47] Indeed, Germany and Italy were politically fragmented and constantly at war; this chaotic situation invited neighboring powers, particularly France, Spain, and Austria, to intervene militarily and fight regularly against each other. At the same time, the constant battling also precluded the formation of a pan-continental empire in Europe. Machiavelli loathed empires and large kingdoms for the very reason that they brought peace: they weakened the moral fiber of the subject peoples. There was again the triangle of Europe, empire, and peace, but this time with *both* empire and peace rejected as useful commodities. Nevertheless, this self-conception of Europe as the "most anti-imperial continent" became a recurring motif in the European history of peace.

It does not mean, however, that the politico-religious notion of Christendom had breathed its last: Roman popes summoned several Holy Leagues from 1495 to 1717 to defend it against the Ottoman Empire, which claimed for its part the caliphate of Islam. In the sixteenth century, the age of Great Discoveries when progress in shipbuilding and navigation made it possible to travel long distances at sea, the dizzying utopia of universal monarchy suddenly took flight again. Following a freak of fate, Habsburg emperor Charles V had just inherited or otherwise taken control of a large portion of Western Europe, notably Spain and Austria. For a brief moment, realization of the vision of a united Catholic society on the continent, finally in peace under the law of Christ, seemed possible. Furthermore, Spain was in the process of establishing a colossal empire in the Americas. Machiavelli lived long enough to witness the fall of the once-mighty Italian Duchy of Milan to the Spanish Army in 1525. Three years after his own death in 1527, his hometown of Florence was besieged and taken, with many of its former republican leaders banished or executed. The Habsburg occupation of Northern Italy cut short, together with the Renaissance, the early conceptions of Europe that had flourished in that region.

It was unsurprisingly in France, England, the Dutch Republic, as well as the northern states of Germany—lands that successfully opposed the Habsburg bid to forcibly unify Europe—that authors of the early modern era took over the task of proposing alternative models to universal monarchy.[48] Those figures also had in common, most of the time, the influence of the Reformed religion on their upbringing. This was quite explicable: in Catholic countries, in a context of censorship, if not outright persecution of dissenters, there was limited scope for criticism of princes. Thinkers could only contribute to the restoration of the power and prestige of the papacy (the Counter-Reformation) or support the Habsburg bid to take over Europe. By contrast, the enormous social, political, and military pressures put on the Protestants galvanized their intellectual energies. To escape their image of heretical rebels, they strove to elaborate new models of legitimacy and political coexistence, thereby forging a new political space in Europe.

Perhaps the most often invoked—often misleadingly—political foundation of the contemporary system of Europe is the Peace of Westphalia, the name commonly used for the treaties of Münster and Osnabrück signed in 1648 to end the Thirty Years' War.[49] It settled thirty years of religious war in the German lands, as well as an eighty-year independence war for the Dutch, both of which ended with a victory against the Austrian and Spanish Habsburgs. In addition to confirming the independence of the Dutch Republic and the Swiss Confederation, these treaties confirmed the *superioritas territorialis* of states within the Holy Roman Empire, a catch-all concept whose purpose was to bring under one roof the preexisting multiplicity of rights and privileges connected with the administration and government of a territory. The notion of *superioritas* was often confused after World War II with what international law calls today "sovereignty"; that is, complete independence and self-government. Clearly the German states of 1648, as junior members of the Holy Roman Empire, were not sovereign in the way we understand that term today. They were not what international relations have come to call "Westphalian states"; that is, fully constituted, independent entities that recognize no other authority than their own (a regrettable and anachronistic misnomer historians might be stuck with, not unlike the term "Byzantine" for the Eastern Roman Empire of the Middle Ages). Furthermore, it is questionable that this "sovereignty" has been the political cure-all it has been touted to be: of all the hundreds of states in German lands in 1648, only two empires plus Luxembourg remained by the end of the nineteenth century; from 1938 to 1945 they formed together a Third Reich, arguably the most powerful and ruthless continental empire Eurasia had known since the Mongol invasion. By 1950, all that remained of this myriad of "sovereign" states was Austria, West Germany, and East Germany, three wrecked states under Allied occupation.

If we can reach beyond the thick veil of myth that political scientists of the mid-twentieth century (as well as constitutional historians of the late nineteenth century) have thrown over the Peace of Westphalia, we can nevertheless consider it a significant prelude to our story: it opened wide a door to reflect on the profound nature of European states and their relation to each other.[50] The treaties themselves, written in Latin—the diplomatic language of the time—were a lengthy catalog (more than 100 articles) of territorial and institutional settlements. They also confirmed the exit of the Dutch Republic and the Swiss Confederation from the empire.[51] The writers identified the differences between the three prevalent Christian confessions (Catholic, Lutheran, and Calvinist) as the chief cause of the conflicts, and they aimed to provide practical arrangements to put an end to them. This meant important gains for the states of the Holy Roman Empire, such as confirming the princes' freedom to exercise their religion in their own state, a guarantee of their personal safety, and equal right to vote at the German Diet. The treaties also referred a number of territorial disputes to arbitration. The main innovation that emerges from them is an equality of rights between princes regardless of religion and of the insertion of this principle into the jurisprudence of the Holy Roman Empire.[52]

By contrast, the treaties of Westphalia are not the beginning of the history of perpetual peace in Europe, because one would be hard-pressed to find, among that successful catalog of practical measures, any lofty conception of a political order of Europe. The assertion that these texts were the "birth of the Westphalian conception of the state" is an ideological reconstitution long after the fact.[53] On the contrary, the image of representatives of German states peacefully conferring within the Diet of the Holy Roman Empire (as well as those of the Swiss Confederation and the United Dutch Provinces) became almost obligatory references for later plans to unite peacefully the European states on an equal footing. The two attributes of a state—territorial sovereignty and being part at the same time of a greater body that guaranteed mutual rights and duties—were thus seen as complementary. Indeed, the rationale of the Westphalian negotiations was to find pragmatic ways to improve the articulation of the two, a necessity that we call today "subsidiarity."

Certainly, by preventing the continuous and arbitrary interference of the Habsburgs in the affairs of Germans states in the Holy Roman Empire, the Dutch Republic, and Switzerland, Westphalia removed a severe impediment to the general political stability of Europe. Yet the fact that the king of France imposed his own signature at the bottom of a treaty—because he had stakes in that region just as in Italy—emphasizes that the Peace of Westphalia was in practice nothing more or less than a settlement treaty for German lands (in a broad sense), made possible by the momentary weakness of the Habsburgs. The outcome was a sort of "Treaty of the Functioning of the Holy Roman Empire" aimed at regulating domestic peace within that institution. Although the Peace of Westphalia was a remarkable diplomatic achievement that shaped later practices *in* Europe, idealizing it as a novelty and as the founding act *of* modern Europe seems a loss of perspective, especially considering that the signatories were adamant about restoring a venerable institution already eight centuries old.

After this blow to Habsburg ambitions, the Holy Roman Empire did obtain a new lease of life, but the dream of Europe living in peace under a universal monarchy and a single Christian religion had collapsed. This failure was a prelude to the brutal decline of Spain and the end of the ambitions of Austria to dominate the continent fully. The European order that remained was a collection of states, a few very large and many small ones, in which no house would be any longer powerful enough to impose its hegemony on all others.[54] It is not yet the beginning of our story, only the last blow to the obsolete (and by then largely deprecated) ideal that Europe, empire, and peace should one day converge into a bright future.

As Randall Lesaffer aptly put it, "Westphalia did not lay the foundation for the modern law of nations. It did however, put an end to the long religious and political crisis within and among the great powers."[55]After it, no power should legitimately expand its dominions by force so as to embrace all of Europe. Any attempt in that direction would, henceforth, be considered an act of defiance against the agreed-on status quo of Europe; it would be reviled as tyranny and would logically prompt a continental coalition to suppress the threat. Westphalia was thus a clear-cut end to the old political order of Christendom, a decapitation. By forever discrediting the dream of *Pax Romana*, the intangible dogma of universal monarchy, Westphalia marked the demise of a dominant and unifying frame of mind and the close of an era.[56]

We cannot, in sum, consider Westphalia the foundation of modern conceptions of Europe, because it established mostly negative prescriptions that prevented interference from the Holy Roman Empire in the affairs of the German states. Not only did the treaties say little or nothing new on how the German states should coexist or cooperate with one another, except by referring to the same traditional institution; they also remained entirely silent on how the European great powers should build peaceful relationships among themselves. Stating that a peace whose sole purpose had been to regulate the internal affairs of the German confederation should be considered an ideological foundation of the "international system" would be an exaggeration, because the venerable Holy Roman Empire was not the blueprint of the European political system later to emerge.[57] Westphalia's true achievement and lasting legacy lay elsewhere: in its intense pragmatism that deliberately cut through the politico-religious disputes that had formerly torn the belligerents apart, in favor of practical arrangements that allowed both sides to have their way. In that regard, we should indeed consider that Westphalia was a precursor of modern peace practices.

So, what then, after Westphalia? The best minds of Europe had a blank slate on which to write ideas about the ideal order of the European continent. In 1651, three years after Westphalia (but without any apparent reference to it), English philosopher Thomas Hobbes published *Leviathan or The Matter, Forme and Power of a Common-Wealth Ecclesiastical and Civil.*

Though Hobbes had a rather dark view of the tendency of humankind toward theft and rapine, he argued that the elevation of a superior authority could channel society to peace, so that property and mutually consensual obligations could be enforced. That principle of order was metaphorically represented by the Leviathan, the strong, graceful, terrifying, and invincible sea monster of the Bible.[58] A reader could mistake this for the medieval concept of universal monarchy, save for a key difference: authority was not to be imposed from the top down, but was to arise from a social contract, built out of the conflicting passions of humans, to impose general peace. Such hegemony could never be that of a Catholic tyranny supported by the pope, as it would have brought some more "abuse of Scripture."[59] But if the principle of order over Europe did not come from an emperor, much less from the pope, from where could come this "common Power to keep them all in awe"?[60] No doubt, the Peace of Westphalia had made this issue less pressing—for the moment. No head of state—that is, outside of the Habsburg dynasty—was still willing or able to contemplate such a project extending its power over Europe.

It is thus paradoxical that the only positive fragment of an idea in the direction of a new European order was a work of "political fiction" that came to be known at the time of Westphalia but referred to alleged events that predated it: the *Œconomies royales* (Deeds of the King) by Maximilien de Béthune, Duc de Sully. Published widely only after the death of Sully in 1641, it purported that French king Henry IV, in association with Queen Elizabeth I of England, had considered an alternative to universal monarchy in the form of a "Universal, Most Christian Republic, composed of all the Kings and Princes of Europe who Profess the Name of Christ," which would defeat the Habsburgs and bring peace to Europe.[61] It would have had two eastern borderlands—Poland in the east and Hungary in the south—to defend itself against the tsardom of Russia and the Ottoman Empire, respectively. This was in line with the political conceptions of Europe at the time, especially because the Ottomans still occupied part of Hungary and laid siege to Vienna one last time in 1683, while the French monarchy had had a long-standing relationship with Poland, which was regularly at war with its rising Russian neighbor.[62]

Henry IV, born a Protestant but converted to Catholicism, had already restored peace and prosperity in France by ending a period of religious troubles and exercising careful rule. The fundamental importance of Sully's narrative for a pan-European alliance was not, however, as a historical source on the reign of the French king (since its reliability is questionable), but as a source of inspiration for authors and thinkers on perpetual peace. New ideas about the order of Europe were greatly influenced by musing about what would have happened if the Good King, instead of being tragically assassinated in 1610, had pursued his alleged grand destiny to its conclusion. This notably influenced the works of the Abbé de Saint-Pierre, and a century after the monarch's death, the philosopher Voltaire would write, "I sing this hero who reigned on France / By right of conquest and right of birth / Who through long hardships learned to govern / Was able to calm the factions and forgive . . . And was the victor and the father of his subjects."[63] Unfortunately, still vague and largely shapeless, unable to foster any concrete solution or practical path, Henry IV's plan proved a mixed blessing by attaching the stigma of "utopia" (a fantasy) to the aim of a peaceful European Republic of States.

That initial debate on the best political order for Europe was thus rooted in the context of the colossal struggle that led the Protestant states of the north—as well as religiously ambivalent France—to escape the double grip of the Catholic union of the throne (the Habsburg states of Spain and Austria) and the altar (the pope). The modern intellectual construction of Europe, as an original creation looking forward, not back to the struggle against the Habsburgs or to the Roman Empire, would have to wait. The second part of the seventeenth century was not yet a dawn, but rather a "political aurora" or "Europe in limbo." It was plagued with many issues, particularly dynastic, which were left without a solution.

The treaties of Westphalia were a diplomatic triumph that closed one of the most violent chapters in modern European history, and fully deserve the qualification of "Peace." Yet precisely because they were peace seeking, the clauses of those documents were grounded in facts and wisely refrained from confronting the Medusa of ideological justifications. With the newly acquired political freedom of the German states to pursue their own version of a secular (but fundamentally Christian) state, so many questions about the European order were still left unanswered and could indeed cause new wars. If the common agreement was that peace should no longer be enforced by the hegemony of a single prince, and that war and peace were a matter of "just behavior," how were the states of Europe supposed to establish peace and prosperity among themselves? And if one power became so powerful that it threatened to resurrect the specter of universal monarchy, how should the others act? With the end of Christendom started the long march of European pacification through nonviolent means. Whichever solution emerged, it would have to deal with two scourges: internecine wars and new attempts at creating a continental empire. Universal monarchy, from a worthy ideal, had become the foil. The political idea of Europe grew out of much trial and error, in search of workable formulas for lasting peace.

This story is, however, far from over. Given that the European twenty-first century may bring a reassessment of a number of nineteenth-century "isms" that our schooling had taught us would be perennial (from nationalism and colonialism to Marxism, socialism, communism, and even capitalism itself), as well as a necessary questioning of the European Union's institutions, revisiting its past should be more useful than ever. Examining the engineering of peace sheds new light on these questions and provides guidelines that could be of help for the establishment of future European-level policies.

Arguing whether the engineering of peace is realist or idealist is likely fruitless: those labels depend on the relative position of the observer at the moment he or she asks the question. In sum, the engineering of peace aims to be a new and pragmatic approach of doing what works toward lasting peace. We may hope that if reconciliation between factions about the future of Europe is ever possible, it may be found in a maxim informing this book's entire argument: *peace is for the strong and war is for the weak*. Military alliances are concluded so that states too weak to resist an empire on their own can survive, whereas peace alliances are fostered by powers already in a position of strength. In this paradoxical statement can be found the fundamental connection between the value of peace and the idea of a strong Europe.

1

The Enlightened Spirit of Peace

BEYOND THE TREATY OF UTRECHT

Since no broader, more beautiful and useful pursuit ever occupied the human mind than a perpetual and universal peace among all peoples of Europe, no author ever deserved more attention from the public, than the one who proposed means to implement such a plan.

—JEAN-JACQUES ROUSSEAU, *ABSTRACT OF MONSIEUR THE ABBÉ DE SAINT-PIERRE'S "PLAN FOR PERPETUAL PEACE,"* 1761

*I*n January 1712, delegations from the major states of Europe streamed through the lowlands of the Dutch Republic to Utrecht on the delta of the Rhine River, to end the War of Spanish Succession, which had devastated the continent for more than a decade. The host of foreign dignitaries who arrived at the little walled city for their congress unsettled its orderly routine. They had to be lodged, fed, and entertained, raising the sensitive issues of protocol that arise inevitably when so many notable persons share a cramped space. Local residents were certainly witnessing the greatest show of their lifetime. After decades of almost uninterrupted conflicts prompted by France, the continental "superpower" of the time, peace was perhaps at hand.

The French word *congrès,* from Latin "go together," can be traced to the end of the seventeenth century: it meant "an assembly of several ministers from different powers who have traveled to the same place to conclude peace, or to conciliate the interests of their masters."[1] The custom of organizing such gatherings after a large conflict had precedents, including the Peace of Westphalia after the Thirty Years' War (1648), and European

29

routines of peace negotiations that were already well established. The War of Spanish Succession had been waged to settle a dispute that had not been possible to resolve otherwise, so the *status quo post bellum* (the condition after the war) constituted the starting point for peace negotiations.

The Peace of Utrecht gave wide circulation to a new political principle—the balance of power—that had evolved in opposition to the dynastic principle of patrimonial states. A first version of this principle emerged in England at the turn of the eighteenth century, and a second gained currency when the concept began to be incorporated into European treaties and continental thought. A competing but equally enduring conception of European peace, based on ideas of institutional union and common norms, arose at the same moment: "perpetual peace." Its best-known proponents were the Abbé de Saint-Pierre, who wrote at nearly the same time as the Peace of Utrecht; Jean-Jacques Rousseau, who wrote during the Seven Years' War (1756–1763); and, finally, Immanuel Kant, who wrote during the greatest cycle of conflict in the eighteenth century: the French Revolutionary and Napoleonic wars (1792–1815). This lesser-known strand of European thought about peace rejected military deterrence as the chief governing principle in the foreign policy of civilized nations, and it was supported by respected Enlightenment-era figures, including Gottfried Wilhelm Leibniz, Voltaire, and Vattel.

The period from the turn of the seventeenth century to 1815 was one of considerable transformation and conflict. It is sometimes called the Second Hundred Years' War, because England and France were on opposite sides in most of the skirmishes.[2] This periodization, devised in the twentieth century, perhaps exaggerates the role of conflict and is moreover Anglocentric, lumping together times, situations, and political regimes that had very little in common save for ongoing strife between the two nations. It has, however, one great merit: it draws attention to the fact that this time, which embraces both the Enlightenment and the French Revolution, was not exactly one of peace and stability for Europe. Yet perhaps it was that incessant conflict that made those years crucial ones for the evolution of thinking about peace; both philosophers and statesmen were driven to end that strife by developing solid ethical, pragmatic, legal, and political principles on which peace in Europe could be founded. The reflections of Enlightenment philosophers would be instrumental in shaping the doctrines of monarchs and political leaders from the post-Napoleonic era to the European union of the late twentieth century. They remain, to this day, foundational for modern political thought in Europe.

The presiding spirit in the century before Napoleon is what I call "the Spirit of Utrecht." It emerged in opposition to the prevailing ideas of universal monarchy in Europe and was characterized by debate between two alternative models of international order: one based on the balance of power and the other centered on the idea of perpetual peace. This debate, which sought peace in Europe in and for itself, was indeed one of the earliest manifestations of the broader spirit of the Enlightenment, in which philosophers, scientists, engineers, and rulers reexamined all aspects of knowledge and craft with a view to improving the human condition. Naturally, war became the focus of philosophical reflection and political experimentation, which was further motivated by the War of Spanish Succession. The Spirit of Utrecht posited that a balance of power had to take precedence over the patrimonial rights and dynastic interests of ruling families. More fundamentally, it reinforced the belief that the political order of Europe should be founded on the law of nations (itself an expression of natural law). This Spirit generated a novel conception of Europe as a "Republic of States," a civilized society with codified rules of behavior. Whether the balance of power alone could stabilize that civilization, or whether new mechanisms of peace should be based on a European Grand Alliance, became one of the defining debates of the Enlightenment. The arguments of that debate would be revisited in each subsequent iteration of the European spirit of peace.

Europe and Its Wars

By the turn of the eighteenth century, "Europe" had become—at least partially—a well-defined geographical conception, delimited by the sea on the north, west, and south. The Holy Roman Empire by then a benign and tolerant entity, stood at its center, with its institutions and a permanent Diet in Augsburg. It was a model of political coexistence for the rest of Europe. By contrast, Europe's eastern edges were less well settled: three vast political formations—the Kingdom of Sweden in the north, the Polish-Lithuanian

Commonwealth in the middle, and the Ottoman Empire in the south—constituted its frontiers. Cartographers were still debating how much of Muscovy should be included in Europe. (St. Petersburg was founded only in 1703.)[3] Since Antiquity, the division between Europe and Asia north of the Black Sea had been commonly set at the River Don, the source of which was barely east of Moscow. Only in 1736, fifteen years after the Russian Empire was officially born, did Russian geographer Vasily Tatishchev take the rather bold step of proposing the Ural Mountains as the notional border for Europe. Given that Tsar Peter the Great wanted to affirm that Russia was part of Europe and should take part in its political order, there was great advantage in stating that its most populous lands belonged to Europe and that vast Asia was at the periphery of it.[4]

The main territorial states—the so-called "great powers" of France, Austria, Spain, England, Prussia, Muscovy, and Sweden—were all monarchies. In general, succession was hereditary, with three notable exceptions: the Polish-Lithuanian Commonwealth, the Dutch Republic, and the Holy Roman Empire—although the empire was arguably not a "power" per se. Dynastic issues still played a central role in the relations between states, through marriages, successions, and recurrent wars. Many of those wars revolved around the historical competition between the French House of Bourbon and the Austrian House of Habsburg.[5]

After a few short years of peace following the wars waged by Louis XIV of Bourbon, the absolute king of France, yet another conflict broke out: the War of Spanish Succession (1701–1714). This time the crisis was only indirectly provoked by the French king; his grandson Philip had unexpectedly inherited the kingdom of Spain after the sickly Charles II, the last Habsburg sovereign, died without male descendants. Spain and France were archrivals; this inheritance would have united Spain and its global empire with the already sizable dominions of France. With France undergoing rapid expansion—territorially, demographically, economically, and militarily—this threatened to resurrect the specter of universal monarchy in Europe. In truth, Louis XIV was not seriously contemplating uniting the two crowns, because such an enterprise would have been difficult to achieve; even the great Habsburg emperor Charles V had been forced to divide his possessions between Spain and Austria. Nevertheless, the consequences of a Franco-Spanish alliance were a dire prospect for the other European powers, prompting a military coalition among England, Austria, Prussia, Savoy, and the Dutch Republic—and igniting a new European conflagration.

Meanwhile, England was also embroiled in its own succession strife. The Jacobites, who were mostly Scottish and Catholic, promoted the claims of the Stuarts to the throne, whereas the opposing Hanoverians supported Protestantism and the German house of Hanover. England stood apart from other European monarchies, however, in being a mercantilist society, rather than a patrimonial one: for its ruling class, real estate was only one of several forms of honorable business and one that should not threaten the others. Parliament took matters in hand in 1701 by passing the Act of Settlement, which determined that, although the Stuart Queen Anne would retain the throne until her death, a Hanoverian would succeed her—on the sole condition he neither be a Catholic nor marry one. Both Louis XIV and the pope naturally opposed this act in the name of divine right monarchy and, as could be expected in such circumstances, supported the claim to the throne of Anne's Catholic younger brother, James.[6] Meanwhile, the parliaments of both England and Scotland consolidated their own legitimacy by approving a formal union in 1707, which gave birth to the United Kingdom of Great Britain.[7] After James failed to overthrow his sister in 1708, the Westminster Parliament solidified its role as an arbiter of last resort by asserting its authority to nullify the inheritance rights of a royal dynasty in the best interests of the kingdom. After this decisive victory against divine right monarchy, the British political class was able to better turn its attention outward, toward the affairs of the Continent.

The great threat from the putative Franco-Spanish Alliance lay with the beleaguered Dutch Republic. Once a prosperous maritime power with global ambitions, the Netherlands had entered into decline. A prolonged conflict against France, which some historians call the Forty Years' War (1672–1712), was not going very well.[8] This conflict had at least the benefit of reconciling the Dutch with their Spanish neighbors in Flanders (roughly modern-day Belgium and Luxembourg), because both were equally threatened by the territorial ambitions of Louis XIV. Furthermore, the Dutch Republic could count on the support of England since William of Orange had become king in the Glorious Revolution (1688–1689). When Spain and France unexpectedly became allies in 1701, the situation turned desperate for the Dutch Republic: Flanders, which had been a convenient Spanish bulwark between France and the Netherlands, suddenly switched sides and turned into a military rear base for a French invasion. To rescue the Dutch from certain defeat, the British and several allied German princes hastily organized a joint military intervention, starting the War of Spanish Succession. The main theater of operations remained in Flanders, but fighting also took place in Germany, in the Americas, and in the western Mediterranean. Unlike the Thirty Years' War of the previous century, each camp experienced successes and setbacks in turn, and neither was able to prevail decisively over the other. France, despite its nominal advantage, was in financial straits and in no position to occupy the Dutch Republic. It soon found itself on the defensive in Spanish Flanders, and the conflict turned into a war of attrition.

The Balance of Power, a New Doctrine for Europe

A singular circumstance of the Congress of Utrecht enabled the European states to focus on reason, rather than implacable military imperatives. Because the War of Spanish Succession had ended in a costly stalemate, there were no triumphant victors imposing their will on humbled losers, as had so often been the case, especially after the Thirty Years' War. Instead, there were only two exhausted sides, both ardently aspiring to peace, so they could move on to more profitable occupations. This unusual situation of two belligerents coming to the negotiating table of their own volition and on a more or less equal footing had a significant consequence: instead of the usual pattern of a victorious side imposing peace terms on the losing one, conditions were present at Utrecht for a truly original and balanced discussion about how to make the state of peace as durable as possible. In early 1713, the two sides agreed to an enforcement mechanism that would prevent any European power from achieving superiority and engaging in wars of conquest: this mechanism was the reestablishment of the *balance of power* between France and other states. The Peace of Utrecht was the first time this term appeared expressly in a treaty as a key principle governing a settlement among the powers. Thus, an unforeseen circumstance at the end of a war triggered a comprehensive, thoughtful approach to establishing lasting peace in Europe.[9]

Over the last three centuries the original conception of the "balance of power" has been so buried under layers of intellectual re-plastering that it has become muddled beyond recognition; it is therefore important to restore its initial meaning. "Balance" referred to, quite simply, the weighing instrument (a scale). The idea was that, to preserve the peace of Europe, "weight" had to be added to or subtracted from two opposing alliances so that they reached the desired state of equilibrium. Scholars customarily refer to the short essay written by David Hume in 1742 as the source of this concept.[10] Yet it was written nearly thirty years after the Peace of Utrecht and in a different context, the War of Austrian Succession (1740–1748).[11] If we travel back almost a half-century earlier, we uncover the original conception, which was both sharply defined and tailored to the political situation of the moment.[12]

The roots of the balance of power were in fact planted long before the Wars of Spanish and Austrian Succession. Instead, they can be traced to a war ruse used in ancient times to weaken a powerful enemy: this strategy was to convince a third party to attack one's enemy. The ancient Roman maxim "divide and conquer" (or "divide and rule") and the Chinese stratagem "kill with a borrowed knife" referred to this tactic.[13] In the insular context of England, discussion of the balance of power concept built on the reflections of political philosophers in Renaissance Italy (especially Machiavelli and Guicciardini, whose works had been translated and printed in English).[14] While the Italian writers had attempted to account for past political independence that was no longer, England at the turn of the eighteenth century was a rising naval power that could more than hold its own in European politics. It needed, however, to protect itself against overbearing neighbors. For this, England needed a political doctrine that would guide it in conducting its continental alliances—specifically, its alliance with France.[15]

These reflections on foreign policy were evolving in parallel with a rational questioning of the traditional pattern of the patrimonial states, which had been the point of reference in Europe since the Middle Ages: some members of the political elite were demanding a limitation of the traditional inheritance rights of princes to lands and their populations.[16] Indeed the term "balance of power" between the Crown and Parliament emerged in England in the context of the Bill of Rights of 1689, which regulated the succession to the throne in the aftermath of the Glorious Revolution.[17] It was as if these two strands of reflection—the art of conducting war alliances and the quintessentially British method of resolving dynastic disputes—were waiting to merge into one consistent vision of a postwar order for Europe.

A document that played an important role in crafting this vision was written by Tory politician and thinker Charles Davenant and aptly titled *An Essay upon the Balance of Power* (1701). Though by no means the only existing text on the topic and certainly not a literary masterpiece (it is rather long-winded and disordered), it has two incontrovertible claims of interest: its being one of the first on the subject and its timeliness.[18] It was written in the brief lull after England emerged from the Nine Years' War (1688–1697) and was again on the brink of war with France. In exquisite detail, Davenant captured the logic of European political alliances against France at this fateful juncture between peace and war. The essay revealed two key facts: the doctrine of the balance of power had not been fully embraced in England in 1702, and yet it was the linchpin of the case for declaring war on France.[19]

At the time of its writing, Davenant was a recently elected Tory representative to the House of Commons. He held that in a world in which no power was able to exercise undisputed domination over others, a sensible way of maintaining a balance would be through the establishment of two opposing configurations of alliances that would cancel each other out, like the two pans of a scale. When one alliance threatened to overcome the other, England would have to throw its weight to the threatened alliance to restore the equilibrium.[20] The image of a balance scale obviously belonged to a metaphorical field of mechanics, and it appeared in other contexts (such as "balance of trade" and the domestic "political balance"). It underpinned a conception of the European states as a *system* in a state of dynamic equilibrium, where changes of alliances, conceived as shifts of mass from one side to the other, were routine. The recourse to this mechanist metaphor was not coincidental: it was the product of an English ruling class adept at natural philosophy (what we would today call science) that had already had a decade to ponder Isaac Newton's laws of motion.[21] Yet Davenant was not philosophizing in the abstract, but pursuing immediate political ends. He boldly advocated preventive war, and the metaphor was in service of his argument.

There was, however, a moral obstacle. France and England were allies at the time, so declaring war would have violated the legal maxim of *pacta sunt servanda* ("agreements are to be respected"). It would be misguided to think Davenant's answer to this quandary was to elevate political immorality to the rank of virtue or to coldly observe Machiavelli's principles of prudence (which a casual observer across the Channel might perhaps ascribe to "perfidious Albion"). On the contrary, Davenant posed as a moralist: he launched into a tirade against the English court aristocracy and business circles, which he considered so self-serving that they would gladly sacrifice the interests of England for financial profit.[22] Davenant thus boldly solved the moral dilemma posed by attacking an ally: maintaining the balance of power had to become the supreme moral rule that justified England's severing its alliance with France. Similarly, it would be anachronistic to conclude that Davenant was involved in some "drive to modernization." On the contrary, this momentous change to England's foreign policy actually relied on the fundamental argument used by the Ancients in their famous quarrel against the Moderns—that society had lost its earlier values of selflessness, frugality, and unity and that it should revert to the models of old. In this instance, resolute action was required to confront both the domestic threat of corruption and the foreign threat to the sovereignty of England. It may seem ironic, but the balance of power was a moralistic argument in the hand of the Ancients against the Moderns.[23]

There was, of course, no dearth of reasons for political antipathy between England and France: in addition to their opposed interests in foreign policy, they diverged in their conception of domestic order, both politically and socially. On the Continent, Catholic absolute monarchy had subjugated the parliaments of Spain and France; it could well obliterate those of England and the United Provinces, two maritime powers that had humbled their kings and remained Protestant against all odds.[24] At the time, the purpose of the balance of power policy was twofold: (1) to protect against hegemony by preventing the union of France and Spain and (2) to promote domestic security; that is, to preserve England's freedoms and prosperity. But was it truly aimed at peace? If that meant finding a political settlement so that everyday business could resume, the answer was ultimately yes. For the time being, however, morality and law were on the side of war.[25]

The conception of the balance of power on the eve of the War of Spanish Succession therefore had two dimensions. The first was that it was an implicit, "natural" phenomenon governing human relations that had already existed for decades; studying it was key to comprehending the stakes and events of European politics. There was, however, an important second dimension, both explicit and prescriptive: it was a maxim of political prudence. If the scale began tipping to one side, England should deliberately shift its weight to the other. On that condition, England could maintain a durable, albeit precarious, peace. It is on those premises that war was declared on France. As Davenant and others repeated insistently, the task of England was "holding the balance of power of Europe" by creating a grand alliance around France.[26] This statement, with a few variations, was to become a long-standing principle of English foreign policy. Notably, it was also the fundamental argument used by another vocal proponent of the balance of power, the Irish deist John Toland, who insisted (also in 1701) that the British Crowns should go to the Protestant Hanoverians instead of the Catholic branch of the Stuarts.[27] There was clearly a parallel between the two contentions of Bourbon versus Habsburg and Stuart versus Hanover. At that time, the debate around the balance of power was inseparable from these dynastic issues.

As could be expected, views on foreign policy—and on the balance of power—evolved somewhat during the War of Spanish Succession. By 1711, the conflict had already lasted for a decade; England had been fighting as part of a grand alliance with the Holy Roman Empire, the Netherlands, Prussia, and Portugal against France, and questions were being raised as to whether this conflict still made sense. The Tory government commissioned a pamphlet from Irish writer Jonathan Swift, titled *The Conduct of the Allies* (1711), to advocate for a peaceful exit from the war. Swift pointedly remarked that the immediate goals of the conflict had already been achieved—Dutch territory was now largely safe—although England found itself in an unbearable situation: its meddling in continental affairs was only serving to advance European allies to its own detriment, at great financial cost. Swift was particularly displeased with the actions of the Dutch, who were expanding their territory by systematically installing garrisons in fortresses captured from Spanish Flanders. Noting that "there is a Ballance of Power to be carefully held by a state within itself, as well as among several states with each other" (and thus Spain and its territories had to be returned to the Habsburgs), Swift argued that pursuing all-out war to defeat Spain was threatening to stack the balance against England itself.[28] Such was the consistency and versatility of this doctrine of the balance of power: it could dictate the moment both to start a war and to stop it.

Swift's work was a remarkable success: ten thousand copies were sold in a month, and several more editions followed in the ensuing months. By this time, the balance of power had become official doctrine of the English government. According to this view, Britain did not seek war, but just as the rules of celestial mechanics forbade any object from resting in static immobility, neither was it seeking peace for itself. The point was to preserve the delicate dynamic equilibrium in the European system, especially against any imperial menace such as posed by the French.

The English desire to sue for peace with France eventually forced the other great powers to the negotiating table. The Peace of Utrecht formally concluded the conflict: France and Great Britain signed the accord on April 11, 1713, and Spain and Great Britain on July 13 of that year.[29] The peace was only a series of compromises, without winners or losers. It was in reality formed of several bilateral treaties, signed between 1713 and 1715, involving France, Great Britain, Portugal, Prussia, Savoy, the Netherlands, Spain, Austria, and the Holy Roman Empire. They covered three aspects: dynastic, territorial, and commercial.[30] Because the dispute over the dynastic rights of the Bourbons to the crown of Spain was the main cause of the war ("the war that this peace must quench was ignited mainly because the security and freedom of Europe could absolutely not allow that the crowns of France and Spain be united on the same head"), primary attention was given to that matter in the first treaty between France and England.[31] Philip V, the grandson of Louis XIV, retained the Spanish throne, but he had to renounce

Europe after the Treaties of
Utrecht, 1713–14

——— Holy Roman Empire

Predominant religious affiliations

☐ Protestant   ☐ Orthodox
☐ Catholic   ☐ Muslim

0   200 km
0   200 miles

Finland

SWEDEN

Lake
Onega

Lake
Ladoga

Åland
Islands

Gulf of Bothnia

Gulf of Finland

St Petersburg

Stockholm

Estonia Ingria

Dagö

Livonia

Ösel

Gotland

Courland

Moscow

Baltic Sea

PRUSSIA

Lithuania

RUSSIAN EMPIRE

Warsaw

POLAND

Volhynia

Galicia Podolia

Budapest

HUNGARY

Moldavia

Transylvania

KHANATE OF CRIMEA

Wallachia

Georgia Karabagh

Black Sea

PERSIA

Bulgaria

OTTOMAN EMPIRE

Albania

Rumelia Constantinople

Aegean
Sea

Chios

Karaman

Syria

Morea

REPUBLIC

Rhodes

Cyprus

Crete

formally his claims to the crown of France, even though that meant violating the laws of France itself.

That first treaty between France and Great Britain naturally also addressed the second dynastic concern: the Stuart claim to the English throne.[32] With France finally acknowledging the Protestant succession of the Hanoverians, a new order was in the making: this recognition helped bring to a close a long period of dynastic and religious contention on the British Isles, initiating a period of political stability that fostered the rise of British power in the world.[33] As a sign of the times, Frederick William was pragmatically acknowledged in the treaties as "King of Prussia," a title he had unashamedly bestowed on himself in 1701. Not only was this a departure from the principle that there should be no royalty in the Holy Roman Empire other than the elected emperor but it was yet another blow to the supremacy of the Habsburgs of Austria, who were "only" hereditary archdukes.

Yet a key element that made the Peace of Utrecht particularly significant for the political history of Europe is the annex that contains the Spanish king's renunciation of the crown of France. This document stated boldly the fundamental aim of the treaties: to "secure for ever [*sic*] the universal Good and Quiet of Europe by an equal Weight of Power, so that many being united in one, the Balance of the Equality desired, might not turn to the advantage of one, and the Danger and Hazard of the rest."[34] In both the Spanish text and in the official Latin version, the metaphor of the "Balance of the Equality desired," explicitly and without doubt, referred to the weighing instrument with two pans. To preserve the peace of Europe, its dynamic system of alliances was adjusted to the desired state of equilibrium by this renunciation, after which the Spanish king expressed the hope that the "needle of the balance would remain invariable." The traditionally acknowledged right of succession that would have granted the throne of France to Philip V gave way to the higher principle of the balance of power—thereby preventing the French House of Bourbon from gaining enough power to subjugate the whole continent.

The French, however, had a very different understanding of the balance of power principle, not least because of the phenomenon of linguistic false friends. The term "balance" immediately evoked the swinging movement of scales, and the word "power" was understood as the capacity of generating a motion (as the power of a horse or an army). In French, the phrase "balance of power" became *équilibre des puissances:* the word *équilibre* meaning "equal weight" and *puissance* primarily signifying the capacity to exert political or legal authority, the might of a state, and, by extension, political "power" itself.[35] As the result, the meaning conveyed in French was "equal force of the [great] powers"; in other words, the international order would have to remain forever a status quo ante—the exact opposite of what the English actually meant.[36]

To make matters worse, a translation back into English failed to reveal the misapprehension: the English word "balance" was a possible (albeit incorrect in that case) equivalent of *équilibre,* and the word "powers" could be used (equally incorrectly) as a translation of the French *puissances.* The two deceptively similar expressions thus created a lasting misunderstanding between French and English speakers, a vocabulary problem that may have prevented many French citizens from grasping the fundamental logic behind the sudden shifts that continue to occur in English foreign policy toward the Continent up to the present day. At least, this fundamental difference of apprehension did not make the two versions entirely incompatible: both sides of the Channel agreed for the moment that an equilibrium should exist between the European powers.[37]

In any case, the new continental concept of "balance of power" reconfirmed a fragmented Europe, evenly split into two blocs. The Holy Roman Empire returned to its earlier steady role, similar to the one it had before the reign of Charles V—as a durable but loose confederation of states, a stabilizing factor in Europe precisely because of its inertia. Even though the empire signed the treaty, Charles VI of Habsburg, who had just acceded to power as Holy Roman Emperor in 1711, sought briefly to reclaim the crown of Spain, with little success.

Another important achievement of the Peace of Utrecht was to cut short the seemingly endless string of territorial annexations initiated by the French Bourbons. The so-called Barrier Treaty of 1715 conferred the formerly Spanish Netherlands (mostly today's Belgium) on the Austrian Habsburgs. Quite importantly, it also provided for large Austro-Dutch garrisons as a "barrier" against any future French expansion. Although these forts afforded limited protection in case of war, the treaty provision established the principle that the eastern borders of France should be limited in the northeast, far west of the natural border of the Rhine River.[38] The Utrecht agreements, following an English plan, created a belt of bulwark states that effectively contained France to the east: from north to south—Austrian Flanders, German states behind the Rhine border, Switzerland and the Alps, and Savoy (now a kingdom by virtue of its acquisition of Sicily), which extended to the Mediterranean Sea. With the exception of Savoy, a few secondary territories, and the temporary expansion after the French Revolution, the geographic contours of mainland France have remained largely unchanged up to our time. The Utrecht treaties also transferred Spain's Italian territories to Austria.[39] Great Britain, by now a great trading power, kept Gibraltar and Minorca (strategic naval bases in the western Mediterranean, wrested from Spain during the war), as well as Newfoundland and Acadia (two of France's Canadian territories, also conquered during the war). In a key commercial settlement, Great Britain secured access to the Spanish colonial trade—including the *asiento,* the bleak monopoly on the slave trade—partly replacing French influence in those territories. Yet, Utrecht brought peace only to Western Europe, as the Great Northern War (1700–1721) was still raging in the east between Russia and Sweden, with the British government studiously hopping between the two sides in obeyance to its newfound principle of foreign policy.[40] Even though the vast region that lay between the Baltic Sea and the Black Sea was considered geographically "in Europe," the great powers clearly still viewed it as a distinct and disconnected political space.

It is often stated that Great Britain was ultimately the winner of the Utrecht settlement. That may have been true in the long term, but as can be inferred from Swift's complaints, that was not how it was seen at the time. Despite new territorial acquisitions and commercial advantages, many members of the English political and mercantile class were dissatisfied that not-unfavorable conditions were granted to France. In fact, Parliament was quite upset with one of the treaty's key authors, Henry St. John (who became Viscount Bolingbroke in 1712), whom they accused of being too lenient at the negotiating table. To emphasize how complicated things were, Bolingbroke was also a Jacobite (a supporter of the Stuart succession to the

FIG. 1.1 Peter Schenck II, *Engraving on the Treaty of Utrecht,* 1714. Peace Palace Library, The Hague.

throne); he was eventually forced to flee to France after yet another abortive attempt by the "Old Pretender" James Stuart to regain power in 1715. Nevertheless, the Utrecht settlement did establish a state of peace in the western half of Europe. All in all, the agreements initiated what J. G. A. Pocock termed the "Utrecht Enlightenment," founded on the force of treaties and guaranteeing a European order indifferent to the official religion of each state.[41]

For the time being, the nature of the European order was more clearly articulated and more peaceful than it had been in the previous century, at least in theory. The chief reason for the "balance of power" clause in the Treaty of Utrecht was to preserve peace in Europe by defusing the succession issues that had triggered the last great war, though whether it would actually have the expected effect remained to be seen. To assess its effectiveness in preserving peace, there are four aspects to be considered—two legal and two practical ones. First, the hope that the treaty would maintain an *invariable* equilibrium in Europe was improbable at best, because the relative power of the states was—as the British well understood—bound to change over time. The use of the word "invariable" was most likely a rhetorical device, just as peace was conventionally described in treaties as *perpetual* and friendship as *eternal.* These were propitiatory phrases employed to express the fervent hope that the treaty would establish a new status quo that would be as durable as possible; the only certainty was that there would eventually be another war.

The second legal aspect was far more consequential: under the terms of the renunciation clause, the internal law of a state (France and Spain in this case) could be subordinated to the "external" law of nations in Europe. Admittedly, there is little indication that the treaties of Utrecht expressed a conscious intent to establish the balance of power in the abstract, as a principle overruling dynastic rights. Yet the legal principle of the balance of power had been carefully articulated to solve the specific issue that had caused the War of Spanish Succession. The Peace of Utrecht established a legal precedent, inaugurating a significant shift from a purely patrimonial view of the European states, where dynastic interests reigned supreme, to a concept of a loose *republic of states,* with a set of agreed-on rules based on common interests—an imprecise idea, but undoubtedly one more civilized than before.[42] The irrevocable renunciation of the Bourbon king of Spain to the throne of France, and the equally irrevocable recognition of the Hanoverian succession wanted by London's Parliament—both clean breaks with the succession rights of divine right dynasties—were two great achievements of the Peace of Utrecht that ushered in the modern history of peace in Europe. By this act, the political configuration of Europe became less tribal. Whether it would be less violent remained to be seen.

A third, enduring aspect of Utrecht's balance of power principle was its acknowledgment of the reality of a politically and religiously fractured continent. In this new reality, no European power would again be in a position militarily to overrule all others. Unfortunately, the balance of power was not only a last-resort principle for cases where one power endangered all others; it was also the path of least effort the rest of the time. The French Bourbons and Austrian Habsburgs remained in competition, continually keeping standing armies and collecting allies; it followed that the outcome would again be a configuration of the great powers into two antagonistic blocs. That situation did not bode well for "perpetual peace and eternal amity" on the Continent.

The fourth and last aspect of the balance-of-power principle was highly significant: Great Britain began to treat its newfound role of maintaining the balance of power in Europe as a rule of conduct. Cabinet officials would use this political wisdom—not unlike engineers use their knowledge of the laws of mechanics—to build better machines. The "trick," which was neither intuitive nor obvious, was that Great Britain should henceforth act as the balancing factor in European politics, dampening potential political conflicts by switching sides if one bloc threatened to overcome the other. As John Campbell wrote in 1750,

> In this lies our great Happiness, that having no Views or Pretensions upon our Neighbours, there is no solid, indeed not so much as a plausible Ground for us to hate them, or they us. This is the true fundamental Principle of our Policy: that in Respect of the Affairs of the Continent, we are not to be governed by any of those temporary or accidental Conveniences, which very often, and that justly too, pass for Reasons of State in other Kingdoms.[43]

Indeed, while the Continentals put their faith in the ability of the treaties to preserve the equilibrium, the British sought henceforth to safeguard it with a prudent policy that consisted of minding their own business (namely, their global sea trade and colonial empire), reserving their interventions on the Continent solely to remedy grave oscillations in the balance of power. In 1849, Prime Minister Lord Palmerston would famously say, "We have no eternal allies and no perpetual enemies. Our interests are perpetual and eternal, and those interests it is our duty to follow."[44] In that prudent restraint toward the Continent may lie a key factor explaining why England (the United Kingdom after 1707) is still the sole European power never to have been conquered since 1700.[45] Even in the direst situations, the United Kingdom was always able to leverage alliances on the Continent or, failing this, to take advantage of diplomatic connivances and even sympathy from populations. Had the United Kingdom engaged in an imperial venture on the Continent to the point of attracting the combined wrath of *all*

Europeans (as Napoleon's France did in 1813–1814), it is not a certainty that even the mighty British Navy could have saved the homeland. This was not likely to happen, however, because of the mercantilist nature of British society: a conquest of the Continent, with the colossal expense and risks it would entail and its dubious returns, appeared much less attractive than the rosy prospects of colonial ventures beyond the seas. Such was the effectiveness of the United Kingdom's foreign policy doctrine toward the Continent in times of trouble that it is still the only European power to have found itself on the winning side of each great alliance since the War of Spanish Succession.

Yet the British doctrine—according to which the balance of power ranked higher than preexisting agreements and alliances—did have a chink in its armor: it undermined the maxim *pacta sunt servanda,* arguably one of the vital axioms underpinning the European Law of Nations. For this reason, a shift in alliances was liable to be considered treachery—unless all parties agreed in advance that the movement of one power into a position of hegemony could be a valid cause for terminating an alliance. Those changes in alliances help explain the survival of the accusation of political perfidy that already existed in French culture against England, which can be found to this day in the pejorative phrase, "perfidious Albion."[46] One of the great diplomatic achievements of the Treaty of Utrecht was that it acknowledged the legitimacy of Britain's decision to break its alliance with France during the War of Spanish Succession. The contractual version of the balance of power, *équilibre des puissances,* certainly lacked the eminently dynamic character of English foreign policy, but it was still adaptable. The Peace of Utrecht thus had two functions: it prevented universal monarchy in the future, and it defined new rights and duties for the monarchs.

A word of caution, however, is in order: the balance of Europe could prevent one power from rising to hegemony, but it did not guarantee that peace would last. War still served as a safety valve and the only means to settle disputes that could not be resolved through diplomacy. The Peace of Utrecht, even though it served as the foundation of a legal order, tacitly acknowledged the legitimacy of war. Although the new European order certainly sought peace as its ultimate goal, at the same time it did not seek to ban war. On the contrary, it harnessed it as the mechanism for resolving disputes, so as to restore the continent to a state of equilibrium. The balance of power provided, as it were, a doctrinal justification to the Roman maxim, "If you want peace, prepare for war": the European states were to keep on the ready for war (and occasionally join allies to wage it) in order to maintain the peace and their own freedoms. Thus, even though the Peace of Utrecht undoubtedly represented an advance in the direction of lasting peace, it was only a limited one—the force of arms remained the last resort and the ultimate arbiter of disputes. As a good case in point, King Frederick William I of Prussia (whose reign started at the time of the Peace of Utrecht) sought "to be alike prepared for War and inclined to Peace," keeping his armies disciplined, constantly trained, and on the ready.[47]

The Plans of Perpetual Peace

The triumphant paradigm of the balance of power was immediately met with healthy criticism. Spurred by disaffection with the endless War of Spanish Succession and its devastation, an alternative school of thought on the European order began to emerge. Instead of aiming to achieve a balance of power, it advocated the creation of a "European Society" or "European Union" of states through a fundamental treaty. The nickname "perpetual peace" was derived from the apotropaic invocation (intended to avert evil) with which peace treaties usually began and that simply meant "lasting peace"—in the same way that the vow of "everlasting love" is commonly used today to ward off death. The debate centered on the best ways to achieve that lofty goal of perpetual peace. In the eighteenth century, several perpetual peace plans were written that sought answers to one central question: How could the great powers establish a European order that would remove the causes of war between them? Indeed, the phrase "plan of perpetual peace" suggested that a state of perpetual war—declared or undeclared—did not need to exist forever. There were so many of these plans written from that time forward that they constituted a literary genre that continued until the mid-twentieth century.[48] And because British diplomats who had brought the balance of power principle to Utrecht had themselves signed their kingdom's commitment to "a Christian and universal peace, and a perpetual and true friendship," British writings on that principle could be considered early specimens of that genre or, at least, close cousins to it.

Three authors achieved the greatest fame in this genre, and they became explicit sources of inspiration for state-sponsored peace plans in later centuries. In contrast to most authors of perpetual peace literature, who agreed on the need to solve interstate conflicts through arbitration rather than war, these three argued for two different solutions: either they advocated (1) a federal model that would establish a superior entity over the states, one endowed with policing powers, or (2) a league of peace based on a humane conception of politics.

The French cleric Charles-Irénée Castel de Saint-Pierre (1658–1743) is one of the first representatives of this literature of perpetual peace and arguably the best known. When the ink was barely dry on the treaties of Utrecht, he published *Projet pour rendre la paix perpétuelle en Europe* (usually translated as *Plan for Perpetual Peace*) in 1713.[49] Saint-Pierre was a member of the Académie Française and, unlike the aforementioned English writers on the balance of power, a resolute partisan of the Moderns against the Ancients.[50] Less known, however, is the fact that he had been perfecting his thesis since at least 1708, while the war was still underway; he had circulated drafts to illustrious correspondents, notably Jean-Baptiste Colbert de Torcy, France's minister of foreign affairs since 1699, for their feedback.[51] Saint-Pierre was pondering whether the allies' lack of "sufficient and durable assurance" that the Bourbon dynasty would allow the conservation of their states and commerce was the root cause of the conflict. This was not, however, a passing issue, but a structural one. "The misfortune of monarchs," he wrote, "is not to be able to achieve true Peace."[52] Saint-Pierre then argued for a change in the generally accepted definition of peace. To him, it was not a state of rest, but rather the flourishing of trade by land and sea; hence, war was a disruption of trade.[53] His insight was that not only unsolved quarrels but also fear and uncertainty—in other words, mutual distrust, particularly with respect to territories—were the true underlying causes of the recent wars in Europe. Fear and uncertainty were also the chief reason for the continuation of conflicts and remained potential causes for more in the future.[54] Hence political peace could only be attained if peace of mind was achieved first, through "sufficient assurances." He strongly doubted, however, that either treaties or the equilibrium of power between France and Austria could ever provide such assurances. Should both prove insufficient, Saint-Pierre observed, "What means do they have to end their differences, and how to put limit to their demands? . . . There are only two of them . . . : either force or the law."[55] Because there was no court of law to arbitrate between the great powers, it was impossible to prevent disputes between monarchs; it was also impossible to end those disagreements without engaging in war. After a war was concluded by a peace treaty, it was again impossible to guarantee the proper execution of the treaty's terms.[56]

To remedy that flaw, Saint-Pierre proposed a different route: pursuing a union of sovereign European states that would provide a legal framework for resolving disputes. As his source of inspiration, Saint-Pierre looked to the ancient Greek federation of cities called *amphyctiones* (Leagues of Neighbors), whose purpose was both "to keep peace among themselves and to safeguard themselves against ambitious neighbors."[57] He cited recent models of European confederations—first and foremost, the "German union" (Holy Roman Empire), the Swiss cantons, and the Seven Provinces of the Netherlands. Saint-Pierre also drew from the famous scheme known as the *Grand Dessein d'Henri IV,* attributed to the Duc de Sully's memoirs to the French king, published in two parts in 1638 and 1662.[58] Using the precedent of this illustrious monarch, grandfather of the current king Louis XIV, Saint-Pierre argued that the principles proven to work on a smaller scale could also be applied on a European scale. In support, he quoted Hardouin de Péréfixe de Beaumont, who was Louis XIV's preceptor and whose seventeenth-century biography of Henry IV contained favorable comments on the idea of a confederation of sovereign states.[59] Saint-Pierre modestly claimed that his own contribution to this "system" was to outline the means to "form this union, to make it bigger, more extensive and perfectly indissoluble, and thus to make peace wholly inalterable."[60]

In addition to the two tutelary figures of Sully and Péréfixe, William Penn, who lived in the British colony of Pennsylvania in America, may also have had an unacknowledged influence on Saint-Pierre. Penn, whose *Essay towards the Present and Future Peace of Europe* was first published in 1693, was a member of the Society of Friends (the Quakers). Inspired by their ideals of nonviolence, Penn proposed the constitution of "*The Soveraign or Imperial*

Diet, Parliament or State of Europe; before which Soveraign Assembly should be brought all Differences depending between one Soveraign and another, that cannot be made up by private Embassies."[61] This diet would have a number of representatives from each European state according to its importance and population, although the will of each state would eventually be represented by one man's vote. There are remarkable similarities between Penn's and Saint-Pierre's texts, including their general ideas, the method used to answer objections, the list of benefits, and the reference to Henry IV's grand design.[62]

Although scholars long considered these similarities to be mere coincidence, more recent research suggests that Penn's work was translated into French shortly after its publication. Indeed, Saint-Pierre might have derived the idea of *projet* (often translated as "plan") from Penn's conception of a "design."[63] At the time, borrowing ideas without acknowledging the source was commonplace. Furthermore, discretion about this influence may even have been a sensible precaution, given that Penn was an English subject and France was then at war with Britain. If Saint-Pierre indeed drew from Penn's essay, then posterity should credit the Quakers as an original source of inspiration for the European tradition of perpetual peace. In any case, Saint-Pierre was accurate in assessing his own contribution to the evolution of the debate on perpetual peace: his work was far more extensive and detailed than that of Penn.

Saint-Pierre's innovation derives from the acuity of what can be called his "geostrategic view of Europe." His objection to the doctrine of the balance of power (which he also called a "system of war") was based on two key premises:

1. "Any peace underwritten under those conditions is merely an armed truce between powers in a situation of near-equality, exhausted and weary, leading to almost continual wars."

2. In particular, "the balance of the two great powers of the time (the Houses of France and Austria) will fail to maintain that peace."[64]

The most radical aspects of his argument were the rejection of war as the standard procedure used by sovereign states to solve their disputes and then its replacement by a legal mechanism. In any case, he argued, the only alternative to war would be hegemonic peace, imposed by a universal monarch, which was impossible to achieve in Europe *because* of the balance of power. No monarch would willingly accept the bid of another for absolute supremacy, and this state of affairs would inevitably lead to war; he cited the general outcry that followed the reunion of the two crowns of France and Spain as ample evidence.[65] The fundamental point is that the balance of Europe was the prerequisite, the context, and motivation for Saint-Pierre's plan of perpetual peace. Without it, the only canonical solution to Europe's problem with war and peace would be a continental empire under a benevolent Augustus.

Saint-Pierre remained, however, a subject of the king of France. His work was constrained by the dominant mindset of European patrimonial societies, for which landed property was the epitome of wealth and power; it followed naturally that territories were the main source of contention and envy between monarchs.[66] Should we also see there, directly or indirectly, the Christian admonition from the fourth chapter of the Epistle of James about lust as the primal motivation for violence, which had inspired the Quakers and William Penn? Conversely, Saint-Pierre believed that if the European states established a status quo ante, confirming every monarch in his possessions "with sufficient guarantee," the source of most conflicts would be removed.

The solution that would neither involve the balance of power nor a universal monarch—which he variously called the European Society (*Société européenne*), European Union (*Union européenne*), European Body (*Corps européen*), or even Great Alliance (*Grande alliance*)—would be a free association of sovereign states with a mechanism to adjudicate their disputes. War would still be part of this system but used only as a last resort as a police action against offending states. This league would need to be based on an irrevocable treaty that set the rights and duties of each state and would be put under the patronage of an arbitration court that would settle disputes. In the event that a recalcitrant state refused to obey its rulings, a common army would make it see reason. Saint-Pierre gave the name *system of peace* to this arrangement, in which disputes would be resolved judicially. He contrasted it to the balance of power established by the Peace of Utrecht that could settle disputes only by war, which he thus called a *system of war*.

In simple terms, Saint-Pierre sought to establish a republic of European states, complete with laws, judges, and an enforcement arm.[67]

A key question for Saint-Pierre was determining the membership and territorial extension of that continental alliance—which meant, in practice, demarcating the eastern borders of Europe. After the Treaty of Utrecht, Saint-Pierre variously counted eighteen or twenty-four sovereignties (states or confederations of states) worthy of participating in the European Society; some were monarchical like France; others were republican like the Netherlands or Switzerland.[68] He argued originally that Muscovy (Russia) and the Ottoman Empire should be members so as to ensure the stability of the whole, which shows that his vision of Europe was purely geopolitical, not based on religious or social parameters. However, he finally decided to give those two states the status of associates only, so as not to alienate his readers.[69] The Latin Christian conception of the European Society, which he had initially tried to set aside, had reimposed itself.

Although the perpetual peace literature is remarkably extensive and, as mentioned, continued until the middle of the twentieth century, the work of Saint-Pierre towers above all others for two simple reasons: it was the most widely circulated in his time and was the one that was quoted—to the exclusion of almost any other—during the eighteenth and early nineteenth centuries. The very concept of perpetual peace is attached to his name. In the dialogue between theory and practice, a not particularly well-written text was far more relevant and influential than other well-argued and eloquent efforts that remained in relative obscurity.

As could be expected, Saint-Pierre's plan drew skeptical attacks as soon as it was published. The German philosopher and mathematical genius Gottfried Wilhelm Leibniz saw great hope for the Continent in the *Plan*, but pointed out a key flaw in a letter to Saint-Pierre: "Men are only lacking the will to deliver themselves from an infinity of evils." Yet Leibniz had a remarkable insight: "But to bring wars to an end, another Henry IV, together with some great princes of his time, would have to welcome your great project. The problem is that it is difficult to get great princes to listen to it."[70]

Saint-Pierre had already provided an answer to this objection, which was a half-nod to the idea (from Hobbes and others) of channeling human passions through law. Perhaps the princes could be persuaded by his repeated appeals to the project's personal *advantages*—increasing commerce and population, securing their borders and their own personal safety, and the like—to contribute to the general interest of Europe. In other words, he hoped to turn the collective egoisms of princes into an instrument of public good. It was a clever strategy, but as can readily be seen, the incentives were not nearly powerful enough to counterbalance entrenched habits.

Looking back, did Saint-Pierre deserve Leibniz's criticism? It would be easy to dismiss Saint-Pierre's plan because of a lack of formal clarity, which is particularly evident to today's readers and was often noted by commentators, particularly its disordered lengthiness, full of many repetitions and variations. Yet this repetitiveness may have been intentional—a strategic attempt to convince princes to support the plan by repeatedly emphasizing its advantages and appealing to their selfish interests. Moreover, his writings were the result of thorough groundwork, not merely a few days' musing. Saint-Pierre went into great detail, refining and expanding his reflections over several years; these changes reflected the results of the survey polls he conducted to find the largest number of possible objections.[71] His work, despite its weaknesses, qualifies as groundbreaking. It is possible that synthesizing this mass of information on a new theoretical subject was beyond his resources. That task was left to later authors.

To make an informed judgment on the significance of Saint-Pierre's work requires determining the accuracy of his diagnosis in relation to historical developments after the Treaty of Utrecht. Later events show that his two premises were largely correct. The first one, that the conditions of Utrecht would lead to a state of perpetual conflict between equal powers in Europe, was prescient. Ambitious monarchies had carved out vast territories in Europe since the end of the Middle Ages at the expense of their neighbors, most of which were cities and small- to middle-sized states. As long as there were so many lesser entities, there would be an ongoing process of "territorial consolidation" to the benefit of the larger predatory states. Because the hunting ground was limited, however, it was inevitable that the great powers would eventually fight one another over the smaller prey. At the same time, the larger states had grown to the point that they were themselves beyond the reach of other apex predators. After the Peace of Utrecht, it was no longer possible for a European great power to pursue a pan-continental empire or to annihilate one of its competitors through war (as Spain had hoped to do with England or France in the sixteenth century). At this point, the great powers could only hope to snatch some territory or commercial advantages from one another.[72] Saint-Pierre convincingly made the point that a European system based on the balance of power was not a guarantee of peace; on the contrary, it made war necessary as a corrective agent, to reestablish the equilibrium when needed. It was thus the essence of what Saint-Pierre called "a system of war."

Indeed, Saint-Pierre's prediction that war would erupt again at the first opportunity was almost immediately fulfilled. Philip V of Spain was unhappy with his lot, particularly the loss of the Italian territories and his exclusion from French succession (Louis XIV had died in 1715). Spurred by his Italian wife Elisabeth Farnese, he sought to reacquire both. This time, Great Britain, the Holy Roman Empire (Austria), the Dutch Republic, and even France—now under a regency—all banded together to make him see reason, in what was called the War of the Quadruple Alliance (1718–1720). This alliance, which made short work of Spain, proved that the other signatories of the Peace of Utrecht had found enough common interest to engage in a European multilateral police operation against a rogue state. This was not only a remarkable achievement of the Spirit of Utrecht but it also made a point in favor of Saint-Pierre's idea of a stable grand alliance.

This concord, however, was short-lived, because France and Great Britain were still at odds about unresolved colonial affairs. The Three Years' War in America (1722–1725), fought between the British and a Native American confederacy backed by France, was clearly a repercussion of the Congress of Utrecht. At the conclusion of the war, no Native American representatives were invited to discuss the ownership of lands being transferred from France to Britain.[73]

Concerning the second premise of Saint-Pierre, the titanic struggle between the Valois/Bourbons of France and the two branches of the house of Habsburg (the Austrian and Spanish) had been an exceptionally important factor in European history from the sixteenth century onward. This competition significantly influenced all the major wars in Flanders, Germany, and Italy, even when it did not directly cause them. In practice, there were three other important rivalries among European powers: a Russo-Austro-Prussian triangle for the domination of central Europe (especially to the detriment of the declining Polish-Lithuanian state), an Ottoman-Austro-Russian triangle for the domination of southeastern Europe, and the overseas Anglo-French competition for colonial empires. Nevertheless, large European wars could only be fought between two coalitions; because France and Austria were the main hereditary enemies, the other powers orbited around that stable axis. They chose sides according to their interests of the moment and their dynastic loyalties. In particular, the Bourbon kingdom of Spain would remain aligned with France for the next several decades; conversely the United Kingdom played a role as what we would call today a "free electron."

In 1733, the War of Polish Succession broke out after Augustus II, a German prince who was also the Elector of Saxony, attempted to make Poland a hereditary instead of elective monarchy by placing his son Augustus III on the throne. When a Polish-born prince, Stanislas I Leszczyński, tried to restore a politically independent regime, Austria, Prussia, and Russia put aside their differences to oust him.[74] Unsurprisingly, this competition set off yet another European war between two alliances, when France and Spain came to the support of Stanislas. The 1738 Treaty of Vienna finally settled these issues: Augustus III maintained his throne, while Stanislas I acquired the Duchy of Lorraine, recently conquered by France, as compensation (it was to be passed to the Bourbon kingdom of France on his death). This treaty was also an opportunity to reshuffle the patrimonial cards for Italy, notably designating the kingdoms of Naples and Sicily for the youngest son of the Bourbon king of Spain, Charles. The war left Poland politically weakened and economically devastated.

There were even more succession feuds in store for Europe. In 1740, a significant swing occurred in the balance of power. Once again, the crisis started because of a succession issue: Charles VI of Habsburg, head of the Holy Roman Empire, had died without a male heir. He left a daughter, Maria Theresa, whose title was contested on the grounds that she was a woman. Frederick II of Prussia promptly invaded Silesia, a strip of land that is today part of western Poland. Not two years after the Treaty of Vienna, Europe was thus split again into two military alliances. France unsurprisingly allied with Prussia against Austria, while Great Britain dutifully supported the sovereignty of the underdog Poland in honor of the balance of power. Fighting even broke out in North America, and naval battles took place in the Mediterranean and the Indian Ocean. At least the balance of power was a safeguard against too drastic changes: the conflict ended in a general military stalemate of the same sort as ended the War of Spanish Succession. The Treaties of Aix-la-Chappelle (or Aachen, 1748) and Nice (1748–1749) concluded, in the words of the first, with a compromise:

I.   There shall be a Christian, Universal and Perpetual Peace, as well by Sea as Land, and a sincere and lasting Friendship between the Eight Powers abovementioned, etc. . . .

II. There shall be a general Oblivion of whatever may have been done or committed during the War, now ended. And all Persons . . . shall be maintain'd or re-established in the Possession of all the Effects, Dignities, Ecclesiastical Benefices, Honours, Revenues, which they enjoy'd, or ought to have enjoy'd, at the Commencement of the War.[75]

These clauses were a return to the status quo ante bellum, while restating the full validity of earlier agreements tracing back to Westphalia in 1648—including the Treaty of Utrecht in 1713. Maria Theresa was confirmed in her throne, and Austria's only concession was relinquishing control of Silesia to Prussia.

The clauses of the Peace of Aix-la-Chapelle were not particularly groundbreaking, but the treaty was a change in form—it was the first European peace treaty signed as a multilateral document. All previous ones, including the Treaty of Utrecht, had been bilateral agreements.[76] There was, in that innovation, more than meets the eye. A bilateral treaty relied entirely on the simultaneous goodwill of two signatories; all it took for the agreement to evaporate was one party's decision to repudiate it. By contrast, a treaty signed by several powers transcended the individual participants, because it established a de facto community of states that subscribed to a catalog of clauses. Each state was now vouching both as a party and a witness to the good faith of the others. Thanks to the Treaty of Aix-la-Chapelle, the balance of military power slowly started evolving toward a balance of diplomacy. Furthermore, as one legal historian recently noted, "The standardization of certain legal technicalities of peace-making, such as the rules of amnesty, restitution and the release of prisoners of war, had reached such a level that general references to these standard practices sufficed, making detailed regulations for each party unnecessary."[77]

A particular element of Saint-Pierre's second premise—the feud between the Bourbon and Habsburg dynasties—however, had limited validity (this was perhaps excusable, because it was so specific). Another eight years and the great powers were at war again, but the unthinkable happened: Austria and France joined forces against other powers. For once, the cause was not a succession dispute, but rather the rising star of Prussia under Frederick II. Maria Theresa of Austria, mulling revenge against her northern neighbor for the loss of Silesia, made an alliance with Russia. All the while, King Louis XV of France had been using a private diplomatic corps, le Secret du Roi, without even informing his own foreign ministers, to advance his dynastic interests in Europe, notably with regard to Poland. An Anglo-Prussian Alliance in 1756 unexpectedly tipped the balance of power; it seems that, in that instance, British diplomacy overcompensated and created the very imbalance it was meant to avoid. In yet another twist of history called the "Diplomatic Revolution," the two incumbent great powers of continental Europe were forced to take a cue from the British: turning their backs on centuries of feuding, the Houses of Bourbon and Habsburg struck an alliance against Prussia and Britain, in what came to be known as the Seven Years' War (1756–1763).[78]

King Frederick II of Prussia, true to character, made a preemptive attack by invading Saxony. The conflict soon expanded across most of Europe, from eastern France to Poland and from Sweden to Sicily. It also had implications for the English and French colonial empires, spilling over to the Americas and India. The multilateral Treaty of Paris, signed on February 10, 1763, by Britain, France, and Spain, ended the conflict by promising (once again) a "Christian, universal and perpetual peace" between the monarchs while restating the full validity of earlier agreements. The terms were, however, an unmitigated disaster for France, which lost its Canadian and Indian colonies to Britain and the rest of its North American possessions to

Spain, keeping only five port cities in India. Spain in turn ceded Florida to Britain. In Europe, however, the treaty was mostly a return to the status quo ante bellum: the war had merely consolidated existing diplomatic practices.[79]

Considering this string of wars in just fifty years, describing the balance of power as an effective way of establishing lasting peace would seem to be a stretch. Despite the ever-renewed promises of "perpetual peace" and "eternal amity," the balance of power repeatedly kept failing to solve a fundamental flaw of patrimonial states: contentious successions. Although the political system initiated by the Peace of Utrecht forbade the merging of France, Spain, and the Italian kingdoms into a universal monarchy, it consistently failed to prevent the infighting of competing dynasties for more power in Europe—and their clashes from wreaking havoc on populations and economies. The system of the balance of power proved its efficacy as a tool for preventing universal monarchy, but it alone was not conducive to peace.

The feudal system of linking political power and family estates, which allowed the rise of such large territorial formations as amassed by the houses of Bourbon and Habsburg, was now showing its age. The Peace of Utrecht did install the idea that successions should not take place if they altered the balance of power in Europe. In the absence of any mechanism to prevent succession disputes, the only solution was a change in the system of military alliances that would restore the balance, and this gave Britain a de facto role as a shifting counterweight. Nevertheless, the great powers, on several occasions, were unable to resolve conflicts other than resorting to war. Furthermore, putting the responsibility on Britain alone to hold the balance of Europe was a tall order: practically speaking, it could not forever assume the burden of intervening in every major conflict. The 1756 rapprochement between the houses of Habsburg and Bourbon was a sign of the age of dynastic feuds drawing to a close; then, in 1770, the two states consolidated their alliance with a marriage between the young Louis XVI and Maria Antonia (who came down in history as Marie Antoinette). Considering that Maria Theresa had thirteen surviving children, of whom five were boys, there was, in any case, very little risk that the Bourbons of France would acquire any rights to the succession of Austria.

Thus, Saint-Pierre's diagnosis that the balance of power was not a "system of peace" was essentially correct, because the European states of the eighteenth century, which were split into opposed military alliances, were forced to live with war with their neighbors always in their sight and to keep armies at the ready. The balance of power certainly demonstrated not only its ability to end wars and thus to restore peace but also its inherent inability to prevent new wars from breaking out. The major flaw in Saint-Pierre's design was the lack, at the time, of any incentive for the monarchs to adopt it. Despite his catalog of advantages and refutations of objections, his attempt to appeal to their self-interest proved unsuccessful. This left a chasm between the turbulent "order" of Europe and Saint-Pierre's envisioned system of peace. After Saint-Pierre, the debate broadly split between cynics, who held that creating a free association of sovereign states was an unreasonable goal (and thus unworthy of attention), and "irenicists," who were still looking for ways of achieving that goal. Standing between these two positions were those who did not believe in Saint-Pierre's design but equally reviled war as an instrument of foreign policy. In sum, even though the reception of Saint-Pierre's *Plan* was initially lukewarm, the publication of his essay constitutes a defining moment for modern political thought in Europe.

The French Antiwar Spirit of the Enlightenment

As the eighteenth century progressed, the question of establishing peace—and creating a new modus vivendi in Europe based on dialogue—became part of the general debate on an underlying philosophical question: What are the rights and duties of the individual in relation to society? Thus the literature of peace plans indirectly contributed to the most disruptive aspects of the Enlightenment—its reflection on the ideal form of domestic government and critique of patrimonial monarchy. However, not all representatives of that school of thought subscribed to Saint-Pierre's plan of perpetual peace. The perfect place for a debate on peace and war was, unsurprisingly, France.

France was nominally a Catholic kingdom, but Protestantism survived there, despite censorship and persecution (especially after the Sun King, Louis XIV, drove tens of thousands of French subjects to Switzerland, the German lands, England, and the Netherlands by revoking the edict of toleration known as the Edict of Nantes, issued by his grandfather Henry IV). Religious dogmatism, however, did more harm than good to his regime. Among the elites, it fostered a spirit of steadfast mutiny against state narrow-mindedness that would give the French Enlightenment a distinctly subversive flavor. The death of Louis XIV in 1715 brought to an end this intellectual agitation, which had a tendency to turn into vindictiveness.

Following in the footsteps of Saint-Pierre, authors of the French Enlightenment devoted much attention to peace and the causes of war. In his 1734 *Reflections on Universal Monarchy in Europe,* Montesquieu wrote, "It was not wars that had made the greatest changes in Europe over the last centuries, but marriages, successions, treaties and edicts."[80] He regretted the inordinate number of professional troops maintained at any time in Europe: "we call Peace this state of effort of all against all."[81] As the War of Polish Succession raged, Montesquieu saw the balance of power rather like an anarchy of disorganized efforts. In *The Spirit of the Laws* (1748), he considered the form of the state and its possible relation to peace and war. These reflections stemmed from his analysis of who owned the state in the sense of who held sovereignty; in a traditional monarchy, "the prince is the source of every power, political and civil," whereas in a republic that sovereignty had to be shared among a subset of the people.[82] The Latin derivation of the word "republic" (*res publica,* "the public thing") could be seen in Montesquieu's definition, as well as in the English term "commonwealth."

Montesquieu did not openly take sides but could not help manifesting impatience toward wars of conquest in Europe. He argued that war negatively affected commerce, not only echoing but also amplifying the arguments of Saint-Pierre and his contemporaries: "The natural effect of trade is that it leads to peace. Two nations negotiating together make each other reciprocally dependent; if one has interest in buying, one has interest in selling; and all unions are founded on mutual needs."[83] This importance of commerce to peacemaking was an interesting notion: Did the bonds of trade indeed "polish and soften barbaric mores," uniting European nations in a community of interest? It was, at this stage, an anthropological observation, not yet the foundation of a foreign policy or of doctrines of mutual coexistence, but in any case, it was a remarkable insight. Colonial trade was also tightly linked to government foreign policy and, as such, also contributed to the establishment of the balance of power. Trade disputes were interwoven into colonial conflicts (in the wake of the Treaty of Utrecht, France signed two bilateral treaties of commerce and navigation with Britain and the Netherlands, and Britain signed a treaty with Spain).[84] Furthermore, inhabitants of other continents certainly could have raised legitimate objections about the "peaceful nature" of European colonial commerce, especially the morally questionable triangular trade with the Americas, which relied on the enslavement of West African populations.[85]

Few publications better represent the progressive shift in the position of French philosophers against war than Diderot's and d'Alembert's *Encyclopédie* (published between 1751 and 1772), a massive, multivolume compendium of contemporary knowledge in which a substantial amount of seditious material was positioned in odd places so as to escape the attention of official censors. The entry on peace was a brilliant example. Designed to appear deceptively inoffensive, it offered a corrosive theory capable of dissolving the traditional order. Rather than defining peace in the traditional way as opposition to war, this entry is remarkable as one of the first attempts in European literature to define political peace as a principle in itself, with war seen as a corruption of that principle:

> Peace is the tranquility enjoyed by a political society; either inside, through the good order that exists among its members; or outside, through the understanding in which it lives with other peoples.[86]

The entry then proceeded to analyze human nature from a "medical" perspective, resulting in a scathing condemnation of war. It is unfortunate that many of the puns no longer register due to the evolution of medical terminology. Here is my attempt to restore the full meaning of that sensational piece into modern English:

> [Thomas] Hobbes asserted that men are incessantly in a state of war of all against all; the belief of that bilious philosopher is as poorly justified as if he had said that the state of pain and disease is natural to man. In the same way as physical bodies, political bodies

(*corps politiques*) are subject to violent and painful pathologies (*révolutions*); even though these infirmities are necessary consequences of human frailty, they cannot be called a natural state. War is the product of the sickness (*dépravation*) of humanity: it is a convulsive and violent disease of the body politic. The latter is healthy (i.e., in its natural state) only when it is enjoying *peace;* it is peace that gives stamina to empires, keeps order among the citizens, confers to laws the force that they need, encourages the increase of population as well as agriculture and trade. In one word, it gives to peoples the happiness that is the purpose of every society.

War, by contrast, depopulates states and imposes disorder. Laws are forced to remain silent in front of the unruliness that it brings; it makes the freedom and property of the citizen uncertain; it interrupts trade and causes its neglect; land becomes uncultivated and abandoned. The most brilliant victories can never repay a nation for the loss of the multitude of its members sacrificed in war; its very victories inflict on its profound wounds that only *peace* can heal.[87]

The author of this piece, the man of letters Étienne Noël Damilaville, who took the sensible precaution of not signing this vitriolic piece, went one decisive step further than traditional arguments for the benefits of peace versus war for European society. He shifted from the mechanical metaphor typical of views on the balance of power to an organic one. The *Encyclopédie* entry degraded war to a morbid condition, a blight on societies; by contrast, it framed peace as a principle of health, fortitude, and power, as well as a cure for a pathology. Although this might sound today as a militant manifesto of pacifism *avant la lettre* (the word "pacifism" would only appear in the middle of the following century), such a reading would miss a key point: this was a frontal attack on the values of the traditional European social order, in which the highest echelon was the nobility, a warrior caste for whom war had been both its *raison d'être* (to protect society) and the foundation of a code of chivalry. Under that traditional value system, the nobility's possession of land was understood to be a reward for their services over the generations. Implicitly, the *Encyclopédie* accused the nobility not only of neglecting the welfare of society but also of actively harming it through their lust to expand patrimonial possessions, which were thus undeserved. Here the diagnosis of war went deeper:

> If reason governed men, if it had its deserved power over the heads of nations, we would not see them indulging inconsiderately in the passions of war; they would not show this doggedness that is characteristic of wild beasts.[88]

The organic metaphor of war as "a disease of the body politic" introduced an element of life and compassion into a subject—foreign relations—that had long been treated in a detached way, as a mechanical subject. It echoed the early words of Saint-Pierre himself: "While pondering on the cruelties, murders, acts of violence, conflagrations, and other ravages caused by War . . . , I started to examine whether war was a disease without any remedy whatsoever, and whether it was utterly impossible to make Peace lasting."[89] In 1740, in a letter to the chief minister of Louis XV, Saint-Pierre had written, "I am only the apothecary of Europe; you are its doctor. Is it not up to the doctor to prescribe the medicine?"[90] Human beings were no longer considered as inert masses that could be acquired and sold, so as to even out the balance of power; they became living and breathing persons who constituted societies and, as such, were entitled to respect for their lives and possessions. The *Encyclopédie* went even further: war was no longer the disease itself, but was the symptom of something deeper. The nobility had become a pathogenic organ, responsible for the ill health and decay of the whole body politic.

This entry on peace also bears a noticeable resemblance to views expressed by the Swiss jurist Emer de Vattel that war was generally an act against nature. Born in the principality of Neuchâtel at a time when it was under Prussian control, Vattel wrote in French, the language of contemporary diplomacy; he is still considered a chief eighteenth-century reference on the law of nations, as Grotius had been in the seventeenth century. Vattel's *The Law of Nations, or Principles of Natural Law* (1758) is an important work recognized for establishing the Law of Nations (what would later be called international law) as a subject in its own right, distinct both from state law and from natural law, yet harmoniously articulated between the two. More remarkable than the originality of the material, however, were Vattel's clarity and the exhaustiveness of his doctrine on the practicalities of war and peace: alliances, neutrality, treaties, commerce in time of war, prisoners, ambassadors, embassies, and so on. Vattel had fully absorbed the English view of foreign policy; he was aware of the construction of the European order around two opposing alliances (Austria and France), with the constant shifting of other powers to support the weaker of the two at any time so as to keep the system in equilibrium. He also approved of the role of England, which wisely had no intention to conquer the Continent—and claimed that it had "the glory of holding the political balance."[91] Vattel's views were founded on German and Dutch thinking about law, enriched by the compassionate considerations of the Enlightenment era. His vision of war was restrictive, justified by strict necessity and limited by morality, as he put it, "The right of making war belongs to nations only as a remedy against injustice: it is the offspring of unhappy necessity."[92] In a way, his claim was reassuring, because it offered a higher principle of enforcement than brute force of arms: Mother Nature herself would punish the offenders, by inflicting unhappiness and misery on them.

In fact, in the *Law of Nations,* Vattel wrote his own tirade against war, which suggests that he might have been an inspiration for the *Encyclopédie* entry on peace:

> Hobbes dared to write that war is the natural state of man. But if—
> as reason would have it—we understand as the natural state of man
> that to which he is destined and called by nature, we should rather
> say that peace is his natural state. Because it behooves a reasonable
> being to end differences by means of reason; it is the peculiarity of
> beasts to solve them by force. . . . Thus, Natural Law obliges [men]
> anyway to seek and cultivate peace.[93]

In a similar vein, he condemned the "breakers of public peace, these scourges of the Earth who, consumed by wild ambition, or spurred by a haughty and ferocious character, take up arms without justice or reason, make nothing of the rest of men and the blood of their subjects,"[94] and cause great damage to commerce, population and finance. Vattel also raised a key principle about the relationship of peace treaties to the domestic law of most kingdoms: the alienation of land was to be subject to the approval of representative bodies belonging to the nation that gave up the land. The main exception to this rule had been France, whose Estates General (the highest assembly of the kingdom) had not been convened for a long time, and in which tacit consent of the nation had been considered implicit in the king's decisions.[95] In other words, the traditional order of Europe had long prescribed that "patrimonial states" should be mitigated by popular representation. This was a valid point both in theory and in practice, which resurfaced later during the French Revolution.

Rousseau's Social Contract for Europe

Saint-Pierre's plan might never have found its important place in European political thought if Jean-Jacques Rousseau had not thought it useful, in 1761, to publish his *Abstract of Monsieur the Abbé de Saint-Pierre's "Plan for Perpetual Peace."* In this essay, Rousseau distilled and improved the work of his predecessor, making it more convincing. His *Abstract* was a profoundly edited text that remained partly truthful to the spirit, but not the letter, of the original *Plan*.[96] And the time was ripe for such a reworking of Saint-Pierre's plan—the Seven Years' War had already been raging for five years.

Jean-Jacques Rousseau was born a citizen of the Republic of Geneva, which made him a natural republican. He therefore agreed with Saint-Pierre's rejection of both universal monarchy and the balance of power.[97] Where Rousseau strongly diverged from his predecessor, however, was in his introduction of a new parallel between legal relations among citizens and those among states. Whereas Saint-Pierre only sought to establish a "higher power" with supra-state prerogatives for the common good, Rousseau provided a reflection on the compact among citizens, which he would put forward in a more elaborate form in *The Social Contract* of 1762.[98] The European states, by adhering to a scaled-up conception for sovereigns of that Rousseauean social contract, would bring together the preexisting civil society of European states into a political entity.[99] He reinterpreted the advantages of perpetual peace proposed by Abbé de Saint-Pierre in that light.

Comparing states to private citizens was a powerful metaphor that Saint-Pierre had also used in his concept of the European Society of States.

Rousseau went further by building, from the bottom up, a comprehensive theory of political order. Each individual would associate with other individuals to form a political body, and each political body would associate with other similar bodies to form a new, larger one. This construction was the complete opposite of the concept of Catholic Christendom of the Middle Ages, whereby the temporal power of Christ was said to extend from the top down—first to the monarchs, then to their vassals, and finally down to their subjects.[100] It thus clearly reflects the impact of his birthplace, Calvinist Geneva, where he was influenced by Protestant thinkers such as Grotius and Hobbes. Rousseau also participated in the political debates of the Enlightenment. He not only professed that the republican form was the most adequate structure for this European federation (which stood to reason) but he also clearly implied that kings derived their legitimacy from their people, not from succession rights. The best way to convey this momentous philosophical shift is to use an expression that Rousseau himself did not use but would soon be used with great success: there should no longer be a *king of France* (who personally owned the land and could bequeath or sell it) but a *king of the French* (a caretaker delegated by his own people).

The social contract was therefore a fundamental amendment to Saint-Pierre's plan. Europe would not merely be governed by a contract between monarchs, but would be a "society of the peoples of Europe" that owed much to Christianity, whose "Clergy and Empire wove the social link."[101] Rousseau wrote, "Thus all Powers of Europe are connected one with another by a sort of system that unites them by a common religion, a common law of nations, by mores, by literature, by commerce, and by a sort of equilibrium that is the effect of all this; and which, although no one is thinking of maintaining it, is not as easy to break as many would think."[102] Yet he complained that the shared features of civilization that brought the denizens of the Continent together were also actively separating them: "their divisions are disastrous to the degree that their relations are more intimate; and their frequent disputes are almost as cruel as civil wars."[103] The simile was strong—by describing European wars as almost like *civil* wars, he was emphasizing the link that unified European society.[104]

In the course of the argument in his *Abstract*, Rousseau made a show of support for Saint-Pierre's plan. He revealed, however, his true beliefs in

Judgment on Perpetual Peace, written in 1756 but only published posthumously in 1782. In that work, he reiterated what others had already exposed as the chief flaw of Saint-Pierre's plan—its inability to answer this question: Why would patrimonial monarchs—on whose goodwill the plan's success depended—forfeit part of their personal sovereign prerogatives to submit themselves to a higher tribunal, especially because they were ruled by passions and jealousies, yearning to "command in order to get richer and to get richer in order to command"?[105] All in all, Saint-Pierre's plan appeared to Rousseau as a "madness of reason." No amount of rational argument would entice princes to do what was best for the general interest. This assumption reinforced Rousseau's belief that, if republican governments could be instituted in all European countries, popular wisdom would bring peace, because ordinary people would not desire war.[106] The discourse about peace was obviously becoming an argument for a profound reform of Europe's "inner nature of rationality, its education and its code of honor."[107] Rousseau, just like the English diplomats before him at the Congress of Utrecht, was very aware that, if one wanted to achieve lasting peace in Europe, one should first curb the patrimonial monarchies.

Rousseau seriously doubted, however, that circumstances would break the princes from belief in their own entitlement, as well as from their habit of waging war. He rejected categorically the idea that a new Henry IV could emerge in reaction to a risk of universal monarchy in Europe. He even doubted that the Good King himself had been entirely disinterested and, in any case, that there would have been any benefit from such an upheaval. Yet Rousseau reckoned that if such a system of peace could indeed be established, it would succeed because its usefulness and force would limit the risks of a secession or a revolt succeeding.[108] A laudable construction, nearly impossible to establish, but indestructible if ever it was achieved—such was Rousseau's judgment of Saint-Pierre's plan.

Yet Rousseau (just like Leibniz earlier) perceived the import of the two triggers that could open the door to an experiment in the direction of a plan of perpetual peace: the endangerment of common liberties and the rise of "a new Henry IV" capable of bringing the states together in an endeavor to defend those liberties. If neither Rousseau nor Leibniz saw these conditions as likely, it was because they lived under the specific political order established in 1713 under the balance of Europe. Based on their experience, it would have been difficult to imagine how this order could ever be overturned. After all, even if it was not necessarily "an *enlightened* age," it was still the "age of *enlightenment*."[109] Even though popular ignorance and social inequalities were considerable liabilities, there was hope that the new course of wisdom Europe had embarked on would prevent a repetition of the worst human catastrophes of the past.

François Marie Arouet, better known as Voltaire, was not as kind to Saint-Pierre's line of thought. In response to Rousseau's *Abstract* of Saint-Pierre's Plan, he immediately published a sarcastic *Rescript* [Reply] *of the Emperor of China*, in which he harshly rebuked Rousseau for including Russia in his plan but forgetting the rest of humankind.[110] Voltaire's question of why Europeans believed they deserved peace and freedom but forgot to extend it to the rest of the world was as profound as it was well founded, because it questioned the morality of colonial wars on other continents. Yet Rousseau's argument for launching the pacification of the world in Europe because of its community of civilization was not worthy of condemnation in itself: it had been merely pragmatic. Voltaire's piece was a squib, and his judgment was obviously clouded by his notorious personal feud with Rousseau; had he known about his rival's *Judgment on Perpetual Peace,* he would perhaps have written differently.

Voltaire's outburst was motivated mainly by his frustration with religious intolerance in Europe, which violated his deep and compassionate view of humankind. In his essay "On Perpetual Peace" (1769), he wrote, "The only perpetual peace that can be ever be established among men is tolerance; the peace imagined by a Frenchman by the name of Saint-Pierre is a pipe dream that will last no longer among princes than among elephants and rhinoceros, or among wolves and dogs. Carnivorous animals will devour each other on the first occasion."[111] The organic (even zoological) metaphor was, once again, used to convey his own emotion of compassion.

For Voltaire, the evil that caused war was not lust for new territories; rather it was religious intolerance. He had already elaborated this view in a *Treatise on Tolerance* (1763), a passionate attack against religious fanaticism, dogmatism, and prejudice, in which he demanded a review of the highly biased trial conducted against Jean Calas, a Protestant businessman from

Toulouse accused of murdering his son (Calas was nevertheless executed on the wheel). Voltaire concluded,

> It does not require great art, or contrived eloquence, to prove that Christians should tolerate each other. I will go further: I tell you that we must look upon all men as our brothers. What! My brother, the Turk? My brother the Chinese? The Jew? The Siamese? Yes, undoubtedly: are we not all children of the same father, and creatures of the same God? . . . This little globe, which is but a point, rotates in space as so many other globes; we are lost in this immensity.[112]

Voltaire, in his vitriolic style, thus slapped the promoters of perpetual peace in the face with sharp questions I can rephrase as follows: Where is this European system of peace of yours supposed to end? and What should be the ideal geographical extension of a peace system? Why not the whole globe, indeed?

After making this decisive argument, Voltaire ended his essay with a prayer to God: "Even though the ravages of war are inevitable, let us not hate each other, let us not tear each other to pieces when in peace, and let us use the instant of our existence to also bless in thousands different languages, from Siam to California, your Kindness that gave us this moment."[113] From the miscarriage of justice against a Protestant in Toulouse, to peace in Europe and in the world, to the peripheral place of ant-like humanity before the broad universe and God, the age of Enlightenment was a time when philosophers found the most universal principles in the most particular cases, and vice versa.

The Capstone: Kant's Essay on Perpetual Peace

As the purpose and art of war changed, the era of the balance of Europe drew to a close. The kingdom of France entered a time of economic and social crisis, which required internal change. To appreciate—and possibly rehabilitate—what the French Revolution of 1789 meant for intellectual history specifically and for the history of peace generally, it is necessary to examine the significance of the word "revolution" in eighteenth-century Europe, because its meaning has been so profoundly altered as to be barely recognizable. Although its literal meaning was (as today) "the return of a heavenly body to its starting point," its political meaning then was "a change happening in public affairs, in the matters of the world."[114] At the time the word had no inherently violent or insurrectionary connotations: witness the precedent of the Glorious Revolution of 1688–1689 in England, when Parliament had disposed of King James II in favor of William of Orange in an unusual but quite orderly process.[115] As if to prove the Enlightenment philosophers right, the spirit of the French Revolution was initially turned toward the harnessing of war. On May 22, 1790, the Constituent Assembly published a "Decree of Peace Declaration to the World," proclaiming that "the French nation renounces to undertake any war in view of achieving conquests, and that it will never use its forces against the liberty of any people."[116]

Unfortunately, this Revolution set deep forces in motion—spurred by rancor, a spirit of retaliation, greed, and fear—to such a point that reform plans were derailed. In a matter of months, the domestic situation in France shifted from euphoria to horror. We need not address the string of circumstances and errors that led to the progressive disaffection of the French with King Louis XVI, save to say that his lack of decisiveness was a key factor. The untimely death of his most steadfast supporter, Honoré Gabriel de Mirabeau, on April 2, 1791—followed by the king's failed attempt to escape from Paris in late June—marked the transition from a peaceful to a warlike revolution. Louis XVI was arrested, and the Republic was proclaimed on September 21. This inconceivable turn of events put France in a state of war with the rest of Europe, both politically and intellectually. While the Terror reigned at home (the king was put on trial and executed on January 21, 1793), the new Republic engaged in a novel type of warfare, in which the nation's survival was always at stake and massive waves of citizens replaced the professional battalions of old. The battles also proved unexpectedly successful, as the French armies took the offensive deep into Flanders, Germany, and Italy. Despite the wanton violence at home, French soldiers were sometimes well received abroad by local populations, perceived as carrying hopes of political reform. On the Continent, the movement of the Enlightenment fractured into two camps, pro and con the French Revolution, that engaged in a quasi-religious war against each other. Just as in the case of the showdown between Protestants and Catholics in the sixteenth and seventeenth centuries, this was a titanic struggle over societal and political conceptions of Europe. Yet it had an even broader scope than the earlier religious confrontations, bringing Russia into the fray.

At the same time as the French marched across Europe, the German philosopher Immanuel Kant wrote his influential treatise, *Toward Perpetual Peace: A Philosophical Sketch* (1795): it belonged to the last wave of eighteenth-century texts on perpetual peace.[117] Born in 1724, just a few years after Rousseau, Kant lived in Königsberg in East Prussia and was known for his moral philosophy. He is also remembered for *What Is Enlightenment?* (1784), which defined that term as man's emancipation from his own state of intellectual minority and the absolute prerogative to think for oneself in all matters, including politics and religion. Certainly, this was one of the most radical statements ever uttered during that period. Now in the twilight of his life, he was in a position to take stock of the abundant literature on perpetual peace and summarize it. However, Kant's own reflection on "peace under freedom" was taking place at a very different time from that of his predecessors—after the French Revolution had successfully challenged the dogma of divine monarchy and already given birth to a republic.[118]

By 1795, however, the crisis had seemed to subside. The "Terrorists" of Paris had been removed from power, and a victorious French Army was occupying the Netherlands. To Kant, there was hope for this messianic revolution, which he was willing to forgive for what was deemed its provisionally necessary violence, as long as it was allowed to establish a rule of law in Europe that had been sorely lacking.[119] His sympathetic feelings were not treasonous: on April 5, 1795, the Treaty of Basel ended the state of war between France and Prussia, which then recognized French control of the west bank of the Rhine. The French republicans had garnered some sympathy in Germany, and Kant had ample reason for musing on whether a new, peaceful European order could emerge out of this "revolution."

Kant's short work *Perpetual Peace* was likely the most accomplished of those written so far on the subject. Rather than presenting a detailed plan like Saint-Pierre's proposal for a European Society, he offered a concise statement of the conditions that should make the aim of perpetual peace possible—which no doubt explains its rather unusual title. It reflected a culmination of philosophical thought about peace during the eighteenth century, summarizing the researches of Saint-Pierre, Leibniz, the *Encyclopédie,* and Rousseau. His text comprised a small number of articles, much like a treaty—as was the norm in the genre of peace plans. Returning blow for blow the arguments of the "practical politician" who looked down on the "political theorist," Kant commanded the respect even of his most skeptical readers.[120]

It is worth noting that, contrary to Saint-Pierre, who had demanded that monarchs sign at once a binding treaty, Kant recommended that states first draw nearer to such a point through "non-action"; that is, states should *abstain* from exerting disruptive efforts. To that end, he proposed six preliminary articles that were *negative prescriptions,* or prohibiting clauses.[121] States would have to refrain from the following:

1. tacitly leaving out of a treaty any matter that might cause future war

2. acquiring land by inheritance, exchange, purchase, or donation

3. keeping standing armies

4. incurring debts for military purposes[122]

5. interfering by force with the constitution or government of another state

6. engaging in discreditable behaviors during war that would make peace impossible[123]

The second clause—against the acquisition of territory by dynastic mechanisms or business transactions—had already been proposed by others, but went much further than the precedent set by the Peace of Utrecht, which stipulated that such methods should be forbidden only if they threatened the balance of power. It is also worth noting that Kant's second clause did not immediately outlaw patrimonial states—notably, Prussia—which could keep the lands they had already acquired. The fifth clause not only clearly outlawed invasions and annexations but also prohibited the imposition of puppet governments and proxy wars.

Kant's prohibiting clauses were an intelligent answer to the flaw in Saint-Pierre's method. Rather than trying to convince patrimonial princes, he listed key preparations that would have to be undertaken before states could even begin to think of coalescing. In another methodological innovation, he distinguished between the ideal and strict formulation of negative prescriptions (*leges strictae*) and recognized that some initial leeway would be needed in applying them (*leges latae*), so as to allow favorable conditions to establish themselves progressively. Notably, Kant did not demand that standing armies be abolished immediately but in due time. This created an explicit articulation between theory and practice. The European powers could work progressively at Kant's program of their own volition—because what, except necessity, could force them to do so?[124]

Could peace really be achieved just by following Kant's maxims? In fact, his preliminary articles only required unilateral decisions from states: they could be implemented even if only one prince (albeit an enlightened one) agreed with them. Yet Kant's preliminary articles did not exclude the possibility of war; they only made it less likely. Their application would only bring humanity to the threshold of peace or, as Kant put it, "the brink of peace." He warned the reader that, because war was in human beings' nature—a belief that echoed Hobbes's view and rejected that of Rousseau and the *Encyclopédie*—an additional positive action had to be taken to prevent it: peace had to be *instituted*.[125] Like his predecessors, Kant believed that achieving peace required the signature of a social contract among states, so they could move away from their "state of nature" (their life in political anarchy) to a civilized "state of society."

There remained, however, the issue raised by Leibniz and Rousseau—patrimonial monarchs would never agree to a collective contract. To address that difficult challenge, Kant posited three additional articles, which he called *definitive*. They, however, should not be understood in the modern meaning of "final" or "unchangeable," but rather in the Latin sense of "that which frames or defines." These three articles were, in Kant's mind, the ones that would truly allow peace to take shape. They covered three types of political relations among human beings: internal to each state (domestic), between the states engaged in a peace league, and between states in the peace league and those states or peoples not yet belonging to the league. He created a three-faceted model, which would come to dominate political thought in the following centuries.

The first, domestic facet was that each participant state would have to be governed by the *rule of law*. Kant believed that only a "republican constitution"—an organization of the state representative of the population and founded on the separation of powers—would be conducive to perpetual peace (according to him, England could be considered "republican").[126] He argued that the citizenry would think twice before committing themselves to wars opposed to their interests. A patrimonial monarch, in contrast, could be lured into war out of greed, because he possessed a country without being truly involved in its labors.[127] It is only at the point of applying this article that he outlawed the patrimonial state of absolute monarchs, which Saint-Pierre still admitted. Obviously, establishing a "republican form" of government would remove the problem of greedy princes refusing to submit to the peaceful inclinations of the citizenry.

The second aspect of the model was the formal act; rejecting the idea of a strong union because European peoples were so different, Kant considered a *confederal alliance* ("federal alliance") the only possible form of organization.[128] Given that the "republics" would represent their peoples by definition, the league of states would become—not by law but in fact—an alliance of peace (*foedus pacificus*) between the peoples. Yet this alliance would guarantee the freedom of the states without making impositions on them. This was a departure from Saint-Pierre's European Society, in which a diet would have imposed the common will on all states and a common army would have enforced decisions. As in earlier models, a court would decide the differences among states. Kant took the idea of a court of arbitration one step further: he rejected not only the role of war in deciding judicial issues but also the legal right of any state or association of states *to* go to war. There would be no monopoly on the use of violence. This radical aspect is noteworthy, because it sharply differentiates Kant's thinking from that of Saint-Pierre and even Rousseau. Several commentators connect Kant's rejection of war to his upbringing in Pietism, a Protestant movement that rejected (not unlike the Quakers) established churches and promoted nonviolence.[129] This possible connection would further confirm the important role of Protestantism in European reflections on peace.

The third facet of the Kantian model was a complete change of attitude toward other states and peoples. As if to answer the blistering criticism that Voltaire had formulated against Rousseau, Kant took pains to frame the relationship between his proposed Alliance of Peace and the rest of the world. Though nothing in the essay itself specifically limited the alliance to Europe, Kant implied that Europe would have to be its starting place. This assumption raised the question of how Europeans should behave toward other peoples. For that purpose, Kant proposed a *cosmopolitan right* ("law of the citizens of the world") to protect individuals outside the signatory states of the alliance.[130] The law would grant rights to human beings even in the absence of a state that could guarantee their citizenship. This notion was both profound and unprecedented. Since Antiquity, the state alone had been the exclusive purveyor of rights; a human being without a state had never been considered as having any rights. This new cosmopolitan law would thus have restricted the right of foreigners (i.e., Europeans) in those lands outside Europe: they would be limited to the right to receive hospitality (i.e., "civilized" treatment). In practice, the cosmopolitan law would have allowed equitable commerce but not colonialism.[131] The purpose of this limitation was evidently to protect non-European peoples against the moral or legal "justifications" that Europeans had always brandished to enslave them. In particular, Kant attacked the notion that "civilized intruders" should consider those lands "without owners, because they counted the inhabitants as nothing"; in other words, he refuted the legal "doctrine of discovery." As justification for this new type of law, Kant introduced a strikingly original view that we would today put under the umbrella of globalization: "The peoples of the earth have thus entered in varying degrees into a universal community, and it has developed to the point where a violation of rights in *one* part of the world is felt *everywhere*."[132] Kant laid out the foundations of *cosmopolitanism,* the view that efforts toward lasting peace should embrace not only Europe but also the peoples of the world at large. This inevitably led to a close questioning of colonial empires.

Perhaps most intriguing, however, is what Kant omitted from these articles of peace. They did not say what should happen just *before* the states were ready to sign the Alliance of Peace. Kant wisely left out, notably, the delicate question of *how* the republican form was to be achieved in each of the future members of the peace alliance. Presumably some kind of revolution would have to occur in each patrimonial state; at the time, when the armies of the French Revolution appeared to be succeeding in Europe, this was within the realm of possibility. Kant's articles also said very little about the functioning of the alliance after it was established. What he wrote were hardly *articles* at all, in the usual sense of clauses of a contract. Drawing on the thinking of Grotius and Hobbes, Kant formulated his articles as political maxims, more natural than legal—and therefore superior to law. His articles therefore had the merit of attracting the reader's attention to the consequences of transgressing them. This may explain the use of "toward" in the title of his essay on perpetual peace: Kant was not offering a plan, but a sketch containing its natural underlying principles.

Kant's alliance of peace was not defined by a list of states or by the European community of civilization. He wrote nothing about which states would be members or what territory it would cover, other than that it would have to operate from a global perspective with regard to other states and peoples. This did not mean, however, that Europe and its civilization completely disappeared from the equation—"our part of the world" appeared beside other continents as a particular case of a theoretical reasoning or rather as the space where the kernel of the alliance of peace was evidently going to form.[133] Because Kant's aim was to reduce the rules for coexistence of states to a minimal list of articles, he removed geographical and cultural constraints from his design. Geography, skin color, religion, language, and myriad other features that seemed so important to Rousseau had no place in these articles for peace, except in the acceptance of inevitable human diversity. As a recent commentator accurately remarked, Kant "does not conceive of the existence of a European people (much less a universal people) as a civil society. Nations are for him *natural* political entities: it is nature . . . that distinguished them in that respect, the one from the others."[134] Presumably, the generalization of this new order beyond Europe would have occurred progressively, by a successive aggregation of states.

The most controversial aspect of Kant's position was what degree of authority his alliance of peace could have had in the absence of military enforcement. He argued that it would have at least a moral force, in the weight of public opinion, based on an inexorable fact:

Men in both their private and their public relationships cannot reject the concept of right or trust themselves openly to establish politics merely on the artifices of prudence;[135] thus they do not refuse obedience to the concept of public law,[136] which is especially manifest in international law; on the contrary, they give all due honor to it, even when they are inventing a hundred pretenses and subterfuges to escape from it in practice, imputing its authority, as the source and union of all laws, to crafty force.[137]

It is important to emphasize that Kant counted on what we would call "peer pressure"—not law—as being the ultimate enforcement agency. His was a universal argument about peace, one that trumped the artificial separation between morality and politics. It was a formula of collective alchemy, a free society of nations that would transcend boundaries between civilizations. Kant created this framework, all without seeking to solve any of the practical issues raised by the map of Europe in his time. With his essay, it is possible to measure the huge distance that political thought about peace had traveled in the eighteenth century—from the propitiatory and plethoric argumentation of Saint-Pierre for a European Union to the self-assurance and formidable conciseness of Kant, with a peace system potentially applicable to the whole world.

Kant's text, published during a lull in the turmoil of the Revolutionary Wars, was well received in Germany, France, and England. It had, however, very little influence on current events. His global conception of humanity and peace was able to interest philosophers and French republicans, but it was too elaborate even for minds that belonged to the "enlightened movement," not to mention the sizable portion of European intellectual elites who had no sympathy for republics. His proposal was a jump into the future, leaving the reflections of the US Constitution and the early French Revolution far behind. To this day, Kant remains a respected and even intimidating figure to the partisans of Machiavelli or *Realpolitik*. His brutally cutting attacks on "prudence" have managed more than once to pierce the armor of the *reason of state,* exposing it for what it so often was: a shroud for intellectual emptiness and a guilty conscience.

Enlightened Reflections on Peace
in Times of War

Kant's thinking proved to have one flaw, which was revealed soon after publication of his sketch on perpetual peace: his belief, built on Rousseau's, that "republics" (representative political systems) would necessarily be more peaceful and less greedy than patrimonial monarchs. In 1795, the same year Kant's essay was published, the French Assembly set a military objective to expand the territory of France to the Pyrenees, the Rhine, and the Alps. The Revolution had inaugurated a new form of war—far less elegant than the "war in lace" of the Ancien Régime—in which ordinary people, much more politicized than in earlier times, eagerly enrolled in patriotic causes, forming large armies where numbers counted more than discipline. The Italian phrase *furia francese* (French recklessness), which dated from the wars of the sixteenth century, came back into vogue. In France itself, conquests were met with cheers, and victorious generals were popular. The French Revolution proved, alas, how assemblies and citizens committed to the "nation" could be just as warlike and thirsty for conquest as patrimonial princes.[138] Europe was realizing that the initially benign Revolution had turned France into a predatory country, intent on war and conquest. The idea that representative governments could be harbingers of peace was increasingly met with scorn; on the contrary, they were seen as the chief cause of trouble. Most of the great minds of Europe who had initially supported the Revolution turned their backs on it. Kant, who died in 1804, was one of the last great philosophers of the Enlightenment to have—albeit briefly—shown sympathy for the Revolution.

Although ideas play a significant role in political and social changes, so do waves of the *longue durée:* the transformation of France and the Revolutionary Wars demolished, within a few years, the status quo established by the Peace of Utrecht. The balance of power, which had evidently failed to keep the peace, had nevertheless proved its validity as a tool for preventing either the Habsburgs or the Bourbons from installing a universal monarchy.[139] By contrast, these philosophical plans of perpetual peace never became reality in the eighteenth century. As a note to Voltaire's skeptical essay on perpetual peace, French philosopher Condorcet wrote in 1784 that "the scheme of a perpetual peace is absurd, not in itself, but in the way it was proposed. There will be no war of ambition or spite when all men will know that there is nothing to be won, even in the happiest wars, except for a small number of generals and ministers."[140] He did pragmatically admit, however, that establishing a European diet (or more specifically a tribunal) might be expedient "to judge different disputes on the restitution of criminals, on the law of commerce, on the principles according which some cases should be decided when the laws of different nations are being decided." This vision contained, in embryo, the rationale of future international courts. He concluded that "it is possible to persuade a prince who has 200,000 soldiers at his disposal that it is not in his interest to defend his rights or pretensions through force; but it would be absurd to ask him to waive his right to do so."[141] How could reason that sought peace ever be stronger than the brutishness of military force? Condorcet summarized, in one sentence, the unresolved riddle left by Enlightenment thinkers for posterity.

In the short term, one thing was certain: European peace was not going to be built through the messianic French Republic that kept warring with its neighbors. The rapid ascent of a young French general, Napoleon Bonaparte, was soon to split Europe once again between Ancients and Moderns. Napoleon and his fellow partisans were the formidable champions of the Roman tradition of hegemonic peace; in front of them stood the defenders of the multilateral Spirit of Utrecht. From this clash of apocalyptic proportions, a new spirit of peace would ultimately emerge.

2

The Spirit of Vienna

A BALANCE OF DIPLOMACY

> That which, in the middle of the last century was considered only as
> the dream of a good man, perpetual peace, became the conception of
> one of the most powerful sovereigns of the continent. The Holy Alliance
> seemed to have every right to this title; it was concluded in the name of
> the holy and eternal laws that establish the nexus of mankind and shape
> its universal society. But diplomacy corrupted this benign inclination
> and turned what should have its been safekeeping virtue into venom.
>
> —ADAM CZARTORYSKI, *ESSAI SUR LA DIPLOMATIE,* 1830

*O*n March 31, 1814, the inhabitants of Paris turned out in large numbers
to watch an unusual show: the mounted Cossacks of the Russian Imperial
Guard passing through the Gate of Saint-Martin on the great thoroughfare
to Flanders, followed by the Prussian cavalry. Never before had the Russian
Army pushed so far west into Europe. Tsar Alexander I, the commander-
in-chief, rode in just ahead of Austrian marshal Karl Phillipp, prince of
Schwarzenberg, on his right and King Frederick III of Prussia on his left.
For the Russian monarch, the privilege of being the first to enter the cap-
ital was a tribute to his army, which had soundly defeated the French *Grande
Armée* three times—in Russia, Germany, and France—and was the largest
and most powerful military force in Europe, probably in the world. When
Alexander passed through the gate, something extraordinary happened: the
Parisians, initially dismayed and silent and then intrigued by his benevolent demeanor, actually expressed cheers of relief.[1] On that day, when the
myth of the powerful French Empire was turned upside down, a bystander

could ask herself a few questions. How could France, the luminary of European civilization "on which the destiny of the world is resting" (according to a popular revolutionary song),[2] cheer a foreign emperor who, not long ago, would not even have been considered European? How could it be that this city, yesterday the capital of Europe, accepted a foreign occupant with such good grace and even treated its commander as a harbinger of peace? And what about the former warlike enthusiasm for Napoleon, who was still making a last desperate stand not far away, in Versailles, with his last sixty thousand men? From a besieged revolutionary state to a continental empire that stretched from the Atlantic Ocean to the Moskva River, and then back to a little pocket of resistance consisting of a few square miles southeast of Paris, French history had indeed come full circle in the course of two decades.

History books on the early nineteenth century, depending on when they are written, are—confusingly—split into two diametrically opposed visions of the post-Napoleonic era. On the one hand, histories of European nation-building written in the late nineteenth century, particularly in France, Germany, Italy, and Spain, depict this moment as a period of regression in the "march of civilization toward progress" and portray "exalted" insurrections later led by national heroes as beacons of hope for the political rights of all citizens.[3] On the other hand, a more appreciative interpretation emerged after World War II, notably spearheaded by Henry Kissinger, in which the allied victory and the subsequent Congress of Vienna marked the diplomatic triumph of the "balance of power" and the foundation of our modern conceptions of world order.[4]

These two interpretations appear to be irreconcilable and for good reason: both are subjective reflections of the ideological necessities of the epochs in which they were elaborated. The first, highly negative, view of the immediate post-Napoleonic order appeared in the context of nation-building in late nineteenth-century Europe, when nation-states sought to displace religious faith as the foundation of political legitimacy and replace it with the new secular mystique of the nation. At a time when "national histories" were forged with great enthusiasm—and often an unabashed lack of objectivity—the post-Napoleonic era was painted in the most unflattering colors under the reductive label of the "Holy Alliance."[5]

The second, more favorable interpretation, was prompted by the start of the Cold War, a moment of deep apprehension in the United States, especially for policy makers educated in the prewar mindset of American isolationism. Balking at the idea that their country had suddenly inherited the ultimate responsibility for "Western civilization," they were thrust into the role of torchbearers of the European diplomatic tradition. In that context, the Realist school of thought, represented by political writers like Hans J. Morgenthau and George F. Kennan, sought inspiration in past European models.[6] Kissinger, in particular, turned to the Congress of Vienna as an intellectual guide in the attempt to organize a new order in Europe after the collapse of its great powers in the wake of World War II.[7] In particular, Austrian chancellor Klemens von Metternich, formerly the *bête noire* of national histories in Europe, was recast as an outstanding role model. These two clashing historical narratives coexisted for several decades: one in the English-language literature of international relations; the other in national histories written in French, German, Italian, and Russian. Looking back, it is easy to see how all these past narratives on the Congress of Vienna were to some degree linked intrinsically to bygone political agendas. Our expanded horizon of experience and our improved knowledge of the post-Napoleonic era—and the specific concerns of our times—prompt us to try to find yet another balance between the two traditional extremes of idolizing and reviling the diplomatic actors of 1814–1815. Looking at them as historical characters instead of mythological statues has another benefit: it actually makes their story more compelling.

This chapter focuses on the "engineering of peace" in this period by viewing the "Vienna Order" as one of several episodes in the long quest for European peace and then distinguishing which of its principles and actions worked and which failed. The allied powers of 1814–1815 sought to achieve two key aims. First, they intended to establish a new peace order out of the apocalyptic adventure of Napoleon or, rather, *against* it, in the hope that no universal monarchy would ever rise again in Europe. Second, the ruling elites wanted to establish a new order against the *canaillocratie,* a term that appeared around 1792 for the tyranny of the *canaille,* or mob—the vile part of the people who behaved like a pack of angry dogs.[8] The phenomenon of the mob explains why the greatest minds of the post-Napoleonic era—

including most French liberals and republicans—felt compelled to identify the Revolution's egalitarian ideology and its "imprudent" extension of political rights to all human beings as the dark source of the evil sweeping over the Continent.

It is important, however, to bear in mind that a constant of post-Napoleonic thought, across the ideological spectrum, was the conviction that the maintenance of peace in Europe relied on keeping political power firmly under the control of restricted circles of social elites. This belief led to definitions of political terms quite different from those today. Authors blamed *democracy* (in a negative sense, as mob rule) for having derailed the Revolution.[9] The excesses of the Terror, in turn, were blamed for spreading warfare outside of France to Europe, opening the way for the accession of Napoleon. After his downfall, liberalism in domestic politics was restricted to opinions or policies favorable to some degree of freedom for the aristocracy and upper bourgeoisie in the exercise of political rights, particularly through parliaments and the press. But except for a few authors, universal suffrage was generally anathema. In European affairs, this approach was embodied, in the heyday of the Congress of Vienna, in the allied powers' policy of giving other states a modicum of voice and leeway to have their own constitutions and laws. On the opposite end of the spectrum was the fringe of reactionary politics represented by anti-constitutionalists and the French *ultras*, who wished to restore absolute monarchy.[10]

Far more influential was the moderate wing of the conservative movement, made up of prudent reformists who did not wish to return to the past but rather to a more orderly state of affairs. In fact, liberals were generally just as attached to order and legality as conservatives. It is, however, true that secret political associations on the left wing of society, such as the Italian Carbonari, were recruiting members of the aristocratic, economic, and intellectual elites to raise funds and stockpile arms for insurrections to oust authoritarian governments or end foreign occupations.[11] Naturally, reactionary propaganda enjoyed portraying all liberals as dangerous mob agitators who sought to reenact the excesses of the French Revolution, just as revolutionists depicted the bulk of conservatives as obtuse reactionaries who wanted to restore the Ancien Régime: both accusations were equally groundless. Yet even those most inclined to insurrection were often profoundly different in spirit from the solidarity of the early French Revolution. If one wanted to sit in judgment on the post-Napoleonic order of Europe for being a "regression," one would also have to condemn most supporters of liberalism for turning their backs on the egalitarian ideals of the French Revolution.

These years saw the birth of the "Spirit of Vienna," the mindset that informed the European order in the years after 1815. Vienna, capital of the Austrian empire, was where representatives from all of Europe convened in September 1814 to redraw the political map of the continent. To best understand the Spirit of Vienna we need to explore the circumstances behind its birth and longevity; its key failures, especially to keep domestic peace; the reasons for its collapse; and, finally, its legacy. It profoundly differed from the Spirit of Utrecht in that the invocation of the balance of power took on a different meaning. As a justification for the military alliance against the threat of Napoleon, it no longer implied that Europe would have to be governed by a system of two opposing military blocs, such as had prevailed during most of the eighteenth century (the "balance of power," a.k.a. the "system of war"). This earlier definition had provided a satisfactory self-regulating mechanism through all the crises and wars of the Utrecht period because no great power was then in a position to overrun the others completely. The balance had provided a legal and practical foundation for maintaining an "acceptable" level of peace on the continent as being the path of least resistance. Unfortunately, the armies of the French Revolution and the Napoleonic Empire had changed all this; they had wrecked the balance of power, making it temporarily unusable. Military balance would be restored only after a long and strenuous effort by a grand alliance of Britain, Russia, Austria, and Prussia.

This Spirit of Vienna was also governed by a growing consensus, by 1814, that the balance of power was a mechanism best left for times of war and that something better was needed for times of peace: a one-bloc system in which periodic parleys would replace military deterrence. One century after the publication of Abbé de Saint-Pierre's *Plan of Perpetual Peace,* ample empirical evidence had accumulated to support his fundamental thesis; namely, that the balance of power, by itself, was an insufficient guarantee of peace. The balance of power principle permanently shifted from being the preferred tool for preventing war and maintaining peace to becoming the last resort against continental hegemony and for a restoration of peace. Indeed, four great powers resolutely turned their backs on this principle to form, for the first time in modern history, a pan-European peace alliance. This required conquering their deeply ingrained distrust of each other. The spirit of this coalition remained aristocratic and hierarchical, as well as Christian, yet it was profoundly different from what had existed before. For the first time in modern history, Europe was under an integrated peace regime that was able to head off the threat of major warfare for a certain time; the concord between the great powers lasted almost four decades until the Crimean War (1853–1856), when Europe returned to a political order that relied on the opposition between military alliances. On the domestic front, however, the record was less positive. The four great powers faced growing public discontent and revolutions, which led them to increasing levels of repression, a phenomenon known as the Reaction. The unsuccessful struggle of liberals to be heard—and the resulting disorders—unlocked a complex chain of events that, within a decade, would profoundly alter the political landscape of Europe. Yet, as we see, the nemesis threatening the European peace alliance would arise from another quarter entirely—the "Eastern Question"; that is, the fate of the Ottoman Empire.

Was the *Pax Napoleonica* Really Peace?

The principle of the balance of power, embedded in the Treaties of Utrecht, was designed to prevent Europe from falling under the power of universal monarchy. Yet it obviously failed to prevent the rise of Napoleon Bonaparte, undoubtedly the most formidable European ruler since Charlemagne. He became far more powerful and effectively controlled more land than had either Charles V of the Holy Roman Empire or Louis XIV of France. Bonaparte acceded to supreme power in France on August 2, 1802, as consul for life. His plans, however, were bigger than for France alone. In December 1804, he proposed a new regime that made him emperor of the Republic, under his first name Napoleon. Presenting himself as a new Charlemagne or Augustus, a providential man who would bring peace and prosperity to France and Europe, he set it as his mission to use military force—war—to impose a new unified continental order, at a time when well-ordered sovereign states numbered in the hundreds.[12] Napoleon's rejection of the Spirit of Utrecht and its commitments to state sovereignty and the balance of power was radical and definitive. He became the most dangerous threat the political order of Europe had known for centuries.

In 1805–1806, Napoleon appeared close to achieving the ideal of the *Pax Romana*.[13] His breathtaking military campaigns crushed Austria and Prussia and led the French Army into both Vienna and Berlin. Napoleon temporarily swung the balance of power in his favor; nothing seemed able to withstand his apparently absolute power and military skill. Success bred success: he was soon routinely able to muster armies of more than one hundred thousand men, five to ten times larger than the average military formations in the War of Spanish Succession.[14]

After finally defeating Russia at the battle of Friedland (1807), Napoleon was able to impose his own order by the Treaties of Tilsit, signed with Russia on July 7, 1807, and with Prussia two days later.[15] The one menace that the Peace of Utrecht had sought to avoid at all costs—a universal monarchy sweeping over Europe—was materializing. Ensuing events were thus perceived as a titanic struggle between a universal monarchy under a French emperor and a loose alliance of independent sovereign states—the former seeking to impose its order over the Continent, the latter strenuously defending their very existence. It was a battle not only of armies for control of a continent but also between two philosophical approaches to the European order: imperial peace versus a multilateral system of powers. The stakes had never been higher.

Nevertheless, an important question bears asking: Once Napoleon had achieved hegemony over Europe, did the territories he controlled actually acquire peace? Could his imperial system have provided a model of coexistence, as some French commentators have asserted as recently as the early 2000s?[16] The *Pax Napoleonica* (if it could be called so) was initially imbued with the liberating ideals of the French Revolution. It came, however, to be perceived by non-French peoples in a very different light—as an authoritarian system that denied state sovereignty.[17] Yet it did produce a semblance of European unity; its economy worked as a broad continental market. This would have been a definite improvement over the previously separate regional markets, save for one problem: it was a war economy, operating in forced autarchy because the century-old trade with colonies across the oceans had been severed. Napoleon also attempted to truncate all continental economic ties with Britain; in fact, that was the very purpose of his system. Yet, this had the opposite effect than intended. Continental port cities suffered heavily, while British ports enjoyed unprecedented expansion as the smuggling of goods became endemic. In continental Europe, textiles, iron, sugar, cotton, pepper, and coffee suffered from drastic price rises.[18] French rule left subject populations with the memory of incessant wars, political repression, economic hardship, and forced military conscription that sent young men to fight in foreign lands. For many German states, particularly Prussia, these impositions created a sense of national humiliation and deep resentment. They responded by eventually rallying against this foreign threat to their freedoms.[19]

Obviously, the notion of Napoleonic *order* should not be confused with that of true *peace,* especially when such an order was imposed on whole nations against their will. For the leaders of the allied powers, it was an apocalyptic experience to be averted at all costs in the future.[20] There was worse: Napoleon inflicted long-term damage on the cause of peace in Europe by seeding anti-French sentiment in the wake of his stunning victories. Taking revenge against France in the wake of the humiliating defeat at the Battle of Jena (1806) became the standard by which the Prussians and many other Germans measured themselves; this did not bode well for the future.[21] For the Spaniards, the French occupation (1807–1814) also became a moment of national awakening. At the same time, both the French occupation and the continuous movement of refugees, armies, and political delegations across the continent confirmed elites in their belief that "Europe" was a geographical space where nations—regardless of their differences—shared a common political fate. European unity and nationalism became the two horses that henceforth pulled the Continent's cart, sometimes in unison, sometimes against each other.

More immediately, the experience of the Napoleonic regime illustrated the frailty of "hegemonic peace." On his path to continental hegemony, Napoleon drew on more than military genius—he included vassal states in his continental system as tools and military reinforcements to acquire more power.[22] Unfortunately for him, this mechanism of forcible integration had only so much elasticity. After the French Empire reached its maximum territorial extent in 1812, a cascade of defections inexorably pulled him back to where he had started. This mechanical effect turned Napoleon's failure in his Russian campaign into the doom of the entire French Empire: it resulted not only in the loss of hundreds of thousands of soldiers—and notably, irreplaceable cavalry—but also, of equal importance, the defection of his allies.[23] The balance of power mercilessly shifted against Napoleon in the gigantic Battle of Leipzig, symbolically called the "Battle of the Nations" (October 16–19, 1813). With a total of more than 600,000 men on the battlefield, it was the largest confrontation in recorded European history up to that time. Napoleon's defeat there was the point at which the hemorrhage of defections became unstoppable. From then on, the French Empire would always fight with disadvantages in numbers of soldiers, horses, and equipment.

The stronger Napoleon's empire had moved forward in the acquisition of new territories, the more swiftly it was then pulled back to its own borders; in this "principle of the maximum elasticity of empires" may lie a mechanical explanation for the contraction of every European power that had attempted so far to unify the continent through force. Although historians have found it easy to pinpoint the mistakes that Napoleon committed in war, his greatest errors perhaps were committed in times of peace or, more precisely, when he repeatedly failed to establish a general state of peace. Even during the negotiations with the Allied powers early in 1814, whenever his military fortunes improved, his demands grew correspondingly to unacceptable proportions.[24] Napoleon engaged in ever more wars, because his preferred way of solving disputes was to enforce his will on other states instead of through generating agreement. This established a form of European order that did not truly qualify as peace. It was, indeed, as if he had violated the natural law of the continent: the so-called *Pax Napoleonica* collapsed in a matter of months because it had not been able to establish among its member states those feelings of mutual benevolence, loyalty, and belonging—in a word, solidarity—necessary for the long-term cohesion of a European political formation. Napoleon's greatest character flaw was what the ancient Greeks called *hubris*—an impatient arrogance that causes a violent revolt against nature and always leads to doom.

Before Vienna: Laying the Foundations

Paradoxically, a preliminary step to formulating a grand alliance that can achieve a long-lasting peace may be a resolution to pursue a military counteroffensive together and to the bitter end, thereby preventing one power from agreeing to a separate peace. On March 9, 1814, in the little town of Chaumont on the road to Paris, the allies signed a treaty of military alliance "to draw closer the ties which unite them for the vigorous prosecution of a war undertaken for the salutary purpose of putting an end to the miseries of Europe, of securing its future repose, by re-establishing a just balance of power."[25] The Chaumont Treaty played a fundamental role in the establishment of long-term peace by precluding any allied power from concluding a separate armistice with Napoleon; its rationale was that the current imbalance of power in favor of the allies rested only on their solid union. The collective resolution to eradicate the threat once and for all explains why, on the last day of March 1814, the allied commanders symbolically entered Paris as a single detachment. A pan-European coalition had thus demonstrated its effectiveness in restoring the balance of power against a ruler like Napoleon—preparing the way to decisive victory in the war.

In crafting the terms of peace the allied powers consciously identified the political regime of Napoleonic France—not the French population—as the root cause of the wars that had spread over the continent. Though Tsar Alexander I did not display any personal animosity to the French people, he categorically refused to leave the deposed French emperor in power or to allow his throne to be given to his son. Napoleon at least maintained his eminent status. In the Treaty of Fontainebleau (April 11, 1814), he signed what amounted to a personal treaty of peace with Russia, Prussia, and Austria, according to which they agreed to the following: he honorifically retained his imperial title and was allowed to retire to the island of Elba, not far from his native island of Corsica, which was constituted as a sovereign territory complete with a miniature court. It is remarkable that Napoleon's emotional abdication of April 11 acknowledged this conclusion: "The allied powers having proclaimed that Emperor Napoleon was the sole obstacle to the re-establishment of the peace of Europe, the Emperor Napoleon, faithful to his oath, declares, that he renounces for himself and his heirs the thrones of France and Italy and that there is no personal sacrifice, not even that of life, which he is not ready to make to the interest of France."[26] On April 20, he bade farewell to his remaining loyal circle of Imperial Guards, who cheered him in tears, despite the overwhelming wave of defections that had struck the French Empire in the previous year and a half. Nevertheless, the adventure did not end too badly for France after all because the allies allowed Napoleon to bow out of the European scene honorably for the sake of future peace. In contrast, Britain refused to be a co-signatory of the Fontainebleau Treaty, claiming that it was unwise to make such concessions to "Boney," the usurper.

In the "Convention for the Suspension of Hostilities with France" of April 23, 1814, the four allied powers declared their intention to "end the miseries of Europe, to found its tranquility on a just repartition of forces between the states comprising it; wishing to give France a government whose principles give the necessary guarantees for maintaining peace and proof of its desire to place itself in friendly relations."[27] By paying homage to the balance of military power and the creation of friendly relations, they took pains to make the outcome of the war look more like an armistice than the capitulation it really was. Thanks in particular to the lobbying of Tsar Alexander I, the victorious powers then took a safe path by recognizing the reinstatement of the Bourbon family allegedly by the French themselves, in the name of the principle of the legitimacy of kings: on April 6, even before Napoleon's abdication, the French Senate had called Louis XVIII, brother of the deceased Louis XVI, to the throne.[28] The succession of the old Bourbon king was not, however, a self-evident choice. Equally valid candidates could have been two former generals in Napoleon's army who had been promoted to royalty: Jean-Baptiste Bernadotte, crown prince of the kingdom of Sweden, and Joachim Murat, king of Naples.

The next step in the diplomatic process was having the king sign a peace settlement. France being the defeated power, it was up to the allies to draft it. On May 30, 1814, the great powers signed, with King Louis, the Treaty of Paris, which had three primary effects: it ended the state of war; recognized the restoration of monarchy in France, albeit in a constitutional form; and set the limits of the post-Napoleonic French kingdom. The Treaty of Paris was, in fact, four nearly identical bilateral treaties, each signed by one of the great powers with France.[29] The thirty-odd articles, already outlined by the earlier convention of April 23, were remarkably magnanimous toward the defeated power. France's borders were maintained as of January 1, 1792; in other words, the allies acknowledged French territorial acquisitions between 1789 and the declaration of war on April 20, 1792, particularly in the northeast (territories that are today in the west of Belgium and in the German Saar region) and in Savoy. During the negotiations, the restored king of France and his minister Talleyrand acted as if they were the victims of Napoleon just as much as the rest of Europe, and the allied leaders had no desire to weaken the king's authority. In the weeks following the Treaty of Paris, Portugal, Sweden, and Spain were invited to countersign it. Together with the four great powers and France, they formed the "Committee of Eight" that was to play a central role at the Congress of Vienna.[30]

The fact that this agreement was followed by the Congress of Vienna is often accepted without comment, but it is worth asking, in terms of the methodology of peace, why there had to be a congress at all. Why did the four great powers not settle all the matters between them in Paris in 1814, as they did in Utrecht in 1713, through the legal instrument of the Treaty of Paris? Why pursue discussions elsewhere and why, of all cities, in Vienna? And why enlarge the circle of participants? From a technical standpoint, the answer lies in Article 32 of the Treaty of Paris: "All the powers engaged on either side in the present war shall, within the space of two months, send plenipotentiaries to Vienna, for the purpose of regulating, in general congress, the arrangements which are to complete the provisions of the present treaty."[31]

To make sense of that general statement, one word is essential: to *complete* the Treaty of Paris. This treaty settlement was limited to the territories west of the Rhine River for a simple reason: the delegates of the four victorious powers recognized that the political map of Europe had been changed to such a degree during the Napoleonic wars that redrawing the borders would be an enormous undertaking fraught with complications and would be far beyond the capabilities of the few in attendance. In addition, legitimizing the government of the restored French monarchy and settling its future borders were matters of some urgency. The Congress of Vienna was not going to be a *peace* congress because the state of war with France had already ended in Paris: its broader purpose was to make a general territorial and political settlement of the rest of the Continent. In fact, the great powers had yet to reach an agreement on a number of points, notably the partition of Poland and the fate of Saxony. The territorial situation in Germany was a complication unto itself, because the rapid redrawing of the map of that region by Napoleon had resulted in the disappearance of many small states and their absorption into others.[32] Facing this maze of issues in Germany and Poland, the great powers took a sensible course of action—they wrote down what they had already agreed on and adjourned the discussions to a more convenient time and place. The new postwar order would be more stable and more durable if they could obtain the consensus of as many states as possible, instead of appearing to impose a hasty and arbitrary *diktat* on the rest of Europe.

Forging Peace

In the fall of 1814, foreign delegations inaugurated the "Spirit of Vienna" by peacefully invading the Austrian capital. The experience replicated that of Utrecht a century earlier, but on a much larger scale. The huge influx of guests posed the usual logistical issues of organizing lodging, food, and transportation for everyone; setting up meeting venues; and catering to rules of precedence and the egos of the participants. A distinctive feature of the Spirit of Vienna, however, was its inclusion in the settlement process of a large number of minor actors from all across Europe. There were two concurrent motivations for this decision: the complication of territorial issues had grown exponentially after the Napoleonic wars, and the more states there were to underwrite the final settlement, the more durable it was likely to be. The choice of venue among the capitals of the four great powers was not very contentious: London and St. Petersburg would have been too far away for many delegations, and there was little argument that Austria should have precedence over Prussia for hosting such an event.

FIG. 2.1 Jean-Baptiste Isabey, *Leading Statesmen at the Congress of Vienna,* 1815.
A. Dagli Orti / De Agostini Picture Library / Bridgeman Images.

Because what seemed like an infinity of details regarding borders and agreements had to be addressed, it was more expedient to delegate their resolution to the diplomats of those governments that had the most immediate interest in them. The Congress of Vienna gave birth to a novel diplomatic configuration. It has been described as four concentric "circles": at the center, the four Allied powers; then the eight signatories of the Treaty of Paris (the four allies plus Spain, Sweden, Portugal, and France), which could be invited to the most important meetings; a third circle of states such as Savoy, Netherlands, Bavaria, Württemberg, and Switzerland, which were invited to those meetings that concerned them; and finally a slew of minor states, which came to present their petitions and possibly to obtain advantages. In addition to these four diplomatic circles, there were many others in attendance, including former Imperial Knights, representatives of the Jewish communities of Germany, bankers, and other special interest groups. It was necessary to collect sufficient information from these various participants about the maze of secondary issues that converged into the main ones and to find a solution for each.[33]

There were many complicated matters to resolve. One notable example was creating a commission for the navigation of the Rhine River between France and the Netherlands, which comprised the German riparian states, but was later expanded to neighboring ones.[34] Here we can see the birth of "technical commissions"—at least fifteen working groups were responsible for different issues at the Congress—which were distinct from and complementary to the work of the diplomats.[35] The public officers and scientists on the various commissions were the direct ancestors of the international officers that are a fixed feature of our modern world. This busy, interconnected system of working groups—comprising individuals from diverse countries and backgrounds, many of whom had never met before—became a beehive of activity. The multilateral nature of the effort to redraft a detailed and realistic map of Europe and its institutions could not help but bring durability and stability to the territorial settlement of the continent. Most importantly, it reinforced the perception of Europe as an actual political community, with a configuration no longer the result of historical accidents, but instead the deliberate product of an engineering process both systematic and meticulous.

In this successful process of political engineering, Germany served as an obvious blueprint: the Holy Roman Empire had died, but not its vast *acquis* (to use a modern word) of multilateral diplomacy. The Congress of Vienna was the moment when the German tradition of political coexistence—of which the Peace of Westphalia (1648) remained the crowning achievement—finally crystallized and merged with the broader, European political system. The allied powers of 1814–1815 brought, for their part, *three* major innovations to the methodology of lasting peace: they separated the peace settlement with France from the general settlement of Europe; they consulted a wide array of states to achieve a consensus; and they tasked a new corps of specialists and knowledgeable public officers with providing realistic solutions to technical problems. On the surface, however, the Congress remained an aristocratic occasion. Around the delegations gravitated large retinues of attendants and servants who had to be kept entertained or to keep others entertained. This resulted in an inordinate number of social functions; indeed, the popularity of waltzing gave the Congress of Vienna its distinct flavor as the "dancing congress." Yet the festivities of Vienna served a key political purpose: they contributed to the negotiation process, by providing access points to the delegations. They also colored the Spirit of Vienna with an exuberant veneer of insouciance that masked the seriousness of the matters at hand and served as an emotional outlet for the exhausted negotiators. It gave individuals without formal roles the impression that they were being included and listened to, making them more willing to agree and cooperate.[36]

All these apparent contradictions between the tight control exerted by the four great powers and the large number of participants are resolved if one considers that the outer circles and the technical commissions, so characteristic of the Spirit of Vienna, were created for consultative and delegated purposes. The inner circle delegated the task of finding solutions to lower-level problems (in traditional top-down fashion), so as to free their own attention and energies for the most important matters—notably, the fate of Poland and Saxony. Two documents demonstrate how the inner circle discreetly retained the final word in each and every case. The first was a secret article of the Treaty of Chaumont that defined five principles for the reorganization of Europe: Germany was to be reinstated as a confederation of independent sovereign states; the Swiss Confederation was to be restored to independence under the guarantee of the great powers; Italy was to be divided between Austria and a series of sovereign states; Spain's monarchy was to be restored; and the Netherlands was to be restored as an independent state under the Prince of Orange.[37] The second document, the "Separate and Secret Articles" between the four victorious powers signed with the Treaty of Paris in May 1814, stipulated that Austria should receive the lands of the former republic of Venice and the kingdom of Piedmont-Sardinia should receive those of Genoa. Just like that, the two ancient maritime republics of Italy, prestigious states of the past, became spoils of war. These secret clauses were obviously meant to exclude other states from the discussion and present these decisions as a fait accompli. Given that Austria was to receive a sizable part of northern Italy, the official language stating that "Italy, beyond the limits of the countries which are to revert to Austria, shall be composed of sovereign states" was misleading.[38]

The Spirit of Vienna, despite its rituals of inclusion, thus had its share of hard-headed "reasons of state": the four great powers managed—behind the scenes—to maintain firm control over the proceedings. Nevertheless, there still was some room for maneuvering by minor states, and more importantly, a countersigning by all the actors involved in the process was peacefully obtained. Ultimately, the Vienna Order was forged by multiple states, some large and some small. It created an articulated system that represented most of Europe—a fact perceived as a welcome change from the unipolarity of the Napoleonic Empire. The greater the number of signatories that subscribed to the final peace settlement, the more stable it would become. Indeed, it might be said, in modern terms, that this show of inclusion was a masterful use of public relations toward political ends.[39]

The relations within the innermost circle are central to this history of peace because they provide a clue to a fundamental question: How could four great powers that had divergent and often competing interests successfully carry out such a massive undertaking? The hierarchy among the four has been variously interpreted. For instance, a number of historians argue that the years 1814–1815 were defined by the tetrarchy of Austria, Britain, Prussia, and Russia (here listed in protocol order).[40] Other scholars, notably Paul Schroeder, have suggested that the Vienna Order was de facto managed by two "hegemonic" powers, Britain and Russia.[41] The reality was a combination of these perspectives. It is legitimate to distinguish between two subcategories in this inner circle. Russia was indeed the undisputed military power on the European continent at this point in time and could field more than a half-million soldiers, as many as the other great powers combined,[42] whereas Britain remained the master of the seas. The two other powers, Austria and Prussia, were at a disadvantage because they had been overrun in 1805–1806. Austria maintained seniority to Prussia by virtue of its larger size and for historical reasons, evidenced by its new status as an empire while Prussia remained a kingdom. Nevertheless, all four allied great powers sat at the same diplomatic table and generally tried to put up a common front before the lesser powers, and each had a seat by right on every major commission and committee.

Even though the peace process was conducted in a hierarchical fashion and its inclusiveness was dictated by expediency and a show of appearances, it was remarkably effective. It also represented a methodological advance over the earlier Spirit of Utrecht, in which only the great powers had a say—not to mention over the Pax Napoleonica, where political decisions had essentially been the expression of one man's will. From this achievement we might draw the maxim, "The more willing parties at a peace settlement, the more solid it will be."

The Great Powers from Allies in War to Partners in Peace

Certainly, establishing an inner circle of the four victorious great powers would not by itself have guaranteed an atmosphere of trust, much less a lasting peace. In fact, they initially lacked a basis for mutual confidence. Despite protestations of friendship, their solidarity was shattered, even before the Congress of Vienna started, by two contentious topics: Poland and Saxony. The crisis involving these two states began simmering during the final campaign against Napoleon. It broke out in earnest in the late fall and early winter of 1814–1815, when Tsar Alexander I announced his desire to extend the control he already held over most of Poland to include the Grand Duchy of Posen (Poznań) and Galicia (today in Poland and Western Ukraine)—territories that belonged to Prussia and Austria, respectively, after the partitions of Poland in the late eighteenth century until they were wrested by Napoleon to create the short-lived Duchy of Warsaw.[43] Alexander won the support of the king of Prussia for his expansionary moves by offering him Saxony, a former ally of Napoleon that included the cities of Dresden and Leipzig, as compensation for Prussia's losses to the east.

The two other powers, Britain and Austria, were alarmed by this scheme, which would have extended Russian borders farther west in Europe and turned Prussia into a Russian ally and a bulwark state. Austria was particularly worried; its foreign minister, Prince Klemens von Metternich, was nervous about the prospect of Russia controlling the heights of Galicia, which would have opened up a main invasion route to Vienna.[44] Austria and Britain went so far as to sign a secret military alliance with the recently defeated France on January 3, 1815, directed against Russia and Prussia. Very quickly, the coalition of the four thus split into two blocs, inching close to a *casus belli*. The four started playing again the eighteenth century's game of the balance of power. But at this juncture, something quite remarkable happened. Both sides, realizing where they were heading, changed course and found an amicable solution: skillful diplomatic maneuvering miraculously helped avoid the worst. In particular, Tsar Alexander deliberately defused the crisis by putting the interests of the entente between the allies above his own territorial ambitions.[45] A major crisis was averted, and reconciliation between the great powers was achieved. The renewed solidarity that emerged from this incident not only overcame prejudices among the four great powers but also inaugurated a major paradigm shift in the European history of peace.

The successful resolution of the Polish-Saxon crisis crystallized a new principle that became a characteristic feature of the Order of Vienna: the inner circle of great powers represented themselves as the legitimate custodians of peace by virtue of the fact that they wielded the power of making war and yet had voluntarily renounced exerting it against each other. Just as the balance of (military) power defined the Utrecht settlement, this one would henceforth be based on a balance of diplomacy.[46] Achieving a reconciliation among the four partners on the Polish-Saxon crisis required them to overcome their natural fears and prejudices and establish a new system of reciprocal guarantees. The creation of a unitary bloc, a novelty in modern European history, was a major achievement that allowed them to wield more power and influence together than they would have been capable of if they remained divided.

Drafting a peace settlement had its own complications. It naturally raised the question of whether it would be accepted by the defeated party, and in 1815, an "oversight" nearly sank the settlement process. Starting the period known as the Hundred Days, Napoleon evaded the surveillance of the British and fled from Elba, landing on March 1, 1815, on the southeastern coast of France. His rapid advance toward Paris—which led to the rallying of the French Army, the collapse of the monarchical government, and his triumphal entry on March 20—was yet another demonstration of the strength of his resolute character and the inability of the restored Bourbons to control the country. Fortunately, advances in communications—optical telegraphs were by then widely used to transmit important dispatches—allowed the shocking news to reach the allies in Vienna in a matter of days.[47]

The great powers signed a declaration on March 13, even before Bonaparte reached Paris. Expressing cold fury, it was the first manifestation of a change from the lenient treatment given to France in 1814. "Bonaparte" (no longer Napoleon) was demoted from an honorably defeated head of state to a bandit:

> In thus violating the convention which established him on the Island of Elba, Bonaparte destroyed the only legal title for his existence. By reappearing in France with projects of disorder and destruction, he has cut himself off from the protection of the law and has shown to the face of the world that there can be neither peace nor truce with him. Accordingly, the Powers declare that Napoleon Bonaparte is excluded from civil and social relations, and, as an Enemy and Disturber of the tranquility of the World, that he has incurred public vengeance. At the same time, being firmly resolved to preserve intact the Treaty of Paris of May 30, 1814 . . . they declare that they will employ all their resources and will unite all their efforts in order that the General Peace, the object of the desires of Europe and the constant aim of their labors, may not be again disturbed, and in order to secure themselves from all attempts which may threaten to plunge the world once more into the disorders and misfortunes of revolutions.[48]

Thus, the allied powers, much disappointed with the Bourbons, instantly regretted their earlier leniency toward defeated France, especially their decision not to station an allied occupation force there—had they taken this elementary precaution, Napoleon's return could not have occurred. Fortunately, they were still remarkably well prepared for the new threat because they had had the wisdom to maintain a legal instrument in force: the twenty-year defensive alliance against France, instituted at the Treaty of Chaumont "to maintain the equilibrium of Europe, to secure the repose and independence of its States, and to prevent the invasions which during so many years have desolated the World."[49] Even more importantly, they had not yet disbanded their armies. Indeed, on March 25, 1815, Britain, Austria, Prussia and Russia signed a treaty, later nicknamed the "Seventh Coalition," in which they appealed to this clause in the Treaty of Chaumont.

The Hundred Days crisis did not even manage to interrupt the proceedings of the congress; on the contrary, commissions and committees worked double time to finish as quickly as possible. On June 9, while a force of the French Army was marching toward Brussels, the Final Act of the Congress of Vienna was signed. This document, centered on territorial settlements and other technical issues, boldly extended the timid innovation of the Treaty of Aix-la-Chapelle (1748): all signatories signed onto the *same* document.[50] Such a multilateral treaty existed in a legal sphere pertaining not to a state, but to a "Republic of States," in the parlance of the eighteenth century. It was more like a social contract, the weight of which relied on many signatories; in other words, on "peer pressure." Although this Republic of States was still shapeless, without even the embryo of a formal government, it had nevertheless been born conceptually. The Final Act, quaintly peppered with the red wax seals of all states of the continent great and small, can be considered the founding act of an informal community of states.

Needless to say, this document was not underwritten as an act of the unreserved free will of all the signatories. It observed the diktat of the initial agreements between the four great powers: Poland remained partitioned, with the largest part going to Russia (Articles 1–14), Genoa and Venice never reappeared on the map (Articles 85–94), and Saxony (Articles 49–50) was partly dismembered to the profit of Prussia. The commissions and committees had gone to great lengths to hear all interested parties and to reach (within the constraints set by the allied powers) acceptable agreements, leaving lesser states with little desire to rebel. Considerable attention was given to facilitating navigation of the great international rivers (Articles 108–117), particularly the Rhine and the Danube. All in all, most participants considered the final outcome advantageous and progressive.

On June 18, battle was joined at Waterloo in what is now Belgium—and ended in disaster for Napoleon. It has been argued that the arrival of the Prussians and bad weather were responsible for his defeat on that day, and that may well be true. Nevertheless, the Vienna Order—and not bad luck—had already sealed the fate of the military campaign. The disproportion between the two forces was far greater than it had been in 1814. The puny French Army was no longer facing a disparate alliance of states whose armies may have been affected by the upheavals of the French Revolution and the Napoleonic Empire, but the juggernaut of the Europe of the Final Act of Vienna. No signatory state was willing to trade the certainties of this new collective contract for the unrest that Napoleon would have brought back in his wake. As Victor Hugo later wrote in his poem *Expiation,* "Waterloo . . . on one side was Europe, on the other was France . . . Victory defected, and fate was tired."[51] Even if Napoleon had won the battle that day, his last legion would sooner or later have been overwhelmed by the even larger armies already on the march. In the event, there was not even a "French campaign" as in the previous year: Napoleon's flimsy regime collapsed like a house of cards, and the allied powers entered Paris in early July 1815 for the second time.

Contrary to popular belief, the Hundred Days had no noticeable influence on the broad settlement agreements of Europe because the Final Act of Vienna had already been signed as the French Army was marching toward Brussels. But Napoleon's campaign did lead to a number of changes in the settlement of France, all for the worse from the French perspective. The second Treaty of Paris, signed on November 20, 1815, confiscated France's annexed territories of 1792, pulling its border back from the Rhine; many fortresses were put back in the hands of bulwark states. Although the new settlement still paid lip service to the French king, its tone was different from that of the 1814 treaty. According to Article V, the Allied powers now needed "an arrangement suitable to ensure them fair compensation for the past and solid warranties for the future."[52] Confidence and goodwill had been partly forfeited: for its collective guilt, France would have to pay the considerable sum of seven hundred million francs for the damage caused by Napoleon's "criminal enterprise" (*attentat*) against Europe, and it would henceforth be occupied for three to five years.[53] Otherwise the new treaty maintained intact all the clauses of the Treaty of Paris of 1814 and of the Final Act of the Congress of Vienna.

Napoleon's impossible adventure nearly marked the end of France as a sovereign state. Some of the allies, installed in Paris again, seriously contemplated partitioning the country among the victorious powers, as had been done with Poland and Saxony. The intervention of Tsar Alexander I

Europe after the Congress of Vienna, 1814–1815

— German Confederation

✶ Local revolts

0   200 km
0   200 miles

St Petersburg

Stockholm

Baltic Sea

R U S S I A

RUSSIAN EMPIRE

KINGDOM
OF POLAND
Warsaw

REPUBLIC OF
CRACOW

Cracow

Galicia

Silesia

Budapest

AUSTRIAN EMPIRE

Hungary

Transylvania

Moldavia

Crimea

Wallachia

Black Sea

Serbia

O T T O M A N   E M P I R E

Montenegro

Adriatic Sea

Salonica

Constantinople

TWO SICILIES

Greece

Aegean
Sea

Ionian Islands
to Great Britain 1815

Cyprus

MALTA

Crete

through his Foreign Ministry and his connections with the French foreign minister Talleyrand averted the worst for France. They were supported by Wellington and Viscount Castlereagh, the British foreign secretary.[54] Most importantly, the episode of the Hundred Days had far-reaching consequences for the practices of peacemaking after war that can be felt to this day. Never again, in the history of European great wars, would the victorious side fail to take the precaution of stationing garrisons in the defeated country or strategic territories. This practice henceforth became an unquestionable practice of multilateral diplomacy, now so self-evident that there is no need to explain its origin.

The British were appalled at how Louis XVIII had abandoned the helm of the state at the first storm, and Castlereagh declined to support his return as a war aim in front of Parliament. Nonetheless, Castlereagh and Wellington remained among the Bourbon king's staunchest advocates.[55] Napoleon, reduced to an outcast and stripped of his former rights and titles, was dispatched to Saint Helena, an island in the southern Atlantic so forlorn its name would likely not have been known otherwise. Joachim Murat, former French general and brother-in-law of Napoleon, who had imprudently abandoned his kingdom of Naples to follow his previous master, lost his title and his life.[56] The Bourbon family was then reinstated in southern Italy in addition to France and Spain. Napoleon's rebellion indirectly reinforced the bonds of solidarity among the four great powers that had been originally established during the 1813–1814 campaign, preserved by the peaceful resolution of the Polish-Saxon crisis and sealed by the Final Act of Vienna.

The Holy Alliance: A Blend of European Mystique and Peace Plans

The Allied powers, having surmounted two severe tests, now strove to achieve even tighter ties than before to secure the peace, as demonstrated by the conclusion of two new treaties. The first had a convoluted history. On September 26, 1815, Emperor Francis I of Austria and King Frederick William III of Prussia signed, somewhat reluctantly, a "Holy Alliance" proposed by Tsar Alexander I. This "alliance" had no application from a diplomatic perspective and was never mentioned in later treaties. Nevertheless, it was important from an intellectual perspective for what it revealed about the "mystical" trend of ideas on Europe typical of the nineteenth century and of the intricate relationship between religion and politics on the continent. The Holy Alliance was Tsar Alexander's moment in European history.

At first glance, this short document, consisting of a preamble and three articles with religious overtones, seems merely to be a declaration of intentions. After an appeal to the "Most Holy and Indivisible Trinity," the preamble requested "Divine Providence," commanding the monarchs to follow "the Holy Religion of our Savior" and to accept the "necessity of submitting the reciprocal relations of the Powers, upon [its] sublime truths." The first article declared that the three monarchs were "united by the bonds of a true and indissoluble fraternity" as "fellow countrymen" called on to protect "Religion, Peace, and Justice." The second article required that the sovereigns and their subjects do each other "reciprocal service," manifest "mutual affection" with "the most tender solicitude," and consider themselves members of the "one family" of Austria, Prussia, and Russia and, more broadly, of "the Christian world" united in the goal of "enjoying Peace." The third article invited all states that wished so to join in this treaty, thereby contributing to "the happiness of nations, too long agitated."[57] This religious phrasing, if somewhat surprising today, was not entirely out of place: many constitutions and international treaties, including the Final Act of the Congress of Vienna, opened with an invocation to God or the Holy Trinity. More importantly, the Holy Alliance's metaphoric use of the Christian family gave it a unique layer of meaning, placing the image of a piously united community squarely into the political sphere alongside "compatriots," "fellow countrymen," "nations," and "subjects." In sum, it proposed a peaceful alliance of hereditary kings and their states, freely extendable to all the Christian states of Europe. As with the Vienna Final Act, the Holy Alliance was ratified by most European states, great and small.

There were, however, two notable exceptions to this general unanimity of support—the Holy See and Great Britain—which had entirely different reasons to oppose it.[58] The Holy Alliance was not well received in London. Castlereagh offered the *bon mot* that the Holy Alliance was a "piece of sublime mysticism and nonsense."[59] The British had two good reasons for their skepticism. First, the principle that a monarch should exert his divine right to lead national politics without restraint did not sit well with the English parliamentary system and, more generally, with the efforts that England, and later the United Kingdom, had invested since the late sixteenth century in attempting to limit the hereditary rights of royal dynasties in Europe. Second, a monolithic European political order would not have been consistent with the British policy of the balance of power, which required a modicum of disunity among the continental states. At the time, the British were chiefly preoccupied with returning to a state of peace favorable to their trade, as well as taking all necessary measures against a possible recurrence of the French menace. In Whitehall, there was neither the need nor the desire to interfere further with the political affairs of the Continent. Nevertheless, Castlereagh did recommend that the British prince regent sign the alliance, both to satisfy and restrain the tsar. In the end, however, the objections of the British cabinet were so strong that the prince regent did not sign.[60]

The papacy's reasons for rejecting the Holy Alliance were more profound because they touched on questions of dogma for the Catholic Church and as such were not open to compromise. Before examining these objections in detail, it is necessary to explain briefly why this treaty was so radical as to be subversive from a religious perspective. It is also necessary to dismiss a curious misconception about the origins of this pact, fostered by Metternich himself: that the Holy Alliance had been a "loud-sounding nothing," a politically worthless "moral demonstration," an "overflow of the pietistic feeling of Emperor Alexander," and was nothing more than the naive invention of the female mystic, Baroness Barbara Juliane von Krüdener, who had supposedly dictated the words of the treaty to the tsar.[61] Like so many myths, this had some element of truth. The baroness, who had had a stormy youth and then converted to pietism in 1804 and started preaching, was indeed convinced that the tsar had a messianic duty to liberate Europe from Napoleon.[62] Furthermore, there is documentary evidence that she did establish a close but short-lived friendship with Alexander I. The problem with this circumstantial "evidence" is that it does not fit with the chronology: the baroness had not met Alexander I before June 1815, by which time the plan of the Holy Alliance was already well formed. The only way she could have influenced the draft in its early stages would thus have been through her correspondence with the tsar, maintained through Roxandra Sturdza, a lady-in-waiting for Tsarina Elizabeth.[63] In her letters and memoirs, Sturdza states that Krüdener never had any hand in the tsar's diplomacy because she had no qualifications to do so. No evidence of her involvement, such as early "drafts," has ever been found in any European archive. The reasonable conclusion is that Krüdener's story was apocryphal and that the tsar's friendship with this "muse" remained confined to his private life. Their relationship was, furthermore, a short one, as the tsar quickly distanced himself from the mystical baroness, who died in disgrace in Crimea in 1824.

In contrast to the apocryphal role of Krüdener, there is ample documentary evidence of the actual drafting process of the Holy Alliance, with early versions still available in the archives. They all point to Alexander I as the mind behind it. He wrote the preliminary notes in pencil and then gave them to his Head of Chancery, Count Ioannis Capodistrias, who rephrased them in diplomatic language. In turn, Capodistrias passed the document to a brilliant and cultivated secretary, Alexander Sturdza (none other than the brother of Roxandra). A few years later, Sturdza wrote a document called "Considerations on the Act of Brotherly and Christian Alliance," which contains precise information on the treaty's genesis, meaning, and reception.[64] Sturdza's testimony confirms, on the one hand, what many historians have claimed—the Holy Alliance was pursuing a religious and counter-revolutionary agenda. Napoleon was the heir of the French Revolution, and his fall marked the end of an era of social and political disorder. Referring to the recent victory of the allies following the Hundred Days, Sturdza asserted, "The *principle of subversion* against all religious and social institutions has just been slain a second time."[65] According to him, this period of European unrest originated in the Seven Years' War and included the American Revolution, the French Revolution, and the Napoleonic era. At the same time, the political view of Europe expressed in the Holy Alliance was also a bold break with the Ancien Régime: between the partisans of absolute monarchy (the "ultras," found in Catholic milieus) and those of republicanism, the Christian ecumenism of the Holy Alliance occupied a middle ground. It was conceived as part of the general program of "defensive modernization" of the post-Napoleonic era—in sum, an *aggiornamento* of society needed to terminate revolutionary disorders. As such, it predictably sparked a storm of criticism from both extremes.[66] In the end, according to Sturdza, Tsar Alexander was simply attempting, with the Holy Alliance, to secure a durable peace in Europe through a *Christian political ecumenism* that would bind its rulers together: it was a combustible amalgamation between the tradition of perpetual peace and a novel trend of Christian spirituality. (This form of thought about Europe, almost forgotten today, continued to thrive for several decades and even inspired the authors of the 1848 Revolutions).[67]

Yet Austria's and Prussia's real problem with the tsar's proposal lay elsewhere: they felt his original version of the treaty was too liberal! Emperor Francis I of Austria, after reading it, asked his minister Metternich to revise it.[68] The latter modified the sentence "the subjects of the three contracting parties will remain united by a true fraternity" into "the subjects of the *three monarchs* will remain united."[69] Similarly, the tsar's initial version stated that the three powers were the three *provinces* of a single nation—a notion the Austrian minister amended to read as three *branches* of the same family. Metternich, who recognized the tsar's attempt to pass off political liberalism under the guise of religious rhetoric (both of which he disliked), was quick to correct this enthusiasm. The paternalist idea of the monarchs as "benevolent fathers," found in the language of the Holy Alliance, was also Metternich's brainchild. Still, the tsar's desire to represent Europe as a "Christian nation" made it into the final version of the text.

It appears, from the original version, that Alexander I wanted to form a European nation that was "essentially one" and living in peace, with the various existing states as *provinces*. It is easy to guess the reasoning behind Metternich's amendments. The original wording would have united the peoples of Europe and elevated them to a position over the heads of the sovereigns. This would have placed unprecedented constraints on the monarchy and sounded uncomfortably like a constitution.[70] The original version even stipulated that the military forces of the respective powers be considered as a single army—130 years before the aborted project of the European Defense Community in the early 1950s. Tsar Alexander I thus initially envisioned a sort of "league of nations," united under the authority of the monarchs; what emerged from Metternich's amendments was a moral alliance of kings, without legal effect. Thus, after the tsar forwarded a line of thought that smacked too much of liberal ideals, Metternich, who felt obliged to ride along, applied the ideological brake.[71]

Among the treaty's intellectual precedents, Saint-Pierre's work on perpetual peace was clearly a reference point for Tsar Alexander. Roxandra Sturdza—who had frequent private conversations with the tsar in 1814 and 1815—later wrote in her memoirs that the Holy Alliance was "the realization of the grandiose concept of Henri IV and Charles Irénée Castel, the Abbé de Saint-Pierre."[72] The idea of a single society of European states had been germinating in the tsar's mind for more than a decade. The circulation of enlightened ideas in aristocratic circles under Catherine II and the presence of French émigrés in Saint Petersburg during the Napoleonic era had fostered a vigorous debate in Russia on what an ideal European order should look like. As a case in point, the scholar Vasili Malinovski, who had worked at the Russian Embassy in London in the 1790s, published an essay, *Reflections on Peace and War,* in 1803 that sought to merge the new Western ideas based on reason with traditional faith.[73] Quite logically, Malinovski considered the French Revolution repulsive and parliamentary Britain a desirable partner. In September 1804, the tsar issued "Secret Instructions," finalized by his close adviser Adam Czartoryski, to his minister Nikolay Novosiltsev. They commanded the latter to forge an alliance with Britain and then to create a European "federation" of peaceful states that would be based on the law of nations and equipped with an army.[74] In this way, the tsar hoped, Europe would become immune from revolutions. These instructions referred explicitly to the Abbé de Saint-Pierre, even if they distanced themselves from his ideas.[75] The tsar's 1804 proposal constituted a plan of perpetual peace in the style of the Enlightenment, but with the difference that it was the product of a ruling monarch, not a philosopher. Predictably, the British cabinet declined to accept the proposal as it stood; in the end, the treaty signed between the two states was more of a conventional military alliance.

On December 31, 1814, three days before the signing of the notorious secret alliance among Austria, Britain, and France at Vienna, Alexander I asked Count Nesselrode, his minister of foreign affairs, to address an urgent note to the plenipotentiaries of Austria, Britain, and Prussia:

> Convinced . . . of the immutable principles of the Christian religion shared by all, it is on this single basis of both political and social order that the Sovereigns, acting as brothers toward each other, will purify their State maxims and guarantee the relationships between the peoples that Providence entrusted to them.[76]

The missive, which was forwarded to the other powers, is interesting in what it tells us about the behind-the-scenes reflections of the Russian delegation and of the tsar, in particular—its wording is also strikingly similar to that of the later Holy Alliance. It shows how intent Alexander I was on mending the rift between the great powers that he had himself caused with his demands over Poland and why he soon backed down from them in the interest of the entente.

By the spring of 1815, uniting the European powers had become a pressing concern with Napoleon's unexpected return. Just before leaving Vienna, Alexander I commissioned a "Projet d'instruction générale pour les missions de Sa Majesté Impériale," dated May 13 / 25, 1815, aimed at strengthening his alliance with his brothers in arms. In this remarkable "Projet," the tsar's immediate concerns curiously merged with his grand designs of old. For instance, he referred to the "grand European family," expressing anxiety that he might have to face a new alliance directed against him, as well as a conviction imbued with mysticism that he was "visibly protected by a superior force."[77] Metternich, a rationalist man of the Enlightenment with prudent reformist dispositions, stated in his memoirs that Alexander's religious vision of a new Europe left him cold. In any case, the tsar commanded enough moral and political influence to persuade the two other continental great powers, as well as most other European states, to sign the compact. The Austrian chancellor helped give credence to the contrived tale of the role of the Baroness von Krüdener by casually mentioning it in his memoirs. Yet because he had participated in the drafting of the alliance and was far too well informed to ignore the tsar's precedent of proposing a European federation, there are reasonable grounds to believe that Metternich deliberately sought to hide his unease about this alarming scheme behind a white lie.[78]

The mystical turn expressed by the Holy Alliance is best understood when placed in the context of the post-Napoleonic era. That many members of European aristocratic circles believed that they had just escaped a near-apocalyptic experience largely explains the wave of mysticism that washed over the continent. In Russia especially, the French invasion of 1812 inspired a groundswell of devotion to the tsar, in which religious fervor played a part. In Germany, a mystical movement also emerged in the years between 1810 and 1820. In the arts and literature, Romanticism expressed this surge of spiritual beliefs in a society searching for new bearings. This mystical movement redefined Europe as a tightly knit spiritual community, without regard for earlier differences between the Catholic, Protestant, and Orthodox confessions and between the established churches themselves. As Alexander Sturdza remarked, the purpose of the Holy Alliance was to restore a "principle of order" in public life after the Revolutionary era, and therefore to "proclaim . . . the sole conservative principles, which had been too long relegated to the subordinate sphere of domestic life."[79]

The Holy Alliance, despite its clumsiness of language and style, was seeking to answer a pressing need of the European elites: how to lay a cornerstone of political solidarity that would be sufficiently strong and stable finally to end the "evil" of the French Revolution—the idea that political legitimacy rested on political representation—and to start a new era of peace. In an attempt to counter the maxim that "legitimacy lies in the people," the Holy Alliance took the bold step of appealing to the Supreme Being as the definitive cosmological argument. The quest for a stable relationship between the great powers explains the intentional but otherwise incomprehensible intrusion of Christian principles into the political sphere.

Needless to say, this highly abstract spiritual conception of Europe was the product of highly educated elites, a world apart from popular religiosity. Eight-pointed stars (a symbol of the Supreme Being), three kings holding hands, interlocked rings, and winged figures wearing crosses and standing on horse-drawn chariots in front of a temple—these contemporary images representing the Holy Alliance were rich in esoteric symbolism. That mystical aspect of the Holy Alliance was unacceptable to the Catholic Church. The Russian authors of that treaty were influenced by Illuminism ("inner light," a Latin cognate of "enlightenment")—a metaphysical philosophy that left behind the skepticism and materialism of Denis Diderot and Paul Heinrich von Holbach to seek new epistemological adventures in *terra incognita*—a world of spiritual rationality beyond the perception of the senses. The German mystic Franz Xaver von Baader (1765–1841) made a substantial intellectual contribution to the religious perspective on European unification. In a pamphlet aptly titled *On the Necessity Created by the French Revolution for a New and Closer Relation between Religion and Politics,* he advocated the establishment of a federation based on the Christian faith; Tsar Alexander I had received a copy of it in the summer of 1814.[80] Baader, although a devout Catholic, belonged to this new mystical strand on the outskirts of the Church of Rome; he envisioned a straight line between individuals and the Supreme Being so close and personal that it created discomfort even among liberal Protestants. Most disturbingly, the intellectual fermentation of these years was favorable to a resurgence of "transcending Christianity," a rapprochement of Christians across denominational boundaries.[81] This religious relativism frightened the established churches, and especially the papacy, which had already issued two bulls condemning Freemasonry in the eighteenth century.[82]

The sincerity of Alexander I's religious faith is generally not questioned, but his political agenda to undermine the power of the Roman Church was also obvious.[83] The Holy Alliance was meant as the spiritual equivalent of a king's deposition. Few historians have noted that, after the thunderous Napoleonic wars, the great powers deliberately evicted one of the most influential actors in European history and one of the highest arbiters of the West European order in a millennium. In Vienna, the Papal State was not even called to be part of the second circle of powers, and its plenipotentiary Ercole Consalvi was forced to resort to ingenuity to fulfill his mission. Observers of the time, however, had anticipated and prepared for the weakening of the pope's position and power. Napoleon had already damaged the prestige of the papacy with his own sacrilegious coronation in 1804; two years later, the abolition of the Holy Roman Empire marked the end of the temporal fellowship between the pope and the Holy Roman Emperor.[84]

When the Holy Alliance stated that "the three sovereigns make up a single nation with the same Christian faith," the underlying meaning was clear: Catholicism, Protestantism, and Orthodoxy were put on an equal footing, making the political organization of Christian Europe "non-confessional."

In summary, the Holy Alliance was the culmination of a long series of political disasters befalling the papacy. Ironically, the final blow came not from the French Revolution or from Napoleon but from the great powers that had defeated him. In 1815, the political role of Pope Pius VII in Europe was reduced to that of sovereign of a small Italian state. This disgrace profoundly wounded the pontiff, and therein lies the reason why the Holy See refused to sign the pact of the Holy Alliance.[85] Representatives of Roman Catholic thought, such as the Jesuits, as well as the political philosophers Louis de Bonald and Joseph de Maistre, angrily attempted to fight back, giving rise to the movement called Ultramontanism (literally "beyond the mountains," the Alps, in reference to Italy). In defiance of the Holy Alliance, they advocated an alliance of European monarchs under the auspices of the pope, as well as a return to the prerogatives of the aristocratic class.[86] Furthermore, Maistre had spent several years in Saint Petersburg;[87] if he mistrusted the tsar, it was not for want of knowing him. Maistre wrote about the Holy Alliance, even before its publication: "Let us note that the spirit behind it is not Catholic, nor Greek or Protestant; it is a peculiar spirit that I have been studying for thirty years, but to describe it here would be too long; it is enough to say that it is as good for the separated Churches as it is bad for Catholics. It is expected to melt and combine all metals; after which, the statue will be cast away."[88] Maistre was exposing what he rightly perceived as a cunning maneuver. By adopting the Christian religion as the guiding principle but diluting it at the same time into an ethereal whole, Alexander I meant to undermine the pope's sphere of influence. Through a process that our age would call "embrace, extend, and extinguish," the Holy Alliance opened the door to a European political sphere that would be free of the influence of the Church (though not free of religion).[89]

This paradigm shift forced supporters of the political role of the papacy to continue their ideological fight with their backs against the wall. On August 15, 1832, Pope Gregory XVI issued a vehement encyclical titled "On Liberalism and Indifferentism." It was a strong restatement of the sole authority of the Catholic Church, emphasizing divine legitimacy and civil obedience, while condemning freedom of conscience as an "absurd and erroneous proposition" (Article 14) and freedom to publish as "harmful and never sufficiently denounced" (Article 15).[90] Indeed, the "source of evil" that the pope called "indifferentism" was "the perverse opinion . . . spread on all sides by the fraud of the wicked who claim that it is possible to obtain the eternal salvation of the soul by the profession of any kind of religion, as long as morality is maintained" (Article 13).[91] That was indeed a fitting description of the great powers' decision to put Catholicism, Protestantism, and Orthodoxy on the same footing. As its title implied, this encyclical condemned *both* liberalism and the Holy Alliance's ecumenism as grave heresies, making the pope's position among the most conservative in Europe.

Yet, alas for the papacy, the metaphorical writing was on the wall: the pope's kingdom in Europe was partitioned and offered to the kings of the Holy Alliance. The papacy had very few supporters left—only France, Portugal, Spain, and a group of Italian states—to support its hopeless bid for relevance in European politics. Unfortunately, none of these states belonged to the inner circle of the victorious great powers. Fighting fire with fire, the Holy Alliance managed to do the impossible: it overturned the mystical alliance of the emperor and the pope, the foundation of the old political order of Europe. A historical giant was slain, and its fall was so quick and sudden that most historians barely noticed. The paradoxical result, with ramifications that would only become clear in the twentieth century, was the liquidation of the Latin Christian order of the Middle Ages, which opened the way to a wholly secularized European political system.

The Congress System as a "Council of the Great Powers"

The second treaty that was devised to reinforce the cooperation of the great powers after the Hundred Days was of an entirely different, more practical nature. The peace, to be lasting, required a continued association of the great powers. For this reason, no fewer than three agreements were concluded on November 20, 1815: the second Treaty of Paris (which revised the peace signed with France in 1814), the act on the neutrality of Switzerland, and finally, the new "Quadruple Alliance" between Austria, Britain, Prussia, and Russia. The latter played a central role in establishing the new European system by maintaining the preexisting military coalition and extending it as a tool for maintaining peace. The treaty's crucial stipulation was Article VI:

> To facilitate and to secure the execution of the present Treaty, and to consolidate the connections which at the present moment so closely unite the Four Sovereigns for the happiness of the World, the High Contracting Parties have agreed to renew their meetings at fixed periods . . . for the purpose of consulting upon their common interests, and for the consideration of the measures which . . . shall be considered the most salutary for the repose and prosperity of Nations and for the maintenance of the peace of Europe.[92]

This treaty was as down to earth as the Holy Alliance was lofty. Most importantly, it inaugurated a practice that had great staying power: regular congresses among a club of great powers, which would act as a grand "Council." Up to then, congresses had been extraordinary affairs, convened only several times in a century and always after a great war. At the time, the political term used in diplomatic correspondence to describe the polity of European states was "Grand Alliance," of which the four great powers considered themselves the guardians. Yet the only formal entity similar to that was the Holy Alliance, of which Britain was not part. This treaty created such a formal entity, the Quadruple Alliance, whose chief promoters were Castlereagh and Metternich.

It is thus that the signatories of the Quadruple Alliance decided to adopt a routine of regular meetings in time of peace, during which they would examine (and solve on their own) important matters in Europe. This was the birth of the "Congress System," meant to perpetuate the Spirit of Vienna: indeed, from late 1815 until 1822, the monarchs and leading ministers of the European states met nearly annually to discuss common matters of interest. They selected different cities in Europe for their successive regular meetings: Aix-la-Chapelle (Aachen), Carlsbad (Karlovy Vary), Troppau (Opava), Vienna again, Laibach (Ljubljana), and finally Verona.[93] This system laid the foundations of conference diplomacy and became a functional example of how powers with different interests could meet regularly to establish common ground for resolving important matters of Europe, thereby preserving peace. The conferences, still called "congresses" at the time, were not perfunctory reunions but substantive meetings, convened to solve specific issues. Given that the four victorious powers almost split into two enemy blocs in late 1814, this was already a remarkable achievement. Moreover, even when their leaders were not meeting in grand congresses, the great powers were hammering out their differences and developing common policies on a variety of issues in several designated ambassadorial conferences—most notably in Paris for the allied occupation of France and in London for continuing discussions on the abolition of slave trade.[94]

It is necessary at this point to dispel the two myths already mentioned about Metternich—that he was a conservative blindly attached to the Ancien Régime and an unthinking supporter of the balance of power. He was a man deeply steeped in Enlightenment thought who pursued the study of both the sciences and humanities, which he also considered the product of natural laws. In contrast to Alexander I, his was first and foremost a rational mind, not at all attracted by either traditional Catholicism or Illuminism.[95] As for the French Revolution, Metternich did not condemn its aims per se but rather its violence and disorder; by contrast, he condemned as "retrograde" those who sought to restore the ancient order. In fact, Metternich's conception of the European order was deeply influenced by Saint-Pierre's *Plan of Perpetual Peace;* even more to the point, he was an admirer of Immanuel Kant and had read his seminal essay *Toward Perpetual Peace.*[96] Metternich believed firmly in an order of Europe based on "Political Equilibrium": a single peaceful "federation" of states, regulated by treaties and ethical principles, that would do away with the deplorable habit that the great powers had of dividing into opposing military alliances. As Kant had written,

> Differences . . . may certainly occasion mutual hatred and provide pretexts for wars, but as culture grows and men gradually move towards greater agreement over their principles, they lead to mutual understanding and peace. And unlike that universal despotism which saps all man's energies and ends in the graveyard of freedom, this

peace is created and guaranteed by an equilibrium of forces and a most vigorous rivalry. [97]

What this equilibrium of "most vigorous rivalry" (*Gleichgewicht im lebhaftesten Wetteifer*) meant, Kant clarified in no uncertain terms:

> Nature unites nations . . . by means of their mutual self-interest. For the *spirit of commerce* sooner or later takes hold of every people, and it cannot exist side by side with war. . . . States find themselves compelled to promote the noble cause of peace, though not exactly from motives of morality. And wherever in the world there is a threat of war breaking out, they will try to prevent it by mediation.[98]

Metternich used the term "equilibrium" to refer to a stable arrangement of powers regulated by international law and operating according to common principles and treaty obligations, something we might today call "a system of collective security."[99] The great powers would achieve this "equilibrium"—and thus lasting peace—if they worked together to channel the autonomy of the states of Europe into a sort of confederation. The frequent meetings of the Congress System should be understood in that perspective. To express a similar notion, British foreign secretary Lord Castlereagh used the term "the Alliance" or "the Union."[100]

Metternich's "equilibrium" should by no means be confused with the balance of power, the military contest between two opposed alliances that had been the hallmark of the eighteenth century; it was actually devised as an alternative to it. Such a misinterpretation, unintentionally fostered by Henry Kissinger at the end of World War II by his description of the post-Napoleonic order as the "era of the balance of power," dies hard. Amid a Cold War shaped by the US antagonism toward the Soviet Union, Kissinger believed that the implicit alliance of the Austrian Metternich and the British Castlereagh against Tsar Alexander's imperial designs was the essence of the Vienna Order (even though Alexander I could hardly be compared to the ruthless Joseph Stalin). Despite attempts by later historians, notably Paul W. Schroeder, to correct this point, the treacherous semantic confusion between the "balance of power" and Metternich's equilibrium (*Gleichgewicht*) has continued to trouble the minds of scholars.[101]

To unravel Metternich's notion of equilibrium, we can call on his adviser Friedrich von Gentz—whose literary talent lay behind Metternich's most famous dispatches—as a witness. In 1818, Gentz described the new political order of Europe as "a principle of general union, uniting all states collectively with a federative bond, under the guidance of the five principal powers . . . ; and so Europe seems really to form a grand political family, united under the auspices of a high tribunal of its own creation, whose members guarantee to themselves and to all parties the peaceful enjoyment of their respective rights."[102] Those words are so strikingly similar to Saint-Pierre's description of the European federation that they were likely a conscious reference. Gentz's use of the word "family," meanwhile, echoed the solidarity bonds of the Holy Alliance. It was a small world: Gentz had been Kant's student and had even published his own peace plan, *On Perpetual Peace,* in 1800 in response to his teacher's essay on perpetual peace.[103] Gentz then proceeded to publish, in 1806, an essay titled *Fragments of the New History of the Political Equilibrium in Europe,* which was obviously aligned with his views on perpetual peace.[104] In sum, the Vienna Order was consciously designed as an informal confederation or what I choose to call "the balance of diplomacy."

As the years passed—and for reasons that will soon become evident—the four great powers left behind the outer circles of lesser powers that had helped them complete the Final Act of Vienna. They constituted themselves as a directorate, the representatives of a cartel of interests that took decisions collegially, as a unitary body. The word "directorate"—a body of directors—is used here deliberately: it refers usually to the French Republican constitution of 1795, which had placed five "directors" at the head of state.[105] By 1818, the international system was becoming increasingly authoritarian again. It was, however, different from the Napoleonic Empire in terms of the concentration of power: instead of a centralized, hegemonic system with one master, Europe was now obeying a board of directors.

The directorate of Europe was far from a static or unitary entity. The two major and two lesser powers (Russia and Britain; Austria and Prussia) were not always in agreement, and their differences contributed to the balance of diplomacy. It is useful to reconstruct the sometimes testy negotiations between those powers, conducted behind closed doors, which can be done by consulting the minutes, correspondence, and memoirs left by the participants. Metternich, in particular, was always worried about the risk posed by a powerful Russian neighbor and became progressively haunted by the fear that constitutional monarchies would come into existence. The Prussian regime, a well-regimented monarchy that had emerged from humiliating enfeeblement precipitated by Napoleon's Empire, equally detested disorder. Britain was the outsider, with only marginal involvement in continental matters, given its preoccupation with maintaining its sea trade with Europe and the colonies. With territories spread all over the world, Whitehall needed to use Britain's human resources as sparingly as possible: if non-interventionism and even liberalism could serve the purpose, they appeared preferable to the high cost of repression. The country's colonial empire and the political preeminence of Parliament explain the frequent political divergences between Britain and its continental partners regarding the appropriate response to the waves of uprisings in Europe.

It is interesting to examine how the four allies successfully managed the reintegration of defeated France into their European system of peace: doing so illustrates the central role they gave to reconciliation in the postwar order. The allies had made it clear, in the wording of the Treaty of Paris of 1814, that they sought friendship with the new king Louis XVIII of France and wanted to put the quarrels of the past behind them. The Hundred Days had done considerable harm to the credibility of the Bourbon regime, but France's saving grace was its supply of great servants of the state. For foreign affairs, Charles-Maurice de Talleyrand-Périgord was a shrewd and experienced diplomat who had long served as Napoleon's diplomatic chief (before falling from grace) and knew his counterparts well. Because of his ambiguous conduct during the Hundred Days, he was soon replaced by Armand-Emmanuel du Plessis, the Duc de Richelieu, a capable aristocrat who had gained the respect of the tsar as a successful governor of the prosperous province of New Russia on the Black Sea and its port city of Odessa for more than a decade (showing again that the European elites indeed formed a small tight-knit world).[106] Finally, at the Congress of Aix-la-Chapelle in 1818, the foreign military occupation of France was declared ended. France then joined the other four states as a full member of the directorate, forming a Quintuple Alliance; from that moment on, it is customarily referred to as a "pentarchy" (five powers). All in all, the post-

Napoleonic order did achieve a remarkable degree of solidarity among the great powers, a strong asset in favor of lasting peace.

The Drift to Reaction: From Making Peace to Keeping the Peace

It is important to bear in mind that the solidarity of Europe's directorate was the preserve of a very small group of individuals representing the great powers, for whom informal and personal bonds played a significant role.[107] The monarchs of Russia, Austria, and Prussia all came from the same generation and had become acquainted with each other on the battlefields against Napoleon. Likewise, senior diplomatic posts were held by aristocrats who shared interests of caste. Individuals who were neither members of the aristocracy nor professional diplomats also had measurable influence. A case in point was Charles Pictet de Rochemont who, as a representative of the Geneva Republic, helped settle issues relating to Switzerland and played a role in the recognition of its neutrality. Pictet, a member of a Protestant family of entrepreneurs and scholars, had an exceptional network of relations in Europe at the highest level.[108] He had made a name for himself among the intellectual elites of Europe as the publisher of and primary contributor to the *Bibliothèque Britannique,* a monthly journal created in 1796, which contained the sum of all scientific and agricultural knowledge available in English; both Metternich and Tsar Alexander were subscribers.[109] Pictet, who met the tsar in late 1813 just before the campaign in France, also became well known to the Russian delegation and was able to promote Swiss interests at every opportunity.

Women also played an informal but significant role in diplomacy, as in the example of the Moldovan-Greek Roxandra Sturdza, who accompanied the Russian imperial retinue in 1814–1815 to the Vienna Congress. Baroness Germaine de Staël is perhaps the best-known instance: the daughter of a finance minister of Louis XVI, she was married to a Swedish diplomat and was Benjamin Constant's close friend. Most importantly, she was a respected writer who staunchly opposed Napoleon's imperial vision of Europe with her own liberal views. In 1812, sensing that her life was in danger, she left her literary salon of Coppet on Lake Geneva to go on a sensational tour of European capitals. Although she was not present at the Vienna Congress, her role as informal diplomat for the Swedish crown prince Bernadotte, whom she had once promoted as a candidate for the throne of France, and her passionate correspondence and writings in defense of the interests of that country kept her high in the mind of kings and diplomats. In 1813, she gave a convincing description of the small interconnected elite society that continued despite the French Revolution and Napoleonic wars and that was a direct offspring of the Spirit of the Enlightenment: "there is still something really beautiful and moral . . . in the association of all thinking men, from one corner of Europe to the other. They often have no relation; they are dispersed at great distances one from the other; but when they meet, one word is enough for them to recognize each other . . . they are really the people of God, those men who do not despair of the human race, and want to preserve its command of thought."[110] That exclusive society of Europeans shaped the Spirit of Vienna.

In the case of the Russian delegation, this personal rapport among the allied leaders was reinforced by the unusual role that Alexander I played in the negotiations—he was personally engaged in them, in contrast to the Austrian and Prussian monarchs, who had delegated their power to their ministers Metternich and Hardenberg, respectively. In Britain, diplomats such as Castlereagh were selected from the ranks of the aristocracy. On the Continent, the loose and porous borders between public and private life, a social legacy of the old patrimonial states, remained a distinctive feature of the Spirit of Vienna. These personal bonds and class interests go a long way toward explaining the Bourbon restoration and reconciliation with France. These features were, however, already beginning to erode. With the emergence of a corps of professional diplomats, as well as public officers sitting on the technical commissions, those who participated in the negotiations increasingly considered their official role as distinct from their private lives.

For the moment, however, the cultural elites of the Continent (except for a privileged minority in high circles), not to mention the population at large, were generally left out of the political processes. This exclusion had important consequences: both Metternich and Tsar Alexander I, conservatives who might have even passed as liberals had they been private persons, started facing increasing discontent as political leaders. Metternich, in particular, saw the aristocratic and bourgeois circles that raised protests as threats to domestic order and thus to his precious peace system. How could a man of such enlightened dispositions have come to embody the Reaction? Certainly, there was a psychological element at work, traceable to the French Revolution. The future Austrian chancellor did not object to freedom itself, but to chaos, which he viewed as the chief impediment of progress. Metternich's personal distrust of popular representation was more pronounced than that of Alexander I. The minister's preoccupation with preventing disorder turned into an obsession, soon overshadowing every other consideration. True to his disposition, he started operating a very effective system of police surveillance and censorship in the Austrian Empire; unfortunately, this had a depressing effect on social life and alienated liberal thinkers in his regime.[111]

An obsessive fear of popular disorder—while understandable in the aftermath of the French Revolution and Napoleonic Wars—was, alas, the chief flaw in the Spirit of Vienna; it explains how the systematic rejection of political representation by Russia, Austria, and Prussia became a considerable liability to the European order. With the appearance of the first public disorder, the task of the congresses became mostly to "keep the peace" among the populations in Europe. Achieving this aim required coordinated and sometimes even brutal interventions by the allied armies. The new European directorate fostered anti-parliamentarian policies at a time when European elites fervently demanded to be heard and when "public opinion" emerged as a political phenomenon.[112]

In 1819, under the influence of Metternich, Austria and Prussia issued the so-called Carlsbad Decrees, which constrained freedom of the press as well as freedom of the universities in the states of the German Confederation, generating a wave of unrest among students.[113] In the 1820s, violent revolts spread throughout Europe, particularly in Spain, Portugal, Naples, and Piedmont. To make things worse, the police forces of the five powers had to deal with small, well-organized secret cells like the Carbonari in Italy, which were made up of bourgeois or educated members and were channeling funds, issuing pamphlets, and collecting weapons for armed insurrections.[114] In Germany, the assassination of the poet August von Kotzebue (a sympathizer of the tsar's foreign policy) on March 23, 1819, was a premeditated, politically motivated act directed against Russia, and it was this atrocity that led to the Carlsbad Decrees.[115] Police forces all over the continent applied a "zero-tolerance" policy that consisted of smashing both hard-core insurrectionists and the general population with the same brutal methods of repression. Alexander I, bitter about what he saw as the failure of his liberal aspirations, suspended the parliament of Poland and abolished freedom of the press there; similar measures were taken across Europe. Unfortunately, such retaliation only fueled the sense of political disenfranchisement, triggering a runaway spiral of tit-for-tat violence. Paradoxically the anxiety of the continental powers to preserve the "peace" at all cost led them eventually to assist each other in campaigns of blanket military repression against their own populations. There was a troubling semantic shift from "peace" as the absence of war to "peace" as "law and order." The specter of general revolution had become a self-fulfilling prophecy.

A turning point in the attitude of the great powers occurred during the Congress of Troppau (1820), where the three conservative eastern powers not only lost the goodwill of the other European states but also the support of Britain. King Ferdinand I of the Two Sicilies (formerly the kingdom of Naples) had just granted his state a constitution after being subjected to a military coup supported by the Carbonari; both Spain and Portugal had also undergone revolutions. To face these "catastrophes," Metternich presented a "preliminary protocol" on November 15, 1820, to the other participants in the Troppau Congress: "States which have undergone a change of Government due to revolution, the results of which threaten other states, *ipso facto* cease to be members of the European Alliance, and remain excluded from it until their situation gives guarantees for legal order and stability."[116] A circular dispatch of Austria, Russia, and Prussia to their diplomatic agents announced, "The Powers exercise an undisputable right in contemplating common measures of safety against States in which the Government has been overthrown by rebellion."[117]

It is hard to disagree today with dissident views at the time that the harshly repressive continental powers had committed an act of usurpation and inaugurated an era of tyranny.[118] Despite the British protestation that "the Powers had not been guided by . . . the desire to interfere with the internal affairs of other governments," such was precisely the conclusion: they had set themselves up as a tribunal entitled to decide on the internal affairs of two European states without even the formality of consulting them. They peremptorily summoned King Ferdinand of the Two Sicilies to the next Congress of Laibach, as if he had been a steward accused of a misdemeanor. This dramatic interference in another state's sovereignty was particularly damaging to the entente with Britain, which maintained good trade relations both with the southern Italian state and Portugal. Allied interventions thus arguably threatened British interests in the Mediterranean and the Atlantic. Lord Castlereagh, visibly exasperated, challenged the philosophical and practical foundations of the continental powers' claims to dictate law.[119]

Progressively, differences started to widen among the members of the Quintuple Alliance. The Congress of Verona in 1822 failed to restore unity. Tsar Alexander I, who had been a mainstay of the entente, organized a final conference in Saint Petersburg in 1824 to revive relations, but momentum toward unity had dissipated. The Troppau Protocol had debilitated European peace, instead of curing its disorders. To this day, the attitude and doctrine of the "Spirit of Troppau," in opposition to the more liberal and inclusive "Spirit of Vienna," have remained a negative paradigm for the interventionism of great powers into the affairs of other states "out of the best of intentions." This episode is also a cautionary tale on the adverse effect of such a policy on preexisting alliances and, more generally, on international peace.

The one-bloc peace system of Europe nevertheless continued to coast along for three more decades, and the term "Concert of Europe" (as in the phrase, "acting in concert"—in accordance, mutually requiring each other's opinions) rose to prominence.[120] Yet the obstinate denial of popular representation—more accurately, the exclusion of educated elites from the political process—was a failing that caused considerable damage to the Vienna peace order and indirectly weakened the original entente among the great powers. It was as deleterious for the European order as it was for the social and national aspirations themselves, since allowing elected representatives to speak up and take the initiative might have gone a long way toward mitigating popular complaints. The self-imposed isolation of the continental great powers may well be the single factor that best explains the "Age of Revolutions," as well as the disaffection of Britain with its partners.

Evolutionary movements, which might have been channeled into peaceful social change, were instead constantly checked and forced to swell until they found their only outlet in revolution. The policy of "keeping the peace" thus became the worst enemy of peace.

Toward a Holy Alliance of the Peoples

Despite the repression, the protest movements in Europe after 1815 were beginning to grow into a new and different form of European awareness. The men who would later lead the Revolutions of 1848 sought broader political representation. In many instances, aspiring members of the lower aristocracy and the educated bourgeoisie simply wanted to play a more active role in political life. In other cases, the protest movements were an expression of national frustration against a foreign power, such as the dominance of Austria over Hungary and Italy, or of Russia over Poland. Yet it is remarkable (and perhaps somewhat counterintuitive) that these men did not try to dissolve the links of solidarity between European states that had been established in the post-Napoleonic era. On the contrary, they inherited a characteristic of the Spirit of Vienna: a mystical vision of Europe that transcended social and political and even religious divides.

A case in point is Giuseppe Mazzini (1805–1872), born in Genoa and often remembered as an Italian patriot who sought to unify the peninsula under a single state. His first *coup d'éclat,* in 1833, was an attempt to liberate his home city (one of the victims of the secret clauses of the Peace of Paris of 1814) from the kingdom of Piedmont-Sardinia. Most strikingly, Mazzini's insistence on the principle of nationality—on the unifications of Italy and Germany—did not at all preclude the dream of also unifying Europe.[121] Indeed, after founding the group *Giovine Italia* (Young Italy), he created *Giovine Europa* in 1834 while he was in exile in Berne, Switzerland. He also inspired the creation of several other national groups, each with its own publications, including Young Germany, Young Poland, and later Young Switzerland, Young France, and Young Austria. Mazzini argued that Switzerland should be the birthplace of European revolutions and, for that purpose, should abandon both its neutrality and the Federal Pact of 1815.

(He was mostly correct: Switzerland was indeed the first state to have a revolution, in 1847–1848, and it did manage to change its constitution, but it held onto its neutrality.)[122] The following year, Mazzini helped to found yet another Roman Republic. On that occasion, the new pope, Pius IX, elected in 1846 to succeed the reactionary Gregory XVI, was poorly rewarded for his more liberal disposition: he was forced to flee his capital when Mazzini's supporters attacked the Quirinal Palace in November 1848. The republican experiment in Rome failed once again: with the intervention of the French and Spanish Armies, the city was retaken on June 30, 1849, and the Papal States restored once more. Profoundly shaken by this misfortune, Pius adopted an ultra-conservative attitude echoing that of his predecessor; the papacy, which had been battered again and again in the previous fifty years, was not to reconcile with republicans for decades to come.[123]

Just like the mystics who had inspired the Holy Alliance, Mazzini was a devout Christian. Emancipated from political obedience to the papacy, he belonged to a vanguard of thinkers inspired by Catholicism but who aimed at social and political reform. After this episode involving the Roman Republic, he published a pamphlet titled "Toward a Holy Alliance of the Peoples."[124] Mazzini stated that the monarchs who had signed the Holy Alliance were aware of their subjects' demands for political representation. Instead of responding to those aspirations, they had purposefully restated that their legitimacy was derived from God, so that they could maintain the top-down hierarchical social order they had inherited from the Middle Ages. Mazzini's proposal, which echoed the ideas of Rousseau and Kant, put forward a reverse, bottom-up view: "It was the European democrats' role to boldly raise a flag bearing the inscription *God and the Peoples* and hold it high against the flag on which the men of 1815 had written *God and the Princes*."[125]

Mazzini indeed believed that true political legitimacy was derived from the people, a concept he termed, as we still do today, "democracy." This word, taken from the Greek *demos* ("the people"), and *kratia* ("power" or "rule"), had, since the 1820s, become more acceptable in continental Europe. Before that, it was used derogatorily to mean "mob rule," and Immanuel Kant even used it to describe a form of despotism.[126] This rehabilitation of the "people" at large was undoubtedly a break with the more elitist groups that had fostered the "revolutions" of the 1820s and a return to the egalitarian principles of the French Revolution. Democracy, rehabilitated in the European political language, was thus redefined as a social contract by which citizens chose their own representatives in elections. Although democratic principles already existed to a limited extent in Britain and even more so in the United States (albeit only for white, male members of its population), they were not yet manifested in continental Europe before 1848.[127] Once the principle of bottom-up legitimacy started to gain wider acceptance, a new issue emerged: whether the right to participate in elections would be extended from a minority of citizens holding substantial property to the whole of the adult male population. With the exception of a few countries like Switzerland and France, it would be some time before the question of universal suffrage truly came to the foreground in Europe.

Finally, in 1848, an extraordinary wave of revolutions washed over European cities from Paris to Warsaw and from Dublin to Naples, remembered as the "Spring of Nations"—producing bursts of panic among governments. In Austria, Metternich's policies had been increasingly failing to the point that the insurgencies nearly toppled the imperial regime; the old chancellor resigned in March of that year and went into exile in England. The new emperor, Francis Joseph I, took the throne at a moment when the Viennese court was in refuge in Olomouc (Olmütz, in Moravia).

In contrast, the Russian Empire stood firm. The successor to Tsar Alexander, Nicholas I, had the throne foisted on him in December 1825 in turbulent times. Honest and diligent, but lacking the culture and sophistication of his elder brother, Nicholas set about ruling the empire according to traditional ideas; that is, with a strong fist. In the crisis of 1848, the solidarity between the eastern monarchs held fast: Nicolas I did not hesitate to lend out the Russian Army to help crush the rebellions threatening his allies. Indeed, the new tsar's military disposition, his repression of the Polish uprising of 1830–1831, and his willingness to lend troops to his Austrian neighbor earned him the nickname of the "policeman of Europe." Almost everywhere, the revolutions ended in disaster: constitutions were revoked, and death sentences and imprisonment were handed out to insurgent leaders. The Vienna Order had been saved in extremis by the solidarity of the great powers, but all the governments of Europe felt the chill in the air. Profoundly shaken, they realized that times had changed and that their policies had to do so too: to restore social peace, they were forced to accept some devolution of power. To that degree, the Spring of Nations achieved its goal.[128]

As already mentioned, the revolutionaries of 1848 did not question the fact that a new order of Europe had been needed after the Napoleonic wars, but they did demand a greater voice in civil society, as well as adjustments to the political map. With the greater political empowerment of the upper bourgeoisie across Europe, the question of maintaining international peace immediately returned to the foreground. The religious motifs of the Holy Alliance were translated into a more democratic language. On August 22, 1849, a "Congress of the Friends of Universal Peace" opened in Paris with representatives from France, England, Belgium, the Netherlands, and the United States (English-speaking peace movements on both sides of the Atlantic kept in close contact). Its proceedings referred to a European grammar of peace typical of the Spirit of Vienna: "the agitation in favor of peace, which had such a development in the last years, was inspired by the wars that drenched our continent in blood at the beginning of this century"; in other words, the recent commotions had resurrected the specter of the Revolutionary and Napoleonic wars.[129]

The proceedings also paid special homage to the "laborious and benevolent sect of the Quakers," referring to their efforts in the United States and Europe, as well as implicitly to William Penn. As might be expected, it also stated that "the utopia of Abbé de Saint-Pierre [has] started to be taken seriously."[130] On this occasion, the poet and writer Victor Hugo, who presided over the debates, read a text sometimes referred to as the "The Idea of Europe." Hugo launched into a passionate attack against all those who dismissed this notion as a naive delusion. First noting that four centuries earlier, anyone would have called the prospect of unifying France "a strange madness and an absurd delusion," Hugo then declared,

> There will be a day when you France, you Russia, you Italy, you England, you Germany, all of you nations of the continent, without losing your specific quality and your glorious individuality, you will coalesce tightly into a higher unit and you will make up the European fraternity, just as Normandy, Brittany, Burgundy, Lorraine, and

Alsace, all of our provinces, merged into France. A day will come where there will be no other battlefields than markets opening themselves to trade and spirits opening up to ideas. A day will come where cannonballs and bombs will be replaced by votes, by the universal suffrage of the peoples, under the venerable arbitration of a grand sovereign Senate that will be to Europe, what the parliament is to England, the diet is to Germany, the Legislative House is to France![131]

To this message urging political union, Hugo added a peaceful ideal, which became a staple of peace movements in the second part of the nineteenth century:

A day will come when cannons will be on display in museums, just as torture machines are on display, while we will wonder how that could ever be! A day will come where we will see these two immense formations, the United States of America and the United States of Europe, facing one another, extending hands across the seas, exchanging their products, their trade, their industry, their art and their genius.[132]

One cannot overstate the Christian ecumenical fervor that informed the participants in the Congress of the Friends of Universal Peace, who were "publicists, philosophers, Christian ministers, eminent writers, [and] several of the considerable public and popular men who are luminaries of their nation." Indeed, an earlier part of the speech, which several sources in France prudently censored for the sake of secularism, stated,

This religious truth, universal peace, all nations connected among themselves by a common link, the Gospel as supreme law, mediation substituted for war, is this religious thought not a practical thought? . . . The law of the world is not and cannot be distinct from the law of God. And the law of God is not war, it is peace (cheers).[133]

The religious spirit was thus still strong in France in the mid-nineteenth century—perhaps just as strong as it had been at the time of the Holy Alliance. Catholic priests and Protestant ministers sat alongside elected MPs. Hugo's words echoed the mystical "high truths" of the opening words of the tsar's Holy Alliance of September 1815. More generally, Mazzini, Hugo, and others seized the Illuministic legacy of Alexander I and made it their own. Although the spirit of the Paris Peace Congress was deeply Christian, it also categorically rejected the Catholic social order of the Middle Ages, which held that political legitimacy flowed from the pope to kings and from kings to their peoples. In the more modern understanding, power had to flow up from the people at large. In the spirit of 1848, the political tradition of Protestant countries effectively found itself in "holy alliance" with grassroots, progressive Catholic movements. It was at this juncture that peace and democracy emerged as strong partners in political advocacy.

A considerable achievement of the International Peace Congress of 1849 in Paris was its reconciliation of the political ideas of religious thinkers in the nineteenth century with those of the Enlightenment rationalists who had supported radical ideas, particularly freedom of conscience and popular representation. For a while, in a pacified France—where competing nostalgias for the Enlightenment, the Revolution, Napoleon, and the Holy Alliance finally appeared to be more or less reconciled—it seemed that everything was for the best. Even the newly elected pope, Pius IX, seemed for a brief moment to condone this evolution. In that moment of grace, Republican France seemed to redeem the failures and disappointments of the rest of Europe.

Unfortunately, it was not to last. On December 2, 1851, Louis-Napoléon Bonaparte, who had been elected president of the young republic, decided to follow in the footsteps of his uncle Napoleon, and he staged a coup that shuttered the national assembly. One year later, he was proclaimed emperor. The brand of "universal suffrage" he invoked to support his authoritarian regime, far from the elevated ideals of Mazzini and Hugo, was a strategy called "populism": a calculated appeal to the selfish interests and prejudices of ordinary people. In practice it was a flirtation with mob rule, the bane of Enlightenment philosophers. Rather than submit to political repression that affected more than 25,000 individuals, Victor Hugo and many others took the path of exile. Very soon, France was pursuing wars of self-aggrandizement with renewed enthusiasm. The birth of the Second French Empire was the last, and possibly the most humiliating, of the defeats that befell the Revolutions of 1848.

The Eastern Question: Nemesis of the Vienna System

Although the solidarity of the continental powers had held remarkably firm during the Spring of Nations, it was finally severed over a matter of external policy: the "Eastern Question," or the competition between the great powers over who would decide on the future of the territories of the Ottoman Empire.[134] The Russian Empire had entertained territorial ambitions over Constantinople and the Straits to the Mediterranean ever since the time of Peter the Great. The same could be said about Austria's ambitions along the Adriatic coast, while France had already attempted to conquer Egypt, and Britain had sought to establish trading posts throughout the Mediterranean and on the southern shore of the Black Sea. Tsar Alexander I, however, had introduced a change in traditional Russian policy by firmly maintaining peace with the Ottoman Empire after concluding the last war in 1812.[135]

Southeastern Europe and the Greek peninsula represented, nevertheless, a "conflict of jurisdiction" between the European system of peace and the rest of the world where colonial rule normally applied. Ignoring the dissenting voices of the Enlightenment, the European powers of the nineteenth century envisioned an increasingly sharper division of the world between "civilized" countries and overseas territories, where colonization was morally justified in view of the "benefits of civilization" and was encouraged because it afforded large opportunities for state aggrandizement and private enrichment. French economist Comte de Saint-Simon aimed "to people the globe with the European race, which is superior to all the races of men; to make it [as] travelable and habitable as Europe, there is an endeavor through which the European parliament will have continually to exert the activity of Europe and always keep it alert."[136] He unequivocally rejected the universal principle that all men were born free and with equal rights, as expressed by the French Revolution. He later wrote that "during the Revolution, the Heads of state . . . established that the Blacks were the equals of the Europeans: this principle was necessarily bad since it is based on a fact the wrongness of which is evidenced by observations."[137] Though this idea should not be confused with the eugenic theories of the late nineteenth century, it was nevertheless a blend of a faith in the superiority of

Christian culture, the naturalism of Comte de Buffon, and the theory of climates, as well as an urge to find a rational justification for the disproportionate role of Europeans in the destinies of the world. Alas, one conclusion was implicit: the new system of peace would include non-Europeans, but it would not represent them.

Colonial enterprises were essentially maritime affairs—crossing the Mediterranean or the Atlantic Ocean was required to reach other continents. Greece was an in-between case. Inhabited by European peoples, it was recognized as the source of civilization, yet it had come to be governed by a "foreign" power that practiced Islam and lived under a separate political regime. Because of the peninsular situation of Greece and the Balkans, military expeditions to southeastern Europe would have to be naval affairs, nearly indistinguishable from colonial warfare in Africa or Asia.

In the context of renewed colonialism, the post-Napoleonic era witnessed the rise of philhellenism, a strong grassroots movement of sympathy for the Greeks, who wished to achieve greater autonomy. Philhellenism posed the question whether the Greeks should be considered equal to other Europeans. References to ancient Greece as the foundation of European civilization were meant to create a dichotomy between Christian Greeks and Asian peoples, such as Arabs or Turks, who were Muslims. Philhellenism was a rebuttal of the ethnic classification of the Greeks by the chanceries of London, Paris, and Vienna as a second-rate people who would benefit from colonial rule.[138] Their lineage with ancient Greece became the chief polemical argument in favor of the Greeks being afforded political rights, as well as political autonomy, within the European system of peace.[139] In practice, demonstrating that the contemporary Greeks were actually different from Turks was a task fraught with difficulties, considering that the two peoples had coexisted for so long and had adopted similar lifestyles. Furthermore, a sizable part of the ruling class of the Ottoman Empire had European, particularly Greek, ancestry. So, where was Europe supposed to end and where was Asia meant to begin, in a political sense? The sublime lyricism of George Gordon, Lord Byron, and references to the Greek heroes of antiquity were thus an attempt to solve the social and political riddle of nineteenth-century Greece by transcending an inconvenient reality.[140]

For the Russian Empire, the stakes were markedly different: being mostly a land empire intent on territorial expansion and access to open water, controlling the Black Sea and the Straits had long been a geostrategic imperative. For Russians, their brotherhood with fellow Orthodox Christians had never been in question, which explains why the Athens of antiquity did not exert the same fascination there as in Western Europe. The Russian moral argument instead was based on the liberation of the Christians of the Patriarchate of Constantinople from Ottoman rule. Empress Catherine the Great contemplated the grand scheme—nicknamed the "Greek Dream"—to re-create an Eastern Christian space in the Levant under the benevolent rule of the tsars. In practice, Russia would give the Greeks a social status akin to other Christian subject peoples such as Ukrainians, Poles, and Armenians. With the benefit of hindsight, we know for certain what the Western chanceries already suspected—that the Russian Empire would have annexed those lands after a few decades of occupation and applied a russification policy, indefinitely postponing any hopes for political autonomy. Regardless of their intellectual aspirations, the conflicting territorial and economic ambitions of Britain, France, and Russia in southeastern Europe were leading them to a clash that was detrimental to the Vienna peace order. Metternich's Austria was, in contrast, taking a prudent stance in the Danube region, seeking to preserve the status quo and keep its powerful Russian neighbor at bay.

The legal status of the Ottoman Empire in the post-Napoleonic order was undefined, in part because the sultan (following tradition) declined the invitation to participate in the peace negotiations of Vienna; thus, the Ottoman Empire was not party to the Final Act of 1815.[141] The sultan Mahmud II would have been well advised to take full advantage of this opportunity to inscribe the territorial integrity of his empire in a multilateral European peace system. Furthermore, the fact that the Holy Alliance excluded the Porte from the "Christian family" could be interpreted as giving Russia license to pursue self-aggrandizement at his expense. In fact, Mahmud II was not invited to add his signature to the charter that was, contrary to Alexander I's promise to Metternich, made public during the Christmas of 1815. The Porte learnt in this way of the declaration of the Holy Alliance and started to "fear that its main goal was a new holy war of the

Christians against Moslems, in other words a new crusade against the Turks."[142] Metternich tried to dispel anxieties in Constantinople by writing a letter to his ambassador in Turkey, aiming to reassure the sultan that "Christian morality commands first and foremost respect for civil laws and the treaties between Powers. It happens that the political situation of the Porte, far from being threatened by this treaty, is party to a system of peace and general benevolence. The religious situation was not challenged; this situation is placed outside of the treaty, just as the law of the Prophet is outside of that of the Christ."[143] Metternich might have been speaking for other powers at Vienna: for example, as long as Tsar Alexander lived, Russia never broke the Peace of Bucharest it signed with the Ottoman Empire in 1812. But the exclusion of the Ottoman Empire from the Vienna Order still left southeastern Europe a gray area for international law and a potential arena for war.[144]

Ottoman worries about the aim of the Holy Alliance may nonetheless have been confirmed by the outbreak of the Greek insurrection in the spring of 1821. In March, a Greek secret society operating out of the Russian port city of Odessa, the Philiki Etairia (Society of Friends), launched an armed rebellion. A troop of young men led by Alexander Ypsilantis, an officer of the tsar's own army, invaded the Danubian principalities of Moldavia and Wallachia, vassals of the Ottoman Empire. The timing was the worst possible: the news reached the great powers at the Congress of Laibach. Preoccupied with the suppression of similar rebellions in Western Europe, they opted for a policy of staunch disapproval. Britain and Austria also feared that any rash move could lead Alexander to change his amicable policy toward the sultan. Peace might indeed have been preserved in southeastern Europe if the Ottoman Empire had not applied the age-old policy of Mediterranean empires: drowning rebellions in blood, deliberately killing subjects and their political leaders as a deterrent. On April 22, 1821, the Sublime Porte staged a public hanging of the Patriarch of Constantinople and instituted a policy of terror against the local Greek population (the so-called Bloody Easter). One year later, it slaughtered the prosperous Greek population on the island of Chios and left the island a desert: three-quarters of its more than 100,000 inhabitants were killed or enslaved, and the rest were forced into exile.[145]

The sheer violence of the repression—which turned into acts of extermination—caused an outcry across Europe. In the West, this response is often considered to be one of the first pan-European manifestations of public opinion in international politics.[146] The response took a different form on Russian soil, where it resulted in a large-scale operation to free the deported Greeks sold into slavery and to accept them as refugees.[147] However, neither the vigor of Western public opinion nor the cost of Russian humanitarian operations managed to budge the great powers from their neutral stance. The real trigger for change in Greece was the death of Tsar Alexander in 1825: under his successor Nicholas I, who did not have the same qualms as his older brother, Russia returned to its historical enmity with the Ottoman Empire. It strove to resume its historical expansion in the direction of Constantinople, starting a new Russian-Turkish war.[148] In response, Britain and France hurriedly dispatched their own navies, lest the Straits and Greece fall into Russian hands. The combined naval forces of three powers annihilated the sultan's fleet at the Battle of Navarino on October 20, 1827.

Indeed, the allies were still fighting together under the banner of the Quintuple Alliance. The balance of power was overwhelmingly stacked against the Ottomans, who were quickly defeated. The question remained of what the great powers would do with the prized Greek peninsula. The allies avoided internal confrontation once more by applying a similar expedient as with the Swiss Confederation in 1815: *if it can't be mine and it can't be yours, then it should belong to none of us.* With the London Protocol of 1828, they proposed the establishment of a Greek state under the nominal suzerainty of the Ottoman Empire. The Sublime Porte, not even consulted, acknowledged the diktat in the Treaty of Adrianople, which concluded the war with Russia in 1829. Significantly, the first president of the Hellenic Republic was none other than Ioannis Capodistrias, head of the tsar's delegation at the Congress of Vienna, who had never abandoned his dream of Greek emancipation (he was unfortunately assassinated within two years). The pan-European Alliance had been preserved, but at what cost? It is not surprising that the Congress System ceased to function by 1823, soon after the start of the Greek crisis. With the European great powers having whetted their appetites for colonial expansion, the situation was hardly conducive to durable peace in the region.

By contrast, the humiliation of defeat and the internal crisis in the Ottoman Empire encouraged liberalization. In the early 1840s, Sultan Abdülmejid I started a series of reforms, known as *Tanzimat* (reorganization) in Turkish. The *Tanzimat* sought to ensure the survival of the Ottoman Empire through the modernization and westernization of the state; its key aims included improving the social integration of non-Muslim populations and abolishing slave markets.[149] Yet as in the case of Russia under Alexander I, there was a wide gap between the intentions of a progressive autocrat and the response of the civil administration, as well as the population in general. Abdülmejid had to contend with the drag of century-old mentalities, which divided society into castes of unequal human beings, with Muslims on top. (This was not peculiar to the Ottomans—the situation of non-Christians was little better in European colonies; slave markets flourished in the American antebellum South, and serfdom was still prevalent in Russia).

The success of the *Tanzimat* might have helped reduce the strength of forces of rebellion and thus contribute to the maintenance of peace in Europe, but this was not to be. France and Britain were cultivating renewed colonial ambitions, while Russia was eager to resume its progression toward the Straits. In addition, the reform process in the Ottoman Empire was costly and required foreign loans, further reducing the leeway of the state. The economically weakened Ottoman Empire was soon labeled the "sick man of Europe." In the late 1840s, a crisis emerged over a protocol that dictated which Christian churches had access to the holy places in Jerusalem. Underlying this crisis was a broader political question: Which European power would be considered the "protector" of the Christian populations in the Ottoman Empire? It is easy to imagine Abdülmejid I's doubts of the sincerity of the foreign powers' solicitude for his Christian subjects, given that these powers ignored his reform efforts and barely concealed their own ambitions of self-aggrandizement. One saving grace had preserved peace so far: because none of the great powers wanted to see the others collect the ripe fruits, none had dared to make the first move. France and Austria preferred to maintain an independent Turkish state with a foot in Europe, rather than letting the Straits fall into Russian hands. Russia steadily advanced its territorial control on the northern coast of the Black Sea, careful not to attract France and Britain into a war. But with greed progressively replacing the desire for peace, the region became the board for an elaborate game of strategy.

The crisis finally erupted in early 1853, one year after Louis-Napoléon Bonaparte, the first president of the unfortunate Second French Republic, seized power and became Emperor Napoleon III. By some twist of fate, a new Bonaparte had risen to power in France who embodied everything averse to a "Holy Alliance"—be it of the kings of 1815 or of the peoples of 1848. In 1852 Napoleon demanded that the Sublime Porte recognize France as the protector of Christian pilgrims in the holy places; as a hint he sent his warship up the Dardanelles. The whole situation was a red rag to Tsar Nicholas I, the traditional champion of the Greek Orthodox, who insisted on Russia being confirmed by the Porte as the protector of the holy places and of all Orthodox Christians in the Ottoman Empire. By asserting himself in the dispute over the holy places, the French emperor triggered the justified fears of the Ottoman Empire, as well as Britain and Russia. The aging tsar Nicholas I turned French intervention into a personal matter for him: having not forgotten Napoleon Bonaparte's invasion of Russia, he was ill disposed toward the latter's nephew, whom he considered a usurper. Nicholas was further infuriated by France's interference in Russian ambitions in the eastern Mediterranean. The solidarity spirit of the Holy Alliance, which had survived the revolutions of 1848, was weakening. The Quintuple Alliance suddenly split in two, with Austria and Prussia taking a neutral stance on the dispute.

The negotiations of 1853, which might have resulted in a compromise if led by the rulers and diplomats of the Congress of Vienna, were dismally botched. The Russian minister of foreign affairs was the aging count, Karl Nesselrode. In the heyday of the Congress System, Russian foreign policy had been mostly managed by Capodistrias, a man of liberal dispositions who had discouraged Russian expansionism in resolving the Eastern Question. Nesselrode, who was present at Vienna and at the later congresses, rose to prominence in the days of the Reaction.[150] His demand for official recognition of the protectorate over Christians in the Ottoman Empire, if realized, would have subordinated the Greek Orthodox Church to Russia. In the Ottoman Empire, where the civil service had traditionally delegated the administration of Christians' daily affairs to their own church, Nesselrode's demand would thus have placed Russia in a position of overruling the central administration. The British ambassador urged the sultan to reject this request. To make matters more difficult, the Russian ambassador to Constantinople, Prince Alexander Menshikov, made a show of arrogance that drove the exasperated Sublime Porte to request military assistance from the other powers.[151]

The diplomatic stalemate was broken by war. In Sinope, on the Anatolian coast of the Black Sea, a Russian flotilla attacked the Ottoman fleet by surprise on November 30, 1853, blowing it out of the water. At the end of March 1854, Britain and France declared war on Russia. In June, after a successful attack on the city of Silistra (in Bulgaria today) that forced the Russian Army to retreat past the Pruth River back into its own territory, the ministries in London and Paris convened to decide on the next steps. Against the advice of their own commanders, the British and French governments decided to attack the Crimean port city of Sevastopol, Russia's primary naval base on the Black Sea. For the Western allies, which had been waging this campaign as a run-of-the-mill colonial war, this was a foolhardy idea. Their troops, already weakened by an epidemic of cholera in the previous months, were unprepared for what they met: a war of the industrial era. They faced a strongly fortified modern city defended by a capable and well-armed garrison and surrounded by a forbidding hinterland. The assailants were not able to storm it, let alone isolate it—a land route remained open at all times with the rest of Russia. As the siege dragged on under miserable conditions, the British population in London started rioting against the war. Finally, the Russian garrison admitted defeat, negotiated a truce, and marched away from the city. The death of the heartbroken tsar Nicholas I on March 2, 1855, opened the way to peace negotiations.[152]

The Peace Treaty of Paris, signed on March 30, 1856, gave the Ottoman Empire a new lease of life. Most importantly, it repaired the omission of the Vienna Order by admitting the Sublime Porte "to participate in the advantages of the public law and *concert of Europe*" (with the admission of the Ottoman Empire, the term had now officially entered the lexicon of European treaties).[153] Sevastopol and all other Russian possessions were returned, and British and French ships gained easier access to the Black Sea for trade. This hardly represented a great change for the region. Despite the foreign meddling, progress on the status of Christians continued in the Ottoman Empire, leading to the Reform Edict of 1856. This law established nominal equality between the subjects of all religions, a welcome step that had the additional advantage of removing a pretext for future Russian aggression.[154]

The Crimean War aptly illustrates how violating the maxim "peace is for the strong, and war is for the weak" could backfire on great powers. There was weakness not only in Tsar Nicholas I's curt and arrogant diplomacy but also in the strategic ineptitude of his foes, particularly their unjustified pursuit of an unproductive and expensive war. In particular, Napoleon III's craving for new military glories, after France had reestablished its place among the great powers, was a form of revanchism after the defeat of 1815. The French government, like the British, was increasingly aware of the other great powers' failings and duplicity and this only increased British and French mistrust. As for the Ottoman Empire, the sultan was in a position of weakness from the very outset, forced into conflict against his will. He was now aware that his empire's very survival could no longer rely exclusively on its armies but needed the ability to manipulate the diplomatic and military balance among the great powers so that they would neutralize each other. It would have taken another kind of strength, from the political leaders on all sides, to find a pacific solution to this crisis.

The Crimean War, often perceived as an unfortunate, if somewhat minor, incident in the history of the nineteenth century, with little influence on the political balances of the continent, in reality marked a historical watershed: the final demise of the Quadruple Alliance of 1815 (Quintuple from 1818, with the addition of France), which had been the mainstay of European peace for nearly four decades—and which might be called in hindsight the "United Kingdoms of Europe." Most of all, it shattered the cherished dream of Tsar Alexander I of establishing perpetual peace in Europe through a Holy Alliance. The curtain thus came down on the Spirit of Vienna and its officially supported ideal of perpetual peace. Even though the Concert of

Europe, which now included the Ottoman Empire, continued during the second part of the nineteenth century with international conferences and negotiated settlements, its momentum was lost. Having taken a step backward to a state of expansionism and mutual hostility, the European powers reverted once again to a balance of military power to guarantee their own survival.

The Vienna Order: From Diplomatic Success to Political Failure

The experience of the years 1814–1815 had demonstrated to the great powers that the balance of power was an effective tool of war, but not a tool of peace. It was true that European princes had managed to overthrow Napoleon's pan-European empire by banding together in a coalition. At the same time, the Polish-Saxon crisis of 1814–1815 convinced them that this same balance of power could not provide a guarantee of peace in the future. Necessity threw them together in the ensuing peacetime as well, as they searched for a durable solution against two threats: the resurgence of imperial France and new revolutions. The reinstatement of the Bourbon dynasty in Paris and the inclusion of France in the peace system were two key steps against these threats.

This desire to create a lasting system of peace explains the flurry of diplomatic innovations, notably the multilateral Final Act of Vienna, the Holy Alliance, and the Quadruple Alliance. Most importantly, these treaties responded to the main objection of Leibniz and Rousseau to the Abbé de Saint-Pierre's plan; namely, that no monarchs would willingly submit themselves to a "system of peace." Spurred by the needs of the moment, Tsar Alexander I consciously took on the role of the "providential man," while Austrian chancellor Metternich attempted to create a system of cooperation that would approximate the alliance of peace imagined by Immanuel Kant. In truth, neither the Holy Alliance nor the Congress System brought any decisive proof that Saint-Pierre's grandiose dream was attainable in Europe. Nevertheless, the Congress System was a deliberate step in the direction of a more unified system for the continent, which demonstrated the benefits of having strong solidarity among the great powers.

The Congress System had, however, two structural flaws that posed as many challenges for peace as they solved: the refusal to increase popular representation and a highly normative attitude toward European states. First, the great powers (with the notable exception of Britain) strikingly failed to answer demands for political representation—they refused to let go of the axiom that the legitimacy of monarchs rested exclusively on inheritance rights to the land. Although Alexander I seemed to genuinely believe that emperors and kings owed their throne to Divine Providence, Metternich was haunted by the fear that parliaments and the press could not help but unleash again the troubles of the French Revolution. The Prussian state, still digesting its massive reforms from 1807 to 1815, was facing a period of political instability, while the kings of France were trying to find their footing under the constitutional constraints imposed on them by the allies. Whatever the premise, the conclusion was in each case the same: the monarch and his administration had to defend royal prerogatives inch by inch against the ever-increasing demands of popular representation. The fear of disorders became, alas, a self-fulfilling prophecy—or worse, a self-inoculated disease that progressively contaminated continental Europe. The staunch refusal to allow the liberal, yet cautiously conservative, elites of the post-Napoleonic era to express themselves was precisely what forced them into desperation and into the ranks of insurgents. What started as a system of peace turned into an age of revolutions.

The second flaw was that the inclusion effort that was so typical of the Spirit of Vienna turned into an enforcement of the principles of the Congress System, and thus into interventions within the internal matters of European states. The Protocol of Troppau of 1820, by which the directorate of Europe decided unilaterally to exclude other powers from the Alliance solely because they had adopted new constitutions, might have appeared barely rational at the time. Yet it negated the inclusiveness of the Spirit of Vienna, which had brought together—with remarkable political agnosticism—absolute monarchies such as Russia, constitutional monarchies such as Britain, and republics such as Switzerland.

In the end, both those flaws could be summed up in the authoritarianism that came to be known as the Reaction. It is thus significant that this increasing intolerance for dissent is what caused Britain's disengagement from active cooperation with the other powers, removing a key motivation for pursuing the Congress System and generally weakening the solidarity among the great powers. Also, it is likely no coincidence that Austria was the great power that edged nearest to collapse in 1848. Only after the passing of that crisis did the continental great powers fully realize that parliaments and the press had been denied their indispensable role as instruments of peace and stability by serving as an orderly outlet, a much-needed relief valve, for the energies of the elites. In the history of peace, the Reaction emerges as a fundamentally unworkable policy and the cause of disorders so grave that they nearly drowned the Vienna Order, particularly in Austria itself.

Within the general picture of the post-Napoleonic order, the initially benevolent and relatively liberal ideology of the Holy Alliance of 1815 pursued by Tsar Alexander I also contained two weaknesses. The first was the principle of "divine legitimacy," which promoted a top-down vision of society and justified the denial of demands for political representation from emerging social classes. The second flaw was the principle of status quo ante regarding political borders, which denied the claims to recognition by a number of populations that had been ignored by the Vienna settlement, notably the Poles, Norwegians, Belgians, Saxons, and Genoese (not to mention the Greeks and other Christian minorities in the Ottoman Empire). The first flaw led to revolutions started by social and economic elites against their own governments; the second to insurrections against foreign occupants, often led by the local aristocracy itself. All that was left to the powers to "keep the peace" was to deploy troops in street battles against insurgents.

The second weakness revealed its significance in the long term. The nineteenth century was an industrial era characterized by great economic and social change, and fixing a status quo ante was proving an impossible task. By the middle of the century, some European states (Britain, Prussia, and France) were achieving greater strength and power, whereas others (Russia, Austria, and the Ottoman Empire) were falling behind. The pressure of these long-term movements up and down created considerable friction between the allies. Russia's return to a policy of expansionism under Nicholas I, the economic decline of the Ottoman Empire, and the reemergence of France under Napoleon III as an expansionist power all caused an imbalance, which fueled the Eastern Question. Ultimately, the Crimean War, which pitted former allies against each other in the struggle over the fate of the Straits and Constantinople, demonstrated that the static peace order of Vienna had finally reached its breaking point. The irony is that the Revolutions of 1848 were not directly responsible for the collapse of the rigid Vienna Order. It was rather the collective failure of the great powers themselves, which had forgotten the lessons of the winter of 1814–1815, to find a balance of negotiation on the Eastern Question in the early 1850s.[155]

A key limitation of the Spirit of Vienna was that its definitions of peace were ambiguous and limited in geographical scope. In particular, the powers that participated in the Congress System ultimately took the definition of peace a little too narrowly, as "law and order"; they tried to keep populations too firmly in hand with the Reaction, to the tragic point of sending troops to shoot at protesting civilians. To make matters even more complicated, the post-Napoleonic era was a turning point when the prerogative to define "peace" for the world became increasingly the monopoly of European powers and, more specifically, of white Europeans. "Colonial peace" outside of Europe during the nineteenth century, which masked the lust for riches and power under the guise of "bringing civilization" to indigenous peoples, constitutes a dark chapter all by itself. From our horizon of experience, it seems paradoxical that European elites who yearned for freedom and political representation for themselves had, for the most part, no desire at all to grant these to native populations with different skin colors and religions.[156]

Closer to our subject of Europe, the great powers' definition of peace continued to exclude the Ottoman Empire, which was still holding a sizable part of southeastern Europe, until the Treaty of Paris of 1856. The very fact that the movement of western Philhellenism sought to include the Greeks among the ranks of "civilized people" in the 1820s by arguing for their ancient genealogy was indicative of how deeply ingrained the preconceptions of human inequality were. It is worth contrasting the indignant reaction of the British press to the Chios Massacre committed by the Ottomans against Greeks in 1820 to its favorable treatment of the British Army's reprisal slaughters against Indians after the Great Rebellion of 1857.[157]

After the collapse of the entente of the five powers on the eve of the Crimean War, the balance of power principle immediately reclaimed its prominence, taking an increasing role in the second half of the nineteenth century. Unsurprisingly, the predatory appetites of the great powers spilled out of Europe. In this new context, competition between them ushered in an Age of Empires intent on colonial self-aggrandizement. Central Asia became the theater of the "Great Game," a fierce confrontation between Britain and Russia. Wherever there were non-European territories left, European expeditionary forces rushed to conquer them, while France, Britain, and other powers "peacefully" competed in the "Scramble for Africa"; that is, by waging war on African peoples.[158]

Indeed, the General Act of the Berlin Conference on West Africa of 1884–1885, signed by the European colonial powers, as well as by the Ottoman Empire (now part of the Concert of Europe) and the United States, was considered an advance for the cause of peace because it established agreement on issues connected with Africa's colonization. Focused on guaranteeing the freedom of trade on the great rivers (the exploitation of natural resources being the primary motivation for these colonial ventures), it required the powers to notify each other of the acquisition of new possessions or the establishment of new protectorates, the only condition being their ability to establish authority over the occupied territories. Given the "sovereign rights or influence" belonging to the occupying powers, they committed to protect their subjects, "care for their moral and material well-being," ensure religious freedom, and suppress slavery.[159] In practice, however, the "rights" granted to African peoples amounted to the protection given by landowners to serfs against specific abuses. Legal interpretations differ on the legal weight of the General Act of Berlin in the framework of international relations and its efficacy on the ground.[160] Yet that treaty is relevant in what it reveals to us of the political implications of theories of racial inequality in an era when "one of the main tasks of anthropology was to define and measure civilization—and its absence—as a justification for and of imperial expansion."[161] African peoples—none of whose representatives were invited to Berlin—were not deemed fit to exert legal and political rights self-evident to Europeans; notably, to own land and to resist foreign occupation. Peace under freedom became increasingly a monopoly of European states or of states of European descent. This triumph of racialism was a regression in the history of peace from the equalitarian ideals of the French Revolution.

By the end of the nineteenth century, the handful of sovereign states that were neither European nor ruled by Europeanized elites—notably the Ottoman Empire, Persia, Ethiopia, Siam, Japan, and China—were all under heavy pressure from outside. In Europe, the emergence of unified Germany and Italy as two new great powers prompted a split of the continent into two blocs: (1) the Triple Alliance of Germany, Austria-Hungary, and Italy (1882) and (2) the Triple Entente of Britain, France, and Russia (1907). This was also a time of prodigious technological advances in steam engines and the production of steel, both of which found immediate military application. In that volatile context, the balance of power was allowed to exert its most pernicious effect: to become the trigger for the runaway arms race that led to the outbreak of the Great War in 1914.

The Spirit of Geneva

SEEKING PEACE THROUGH A LEAGUE
OF NATIONS

Europe is not made of isolated states, one independent from the other.
It forms a harmonious whole. Destroying one part of it, is offending the
others. Our salvation is to be good Europeans. Outside of this, it is all
ruin and misery.

—ANATOLE FRANCE, 1922

*T*he Hall of Mirrors of the Palace of Versailles, the former residence of
Louis XIV turned national museum, was packed at 3:00 P.M. on that fateful
day of June 28, 1919. After a seven-month process, many diplomatic delegations were gathered to sign the peace treaty that was to close the Great War
with Germany. The weather was exceptionally cold for the season, and the
atmosphere just as chilly; the mood was not one of reconciliation. The
choice of location was highly symbolic: the very place where the Second
German Empire had been proclaimed in 1871, just after France had suffered
humiliating defeat and occupation.[1] British diplomat Harold Nicolson recounted in his diary: "Isolated and pitiable, come the two German delegates. Dr. Müller, Dr. Bell. The silence is terrifying. . . . They keep their
eyes fixed away from those two thousand staring eyes, fixed upon the ceiling.
They are deathly pale. They do not appear as representatives of a brutal
militarism. . . . It is all most painful."[2] After the signing ceremony, "the
Germans were conducted like prisoners from the dock, their eyes still

fixed upon some distant point of the horizon."[3] An American witness, US
secretary of state Robert Lansing, gave a similar account:

> It was as if men were being called upon to sign their own death-
> warrants, fully realizing that they were at the mercy of those whom
> they had wronged beyond the possibility of pardon. They seemed
> anxious to get through with it and be off. . . . With pallid faces and
> trembling hands they wrote their names quickly and were then con-
> ducted back to their places.[4]

Indeed, the setting of the room and the atmosphere evoked a court rather
than a negotiation venue.[5] It is worth asking how it came to that point.

As we turn now to the efforts of the great powers to reestablish and
maintain lasting peace between the Great War and the outbreak of
World War II, some differences between the treaty concluded at Versailles and earlier peace treaties become immediately apparent.[6] The victorious Allies seemed to convey a sense of exclusion and retribution,
which was quite different from the victors' attitudes at Vienna. Indeed,
the French president Raymond Poincaré had opened the Paris Peace
Conference six months earlier in the same Hall of Mirrors, with the following words:

> This very day forty-eight years ago, on January 18, 1871, the German
> Empire was proclaimed by an army of invasion in the Chateau at Ver-
> sailles. It was consecrated by the theft of two French provinces; it
> was thus vitiated from its origin and by the fault of the founders; born
> in injustice, it has ended in opprobrium.
>
> You are assembled in order to repair the evil that it has done and to
> prevent a recurrence of it. You hold in your hands the future of the
> world.[7]

As Poincaré's historical reference implied, the place and time of the signing
ceremony were carefully chosen for their symbolic value. That ceremony
was one more link in a chain of acts of mutual defiance between France and
Prussia—which stretched from Louis XIV's enmity with Prussia during the
War of Spanish Succession in the early eighteenth century and included the

FIG. 3.1 William Orpen, *The Signing of Peace in the Hall of Mirrors, Versailles*, 1919.
Art. IWM 2856, Imperial War Museums, London.

king of Prussia's national call to arms, "To My People" (1813), to avenge the crushing French victory of Jena in 1806.[8]

Paris Peace Conference produced not one, but five treaties signed in and around Versailles between June 1919 and August 1920 to make peace with Germany, Austria, Hungary, Bulgaria, and the Ottoman Empire; together the five are called the Treaties of Paris.[9] What many witnesses could not see at the time, however, was that the Peace Conference would fail to "repair the evil and to prevent a recurrence of it," as Poincaré had hoped when opening the negotiations. We can therefore talk about a Paris Conference (because discussions took place in that city) and the Treaty of Versailles (because it was signed in that suburb), but unfortunately "Peace of Versailles" is a misnomer. Some of the core territorial issues at stake, notably for Germany, Hungary, and Italy, did not find an amicable resolution in the following two decades. Even more harmful, two nationalistic attitudes came to the fore in the interwar period that were antipathetic to peace: *revanchism,* the desire to obtain revenge for past slights, and *irredentism,* the claim to recover territories. These fostered a dark myth of the Treaties of Paris that holds sway to this day and obscures our understanding of the events; fortunately, several recent publications have contributed to dispelling that myth.[10]

The Paris Conference was also radical in a positive way: peace was not to be solely achieved through the signing of treaties or deliberations at conferences, but was to be instituted through an international organization, the League of Nations. In 1917, Lord Robert Cecil, British Under-Secretary for Foreign Affairs, had talked about establishing a "peace machinery when this war is over."[11] The mechanical metaphor of the international order, with its "systems" and its "balance of power," was moving well into the practical realm of engineering. The League of Nations gave birth to the Spirit of Geneva, the phrase immortalized by the Swiss writer Robert de Traz in his 1929 bestseller *L'Esprit de Genève.* De Traz wrote another book in 1936, *From the Alliance of Kings to the League of Nations,* in which he compared the peace systems of 1815 and 1919.[12] The Spirit of Geneva he described was so contrary to the Spirit of Versailles that it was as if the victorious Allies had adopted an entirely new attitude toward peacemaking in the space of a single decade. In the years between the signing of the treaties to end the Great War and the beginning of World War II, the international community engaged in a continuous—and eventually doomed—struggle to correct the excesses of Versailles and bring about peace.

There is a second myth about this interwar period: that the League was intrinsically a "failure." In 1939, one of the English authors of the Treaty of Versailles, Lord Lothian, called the demise of the League of Nations "the greatest disappointment from which mankind has suffered since the Great War."[13] The League, boldly designed as the world's "machinery of peace," aimed at nothing less than the eradication of war; its proponents thus keenly perceived each new war as an existential setback. In the face of those hopes, the eventual disintegration of the League of Nations under the cumulative onslaught of the Italian, Japanese, German, and Soviet imperialisms was understandably perceived as catastrophe. Yet the League of Nations had its remarkable successes, such as the Locarno Agreements (also known as the Pact of Locarno) of 1925. It generated, in its heyday, sympathetic and even fervent public opinion, as well as media interest.

After World War II, the League of Nations was forgotten and its impact discounted, and this negative perception persisted until the late twentieth century: as one biographer of US president Woodrow Wilson wrote nearly twenty years ago, "The League stands now as a kind of noble irrelevance, little researched and not much admired."[14] Denying the League's contributions to the history of peace may also have been politically expedient for the United States and the Soviet Union, because this international institution was a considerable inconvenience for both of them, for reasons discussed later; history books on both sides of the Iron Curtain reflected this attitude.[15] Since the end of the Cold War, the League has undergone a process of rehabilitation.[16] In fact, assuming that it was "irrelevant" for the very reason it had "failed" is a fallacy. Reexamining the story of the League of Nations with a fresh perspective also provides an opportunity to critically reassess narratives written in an earlier era.

This chapter examines another key question: Why should the League of Nations be included in a *European* history of peace? Was it not, after all, meant to be a worldwide organization aiming at *world* peace? That is true, yet for all its universal goals, the structure and scope of the League were informed by Europe's peace experiments of the nineteenth century: it was no coincidence that the Congress of Vienna attracted renewed historical attention during World War I and immediately afterward.[17] US president Wilson promoted the League of Nations primarily to prevent European conflicts that could also involve the United States and secondarily to address colonial issues. Its overall mission was to remedy the failure of a continental system based on the balance of power to preserve peace; its particular aim was to prevent an attempt at revenge by the defeated Central Powers. By necessity, the League often concentrated on disputes between European states. Furthermore, of the fifty-seven members of the institution in 1926, all but six—China, Haiti, Iran, Japan, Liberia, and Thailand—were either European countries or countries formerly under colonial rule or, in the case of India, governed by a European power. Considering that the United States eventually refused to join and that all members of the League's decision-making body, its Council, were European except Brazil and Japan, it is clear that European states were massively overrepresented.[18] Unsurprisingly, the League sat in a European city, Geneva.

Finally, the League spawned a pan-European movement, notably with the Locarno Agreements of 1925, which sought to heal the wounds from the Treaty of Versailles and lay the foundations of a fresh continental union. Although in theory a global organization, it was in practice a typical product of Europe in this clash between the universal and the particular. It also established key patterns that would later shape the European Communities of the Cold War era. In any case, one question is paramount: Why and how did the European tradition of international relations that had supported the orders of Utrecht, Vienna, and Geneva suddenly collapse in the late 1930s in the face of totalitarian conceptions of the international order?

The Great War: Civilization's Suicide

By 1918, peace was in urgent need of redefinition, because the nature and scale of war had fundamentally changed, and for the worse. The technological revolution of the second part of the nineteenth century had produced generalized firearms loadable from the breech, which massively increased the rate and power of fire. Metal cartridge rifles for infantry, large artillery guns loaded with prepackaged metal ammunitions, and automatic machine guns were able to mow down dozens of soldiers at a time. By contrast, military engagement doctrines had not significantly evolved and still relied on massive infantry assaults. To make matters worse, dramatic population increases in the combatant countries meant that the number of soldiers at the Battle of the Marne in September 1914 was about five times higher than in the "colossal" battle of Leipzig a century earlier. As a result, the first clashes of the Great War became an open-air slaughterhouse: within a week, a half-million men were killed or wounded.

The great powers had grossly underestimated the nature, scale, and scope of the war they had begun; they mistakenly relied on a belief in maneuver warfare, seeing the war as a fast-paced beast that they could master and control. Even though the slogan "the war will be over by Christmas" is apocryphal, it did sum up the mood at the time.[19] The dominant conception of warfare—as Clausewitz had written in the previous century—was still "nothing but a duel on a larger scale," intended "to compel our enemy to do our will."[20] Alas, this perspective failed to take into account the following warning from the great strategist: the improved social conditions of "civilized" states in peacetime, which sought to make wars less destructive, were different from those that prevailed on a battlefield, and "to introduce the principle of moderation into the theory of war itself would always lead to logical absurdity."[21] The increased capabilities of the belligerents to obliterate each other had an immediate effect: opposed armies had no choice but to dig themselves in. On the French and Italian fronts, this became "trench warfare," a mutual siege where the advantage invariably went to whoever was already holding the ground and where the fate of countries, not cities, was at stake.[22] By Christmas 1914, on the Western Front winning did not confer a tactical advantage, but left everything to lose strategically for the belligerents, with only the Eastern Front remaining open for maneuver warfare. As if to confirm Clausewitz's principle that "the only limiting factors are the counterpoises inherent in war," military operations were carried out without question, no matter the cost and regardless of initial war aims; inaction was considered treasonable.[23] None of the belligerents were thus able to terminate the fighting when they wanted.

Nevertheless, several voices continued to advocate for peace throughout the Great War, despite the apparent futility. On September 15, 1914, French writer Romain Rolland wrote an essay protesting the war, "Above the Fray."

He lamented that the enthusiasm of young Europeans was being wasted in a "sacrilegious mêlée," and he advocated the creation of a "High Moral Court" to judge war crimes and to be staffed by magistrates from neutral countries.[24] The 1914 Christmas truce could be counted as a step in the direction of peace, though it amounted only to a fraternization episode among combatants (there was no political intention on either side to end the war).[25] More significant were the efforts led by Pope Benedict XV who, on March 4, 1917, mourned the "suicide of civilized Europe." He declared the neutrality of the Holy See and attempted from that perspective to mediate peace. Despite Benedict's failure to alter the course of the war, his diplomatic efforts were matched by humanitarian action, such as attending to prisoners of war, the exchange of wounded soldiers, and food deliveries to needy populations in Europe.[26]

The endless deadlock of the Great War thus continued, to the point of breaking the long-lasting cultural taboo on the murder of civilians. The immobility of the forces on the front was exceedingly frustrating, given that fast steamships, train convoys, and more recently dirigible airships had reduced travel times between European capitals from days to hours. As a result, civilians were only a few hours away from the front, and by working in factories to supply the frontlines, they became parties to the war effort. To break the insufferable deadlock, the temptation for the military to target civilians became irresistible. The German Army committed premeditated atrocities against civilians in 1914 in an episode called the "Rape of Belgium."[27] And the German High Command coined the term "total war"—the willingness of belligerents to achieve victory at any cost—in the context of the first strategic bombings of civilians in London by zeppelins in 1915.[28]

Civilians' perception of warfare was transformed by the realization that they could be killed at any moment, even in cities far from the front. Although the war, like past conflicts, initially asserted itself mostly through shortages and hunger, its impact came to include violent death at home. Despite the claim of one historian that the Napoleonic wars comprised the first "total war" because of their intensity and scale, their military operations were more or less constrained by a moral code of respect that both the allied powers and Napoleon owed to civilian populations, which condemned excessively cruel behavior as an *atrocity*.[29] In contrast, the Eastern Front was the scene of many atrocities from both sides against civilians, as well as of deportations, and the Ottoman Empire engaged in large-scale massacres of Armenians and other populations. During the Great War, the necessities of modern warfare ushered a new level of inhumanity into war.

For the combatants, trench warfare was both a mentally and physically devastating form of conflict, and it soon became a chief cause of popular disaffection with war itself. From April to June 1917, several mutinies broke out in the French Army, in which pacifism—understood as a disavowal of the conflict—played a role. In Russia, 200,000 protesters (many of whom were women) took to the streets of St. Petersburg in early March 1917 to demand more food and the return of soldiers from the front; the army's refusal to quell the protests precipitated the fall of the tsarist regime. In October, hundreds of thousands of Italian soldiers deserted after the defeat at Caporetto (Kobarid, in today's Slovenia). The large number of casualties and the privations of the war economy also started taking their toll on the morale of civilian populations, leading to hunger riots. By 1918, a whole generation of young Europeans had become disgusted with the business of war; many art forms, including painting, sculpture, and literature, portrayed war in the bleakest tones. The aged French writer and literary critic Anatole France summarized these feelings in 1922 with a scathing statement: "we believe we are dying for the fatherland, [but] we are dying for industrialists."[30]

To add to the war's impact, it was truly global, because most of the world's sovereign states had taken sides. Historians have pointed out that the Seven Years' War of the eighteenth century was also "global,"[31] because it was fought in Europe, in the colonies, and over all the oceans—yet those colonial battles never reached the dimension of the clashes of 1914–1918. German submarine warfare against commercial shipping in the Atlantic, for instance, was seen as "a warfare against mankind . . . a war against all nations," as President Wilson put it.[32] Although most of the fighting did take place in Europe, millions of soldiers were conscripted from French and British colonies. All in all, the conflict was murderous, total, persistent, and profoundly distressing. With human, economic, and psychological impacts at a global level, it truly deserved to be called the Great War or the World War.[33] Wilson vividly expressed, in a 1919 speech, the disheartening realization that the very progress made in learning and technology that was the pride of Europeans had also led to more destruction on the battlefield:

> Is it not a startling circumstance for one thing that the great discoveries of science, that the quiet study of men in laboratories, that the thoughtful developments which have taken place in quiet lecture-rooms, have now been turned to the destruction of civilization? The powers of destruction have not so much multiplied as gained facility. The enemy whom we have just overcome had at its seats of learning some of the principal centers of scientific study and discovery, and used them in order to make destruction sudden and complete; and only the watchful, continuous co-operation of men can see to it that science, as well as armed men, is kept within the harness of civilization.[34]

The only way to counteract the industrial advances of warfare would be to achieve comparable progress in the methodology of peace. It was perceived as a race between civilization and barbarism.

The Paris Peace Conference: Chaos and Precipitation

If modern European history is any indication, the greatest political changes have not been caused by war itself but by the nature of the peace agreements that followed. This, in turn, largely depended on which members of the victorious alliance had the upper hand *after* the ceasefire. For example, in 1917 the Central Powers managed to overrun Russia, then in the throes of the Bolshevik Revolution. The will to fight having left the Russian Army, most of Belarus and Ukraine fell easily. A small contingent of Germans went as far as Georgia in the Caucasus, joining forces with the Ottoman Army; the Black Sea fell entirely to the Central Powers. On March 3, 1918, Germany imposed the Treaty of Brest-Litovsk on Russia, with draconian conditions. Russia relinquished Belarus and Ukraine, Germany acquired the Baltic States, and the Ottoman Empire acquired the provinces of Kars and Ardahan in Eastern Anatolia. Russia was brought to its knees.

It was not, however, the first time in European history that the victorious empire of one day became the vanquished of the next. The entry of the United States into the war in 1917, with a force that eventually grew to two million men, threatened to tip the balance of power by the summer of 1918. On the battlefields, maneuver warfare finally replaced trench warfare, as the Germans staked everything in a last offensive against France. When the German soldiers started to run out of steam, their movement turned into retreat and then into rout. In that context, armored tanks—invented by the British but perfected by the French—were a capital innovation that would later come to dominate military tactics. The misfortune that befell Russia repeated itself. By the end of 1918, the Central Powers, their armies exhausted and suffering dwindling morale, witnessed mass protests in cities across Germany, in Vienna, and Prague. Almost simultaneously, both Austro-Hungary on the southern Italian front and Germany on the Western Front caved in. Each sued for an armistice, signed, respectively, in a mansion near Padua (November 3), and in a train wagon in the forest of Compiègne (November 11). In the latter case, the agreement stated in crisp military style: "Cessation of hostilities by land and in the air six hours after the signing of the armistice."[35] Because the sea blockade was maintained, the armistice did not apply to the seas.

The attitude of the victorious Allies in Versailles was much less amicable than at the Congress of Utrecht or the Paris peace negotiations of 1814 because of hostility toward the defeated powers. Even though the spirit of this moment is symbolically attached to the Hall of Mirrors, the negotiations took place at the French Foreign Ministry, on the Quai d'Orsay in Paris. The hierarchical structure of the delegations, representing what historians call "the Allies," was odd. From the Triple Entente of Russia, France, and Britain, Russia was absent because the tsarist state has collapsed; the only formal "Allies" left were thus Britain and France. The United States was self-styled as an "Associated Power" to stress the independence of its foreign policy despite its close military cooperation with the Allies. Woodrow Wilson, like Alexander I in the early nineteenth century, was an outsider, because he was head of a remote state. Although he was personally involved in the negotiations, poor health forced his absence from some of the debates.

Italy was a minority partner, and a troublesome one, given that it had switched sides in 1915. As a reward for entering the war on the side of the Allied Powers, France, Britain, and Russia had promised Italy, by a secret Treaty of London, that it would acquire territory over Austria-Hungary and a "just share" of southern Anatolia "in the event of total or partial partition of Turkey in Asia."[36] The problem was that the treaty never had the effect of formally allowing Italy to "join the Triple Entente," as is often stated. It was merely a "military convention" that associated Italy with the individual members of that alliance (the term "Triple Alliance" did not appear in the treaty). Italy's position was that the treaty was a solemn and binding agreement on equal terms, but it had made a fools' bargain. Its government had joined the war effort for motives of self-aggrandizement, only to find that the two remaining Allies, France and Britain, no longer felt compelled to honor their less-than-honorable promise to a power they considered only a junior partner; in addition, Wilson firmly opposed it, for reasons that soon became obvious. This was catastrophic for the Italian government, which had drawn its whole population into the war based on the promise that it would annex Istria and Dalmatia. After extracting a huge human toll from its soldiers, it then had only the acquisition of South of Tyrol to show for it. Honor bound to keep its side of the bargain at all costs and threatened with nationalist insurrections if it did not comply, the Italian delegation in Paris had its back against the wall.

Finally, Japan had declared war on Germany in the Pacific on the basis of a military alliance concluded with Britain in 1902.[37] The net result was that the "Five Powers" that congregated at the Paris Conference— Britain, France, the United States, Italy, and Japan—formed a discordant assemblage of co-belligerents, called "Principal Allied and Associated Powers" for lack of anything better. They were not acting in concert, by any stretch of the word. In reality the Paris Conference should have been only a "preliminary peace conference," after which a proper peace conference could have taken place with the defeated powers—but that was not to be.

The negotiation was initially directed by a Council of Ten, made up of two members from each victorious power—the heads of government and foreign ministers of Britain, France, Italy and the United States, as

Europe after the Treaty of Versailles and Related Treaties, 1919–20

	Victorious powers
	Allied occupation of the Rhineland, 1919–30
	Territory ceded by Germany after the Versailles Treaty
	Former borders of the German, Austro-Hungarian and Ottoman Empires in 1914
	Former Russian Empire
	Neutral countries during World War I
①	Curzon Line
②	Eastern border of Poland after Russo-Polish War, 1921
③	Occupied or claimed by Greece, 1919
④	Greek-Turkish border 1922

FINLAND

Leningrad

Helsinki

Tallinn

ckholm

ESTONIA

Riga

LATVIA

anzig
ty under
f Nations)

LITHUANIA

East
Prussia

① Warsaw

②

P O L A N D

U   S   S   R

LOVAKIA

na

Budapest

HUNGARY

R O M A N I A

Belgrade

Bucharest

Black Sea

KINGDOM OF
SERBS, CROATS
AND SLOVENES
ater YUGOSLAVIA

Serbia

BULGARIA

Sofia

③ Istanbul
(Constantinople)

④

ALBANIA

atic Sea

Aegean Sea

T U R K E Y

G R E E C E ③

Athens

(Italian occupied)

CYPRUS
(British)

0   400 km

0   400 miles

S e a

CRETE

well as two Japanese representatives; it was supplemented by "delegates and technical advisers," and a secretariat general, numbering sixty persons in total. The negotiations laboriously plowed on, trying to reconcile contradictory agendas with the chaotic situation of Europe, but achieving precious little. By the end of March, Wilson and the three prime ministers—Clemenceau (France), Lloyd George (Britain), and Orlando (Italy)—had taken matters into their own hands. Negotiating behind closed doors, they formed a Council of Four, which reduced the Council of Ten to a subordinate body. Japan, having solved its own issues, rarely participated: the Four Powers were now France, Britain, Italy, and the United States. These negotiations were characterized by improvisation and informality; the men met in Wilson's private residence and initially did not even take notes, until a British diplomatic secretary forced himself into the meetings and brought a semblance of order to them.[38] On April 24, 1919, the Italian delegation left the conference in protest over the Adriatic question, only to return ten days later. The four representatives finally hammered out a half-baked treaty by the end of May. Their agreement was so tenuous, however, that any thoughts of a proper peace conference were laid aside. The real—and sad—reason why Germany was not consulted was that the victorious powers were too disunited to put up a common front, and they were running behind schedule.

The one-sidedness of the treaty clauses was not really the intention of the United States, Britain, or France for that matter. In a speech to Parliament on January 5, 1918, Lloyd George had made a statement about Britain's involvement in the war:

> The destruction or disruption of Germany or the German people has never been a war aim with us from the first day of this war to this day. . . . We were forced to join in this war in self-defense. In defense of the violated public law of Europe, and in vindication of the most solemn treaty obligation on which the public system of Europe rested, and on which Germany had ruthlessly trampled in her invasion of Belgium, we had to join in the struggle or stand aside and see Europe go under and brute force triumph over public right and international justice.[39]

The conditions unilaterally imposed at Versailles on Germany were clearly unfavorable, particularly the redefinition of its borders, which entailed the loss of the Saar coal mines, the insertion of a corridor between the main body of German and Eastern Prussia to give Poland access to the sea, and the loss of its colonial empire. The treaty also provided for demilitarization and unrestricted intervention in the German economy for both the Allies and the United States, without reciprocity. Symbolically, however, Part VII, "Penalties," stood out for its harshness. Its first article (Article 227) demanded that "the Allied and Associated Powers publicly arraign William of Hohenzollern, formerly German Emperor, for a supreme offence against international morality and the sanctity of treaties." The article conceded that a tribunal would have to be constituted to enforce "guarantees essential to the right of defense." Article 231 stated that Germany accepted responsibility "for causing all the loss and damage of the war . . . as a consequence of the war imposed . . . by the aggression of Germany and her allies."[40] Accepting responsibility was to be understood in legal terms— it meant that Germany was required to pay financial reparations for damages—and the next article clarified that it specifically applied to civilian losses. The German delegation, which had predicated its negotiation strategy since the opening of the peace talks on defining mutual responsibilities for the war's losses, perceived this as a "Guilt Clause."[41]

The German plenipotentiary Count Ulrich von Brockdorff-Rantzau, protested, stating that Germany had expected a "peace of justice" and a "peace proposal based on the agreed principles." He added that a "people of 70,000,000 suffers but does not die."[42] Brockdorff-Rantzau then maintained an attitude of outrage and defiance. Although this was perhaps understandable, it lost Germany the sympathy of Wilson's delegation. On June 16, the Allies gave Germany an ultimatum: either sign the treaty as it was by June 23, or they would consider the armistice lapsed. Nearly forty Allied divisions were made ready to invade Germany, and additional forces were prepared to resume the blockade of the country.[43] These actions seemed quite contrary to the spirit of the armistice, because the Allies had committed to "give consideration to the provisioning of Germany during the armistice to the extent recognized as necessary."[44] The German delegation answered that "they regard it as their duty . . . to point out with all possible emphasis that the carrying out of this agreement must throw the German people into anarchy and famine."[45] It was not an idle statement, because the country was still suffering from food riots that destabilized the legitimate government and bolstered the strength of both pro-Bolshevik and radical right-wing groups. The Allied ultimatum was not limited to the defeated powers: the Entente (namely France and Britain) also demanded that neutral states stop all commerce with Germany in the event of the blockade. Sweden, Denmark, and Switzerland lodged formal protests against this demand.[46] Brockdorff-Rantzau, who wanted to continue wrangling with the Allies, soon realized the German government would not let him do so; he resigned to avoid submitting to what he termed a *diktat*. That keyword had been uttered. The "dictated peace" would become the object of bitter debate in 1919 and then play an enormous role in Hitler's political campaigns and eventually in the Third Reich.[47]

The other defeated powers held their signing ceremonies in stately, though more modest, locations than the Versailles Palace. Austria held its own ceremony ten miles north in the Palace of Saint-Germain-en-Laye. For the Habsburgs, who once aspired to a universal monarchy in Europe and overseas, the outcome of the war was devastating. On November 11, 1918, Emperor Karl I wrote a renunciation document acknowledging "the decision that Germany-Austria is making about its future system of government" and proclaiming his abdication.[48] It was a ghostly echo of the dissolution of the Holy Roman Empire by his ancestor Francis in 1806, under similarly tragic conditions.

The death of the Austro-Hungarian Empire was formally pronounced on September 10, 1919. The Habsburg monarchy did not get so much as a burial ceremony, because the Treaty of Saint-Germain was both a peace treaty and a settlement treaty. It acknowledged the existence of Austria, Czechoslovakia, and the Kingdom of Serbs, Croats, and Slovenes (which would become Yugoslavia), and defined their respective borders. Karl I had assumed Austria would be merged with Germany, but the Allies vetoed the idea. Central Europe thus was beginning a process of balkanization. The Treaty of Saint-Germain dealt, however, only with the western half of the former Austro-Hungarian monarchy. The fate of the kingdom of Hungary, which finally emerged as an independent state in February 1920, replacing short-lived communist and counterrevolutionary regimes, was settled on July 31, 1921, when it also formally ended its state of war with the Allies.

Hungary's ceremony was held in an annex of Versailles, the Grand Trianon. Unlike the successor countries, which were seen as new creations, Hungary had been a kingdom within the "dual monarchy" and was thus considered a defeated country: in a similar provision to those of the Versailles and Saint-Germain Treaties, Article 161 of the Treaty of Trianon affirmed Hungary's "responsibility . . . for causing the loss and damage . . . as a consequence of the war imposed . . . by the aggression of Austria-Hungary and her allies."[49] Ultimately, Hungary paid dearly for the considerable advantages it had reaped from the Austro-Hungarian Compromise of 1867, when it had gained control over a full half of the empire located east of the Leitha River, Transleithania, which formed a downward-facing crescent with Hungary at the center and Slovakia on the north. It extended southwest to Croatia on the Adriatic coast and southeast to Transylvania in the Carpathian mountains.[50] After signing the Treaty of Trianon, Hungary lost two-thirds of its territory within Europe: Transylvania was ceded to Romania, Slovakia to the new state of Czechoslovakia, and Croatia and Slovenia to the newly created Kingdom of Serbs, Croates, and Slovenes. Hungary also waived all rights to former colonial possessions of the Austro-Hungarian Empire. The dismemberment of the kingdom left substantial Hungarian populations living outside of Hungary, particularly in Czechoslovakia, Romania, and Serbia. In an odd contradiction to Wilson's principle of self-determination (the "freest opportunity of autonomous development"), many were displaced without recourse to plebiscite. For Hungarians, the treaty was received as a national tragedy.[51] Bulgaria signed its own treaty on November 27, 1919, in Neuilly-sur-Seine's townhall.

The disorganized Paris Peace Conference ended as it started, reversing the progress made toward peacemaking of the post-Napoleonic era. The treaties were drafted unilaterally, hurriedly, and without attention to detail. Rather than being guided by ordered agendas or technical commissions, the treaty provisions acknowledged faits accomplis on the ground (particularly proclamations of independence) for the lack of better alternatives. The trend in peace negotiations over the past century had been toward professionalization, accompanied by delegation and specialization, and progressively building a broad consensus through several carefully crafted treaties. The Principal and Allied Powers, which lacked a shared organic vision in the first place, took the route of drafting a settlement treaty with each defeated power, as if various parts of Europe could be treated separately from the others, and hoping that the general outcome would somehow be coherent. Unfortunately, this waterfall approach—using the settlement of Germany to determine that of Austria and then Hungary, which in turn determined that of Bulgaria and then the Ottoman Empire—only increased the likelihood of irreversible mishaps.[52]

A methodical approach to establishing lasting peace was all the more necessary, because the situation in Europe was much more chaotic and volatile than in 1814. After the collapse of four major empires, a massive transformation was underway, from states held together by allegiance to a dynasty to new states, most of them based on ethno-nationalism coded as popular sovereignty. A new phenomenon was on the rise that would continue to threaten peace for the next two decades and eventually cause a second world war: *irredentism,* movements that sought the return of a territory to a nation. The word, rooted in the Latin *irredenta* (not returned), was coined by the Italians who wanted territories in Croatia to be returned to Italy, notably the city of Fiume (today's Rijeka); a strong irredentist movement also developed in Hungary over Transylvania.[53]

To cope with that volatility, the only effective option for the victorious powers (even supposing it were possible) would have been to carefully follow the lead of 1814–1815: first, focusing intensively on restoring the state of peace with the utmost dispatch *and,* second, when a semblance of order was restored, calling a pan-European congress to carefully redraw the continent's map with the assistance of technical commissions. Instead, the Paris Conference dived without preparation into the question of territorial settlements, quickly becoming lost in a vast morass. Wilson, Clemenceau, Lloyd George, and Orlando, already out of their depth (as anyone else would have been) and driven to exasperation by the urgency of the need and the lack of progress, took the exact opposite route from that taken by their predecessors in 1814: the leaders took matters into their own hands by summarily excluding allies, defeated powers, and neutrals alike from the decision-making process. That final, desperate attempt to sever the

"Gordian knot" was only the last of a long series of choices that had already doomed the peace process to failure.

An example of an unresolved territorial issue was the Polish Question, left unsettled from the Vienna Order. The Treaty of Versailles restored Poland to complete independence from Germany, with the exception of East Prussia (which remained German) and the Free City of Danzig. In the Treaty of Trianon, however, no settlement was reached for the territories that were formerly part of the Austro-Hungarian and Russian Empires: Article 89 of the Treaty of Saint-Germain with Austria recognized the frontiers of Poland "as may be determined by the Principal Allied and Associated Powers,"[54] which was inconclusive at best. In addition, the Bolshevik state, having no control over the Polish territories formerly controlled by the Russian Empire, and furthermore at war in Ukraine against a French Army, was not called to sit at the negotiation table. Poland would continuously be at odds with the Soviet Union after the latter country reasserted control over Ukraine in 1920.[55]

The history of the Black Sea and Anatolia after the end of World War I was similarly complex and tragic. At the end of the war, Britain, Italy, and France occupied Constantinople, the Straits, and all territories outside of Anatolia, while Greek forces landed in Anatolia in May 1919 in the Smyrna District (Izmir). The fate of the region was discussed without the involvement of the United States and was formalized in the Treaty of Sèvres, signed in the historical Sèvres porcelain factory a few miles east of Versailles, on August 10, 1920.[56] This treaty essentially created a colonial partition: the Straits were to be placed under an international mandate, whereas Greece would obtain most of the remainder of Thrace, including Adrianople, as well as the Smyrna District. The ailing Ottoman Empire was eventually abolished on November 1, 1922, but the strife was not over: led by Kemal Atatürk, a Turkish successor state with its capital in Ankara refused to acknowledge the new status quo. Paradoxically, an attempt by Greek army to expand its territory by annexing western Anatolia into Greece broke the deadlock by causing a rift between Britain and its French and Italian allies. Both France and Italy began to show increasing sympathy for Turkey, and the Greek expedition ended in disaster. On July 24, 1923, the Treaty of Lausanne closed the issue by recognizing Turkey's control over Anatolia and

Adrianople in Europe—but not without the tremendous loss of civilian lives and massive deportations. This human tragedy, remembered in Greece as the Great Catastrophe, forever changed the hitherto multicultural demography of Asia Minor.[57]

The Third Feature of the Treaty of Versailles

The Treaties of Paris, in addition to being both peace and settlements treaties at the same time, had a third notable feature. On Monday, February 3, 1919, two weeks into the Paris Peace Conference, the first meeting of the Commission on the League of Nations took place in a former Parisian palace, then the Hôtel de Crillon. On that occasion, Woodrow Wilson presented the first draft of the Covenant of a future League of Nations.[58] The commission was more inclusive than the main group discussing the German treaty: it had fifteen members, all of whom had been engaged in the war effort. The United States, the British Empire, France, Italy, and Japan had two members each, whereas Belgium, Brazil, China, Portugal, and Serbia had one each. The initiative was not driven solely by the US government, as commonly thought; a French delegate, Léon Bourgeois, presented an original draft on behalf of his government, whereas Italian lawyer and statesman Vittorio Emanuele Orlando presented a counterproposal.[59] The commission soon expanded to include representatives from Poland, Romania, Greece, and the Czecho-Slovak Republic; unlike the Spirit of Vienna of 1815, however, there were no representatives from either the defeated powers or the neutrals. Yet even the German government (though not invited to the meetings) sent its own proposal for bylaws for a "permanent peace . . . by obligatory settlement of international differences"; it contained a clause to the effect that all belligerents of the war and the neutrals should be members by right and, in contrast to the US draft, provided for enforcement, including military measures. It also featured a detailed International Workers' Charter that specified the rights of residence and social insurance.[60]

Representatives met in the evenings so as not to interfere with the meetings of the Peace Conference. The moonlighting operation proceeded efficiently: it took only fifteen sessions to complete the Covenant, which was ready on April 11, 1919. The United States and Britain played the most significant roles in developing this document, which represented, by and large, a consensus between the two delegations. Unfortunately, a clause on racial equality brought to the table by Japan was rejected by the other four powers.[61]

The US government had to travel a long path to enable it to propose a League of Nations at a peace conference in Paris. For more than a century, the Monroe Doctrine had defined North and South America as a separate zone of influence, in which European powers had no rights of intervention or colonization; conversely, it considered Europe outside the scope of US interests.[62] Guided by that spirit, in December 1914 Wilson was mulling over the possibility of establishing a Pan-American Alliance based on "mutual guarantees of political independence under republican form and mutual guarantees of territorial integrity."[63] Such an idea would have been compatible with the Monroe Doctrine, whereas an alliance that involved Europe would not.[64] It was Edward Grey, British foreign secretary until 1916 and a prominent member of the Liberal Party, who initiated the idea of a world alliance. He sent "emphatic" letters to Colonel Edward Mandell House, a longtime friend of Wilson and his adviser on foreign affairs, advocating that the future peace of the world "depended upon a general and permanent conference of the nations, the substitution of international organization in place of the existing anarchy, international concert instead of national individualism."[65] Simply stated, Grey was building on the traditional tenets of perpetual peace—a "conference system" not unlike that of the post-Napoleonic era, institutionalized by an international league of peace, and a world order based on cooperation instead of military competition.

A key factor that contributed to Wilson's shift in policy toward Europe was the evolution of German submarine warfare. In 1916, attacks by German submarines on Allied merchant ships just off the US coast had been rare but nonetheless had the effect of making the European war a matter of US domestic interest. On May 27, 1916, Wilson addressed the First Annual Assemblage of the League to Enforce Peace, delivering what he considered to be the most important speech of his career. After observing that secret diplomacy and a general lack of political openness (even on the part of the United States) were key causes of the unexpected outbreak of war, he set forth three principles: all people should have the right to choose the sovereignty under which they lived; small states should benefit from the same guarantees of sovereignty and territorial integrity as larger ones; and "the world has a right to be free from every disturbance of its peace that has its origin in aggression and disregard of the rights of peoples and nations."[66] He went on to define his two aims regarding the war itself—first, a settlement among the belligerents as they deemed fit (the United States had no demands for itself); and second, a "universal association of the nations" to maintain the security of the seas and protect against future aggressive wars. Initially, this expansion of the Monroe Doctrine to Europe did not imply that the United States should join the war effort. It certainly implied, however, that the United States would obligate itself to support this association after the war, through a more active approach to international policy.[67] This change of approach was a prelude to the "Wilsonian moment" of Europe.

In January 1917, the German diplomatic service unintentionally gave the United States the justification to enter the war. A telegraphic dispatch to Berlin's representative in Mexico City was intercepted, which revealed that Germany intended to start unrestricted submarine warfare—to sink US merchant ships. It also would be directing the German ambassador to exploit the ongoing border war between Mexico and the United States: should the United States be drawn into the Great War, Germany and Mexico "would make war together and make peace together."[68] The US government decided to promptly release this information to the press, causing outrage among the American public (a move reminiscent of the "Ems Telegram Affair" of 1870, when the Prussian government leaked a diplomatic dispatch to the press with the same effect, a few days before declaring war on France).[69] Wilson nevertheless reasserted, in an address to the Senate, his hope of joining a peace agreement between both sides of the conflict in Europe: "No covenant of cooperative peace that does not include the peoples of the New World can suffice to keep the future safe against war; and yet there is only one sort of peace that the peoples of America could join in guaranteeing."[70] Yet, when Germany confirmed that unrestricted submarine warfare would start on February 1, 1917, the United States broke off diplomatic relations. The divorce became final when German submarines sank a US merchant ship off the coast of Cornwall two days later; in just a few months, US public opinion had changed from isolationist to prowar. Faced with this blatant *casus belli,* Wilson asked Congress to declare war on Germany. His request was granted on April 6, 1917.

It was in May of the same year that Wilson answered the ceasefire proposal from Pope Benedict XV as follows:

> The object of this war is to deliver the free peoples of the world from the menace and the actual power of a vast military establishment controlled by an irresponsible government which . . . proceeded to carry the plan out without regard either to the sacred obligations of treaty or the long-established practices and long-cherished principles of international action and honor.[71]

In other words, he did not see the point of negotiating with a foe who would not keep his word. Nevertheless, the entry of the United States into the war did not fundamentally alter the Wilsonian doctrine. Defeating Germany had become necessary, but it was only a step on the way to establishing the new system of peace he had conceived.

Wilson was reluctant to open a public debate at home that might, in his view, compromise the success of his enterprise. He was not, however, trying to impose original views; he was building on preexisting theories and was gratefully taking advice from a specialized circle that could provide well-elaborated contributions. Colonel House played the "role of a commission all by himself," meeting with British diplomats, as well as with US diplomat David Hunter Miller, and with American peace societies; House also provided Wilson with a synthesis of their reflections. The British, who had their own plan, forwarded it to House in early January 1917.[72] In this fashion, the Wilson-House-Miller trio prepared the official US draft of the League while the United States was waging on Germany, with the tacit approval of London.[73]

On January 8, 1918, Wilson addressed a joint session of Congress in a speech on war aims and peace terms, introducing the program now remembered as the Fourteen Points. The first five points covered general principles, calling for a ban on secret diplomacy, freedom of the seas, freedom of commerce, reduction of armaments, and a (moderate) call to settle colonial issues. Wilson next laid out his conception of how to settle European territorial issues after the war. He notably proposed to restore the sovereignty of Poland, lost at the end of the eighteenth century, and offered autonomy to the non-German peoples of the Austro-Hungarian Empire—he did not use the term "independence," because offering terms of peace to Austro-Hungary that required it to accept its own dismemberment would have been absurd. Point XIV is particularly relevant, because it is the earliest mention of the League of Nations: "A general association of nations must be formed under specific covenants for the purpose of affording mutual guarantees of political independence and territorial integrity to great and small states alike."[74] The conclusion to the speech was so important that one might call it the "Fifteenth Point":

> We have no jealousy of German greatness, and there is nothing in this program that impairs it. We grudge her no achievement or distinction of learning or of pacific enterprise such as have made her record very bright and very enviable. We do not wish to injure her or to block in any way her legitimate influence or power. We do not wish to fight her either with arms or with hostile arrangements of trade if she is willing to associate herself with us and the other peace-loving nations of the world in covenants of justice and law and fair dealing. We wish her only to accept a place of equality among the peoples of the world—the new world in which we now live—instead of a place of mastery.[75]

After the Armistice, Wilson sought to make it clear that the United States had entered the war with no intention of intervening in the politics of Europe or any other part of the world.[76] In retrospect, this echoed the statement of 1815 that the allied powers were not fighting France but only the government of Napoleon.[77] Wilson also argued for the necessity of the League of Nations to maintain world peace, the matter in which the United States was most concerned. His conclusion made clear that the Covenant of the League was, in his mind, distinct from the rest of the Treaty of Versailles and much more significant than it, because its purpose was not to make peace but to maintain it:

It is a solemn obligation of our part, therefore, to make permanent arrangements that justice shall be rendered and peace maintained. This is the central object of our meeting. Settlements may be temporary, but the action of the nations in the interest of peace and justice should be permanent. We can set up permanent processes. We may not be able to set up permanent decisions. Therefore, it seems to me that we must take, so far as we can, a picture of the world into our minds.[78]

Following this speech, he secured the unanimous agreement of the Paris Peace Conference that the League of Nations should be an integral part of the Treaty of Versailles. This became known as the "Wilsonian moment."[79]

Even though the bylaws of the League of Nations were incorporated into a peace treaty, there was a world of difference between the spirit of the League and that of the five Treaties of Paris. Those documents appear today much like the composite statues sometimes displayed in older archaeological museums—made up of separate pieces of varying color, material, and handicraft and hastily patched together to form an assemblage so mismatched that even a casual observer instinctively feels that something is amiss. One found, lumped together, the restoration of the state of peace with war reparations, the territorial settlement of a sizable part of Europe, followed by the League of Nations provisions establishing a multilateral peace organization based on the free participation of states.

Britain's support for Wilson's vision of peace was qualified by some reservations. The Foreign Office could not have reasonably subscribed to the first point of Wilson's program, a ban on secret diplomacy, because it was bound by two secret pacts of 1915–1916: the Treaty of London, which granted territories to Italy from the Balkans, and the Sykes-Picot Agreement with France, which laid out a plan for the dismemberment of the Ottoman Empire. As was the case with the secret partition clauses of the Treaty of Paris of 1814, Britain wanted to support both the League and its own secret pacts. Britain and France also had an eye on the German colonies in Africa and the Far East. The more cynical diplomats in London and Paris may have thought that the League offered an expedient cloak of respectability for those who still wanted to indulge in colonial self-aggrandizement. In any case it was the clear policy of the governments of Britain, France, and Italy that the lofty principles of the League would have to wait until their territorial war aims had been satisfied.

It is indeed worth comparing the European Allies' lingering territorial ambitions with Wilson's diagnosis of the war's causes in his address to them at the end of January 1919:

> We are here to see, in short, that the very foundations of this war are swept away. . . . Those foundations were the private choice of small coteries of civil rulers and military staffs. Those foundations were the aggression of great powers upon small. Those foundations were the folding together of empires of unwilling subjects by the duress of arms. Those foundations were the power of small bodies of men to work their will and use mankind as pawns in a game. And nothing less than the emancipation of the world from these things will accomplish peace.[80]

Wilson followed up with the claim that "no right anywhere exists to hand peoples about from sovereignty to sovereignty as if they were property."[81] At a time when states were no longer the patrimonial property of a family, Wilson recognized small cliques as illegitimate appropriators of the state and of other human beings. He thus promoted the right of self-determination of peoples (somewhat like the Holy Alliance of the Peoples that Giuseppe Mazzini had hoped for). Certainly, it was contradictory that Germany, while forced to undersign the creation of the Covenant of the League of Nations, was eventually barred from membership and that the Austrians, whose Constituent Assembly had voted in favor of uniting with Germany, were denied that right.[82]

That the Treaties of Paris had three functions—serving as peace treaties, settlement treaties, and the founding acts of a peace institution—goes a long way to explain the US Senate's refusal to ratify them. Not unlike Tsar Alexander I before him, Wilson's geographical distance from his own country made it difficult for him to consult with his own government on a regular basis, and this forced him to take great initiative when negotiating the Treaty of Versailles. But unlike Alexander, Wilson was not an autocrat able to ratify a treaty on his own: the other participants in the diplomatic negotiations may have discounted the fact that the US president had not always been representing mainstream opinion in his own country, and particularly that of the US Congress. Indeed, so intent was Wilson on constructing a postwar order in Europe that he failed to rally US public opinion behind his efforts. In the midterm elections of 1918, the Republican Party won the majority in both the House and Senate—making Wilson's situation as a Democratic president precarious. One of his archenemies, Henry Cabot Lodge, became majority leader and chairman of the Senate Foreign Relations Committee. Lodge was hostile to the Fourteen Points, instead supporting the position that it was necessary to crush Germany militarily and economically; he also admitted to a profound personal hatred of Wilson. Not surprisingly, he staunchly campaigned against the United States joining the League of Nations.[83]

Lodge's generally militant view of foreign policy also contributed to his opposition to the League. He had supported the Spanish-American War in 1898, which resulted in the United States incorporating Puerto Rico and extending its domination over Cuba and the Philippines (crushing, in the process, the first Philippine Republic). In the same year, the United States also annexed Hawaii. Unlike Lodge, Wilson had been reluctant to see his nation embark on an imperialist course, even though he eventually supported the idea that the United States should acquire Puerto Rico and the Philippines so as to "train them in self-government."[84] Lodge may have taken the statement in the Fourteen Points that "the day of conquest and aggrandizement is gone by" as a direct attack on his own political stance. Yet Wilson's conviction of being in the right, compounded with his isolation as head of a wartime state, may very well have contributed to eventual political defeat. In particular, he refused to let Republican senators accompany him to Paris, which might have allowed him to keep them under control, get them engaged in peacemaking, or even to appease them. Excluding them could not help but alienate Lodge and his friends even more from presidential policy at the Paris Peace Conference.

Later, while Wilson toured the United States to convince the public of the soundness of the Treaty of Versailles, his inflexible attitude toward his political opposition achieved the same negative effect: on November 19, 1919, for the first time in its history, the US Senate rejected a peace treaty.

Technically, this rejection of the treaty meant that the United States was still in a state of war with Germany. After this political fiasco, the president's team realized that it had lost credibility in Europe and would not be able to influence the impending settlement of the Ottoman Empire.[85] Although the opposition of Lodge and his supporters has been abundantly rationalized in US historiography, his attitude was just as colored by emotion as Wilson's; Lodge seemed to have been motivated by national pride as well. His statement—"I have loved but one flag and I cannot share that devotion and give affection to the mongrel banner invented for a League"—was tainted by a slur against people of mixed descent.[86]

Wilson's gamble of incorporating the Covenant of the League into the Treaty of Versailles worked well when he was negotiating with the Allied Powers, because it facilitated the British and French parliaments' acceptance of it as part of the peace package. Wilson was aware that he had to seize this opportunity, because it might not present itself again. By contrast, it turned out to be a tragic impediment on the domestic front; the Senate could reject the entire treaty because of the opposition to the League and because it was not under any immediate obligation to underwrite the peace treaty signed between the Allies and Germany. Given the founding history of the United States, the political passion on both sides makes sense. The nation was born at the end of the eighteenth century after splintering from Britain, and its early foreign policy was focused on carefully severing political links with Europe; a debate about committing the country to a long-term relationship with Europe through the League was bound to be distressing. In the end, the Senate maintained the status quo ante of the Monroe Doctrine. To make matters worse, Wilson's project was opposed not only by those—like Lodge—who supported harsh peace conditions for Germany and objected to the Covenant of the League but also by those who condemned the conditions of the peace treaty itself—notably German Americans and Italian Americans. Had the two issues been separated, Wilson's middle-ground position might have been easier to defend in the Senate. Regardless of the merits of the debate, US political leaders had made a show of disunity in front of the world. In Europe, the news of the repudiation was met with dismay and embarrassment for Wilson, as if an eager groom had suddenly gotten cold feet. In the end, the state of war was terminated by a separate US-German Peace Treaty signed in Berlin on August 25, 1921. Wilson, already weakened and ill after suffering a series of strokes, retired from politics at the end of his term and died in 1924.

Intellectual Origins of the League's Covenant

It is worth turning to the first part of the Treaty of Versailles, the Covenant, whose principles raised such hope in Europe and such contention in the United States. It is terse, and its tone is administrative, rather than ideological. Indeed, its statement of principles is remarkably short:

> TO PROMOTE international co-operation and to achieve international peace and security by the acceptance of obligations not to resort to war, by the prescription of open, just and honorable relations between nations, by the firm establishment of the understandings of international law as the actual rule of conduct among Governments, and by the maintenance of justice and a scrupulous respect for all treaty obligations in the dealings of organized peoples with one another.[87]

As proposed, the League differed from earlier international systems in its dual structure, having both a political arm (a Council and an Assembly) and a judicial one (an International Court). It was designed to be a permanent organization, with a founding treaty. This approach derived from the application of a key assumption of the tradition of perpetual peace, which Kant had formulated in this way: "the state of peace must be established [by a peace alliance]." Practically, it echoed the Hague Permanent Court of Arbitration, as well as the International Telegraph Union, the Universal Postal Union, and other organizations that institutionalized the technical commissions inaugurated by the Treaty of Paris in 1815. Most importantly, it served as an umbrella over all of these bodies so they would fit within a general framework. Unfortunately, disarmament provisions were dropped from the Treaty of Versailles (except in the case of Germany), and the League of Nations was established with that important pillar missing. Nevertheless, because the arms race was seen as the chief factor that caused the Great War in 1914, the issue of disarmament remained central to the League's debates.

We may ask why this document, given its administrative focus, was called a covenant. Of Latin origin, "covenant" is a rather formal word meaning literally "coming together." In addition to its legal designation of an agreement of conduct between two parties, it also has strong religious connotations. It is the term used in English translations of the Bible (Jeremiah 31:31–33) to indicate the agreement between God and the people of Israel, materialized by a mutually binding document, contained in the Ark of the Covenant; it is also used in modern English translations of Christ's Last Supper: "This cup is the new covenant in my blood."[88] Another interpretation of "covenant" belongs to the same metaphorical register as "the bonds of a true and indissoluble fraternity" that had united the monarchs of the Holy Alliance in 1815.

Indeed, Woodrow Wilson's biographers agree he was a devoted Presbyterian. There is no universal agreement, however, on whether it was truly his religiosity that motivated him to infuse his foreign policy with such a high tone of morality. Some historians dismiss religion as an influence on his domestic political policy and even more on his foreign policy.[89] By contrast, John Mulder, one of the editors of Wilson's papers and the author of what has been described as a "religious" biography of the president, asserts that covenant theology was indeed a template for Wilson's view of the world.[90] Wilson also held Giuseppe Mazzini in high regard; both shared a conception of liberal republicanism based on Christian faith, traceable to the Reformation-era idea that free and civilly responsible citizens were the exclusive source of leaders' political legitimacy. This was the foundation of the internationalist conception Mazzini had aptly expressed as the "Holy Alliance of the Peoples."[91]

Yet in sharp contrast with the militant religious declarations of Tsar Alexander's Holy Alliance, the text of the Covenant is fully secular. It does not take God as the source of rightfulness or political legitimacy; rather, it seeks to establish the preeminence of international law. Most importantly, international politics in Europe had operated outside of established churches since 1815; any references to religion in the Covenant would have had to be expressed in abstract and consensual terms. As the historian John Milton Cooper argues, religion should be considered a source of personal inspiration for Wilson and not an overt element of the Covenant; the president kept his metaphysical conceptions carefully out of the legal sphere. In other words, Wilson saw natural law and divine law as one and the same and considered them to be the implicit foundation of human laws. Like many US politicians even today, he was able to use religious metaphors very effectively in conveying his ideas to constituents.[92]

The term "covenant," however, did not make it into the French version of the text, because its meaning would have been lost in translation.[93] Its etymological equivalent, "convention," lacked the necessary solemnity: it was so mundane that it was used to refer to practical and often secondary agreements between states. Furthermore, the French government—which supported the idea of a secular society, with the separation of church and state—might not have welcomed any word with ostensibly religious connotations.[94] The word *pacte,* from Latin *pactum,* was used instead, no doubt because it had the necessary connotation of a solemn act and had long been part of the secular vocabulary of international law, particularly for military alliances. Its use was a linguistic compromise in the best tradition of diplomacy.[95]

The intellectual influences that eventually coalesced to form this covenant were quite varied. During the Great War, there was a flurry of essays, legal texts, and pamphlets proposing peace plans. Many authors, notably E. B. Copeland from California and the lawyer Paul Otlet from Belgium, referred to the perpetual peace literature, citing or echoing Henry IV (or rather the Duc de Sully), William Penn, the Abbé de Saint-Pierre, Jean-Jacques Rousseau, and Immanuel Kant, as well as the Holy Alliance of 1815. The internationalist movement actively rehabilitated the Congress of Vienna "in the name of peace and justice," noting it had been "anathemized of late as history's choicest demonstration of unprincipled national selfishness."[96] Copeland also made reference to the two Hague peace conferences of 1899 and 1907. These wartime essays were focused not only on how to establish peace but also on how to preserve and maintain it once achieved. Otlet, for his part, supported a world organization that would also include the neutrals and the Central Powers, fearing that the Allies would found the new League of Nations as only a treaty of alliance among themselves; his proposal therefore came nearest to that of the Abbé de Saint-Pierre. He included a detailed "world constitution" and a "catechism" of objections to the plan and their answers.[97] What makes Otlet's proposal interesting is its inclusion of separate sections on the rights of states, nationalities, human beings ("men are born and live free, equal in rights and are in solidarity one to each other"), associations, and religious organizations.[98] The League of Nations Archives in Geneva contains a fascinating collection of about forty plans written in those years, all of which were sent to Wilson or to his office, even after his death. Most of their authors were lawyers and economists who thought carefully about issues of peacemaking in Europe.[99]

The British government also contributed to the intellectual foundations of the League, producing research of its own. In December 1916, Robert Viscount Cecil, a Conservative who had recently been appointed Undersecretary of Foreign Affairs, took over the project of establishing a league for peace where his predecessor Edward Grey had left it—including lobbying the Americans through his correspondence with Wilson's adviser, Colonel House. Grey had attempted to reach a treaty of "mutual reduction of military expenditure" with Germany in 1911, even promoting the establishment of a system of international arbitration in conjunction with then-president William Howard Taft.[100] On September 3, 1917, Cecil wrote to Colonel House suggesting that the time was ripe for creating commissions to explore formation of a League.[101] In November, Cecil requested his senior, Foreign Secretary Arthur Balfour, to set up a commission to examine proposals for a future peace organization. Lord Phillimore, a lawyer and a senior judge, was tasked with chairing a committee that would prepare a compendium of schemes for a league. Established on January 3, 1918, the committee professed to have "carefully considered" the various private schemes for a league and claimed to embody in its recommendations "their leading ideas" while avoiding "their more obvious stumbling blocks".[102] The Phillimore committee met nine times before submitting its interim report to Balfour on March 20, 1918. Phillimore had published in 1917 an analysis of past peace schemes along with a plan of his own that embodied a moderate, practical approach to the question.[103] His historical essay would be attached to the committee's report along with a handbook prepared for use by the British delegation to the Paris Peace Conference. After being circulated only internally, the handbook appeared in a separate edition in 1920 under the title *Schemes for Maintaining General Peace*. The guide decisively molded governmental thinking in both the British and the American delegations and influenced much of the covenant's ultimate shape.

Phillimore distinguished four types of schemes for international peace: (1) a "Universal Superior," or a universal monarchy on the ideal model of the *Pax Romana* under Augustus; (2) a Federation of States, or a supranational state on the model of the United States or Switzerland, an idea traced to the Grand Design of Henry IV of France and the Abbé de Saint-Pierre; (3) systems based purely on arbitration, traced to Pufendorf and Vattel and, of course, the two Hague Conventions and the Permanent Court of Arbitration; and (4) composites of the last two solutions, which would separate "justiciable" issues best resolved by a court from those best resolved through political debate.[104]

Whereas the first and second schemes should be well known to readers by now, the third one was inspired by the prototype of the Hague Permanent Court of Arbitration and its paradigm of "peace through law." In May 1899, the first international peace conference focused on armaments reductions took place in The Hague. It was convened under the initiative of Tsar Nicholas II, who was concerned that the Russian Treasury would not be able to keep up with the demands of an ongoing arms race in Europe.[105] Although the conference failed to achieve the desired reduction in armaments, it had an important side effect. The great powers, "animated by a strong desire to work for the maintenance of the general peace," resolved that "with a view to obviating, as far as possible, recourse to force in the relations between States, . . . to use their best efforts to insure the pacific settlement of international differences."[106] The participating states instituted a Permanent Court of Arbitration for the friendly settlement of disputes.[107] There was, however, no obligation to make recourse to it nor any enforcement mechanism for its decisions. The second Hague conference in 1907, this time convened under the initiative of the US government, expanded on the technical achievements of the first. Yet putting together an international *political* organization after the Great War was going to be a far more complicated and delicate enterprise, with challenges even more daunting than those of post-Napoleonic Europe. The stumbling block to limiting the right to make or not make war was clearly going to be the belief in the absolute sovereignty of states.

After discarding the first and second schemes, which were politically impracticable, the handbook focused on whether to settle international disputes through a judicial or political process—in other words, whether by an international court (typically that of The Hague) or a new "federation" of states. It concluded that the purely judicial model was "defective and weak," because no state could be ever compelled to take recourse to a court or to respect its decisions.[108] The fourth scheme appeared to be the most convincing. Following up on it, the Phillimore report thus provided a detailed rationale for the League's system of two *mandatory* mechanisms for the peaceful resolution of conflicts: a judicial mechanism for cases that a court was competent to hear and a political mechanism based on a council of great powers to resolve other issues. On how a League would limit a state's recourse to force of arms, the report proposed an original solution: a moratorium on war activity through a judicial "injunction" against any state involved in a quarrel. By contrast, rearmament would not be forbidden to a state that felt threatened by another, because determining what constituted rearmament would be too difficult. A party would be allowed recourse to war unilaterally only in cases when it had already experienced aggression from another party that had not heeded the injunction.[109]

There remained, however, an unresolved issue. The handbook used the term "federation of states" loosely, encompassing a wide range of structures from (in today's terms) an alliance to a confederation, and even to a nation composed of states like the United States. Its discussion of the supranational character of the new League (or the lack thereof) also remained cursory. This fuzziness was understandable in the legal context of the British Empire, a naval power that had developed outside continental Europe and ruled over nearly one-quarter of the world's population. The British government's notion of statehood was ordered in a hierarchy of three levels: the United Kingdom at the top, a second tier of states with their own legislatures (Ireland, Canada, Newfoundland South Africa, Australia, and New Zealand), and then the colonial administration of the Indian Raj and other dependencies directly governed by British public officers. This political balance, held together by loyalty to the Crown, was dynamic and in constant evolution—even veering toward revolution in Ireland—with a general tendency toward self-government as a step toward "progress" and social justice. The advantages of such an assemblage appeared self-evident to English political circles, as well as to the Peace Society, an organization for the promotion of peace that was active in Britain from 1816 until the 1930s.[110]

By contrast, continental states had held clearer, stronger positions on issues of external interference ever since the Treaty of Westphalia (1648). In more recent times, they considered statehood to be a binary proposition: either a European state was considered sovereign, or like Poland after the partitions of the late eighteenth century, it was not. Similarly, the US political system had undergone a war of independence and a later civil war that confirmed the need for a strong federation, rather than a confederation with more power devolved to the states; it also strongly relied on the Monroe Doctrine's principle of non-interference with the European great powers. Thus, the question of what form the new peace "league" would take would be a challenge for all European states that joined the future organization and a stumbling block for the United States.

More generally, Phillimore's analytical approach reflected a legalistic bent, as if the proponents of the various schemes for maintaining peace had been called to the bench to state their case and he, as a judge, had issued a decision. Unfortunately, the issue was not really susceptible to an a priori intellectual adjudication; only experimentation, together with a fair amount of diplomatic negotiation, could settle the matter. This report, kept secret until its publication in 1920, remains nevertheless a fascinating survey of the main conceptions of how to set up a peaceful international order. It also shows that, at the time, the British commission's belief in the sacredness of international law aligned with that of Wilson. In reality, the articles of the Treaty of Versailles indicate that the attitude of Britain and France toward the League was not so different from that of Metternich's Austria toward the Holy Alliance a century earlier: it was something that was best, for the moment, left to theory.

The peacemakers of 1919, for that matter, keenly perceived the link between the League of Nations and its predecessor—just as some cultured elites of 1815 had discerned the parallels between the Holy Alliance and

Saint-Pierre's plan. In 1919, Guglielmo Ferrero, an Italian historian who had written about the Congress of Vienna, published an essay in English titled *Problems of Peace: From the Holy Alliance to the League of Nations, A Message from a European Writer to Americans.* He claimed notably that "in 1914 there were still two Europes; in 1919 there is only one," echoing the reflections of Gentz on the Vienna Order a century earlier.[111] Ferrero formulated three necessary conditions for peace:

> The first is that all the States forming part of the League should undertake to recognize and to deal only with legally constituted governments. Secondly, they should pledge themselves to respect nationality; that is to say the language, the religion, and the culture of every people. Thirdly, they should undertake to reduce armaments to the lowest limits, and to admit the principle of reciprocal inspection.[112]

This last principle would become one of the leitmotifs of the League: given that arms races triggered wars, disarmament treaties were a necessary means to prevent them.

Similarly, Robert de Traz expanded on the League of Nations as a legacy of the Vienna Order in his 1936 book, *De l'Alliance des rois à la Ligue des peuples* (From the Alliance of Kings to the League of Nations). He noted that the leading personalities in both instances were outsiders to traditional European politics: a Russian in the case of the Holy Alliance, and an American in the case of the League of Nations. Despite the fact that Alexander I was an autocrat and Wilson was president of one of the most advanced republics in the world, they had intriguing commonalities. In particular, they each held an elaborate vision for peace that made them appear as political prophets in Europe yet caused them to be disowned in their own countries. Both also represented an emerging great power, an outsider to the ranks come to pacify or arbitrate in European matters. Both intervened in European affairs after the Continent had narrowly escaped imperial domination. Both the Holy Alliance and the Covenant of the League of Nations had the purpose of establishing lasting peace. Finally, Alexander I and Wilson were both highly complex characters: religious and morally elevated but not free from contradictions and even character flaws.[113]

By contrast, the League of Nations did introduce a fundamentally new element that separated it from the Congress System of a century earlier: it was an independent entity able to adopt attitudes and policies distinct from those of the great powers. It could place obligations, at least in theory, on the great powers themselves, although without questioning their sovereignty. Its process was much more structured than the Congress System, which had essentially been a series of ad hoc diplomatic meetings. Most importantly, its formal independence was a radical innovation that remains unique in diplomatic history, especially because such independence was later purposefully struck from the Charter of the United Nations.

Several historians have pointed out that Wilson's liberal internationalism had traits similar to some found in Kant's philosophy, a fact not lost on Wilson's contemporaries.[114] When Wilson stated in his "Fourteen Points" speech that "the day of conquest and aggrandizement is gone," he was taking a page from the Enlightenment philosophers on perpetual peace. In particular, his condemnation of states that considered people as property mirrored Kant's idea that

> a state, unlike the ground on which it is based, is not a possession (*patrimonium*). It is a society of men, which no-one other than itself can command or dispose of. Like a tree, it has its own roots, and to graft it on to another state as if it were a shoot is to terminate its existence as a moral personality and make it a commodity.[115]

Arguably, the League of Nations belongs to a Kantian model, because it did not have executive power to order military intervention against recalcitrant states, a power recommended by the Abbé de Saint-Pierre and frequently used by the Congress System; a member could, however, be excluded from the League.[116] Yet it is important to note that neither the speeches of Wilson nor the papers of Colonel House mention Kant, suggesting that even though the German philosopher was evidently known to the authors of the League, his essay on perpetual peace was not considered an explicit reference. Most likely, Wilson and the other League founders "reinvented" it in the course of their negotiations. Unless a more direct link is uncovered, the most likely explanation is that there was a convergent evolution of ideas.

Another stance shared with Kant's philosophy was Wilson's stalwart position during the February 1919 negotiations in Paris that he did not want the League to have its own army. The French government, more in line with Saint-Pierre, insisted that the League of Nations should have one—and, furthermore, that it should be able to mandate the disarmament of its members. This created tensions in Paris, because both the US and British delegations felt the French proposal was targeting Germany and would serve more to enforce the reparations stated by the Treaty of Versailles than to advance world peace.[117] Furthermore, both Britain and the United States strongly relied on their respective military navies as chief instruments (and symbols) of their independence and security; their representatives in Paris would have had to contend with strong opposition back home to subjecting these forces to international jurisdiction. Just as an institution of peace would have been impossible in 1815, a common army was not a realistic proposition in the context of Versailles. Kant had triumphed over Saint-Pierre on the point of the common army, but was he right to believe that "Common Power" and—in the extreme—economic sanctions would be sufficient to deter rogue states from using military power? Could peer pressure actually be strong enough to prevail against such states? This was one of the key challenges for the League of Nations.

Geneva from Local to Global

The first official meeting of the newborn League took place in Paris on January 6, 1920. The next general meeting took place in Geneva on November 15 of that year. It was assumed that the League's seat would be in Europe, but the choice was the result of a long negotiation in Paris in early 1919, which essentially worked by the elimination of candidate cities. The selection criteria were exactly opposite to those the French had used to select Versailles as the location for the signing ceremony. William E. Rappard, an American-born Swiss academic who participated in the diplomatic discussions, recounted in 1945 that one of the initial ideas was indeed to establish the League in the capital of a power that had won the war: the French naturally proposed Paris, whereas the Belgians proposed Brussels.[118] The

British and US delegations, however, saw the situation in a different light. President Wilson, with the support of Lord Cecil, stated that the seat of the League should not be a prize awarded to a victor. Rather, it should be the place most favorable for the serene and impartial deliberations of this new body.[119] Certainly, if a country had a right to be partial after the war, it was Belgium, because of its sufferings under German occupation. Hence, countries that had remained neutral during the war became a natural choice: this left the Netherlands and Switzerland. A strong movement to establish the League in Geneva emerged. Aptly called the "Lobbies of Geneva," it was supported by the Swiss federal government, with Rappard as its figurehead. These lobbies benefited from Rappard being on good terms with the US president—a friendship reminiscent of that of Pictet de Rochemont with Tsar Alexander I a century earlier.[120]

The Netherlands and Amsterdam had two downsides in Wilson's eyes. First, Amsterdam was a capital, whereas Geneva was not, although that inconvenience might have been fixed by selecting The Hague instead. The more serious drawback was that the Netherlands had a monarchy. This was a disqualifying factor for Wilson, who did not consider it suitable to have a republic of nations deliberate "at the footsteps of a throne"; it was also unlikely to generate a favorable response from the US public. In Switzerland, the capital city of Berne was also considered, but it was German speaking, and French was after all still the cardinal language of diplomacy. This left but two candidates: Lausanne and Geneva.

The latter had a special claim: it was the seat of the International Committee of the Red Cross (ICRC), founded in 1863 by Genevan businessman and philanthropist Henry Dunant, whose ideas had considerable influence. In spite of its name and its involvement in humanitarian diplomacy and field operations all over the world, the ICRC was and still is exclusively composed of Swiss nationals; its flag is the Swiss one with inverted colors.[121] Dunant's contributions were highlighted again at the beginning of the twentieth century when he was awarded the very first Nobel Peace Prize in 1901. During the Great War, the Red Cross played a major role in tracing missing persons and restoring contacts between war prisoners and their families.[122] For an idealistic Presbyterian such as Wilson, the sixteenth-century reformer John Calvin, Jean-Jacques Rousseau, and Henri Dunant were three significant names attached to Geneva. In the end, that city was selected thanks to the lobbying of the US president. As Robert de Traz put it, the League "preferred this neutral city, with its neutrality at once active and benevolent, to belligerent Brussels, or revolutionary and defeated Vienna."[123]

The spirit of the League of Nations was undoubtedly connected to its host city, the "Protestant Rome" that had been home to Calvin. De Traz publicized the term *Spirit of Geneva* in his book of the same title, first published in French in 1929:

> This Spirit of Geneva, still intermittent, local, and displayed by but a few persons, is a spirit which comprises a desire for liberty and universality, a confidence in man, provided he submit to rules, an inexhaustible curiosity as to ideas and people, a compassion for all miseries combined with an urge to invent, to ameliorate, to administrate with method.[124]

Quoting the bon mot of Talleyrand, he added, "There are five parts of the world: Europe, Asia, Africa, America, and Geneva." De Traz was well aware that he was helping turn Geneva into a symbolic place, distinct from the real city:

> This spirit, I say, escaping suddenly from its natural representatives, grows gigantic, adopts new significance even at the risk of weakening itself, and becomes the ideal of innumerable foreigners of all races who, scattered over the world, are often ignorant of Geneva's part in history. It ceases thus to be an exclusive attribute of the Genevese, and it is invoked by most nations on earth. The very name "Geneva" comes thus to transcend any local or particular significance, and it is transformed by a strange experience into a symbol.[125]

Indeed he contrasted the Spirit of Geneva with what he condescendingly called the "Genevese Spirit," the petty and self-centered bourgeois mentality that infused local politics.

The dichotomy between the mythical "international city" and the real town of a little more than 100,000 inhabitants was perhaps what gave the Spirit of Geneva its signature modesty. Far from the monarchic pomp and glamour of Versailles, the elaborate military protocols of London or Washington, or even the ornate bourgeois Peace Palace of The Hague, the first meetings of the General Assembly took place in an austere building located in a residential neighborhood: the *Salle de la Réformation* (Reformation Hall), also called the *Calvinium,* originally a meeting hall for local Protestant societies. The reason for the choice was expediency: it was the only space large enough to hold a gathering the size of the General Assembly. Everything else was pocket-sized: the secretariat of the conferences was hosted in the adjacent Hôtel Victoria for travelers.[126] The heads of state and diplomats of 1815, before convening in Vienna, had already achieved a sense of fellowship through links between members of aristocratic families, who met informally in the private salons of Vienna and at sumptuous social functions. In contrast, in the 1920s, the cream of international diplomacy was meeting in a provincial hotel, an unassuming hall, and ordinary cafes. Nevertheless, the mingling of diplomats deliberating the future of the world with townspeople attending the nearby municipal market worked quite well. The only touch of grandeur in Geneva was the nearby lakeside quays where the nearly 300-foot high fountain was located.

As behooved a proper institution, the League had its own budget. In late 1920 it used its funds to purchase a luxury hotel—the Hôtel National on the opposite bank of the lake—to host its Secretariat and Security Council. The decorous building was located in a fashionable neighborhood, with a romantic view of Mont Blanc, though it paled in comparison to the princely residences of Paris, London, Vienna, and Berlin. In 1924, it was renamed Palais Wilson in homage to the late president. The Secretariat began generating a large corpus of paperwork needed for agreements on trade, public health, and other fields. Because the League of Nations was a complex formal entity, lawyers and "technicians" were to play a considerably greater role than they had in the previous century, expanding a tradition inaugurated in Vienna. The Spirit of Geneva was troubled, to be sure, by the awkward fact that the League was the brainchild of an American president who was then disavowed by his own country; as a result, US delegates were conspicuously absent. Nevertheless, the League initially seemed to be doing its intended work.

The Spirit of Locarno

As mentioned, the League was functioning without one of the greatest powers of its time, the United States; Germany was also not a part of it. The Treaties of Paris contained the territorial clauses customary for a peace treaty, as well as clauses related to war reparations and the resumption of commerce. Yet they could hardly be seen as bringing about peace, assuming the word meant that all parties considered themselves sufficiently satisfied with the settlements (especially on territorial issues), so that reconciliation—and thus pacification—could take place.[127] From that perspective, the Treaties of Paris were markedly different from the Treaties of Utrecht (1713) and the Final Act of Vienna (1815): they did not settle the prewar disputes but merely repressed them. By forcing German politicians and citizens to swallow their anger at a fait accompli, the Western Allies were embarking on a risky route. Both the US and the Soviet press likened the situation to a volcano on the verge of eruption. Although the excessive rigidity of the status quo ante had also caused the collapse of the post-Napoleonic order of 1815, the structural threat to the Peace of Versailles was potentially more serious because the situation allowed no outlet for the Germans. For the time being, the volcano lay relatively dormant—and perhaps the hopes of peace raised at Versailles could still be achieved.[128]

One key step toward pacification was the 1924 "Protocol for the Pacific Settlement of Disputes," proposed to the League of Nations by the prime ministers of Britain and France, Ramsay McDonald and Edouard Herriot, respectively. This proposal brought the League closer to the principles set out by Saint-Pierre, as its second article illustrates:

> The signatory States agree in no case to resort to war either with one another or against a State which, if the occasion arises, accepts all the obligations hereinafter set out, except in case of resistance to acts of

aggression or when acting in agreement with the Council or the Assembly of the League of Nations in accordance with the provisions of the Covenant and of the present Protocol.[129]

The states would also recognize "ipso facto and without special agreement" the jurisdiction of the Permanent Court of International Justice (later the International Court of Justice).[130] Any state that resorted to war in violation of this agreement or the Covenant was an "aggressor." This text, informally called the Protocol, generated considerable hope and was approved unanimously by the delegates on October 2, 1924. It seemed to have the potential to strongly reinforce the authority of the League.

Unfortunately, the enthusiasm was short-lived: the Assembly's vote was not binding, and the Protocol needed to be ratified by each state.[131] A general election in the United Kingdom brought to power a new government led by Stanley Baldwin. Parliament refused to ratify the Protocol, for a number of reasons connected with Britain's status as a maritime power with the biggest naval fleet in the world. This treaty was seen as harmful to the interests of the British Commonwealth because it would have allowed foreign interference in its domestic policies, increasing the danger of Britain becoming embroiled in war over European frontiers. Paradoxically, the awareness that the order of Versailles was unjust is what drove the British political class to retain its right to make or not make war. These politicians also feared that the Protocol might lead to ill will between Britain and the United States, further reducing the chances that the latter would one day enter the League; at least in theory, the Protocol might have forced the British Navy to prevent US ships from doing commerce with an "aggressor" power.[132]

This concern was understandable, because it was founded on recent memories of international aggression: the German attacks on US shipping during the Great War had prompted the United States to enter the war. Resonances or echoes even went as far back to the "Alabama Affair" during the American Civil War; this was a dispute between the United States and Britain over Confederate raider ships operating from British ports. This affair, settled through a tribunal of arbitration in Geneva in 1871–1872, had ended with Britain giving financial reparations to the United States.

Although Britain had international, and particularly maritime, law on its side in the 1920s, the trauma remained—especially because establishing the legality of a ship's seizure in court would be an uncertain process. Looking back, we might wonder: Had a diktat not been imposed on Germany, and had the United States joined the League in the first place, could the spirit of the Protocol have become reality? In any case, this effort to reinforce the Covenant shows that the delegates were aware that the state of peace was fragile and that the League, as it was then constituted, would not necessarily be in a position to prevent member states from unilaterally resorting to war in times of crisis.

The delegates faced this question: If war should arise, despite the best efforts of the League of Nations, could peacetime agreements at least mitigate its worse effects? As stated, the Great War had exposed the conundrum that the same progress that had fostered better conditions in times of peace also made it possible, in times of war, to kill more human beings in more atrocious ways. After the war, banning particularly inhumane weapons gained support. In 1925, the Assembly of the League signed the "Protocol for the Prohibition of the Use in War of Asphyxiating, Poisonous or other Gases, and of Bacteriological Methods of Warfare," usually called the "Geneva Protocol."[133] It may seem paradoxical that states would have committed in advance of war to legal agreements about the conditions of war, which was—by definition—the abandonment of legal restraint in favor of force. Yet such a mitigation agreement had three essential effects: before a war, to deter states from openly investing in inhumane methods of killing; during a war, to enhance the likelihood that an alliance would form against a state that had resorted to those methods; and after a war, to influence the conditions of peace to the detriment of states that had violated the agreements.

Indeed, the protocol prohibiting chemical and bacteriological weapons was ratified by most states, with the exception of the United States and Japan. Several states added a reserve clause that should an enemy state use those weapons against them, the treaty would cease to be binding—still leaving the risk that any belligerent could open a Pandora's box. Yet the agreement was well respected. After its entry into force in 1928, the only country to violate it was Italy (during its invasion of Ethiopia in 1935); even during World War II, no belligerent dared violate it on the battlefield. Despite the failures and flaws, these initiatives opened what historians have termed the "Golden Age of Geneva."

A next step toward pacification occurred the same year, six years after the Treaty of Versailles, under the leadership of three men: Aristide Briand of France, Austen Chamberlain of Britain, and Gustav Stresemann of Germany. It was aimed at peacefully resolving the ongoing territorial demands of Germany, particularly to regain control of the territories of Upper Silesia and the "Danzig Corridor" (eastern Pomerania), which had been forcibly ceded to Poland under the Peace of Versailles. France and Belgium had also occupied the industrial Ruhr region in 1923, after Germany failed to pay war reparations—President Poincaré justified the French occupation by noting that Germany had defaulted on its obligations, because it had no intention to fulfill them in the first place. After the British government failed to agree on economic sanctions, Poincaré concluded that only the use of military force could secure German cooperation.

Yet hyperinflation had brought Germany's economy to its knees, thus compromising its ability to pay war reparations. The Ruhr occupation also motivated a change in public opinion, particularly in Britain, about the soundness of the war reparation clauses and, by extension, the territorial clauses of the Treaty of Versailles. The French policy of keeping Germany in check, as embodied by Poincaré, had evidently backfired.

The great powers met in London, where they pressured the French government into abandoning its position. This led to the Dawes Plan, signed on July 24, 1924, which eased the repayment schedule of the German debt and included a loan from the United States to Germany. In addition to stabilizing the German currency, the Dawes Plan was a clear indication that some clauses of the Treaty of Versailles should be revised. Furthermore, Poincaré's unpopular financial policy led to an election victory for a left-wing coalition in France; his resignation in 1925 heralded a wave of marked political change in Europe.[134]

The individuals who led this evolution in the foreign policy of the European great powers were not newcomers. Aristide Briand, foreign minister of France from 1925 to 1932, had already served several times as prime minister and was a reporter of the commission charged with creating the law of separation between church and state in 1905. Austen Chamberlain, who served as Secretary of State for Foreign Affairs under Stanley Baldwin, was leader of the Conservative Party, had served as Secretary of State for India, and had twice been Chancellor of the Exchequer and Leader of the House of Commons. In Germany, Gustav Stresemann was a moderate conservative and a prominent member of the German People's Party, who had opposed the Treaty of Versailles along with the greater part of the political class. He briefly became chancellor in 1923 when hyperinflation was at its peak. After his coalition collapsed, he served as foreign minister under successive governments until his early death in 1929. All three men were old hands at pragmatic politics, with fairly open minds toward exploring new approaches.

Chamberlain opened the Locarno Conference on October 5, 1925, in the large, drab meeting rooms of the local courthouse in the Swiss city of that name; the room featured a portrait of Castlereagh, the British diplomat of the Vienna Order.[135] For all his experience, Chamberlain retained his high ideals that he voiced with a rhetorical flourish, expressing the hope that the beautiful scenery of Switzerland, with its happy and majestic valleys, would "ensure a successful issue to [their] labours" to eliminate once and for all the division of Europe into rival camps.[136] Yet he did not lose sight of his negotiating mandate, also pointing out that British security interests did not include guaranteeing the territorial arrangements in Eastern Europe.[137] The ultimate prize was even bigger: binding Germany into a new European settlement. With this in mind, Chamberlain claimed that the Locarno treaties "which bring Germany into the League [and] make her again a member of the European family, . . . will mark in history as the dividing point between the era of war and the era of peace."[138] To which the German chancellor Stresemann added, "The States of Europe at last realise that they cannot go on making war upon each other without being involved in common ruin. . . . The attempt to create a new and better Europe by methods of compulsion, dictation and violence has been a failure. Let us try to achieve this object on the basis of peace and equal rights and liberty for Germany."[139]

The "Rhineland Pact" that emerged from the initial discussions was a friendship treaty among Germany, France, Belgium, the United Kingdom, and Italy. It guaranteed the inviolability of the territorial clauses of the Treaty of Versailles regarding Germany's western border, renounced war (except in cases of self-defense or obligation under the League), and committed to international arbitration on the question of Germany's eastern borders. The Locarno negotiations marked an important turning point: for the first time since the end of the Great War, the Allied Powers were seeking to settle differences in talks that included the defeated party, Germany.[140] It was, finally, a return to multilateral diplomacy. Because the Locarno Agreements appear to have corrected the key flaws in the postwar order, the pact opened a period of hope known at the time as the *Spirit of Locarno*. It was both a direct offspring and an upbeat variation of the Spirit of Geneva, as well as a descendant of earlier plans of peace: revealingly, the papers of the Treaty of Locarno kept at the the League of Nations Archives contain copies of Kant's essay, *Toward Perpetual Peace,* in both German and English.[141]

The Pact of Locarno indeed made possible a major, positive change for the League of Nations. On February 8, 1926, the German chancellor Stresemann officially applied both for Germany's membership in the League and for a permanent seat on the Security Council. On September 8, the General Assembly formally assented to both requests. How this development was perceived in Geneva can be seen in an editorial by Swiss historian and journalist, William Martin. Published in the *Journal de Genève*, the article aptly titled "The Session," is infused with joyful optimism:

> This is not first time that after a great war peoples who had been enemies are getting closer again, . . . [the] history of the world is made of such reconciliations. Yet they never had such solemnity, such greatness, nor had they presented such guarantees of durability. Wars were followed by peace, then alliances against a new enemy. What is happening today is something else and much more. It is a formal promise of forgiveness and cooperation toward a constructive work. We could not have wished for a pact to be concluded with more truth and . . . with more tact.[142]

Martin's style in this editorial and his use of an antonomasia in the title ("*The* Session," as if to emphasize that it would stand out from all others before and after) were quite different from his usually dispassionate style.

The two "pilgrims of the peace" Briand and Stresemann were widely acclaimed on the international scene. On December 10, 1926, both were awarded the Nobel Peace Prize for their actions to bring about reconciliation between Germany and France. On that occasion, the speech delivered by Norwegian explorer and humanitarian Fridtjof Nansen expressed his awareness that the Treaty of Versailles could be a liability in the future:

> A peace settlement following a ruinous war can easily degenerate into the imposition by the victors of more or less humiliating conditions upon the vanquished. Such terms, in their turn, can easily bear fruit which will in time ripen into a fresh war. The Peace of Versailles can certainly not be said to constitute an exception to this rule.

But on a more optimistic note, he added,

> The League of Nations is no longer a remote or abstract idea. It is a living organism. Its institutions are now an essential part of the machinery of world control. If we can put the full force of the combined power of individual governments behind these institutions, behind the policy of disarmament, behind all the policies pursued by the League, then we shall put an end to war.[143]

As everyone present recognized, any sensible peace policy, to be effective, would, however, need to include the one founding power of the League of Nations that had declined to join: the United States. To compensate for the US absence, Briand proposed an agreement that would outlaw war between France and the United States. At first, President Calvin Coolidge and his secretary of state Frank B. Kellogg disliked the idea, because a bilateral agreement might have been perceived as a de facto military alliance between the two countries.[144] In an appeal to inclusion reminiscent of the last article of the Holy Alliance of 1815, the two countries then decided to invite others to sign onto the agreement, thereby making it a truly multilateral treaty. In its final form, the so-called Kellogg-Briand Pact stated that the signatories "condemn recourse to war for the solution of international controversies, and renounce it, as an instrument of national policy in their relations with one another," and that "they agree that the settlement or solution of all disputes or conflicts of whatever nature or of whatever origin they may be, which may arise among them, shall never be sought except by pacific means."[145] The importance of this text—which the US Senate ratified overwhelmingly in 1928—should not be underestimated. By establishing the illegality of the recourse to war as a solution to differences, it indirectly "proved" the basic premise of international legalism: unresolved disputes should be brought before an international court. Because both Britain and the United States underwrote this treaty, it plugged the hole that had been left open in the Protocol of Geneva when Britain had refused to ratify that document; it thus also remedied to some degree the absence of the United States from the League's legal framework. For his achievement, Kellogg was awarded the Nobel Peace Prize in 1929, together with Archbishop Nathan Söderblom, who had organized a Universal Conference on Life and Work in Stockholm in 1925. That ecumenical conference had mobilized Christian churches to support the League's system of international arbitration; the culmination of these efforts was the foundation of the World Council of Churches in 1948, with its seat in Geneva.

In a speech on December 10, 1930, Johan Ludwig Mowinckel, prime minister of Norway and the awarding member of the Nobel Prize Committee, made the following declaration about the Kellogg-Briand Pact: "Seldom has an inscription been as appropriate as that which the town of Le Havre inscribed on the box holding the gold pen it presented to Frank B. Kellogg as he stepped ashore on his way to Paris to join France and other leading world powers in signing the pact on August 27, 1928: *Si vis pacem, para pacem* (if you want peace, prepare peace)."[146] Although Mowinckel knew that "theory should not be mistaken for reality," especially given the reservations of several states and the ongoing question of German reparations, he concluded that this achievement would cause the Spirit of Geneva to live among the people. Quoting de Traz, he added that, even though this spirit was "still weak, disputed, even despised, at every moment in danger of perishing—no catastrophe can destroy it forever, for it bears mankind's indomitable hope, that of resurrection."[147]

Two Unification Plans

The early years of the 1920s were so favorable to projects of European unification that just after World War II ended, Winston Churchill paid homage to Aristide Briand and Count Richard N. Coudenhove-Kalergi, who became figures of almost prophetic dimensions.[148] Unlike Briand, Coudenhove-Kalergi had an unusually diverse background. His family tree had two main branches: the Coudenhove side of the family was from Austria, and the Kalergis were a wealthy Greek family from Crete, with roots in the Byzantine Empire. The count's father was an Austrian diplomat and his mother was Japanese. In his book *Pan-Europe* published in German in 1923 and in English in 1926, he sought to solve what he termed the "European question"—the absence of unity among the nations of the continent—which was made more urgent by the rise of three strong blocs: the United States (and the Pan-American Union), the British Empire, and the Soviet Union. He believed that the root cause of Europe's woes was the senility not of its people, but of its political system, which required radical change.[149] He perceived that the competition between great powers—the balance of power—would result not only in disastrous economic competition but also in mutual destruction, thus ending the organization of Europe. His solution was the idea of "Pan-Europe," which he defined as "Europe in a political sense." As he asked, "Can Europe in its political and economic disunion maintain its peace and independence in the face of growing non-European world powers—or is it compelled to organize itself into a confederation of states in order to save its existence?"[150]

Arguing for the latter alternative, he claimed that Europe was facing a political turning point because of five factors: (1) the expansion of the British colonial empire outside of Europe; (2) a similar expansion of the Russian continental empire toward Asia; (3) the emancipation of East Asia, with the rise of Japan as a great power; (4) the rise of the United States; and (5) the comparative decline of continental Europe, with the end of the Austro-Hungarian monarchy and the defeat of Germany, leaving only two powers, France and Italy (whose position was now insecure). As a result, Europe was no longer the center of the world but on its periphery.[151] To remain influential among those five "planetary fields" (his term), Europe should be unified into a strong body: a political entity consisting of all European continental states that would also include the African colonies. His chief concern was Soviet military aggression, even though Russia had not fully recovered from its own internal turmoil; it did not matter to him whether the Bolshevik Revolution ultimately succeeded or a reaction took place. He was worried that the Treaties of Paris had already led to the resurrection of eastern states (Poland, Romania, and Bulgaria) that were in no position to resist a Russian invasion. Furthermore, if Germany were not reconciled with the other powers, it would be liable to side with the USSR to the point of agreeing on a partition of Poland—on all these points, he was truly perceptive.

Concerning the eastern frontier of Europe, he asserted that the Ural Mountains could not be considered a political limit, because the demarcation between East and West was debatable; Europe's frontier was, worryingly, now at the Russian border. He believed that the Bolshevik Revolution had severed Russia's link with Europe, setting the European border again on a north–south line east of Finland, the Baltic States, Poland, and Romania.[152] He worried about the future of Russian culture: it might either become more Asian in nature after the destruction of westernized elites during the Bolshevik Revolution or else resume its interrupted Europeanization by extending Europe's cultural domination as far east as the Pacific Ocean. Coudenhove-Kalergi advocated a European Security Pact to prevent the "Russian invasion" of Europe.[153]

Yet Coudenhove-Kalergi was also critical of the League of Nations. Although he approved of its mission, he considered it "inorganic" and a "utopia," and he felt it had already compromised its credibility by capitulating to Poland in the crises of Upper Silesia, Lithuania, and Eastern Galicia.[154] Furthermore, he argued that the League of Nations was drawing in non-European states to weigh in on European issues, even though the United States would never have tolerated the League's intervention on American issues, nor Britain on its colonial issues. Pan-Europe, formed after the federated model of the United States, would be dedicated to self-help through unification within a political and economic administrative union.[155] After its formation, the world would be divided into five separate political continents: Pan-America, the British Empire, the Russian Empire, Pan-Asia, and Pan-Europe.[156] He considered it necessary for Europe to pass from a "national period" to a "continental period," bringing along with it a new form of patriotism. Coudenhove argued that the imminent economic and political pressure of "Pan-America" (with the United States as the most prominent actor) and the Komintern (aligned with the Soviet Union) would necessitate Europe's unification. He went as far as proposing a customs union between France and Germany to reunite the German coal and the French iron ore industries—an idea actively pursued in the days of the League, but that would not materialize for another thirty years.[157]

Coudenhove's proposal can be added to the list of significant European plans for perpetual peace. He explicitly inscribed his idea of European unification in the canonic tradition, tracing it to, among others, the Quakers, the Abbé de Saint-Pierre, Rousseau, and Kant.[158] He also identified three attempts to unify Europe in the nineteenth century. The first, paradoxically, was Napoleon's project of European unification, though he obviously disapproved of its method. "Had Napoleon won at Leipzig," he speculated, "Europe would in all probability have been a federation to-day. French hegemony would scarcely have survived the death of Napoleon, but the political and economic union of the Continent would probably have survived that hegemony."[159] The second was the Holy Alliance, which "bound together the European world of nations, including Russia, in a united front against war, imperialism and revolution." He found the Holy Alliance problematic, because "it was a league not of peoples, but of rulers." The third attempt was Mazzini's Young Europe movement, which "made its appeal direct to the peoples" and was "in more than one sense the precursor of the Pan-Europa movement." However, he judged Mazzini's attempt a failure, with far-reaching consequences: "Nationalism became divorced from the European idea, came into conflict with neighboring nationalisms, and pursued the path of chauvinism which ended in the World War."[160] He did not see ethnonationalism as a natural offspring of 1848, but as a destructive deviation.

Here was a change of tone compared to that of earlier plans: far from the optimism of the eighteenth century or even the faith in European progress of the nineteenth, Coudenhove-Kalergi's view of the future was grim: he saw an impending demise that only Pan-Europe could avert. Peace was no longer a goal to be pursued for itself, but a necessary condition for the continued freedom of Europeans. This shift in perspective (which inserted itself in the general debate on which great powers would come to dominate the world and which would succumb), was motivated by a conviction that the states of continental Europe had irremediably lost world dominance in the Great War.[161] For the first time, the European great powers had to worry about being dominated by external powers. To avert that fate, he advocated a "European Monroe Doctrine" that he defined as "Europe to the Europeans." His claims that no European power was in a position to compete with the United States or Russia and that a new war would subject Europe to their vassalage were far-sighted. His clarity of vision was quite remarkable: he even recognized the risk of a German-Soviet pact, to the detriment of Poland, as a preliminary to the disaster of a new internecine war. After the publication of his book, the Pan-Europe idea took on a life of its own. Coudenhove-Kalergi also published a monthly journal called *Pan-Europa* to promote his ideas to a large audience. The Pan-European Union, founded in Vienna in 1924, became one of the most active pro-European organizations in the interwar period and is still active today (to the Nazis, this movement, which regarded Hitler's expansionist program as doomed from the start, was anathema, and it was banned when they came to power).[162]

Pan-Europe belonged to the realm of ideas, but the Pact of Locarno and the admission of Germany to the League of Nations opened the way to another advance in the direction of peace on the plane of politics. On September 5, 1929, Briand proposed that the Assembly of the League of Nations establish "a sort of federal link" between the peoples geographically grouped in Europe. He advocated the possibility of "contacting each other, to discuss their interests, take common resolutions, establish between them a solidarity link which would allow them . . . to face serious circumstances should they occur."[163] It is significant that this association would operate in the economic field, where the need was most pressing. Stresemann threw his weight behind the project. As he explained a few days later to the Assembly, although the Treaty of Versailles had created many new states, it had given no thought to integrating them into a European economic system; he lamented that, even though the duration of travel between Germany and Japan had been reduced, rail trips in Europe were slowed by hour-long formalities at each border.[164] Thus the economic focus of European unification was rooted in the unintended political balkanization that had occurred in the aftermath of World War I.

The first reactions to Briand's proposal of "a sort of federal link" being positive, the French government sent surveys to the twenty-seven European member states of the League to get more detailed feedback. The head of cabinet Alexis Léger—better known under his pen name of Saint-John Perse—wrote a "Memorandum on the Organization of a Regime of European Federal Union" on May 1, 1930. This "European Union" would exist within the framework of the League (according to Article 21 of its Covenant, which explicitly provided for such institutions) and operate in coordination with it. It was to be founded with a pact, with the presidency taken by each member country in turn, to avoid the undue preeminence of one country over another. It proposed a structure not so different from that of the League: a "European conference" representing the governments, a "Permanent Political Committee" with a few selected members, and a "Secretariat." Economic issues would be subordinated to security issues, which in turn would be subordinated to the political goal of a union; its purpose would be to "pull together the economies" and establish a "common market."[165] It was inclusive as far as Europe was concerned, but neither exclusive of nor directed against any other country or organization. "To Unite to live and prosper: such is the strict necessity now facing the Nations of Europe," concluding that this initiative would benefit "the European community as well as mankind."[166]

The European economic and political environment was changing rapidly: after the Wall Street crash on October 24, 1929, the Great Depression washed over Europe, and national governments soon started adopting protectionist measures. When Stresemann died of a stroke on October 3 at age fifty-one, the project for a European Union lost a key advocate in Germany, with his successors having to contend against the growing belief that it was merely a way for France to ensure its supremacy in Europe. A Commission for the Study of a European Union started work in September 1930 and met for five sessions until it was dissolved in 1932, but it was obvious that the Secretariat of the League now considered it an inconvenience. Despite the lack of success, the "Memorandum" and this commission marked the most formalized political advance made to this point toward European unification. It also standardized terms, such as "European Union," "European community," and "common market," that would be reused later in the twentieth century.

Peace, Betrayed

The successes of the Spirit of Geneva were unfortunately short-lived. Every permanent member of the Council of the League struck serious blows at its legitimacy, one after the other. The first to do so was Japan, a founding member of the League. It turned to militarism and totalitarianism when, in September 1931, it invaded Manchuria in northern China, marching to the Great Wall. The League of Nations entrusted a commission made up of four representatives from permanent Council members (Britain, France, Germany, and Italy) and one American diplomat to address the matter. Reporting its findings on October 2, 1932, the commission blamed Japan for its aggression and recommended that it withdraw its troops from Manchuria. On February 24, 1933, the General Assembly adopted the report by a vote of 42–1, with Japan casting the sole negative vote. That day, the agitated and indignant Japanese delegate Yōsuke Matsuoka shocked the Assembly by announcing that it refused to accept the League of Nations' resolution; he walked out, never to return. This was a test of fire, the dreaded worst-case scenario contemplated by the Abbé de Saint-Pierre and Kant: a member of the Society of States had refused to abide by its decisions, leading to secession. The outcry in the international press and public opinion was considerable, but there was nothing the League could do.[167]

The second power to violate the spirit and aims of the League was Germany. After the hyperinflation of the early 1920s, the country was financially devastated in 1929 by the Great Depression; unemployment rose while industrial production collapsed. The National Socialist German Workers' Party (NSDAP), better known as the Nazi Party, came into power in January 1933. It brutally crushed all political opposition, and the rearmament of Germany accelerated. On October 19, 1933, in a curt letter, Foreign Minister Konstantin von Neurath informed the League's general secretary, Joseph Avenol, of Germany's withdrawal.[168] The next month, at the first national election since the Nazi Party came to power, it won more than 90 percent of the vote.

The third defector was Italy: in October 1935, after an incident at the border between Italian Somalia and Abyssinia (Ethiopia), the dictator Benito Mussolini sent 400,000 troops to invade Ethiopia, in a ruthless war in which Italy used poison gas in clear violation of the Geneva Protocol against Chemical Weapons of 1925. Abyssinia, admitted to the League in 1923, was the only state on the African continent that had retained its sovereignty during the late nineteenth-century Scramble for Africa. On June 30, Emperor Haile Selassie came to Geneva to deliver a speech to the League of Nations, in which he asked it to intervene against Italy on his country's behalf:

> I ask the fifty-two nations not to forget to-day the policy upon which they embarked eight months ago, and on faith of which I directed the resistance of my people against the aggressor whom they had denounced to the world. Despite the inferiority of my weapons, . . . my trust in the League was absolute. I thought it impossible that fifty-two nations, including the most powerful in the world, should be successfully held in check by a single aggressor. Relying on the faith due to treaties, I had made no preparation for war.[169]

One of the most troubling events in the history of the League took place at this point. In December 1935, French prime minister Pierre Laval and British foreign secretary Samuel Hoare devised a secret treaty with Mussolini, offering their support for his partition of Ethiopia in exchange for his continued opposition to Nazi Germany, which was then attempting to annex Austria. When the draft of the treaty was leaked to the press, it caused an enormous scandal. Laval and Hoare were forced to resign, and the matter nearly cost the British prime minister his position.[170] As the fourth and fifth perpetrators in this string of treasons, Britain and France thus delivered a final blow to the reputation and credibility of the League: two founders and mainstays had been caught in an act of secret diplomacy with a country that had violated the League Covenant by causing a war of aggression. Even worse, Britain, France, and Italy were three of the four members of the original Council of the League; Japan, which had already walked out, had been the fourth. Italy withdrew from the League on December 13, 1937.

The disgrace deepened when the new prime minister of Britain, Neville Chamberlain, concluded in 1936 that the League had lost its power as an instrument of world peace:

> Surely it is time that the nations who compose the League should review the situation and should decide so to limit the functions of the League in future that they may accord with its real powers. If that policy were to be pursued and were to be courageously carried out, I believe that it might go far to restore the prestige of the League and the moral influence which it ought to exert in the world. But if the League be limited in that sort of way it must be admitted that it could no longer be relied upon by itself to secure the peace of the world.[171]

After Adolf Hitler took power in 1933, he set as the ultimate aim of Germany's foreign policy the acquisition of *Lebensraum,* a vast "living space" in Central and Eastern Europe where German colonists could settle and rule over the "inferior races." Even though the Nazis were careful not to specify African or Arab peoples (their racist biases had a certain opportunistic flexibility), their elevating the German race to the highest status and extending colonization to the peoples of Europe itself were extrapolations of earlier Social Darwinist arguments, which were used to justify overseas colonialism before World War I.[172] In the face of Germany's aggressive rearmament and its increasingly belligerent attitude, France and Britain set aside the modern ideal of peace under international law in favor of an older, time-honored practice—that developed by the Byzantine Empire, Muscovy, and later Venice—of paying tribute to an aggressive power to save the expense of a war; in other words, they used the strategy of appeasement.[173] After Mussolini withdrew his opposition to the annexation of Austria and France and Britain declined to intervene, the *Anschluss* became a reality on March 11, 1938. Germany invaded its smaller neighbor only one day before a general referendum on the merger of the two countries was to take place; after the coup, the Nazis immediately engaged in the repression of political opposition and Jews. Hitler then turned his sights on the Sudetenland in

Czechoslovakia, where the majority of the population was German speaking. This manifestation of irredentism sparked an international crisis. In September, British prime minister Neville Chamberlain and French prime minister Edouard Daladier met in turn with Hitler at his residence outside of Berchtesgaden in Bavaria; one sign of the times was that no representative of Czechoslovakia was invited. The British and French diplomats agreed to the cession of the Sudetenland to Germany; to counterbalance this concession, they hoped to create a series of interlocking pacts with other European countries, particularly Poland and the Soviet Union.[174]

Czechoslovakia was not in a position to resist annexation, and the Sudetenland contained its defensive fortifications; Hitler immediately seized the opportunity to claim control over the rest of the country. At Mussolini's suggestion, a conference including France, Britain, and Germany was held in Munich on September 29. By that point, guilty-faced members of the French and British delegations had lost the moral high ground. By following the policy of appeasement, they had shown that the land and population of Czechoslovakia were still property that could be bought or sold: the long process of transformation from hereditary patrimonial monarchies to the ethnonationalist state now was completed, with the triumph of what I call the "patrimonial republic": the absolute landlord was the Aryan race, under the guidance of its leader Adolph Hitler. Germans would occupy their assigned superior place, and the *Untermensche* would become slaves of the state.

Repeating their strategies instituted earlier at the twilight of the Ottoman Empire, other European states then resorted to scavenging: Poland annexed the Czechoslovakian railway junction of Bohumín, and Hungary took a part of Carpatho-Ukraine.[175] The year when the stately Palace of Nations in Geneva was finally inaugurated as the seat of the League was paradoxically the pivotal moment when the addiction to self-aggrandizement was reaffirmed in the life of European states. While the Western press was proclaiming that "peace had been saved," Germany dismembered Czechoslovakia by annexing Sudetenland in March 1939, imposing a Bohemian and Moravian Protectorate on the rest of Czechia, and leaving a rump Slovak state that had lost considerable territory to Hungary.

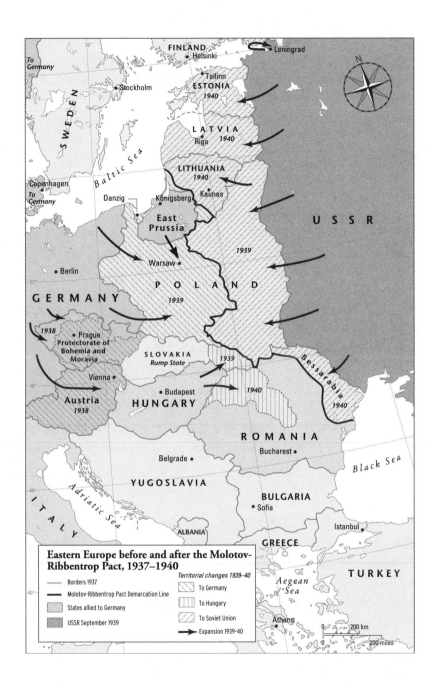

Eastern Europe before and after the Molotov-Ribbentrop Pact, 1937–1940

Borders 1937

Molotov-Ribbentrop Pact Demarcation Line

States allied to Germany

USSR September 1939

Territorial changes 1939–40

To Germany

To Hungary

To Soviet Union

Expansion 1939–40

The Soviet Union, which replaced Germany in 1934 as a permanent member of the League Council, was the last to commit treason. Before the German invasion of Poland, the Soviet Union had secured its own "sphere of influence" in Eastern Europe, thanks to secret clauses of the Molotov-Ribbentrop Pact of August 23, 1939. When Germany attacked Poland from the west on September 1, and the USSR attacked from the east on September 17, the Soviet Union entered the war in collusion with Nazi Germany, in a game of territorial aggrandizement. Together they defeated and partitioned Poland. A political cartoon of the time shows Adolf Hitler and Joseph Stalin meeting over the corpse of a Polish soldier, addressing each other with insulting remarks in a most courteous manner. Neville Chamberlain, still temporizing on September 1 in the hopes of appeasing Hitler, left Parliament puzzled that evening—despite the commitment of Britain to declare war on Germany if such an eventuality happened. On September 3, both Britain and France declared war against Germany. Yet the League continued its work, as the invasion of Finland (part of a secret clause in the Soviet alliance with Nazi Germany) caused a surge of activity in Geneva. On December 14, the General Assembly voted to exclude the Soviet Union, on the initiative of France and Britain, which were by now both committed to the war. This event, which prompted an infuriated re-action from TASS (the Soviet press agency), stung Stalin as a public humiliation. It would have indirect consequences for the world that reverberate to this day.[176]

Interwar Order: Beyond the Myths

To draw useful lessons from the pursuit of lasting peace in Europe during the interwar era, it is necessary to do away with two misconceptions, which have long clouded understanding of this period: one is about its start and the other about its end. The first is the belief (often accompanied by indignation and resentment) that the victorious powers of 1919 had come to the Paris Peace Conference with the wrongful purpose of weakening Germany, Hungary, and the other defeated powers. The second (outwardly condescending) myth is that the League was a flawed device and that its inability to respond to military force with military force was the factor that ultimately precipitated World War II.

What helped give rise to the first misconception was the passionate denunciation by British economist John Maynard Keynes, written one year after the Treaty of Versailles was signed, of its treatment of Germany. He strikingly compared it to a "Carthaginian Peace," referring to Rome's imposition of peace conditions on Carthage after the Second Punic War in 201 BCE—Carthage's refusal then to accept the draconian terms triggered a third war and the eventual destruction of the city.[177] Keynes made several insightful points when denouncing the economic consequences of the Treaty of Versailles, but he overstated the negative effects of some provisions, such as Germany's reparations: save for the food shortages, its economic and industrial infrastructure were still in better shape than those of northern France, Belgium, and Poland, and its soil had barely been stressed by combat.[178] Keynes's thesis falls into a straw man fallacy, however—impugning the victors' motives and character by portraying them as Ancient Romans indulging in a war of extermination.[179] No delegation of a victorious power spoke of "treating Germany as Carthage" during the peace conference, for the reason that there was no such intention.

The myth of Versailles—which ascribes the problems with the treaties to wrongful intentions—undermined the League's legitimacy in Europe and, by reflection, legitimized authoritarian governments, especially those in Central Europe, that promised to take matters into their own hands and "redress wrongs" by the use of force. Anchoring its election campaign in the woes of the economic crisis and the promise to reject the Treaty of Versailles, the Nazi Party had a solid platform for success in the elections of July 1932 and enough leverage to stage the coup that in January 1933 ended not only democracy in Germany but also hopes for a durable peace in Europe. The same anti-Versailles propaganda was even used to justify Nazi Germany's self-aggrandizement during both the Sudetenland crisis in Czechoslovakia and the invasion of Poland that started World War II.[180]

As for the argument that the Treaty of Versailles was the work of a small group of "traitors of the German People," suffice it to say that Germany benefited from male universal suffrage from the foundation of the empire in

1871 all the way through Hitler's rise to power. A wide cross section of German citizens had voted into power the parliament that supported Germany's "war against the world." The same electors brought into office the MPs of the German republic who formally ratified the "diktat" of Versailles in the Berlin Reichstag Palace on June 22, 1919, with a majority of more than 60 percent of those present.[181] Hungarian historiography has also propagated a self-victimization narrative about the Treaty of Trianon, yet its parliament ratified it unanimously on November 13, 1920.[182] Similarly, the irredentism of postwar Italy and its claim of betrayal by the Paris Conference were based on the morally dubious bargain it made with the Allies in 1915, which allowed Italy to enter the Great War as a mercenary state. As in Agatha Christie's *Murder on the Orient Express,* written in 1934, the indignant witnesses could well lay the blame on each other, but they had all contributed to the deed.

To begin to make sense of what really happened, it is first necessary to step back and examine the events in the broad context of Europe at the end of 1918. Large parts of the continent were multiethnic patchworks of populations that had lived for ages under four dynastic empires: the Russian, Austro-Hungarian, German, and Ottoman Empires. Their disintegration left a power vacuum that threw these regions in political chaos. Most importantly, the defeat of the four empires in the Great War was only the last shock, and the actual causes of their collapse were structural. These multinational formations were weakened over the decades by societal upheavals of unprecedented scale: notably, unsatisfied demands for the improvement of social conditions ("the social question") and the political representation of ethnic groups ("the national question").[183] That fact must be kept in mind, rather than blaming the Paris Conference for not bringing about peace in Eastern Europe, leaving Germany in a politically unsustainable situation, and creating a profound sense of resentment in Hungary. It is pointless to assign abstract blame to the "doctors" of the Paris Conference for the preexisting condition of Europe. Similarly, the debate of whether things could have gone differently belongs to counterfactual history and is not of interest here.

Instead, a more productive focus is on what was actually in the sphere of responsibility of the diplomatic delegations in Paris: namely, the proceedings of the conference that produced the Treaty of Versailles. That conference was certainly not a high point in the history of European diplomacy: human passions, not cynical motives, were allowed to derail the peace process. Engulfed by the European "sea of events," the Paris Conference never managed to assert control over them. The delegations, in their effort to cope with the chaotic situation that changed day by day, found themselves making choices they had not foreseen, going in directions they had not intended.

The engineering of peace, which is based on a detailed analysis of the peace negotiations, raises this question: With the benefit of hindsight, is it possible to identify specific instances of errors or miscalculations from the Four Powers, from which we could draw useful lessons? The answer is, fortunately, yes. The crucial observation, in that regard, is that the victorious powers did not apply precautions and best practices of the engineering of peace, which their predecessors of 1814–1815 had consciously and carefully used to build the monumental and stable edifice of the Final Act of Vienna. Two major deviations from that preexisting rulebook are largely sufficient to explain the internal difficulties of the Paris Conference. The first was a lack of preparation, so that the victorious powers arrived at the peace negotiations with a disunited front; and the second was the methodological error of not separating the urgent priority of signing the peace with the defeated powers from the important but far more complicated redrawing of Europe's map.

The first error occurred at a crucial moment that is generally overlooked by both historians of diplomacy and by military historians, because it happened in a time of limbo, when the fate of arms had already been decided but the ceasefire had not yet been signed. In this two-week period at the end of October and the beginning of November 1918, the governments of Britain, Italy, and France were caught off-guard by nearly simultaneous armistice offers by the Ottoman, Austro-Hungarian, and German Empires.[184] In that eleventh hour, the victorious powers committed a misstep that started the peace negotiations on a wrong footing and compromised their proceedings. The allied empires of Central Europe knew that their routed armies were within days of being decimated and that their military commanders would soon be in no position to discuss conditions. In what could be seen as a last stroke of genius (or simply common sense), they each engaged in the same evasive maneuver: politically engaging one of their enemies in separate armistice negotiations. Each victorious power immediately attempted to seize the offer proposed to it for its exclusive profit, treating the conditions separately from the others. In the agitation of the moment they entirely failed to coordinate and centralize their efforts: the British Navy negotiating with the Ottomans (and excluding the French); the Italian Army dealing on its own with the Austro-Hungarians; and the French Army dealing with the Germans without the British. In that respect, this last maneuver of the Central Powers was a perfect success. The three Western powers broke ranks and rushed headlong into separate peace treaties, without realizing that, if they had only coordinated their efforts for a few more days, they would soon be in a position to reap the only prize that could have justified the sacrifices of the Great War: three capitulations. In that moment, they forgot that the whole object of the four years of war against the Central Powers had been "to compel our opponent to fulfil our will" (as Clausewitz might have said), which could only reasonably be interpreted as obtaining surrender from them. Unfortunately, the Four Powers had not taken the precaution beforehand to formally agree on war aims and the principles of a postwar order (despite Wilson's Fourteen Points). Once this window of opportunity was missed and the armistices granted, there was no turning back.

For reference, the four Great Powers of 1814 had thoroughly considered this exact issue at a high political level and reached an agreement with each other at the Treaty of Chaumont:

> The High Contracting Parties reciprocally engage not to treat separately with the common Enemy, nor to sign Peace, Truce, nor Convention, but with common consent. They, moreover, engage not to lay down their Arms until the object of the War, mutually understood and agreed upon, shall have been attained.[185]

Had the "Allies" of 1918 gone through a similar process of mutual clarification before negotiating in Paris, they would likely have agreed on the necessity of this "Chaumont clause"; namely, that surrender was the only thing they could sensibly accept each time, in the presence of all high commands of allied armies on the front. According to the rulebook, a parade of military troops should have marched under the triumphal arches of capital cities (as in Berlin and Vienna) to symbolically declare that they had lost the war. The Allies should also have immediately requested that a military force be sent to occupy the nerve centers of those countries; this failure is surprising, because the lesson should have been well learned in 1815 after Napoleon's Hundred Days, and Germany had applied this measure in 1870 against defeated France.[186] The delegations then arrived at the Paris Conference under the motley banner of "Principal and Allied Powers" and immediately proceeded to obstruct each other—clearly violating the Chaumont requirement of acting *in perfect concert* during all ceasefire and peace proceedings. Indeed, thoroughly agreeing on common war aims and accepting nothing but Germany's formal surrender would once again be the guiding principle for the Allies in 1945, having learned from this experience.

The second, equally crucial error is that the Four Powers neglected to use the one innovation that had successfully redefined the map of Europe in 1815: separating the urgent issues of signing peace with the defeated powers from the general redefinition of the map of Europe and the founding of a new political order. In truth, organizing such a conference with Germany to consolidate the treaty clauses had, indeed, been the original intention, but as mentioned, the Four Powers did not trust each other enough to go through such a process. As a result, the Paris Peace Conference found itself bogged down in a morass of unsolvable issues; to make things worse, they eventually took everything into their own hands in an effort to speed up the proceedings. By the time the "peace treaties" that concluded the war with the German, Austro-Hungarian, and the Ottoman Empires had been hashed out, those states had already ceased to exist (whereas the immediate concern of the allied powers of 1814 had been to occupy Paris so as to prop up a French government that could sign a peace treaty as fast as possible). The victorious powers of 1919 found themselves, after several months of grueling work, in the detestable situation of signing the peace treaties with successor states that objected to reparations clauses and territorial losses, for the good reason that they had not started the war.

In addition, separating Europe into five areas, one per defeated power, made sense if doing so would end the state of war with each. Yet, it was woefully inadequate for a global territorial settlement of Europe, because none of these regions existed in a vacuum. This was especially true considering that Europe had become considerably more complex and diverse than a century earlier, leading to multiple demands to redraw borders along ethnic lines, which made for volatility far worse than that in 1815. To confront this challenge, the Paris Conference lacked, unfortunately, a high-level blueprint for the Continent that would also allow it to keep track of details; as a result, it constantly operated at an in-between level that afforded neither the view of the forest view or of the trees. Operating from that perspective would have presumably required assembling the Allies, the defeated powers, and the neutrals in a second, general settlement conference for Europe that also would have involved a wide cross section of European professionals such as lawyers, bureaucrats, engineers, and industrialists; its product would be a settlement treaty undersigned by all the states of Europe. We might speculate whether such a conference would have been possible, but it can be stated with certainty that the absence of any such organized settlement process weighed heavily after the Great War because of the inadequacies and the lack of consensus on the existing negotiations. In retrospect, the attempt by a few plenipotentiaries and their secretariats to resolve, all by themselves, the colossal territorial tangle of postwar Europe with five geographically distinct treaties was bound to produce a substandard and controversial result—and one that came too late. These two errors may be treated as culpable negligence, because the Four Powers should have known better (a verdict that rules out the possibility of malicious intent).

By contrast, Woodrow Wilson's unorthodox decision to exploit the momentum of the Paris Conference by inserting the League's Covenant in the peace treaties cannot be considered a design error, because it was then still a novel approach. It can even be seen as the right decision as far as Europe was concerned, because the League of Nations was indeed established and did become operational. However, the chances of having the Covenant ratified by the US Senate were low because of the firm, dominant American belief in the virtues of isolationism, and Wilson should not have conditioned the US signing of the peace treaty on the Senate's approval of the League. Not without merit, the Office of the Historian of the US government stated, "Wilson's insistence that the Covenant be linked to the

Treaty was a blunder" because he had engaged his country in a leap of faith that the US Senate was ultimately unwilling to support.[187] As the Spanish diplomat and pacifist Salvador de Madariaga later wrote,

> The only reason why America did not ratify the Covenant is because of the slow movements of the Senate. If every other nation had had such a slow body for ratifying the treaties, very few of them would have ratified the thing. If anyone had noticed what was inside, few would have ratified it. If the Covenant were put today as a fresh proposition to any nation in the world, it would not have a chance anywhere.[188]

In any case the outcome of a League of Nations made up of European states but not the United States was better than no League at all, and Wilson's gamble is what ultimately allowed this invaluable experiment for the engineering of peace to proceed. [189]

Let us turn now to the end of the interwar period and to the second major misconception about the League of Nations; namely, that its inability to respond to military force with military force was the key factor that ultimately precipitated World War II. Though this was recognized at the time as a significant obstacle to the League's effectiveness, arguing that the League would have been a "failure" merely because it was unable to muster an army to stop Italy's invasion of Ethiopia or Japan's incursion into Manchuria does not stand up to examination. This claim is even astonishing, considering that the peace organization often cited as a counter-example for its "robustness"—the United Nations—has never activated Article 43 of its Charter, which requires member states to put military means at its disposal. Even if it had, the UN could not have mobilized enough military resources to stop the Soviet Union's aggressions against Hungary in 1956 and Czechoslovakia in 1968—and, in any case, Moscow's right of veto eliminated the possibility of any debate at the General Assembly. In sum, expecting that any *peace alliance,* yesterday or today, could be provided with enough hard power to stop a major imperial power already set on war is idealistic. As European powers learned repeatedly—and again in 1939—the only workable course of action to redress matters at that point is to assemble a *military alliance* in an attempt to restore the balance of power and to prepare for a war that could last for a long time.

In reality, the peace system of the League collapsed because the governments of France and Britain turned their backs on the principle inscribed in its Covenant. Ceding to the anti-Versailles mindset—which on their part came to be known as *mea culpism*—they agreed to forgive transgressions against the international order committed by two totalitarian governments, Italy and Germany, that were in the process of self-aggrandizement.[190] In particular, the contradictory efforts from several states to appease Hitler during the Munich Agreement in 1938 proved counterproductive and were consequently derogatorily termed the "Spirit of Munich." For posterity, this experience showed that appeasement was a second-rate political instrument that sought to buy an immediate truce at the cost of a future war: it is an ironic lesson that appeasement achieves a result opposite to that of a peace process. As Winston Churchill argued on February 22, 1938, Chamberlain was wrong to have indulged Mussolini, because he was simultaneously abandoning the tried-and-true method of maintaining peace or a peaceful co-existence between states and compromising the regional balance of power:

> The old policy was an effort to establish the rule of law in Europe, and build up through the League of Nations, or by regional pacts under the League of Nations, effective deterrents against the aggressor. . . . a firm stand by France and Britain, with the other Powers associated with them at that time, and with the authority of the League of Nations, would have been followed by the immediate [German] evacuation of the Rhineland without the shedding of a drop of blood; and the effects of that might have been blessed beyond all compare, because it would have enabled the more prudent elements of the German Army to gain their proper position, and would not have given to the political head of Germany the enormous ascendancy which has enabled him to move forward. . . . Austria has now been laid in thrall, and we do not know whether Czechoslovakia will not suffer a similar attack.[191]

In contrast with the ineffectual policy of the French and British delegations at Munich, the General Assembly of the League did issue condemnations of the aggressions of Japan against China, Italy against Ethiopia, and the Soviet Union against Finland in September 1939.[192] Yet the League did have a fundamental structural weakness: it lacked any way to enforce recourse to the International Court in those cases, at which point it only could have authorized military actions against the offenders.

It follows that the League operated exactly as designed. The Assembly gave the floor to a small country like Ethiopia to publicly confront and accuse Italy, a member of the Council, and did not shrink from deciding to expel a world power from that same Council. In fact, Churchill later laid the fault for letting the war happen on the Four Powers themselves: "The League [of Nations] did not fail because of its principles or conceptions. It failed because those principles were deserted by those states which brought it into being, because the governments of those states feared to face the facts and act while time remained."[193]

Indeed, the League of Nations was an ambitious and innovative machinery of peace. It managed to bring several international mechanisms under one roof, having an Assembly, a Council, and a Secretariat. Its main achievement was that it continued to function for two decades in a complex and challenging environment. That advance is to be compared to the Congress System of the previous century, which actively functioned for less than a decade and then continued to exist by inertia (and brought its full measure of disappointments to the Age of Revolutions). The League of Nations was engineered to be an entity mitigating the unilateralism of the Treaties of Paris, and it acted accordingly. Indeed, most of its efforts to solve territorial disputes over two decades can be interpreted as conscious attempts to fix the flaws and omissions of these treaties—particularly the lack of proper settlement of Eastern European borders because of the absence of the Russian state at the Paris Conference. The League thus accumulated considerable experience as a facilitator on technical issues regarding several states; it built on the tradition of civil commissions inaugurated a century earlier at Vienna with the Rhine Commission and considerably expanded on it.

Yet the League of Nations is remembered as a "great disappointment." In its final years, the League went from one setback to another until the outbreak of World War II. As an organization, it lived in limbo until 1946, when its assets were transferred to the United Nations. Extraordinarily high hopes had been attached to the League—namely, that it should ensure peace forevermore in Europe—especially after the Locarno Pact. But it would be irrational to judge the "success" of the League against such an impossibly lofty standard. It would be better to focus on the few precious years of peace that it did afford (once again, this is to be compared with the period from 1945 to 1989, when the military frontier of the Iron Curtain did not see a day of actual peace). As André Maurois remarked in his preface to the 1935 English translation of de Traz's *The Spirit of Geneva,* "The League of Nations can no more guarantee peace than the doctor can guarantee a cure. But is that a reason for doing without the doctor?"[194] Here, again, was the powerful organic metaphor of war as an international disease. The League did its best to assist Europe's recovery after the Great War, after the collapse of empires (the "preexisting condition" of Europe), and the shock treatment inflicted on Europe with the Treaties of Paris; after initial successes that entertained hopes of recovery, the patient still succumbed.

Finally, a word is needed on what might well be the real reason why the League earned its bad reputation. Paradoxically, it fared too well in some areas: it publicly exposed the great powers and thereby challenged balances of power that they were comfortable with. The League of Nations provided a diplomatic arena in which any small country could step forward and exert unbridled freedom of speech, at a level unthinkable during the Cold War and still unwelcome in our day and age. For that reason, it carries memories of painful public embarrassment for great powers. During that era, the United States was constantly being reminded of its refusal to honor Wilson's commitment to participate in the League, with the consequence that its reputation as a trustworthy international partner was diminished. Incredulous and indignant delegates of the empires of Japan, Germany, and Italy were called in front of the Assembly and publicly humiliated. France and Britain, the two greatest colonial powers of the time, had their dereliction of duty publicly exposed in 1935. The exclusion of the Soviet Union from the League in 1939 may be considered a last assertion of power, one that left a profound scar on the Soviet psyche.[195]

To make up for a lack of an army, the League of Nations thus had, as Kant had shrewdly contemplated, a weapon: its caustic outspokenness. It carried a noteworthy power with it, because it could mete out severe moral punishment to great powers where it hurt the most—to their pride. The mighty armies of Italy, Germany, Japan, and the Soviet Union were powerless to protect their own envoys from being called in front of the Assembly and dressed down. Our day and age owes the international condemnation of these past empires to the League of Nations' habit of calling a spade a spade. The powerful military alliance that fought and defeated the Axis powers in World War II also relied, for its legitimacy, on condemnations issued by the League, and in that regard it contributed to the final victory. Although its Assembly certainly did not provide a definitive answer to the question, *Qui custodiet ipsos custodes?* (Who will watch the watchmen?), it undeniably got closer to making the great powers accountable, by making indelible marks on their record. This may explain why, at the end of World War II, the Spirit of Geneva was regarded with wariness in the circle of victorious powers and "best left forgotten." Let us follow their process of creating a new world order that would not allow things to get out of hand again.

4

The Postwar
European Spirit

BREAKTHROUGH TO UNIFICATION

The work, my friends, is peace. More than an end of this war—an end to
the beginnings of all wars.

—FRANKLIN D. ROOSEVELT, LAST UNDELIVERED SPEECH,
PREPARED FOR JEFFERSON DAY, 1945

*O*n July 17, 1945, a conference on the future of Germany opened between
the United States, Britain, and the Soviet Union in Potsdam. The location
was the Cecilienhof, a fairly modest Tudor-style residence that had been
built during World War I as a cozy getaway for the Prussian crown prince.
This was not going to be a *peace* conference, however. During the Versailles
Conference in 1919, the Allies had made the questionable decision to
exclude Germany from all deliberations. This time, there was not even a
sovereign state left to sign a peace treaty: just like Poland at the end of the
eighteenth century, Germany as a nation-state had ceased to exist. This
conference would be about the conditions of partition and military occupation of a de facto stateless land.

Establishing a new postwar order under these conditions raised profound
moral and practical questions about the meaning of "peace." German military representatives had agreed to the unconditional capitulation of the
German Reich in the form of an Instrument of Surrender, which took effect at midnight on May 8, 1945. Although signing that document marked
the final silencing of the guns, Europe was far from being in a state of peace.

The expression *Stunde Null,* or "Zero Hour," became broadly used in Germany to refer to a rupture with the past and the start of a new time of uncertainty, with no assurances about the future.[1] As the world awoke to the systematic nature of the Holocaust, the country was, if not actually starting from zero, certainly at an all-time low. Germans, particularly the young, experienced a bleak dawn characterized by shame and guilt. Wartime cruelty had, however, not been unique to the Germans: Russians, Romanians, and many others had committed crimes that could not be attributed to the "messiness" of war but explained only by a maniacal resolve to destroy human lives.[2] Even the Royal Air Force had embraced the idea of killing tens of thousands of civilians through obliteration bombings of cities, a prospect that would have horrified the military forces of World War I.[3] European peoples had crossed, for the second time in the twentieth century, a new threshold toward total war.

And once again, the chaos of a continental war had thrown the pursuit of European order off course. Yet the situation after 1945 was even more dire than after the Great War. There had always been an implicit assumption that peace treaties would follow war and that European powers would recover stronger than before: certainly, they had even survived the "suicide of Europe" of the previous Great War. But this time was different, because all that Europe had to offer in 1945 were the two evils it had sought to overcome ever since the War of Spanish Succession: a continent hopelessly divided into two opposed military blocs and the eastern part firmly in the grip of a large authoritarian empire that aspired to European dominance. The demoralized political classes of Paris, London, Berlin, and Rome were ushered into an alien world order in which the United States and the Soviet Union had far more important concerns to attend to in Europe than the Europeans' own conceptions of perpetual peace.

Worse still, Western European countries where democracy survived had to steer a path toward reconstruction while coping with a world where the League's successor, the United Nations, was in no position to alleviate the plight of those peoples dominated by the Soviet Union—or, indeed, the plight of those west of what would become the Iron Curtain. New peacetime institutions needed to arise in the 1950s from the rubble of Western Europe to make up for the collapse of the UN's grandiose aim of bringing perpetual peace to the world. These new institutions might be grouped into two categories: the *Atlanticist* (or transatlantic) organizations, fostered and financially supported by the United States, such as NATO and the OECD; and the *Europeanist* institutions created by the direct initiative of European states, such as the Council of Europe and the later European Communities.[4] Although aligned in principle, these two types of organizations differed in one significant way: Atlanticist institutions reflected the plans and programs of the United States regarding the rebuilding of postwar Europe, whereas Europeanist ones were designed by Western Europeans themselves to achieve their own long-term solutions for peacetime. The Cold War would made it necessary for the US constructions to exist for some time to come.

The efforts to reconstruct the continent were informed by what was then called explicitly for the first time "the European Spirit."[5] This European Spirit emerged in two waves, the first after 1945, the second after 1989. They were distinct but in the end they overlapped, as one transformed into the other: I call one "the Postwar European Spirit," the other, "the Spirit of Enlarged Europe" and I treat them in successive chapters. Focused squarely on unification of the continent—though it ultimately only suffused the Western part of it, under the US umbrella—the initial, Postwar, European Spirit cannot be tied to one city like the earlier ones, but instead to a narrow strip along the left bank of the Rhine River between Germany and France, on which are located the cities of Brussels, Luxembourg, and Strasbourg. The earlier Spirits of Utrecht, Vienna, and Geneva had all arisen from the upheavals of a great war; but this time, the great powers of the continent had exhausted themselves in one fratricidal war too many. This new European Spirit carried the grief of an irreparable loss, which would be handed down to successive generations.

The Postwar European Spirit led to the creation of supranational institutions as early as 1950, in a process conventionally described in English as European "integration," "construction," "unification," or "cooperation." Although apparently descriptive, each of these terms has "its own resonance and means of duress."[6] The original term (used by the promoters of the European project) comes from the French *construction européenne,* generally translated as "building Europe." I will use the term "construction" here to distinguish this specific unification process from previous ones, in which European states did not relinquish sovereignty to a higher, supranational body. The promoters of this new spirit, like their predecessors, made reference to a philosophical and political heritage that could be traced to the Enlightenment. It was initially carried by the first French Revolution, which declared peace to the world in 1790, but was then betrayed by the second Revolution of 1792, which declared war on the rest of Europe. As French prime minister Robert Schuman noted in London on May 5, 1949, "Our exponents of revolution conveyed beyond our frontiers the new message of freedom, which became the common property of mankind today. In their zeal they did not always contrive to keep within the bounds of peaceful methods. We will not be subject to any such temptation."[7]

The Twin Tragedies of Europe

The disaster caused by World War II affected more than Germany: it ended the era of European supremacy. In France and Britain, the postwar celebrations of the victory of May 8, 1945, were leavened by elements of dread and denial. On that day their rank as global powers was already a thing of the past. The United States and the Soviet Union had inherited the mantle of world leadership as superpowers: they were the actual victors who had turned the tide of war and forced Germany to surrender.[8]

The loss of international status was particularly problematic for Britain, for whom the war had been a pyrrhic victory. Historian Peter Clarke evokes this fact in stark terms: "We simply need to recognize that their finest hour in 1940–1941, when the citizens of the British Empire were inspired to resist the Nazi menace at all costs, left bills to be paid later. Defeat would obviously have spelled the end of the Empire. But so did victory, as the British were to discover soon enough."[9] The most formidable naval force in the world in 1939 had been the British Royal Navy; by 1945 it had been overtaken—and left far behind—by the US Navy. Exhausted by the war effort, financially bankrupt, and dependent on the United States for the basic necessities of life, especially food, the United Kingdom was but a ghost of the great power it had been six years earlier.

On the continent, material conditions were far worse. If the Napoleonic wars had seemed apocalyptic to the Europeans of 1815, conditions during the first months of 1945 were bad beyond words. Cities were devastated and economic resources completely exhausted. Warsaw was in ruins and its population depleted; the economies of Belgium and Netherlands were destroyed after being occupied for four taxing years. A pervasive lack of food would plague the Europeans for many years after war's end. Food rationing would continue until the early 1950s, while the US dollar replaced the British pound as the world's reserve currency. As Tony Judt wrote, "Surviving the war was one thing, surviving the peace another."[10]

The extent of this "Tragedy of Europe" was well described by Winston Churchill in a speech delivered in September 1946 in Zurich shortly after he was ousted as prime minister:

> I wish to speak to you today about the tragedy of Europe . . . Over wide areas a vast quivering mass of tormented, hungry, care-worn and bewildered human beings gape at the ruins of their cities and homes, and scan the dark horizons for the approach of some new peril, tyranny or terror. Among the victors there is a babel of jarring voices; among the vanquished the sullen silence of despair.[11]

Dark clouds were indeed gathering on the horizon, as a new Russian Empire had materialized in the form of the expansionist Soviet Union. It became increasingly clear that the "liberated" countries of Eastern Europe, including Poland and Czechoslovakia, would not be restored to their status quo ante: their governments in-exile that were set up in London after the German invasion would be denied the right to retake possession of their respective countries. Those countries would instead be summarily subjugated as vassal states. This is why Churchill wanted to find a "sovereign remedy" in the unity of Europe:

> It is to recreate the European fabric, or as much of it as we can, and to provide it with a structure under which it can dwell in peace, safety and freedom. We must build a kind of United States of Europe. In this way only will hundreds of millions of toilers be able to regain the simple joys and hopes which make life worth living. The process is simple. All that is needed is the resolve of hundreds of millions of men

and women to do right instead of wrong and to gain as their reward blessing instead of cursing.[12]

In particular, Churchill made the astonishing observation that for this remedy to be realized, reconciliation had first to occur between Germany and France. Significantly, he referred to the two precedents of the interwar period:

> Much work has been done upon this task by the exertions of the Pan-European Union, which owes so much to the famous French patriot and statesman Aristide Briand. There is also that immense body which was brought into being amidst high hopes after the First World War—the League of Nations.[13]

Let it be clear, however, that Churchill was advocating an alliance of the countries on the Continent and that he did not conceive the British Empire as being part of a Pan-Europe. Just five months before, in his speech titled "The Sinews of Peace," given at a college in Fulton, Missouri, he gave new life to a now-famous metaphor: "From Stettin in the Baltic to Trieste in the Adriatic, an *iron curtain* has descended across the Continent."[14] The term was used in the late eighteenth century to refer to a protective metal sheet lowered in case of fire on a theater stage. Later, in the 1920s, the terrrm "Iron Curtain" was applied to the Soviet Union in the sense of an "impenetrable barrier" to refer to its isolationist policies.[15] Churchill continued,

> The Russian-dominated Polish Government has been encouraged to make enormous and wrongful inroads upon Germany, and mass expulsions of millions of Germans on a scale grievous and undreamed-of are now taking place. The Communist parties, which were very small in all these Eastern States of Europe, have been raised to pre-eminence and power far beyond their numbers and are seeking everywhere to obtain totalitarian control. Police governments are prevailing in nearly every case, and so far, except in Czechoslovakia, there is no true democracy.[16]

It was quite in character for the seasoned British politician to meet the Soviet Union's threat to Eastern Europe with defiance and to warn his audience not to underrate the "abiding power" of a slowly decolonizing Britain. Unfortunately, there was little that could be done by the time he spoke. After declaring war on Germany in September 1939 to honor its commitment to assist Poland, Britain had consumed itself; it was unable to prevent its former Polish ally from being overrun by the Soviet Union.[17] Considering that the motivation of the United Kingdom for entering World War II was to defend Poland from German invasion, seeing it after the war wholly occupied by the Soviet Union could hardly be looked at as a victory. Every day brought new evidence that the once-mighty European powers had condemned themselves to a future of vassalage—or "alignment," to use the euphemism that had come into vogue.

The Spirit of Yalta: From Eagerness to Discomfiture

The military standoff in Central Europe after World War II was largely the effect of a freakish diplomatic deadlock between the United States and the Soviet Union. A new peace spirit fostered by the US government emerged in the last months of the conflict, the "Spirit of Yalta." As soon as the wartime tide turned in favor of the Allies, the US government logically assumed that a peace treaty would conclude the conflict and establish a collective postwar order in Europe, following the time-honored patterns of 1815 and 1919. The unexpected vicissitudes of the Spirit of Yalta helped shape the Postwar European Spirit.

The peace process began in a well-organized manner with a united front, the Allies obviously having learned their lesson well from the catastrophic disunity of the Paris Conference after World War I. In late 1943, as the tide of battle started turning in their favor against Germany and the Axis powers, the Allies began setting out their own "Chaumont clauses" to end the war together and to ensure preliminary agreement on the future international order. Following an Allied intergovernmental conference in Teheran in December, Franklin D. Roosevelt, Winston Churchill, and Joseph Stalin issued a joint declaration announcing that the old dream of perpetual peace was on the verge of being realized:

> We express our determination that our nations shall work together in war and in the peace that will follow. . . . And as to peace—we are

sure that our concord will make it an enduring peace. We recognize fully the supreme responsibility resting upon us and all the United Nations, to make a peace which will command the good will of the overwhelming mass of the peoples of the world, and banish the scourge of war for many generations.[18]

In February 1945, a second intergovernmental conference took place at Yalta in Crimea. On March 1, 1945, Roosevelt then reaffirmed the same conviction to Congress that lasting peace was at hand, stating that Yalta's conference had been

> a successful effort by the three leading Nations to find a common ground for peace. It ought to spell the end of the system of unilateral action, the exclusive alliances, the spheres of influence, the balances of power, and all the other expedients that have been tried for centuries—and have always failed. We propose to substitute for all these, a universal organization in which all peace-loving Nations will finally have a chance to join.[19]

The US president was, of course, announcing the foundation of the United Nations Organization, "a permanent structure of peace upon which we can begin to build, under God, that better world in which our children and grandchildren—yours and mine, the children and grandchildren of the whole world—must live, and can live."[20] In a later speech, which he never lived to deliver, the president planned to declare, "Today, as we move against the terrible scourge of war, as we go forward toward . . . the contribution of lasting peace, I ask you to keep your faith."[21]

After Roosevelt's untimely death on April 12, 1945, the new president, Harry Truman, quickly came to the conclusion that his predecessor's faith in Stalin's Soviet Union had been misplaced. On the contrary, Truman believed that Stalin's agenda from the outset had been determined by "exclusive alliances," "spheres of influence," and especially the "balance of power." The first cracks between the USSR and the Western Allies appeared even before Germany's capitulation, when it became obvious that Stalin, despite his signing the Declaration on Liberated Europe at the conclusion of the Yalta Conference, intended to establish communist governments in each Eastern European state already occupied by the Red Army.[22] Nevertheless, Truman chose to proceed with Roosevelt's grand plan of transforming the military alliance of the Declaration of the United Nations (January 1, 1942) into a new peace organization that would replace the defunct League of Nations. When the United Nations Conference on International Organization opened in San Francisco on April 23, 1945, the US and Red Armies were about to join forces on the Elbe River, and the final Soviet offensive on Berlin had already started.[23]

The solemn signing of the UN Charter on June 26, 1945, in the presence of delegates from fifty countries, was the key moment of the Postwar European Spirit. The aim of the new organization was "to maintain international peace and security; and to that end: to take effective collective measures for the prevention and removal of threats to the peace, and for the suppression of acts of aggression or other breaches of the peace, and to bring about by peaceful means, and in conformity with the principles of justice and international law, adjustment or settlement of international disputes or situations which might lead to a breach of the peace."[24] Structurally, the UN was clearly based on the League of Nations' blueprint, with a General Assembly, a Council (renamed the *Security* Council), and a Court of Justice.[25]

In practice, however, there was a substantial difference between the two entities: whereas the Hague peace conferences of 1899 and 1907 had tried to establish a world of "peace through law," and the League of Nations had been a relatively egalitarian system that entrusted considerable power in the hands of its Assembly, the UN was a directorial system in which a circle of great powers would call the shots. Its Charter stipulated, somewhat confusingly, that "decisions of the Security Council on all other matters shall be made by an affirmative vote of nine members including the concurring votes of the permanent members."[26] Any "non-concurring" permanent member— namely the United States, Britain, France, USSR, and China—had discretionary power to render any decision of the General Assembly null and void. In practice, the permanent members of the Security Council had the power to sideline the General Assembly at their discretion, even on matters that concerned themselves directly.

The motivation for this decision-making structure is clear: the victorious powers of World War II wanted to guarantee their own independence and influence, and they did not trust each other. With the veto power, each was given the right to throw a wrench into the UN decision-making process whenever it threatened its own interests, thereby forcing the machinery to come to a halt. For Stalin, it was the indispensable guarantee that smaller countries would never be allowed to take control of the stage and threaten the Soviet Union's position in international organizations, as Finland had done (in relation to the League) in 1939.[27]

In retrospect, we may wonder why the notion of an unlimited veto power did not immediately strike the British and US governments as problematic because it would necessarily make the UN ungovernable. They should have been especially aware of this effect, because the past offenders in the League of Nations—Japan, Italy, Germany, and the USSR—had all been members of the League's Council when they had committed their bellicose actions that subverted the organization. Preventing abuses of power is a problem intrinsic to any organization, and a peace organization was no exception. This posed the key political question, *Qui custodiet ipsos custodes?* (Who will watch the watchmen?); namely, the accountability of great powers toward the international community. It is significant that, instead of taking the route of increasing that accountability, the victorious powers decided to take the opposite one of reducing it to naught. To the representatives of democratic countries, the domestic safeguards of the rule of law may have appeared sufficient. One of the Security Council members, however, was a totalitarian power. Not only did the UN Charter not answer the accountability question that had plagued the League of Nations but it also made it inherently impossible to discipline great powers, placing them outside the restraints of international law.[28]

The US government supported this veto power, but it did recommend a safeguard that would have prevented a member from voting on issues that concerned itself directly. Both Churchill and Stalin opposed this proposal, the latter arguing that "situations when some powers are put in opposition to others" would undermine the cause of universal security.[29] We now know that this argument was a sophism on the part of Stalin, because he had been in opposition to the Western powers all along. As for Britain, Foreign Secretary Anthony Eden attempted to warn Churchill that striking the proposed safeguard clause was a bad idea, but he was overruled.[30]

Beyond the abstract argumentation, inserting the safety valve of veto power to limit the decision-making power of the General Assembly was obviously an example of the pursuit of *Realpolitik*. For the United States, it was a non-negotiable condition for Senate ratification, and without that ratification, the UN would have met the same fate as Wilson's League of Nations in 1919. For Britain and France, no match for the Soviet Union and the United States, their veto power appeared to guarantee both their sovereignty and their right to a continuing say in world affairs. As stated earlier, Stalin was worried that the USSR could be expelled from the UN for breaches of international law, as it had been from the League of Nations in 1939. At San Francisco, the Soviet plenipotentiary Andrei A. Gromyko threatened to block Soviet participation unless the unanimity rule for the permanent members of the Security Council was enshrined in the UN Charter. Gromyko also demanded that the seat of the United Nations be located in New York instead of Geneva, thereby tying the United States more firmly to the new organization.[31]

Thus, only six years after the Soviet Union's ignominious expulsion from the League of Nations, Stalin achieved a great diplomatic success. The Soviet Union was universally recognized as a legitimate and permanent member of the Security Council, with de facto immunity from the principles of international law that the United States had sought to impose; it was also given free rein in Eastern and some parts of Central Europe. By the end of October 1945, a majority of states in the world had ratified the UN Charter, giving it full force under international law.[32]

The flaw in the UN's peace engineering was simple yet fatal: there would be no recourse for a country aggressed against by a permanent member of the Security Council.[33] Stalin would be able to carry out his domination plans in Central Europe with the certainty that the legitimacy of the Soviet Union could, in practice, not be legally challenged. He furthermore correctly assumed that once the Western Allies had given their word in a ratified treaty, they would not dare go back on it. The negotiation process between the victors of World War II resulted in a United Nations that would be an exclusive club of great powers with a muzzled assembly. Members of the Security Council would have no choice but to save face and adopt peace rhetoric that would extoll the "success" of that organization, despite the evidence to the contrary.

By the time the Third Reich surrendered, the political situation in Europe had grown Kafkaesque. Nevertheless, the United States and the United Kingdom still clung to the hope of reaching the coveted peace treaty by somehow making Stalin accountable for his promises. To that end, they set out to keep the Soviet Union's expansionist aims in check. Article I of the Potsdam Agreement, which was signed by all three powers on August 1, 1945, established a Council of Foreign Ministers tasked with the preparatory work for the peace settlements. There were to be five meetings from 1945 to 1947. Article II defined the conditions of the joint military occupation of Germany by the three powers, particularly the dismantling of the Nazi apparatus and of the facilities of war production. The Potsdam Agreement also laid out the conditions for the occupation of Austria, provided that a government of national unity would be formed in Poland, and permitted the termination of the "anomalous" position of the Axis allies—namely, Italy, Bulgaria, Finland, Hungary, and Romania—by peace settlements.[34] However, it failed to harness Stalin's ambitions. The United States and Britain were unable to prevent Germany's loss of Lower Silesia and the eastern parts of Pomerania to Poland, and of East Prussia to Poland and the Soviet Union; they also acceded to the Soviet demand to expel German populations from Poland, Czechoslovakia, and Hungary—not because they approved of this order but because they hoped, as a last resort, that the Council of Foreign Ministers would mitigate its effects.[35] More than twelve million Germans were forced to leave their homes, making this one of the greatest population transfers in European history and a tragic epilogue to the war. The death toll among the refugees, estimated to be at least a half-million individuals, was added to the final count of civilian victims of Nazism and the World War.[36]

How Stalin's decisive postwar victory came about is a complicated story, but it is a testament to his exceptional abilities as a smooth talker. At first glance, one might see a parallel with the Munich conference of 1938, because the Potsdam Agreement was indeed an instance of a single totalitarian state prevailing over a coalition of democratic Western Allies. Yet the similarity stops there: this time there was no vocally angry counterpart (Hitler had

Europe after the Yalta Agreements, 1945

Soviet Union from May 1945

Soviet occupied or controlled

Occupied by Western forces or with pro-Western sympathies

Neutral

----- Pre-war borders and Allied occupation zones of Germany

—— Western limit of Soviet occupation or influence mid-1945 (Iron Curtain)

☐ Original members of NATO 4 April 1949

★ Members of Warsaw Pact, 1955

0   400 km

0   400 miles

FINLAND

Helsinki

Leningrad

Estonia

Moscow

Latvia

Lithuania

to USSR

to Poland

U S S R

★

Warsaw

Kiev

O L A N D

★

oland

Cracow

SLOVAKIA
p February 1948

a

Budapest

Odessa

U N G A R Y

★

Yalta

R O M A N I A

Bucharest

Black Sea

Y U G O S L A V I A
slav–Soviet rift 28 June 1948
becoming non-aligned

★

BULGARIA

Istanbul

ALBANIA

Adriatic Sea

GREECE

Aegean Sea

Civil war
1946–49.
Pro-western Forces
gain control

Athens

T U R K E Y

S Y R I A

Cyprus
(British)

Crete

LEBANON

n

ta (British)

S e a

aggressively advertised his territorial claims in *Mein Kampf,* in speeches, and on the radio), and consequently, there was no one to "appease." On the contrary, Joseph Stalin wore a mask of warm friendliness, careful at all times to speak reassuringly without committing himself formally; his demeanor allowed his partners to believe what they wished. At Yalta, the Soviet leader repeatedly asserted "that the three Great Powers which had borne the brunt of the war and had liberated from German domination the small powers should have the unanimous right to preserve the peace of the world."[37] The claim has been made that Roosevelt, fatally ill at that time, was duped by Stalin's social graces and half-promises; intent on accomplishing the broad aim of a lasting peace, which he thought would be the crowning achievement of his political career, he lost his grip on the negotiations.[38] The accuracy of this argument is far from certain. Although the strength of Roosevelt's desire to secure his legacy is not in doubt and his illness did weaken his spirits, the president was also a consummate politician and a charmer; having seen through Hitler's intentions and led his country to victory against the Third Reich, one could not plausibly think he was easy prey for Stalin. As for Winston Churchill, he already had misgivings at Yalta and later claimed he would have been willing to take action to enforce the Potsdam Agreement had he remained in power. He was likely sincere in making this claim, although it is questionable whether Britain would have had the hard power needed to resist Stalin. In any case, the Soviet Army was on the ground, and the Americans were not willing to reignite the war. Finally, Truman agreed at Potsdam, on the counsel of his adviser Joseph E. Davies, a former ambassador to Moscow and a known Sovietophile, to recognize the legitimacy of the governments installed by Stalin in Eastern Europe.[39] That decision not only overthrew the governments-in-exile of these countries then in London; it fulfilled Stalin's aim of dividing Europe into two spheres of influence. Despite this outcome, neither Roosevelt, Churchill, nor Truman can be credibly charged with ineptness or, worse, being party to a "sellout" or "Western Betrayal," as their conduct would afterward be characterized.[40] The explanation is simpler: the victory in that wrestling match between formidable opponents belonged to Stalin, who was the superior negotiator thanks to the devices of his toxic personality. Devoid of moral qualms and knowing how to exploit those of others, he patiently coaxed his challengers into granting additional concessions on Eastern Europe, eventually leading them into the blind alley of the Potsdam Agreement. This may count as a textbook case of "coercive diplomacy" of a particularly dangerous nature: one that, instead of wielding military force, entices and deceives before resorting to a fait accompli, thus leaving adversaries blaming one another or believing they deserved their misfortune.[41]

Disagreements between the Soviet Union and the other powers, particularly over Eastern Europe, flared up at the very first UN Security Council meeting on January 17, 1946. Andrei Gromyko, now the Soviet Permanent Representative in New York, earned the nickname of Mr. Nyet ("Mr. No"), or "Grim Grom," for wielding his veto power in the United Nations Security Council on more than twenty occasions.[42] The Western powers on the Security Council faced an arduous situation, perhaps the most difficult encountered so far in the engineering of peace: caught in a trap, they were forced to coexist with another power that did not share their values, was not in a mood to cooperate, and could decide to put a stop to their activities at any time. Infuriatingly for the US government, which was on its own ground in New York and effectively directed most of the UN's activities, the USSR's position was unassailable—nothing could be done about it.

In contrast to proceedings in the Security Council, the first session of the United Nations General Assembly (UNGA), which took place in London in 1946, passed a remarkable number of resolutions, including a call to end racial and religious persecution, the establishment of genocide as a crime, the launching of an organization for the care of refugees, and the reinforcement of the primacy of international law.[43] On December 11, 1946, the General Assembly unanimously adopted the draft of the Universal Declaration of Human Rights, the final version of which was issued in 1948. Unfortunately, UNGA—tasked with representing all of humankind—was largely consultative, because it took just one member of the Security Council to veto its resolutions. If the USSR did not object to many of its resolutions of principle, it was for a good reason: the Soviets preferred to concentrate their vetoes on matters of practical import, rather than on conceptual documents that were dead letters as far as they were concerned. Despite the aims of the United Nations, the maxim "might makes right" once again became the final word in international relations. To the credit of the United States, it did not use its veto power until 1970. Even so, the UN Headquarters, built in New York in 1952, became a temple dedicated to a faulty piece of machinery, condemned to run forever in idle for lack of a proper clutch.

The frustration of the US government because of its failure to achieve its peace goals explains its fundamental shift in foreign policy after World War II. Harry Truman felt he had no choice but to break abruptly with the Spirit of Yalta, and consequently he adopted the balance of power principle—the very paradigm of eighteenth-century European politics that Roosevelt claimed had died at Yalta—as the cornerstone of what came to be known as the "Truman Doctrine." On March 12, 1947, Truman declared his position in an address to a joint session of the US Congress:

> To ensure the peaceful development of nations, free from coercion, the United States has taken a leading part in establishing the United Nations. . . . We shall not realize our objectives, however, unless we are willing to help free peoples to maintain their free institutions and their national integrity against aggressive movements that seek to impose upon them totalitarian regimes. This is no more than a frank recognition that totalitarian regimes imposed on free peoples, by direct or indirect aggression, undermine the foundations of international peace and hence the security of the United States.[44]

Truman thus accepted that the United States could no longer rely on the unified order that the founders of the United Nations had envisaged to establish lasting peace. In practice, US foreign policy required far more active steps, including military aid, to prevent a number of European states from falling prey to communist insurgencies supported by the Soviet Union or from direct invasion. Truman called on the United States to play the role of protector of independent states against these menaces:

> It must be the policy of the United States to support free peoples who are resisting attempted subjugation by armed minorities or by outside pressures.
> . . . We must assist free peoples to work out their own destinies in their own way.

. . . Our help should be primarily through economic and financial aid which is essential to economic stability and orderly political processes.[45]

The Truman Doctrine emphasized economic interventionism over political imposition, in an attempt to distance itself from the hallmark combative strategies of the Soviet Union. Truman's pledge to the United Nations was not, however, absolute, because "the world is not static, and the status quo is not sacred."[46] This speech served as a "call to arms," rejecting changes to the status quo that violated the letter of the UN Charter "by such methods as coercion, or such subterfuges as political infiltration." Truman concluded by emphasizing the motivation for his doctrine: "If we falter in our leadership, we may endanger the peace of the world—and we shall surely endanger the welfare of our own nation."[47] In its principles at least, the Truman Doctrine was non-imperial, but it certainly acknowledged that US diplomacy had failed in 1945 in its aim to put the world on a path to lasting peace.

Even with the benefit of hindsight, it is hard to see what else Truman could have done other than resorting again to the balance of power principle after the first round of diplomatic wrestling against the Soviet Union had gone so badly. Nevertheless, he did make one conscious choice: accepting the fait accompli of the UN Charter and the Security Council without questioning its legitimacy. Security Council meetings became one of the chief battlefields of the Cold War, where strategy translated into elaborate palace intrigues and the two superpowers exchanged barbs instead of bullets. The moral damage was significant—the centuries-old dream of achieving a lasting peace had been dragged through the mud, and there was little that European states could do about it. In retrospect, the United States might have been wiser to do without a world peace organization, rather than coping with one that was ungovernable and that constantly fettered its foreign policy.

Peace through Economic Recovery: Marshall's Plan

In the meantime, just as pressing as the threat of Soviet domination was the need to repair the devastated European economies. Thanks to a US bailout, the British Treasury barely averted bankruptcy in 1946. Whereas food rationing ended in the United States within a year of the war, food shortages continued much longer in many European countries. In the particularly harsh winter of 1946–1947, hunger drove thousands of Germans to protest in the streets. In France, rationing lasted until 1949; in West Germany until 1950. Economically depleted Britain had to endure rationing for more than nine full years after the war, until July 3, 1954, a date remembered as Derationing Day.[48] In East Germany, which the Soviet Union had stripped of industrial equipment as "reparations," rationing continued until 1958. In Poland, meat was rationed and shops never fully restocked until the communist regime ended in 1989.[49]

This situation provided an opportunity for a most original and effective "peace plan." In Washington, there was keen awareness that European states were in desperate need of supplies and financial resources not only to recover from the devastation of the war but also to kickstart and protect their political sovereignty. In particular, the fate of the West German economy had to be decided. Initially, the prevailing approach among the Western Allies was akin to that of Versailles in 1919: curtail Germany's economy and cap its heavy industry. Indeed, US secretary of the treasury Henry Morgenthau proposed a plan in 1944 that emphasized not just German disarmament but also "the total destruction of the whole German armament industry, and the removal or destruction of other key industries which are basic to military strength."[50] Fortunately for the Germans, and likely for peace in Europe, US foreign diplomacy was entrusted in 1947 to a hands-on kind of individual—George C. Marshall, the US Army chief of staff from 1939 to 1945 who, working as a competent strategist and logistician, had played a major role in the industrial war effort, earning himself praise as the "architect (or organizer) of victory."[51]

On June 5, 1947, Marshall, in his new capacity as secretary of state, presented his program for Europe to the graduating class at Harvard University. His analysis of the plight of the continent was entirely pragmatic: "It has become obvious during recent months that this visible destruction [of cities, factories, mines and railroads] was probably less serious than the dislocation of the entire fabric of European economy.... But even given a more prompt solution of these difficult problems, the rehabilitation of the economic structure of Europe quite evidently will require a much longer time and greater effort than had been foreseen."[52] Because of their lack of infrastructure, cities were no longer able to produce necessary goods. Instead of investing in their own reconstruction, ailing states were forced to divert their meager financial resources to import necessities. It was thus logical "that the United States should do whatever it is able to do to assist in the return of normal economic health in the world, without which there can be no political stability and no assured peace."[53] The United States was going to kickstart the European economies in order to provide the initial conditions for lasting peace. This was an example of the "engineering" of peace in the true sense of the word.

Certainly, the Marshall Plan did not contradict the aims of the Truman Doctrine, which also prescribed economic interventionism. It had, however, a broader scope, because it proposed the development of peaceful economic relations across political boundaries. The United States would help all European countries, regardless of their role in the war and of their current alignment with Washington or Moscow. Indeed, Marshall stated, "Our policy is directed not against any country or doctrine but against hunger, poverty, desperation, and chaos. Its purpose should be the revival of a working economy in the world so as to permit the emergence of political and social conditions in which free institutions can exist."[54] Contrary to the Truman Doctrine, which acknowledged the "system of war" between the United States and the Soviet Union, the Marshall Plan thus presented itself as a genuine doctrine of peace.

Marshall added a proviso: "Any government that is willing to assist in the task of recovery will find full cooperation, I am sure, on the part of the United States Government. Any government which maneuvers to block the recovery of other countries cannot expect help from us."[55] There was no threat of retaliation, only self-restraint from action. In the summer of 1947, the Soviet Union made such a blocking maneuver, forbidding European countries under its control to participate in the plan. The Soviet leadership, which promoted a planned economy, had obvious ideological reasons to reject the Marshall Plan. Rapid economic recovery, bolstered by US aid, would have favored the emergence of private enterprise, and an influx of goods and services would have raised questions about the effectiveness of communist planning in its early stages in Central Europe. Simply put, a showcase of US industrial capacity would have placed the Soviet system in an unfavorable light.

Indeed, economic differences between the countries supported by the United States on the one side and the Soviet Union and its satellites on the other side became increasingly apparent. After the US Congress passed a grant of $17 billion in April 1948, the Marshall Plan was an unmitigated success wherever it was implemented. Much of the help went to Britain, while new tractors started to dot the French countryside, a remarkable sight in the postwar period.[56] On April 16, 1948, the United States launched the Organization for European Economic Co-operation (OEEC) to distribute aid from the European Recovery Program (the formal name for the Marshall Plan). Headquartered in Paris, the OEEC had eighteen member countries. As could be expected, the United States tightly controlled expenditures and required Europeans to buy American-made equipment. The recovery of the Western-occupied parts of Germany was especially spectacular compared to the sluggish reconstruction of the Eastern communist part. The Marshall Plan came to an end on December 14, 1960; at that point the OEEC became the Organization for Economic Co-operation and Development (OECD) and admitted the United States, as well as Canada and Japan, as peer members. The economic assistance by the United States had shaped the institutional landscape of Europe, fostering a sense of shared achievement among the beneficiary states.[57]

Nevertheless, the "balance of power" would remain a byword for the political situation in Europe as the rift between the Western Allies and the Soviet bloc deepened. Stalin initially aimed to unify Germany under a single state, as he had announced to German communist leaders in 1945.[58] Yet popular opposition was fierce, and the following year, local elections in Berlin delivered a crushing defeat to the Communist Party, particularly in the Soviet-occupied area. Furthermore, the Marshall Plan was acting as a political magnet, drawing favorable public opinion in Germany and Central Europe. When the four occupying powers—Britain, France, the United States, and the Soviet Union—convened for the fifth session of the Council of Foreign Ministers in London on December 15, 1947, they failed to come to a consensus about the status of Germany.

Faced with the ever-increasing intractability of the Soviet Union, the three Western Allies finally concluded that negotiations with them regarding Germany had reached a dead end: Stalin would never sign a peace agreement except on his own terms. The Allies accordingly decided to give up on the Soviet-controlled area and to make the best of what remained.[59] In early 1948, they convened a conference in London with the Benelux countries (Belgium, the Netherlands, and Luxembourg) to pave the way for German participation in the international Western order, outside of the Soviet sphere. The conference closed on June 2 with the decision to unify the areas of Germany under their control into a federal state. The Western Allies started to break free of Stalin's diplomatic quagmire; even though they had to write off Eastern Europe and part of Germany, they could at least take back the political initiative in that part of the Old Continent they controlled.[60]

Yet it was only a matter of time before a crisis would erupt. In mid-June 1948, the Deutschmark was launched; within a few days, the new currency started pouring into Berlin. In response, the Red Army started blockading all land access to the city, and the Soviets announced the introduction of their own currency—the East German "Deutsche Mark"—in their zone. The skies, however, remained open. The Soviet Union, still playing along with the legalistic facade, had formally agreed in November 1945 to allow three twenty-mile-wide air corridors to Berlin and did not risk downing airplanes flying in those spaces: doing so would have handed a *casus belli* to the Western Allies. The Soviets, calculating that Berlin could not be supported by air, counted on a siege instead.

The plan backfired. Not only did the United States have more than ample airlift capabilities to resupply the city but this effort also turned into a publicity stunt, as American and British films extolled the success of this logistical operation during the harsh winter.[61] On May 12, 1949, the last remnants of the blockade were lifted; the Federal Republic of Germany was born two weeks later, on May 23. On November 22, 1949, the Western Allies signed the Petersberg Agreement (named for the hotel outside of Bonn where it was signed) with the newly elected chancellor, Konrad Adenauer, which paved the way for West Germany's participation in international processes. The reborn state was henceforth able to become a member of the Council of Europe and to enter into bilateral agreements with the United States, so as to receive Marshall Plan relief. It was also allowed to engage in international trade and consular activities.

This was significant progress, but because the Soviets continued to refuse to underwrite a treaty for the whole of Germany, courts continued to consider the country still legally at war for most purposes.[62] It was another facet of the diplomatic conundrum for the Western Allies: signing a separate peace treaty with the Federal Republic of Germany would not have been acceptable, because it would have legalized the partition and abandoned the country's eastern part to Soviet domination. In an irregular procedure, they resolved unilaterally to end the state of war with Germany: the parliaments of France and the United Kingdom both passed a bill to that effect on July 9, 1951, and the US Congress did so a few months later, on October 24, more than six years after the capitulation of the Third Reich.[63] Germany was thus placed in a curious limbo: not at war but not at peace either. For the first time in modern European history, no peace treaty ended a large war; these were dark times for legality.

Tragedy also continued to unfold behind the Iron Curtain. After a rigged referendum and the repression of political opposition in Poland in 1946, the country came under communist rule the following year. Hungary became a Soviet-dominated "People's Republic" in 1949, after the Soviet Union used the "salami" technique, which consisted of evicting political parties and opponents one after the other. In Prague, which had both a strong democratic tradition and a strong Communist Party (scoring 38 percent of the vote in the 1946 national elections), a coup was staged in 1949 with the support of the police and the Red Army, bringing Czechoslovakia under Soviet control.

In applying the Truman Doctrine, the United States endeavored to restore the balance of power in Europe by leveraging the existing system of alliances. One such agreement was the Treaty of Dunkirk. The United Kingdom and France signed this on March 4, 1947, as a treaty of alliance and mutual assistance in case of Germany's possible resurgence. On March 17, 1948, France, Britain, and the three Benelux countries signed the Treaty of Brussels. It was, on the surface, focused on economic cooperation, but an article specifically provided for aid and assistance if a signatory was attacked. Although the potential attacker could be interpreted as either Germany or the Soviet Union, the real target was obviously the latter, because the new German state did not yet have an army. Additionally, this treaty created a dispute-resolution mechanism by pacific means through the International Court of Justice at The Hague; at least in Western Europe, the ailing spirit of peace through law was still surviving.

On April 4, 1949, while the Berlin Blockade was still ongoing, the foreign ministers of the United States, most Western European states, and Canada—twelve countries in total—gathered in Washington to sign the North Atlantic Treaty, giving birth to the North Atlantic Treaty Organization (NATO).[64] The absentees included Germany and Austria, both partly occupied by the Red Army; Spain, an outcast under Fascist rule; Finland and Sweden, both of which elected not to participate because they were uncomfortably close to Russia; and finally Switzerland, which maintained its permanent neutrality, first recognized by the great powers of 1815, including Russia.

Historians tend to focus on the North Atlantic Treaty's practical commitment to military assistance, rather than the cryptic peace rhetoric in which it was couched. The treaty's opening statement expressed faith in the United Nations, as well as a wish "to live in peace with all peoples and governments." The document called for its signatories to "maintain and develop their individual and collective capacity to resist armed attack." It was, plainly, a pact of mutual assistance in case of foreign aggression. There was, in principle, a commitment to settle international disputes "by peaceful means in such a manner that international peace and security and justice are not endangered, and to refrain in their international relations from the threat or use of force in any manner inconsistent with the purposes of the United Nations."[65] Although consistent with the principles of the Kellogg-Briand Pact of 1928, this last clause was of little practical use, however: NATO's raison d'être was to respond militarily to a Soviet attack, and it was evident to the latter that this was no peace alliance.[66] Realistically, NATO's aim to "safeguard the freedom, common heritage and civilization of their peoples, founded on the principles of democracy, individual liberty and the rule of law" was born less out of sincerity than to save appearances for the United Nations.[67] What really mattered at that point was that Western

European nations were in dire need of a military alliance to restore the balance of power against the Soviet Union.

In Moscow, news of the military alliance was received with anger. From then on, the Soviet Union resolved to openly obstruct the UN by practicing its right of veto even more frequently, and by the end of 1949, it had already used it forty times.[68] The Cold War took a turn for the worse when the Soviet Union detonated its first atom bomb in Kazakhstan on August 29, 1949—several years before the Western Allies expected the Soviet Union to be in a position to do so. The US public began to see the specter of the nuclear destruction of their cities as a real possibility. For the first time, American civilians practiced taking shelter from bombs ("duck and cover" drills).[69] A new expression came into prominence: the "balance of power" became the "balance of terror."[70] The Soviets' nuclear capacity made clear that the relative weight of armies was no longer the decisive factor in warfare and dashed the hopes of those who still wanted Eastern Europe to be liberated from the Soviet Union by conventional war. Paradoxically, the arms race and the ineffable prospect of nuclear apocalypse provided even more reason for the two superpowers to pursue their eerie diplomatic ballet at the UN in the name of "peace."

Back in Europe, the Eastern Question manifested itself in a new guise. After World War II, the Soviet Union expanded its control as far south as Bulgaria, at the border with Greece, where it then proceeded to foster communist insurgencies in both countries. Once again, Russia was threatening to overrun the Straits and get full access to the Mediterranean Sea. The status of the Straits had, however, changed: a new legal regime, entered in force in 1936, gave their control back to Turkey. Although the right of passage for ships through the Dardanelles and Bosphorus remained largely guaranteed, Turkey, if involved in a war, had the right to deny passage to warships at its sole discretion.[71] The United States, realizing the value of engaging in a military alliance with Turkey—then it would keep the Soviet Black Sea Fleet bottled up in case of war—and Greece, because of its border with both Bulgaria and Turkey, pushed the two states to join NATO in 1952. This effectively did away with the threat of invasion. Cut in two by the Iron Curtain, the Black Sea became a "frozen sea," because traffic could no longer flow from the northern and western shores to the southern shore of Anatolia. Most sea connections between the two "worlds" were interrupted, with the notable exception of long-distance trade through the Straits (especially from the port of Novorossiysk).[72] Finally, the potential contribution of West Germany to the common defense could no longer be ignored. When that country joined NATO in 1952, the Soviet Union reacted by creating its own Warsaw Pact with its satellite states.[73]

The Semi-Success of the Council of Europe

The UN's diplomatic quagmire was setting the stage for the development of postwar institutions in Western Europe. Divided in two by the Iron Curtain, with opposed armies permanently mobilized, the continent was a "system of war" in the terms of the Abbé de Saint-Pierre. Europe had shifted rapidly from World War II to the Cold War, without a perceptible break between the two.[74] How, in an international environment that had never been so averse to continental unification, could a new European Spirit possibly come to light?[75]

The burgeoning solidarity of states on the continent was motivated, of course, by the direness of their conditions, which was pushing national pride into the background. The strong desire for reconstruction, defense against the Soviet menace, a return to political significance, improved standards of living, reconciliation, and peace quickly crystallized into a redeeming dream of closer union. The first manifestations were grassroots federalist associations, inspired by the two dominant political movements of the time: Christian Democracy and socialism. In September 1946, activists from fourteen countries met at the bucolic village of Hartenstein on Lake Lucerne, Switzerland, where they issued a manifesto calling for the creation of a "European community" imagined as a part of the UN. This "federation," to which states would delegate "economic, political and military attributes of their sovereignty," would forego imperialism and refuse to be the instrument of a foreign power; it thus broadly fit into the Abbé de Saint-Pierre's archetype, though it did not provide for a court.[76] It led to the creation of the European Union of Federalists, an association with 100,000 members by December 1946. Six months earlier, the Socialist Movement for the United States of Europe had been founded in June 1946. The two associations merged in November 1947 to form the International Committee of the Movements for European Unity (ICMEU).[77]

In September 1947, Richard Coudenhove-Kalergi, the author of *Pan-Europe,* played an instrumental role in organizing a conference of the first European Parliamentary Union (EPU), comprising elected members of national parliaments.[78] The picturesque locale of the Swiss mountain village of Gstaad, where the EPU met, was yet another manifestation of the mystique of this mountainous country of Switzerland that was federalist, neutral, and untouched by war and had been the seat of the League of Nations. About nine months after this meeting, on May 7, 1948, Winston Churchill himself opened the Congress of Europe at The Hague organized by ICMEU, where some 800 activists from twenty-five countries discussed the program for European unity.[79] The Congress of Europe, which revived the legacy of the peace congresses of the nineteenth and early twentieth century, was a nongovernmental conference. Yet its purpose was to lay the foundations for an international organization that would draw states in and provide a venue where members of civil society could directly influence their governments. Among the influential participants were former heads of states, businesspeople, representatives of trade unions, and elected representatives in parliaments. The group included several individuals who would play a role in future events: Robert Schuman of France, Konrad Adenauer of Germany, and Paul-Henri Spaak of Belgium. Collectively, these men would represent the Postwar European Spirit.

The Congress of Europe issued an audacious "Political Resolution" stating that "the time had come when the European nations must transfer and merge some portion of their sovereign rights so as to secure common political and economic action for the integration and proper development of their common resources." Moreover, "any Union or Federation of Europe should be designed to protect the security of its constituent people, should be free from outside control, and should not be directed against any other nation."[80] Unlike the participants in the Paris Conference of 1919, those who took part in this congress had no qualms about including Germany in the new peace order, stating that its "integration in a United or Federated Europe alone provides a solution to both the economic and political aspects of the German project" (namely the reconstitution of a German state).[81]

In his opening address, Churchill echoed his call for Franco-German reconciliation from his Zurich speech of 1946: "Europe requires all that Frenchmen, all that Germans, and all that every one of us can give. I therefore welcome here the German delegation, whom we have invited into our midst. . . . *United Europe provides the only solution to this two-sided problem* and it is also a solution which can be implemented without delay."[82] This political resolution also demanded the convening, "as a matter of real urgency," of an assembly chosen by the parliaments of the participating nations, an institution it called the Council of Europe. In addition, it demanded a Charter of Human Rights in the wake of the UN's International Declaration of Human Rights, as well as a court to protect those rights.

Denis de Rougemont, a Swiss intellectual and journalist who had taken a firm stand against Germany at the start of World War II and who served as a Swiss emissary to the United States, was given the task of writing a "Message to Europeans," which was read at the congress's closing session, held in The Hague. The document vividly described the predicament of the Old Continent: "Europe is threatened, Europe is divided, and the greatest danger comes from her divisions. Impoverished, overladen with barriers that prevent the circulation of her goods but are no longer able to afford her protection, our disunited Europe marches towards her end. Alone, no one of our countries can hope seriously to defend its independence. Alone, no one of our countries can solve the economic problems of today."[83] Without naming the Soviet Union, de Rougemont's vibrant "Message" made it clear that European disunion was a liability.

De Rougemont then proceeded to describe what was occurring beyond the Iron Curtain: "Without a freely agreed union our present anarchy will expose us tomorrow to forcible unification whether by the intervention of a foreign empire or usurpation by a political party."[84] As so many times before, the threat of a continental empire was the spur for greater union. This time, however, European states did not have the option of a military alliance, given the superiority of the Red Army. Their shared sense of powerlessness and insecurity, as well as their existential fear of oblivion, goes a long way toward explaining the particular turn of this new spirit, which saw redemption only in a powerful federation of sovereign states.

National governments watched this Congress of Europe warily, because they did not yet know how their parliaments and publics would react. One thing was obvious: they did not share the participants' bold enthusiasm for a federalism that would require them to hand over part of their sovereignty. Therefore, the national leaders took into their own hands the political process of instituting the Council of Europe. On May 5, 1949, the Treaty of London issued the Statute of the Council of Europe. Ten countries from Western Europe—Belgium, Denmark, France, Ireland, Italy, Luxembourg, the Netherlands, Norway, Sweden, and the United Kingdom—reaffirmed their belief that "the pursuit of peace . . . is vital for the preservation of human society and civilization." All the Council's founding states were outside of the Soviet sphere of influence; neither West Germany nor Austria was initially included, because their status had not yet been determined. The national leaders, however, had no intention of implementing the ambitious program of the Congress of Europe. The Statute of the Council of Europe simply stated the signatories' purpose "to achieve a greater unity between its members for the purpose of safeguarding and realizing the ideals and principles which are their common heritage and facilitating their economic and social progress." With references to a sovereign federation struck from the text, the Council of Europe would merely be a venue for "discussion of questions of common concern and . . . agreements and common action."[85]

French prime minister Robert Schuman played a key role in this process, together with his chief of cabinet Jean Monnet. Paul-Henri Spaak, a Belgian socialist who had several times served as prime minister and foreign minister of his country, was elected president of the Consultative Assembly (now known as Parliamentary Assembly) of the Council of Europe.[86] In terms of its power, the Consultative Assembly, as its name implied, was only a deliberative body. It thus resembled a scaled-down UN General Assembly, with two advantages: it was made up only of like-minded states that adhered to the rule of law, and it was not at perpetual risk of seeing the fruit of weeks of collective work subjected to the laconic *nyet* of the Soviets or of another state's veto power.

Within the framework of the Council of Europe and in the wake of the Universal Declaration of Human Rights of 1948, a Convention for the Protection of Human Rights and Fundamental Freedoms was signed in 1950. A new European Court of Human Rights immediately assumed considerable authority as the last judicial recourse of individuals in member states. The newly created Federal Republic of Germany joined the organization that same year.

The seat of the Council of Europe, the French city of Strasbourg in Alsace-Moselle (known as *Elsass-Lothringen* in German from 1871 to 1918), was chosen in view of much needed Franco-German reconciliation. Although this region's loyalty went to France, it was not quite the France of Paris: it had been progressively acquired by French kings in the seventeenth and eighteenth centuries, belonged to Germany between 1871 and 1919, and then returned to France after World War I (though it was de facto reannexed to Germany during World War II). Instead, this region was a symbolic common ground. Although part of France, it retained German linguistic traditions and remained attached to a specific legal status inherited from the Prussian era, including a religious concordat with the Catholic Church that would have been unthinkable elsewhere in secular France. The Christian Democrat Robert Schuman was himself a manifestation of this mixed identity and mutual empathy. Born in Luxembourg with German citizenship, he studied at the University of Strasbourg in the years preceding World War I, at the time of German rule. This German-born, German-speaking, and German-educated man who had campaigned for the return of this region to France in 1919 was now French prime minister and strove to transcend the Franco-German rift by elevating Strasbourg to the rank of a European center.

In 1955, the Council of Europe adopted the Flag of Europe. Designed by the Alsatian artist Arsène Heitz, the flag featured twelve stars placed in a circle against a blue sky. Officially representing "unity, solidarity and harmony among the peoples of Europe," this image was a well-known symbol called a "circle of stars." It had both political precedents, having been used on the very first US flag, and religious precedents, as a Christian symbol for the Virgin Mary.[87] In secular France, where religious symbols had been banned from public life since the Third Republic, the flag's design sparked a controversy over the alleged intentions of its creator and its sponsors. In other countries—notably, Germany and Italy where religious symbols, especially those of Christian Democracy, had been imported into the political sphere—this affinity was instead perceived as a curiosity.[88]

It is worth mentioning that this *European* Spirit was not called such because it was a Spirit *of* Europe (reflecting geography or culture), but because it manifested itself *in* Europe. The founding members, not unlike the Abbé de Saint-Pierre, Rousseau, and Kant, faced the challenge of defining the boundaries of their action: Where did Europe begin and end? The answer they reached represented a U-turn from the traditional definition of a national identity, which is based on having a unified geography, language, and culture. Schuman's answer was not normative, because it did not refer to any of those criteria. On the contrary, he defined "Europeanness" inclusively:

> There have been—and still are—learned disputes as to the geographical bounds of Europe. But Europe cannot possibly wait for definition, for the end of that controversy; she does, in fact, define her own bounds by the will of her peoples. . . . Today we are laying the foundations of a spiritual and political co-operation from which there will arise the European spirit [*l'esprit européen*], the promise of a broad and lasting supranational union.[89]

The fact that this European Spirit was conceived in Western Europe and would, its proponents hoped, expand from there, was incidental to its defining goal: creating lasting peace among free equals. Nothing in the Council of Europe's bylaws prevented, in theory, an Asian or African nation from becoming part of it (and indeed, at that time Algerians lived in a French *département*). Today, when the membership of the organization spans the Eurasian continent all the way to Kamchatka on the Pacific Ocean, imagining that the European Spirit had been meant to apply exclusively to "Europeans" appears as reductive as concluding that the Spirit of Vienna or Spirit of Geneva had never been intended to expand beyond the confines of their respective cities.[90]

Europe as a Multicellular Organism:
The Achievement of the Schuman Declaration

Among the promises that the Council of Europe was not in a position to fulfill was Franco-German reconciliation. German citizens—at least, the elites who had come to power after denazification—had little interest in revanchism; the country, defeated and politically subjugated, while perhaps eschewing an explicit sense of collective guilt, nevertheless embraced a sense of collective shame and responsibility that made for a very different mood than in 1919. Not even the country's considerable territorial losses to Poland, which Germans were reluctant to recognize, stirred anyone but a minority to irredentism.[91] In fact, the country in greatest need of pacification was France. The painful memory of the defeat in June 1940 at the hands of Germany lingered, not least of the ceremony in which the armistice was signed in the same wagon in Rethondes in which France had received Germany's armistice in 1919. There was, however, something deeper at work: the French ruling classes dove into "the Purge"—distancing themselves as quickly as possible from the taint of "collaboration" with the Nazis. What made it particularly traumatic was both that the Vichy regime had officially committed to cooperation with the Germans and that collaboration was so widespread; a large number of civil servants (particularly in the police forces) had been compromised, forcing the new government to conduct an expulsion policy that could carry the penalty of "national indignity."[92] In the climate of general suspicion that followed the liberation, any manifestation of friendship with Germany was liable to be perceived as a continuation of treasonous links with the former occupier. In any case, France's immediate priority was its own reconstruction, and it saw German rearmament—not the Soviet menace—as the primary geopolitical risk.[93]

Moreover, the old Franco-German feud of the 1920s was threatening to flare up again. In the immediate aftermath of the war, France sought to occupy, as it had already done with the Rhineland, the Saar and Ruhr regions of West Germany, which provided the coal and the steel that had been essential to the German war effort. The recovery of the German *Konzerne,* the large industrial trusts that had sustained the Nazi war machine, was also worrying. On September 8, 1945, the Economic Affairs Department of the French Foreign Ministry issued a memo outlining a plan to detach both the Saar and Ruhr regions from Germany: "France considers it to be an essential element of its security and believes that steps must now be taken to prevent those regions from once again becoming an arsenal, a transit area and a base for attacks on its border or the borders of its Western European Allies."[94] The memo proposed creating a protectorate of the Saar that would share a customs union with France and placing the Ruhr under the jurisdiction of an international committee made up of representatives of the United States, Britain, and France. These two steps, the French envisioned, would reduce the risk of German rearmament by denying it access to raw materials (the coal mines of Upper Silesia had already passed to the control of Poland), while also strengthening French industry.

The man behind this plan was Jean Monnet, the indefatigable French civil servant who helped devise the Council of Europe's Assembly. During the war, Monnet had supported de Gaulle's Free France movement and acted as a liaison between the British and US governments, coordinating the provision of war supplies to England.[95] Born into a family of cognac merchants, he was a man of business, industry, and logistical acumen. Indeed, using his great diplomatic skills, he later enabled France to obtain in 1947 the protectorate of the Saar and to have a seat in the tripartite commission overseeing the Ruhr, in exchange for its agreeing to the creation of a West German state. Yet this policy of keeping Germany at bay by preventing its full economic development was more in the spirit of Versailles than in the spirit of reconciliation. Indeed, growing differences about the future of Germany started straining France's relations with the United States and Britain—to the point that the idea was raised that France should withdraw from the occupation powers. France's posture was unsustainable, and a policy shift was needed.[96]

As months passed, the specter of a hypothetical German resurgence paled in comparison to the verified threat of the Red Army. More than 1,500,000 Soviet soldiers were stationed as far west as Magdeburg in Germany, 450 miles from the French border, and in eastern Austria. The Berlin Blockade of 1949 had convinced the French of two things: the Soviets meant business, and the Germans were powerless.[97] French politicians then found themselves in a quandary. If they allowed Western Germany to keep its steel industry, it could rearm and again become a danger to France; conversely if deprived of its steel industry, it could become easy prey for the USSR. Hence agreeing to a West German state was not enough; such a country would also need the means to sustain itself.

Facing a seemingly unresolvable dilemma, Robert Schuman adopted a workaround that predecessors in the history of European peace had earlier used to secure critical regions such as Switzerland or the Straits against hostile exploitation: as it were, "if it cannot be mine and it cannot be yours, it should be neither mine nor yours." This time, Schuman applied a new twist to this formula: "if it cannot be mine and it cannot be yours, then it should be ours to share." Because the steel industry of the Saar and Ruhr could not belong to either Germany or France, Schuman proposed to entrust it to a supranational organization, of which both France and Germany would be members. He pursued this unorthodox idea quietly, without even notifying the French government, although he tasked the indispensable Jean Monnet with leading the effort.[98]

Schuman realized this approach could actually work: it would move France and Germany from antagonists in a "state of nature" into a new social contract. Witness the fact that the mistrustful French government, when apprised of the idea in early May 1950, agreed to support it. On May 9, the French foreign minister delivered a speech that came to be known as the Schuman Declaration. Referring to World War II and the Soviet menace, he stated,

> World peace cannot be safeguarded without the making of creative efforts proportionate to the dangers which threaten it. The contribution which an organized and living Europe can bring to civilization is indispensable to the maintenance of peaceful relations. In taking upon herself for more than 20 years the role of champion of a united Europe, France has always had as her essential aim the service of peace. A united Europe was not achieved, and we had war.

At this point he described a process of unifying postwar Europe that turned out to be a breakthrough:

Europe will not be made all at once, or according to a single plan. It will be built through concrete achievements which first create a de facto solidarity. The coming together of the nations of Europe requires the elimination of the age-old opposition of France and Germany. Any action taken must in the first place concern these two countries.[99]

With one simple statement—"Europe will not be made all at once, or according to a single plan"—Schuman overturned the most fundamental assumption underlying the hundreds of perpetual peace plans since the early eighteenth century. Indeed, why expect that a "big bang" treaty should give birth to a fully formed European Union? Schuman was not merely saving the territorial integrity of Germany while promoting Franco-German reconciliation, not to mention the entente between the Western Allies.[100] His small-steps approach answered in the simplest way Leibniz's objection that no sovereign would accept a perpetual union contract: it stated that there would be no such agreement. Instead there would be "concrete achievements which first create a de facto solidarity," in this case the pooling of the essential resource of steel.

Schuman went on to propose that France and Germany jointly control the steel industry in the Ruhr. Because coal and steel were essential materials for war, placing these resources *in common* would be the bold step that might achieve a remarkable result: "The solidarity in production thus established will make it plain that any war between France and Germany becomes not merely unthinkable, but materially impossible." It would also undermine the trusts that had kept national markets hemmed in, particularly the German *Konzerne* that had profited from the policies of Nazi Germany. Those nonstate actors were potential enemies that both France and Germany would have to guard against. Finally, this was one of the first signs of a momentous shift in language: the term "Europe" now appeared unqualified (on its own) in an official speech, no longer as a geographical space or as a community of civilization, but as a political entity to be *made*.

Schuman concluded his declaration by describing the body that would become the European Coal and Steel Community:

[This treaty] proposes that Franco-German production of coal and steel as a whole be placed under a common High Authority, within the framework of an organization open to the participation of the other countries of Europe. The pooling of coal and steel production should immediately provide for the setting up of common foundations for economic development as a first step in the federation of Europe, and will change the destinies of those regions which have long been devoted to the manufacture of munitions of war, of which they have been the most constant victims.[101]

Schuman's approach, which we might call functionalism, consisted of advancing toward a large, well-formulated aim without a predefined plan of action, while relentlessly pursuing any opportunities in the desired direction as they presented themselves; events alone would reveal the implicit "grand plan." Each of the successive agreements in the direction of a European federation (his own term) would create organic bonds that would progressively tie the countries together. With this apparently innocuous focus on "concrete achievements which first create a de facto solidarity," Schuman created the first workable formula for European unification—a political superglue to cement European countries together.

By introducing an effective change in the process of engineering peace, this declaration marks a watershed in the *longue durée* of European history. In earlier plans of perpetual peace, Saint-Pierre, Rousseau, and Kant had all imagined that a congress of states would sign a treaty that would institute a grand peace alliance, under which all Europeans would live happily ever after. This assumption also informed Tsar Alexander I's Holy Alliance. A century later, the same hope that the League of Nations would cure the evils of the world led Woodrow Wilson to fight to insert its Covenant into the Treaty of Versailles. Franklin Roosevelt did not even want to wait for World War II to end before organizing a solemn ceremony for the foundation of a United Nations Organization. Unfortunately, none of these plans worked out as intended. Even the ambitious federalist movements, which attempted to create a Council of Europe immediately after World War II, only succeeded in creating a consultative organization that was anything but federal.[102] In sum, there was a serious flaw in the structure and organization of general peace pacts: only in a handful of instances have sovereign states voluntarily signed such agreements and only when their very existence was threatened. It was never realistic to expect that a number of leading nation-states, having experienced the intoxicating taste of sovereignty, would suddenly relinquish it, and all at the same time.

Although Schuman applied a functionalist approach to the peace-building process in Europe, he did not originate this political philosophy. Functionalism as a political conception was first formulated by David Mitrany, a Romanian-born Yale academic, in his 1943 manifesto, *A Working Peace System*. During World War I, Mitrany had participated in the grassroots campaign for a postwar international peace organization, and he hoped that aim would be realized after the current war ended. He theorized the creation of a peaceful world order inspired by the biological survival mechanisms of living cells.[103] The functionalist approach adopted the metaphor of vines and other creeper plants, which relentlessly conquer space in all available directions through cellular division and aggregation. By undergoing such processes of growth, they can withstand a considerable amount of constraining, cutting, and uprooting without losing their vitality. In other words, they have a special ability to survive in ever-changing environments. This view of international relations was also innovative, because it marked a shift from the mechanistic metaphor that had given birth to the balance of power and, its opposite, the "machineries of peace."

Functionalism (from "function," ultimately from Latin *fungere*, "to do, to work") was a doctrine that encouraged individuals and, by extension, states to act as living organisms in their struggle for survival; that is, "doing what works." Rejecting the assumption that treaties and international law could guarantee international peace ("protected peace"), particularly the status quo ante of borders, Mitrany advocated instead a modus operandi that would allow for what he called "peaceful change."[104] This required a "spreading web of international activities and agencies" and cooperation at all political levels: municipal, regional, state, and so on.[105] To Mitrany, functionalism was distinct from federalism. International organizations would not develop best according to any grand design of international institutions, but would instead achieve "organic" growth through continuous forays into new areas (through a "web" of efforts) using already available resources.

Whereas the *Plan* of the Abbé de Saint-Pierre sought to establish an immediately "perfect" system that would guarantee a peaceful status quo ante forever, Mitrany's theory advocated incremental growth. It is difficult to overstate the importance of this paradigmatic shift—it questioned all assumptions about lasting peace that had been made so far.

Schuman's functionalism added a dimension to Mitrany's purely opportunistic approach to institution building. He inserted existing European political entities of all levels (supranational, national, regional, municipal) into the model and formulated a rule of behavior for how they should operate harmoniously with one another. For this, he found inspiration in the Catholic Church, which had developed a management principle for the administration of its own matters: *subsidiarity*. According to this principle, decisions should always be made at the lowest possible level, rather than by a central authority. For the ancient Romans, *subsidium* had been a military term meaning the "troops in the rear line of battle"; hence, the abstract sense of "help, relief, protection." In the modern Christian philosophy of human free will, subsidiarity had evolved to mean "initiative."[106]

The functionalism based on subsidiarity was distinct from the federalist theories, and particularly the federalism of the United States. By refusing to proceed according to an initial "big plan," it rejected any notion of a manifest destiny for "political" Europe; it instead embraced an unpredictable road, with challenges to be met as they arose. Without repudiating the aims or the *acquis*—the accumulated wisdom—of the European tradition of perpetual peace, functionalism was thus paving the way to greater integration. There was an added virtue to the organic metaphor of plants. Mechanical contraptions like covenants and constitutions ("machineries") are born fully formed and therefore limited by their original design: because they cannot repair themselves, they eventually break apart from fatigue or obsolescence. Whenever the status quo breaks, so would the machinery, but plants are organisms capable of responding to changing conditions and even repairing damage inflicted on them. This metaphorical shift was also a sign of changing times. Whereas the English paradigm of the balance of power in the early eighteenth century was shaped by Newtonian physics, the political intuition of postwar functionalism took its inspiration from cell biology. Here was a new, adaptable, and distinctively modern form of peace engineering for Europe. Schuman's declaration is generally pinpointed as the starting point of the European integration process, which would lead eventually to the European Communities and later to the European Union.[107]

Schuman and Monnet were only two of the individuals who contributed to this new European Spirit of the 1950s; together with their peers from various nations, cosmopolitan in background, often Catholic in religion, and predominantly Christian Democrat in politics, they were later labeled the "Founding Fathers of Europe."[108] The German Konrad Adenauer was vice mayor of Cologne before World War I and became its mayor afterward. As a Center Party politician, champion of democracy, and observant Catholic, he was in strong disfavor with the Nazi regime. The Italian Alcide de Gasperi was born in the province of Trentino, which during his childhood belonged to the Austro-Hungarian Empire. Gasperi studied in Vienna, spoke perfect German, and was an anti-Fascist who had obtained protection from the Vatican for several years. The "Founding Fathers" also included representatives from other political parties, notably Paul-Henri Spaak, a Belgian from the Socialist Party. These men placed the cause of European integration above party loyalty. If Christian Democracy was so prominent in that effort—as Adenauer pointed out—it was for a practical reason: in Germany and Italy, its members had been among the last to resist the onslaught of totalitarianism, never accepting defeat or assimilation.[109] In Germany, the Christian Democrats were a new conservative party whose leaders emerged from the Nazi era with a relatively clean slate, and that appealed to Catholics and Protestants alike.[110] Yet, the reader should keep in mind that even though the label "Founding Fathers of Europe" (especially in French literature) was used to honor these leaders, it is misleading. The meaning it carries is problematic because it suggests a teleological fallacy—that there was some destiny or grand design that all Europeans would inherit and carry forward, which was precisely not the case. What distinguished the Postwar European Spirit was the absence of a grand plan and, in its place, only a set of aims carried out by a desperate few political leaders, who felt compelled to reconstruct Europe after the devastation of World War II.

Six countries signed the treaty of the European Coal and Steel Community (ECSC) in Paris on April 18, 1951. Three of the signatories were historically significant powers of Western Europe—France, Germany, and

Italy—two of which had been defeated in World War II. The other three signatories—Belgium, Luxembourg, and Netherlands—were constitutional monarchies created out of the Vienna Order as buffers against France in the wake of the Napoleonic wars; at the outset of both world wars, they had served instead as buffers against Germany. On September 5, 1944, before their own territories were even liberated, the three governments-in-exile of these smaller countries had signed a convention in London creating the Benelux Customs Union, which was ratified in 1947. The core of the European postwar project is thus to be found in this obscure treaty between three second-tier countries.[111] Just five years after the war, a new role emerged for them: Benelux, which showed equal affinity with both French and German culture, would be the political emulsifier helping reconcile the two previously antagonistic nations. Considering that Belgium, the Netherlands, and Luxembourg were ruthlessly invaded by Germany just a decade earlier, their willingness to associate with their former occupier was an extraordinary act of reconciliation.

This configuration as a six-member alliance raised one of the age-old diplomatic problems bedeviling any European peace alliance or confederation, including the Holy Roman Empire: how to determine where the headquarters should be located. Paris, Berlin, and Rome were all capitals of previously antagonistic great powers and therefore unsuitable. The logical choice was the narrow "European peace strip" on the west bank of the Rhine River, stretching from the North Sea to the Swiss border. Consisting of Belgium, Luxembourg, and a sliver of French territory, it contained three eligible cities: Brussels, Luxembourg, and Strasbourg. This area was desirable because of the status of Belgium and Luxemburg as neutral territories between major European states and for some practical reasons, such as good communications and transport links; unsurprisingly, the line stretched farther south to French-held but German-speaking Alsace-Moselle. Thus, Strasbourg had been selected earlier as the seat of the Council of Europe.

In these years, the process of European unification was compared to a building site, with the term "European construction" coming into vogue. This metaphor was not incompatible with the functionalist concept of living organisms seeking to unite their efforts: plants and animal species do build structures "organically," and humans had long built shelters without the need for architects and drawing boards.[112] Significantly, Schuman himself stated in his famous declaration, "Europe will be *built* through concrete achievements."

In 1958, a German scholar working in the United States, Ernst Haas, wrote about the experience of the ECSC in a book that became a classic reference, *The Uniting of Europe: Political, Social, and Economical Forces, 1950–1957*. It proposed a pragmatic theory that Haas called neo-functionalism, which he positioned between the two dominant theories of international relations of the time: the realist theory of Hans Morgenthau and others, which posited that nation-states sought to achieve maximum sovereignty and power, and the idealist theory that invoked the supremacy of international law ("peace through law"), which he traced to Immanuel Kant and which he considered as somewhat naïve. As Haas later observed, the "ECSC experience has spawned a theory of international integration by indirection, by trial and error, by miscalculation on the part of the actors desiring integration, and by manipulation of elite social forces on the part of small groups of pragmatic administrators and politicians in the setting of a vague but permissive public opinion."[113] The popular neologism "supranational" applied specifically to the ECSC and referred to an original form of integration that was a hybrid between an international organization and a federation. Haas recognized that the difference between the two was not a straightforward one to delineate.[114]

Even though this "functional" approach to unifying Western Europe was a breakthrough, it was no guarantee that events would unfold smoothly. As could indeed be expected with any living organism, the trial-and-error method was bound to meet resounding failures along the way, which served as cautions for the future. One such debacle in 1952 was the proposed European Defense Community (EDC), a plan to create a common Western European army from the militaries of West Germany, France, Italy, and the Benelux countries. The trigger was the Cold War crisis erupting on the other side of the Eurasian continent.

In 1950, the North Korean Army, with Soviet equipment and training, launched a conquest of South Korea; the Soviet Union stopped short of directly involving the Red Army so as not to provide justification for a US declaration of war. Fearing that the collapse of South Korea would threaten

Japan, Truman sent US troops as part of a force sponsored by the United Nations. The UN was able to decide to counter this aggression because of a serious miscalculation on the part of the USSR: at that moment it was boycotting the international organization and so was unable to exercise its veto power at the Security Council. In the crisis atmosphere that ensued, an open military clash in Europe was becoming a real possibility.[115]

With the Cold War as the priority of its foreign policy, the United States provided closer attention and military reinforcements to NATO than to any other sphere. Yet given the numerical superiority of the Soviet Army, US support would not be sufficient; the Western Allies thus had to consider the difficult question of rearming West Germany, only five years after the end of the Third Reich. As was the case earlier with the possible growth of the German steel industry, the French government was alarmed by this idea. To allay French fears, Jean Monnet sought to capitalize on the success of the ECSC and conceived of the idea of a supranational army in the summer of 1950, urging French prime minister René Pleven to promote it. Pleven presented the idea first to the French Council of Ministers and then to the National Assembly.[116] Initially, the idea was met with considerable skepticism in Europe for three reasons. The first objection, strongly voiced by the British, was that it would create a supranational institution that would limit national sovereignty. Second, Monnet's proposal would actually put restrictions on the size of the West German army; this provision was resented by the Germans and opposed by the Dutch, who feared a Russian invasion more than anything else and wanted a strong defense on the Elbe frontier. President Truman was similarly displeased: he was counting on NATO to oversee Europe's military defense and believed that such a limitation on the West Germany military conflicted with the strategic requirement to defend the Elbe border. The third objection, prevalent in France, was the exact opposite of the two others: French politicians still feared a return of German expansionism, a danger they believed to be even more immediate than a Russian invasion. Obviously, stark differences in ideology and geographical viewpoints still had to be reconciled.[117]

Once again external circumstances—the Korean War and the increased risk of war with the Soviet Union—forced a change of perspective. The same Group of Six that created the ECSC successfully kickstarted the European

Defense Community with the signing of a treaty in Paris, yet this did not prevent the outbreak of a fierce ideological battle in France. Although the quarrel was ostensibly about the appropriateness of German rearmament, the underlying motivation was more profound and was reminiscent of the UK's dilemma with its own Commonwealth, as France still had its own colonial empire. Parts of the French political class still adhered to the prewar conception of the state and felt strongly that the country was still powerful enough to wage war in Europe and abroad and that it could more than make up for the absence of Germany in a coalition against the Soviet Union.[118] The ratification process dragged on, with the French parliament set to discuss it more than two years after the treaty was signed. And then, a piece of procedural chicanery removed the treaty from the parliament's agenda on August 30, 1954, in what later came to be known as "the Crime of August 30." As one member of parliament, Paul Reynaud, put it, "For the first time since there is a Parliament in France, a treaty has been repelled, without giving the author of this treaty, nor his signatory, the floor to defend it."[119] Ironically, the scuttling of the EDC, of such consequence for Western Europe, was caused by a purely procedural maneuver to defeat a ministerial proposal, and for mostly domestic reasons: momentum toward creating a common army was halted in France for partisan and nationalistic reasons.[120]

Seen from a Europe-wide perspective, however, the EDC failed because Franco-German reconciliation had not yet taken place. A military alliance would have been quite a leap forward, but the setback was so traumatizing to the French government and its partners that such an idea would not be considered again for decades. Yet, by opposing the EDC, the French achieved an effect opposite to what they had intended: while the threat of Western German revanchism proved to be a mirage, they ended up reinforcing the subordination of Europe's defense to NATO and thus to the US supreme military command for decades to come. And with military autonomy being a cardinal condition for the exercise of sovereignty, they unwittingly but irreparably forfeited the independence of Western European states—including France—to the United States. To make up for the fiasco, the 1948 Treaty of Brussels was amended on October 23, 1954, to give birth to the Western European Union (WEU) as a Europeanist counterpart to the Atlanticist NATO, but it did not amount to much compared to its half-sibling.[121] The scuttling of the EDC may be one of the worst cases of political shortsightedness in the history of postwar European unification. It was, in any case, an early warning sign that the road to achieving European peace and unity was going to be neither linear nor smooth.

Nevertheless, "the crises of empire"—the progressive abandonment of colonial dominions and the acceptance that the United States and the Soviet Union were the world's two superpowers—were two key factors in the increasing momentum of Western European countries toward continental unification. Except for little Luxembourg, all the founding members of the ECSC had had overseas possessions at some point. Germany lost its colonies after World War I, and Italy's one remaining colony was dismembered when Libya became independent in 1949; in the 1950s the much larger Dutch and French colonial empires also started to crumble. In the course of the often-violent processes of decolonization, it was difficult for any involved European country to participate serenely in a peace process on the Continent. As funding for those overseas wars became more and more difficult to procure, public opinion in the imperial nations grew increasingly disaffected with colonial commitments.[122]

The first violent anticolonial insurrection occurred in the Indonesian archipelago, immediately after the surrender of Japan in August 1945. The Netherlands' attempt to reconquer their former colony, in what was termed a "police operation," was badly received domestically and internationally. In 1949, US secretary of state Dean Acheson intervened and demanded that the Dutch government reach a settlement with its former colony. Several years later, the faith of the French political class in their country's military capability proved sorely misplaced when the French Army found itself in severe difficulty in Indochina, where the Viet-Minh rebellion took on a geostrategic dimension after Communist China threw its weight behind it. Hampered by a lack of public support, the French government was forced to accept US logistical aid. Even with that support, the French expeditionary corps was surrounded and capitulated at Dien Bien Phu on May 7, 1954. In consequence, France was forced to grant independence to Laos, Cambodia, and Vietnam in the Geneva Agreements of July 21, 1954. After that humiliation, France lost faith in its own capability to wage an overseas war on its own. One would think that alone would have eliminated the key French objections to a Western European army, yet its military disgrace was not sufficient to save the EDC from oblivion.

The crises of empire deepened when the European colonial powers failed to maintain their presence not only in remote colonies but also on the southern shore of the Mediterranean. Algeria, almost four times larger than France, was nominally part of it and was featured as such on early maps of the ECSC; it was also a colonial society in which local populations were still denied political rights. In 1954, the Algerian liberation war broke out, and the massacres and atrocities committed on both sides caused a profound moral crisis in France, contributing to the downfall of its government. In 1958 a new constitution was enacted, creating a presidential system, the so-called Fifth Republic: war hero Charles de Gaulle served as its first head of state. Algeria's independence was but one more trauma that challenged the alleged universality of French civilization.

It was the accession of Egypt to sovereignty, however, that forced the French and British to reconsider the way they conceived of themselves and to reexamine their national identities. Egypt had been a nominally independent monarchy since the British government enacted a unilateral declaration of independence in 1922. This declaration, however, exempted the Suez Canal, a vital communication and supply line between the Mediterranean and the Indian Ocean: the United Kingdom had every intention of firmly holding onto it, even though British troops had withdrawn from there by 1947. A coup overthrew King Farouk in 1952, replacing him with a group of nationalist officers led by Gamal Abdel Nasser, who claimed the Suez Canal for Egypt and nationalized the Company of the Suez Canal. This resulted in a grave geopolitical crisis: the right of British and French ships to cross the canal, hitherto guaranteed by an international treaty, could then potentially be obstructed at any time.[123]

In response, Britain and France struck a secret alliance—as was customary in earlier times—to carry out a punitive military expedition that also involved the newly founded state of Israel. Despite its military success, the operation quickly turned into a political debacle. British public opinion was split on the matter, and the reaction of the UN was decisively negative; both the Soviet Union and the United States urged suspending the operation. In theory, the United Kingdom and France could have vetoed this action by the UN, but in practice the USSR brandished a nuclear threat, while the United States wielded an economic cudgel.[124] When Britain, then struggling with public debt, next required a loan from the International Monetary Fund, the United States curtly denied it and threatened to sell its British bonds; the pound sterling was then attacked on the foreign exchange market.[125] The cruel lesson was that colonial pride was not for paupers: European powers were no longer free to decide their policies on other continents. With the British and French governments humbly bowing to the superpowers, a page in the history of the Old Continent was turned. From then on, any military operation conducted by either Britain or France would have to be either requested or endorsed by Washington. Thus, the Suez crisis abruptly closed the era of the fully sovereign European nation-state with a global reach, and this painful realization opened the way to the European drive for unification.

Meanwhile, on the European continent, a drama was unfolding on the eastern side of the Iron Curtain. In October 1956, a general uprising against Hungary's communist government, which had started during the summer as a student protest, swept through the country like wildfire. In response, on November 1, more than one thousand Soviet tanks entered the country, tangling with the Hungarian Army, as well as civilians. To give an idea of the scale of this confrontation, the German Wehrmacht had used only 300 tanks to suppress the 1944 uprising in Warsaw and leave the city a field of ruins. Although the Soviet intervention was not nearly as bloody, it drove 200,000 refugees, many of them intellectuals, onto the roads during the unusually cold winter. This event deeply resonated with public opinion in Western Europe. Yet, in contrast to the crises of 1938–1939, which had provoked interventions by the French and British governments, the assault on Budapest found both Western European powers seemingly paralyzed.[126] The UN was helpless, even more than the League of Nations had been during the crises of 1930s: during the Security Council meeting of October 30, the Soviet Union vetoed a protest letter and arguments by the United States, Britain, and France against the intervention, and it refused to refer the matter to the General Assembly.[127] The writing was on the wall: diminished by the war and the collapse of their colonial empires, the countries of Western Europe—especially the "victors" of World War II, Britain and France—had no choice but to bite the bullet in this postwar "peace-time." If they still wanted to count as players on the international scene, they would somehow have to regroup their forces.

Conjuring the Fear of Falling Behind: The Economic Community

After the failure of the European Defense Community and especially the setbacks of 1956, even the good Abbé de Saint-Pierre might have despaired that a European unification project would ever see the light of day. Yet the Schuman doctrine of small steps was able to exploit the one avenue that was still open: economic integration. Earlier, during the ECSC conference of 1955 in Messina, Sicily, the foreign ministers of the six member countries had discussed the possibility of relaunching European construction by creating a customs union. This was not a novel idea. Germany formed its own *Zollverein* (customs union) in 1833, at a time when it was still a very loose confederation of states, the German Bund; the project was inspired by the abrogation of the tariffs in German states under Napoleon. The Grand Duchy of Luxembourg, though never part of the German Reich, was a member of its customs union until 1919. And, of course, there were the Franco-German efforts of the interwar period, culminating in Briand's and Stresemann's proposal of a European Federal Union.[128] The ECSC foreign ministers did, however, have the notion of also pooling their valuable atomic energy resources in a common European body. In Messina, the ECSC members appointed an intergovernmental committee led by the Belgian Paul-Henri Spaak (the "Spaak Committee"), with a steering body made up of the foreign ministers, to lead the initiative.[129] The United Kingdom also sent a representative, Russell Bretherton, a prudent civil servant and economist. As Bretherton noted, his government refused to participate actively in the negotiations for the expected reasons: Britain wished to preserve its freedom of movement, and the question of the economic relationship between the Commonwealth and Europe remained unresolved. Britain was especially hostile to the idea of committing its strategic atomic resources to a supranational body.[130]

The Spaak Committee presented its report on September 6, 1955, in the Dutch city of Noordwyk, near The Hague. Negotiations continued during the fateful year of 1956 and led to the Treaty of Rome, signed on March 25, 1957, which instituted both the European Economic Community (EEC) and the European Atomic Energy Community (Euratom), becoming effective January 1 of the following year. The agreement was detailed, although it deliberately focused only on economic subjects. Its purpose was to promote the harmonious development of economic activities and to raise the standards of living in the member countries. It would facilitate the free flow of goods and services throughout the member countries by eliminating custom duties and establishing common agricultural and transport policies; it aimed to establish a common market within twelve years. Its organs were an assembly of national delegates selected by the countries' parliaments, a council with one delegate from each member country, a commission that was effectively the secretariat, and a court of justice, to which the commission could refer any member country.

The new European institution, the European Economic Community, was not exactly aligned with Saint-Pierre's paradigm, nor did it have the typical features of a federation, because it was largely governed by an unanimity rule: the disagreement of any one country on any new political decision would be tantamount to a veto. Yet the EEC was far more than a free-trade area, because it had an attached supranational enforcement mechanism. The judicial body with mandatory jurisdiction over interstate disputes was a crucial device, one the League of Nations had not been able to activate and the United Nations had cut off. The word "peace" did appear in the treaty, though only in the preamble, in the modest statement that the signatories were "RESOLVED to strengthen the safeguards of peace and liberty by establishing this combination of resources."[131] It was, nonetheless, a bureaucratic restatement of the rationale and method of European unification expressed in the Schuman Declaration.

On the day the Treaty of Rome was signed, French minister of foreign affairs Christian Pineau confirmed in his public address at the signing ceremony that "too many recent events" (of 1956) had changed the attitudes of those who had so far been the "most reluctant" about the European construction. He also emphasized their painful losses in the war: "The experience of the last war showed, particularly for France and Germany, that a disunited Europe automatically made the powers in conflict lose ground,

FIG. 4.1 Signing of the EEC and Euratom Treaties, Rome, 1957. European Commission Audiovisual Library.

both politically and economically, in front of the great powers on the other side of the Atlantic and in Eastern Europe."[132]

This was, in a nutshell, the argument that Count Coudenhove-Kalergi had formulated in the 1920s. The tragedy of war-torn Europe, as well as the encroachments of the Soviet Union and the United States, had generated the decisive impulse for European countries to unite. Pineau also proclaimed the common "desire to associate other countries to the European construction, particularly Great Britain," respecting its aims and purposes:

> The Second Project, also of British origin, consists of incorporating the specialized assemblies extant in Europe into the larger framework

of the Council of Europe. As a side note, it was that British initiative that led us, to a large degree, to reduce and not enlarge the number of Assemblies that could be incorporated into that structure.[133]

Indeed, the British government at the time was considering an expansion of the functions of the Council of Europe, in the form of a Free Trade Area (FTA), a British "Greater Europe" free-market project, that would cover Western Europe (known as "Plan G").

The formation of the European Economic Community coincided with profound political changes in London and Paris. In Britain, the Conservative Harold Macmillan became head of the cabinet in January 1957 in the wake of the Suez fiasco; in June 1958, Charles de Gaulle came to power in France with the mission of implementing the constitution of the Fifth Republic. De Gaulle, who did not share his predecessors' unreserved enthusiasm for European associations, inaugurated a more assertively independent foreign policy, abruptly ending negotiations with the British on the Free Trade Area in November 1958.[134]

After France ended these negotiations, the new cabinet in London had legitimate reason to worry about the EEC. If it proceeded, the still ailing British economy might be at a disadvantage in trade exchanges with the Continent. In response, Britain did what it had done so often before—counter-balance an alliance of continental states with one of its own making. It developed a treaty parallel to the Treaty of Rome that would remove trade barriers and create closer ties with both the US-sponsored OEEC and the continental EEC. With agreements to reduce tariffs, which allowed each country to manage its own economy—particularly its imports—the treaty would be less restrictive than that of the EEC. Britain rounded up six countries on the edges of Western Europe to support its proposal: its historical associate, Portugal; three Scandinavian countries, Sweden, Denmark, and Norway; Austria, which had been forced to remain neutral because of its position within Central Europe under Soviet control; and Switzerland—which was also attracted to the free trade agreement because, in contrast to a customs union, it would not affect its freedom to determine tariffs, thereby allowing it to preserve its sovereignty and its precious permanent neutrality.

On January 4, 1960, the European Free Trade Association (EFTA) was established by a Convention signed in Stockholm. Its stated purposes were to promote the "sustained expansion of economic activity, full employment, increased productivity and the rational use of resources, financial stability and continuous improvement in living standard"; to "ensure trade between member states take place in condition of fair competition"; and "to avoid significant disparity . . . in the conditions of supply of raw materials." In the spirit of free trade, it also sought "to contribute to the harmonious development and expansion of world trade and to the progressive removal of barriers to it."[135] This last sentence expressed the need to favor exchanges with the former colonies of Britain and Portugal. There were now *three* systems of international institutions in Western Europe: the Council of Europe as an umbrella organization; the Club of Rome with its six members of the EEC; and the British-sponsored EFTA with seven. If one included the US-led system of alliances, the NATO and OEEC, then there were four. Although each of these systems represented undeniable progress, together the result was closer to alphabet soup than to a unitary political system.

Despite all these institutions, reconciliation between France and Germany would not happen without direct diplomatic efforts between them. The inclusion of West Germany in the Council of Europe, as well as the foundation of the ECSC in 1950 and the EEC in 1957, helped narrow the gap between the two countries. Yet the failure of the European Defense Community in 1954 was a wake-up call that rapprochement had its limits because of the power of old grudges between France and Germany that went all the way back to Louis XIV and the Napoleonic wars.[136] In addition, Adenauer was troubled by the militant past of French president Charles de Gaulle who had relentlessly fought Germany during World War II, had conceived of a plan to partition that country, and had been one of the strongest opponents of the EDC.[137]

In contrast, immediately after the inauguration of France's Fifth Republic on September 4, 1958, de Gaulle opened discussions with his German counterpart, whom he hosted at his private residence in Colombey-les-deux-Eglises on September 14–15. On November 26, it was de Gaulle's turn to visit Adenauer in Bad Kreuznach, a small spa town in Rhineland-

Palatinate. From there, negotiations progressed steadily; the two leaders' personal relationship prepared the ground for political reconciliation. This process culminated in the Élysée Treaty, signed on January 22, 1963, whose avowed purpose was to "seal the reconciliation between France and the Federal Republic of Germany."[138] The treaty established a sort of bilateral "Congress System" for Western Europe: there would be consultations between the two countries about foreign policy and defense at least every three months with a view to aligning their respective strategies and tactics, and importantly, there would be instituted a variety of youth education programs. Indeed, it was through the younger generation—with foreign-language instruction, the establishment of equivalences of academic diplomas, scientific cooperation, and student exchanges—that reconciliation between the two peoples would occur and grow. By all accounts, this initiative was a success: it created a new Franco-German bond that would have a profound impact on the evolution of the EEC.

The United Kingdom and Europe: A Love-Hate Relationship?

One state was still missing from the European construction: the insular power, the United Kingdom. While continental Europe struggled to rebuild itself, the British political class faced its own dilemma—how to strike a balance between its overseas interests and its interests on the Continent. Since the early eighteenth century, the doctrine of the balance of power had provided a reassuringly consistent answer. In the days of the Congress System, Britain remained aloof from territorial and social issues on the Continent, intervening solely when its own interests were concerned. After World War I, the League of Nations answered Britain's dilemma by facilitating greater autonomy for the colonies, which had been expanding in population and power (even as the League preserved colonialism with the mandate system): in 1926, the British Empire began bending in the direction of greater colonial autonomy with the creation of the Commonwealth of Nations. After World War II, the far-flung subjects of British imperial rule were passionately motivated to realize their economic, political, and social aspirations.

Back in Europe, the British had always been guided by a well-rounded set of policies, suitably updated, that not only balanced the relationships between Europeans but also Britain's relations with its overseas territories. But with barely enough financial resources to feed its own population, the United Kingdom was no longer able to fund its military and administrative presence overseas. Whitehall, with a sense of urgency, instructed the new viceroy, Lord Mountbatten, to shepherd Indian independence in 1949. By granting India its independence, the British were following the path of severing close ties with distant colonies and refocusing attention on postwar domestic issues. However, the move to independence was not smooth. British higher education had unintentionally infected young Indians with the same plague that had just devastated Europe: principles of ethnonationalism took hold among the young political leaders in the Indian Congress and the Muslim League, many of whom were educated in London or in British schools across the empire. The new nation's political leadership—in a move underwritten by Britain—partitioned the subcontinent into India and Pakistan. As similar partitions had invariably done previously in Europe, this one led to the brutal destruction of traditional social orders and threw the region into violent conflicts.

In 1950 the British government politely declined the offer to subject their own steel industry to a European central authority when France, which was leading that initiative, presented the deal as a take-it-or-leave-it proposition. Whitehall understood full well that the establishment of the European Coal and Steel Community might be just the first step toward a supranational unification of Europe.[139] One cartoon in the French press portrayed Britain as a bass drummer, sitting on its own instrument and refusing to play, with the rest of the orchestra saying "Pity, let's start without them." Another depicted Britain rowing away from a ship named "Europe."[140]

France's unexpected proposal of the European Coal and Steel Community was presented at a time when the British government was still figuring out how to strike a balance between its former colonies and continental Europe.[141] As the French ambassador wrote to Paris, "No responsible politician here will agree to consider the possibility of the United Kingdom joining a European federation without knowing how participation in the Federation would be reconciled with the continuing existence of the Com-

monwealth."[142] European leaders had more than welcomed British membership in the Council of Europe in 1949, which was promoted by Winston
Churchill as an international alliance, a venue for common projects, and
quite possibly a preliminary to a free trade agreement. However, joining the
European Coal and Steel Community would have been a bold step. Despite
the flowery rhetoric in speeches ("United States of Europe"), most British
political leaders did not seriously contemplate the federal constitution of the
United States as a model for a European system, at least not with the United
Kingdom becoming part of it. The governing Labour Party declared, "The
European peoples do not want a supra-national authority to impose agreements. They need an international machinery to carry out agreements
which are reached without compulsion."[143] The careful choice of words
("machinery") no doubt meant that the British government was skeptical
about this new passion of the Continent for multicellular biology: it still preferred to view the international system more like a steam turbine.

Winston Churchill, who returned to power as prime minister from
1951 to 1955, vowed to prevent further dissolution of the British Empire.
Yet British colonies achieved independence one after the other and sometimes through violent revolution, as in Kenya and Malaya. When twenty-
five-year-old princess Elizabeth II ascended the British throne in 1952, she
became the nominal ruler of a union of nations that staunchly kept the
trappings of a world power. But just as English absolutism became a monarchy of appearances by the end of the seventeenth century, so now Britain
was turning into a ghost of an empire with hardly any colonies left to rule.

These transformative developments motivated the British to experience a
change of heart about the European Question. As time went by, the foundations of British resistance to joining the European Communities—the
twin beliefs in the Commonwealth and in free trade that had inspired its
rejection of supranational institutions—weakened.[144] More disquiet-
ingly, the economic balance of power was swinging in favor of the biolo-
gists: the success of the EEC and of Franco-German reconciliation meant
that an economic juggernaut was emerging in Western Europe, which
Britain and its EFTA coalition could not hope to counterweigh.

After his reelection in 1959, Tory prime minister Harold Macmillan set
up a commission to reevaluate the relationship between the six members

of the EEC and the seven members of EFTA, known as the "six–seven" relationship.[145] Macmillan, a level-headed observer of politics, concluded that because the EFTA and EEC were not only failing to counterbalance each other but were also drifting farther apart, the UK economy would soon stand at a disadvantage with the members of the Common Market. The Macmillan cabinet did not take a position on whether to join the EEC or merely to obtain some form of "identification" (meeting the standards of the EEC without joining it). Its US ally, on whom Britain strongly relied both politically and economically, did not have any objections to moves in that direction, so long as they reinforced the Western European bloc against the Soviet Union. Indeed, US support for British participation in the EEC became enthusiastic after John F. Kennedy took office as president in January 1961. The government in London thus started actively negotiating with Paris and Bonn to secure their agreement for British membership.

Franco-British reconciliation was required in this process as well, because de Gaulle felt the urge to settle a few historical differences. What then happened was akin to what the French call a *dépit amoureux,* or a lovers' tiff: when Britain, the object of desire, was finally ready to yield to the advances of France, the latter adopted a posture of heated rejection. De Gaulle reproached the British for evading the Treaty of Rome negotiations and then for asking to join on their own conditions. This was the same de Gaulle who, in the last days of the debacle of June 1940, had made a proposal for an indissoluble alliance between France and Britain, which Churchill had considered seriously but which was ultimately pointless after the collapse of the French Republic.[146] One cannot help but think of the similar offer that Russia's Tsar Alexander I made to Britain in 1804, in another set of equally dramatic circumstances.

De Gaulle's perception of the British Commonwealth as a threat to renascent French industry played an important role in his opposition. On January 14, 1963, he cut short all negotiations in a public interview in front of 800 journalists by questioning with acerbic irony the readiness of Britain to accept the rules of the Common Market.[147] In contrast, de Gaulle praised his rapprochement with Adenauer's Germany, France's former foe: "a mutual discovery is occurring for two neighbors who realize how much the other is attractive; for the first time in a long time, Gauls and Germans notice their mutual solidarity, strategically and economically."[148] In London, this open snub toward a former ally—who had, after all, faithfully supported the Free France during the war—and one that moreover was combined with the favorable treatment of the enemy of yesteryear, left much rancor.

The French president's position reflected a complex mix of stances: although he was arguably a Europeanist and a strong supporter of Franco-German reconciliation, he was also wary of a supranational European order and profoundly hostile to US influence on Europe. De Gaulle feared that the inclusion of the United Kingdom in the EEC would lead to institutional overstretch—"We would build, as eleven. Then as thirteen. And then perhaps as eighteen."—and result in a colossal Atlantic Community dependent on and led by the United States.[149] He further worried that this larger Atlantic Community would quickly absorb the Community of Europe: "This hypothesis is perhaps perfectly justifiable in the eyes of some, but it is not at all what we have wanted to do and what France is doing, which is a specifically European construction."[150] In sum, de Gaulle felt that the Anglo-American "special relationship" would act as a Trojan horse, reducing the sovereignty of European states. Because the EEC was governed by a unanimity rule and de Gaulle vetoed the Britain's application, its application to enter was rejected without appeal. Despite this rejection, political sentiment in London in favor of closer connection to Europe was growing across political boundaries, and the newly elected Labour government of Harold Wilson submitted another application in 1964. The lengthy negotiations ultimately broke down in 1967 and for the same reason: as long as the mercurial French president remained in power, every step in this direction would be rebuffed. As de Gaulle declared, "It is common knowledge that England [sic], as a great state, and as a nation true to itself, would never agree to dissolve itself in some utopian construction."[151] True to his anti-Atlanticist stance, the French president also pulled France out of NATO temporarily on June 21, 1966.

Profound societal changes were nevertheless underway: just as the Revolutions of 1848 forced institutional changes in nineteenth-century Europe, the Western European social protests of May 1968 indirectly gave further impetus to the European construction process. In France, students, trade unionists, and feminists, as well as opponents of the Vietnam War, all took to the streets. After his reelection in June, the aging de Gaulle, at that point perceived as an ultraconservative, staged a citizens' referendum to dissolve the Senate and decentralize the state. French citizens resoundingly rejected his proposal on April 27, 1969; on the following day the president became, as happened to Prince von Metternich in 1848, *un homme de trop* (a superfluous man) and resigned. While the protests spread across Europe, notably in Britain, Germany, Italy, and Spain, nowhere was the government as shaken as in France. Most importantly for the history of European unification, de Gaulle's resignation removed the principal obstacle not only to Britain's entry into the Common Market but also to the entry of Norway, Ireland, and Denmark.

Western Europe was not the only part of Europe to be affected by protests, however. On the other side of the Iron Curtain, uprisings also took place, motivated chiefly by economic hardship and issues of political sovereignty. The Soviet Union was not prepared to countenance challenges either to Marxism or to Soviet rule, and the Soviet-sponsored Polish government got things back in hand in the traditional, authoritarian way. In August, a quarter-million men and two thousand tanks from the Warsaw Pact entered Prague, twice as many as were used in Budapest twelve years earlier.[152] In Western Europe, which received a wave of 70,000 Czech emigrants, this came as another wake-up call. As during the 1950 Korean Crisis and the 1956 Hungarian Revolution, this brutal reassertion of Soviet supremacy gave increased momentum to the European construction project. Three other countries, in addition to the aforementioned United Kingdom, applied for membership in the EEC: Denmark, Ireland, and Norway. All except Ireland were already members of the EFTA. The citizens of Norway rejected the proposal to join the EEC in a referendum in 1972, so in the end, only three new members were admitted. Britain was the only country not requiring its people to vote on admission, but this omission was corrected in 1975, when more than two-thirds of the voters (67%) gave their approval. The EEC was thereafter nicknamed the "Europe of the Nine." It was at this point that the word "Europe" experienced a semantic shift: when used in a political context, it started to become broadly synonymous with the EEC, at least in Western Europe.[153]

As Schuman aptly proclaimed in a 1970 address, "Great Britain was lucid enough to tell the democracies of Western Europe: 'Unite.' She was not ambitious enough to say: 'Let us unite.' The Community was thus built according to the wishes of Great Britain, that is to say without Great Britain."[154] Genuinely wanting to be part of Europe because it belonged to the same family, but without being fully part of it—this was Great Britain's quandary. *To be, or not to be, that is the question*—this Shakespearean expression became a trope for Britain's European Question.[155] With Britain as an EEC member, however, the European construction acquired its long-awaited momentum. Western Europe was still a construction site, but the Postwar European Spirit was at last on the verge of realization.

The European Communities: A Western System of Peace within a Global System of War

One should not lose sight of the fact that the success of the Western European method of peace during the postwar period made it in effect a system of peace within a global system of war. This observation challenges the traditional narrative that the UN made more progress toward peace than did the League of Nations. If the latter justly deserves to be considered a failure because it ensured peace between the great powers for only two decades, then the same standard of judgement should be applied to the UN. Its Security Council maintained only a form of armed truce in Europe during the four decades of the Cold War, when two considerable armies were mobilized on both sides of the Iron Curtain. For a world organization that Franklin D. Roosevelt intended would "save the succeeding generations from the scourge of war," "reaffirm faith in fundamental rights," ensure "justice and respect for the obligations arising from treaties," and "promote social progress and better standards of life," the hegemony of the Soviet Union over half of Europe cannot be considered as a genuine success.[156] The UN official website today portrays Andrei Gromyko as a man who represented the Soviet Union with "style and dignity," stating that those who dealt with him had "respect, even affection for him."[157] This diplomatic "affection" for a man assigned by Stalin to defend the deportation of more than ten million ethnic Germans and the imposition of communism in Eastern Europe seems to be a problematic instance of historical casuistry.

Yet the UN has had two significant merits as a peace organization. First, it provided a permanent meeting ground for the two superpowers so that they could quarrel verbally instead of fighting on a battlefield; perhaps having that forum prevented the arms race of the Cold War from resulting in nuclear conflict. Second, the UN had far more opportunities than the League of Nations to function as an active "peacekeeping" force in war zones, an activity in which the UN achieved an honorable track record during the Cold War. Unfortunately, it was unable to prevent regional wars, and the obligation stated in its Charter that all member states should put military forces at its disposal largely was not activated; in that respect, it had a similar "flaw" to the League of Nations. However, its creation in 1948 of a system of peacekeeping missions conducted by multinational troops that came to be known as "Blue Helmets" was a successful innovation.[158] Let us observe, once again, the semantic shift from the diplomatic activity of "making peace" between states to police operations conducted by the military to "keep the peace" against disorder, a shift that also occurred in the post-Napoleonic era when the initial liberalism of the Congress System gave way to the Reaction. The almost immediate fallback to military police operations was a sign of the UN's inability to realize the loftier goal of a lasting peace between states.

Indeed, it should be clear by now how much the failure of the Spirit of Yalta—that is, the destruction of Roosevelt's peace plans caused by the Soviet takeover of Central and Eastern Europe—was a major incentive for what I call here the Postwar European Spirit and the European construction that began in 1950. As Robert Schuman wrote in 1963,

> The major problem threatening peace is that of East-West relations, between the West and the Soviet Bloc. This is today's problem in the highest sense of the word, not only because of its intrinsic difficulties, but because it is closely related to all the other outstanding problems concerning Germany, Austria, the Balkans, the Middle and the Far East. Moreover, it dominates the whole

issue of military spending and consequently of our financial and economic position.[159]

In three visionary sentences, Schuman captured the essence of Europe's peace problem and its relation to the issues of the Cold War. As the likelihood of a new conflict between France and Germany diminished, Western European leaders became increasingly aware that the Soviet Union was their gravest threat. In the early 1960s, daily life under Soviet domination had become less brutal than under Stalin or the Nazis, yet the USSR sought all the same to impose an imperial (or hegemonic) peace order over much of Europe: it was exactly what all European states had collectively resisted since the Treaty of Utrecht and against which they had been allied ever since. At a time when the former European great powers of France, Britain, and Germany had dwindled into political insignificance, the European construction was a key response to the Soviet presence in Central Europe. The two facets of foreign and economic policy were so closely intertwined in political discourse as to be inseparable. The Cold War and the threat of a "new tyranny" (to use Churchill's phrase) were thus more than just the international context for the postwar unification of Europe: they provided a large part of its motivation and internal impetus.[160]

Another key internal factor also opened the way to that unification: the postwar European method, which was the combination of two "peace tools" that put an end to the balance of power as the principle regulating the coexistence of states within Western Europe and to war as a dispute-resolution procedure. The first of these tools was already contained in Churchill's seminal Zurich speech of 1946: "If Europe is to be saved from infinite misery, and indeed from final doom, there must be an act of faith in the European family and an act of oblivion against all the crimes and follies of the past."[161] It was here that the former wartime leader invoked the "astonishing" first step of reconciliation between France and Germany. Such reconciliation was of course already part of the European peace toolkit. In 1815, the allied powers invoked it in their treatment of France. In contrast, little more than a century later, the Allies deliberately cast aside a conciliatory approach in 1919, with fateful consequences. By then, "reconciliation" had taken on a completely new meaning: changing the minds of entire populations.

Four years later, when Schuman stated that "Europe will not be made all at once, or according to a single plan," few observers really understood the significance of his observation. The efficacy of this second peace tool, functionalism, still escapes many observers today. The original Council of Europe failed to become a federal institution because it was an attempt, like all previous ones, to become "at once, and according to a single plan." To jump the hurdles of securing ratification by each nation, it had to be limited to a declaration of intentions (though this was at least implemented by useful institutions such as the European Court of Human Rights). The European construction made a clean break with this approach. Without doing away with the cherished dream of the good Abbé, it provided the twist that finally made it feasible: it adopted functionalism as its method. It followed the humble but highly effective growth path of the vine that grew organically, seeking to exploit any "concrete achievements that create a de facto solidarity." Of course, functionalism had to be combined with the first peace tool, reconciliation; it stands to reason that, before pooling their most strategic resources, France and Germany had to abandon first their primordial instincts that one's life should be the other's death and then proceed on a pathway toward mutual trust. The "pooling of resources," the biological process that allows multicellular organisms to grow vastly larger and more powerful than monocellular ones, was the watchword of the European Coal and Steel Community in 1950. The organic growth of the EEC from six to nine, and then twelve members, steady though not easy, is evidence enough that this new political "organism" had far greater flexibility, resilience, and potential than the "machineries of peace" of the past, such as the League of Nations or the dream of a European federation, the latter of which only existed in philosophical writings and stillborn plans.

It is important, at this point, to underscore a key fact: the US government did not take a controlling hand in planning, founding, or changing the European Communities—a commendable approach, given that the Soviet Union did not refrain from imposing its own ideology and instructions on its "brother" countries of the Comecon (the rival economic organization of Soviet bloc nations created in 1949). Quite to the contrary, the underlying rationale of the Common Market was the idea that the European nation-states had become too small for the needs of a modern economy, and the disastrous ideologies of national autarky (much in vogue in the late 1930s) had proved a dangerous delusion. The Common Market was certainly also meant to compete with US economic dominance. Its establishment required both national and supranational intervention to dismantle national trusts and other impediments to the free circulation of goods. In this idea, contained in particular in the German "ordoliberalism" developed by Walter Eucken and his colleagues at Freiburg University—and not only by proponents of American liberalism—lay the motivation behind the creation of a Common Market.[162] The European model was not derived from political mimesis of, or pressure from, the ascendant postwar United States. Rather, it was meant to compete with US economic dominance and was even directed against it—a fact that became obvious during the "Chicken War" of the early 1960s between the EEC and the United States, waged around the issue of agricultural imports.[163]

Similarly, the promoters of the European construction could not fail to notice the increasing ideological chasm opening between the two sides of the Atlantic. Most notably, Jean Monnet and Paul-Henri Spaak had both lived for considerable periods of time in the United States and were especially concerned with the US turn to the Truman Doctrine and the rise of the eminently un-European notion of a "superpower." These Europeanists pragmatically welcomed the Marshall Plan, not because they saw it as a tool for peace but because they perceived the need for reconstruction and a balance of power against the Soviet Union. They believed that US leadership was necessary for the time being, under the wider umbrella of NATO. However, to infer from that cooperation that the Western Europeans adhered to the core principles of American liberalism and to the desirability of the balance of power as an instrument of peace would be incorrect. Later, transatlantic circles, such as the Bilderberg Group of the Netherlands (established in 1954) and the Davos Forum in Switzerland (founded in 1971 by German businessman Klaus Schwaab), did indeed promote a particular brand of American-inspired economic liberalism that reinforced ideological ties between the United States and Europe, as well as with other regions. Yet given that those clubs played almost no role in critical geopolitical events, there is little reason to subscribe to suggestions of an "American conspiracy" to influence the European integration process. The roots of the

European construction were endogenous, and nourished from springs within Europe itself.[164]

Indeed, if these circles truly had been broadly influential, that might have been counterproductive, because their "capitalistic" view of the economy, as well as the elitist character of their meetings, did not align with the values of equality and solidarity proudly proclaimed in the European treaties or generally in the press of the member states. Indeed, most political classes of Europe, including those who called themselves "liberal," had been leaning toward social democracy since the early 1950s. Differences in worldview between the European capitals and Washington were very obvious when de Gaulle was in power, yet they were perceptible among all the major figures who participated in the history of European construction. In truth, what most brought the Americans and the Europeans together after World War II was a pragmatic consideration: a brotherhood born from the alliance against the Axis continued to exist during the Cold War because of the military threat posed by the Soviet Union.

By contrast, the progressive expansion of the EEC from six to twelve members in the grim context of the Cold War, without any grand plan or manifest destiny, and the effective reconciliation of Germany and France, stand out as the two most remarkable successes in the engineering of peace. In 1981, Greece joined as an "additional passenger" despite the fact that its economy was considerably lagging behind the rest of Europe. The admission of Greece, which had been governed until recently by a junta of colonels, was met with much skepticism: Was there any rhyme or reason for the addition of a remote country at the extreme tip of southeastern Europe that did not have any land connections to the other EEC states? From reading the public discourse about Greece joining the EEC, one could think that the prime motivation was cultural affinities, particularly the fact that Athens was "the cradle of democracy" and that public opinion in Western Europe was experiencing a repetition of philhellenism, the popular movement of sympathy for the Greeks in the 1820s.[165] In reality, and just as with this precedent, securing the Straits was the focus of Western European governments: the EEC members resolved to extend a protective umbrella over Greece to avert the loss of a key bulwark against Soviet influence in the Eastern Mediterranean. Out of this consideration, the others followed. The method would be an original one. Instead of using subsidies or military intervention, the EEC would sustain Greece "through the development of [its] economy under democratic institutions."[166]

In 1986, Spain and Portugal also joined the bloc. Like Greece, both of these southern European countries emerged from military dictatorships. Yet the rationale was more economically focused this time—they were actually connected to the EEC by land (and thus in no risk of being threatened), and their economies were on the rise. With these three additional members, the EEC reached, for the first time in its history, a plateau on which it became a sizable actor: it had, for the time being, reached the geographic limits imposed by the Cold War's Iron Curtain. This European supranational organism appeared to be a hybrid of a federation and a confederation, in Kant's terms. Yet it was sui generis (one of a kind), neither one nor the other: a sort of political platypus. How it gave birth to an actual European Union after the collapse of the Iron Curtain, giving way to a very different Enlarged European Spirit, is the subject of the next chapter.

5

The Spirit of
Enlarged Europe

THE FLIGHT OF THE MONARCH BUTTERFLIES

> My name is Samantha Smith. I am ten years old. . . . I have been
> worrying about Russia and the United States getting into a nuclear
> war. . . . I would like to know why you want to conquer the world or at
> least our country. God made the world for us to live together in peace
> and not to fight.
>
> —SAMANTHA SMITH TO YURI ANDROPOV, 1982

*I*n November 1982, an American schoolgirl, Samantha Smith, caused a
worldwide sensation by writing an unusual letter to the head of the Soviet
Union. It posed, in a few short sentences, the age-old issues of war, empire,
and tyranny. Yuri Vladimirovich Andropov, general secretary of the Communist Party, wrote her an even more surprising reply that signaled changing
times and even anticipated the European order that would take place within
a decade:

> Yes, Samantha, we in the Soviet Union are trying to do everything
> so that there will not be war on Earth. . . . In America and in our
> country there are nuclear weapons—terrible weapons that can kill
> millions of people in an instant. But we do not want them to ever be
> used. That's precisely why the Soviet Union solemnly declared to the
> entire world that never—never—will it use nuclear weapons first
> against any country. In general, we propose to discontinue further

production of them and to proceed to the abolition of all the [nuclear] stockpiles on Earth.[1]

And to the girl's naïve question—"Why do you want to conquer the whole world or at least the United States?"—he replied, "We want nothing of the kind. . . . We want peace for ourselves and for all peoples of the planet."[2]

Samantha Smith was hailed as a hero throughout the Soviet Union; she appeared on stamps, and riverboats were named after her. In the United States, her story also attracted much attention from the media, especially after she accepted an invitation to visit the USSR with her parents.[3] The governments of both superpowers played along, enjoying the détente with little risk, knowing they would be able to dismiss it all as childish talk at any moment. Many, of course, questioned the sincerity of a man who had spent fifteen years as head of the feared KGB agency and was well versed in propaganda techniques and the repression of dissent.

Even more importantly, the Soviet Union had been fighting the Cold War for almost four decades, ever since signing the Yalta Agreements. Though there were no pitched battles in Europe between the two blocs after 1945, their massive armies were always on the ready along a line from the Baltic to the Adriatic; this created a dynamic that could not be directly compared to any of the previous episodes we have examined. The Cold War was an unexpected return to the practices of traditional European frontier wars between two organized states, such as those between Habsburg Austria and the Ottoman Empire from the fifteenth to seventeenth centuries, which required a permanently manned military border.[4] Far from being a genuine state of peace, it was a frozen conflict, a territorial struggle between two obstinately antagonistic powers. The Cold War took on the character of a war of attrition, because it lasted for decades, albeit waged at a political and economic level; time replaced violence as the chief destructive agent, and the party whose morale, manpower, and resources ran out first would be the first to cave.

It might seem surprising that the fifth episode in the story of *European* unification should open with an exchange of letters between a Soviet premier and an American schoolgirl. Yet underneath the deep layers of hypocrisy in the propaganda war between East and West, there was something in this correspondence's focus on peace that struck a chord of truth in both the Soviet Union and the United States. Andropov's response reflected a surprising change of rhetoric, in contrast to earlier testy exchanges between diplomats with their mutual threats of annihilation.[5] The Soviet leadership had a secret reason for its change in attitude: its social and economic fabric was fraying. This posed an existential threat to a regime whose raison d'être had been to build a communist utopia, complete with a new, more efficient model of government and a more equitable distribution of wealth. While the residents of Western Europe were enjoying the abundance offered by their consumer societies, in the communist world the shelves of shops remained despairingly empty, and citizens had to haggle on the black market to obtain basic goods. Decades after World War II, corruption was rampant at all levels of society. Even Poland and Eastern Germany, about whose relatively higher living standards Soviet citizens fantasized, were destitute compared to the West.

This derelict economic scene behind the Iron Curtain was the backdrop to the Spirit of Enlarged Europe—one that, like the earlier spirits, arose in the aftermath of a prolonged conflict against an imperial power. This spirit not only had its own intellectual roots but also a sense of drama that was absent from the Postwar European Spirit. It was like a massive flood that swept away everything in its path, washing out communist governments as if they were straw huts. Once the political structures dam broke, the flood became subject only to the chaotic dynamics of fluids. This upheaval, commonly called the "Autumn of Nations," eventually forced the formidable Red Army to retreat to the higher ground of the Soviet Union and ultimately brought peace to most of Europe.

The Spirit of Enlarged Europe expanded the European construction eastward as far as the border with Russia to the north and the Black Sea to the south. Tracing its genesis and development requires an unusually wide canvas; indeed, it would be impossible to understand this twist in the story of European unification without acknowledging the crucial role played by the East—particularly Russia—because it was during Andropov's short tenure that the first stirrings of a massive wave of reforms emerged. At the end of the 1980s, Mikhail Gorbachev's policies of *glasnost* (transparency) and *perestroika* (restructuring) facilitated a final peace settlement for Germany, which in turn made possible the territorial settlement of Poland's western border and of Russia's enclave of Kaliningrad (formerly Königsberg in eastern Prussia). That these two conditions for the Soviet turnaround would ever be met, as had been hoped for since the end of World War II, seemed like a fantasy at the height of the Cold War.[6] In this chapter we see how protests against Soviet occupation molded the conscience of the peoples of Eastern Europe and how Gorbachev fostered the Enlarged European Spirit by giving it intellectual justification and legitimacy inside the Eastern bloc. Most importantly, we learn how and why this upheaval coincided with the birth of the first actual "European Union," the very entity called for by the Abbé de Saint-Pierre and his followers, and how it expanded eastward until it covered most of the continent. Thus this chapter shows how the European Union, from its birth as a frail Western European creature, grew to become the largest, most viable political organism ever to exist in Europe.

An Epic Peace Spirit

What was the nature of this Enlarged European Spirit? Some critics consider it a "subaltern" and unrefined form of the European Spirit with a simplistic script; others do not see it as a spirit at all.[7] However, it unquestionably had a profound influence on the European project. For a brief period of time, it was distinct from the Postwar European Spirit, but when the two streams converged, it brought with it an appeal to the emotions that proved able to motivate populations well beyond the circles of culture and power. A wide canvas is necessary to embrace this spirit and reconcile it with earlier ones, creating a broad narrative of the idea of Europe over the *longue durée*. Regrettably, its story has so far remained largely confined to national narratives of such Central and Eastern European countries as Poland and Hungary.[8] The task, then, is to reintegrate its parts, over time and over space, to see it whole for once.

Western European political discourse still projects the image of a European bloc that laboriously developed from West to East. Although this is an accurate view of the EU's enlargement process, looking at the move to unification from the perspective of social and economic history presents this image in reverse: a powerful wave of Central and Eastern European peoples flowing westward. Demographic data certainly reflect this movement toward Western Europe, especially by young people looking for jobs and opportunities, who quickly left behind the Russian *lingua franca* of the Soviet era for the English pidgin of the Continent.[9]

The Enlarged European Spirit amazed the world as a dizzying and slightly disquieting phenomenon like the hatching of monarch butterflies in California, in which millions of winged creatures swarm the sky to start a long exodus. In 1989, simultaneous peaceful revolutions, which had hitherto lived separately underground as in a larval state, emerged against communist regimes. That these revolutions all occurred at approximately the same time has to be attributed to the warming of political conditions in the Soviet bloc with perestroika. In those times of upheaval, intellectual considerations mattered less than the impetuous course of events. Nevertheless, we need to analyze the political catastrophe that befell the communist regimes rationally to understand how and why it occurred and to draw useful lessons for the engineering of peace.

This Enlarged Spirit, so new and different, also requires that we alter our traditional understanding of the chronology and periodization of European history. Although Americans and Western Europeans perceive World War II and the Cold War as two distinct periods, the picture is blurred for many Eastern Europeans. For Poland, World War II started with a coordinated invasion by the German Wehrmacht from the west and the Soviet Army from the east. In Finland, the Baltic Republics, and Romania, war began with an invasion by the Red Army followed by a counter-invasion by the Axis forces in 1941. That the Soviet Union and Nazi Germany turned against each other only two years after signing a non-aggression pact in 1939 does not alter the fact that both invaders were totalitarian states, detested by the occupied populations.[10] The popular movements of 1989 in Eastern Europe should thus be seen as the last convulsions of a half-century of conflict that started when World War II began. To provide a common temporal frame for all these countries that lost their sovereignty and fully recovered it only in 1989, I use the shorthand term "the Fifty Years' War" (1939–1989).[11]

Making sense of the latest, and last, of our "Spirits" demands an expansion of horizons eastward. In fact, in this period, the "East" encompasses three distinct geopolitical regions, each with its own peculiar historical heritage and aspirations. The first is Central and Eastern Europe. Its populations aimed for a "return to Europe": that is, for the reestablishment of connections severed by the Iron Curtain. The second is southeastern Europe (or the Balkans, though these two terms do not necessarily overlap), which had its own social forces and issues, and whose peoples desired to rebuild the state by means of free elections and reforms. The third is the traditional realm of the Russian Empire, which experienced the collapse of the Soviet Union as a trauma. All three looked to Western Europe: the seat of the European Communities, which had drawn on the *acquis* of the Postwar European Spirit of the 1950s. The struggle to reform the "West" at this moment inevitably entailed contention over the shifting boundaries of the "East."[12]

It is necessary, finally, to dispel a common misconception: the Enlarged Spirit was not rooted in the literary and philosophical traditions of Western Europe, much less in American liberalism. The inspiration for unification did not come directly from the elevated aims of the Abbé de Saint-Pierre, Immanuel Kant, Tsar Alexander I, or President Woodrow Wilson. The motivations were, often literally, "bread-and-butter" ones connected to a keen sense of political frustration. They were steeped in regional memories and accentuated by day-to-day economic necessities. What most grassroots people wanted more than anything was simply a return "to a normal life" in a "normal country," to use the words of the Polish dissident Adam Michnik.[13] Why, then, does this spirit deserve to be called "European"? Because after those movements simultaneously hatched in 1989, they swarmed the same enemy—communist regimes—before seeking to coalesce into a unified European order. The collapse of East Germany cannot be understood without considering events in Hungary, which in turn precipitated the Romanian revolution.

"A Common European Home"

The Spirit of Enlarged Europe did have an institutional foundation, which was established in the early 1970s: the Conference on Security and Cooperation in Europe (CSCE). Under the auspices of the CSCE, there was a series of diplomatic conferences in several European cities, which involved states from both sides of the Iron Curtain. On these occasions, neutrals such as Switzerland, Austria, and Finland played a key role as providers of "good offices" (services rendered as mediators).[14] Both the Western allies and the Soviet Union eagerly participated in these diplomatic efforts, which eventually led to the Helsinki Accords and the Organization for Security and Co-operation in Europe (OSCE). The OSCE was a novel brand of peace organization that was in the spirit of the UN: unlike the opposing military alliances (NATO and the Warsaw Pact) and economic organizations (the European Communities and the Comecon), the OSCE was a truly pan-European organization that transcended the divide of the Iron Curtain.[15]

The preamble of the Helsinki Final Act of August 1, 1975, which formalized the Accords, described the signatories' intentions in an elevated tone: "motivated by the political will, in the interest of peoples, to improve and intensify their relations and to contribute in Europe to peace, security, justice and cooperation as well as to rapprochement among themselves and with the other states of the world."[16] Its ten principles were drawn directly from the toolkit of perpetual peace: sovereignty, rejection of the use of force, peaceful resolution of disputes (i.e., commitment to the use of mediation, arbitration, or a legal court), territorial integrity, respect for human rights, self-determination, cooperation between states, and good-faith observance of obligations under international law. Although this agreement is often noted for its contribution to the field of human rights, it was first and foremost a multilateral agreement on political coexistence in Europe.[17] It could be considered something of an extrapolation of Schuman's principle of 1950, according to which only a "small steps" policy would yield results; this time, it was applied to both sides of the Iron Curtain.

The Helsinki Accords also introduced a counterintuitive notion to the European political landscape: the "indivisibility of security." This held that the security of each state was inextricably linked to the security of all other states; in other words, all the states of Europe (on both sides of the Iron Curtain) had to cooperate. International lawyers view the Helsinki Final Act as the foundation for a new pan-European system; in no way was this treaty in a position to end the Cold War, but it had the potential to alter the rules of the game.[18] The Helsinki process thus brought something far more substantial than the hollow invocations of peace in the North Atlantic Treaty and the Warsaw Pact: after all, this was still the Cold War, when the United States and USSR each wished to tip the balance of power in its own favor.

The motivation for the United States and Western Europe to participate in the Helsinki Accords was quite simple: these agreements advanced the short-term aim of improving human rights in Central and Eastern Europe and, in the longer term, of achieving a peace settlement in Europe. Why, however, was the general secretary of the Communist Party, Leonid Brezhnev, willing to underwrite such an agreement? After all, it upheld "the sovereign equality and individuality as well as all the rights inherent in and encompassed by its sovereignty, including in particular the right of every state to juridical equality, to territorial integrity and to freedom and political independence"—the very antithesis of the USSR's policy.[19]

Indeed, two weeks before the Accords were signed, Soviet premier Alexei N. Kosygin formulated what came to be known as the "Brezhnev Doctrine" or the "limited sovereignty doctrine."[20] In response to suggestions that the joint military operation of 1968 against Czechoslovakia had "run counter to the Marxist-Leninist principle of sovereignty and the rights of nations to self-determination," he declared,

> The peoples of the socialist countries and communist parties certainly do have and should have freedom for determining the ways of advance of their respective countries. However, none of their decisions should damage either socialism in their country or the fundamental interests of other socialist countries, and the whole working-class movement, which is working for socialism.[21]

The Soviet Union was at this time in the midst of a major crisis. The brutal repression of the Prague Spring had taken a grave toll. Moscow lost the support of many sympathetic left-wing intellectuals in the West who had so far generally supported the Soviet Union. Worse, it lost control over a number of Western Communist Parties that, fearful of losing their electoral base, turned away from the USSR to embrace "Eurocommunism."[22] A public relations campaign was necessary to repair the damage. To Brezhnev—who welcomed the savings to the military budget mandated by the new disarmament agreements, leaving more resources to address internal security and economic issues—allowing the international community limited leverage over the Soviet Union through the Helsinki Accords seemed a small price to pay. Soviet leaders had already abandoned Stalin's hopes of advancing farther into Western Europe—signing the Helsinki Accords was effectively a maneuver to gain strategic advantage in the Cold War by relieving the the financial burden of keeping the Red Army on the Western front.[23]

Moscow's strategy of pretending that its agreement was all about sovereignty and human rights was thus a ploy aimed to score points with Western public opinion while gaining acknowledgment of the status quo of Eastern Europe's military occupation. To avoid making real commitments to sovereignty and human rights, Soviet leaders relied heavily on the semantic tool known in Russian as *dubovyi iazyk,* literally "oak tongue" or "wooden language," which was deployed throughout the Brezhnev Doctrine. Rich in vague yet substantive-sounding phrases ("proletarian revolution," "imperialistic forces") and passive formulations, but lacking in references to time and space ("tomorrow" meant "the future"), it was a collection of general statements presented as formal conclusions. Its undeniable political power relied on the unexpressed maxim that any lie upheld with impunity is as good as the truth. As such, the wooden tongue was an act of political violence directed not only toward listeners but also at day-to-day reality itself.[24]

Brezhnev's gambit, however, failed in gaining an advantage, because his Western political counterparts eagerly jumped on the financial distress of the Soviet Union to press for liberalization, creating a climate of political blackmail against the USSR. In what came to be known as the Helsinki Process, gradual advances were made on matters of commerce, as well as on the treatment of political opponents and the right to emigration.[25] Nevertheless, conditions for the populations within the Soviet bloc did not substantially improve either politically or economically. On the contrary, worrying signs of the system's deterioration were growing in number and strength. When Brezhnev's successor Andropov requested in 1983 a report on the economic development of the USSR in qualitative, rather than quantitative terms, the results were bleak.[26] Whereas Khrushchev had declared at the 21st Party Congress in February 1959 that by 1965, "the Soviet Union [will] outstrip the United States in [the] volume of production," Soviet economic output was instead surpassed by both West Germany and Japan.[27] Clearly, meaningful improvement would require a major generational shift.

In the early 1980s, the Soviet government's fear—concealed at first, but then increasingly publicized—that its nation was weakening internally and losing its grip over its satellites, ushered in a policy change: a spirit of overture arose, as freedoms increased and the opening to the West widened. In 1985, fifty-four-year-old Mikhail Sergeyevich Gorbachev acceded to the position of general secretary. Andropov had shrewdly recommended Gorbachev as his successor, but circumstances had temporarily put in his place an elderly conservative, Konstantin U. Chernenko, who died within a year, opening the way for the new man.

Gorbachev's challenge in international affairs has to be placed in the context of the Soviet invasion of Afghanistan in 1979, which led to the United States' immediate reversal of the détente policy from the first years of President Jimmy Carter's administration. In direct response to the invasion, the United States boycotted the 1980 Olympic Games in Moscow. The new president elected in 1981, Ronald Reagan, initially did not think much of the Helsinki Accords.[28] On March 23, 1983, shortly after labeling the Soviet Union an "evil empire," he announced plans to develop a Strategic Defense Initiative (SDI), in which satellites would take down Soviet nuclear missiles before they reached US soil. This gladiatorial announcement alarmed both the United States' Western allies and the Soviet Union. The resulting diatribe between the two superpowers threatened to derail the meticulously maintained peaceful façade of Helsinki.

The Soviet Army was still bogged down in an unwinnable war in Afghanistan. To make matters worse, in November 1983, Soviet military leaders mistook a NATO command post exercise joined by the US military as the prelude to an actual nuclear attack. This incident introduced a new format of coded communication and radio silences between the United States and the Soviet Union, which caused their relationship to deteriorate.[29] The net result of Reagan's Strategic Defense Initiative would reinforce the resolution of the new Soviet leader to break free of the straitjacket of the Cold War—a crucial decision that would facilitate later events. Not only did Gorbachev decide not to pick up the gauntlet Reagan had thrown down but he also began to engage more deeply in the Helsinki process, in the face of opposition at home, to activate the real reform he had in mind.[30] On May 17, 1985, the Soviet premier delivered a sensational speech in Leningrad that broke with decades of rhetoric about the superiority of communism to other political systems:

> We are now spending, comrades, significantly more raw material, energy and other resources per unit of national income compared to many other countries. . . . In other words, resources are becoming ever less accessible and more expensive. . . . So the issue is: we squander countless resources in each sector, but nobody is going broke. It only seems that way. In a family you do feel this, when it comes out of your own pocket, but out of the state's pocket, nobody feels it. We must arrange things so that this is felt.[31]

Gorbachev implied that one of the basic tenets of communism—collectivization of the economy—had been implemented too drastically. He later, in 1990, revealed that the Soviet Union would undergo a sweeping change, overturning Brezhnev's conservative policies:

> But back in March–April 1985 we found ourselves facing a crucial, and I confess, agonizing choice. When I agreed to assume the office of the General Secretary of the Communist Party of the Soviet Union Central Committee, in effect the highest State office at that time, I realized that we could no longer live as before and that I would not want to remain in that office unless I got support in undertaking major reforms.[32]

He noted that government leadership was aware that the Soviet bloc was suffering from *zastoi,* roughly translated as "stagnation." Its root causes were collectivization, pervasive bureaucracy, "militarized industries that siphoned off our . . . intellectual resources," and "the unbearable burden of military expenditures that suffocated civilian industries and undermined the social achievements of the period since the Revolution."[33] Gorbachev thus diagnosed the greatest liability of the Soviet Union: the diversion of economic resources to military spending for too long. Having left its civilian population living in relative poverty compared to the West, the USSR was on the verge of bankruptcy. Decades of militaristic obsession with empire and war had turned the Soviet Union into an antiquated organization led by conservative old men in charge of decrepit production facilities.[34] Given the superior economic vitality of the West, it was a losing game. The remedy required ending the Cold War and working toward international peace.

In an astonishing admission by a Soviet leader of sins of the past, Gorbachev advocated a shift from violent to peaceful means to resolve domestic differences:

> Steering a peaceful course is not easy in a country where generation after generation of people were led to believe that those who have power or force could throw those who dissent or disagree out of politics or even in jail. For centuries all the country's problems used to be finally resolved by violent means. All this has left an almost indelible mark on our entire "political culture," if the term is at all appropriate in this case.[35]

Gorbachev was also turning his back on the dogmatic opposition between the socialist and capitalist blocs. He wrote in *Pravda* in October 1985, "We are not conducting a Metternichian 'balance of power' policy, setting one state against another, knocking together blocs and counter blocs . . . but a policy of global détente, strengthening world security and developing international cooperation everywhere."[36] Gorbachev's reference to Metternich was less historically accurate—the Austrian chancellor believed in a system based on an equilibrium, not a raw balance of power—than a jibe aimed at the realist post–World War II school of international relations inspired by Henry Kissinger, which had exalted Metternich's policies as a paradigm for relations with the USSR.[37] Indeed, this preconception explained Washington's incredulous reaction to Gorbachev's change in Soviet foreign policy.

The die was now cast. Gorbachev's desire to bring an end to the Cold War was only strengthened by the disaster at the Chernobyl nuclear facility in April 1986. In his UN speech on December 7, 1988, he paid tribute to the Universal Declaration of Human Rights. Insisting on the "compelling necessity of the principle of freedom of choice"—thereby disavowing the Brezhnev Doctrine—he announced that the USSR would reduce its military presence in Eastern Europe, especially East Germany, by withdrawing 50,000 troops and 5,000 tanks. "All remaining Soviet divisions . . . will be given a different structure . . . which will become unambiguously defensive, after the removal of a large number of their tanks."[38] The message was unequivocal: no longer would Soviet tank divisions suppress street disorders in Eastern Europe, and the communist regimes of the "sister republics" of the Warsaw Pact would be left to their own fates.

The biggest surprise of all was yet to come. On July 6, 1989, before the Council of Europe in Strasbourg, Gorbachev presented an elaborate doctrine of European peace that left the audience thunderstruck. He referred to previous attempts at European unification, both imperial and voluntary, as well as to the words of Victor Hugo at the Congress of Peace in 1849: "you will, without losing your distinguishing features and your splendid distinctiveness, merge inseparably into some higher society and form a European brotherhood."[39] Gorbachev's innovative proposal recognized that Europe was composed of two different systems, but he nevertheless advocated the development of a united continent that would reconcile them:

> The idea of European unification should be collectively thought over once again in the process of the co-creation of all nations—large, medium and small. . . . Yet the difficulty lies elsewhere—it lies in the rather widespread belief (or even in the political objective) that what is meant by overcoming the division of Europe is actually overcoming socialism. But this is a course for confrontation, if not something worse. There will be no European unity along these lines.[40]

Actually, Gorbachev's claim for a united Europe should have been only mildly surprising, because it was taking the principles of the Helsinki Accords to their logical conclusion—for its security to be "indivisible," Europe had to be indivisible as well. More shocking was his announcement that the Soviet Union was going to pivot from the Brezhnev Doctrine of limited sovereignty: "any interference in internal affairs, any attempts to limit the sovereignty of states—whether of friends and allies or anybody else—are inadmissible." Echoing the analogy of the European construction, he proposed the idea of "Europe is our home" and a "restructuring of the international order existing in Europe that would put common European values in the forefront and make it possible to replace the traditional balance of forces with a balance of interests."[41] In place of military confrontation he substituted compromise through negotiation. The decisive factor was no longer power but persuasion.

Not only was the term "balance of interests" well chosen but also Gorbachev's metaphor of the "common European home" resituated the Soviet Union, whose land area was the Russian Empire's historical sphere of influence, squarely within the geography of Europe:

> The philosophy of the concept of a common European home rules
> out the probability of an armed clash and the very possibility of the
> use or threat of force, above all military force, by an alliance against
> another alliance, inside alliances or wherever it may be. It suggests a
> doctrine of restraint to replace the doctrine of deterrence. This is not
> just a play on notions, but a logic of European development imposed
> by life itself.[42]

The reference to restraint encourages a comparison with what I earlier called the "balance of diplomacy" of Tsar Alexander, who showed unusual empathy for both sides when attempting to bridge the historical chasm between Russia and the rest of Europe. In this speech Gorbachev also rephrased Kant's principle of "peace . . . created and guaranteed by an equilibrium of forces and vigorous rivalry."[43] In fact, the formulation of a "balance of interests"—the active search for the most acceptable compromise between sometimes contradictory interests—was a concept that any lawyer or judge could easily comprehend.[44]

Once again, Gorbachev made it clear that the chief driver of perestroika and the pursuit of a European system of peace was the need to escape the wholly unsustainable system of war in which the Soviet Union found itself. The Cold War had diverted a disproportionate amount of economic resources to armaments, while the domestic economy of socialist countries, plagued by inefficiency and waste, had been left behind. In other words, the Soviet Union had to quit the Cold War *and* reform the economy of its bloc of nations, or it would be doomed. On that day in Strasbourg, Gorbachev announced a reduction of military expenditures "by one and a half to two times." He made a plea for mutual disarmament and the departure of "all foreign troops from the territories of other countries," suggesting that both US and Soviet troops leave Europe. The speech was received enthusiastically and, at the time, perceived as a "historic event."[45] By launching the concept of the "common European home," Gorbachev unexpectedly inspired the Enlarged European Spirit. It seemed that the former belligerents of the Cold War were finally heading toward a peace on equal terms, much like the Peace of Utrecht in the eighteenth century. Yet none of the players suspected how quickly the situation would change.

The years 1989 and 1990 became as crucial turning points in the quest for lasting peace in Europe as the years 1713, 1815, and 1919. Only two months after the signing of the Settlement Treaty that reunited the two Germanies (more on which later), peace negotiations began for the rest of Europe. An OSCE summit took place in Paris on November 19–21, 1990, in which gathered the European states (including the neutrals), together with Canada, the United States, and the Soviet Union. The participants issued the Charter of Paris for a New Europe (also known as the Paris Charter), which opened with a bold declaration:

> We, the Heads of State or Government of the States participating in the Conference on Security and Co-operation in Europe, have assembled in Paris at a time of profound change and historic expectations. The era of confrontation and division of Europe has ended. We declare that henceforth our relations will be founded on respect and co-operation. Europe is liberating itself from the legacy of the past.[46]

For a brief moment, and for the first time since the Congress System of the post-Napoleonic era, the states of Europe formed a grand alliance of peace that embraced the whole continent, from France and Britain all the way to Russia.

The partners committed to "refrain from the threat or use of force against the territorial integrity or political independence of any state" and to "settle disputes by peaceful means."[47] This agreement, once again, reconnected with the tradition of perpetual peace through law and the recourse to arbitration or courts. In the same vein, the Paris Charter reasserted "the essential contribution of our common European culture and our shared values in overcoming the division of the continent."[48] The document emphasized the altered circumstances in the aftermath of the USSR's change of heart. It had one important limitation, however, that made for a missed opportunity for a grand European settlement: the Paris Charter did not result in a formal treaty, which would be followed by parliamentary ratification. As merely a declaration of intentions of state representatives, it failed to mandate any obligations for the states themselves, nor did it create any precedent in international law. Even though the 1990 OCSE summit in Paris was called the "peace conference" of the Cold War, it never produced a signed global peace treaty.[49]

Nevertheless, a striking recognition of the Soviet Union's contribution to the ongoing peace process came on October 15 of that year, when the Norwegian Nobel Committee awarded its Peace Prize to Mikhail Gorbachev for "his leading role in the peace process which today characterizes important parts of the international community."[50] The committee acknowledged that several factors had encouraged "dramatic changes" in the relationship between East and West, but it wanted personally to honor Gorbachev "for his many and decisive contributions. The greater openness he has brought about in Soviet society has also helped promote international trust."[51] Gidske Anderson, the chairperson of the Norwegian Nobel Committee, insisted that the end to the balance of power had inaugurated the peace process: "East and West, the two mighty power blocs, have managed to abandon their life-threatening confrontation and have, instead, embarked on the long and patient road to cooperation on the basis of negotiation."[52]

In his acceptance speech, Gorbachev responded by lyrically announcing the rallying of Soviet Union to perpetual peace, the intellectual tradition that had provided an alternative to the balance of power: "Immanuel Kant prophesied that mankind would one day be faced with a dilemma: either to be joined in a true union of nations or to perish in a war of annihilation ending in the extinction of the human race. Now, as we move from the second to the third millennium, the clock has struck the moment of truth."[53] He noted that the OSCE summit in Paris established a "framework for a Europe based on the rule of law, stability, good relations between neighboring countries and humane attitudes" and expressed his hope that "such a Europe will be understood and accepted by nations and governments in other parts of the world as an example of universal security and genuine cooperation."[54]

Quite apart from the exchange of congratulatory speeches, the public acquiescence of a Soviet leader to the tradition of perpetual peace was an astonishing turn of events in European history: the equivalent of a reversal of fortunes in times of war. In awarding the prize to Gorbachev, the Nobel Committee recognized his leading role in the creation of a system of peace that spanned Eurasia from the Atlantic Coast to the Urals, all the way east to Kamchatka.

Central and Eastern Europe: Home Again

The social movement undermining the communist regimes in Eastern and Central Europe had been going on for some time, but it was only in 1989 that the spectacular "flight of monarch butterflies" took place. The peoples of these regions were longing for a return to better times, when they had belonged to the community of Europe and had participated in its circulation of people, goods, and ideas. Most of these Central and Eastern European countries acquired independence during the late nineteenth century or after the Treaty of Versailles, as the empires (Ottoman, Austro-Hungarian, German, and Russian) splintered. Freedom for them not only meant freedom from political oppression and want but also the freedom to speak, travel, engage in political activity, and acquire possessions. Until 1989, local communist governments, aware of their fundamental unpopularity, were able to count on using the last resort against popular discontent: the tank divisions of the Warsaw Pact. After Gorbachev announced that he would not follow the precedents of 1956 and 1968, consternation and anxiety gripped the communist nomenklatura in Central and Eastern Europe. They realized that their world was about to end. The Soviet policy shift inaugurated a period of rapid political change that resulted in the end of communist rule, termed the "Autumn of Nations" (or "Autumn of the Peoples") alluding to the "Spring of Nations" of 1848.[55] These events were also called "revolutions," although they were not marked by the violence of the French or Russian Revolutions. As Adam Michnik later confessed, "My obsession has been that we should have a revolution that [does] not resemble the French or the Russian, but rather the American, in the senses that it be for something, not against something. A revolution for a constitution, not a paradise. An anti-utopian revolution. Because utopias lead to the guillotine and the gulag."[56] They were revolutions in the more traditional sense of the word as "a return to normality" or "a positive change of regime." This mostly peaceful process, which sought to restore the rule of law in the totalitarian regimes imposed by the Soviet Union, may with equal justification be called a "Democratic Restoration," or to use Jürgen Habermas's terms, "rectifying" or "catch-up" revolutions.[57]

This movement was not, however, defined by abstract intellectual slogans; its demands focused on two basic needs that the communist regimes had failed to satisfy sufficiently: food and political freedom. At a time when shops in the European Economic Community were overflowing with produce, food rationing remained a fixture in the East. Frustrated citizens demanded the right to take the future into their own hands by having the freedom to engage in more private enterprise, as well as gaining greater freedom of speech and political action. These claims were not, however, focused on building a "better Europe," much less "a better world," but rather on the immediate desire for decent living conditions. It is true that dissident elites longed for a "return to Europe," but theirs was not a political program. It was rather a return to the idealized Western polity, which they regarded as providing the freedom and abundance that they had lost under the Nazi and Soviet occupations.[58]

Thus, initially disparate and mostly national movements had been gnawing at the foundations of their respective regimes for some time. In the spring of 1988, strikes broke out—once again—in Poland. They were led by Lech Wałęsa, the already famous head of the Solidarity Citizens' Committee (Solidarność), which had staged spectacular strikes in the early 1980s. Again, the government resorted to the time-honored way of communist regimes—with tank divisions and martial law. However, these actions did not end the strikes, and as they continued well into September 1988, the Polish Communist Party (PZPR) felt that it might be wise to make a few concessions to placate the population. The party's heads invited the leadership of Solidarity to engage in talks, hoping to convince them to adhere to rules that would preserve the essential prerogatives of the party. The ensuing "roundtable" lasted from February 6 to April 5, 1989; it led to the legalization of independent trade unions and the formation of a Senate elected on the basis of universal suffrage, which would supplement the historical parliament (*Sejm*). The PZPR had, however, clearly underestimated its own unpopularity; the free legislative elections on June 4, 1989, turned into a blowout. Solidarity swept 99 of 100 seats in the Senate, as well as all of the freely allocated seats (which made up 35% of the total number of seats) in the Sejm. The foundation of the communist regime had always rested on the axiom that the single party represented the will of the Polish people; as soon as that was exposed as a fantasy, the whole state apparatus started to fall apart. After the Polish government realized that Moscow had abandoned it to its fate, it surrendered without a fight.[59]

Poland then staged an eminently symbolic conclusion to the Fifty Years' War that emphasized how World War II and the Cold War were intertwined in a single process. On December 22, 1990, Ryszard Kaczorowski, the last president of the Polish government-in-exile—which had resided in London ever since it was founded in September 1939—solemnly returned the insignia of the Polish Republic to Lech Wałęsa, in his new role as president.[60] The Soviet-imposed Polish People's Republic having been thus abolished, this ceremony established a solemn link between the Second Republic—destroyed in the first days of World War II—and the newly constituted Third Polish Republic. It was the close of a circle, Poland's eventual victory against the joint Nazi-Soviet aggression of September 1939, and the return of the country to a state of peace.[61]

The second country to experience turmoil was Hungary. Where popular demands in Poland were mostly economic in nature, Hungarian demonstrations were politically and nationally focused. Some protests commemorated the 1956 insurrection in Budapest, and others manifested solidarity with Hungarian minorities in Romania's Transylvania. Mass demonstrations took place throughout 1988, to which the government and police chose not to react with the violence of the past. The government was already letting its citizens travel to the West and—even before Gorbachev's bombshell at the Council of Europe—started dismantling the barbed-wire fences on the border with Austria. On August 19, 1989, an official celebration of free borders took place at the city of Sopron, on the formerly closed Austro-Hungarian border. There, representatives of both countries staged a "Pan-European picnic" and shook hands, symbolically breaching the Iron

Curtain. This moment of reconnection was staged as the popular version of a peace agreement between the two countries. By the end of October, the Communist Party had relinquished its control over public life, and the parliament had adopted a new constitution that marked the death of the People's Republic of Hungary.[62]

In Czechoslovakia, liberation came later; large demonstrations took place on International Students Day, November 17, 1989. The initial student movement grew into huge popular rallies that involved workers, leading to a general strike by November 27. Parliament, yielding to popular pressure, started to dismantle the constitutional provisions that had maintained the one-party system. This "Velvet Revolution" (so called because of its peaceful character) brought to power Václav Havel, a former writer and dissident, and his Civic Forum movement. Aptly named, Havel's movement brought together the country's citizens to dislodge a communist regime controlled by a foreign power.[63] Czechoslovakia was the first country to have suffered German aggression in 1938, one year before the start of the Fifty Years' War; in 1989, a new period of sovereignty, civic liberty, and peace thus began for that country. In diplomatic terms, what happened to the states of Poland, Czechoslovakia, and Hungary did not qualify as a *thaw,* as in the 1970s; it was rather a *debacle,* a word that evokes the tumultuous flooding caused by the breakup of ice on a frozen river.[64]

A Star Is Born: The Unexpected Reunification of the Two Germanies

The case of the fall of communism in the German Democratic Republic (GDR) merits separate consideration, not because the internal dynamics that brought it about were any different from those of its sister republics, but because the GDR had essentially been a "semi-country," a part of a larger one. As long as the Cold War balance of power was maintained and the Iron Curtain kept the two sides apart, a peaceful settlement of Germany remained an impossibility. The German Question was the most intractable issue arising from the conflict between the two blocs in Europe.[65] Three factors, all connected to the economic crisis in the communist countries, led to a debacle there.

The first factor had been at work for some time: East Germany simply had no money left in the public purse to pay for its armed forces, public services, and pensions, and it was increasingly in debt to Western countries. In contrast, West Germany had developed since the war to become one of the world's most prosperous economic powers. Its currency was among the strongest on the planet; by 1989, the gross national product (GNP) per capita of West Germany was twice that of the Soviet Union, while its total GNP was roughly the same, despite the enormous difference in territory and military power. The economic decrepitude of East Germany equally contrasted with the prosperity of the rest of the member states of the EEC.[66]

A second factor was the East Germans themselves, who watched West German TV and were fully aware that not all was going well on their side of the wall; this consciousness had been undermining the foundations of the regime for some time. Watching ads in German for Mercedes, BMWs, and Audis did not please viewers in a country with a GNP per capita one-third lower than West Germany's and where the wait to purchase an automobile averaged thirteen years.[67] The third precipitating factor was the news of the Kremlin's disengagement policy, which left the East German government with sole responsibility to maintain "order and security" along its more than 800-mile "Inner Border" with West Germany. The aging general secretary of the East German Socialist Party, Erich Honecker, defiantly vowed to remain faithful to Marxist teachings. Still, the Berlin Wall endured as a haunting symbol of the Cold War divide. The president of West Germany, Richard von Weizsäcker, famously quipped, "The German question would remain open as long as the Brandenburg Gate remains closed."[68]

By the late 1980s, US President Ronald Reagan had warmed to the idea of a possible rapprochement with the USSR. Seeking to complement John F. Kennedy's performance of 1963 in West Berlin with one of his own, Reagan delivered a speech on June 12, 1987, in front of the Brandenburg Gate. In the presence of West German chancellor Helmut Kohl, he tied together themes of economic prosperity, peace, and freedom, pointedly remarking that the tide had turned:

> In the 1950s, Khrushchev predicted: "We will bury you." But in the West today, we see a free world that has achieved a level of prosperity

and well-being unprecedented in all human history. In the Communist world, we see failure, technological backwardness, declining standards of health, even want of the most basic kind—too little food. Even today, the Soviet Union still cannot feed itself. After these four decades, then, there stands before the entire world one great and inescapable conclusion: Freedom leads to prosperity. Freedom replaces the ancient hatreds among the nations with comity and peace. Freedom is the victor.[69]

Reagan then proceeded to link peace to prosperity, with a call to Gorbachev that became world famous:

General Secretary Gorbachev, if you seek peace, if you seek prosperity for the Soviet Union and Eastern Europe, if you seek liberalization: Come here to this gate! Mr. Gorbachev, open this gate! Mr. Gorbachev, tear down this wall![70]

Reagan's speech was well argued and well delivered, but something was missing: an authenticity, a special rapport with the Berliners that belonged to an earlier era and another US president. In fact, Reagan's harangue was somewhat out of place, because (as would soon become public knowledge) Gorbachev then had no intention of "tearing down the wall" for the same reason that he was not going to fail to support the government of East Germany. The speech did, however, create additional discontent among the citizens of the beleaguered East German state. A much more popular expression of solidarity was delivered a year later on July 19, 1988, when rock star Bruce Springsteen gave a giant three-hour concert in East Berlin, the largest in the history of the GDR.[71]

That moment of solace, however, did not halt the rising wave of popular unrest—far from it. Communal elections on May 7, 1989, became the turning point of the struggle against the regime. When 100,000 East Germans answered the opposition's appeal and publicly protested the elections, the government's only recourse was police repression. But opening fire on the protestors would have started a long struggle, for which the state would sooner or later have run out of resources. Pressure mounted once again in August 1989, when the dismantling of the border fences between Hungary and Austria allowed groups of East Germans to escape to the West. The GDR's attempt to seal the border with Hungary only managed to divert the flow of emigrants through Czechoslovakia.[72]

Then a most curious thing happened, which became a highlight of the Enlarged European Spirit: tens of thousands of Germans publicly declared their love for a Soviet leader. On October 7, 1989, during the solemn celebrations of the fortieth anniversary of the GDR, Soviet premier Mikhail Gorbachev was greeted with shouts of "Gorby, liberate us!" In an interview conducted after the celebrations, he declared, "Danger awaits those who do not react to the real world; if you move with the currents of the real world . . . then you have no reason to fear difficulties."[73] This was a warning for Erich Honecker, who had been in power for eighteen years and lived in denial of the existential threats to his regime. The aging Honecker finally resigned on October 17, after falling critically ill during the events of July 1989—a large wave of refugees left the GDR for Austria via Hungary, many more wanted to leave the country, and there was increasing discontent. Much like conservative leaders after the insurrections of 1848 and 1968, many of Honecker's fellow communist leaders were forced to bow out as well, prompting a generational shift.

Finally, the dam broke on November 9. As the new heads of the GDR were contemplating a modest relaxation of restrictions in the use of the crossing points to West Germany (as well as those to West Berlin), a bungled televised news conference left East Germans with the impression that those new regulations had immediately gone into effect.[74] After dusk, thousands of people crowded in front of the checkpoints on the eastern side of the Berlin Wall. Border guard officers, paralyzed by the lack of instructions to respond to the crowd, caved in and gave the order to let people through. The communal spirit on that day was indescribable, as jubilant East Germans strolled into West Berlin and others drove tiny Trabant cars through its streets, all greeted with flowers and champagne. In the following days, Berliners used all the tools they could find to chip away at the wall, creating informal gates. Television crews selected the most spectacular spot. They filmed exhilarated youths standing at night on top of the Berlin Wall, in front of the barricaded Brandenburg Gate, two vivid symbols of the Soviet occupation. For public opinion worldwide, the dismemberment of the once-

mighty Berlin Wall, which had stood for nearly three decades, went beyond an easing of travel restrictions for East Germans: it symbolized the
end of the Cold War. A new spirit was on the march.

The West German chancellor, Helmut Kohl, saw the opportunity of a
lifetime: on November 28, he took the gamble of announcing a "Ten-Point
Plan for German Unity" at the Bundestag, the West German parliament.
Although he still situated the future of Germany within the context of East–
West relations, one of its politico-economic systems had definitively de-
feated the other:

> The development of inter-German relations remains embedded in
> the pan-European process, and that always means in East-West rela-
> tions. The future architecture of Germany must conform to the
> future architecture of pan-Europe. In this regard, the West has set
> the pace with its concept of a permanent and just peaceful order of
> Europe.[75]

The message was clear: the collapse of the Iron Curtain opened the door
to a settlement of the German Question and, in turn, to a state of peace for
all of Europe, and this effort would have to be pursued in cooperation with
the Soviet Union. Kohl also appealed to Gorbachev's principle of a "common
European home" to overcome the division of Europe. He saved, however,
his most important and contentious point for the end:

> With this comprehensive policy we are working toward a state of
> peace in Europe in which the German people can regain their unity
> in free self-determination. Reunification—that means re-attaining
> the national unity of Germany—remains the political aim of the gov-
> ernment of the Federal Republic.[76]

The cat was out of the bag. The support for German reunification from
both sides of the former wall emboldened Kohl to act without consulting
the victorious powers of World War II. The new East German leader, Egon
Krenz, announced free elections, which took place on March 18, 1990, and
resulted in an overwhelming victory for the Christian Democrats—echoing
the Christian Democratic victories in Germany after 1945 in the wake of
the fall of Nazism. Shortly thereafter, the two states signed the Treaty

establishing a Monetary, Economic and Social Union, which entered into force on July 1, 1990. In one fell swoop, Germany's "Inner Border" was officially abolished. In his memoirs, Kohl would recall this treaty as "the greatest achievement of German economic history" and a unique opportunity "to serve the peace of the world in a united Europe."[77]

This policy of fait accompli to achieve a postwar settlement of Germany was successful at the international level, despite initial skepticism from foreign governments. The superpowers were in the end both favorable to it: the United States had always staunchly supported German reunification, and Gorbachev ultimately acquiesced to the idea. The new governments of Poland and Czechoslovakia were another matter, because they feared that the newly reunified nation would reopen the question of its eastern territories lost in 1919 and 1945 (including Pomerania, East Prussia, and Silesia).[78] This fear was understandable, because German irredentism had led in the past to the invasion of Czechoslovakia in 1938 and of Poland in 1939; indeed West German maps of the 1980s still marked those territories as being "under Polish administration." Clearly, reunification would require more than a bilateral treaty between Germany's two halves. The two eastern neighbors demanded, as a condition of their acquiescence, that their own integrity be preserved in perpetuity under the blanket of a new *Pax Europeana*—an extension of the Western European system of treaties to the East, which would provide a long-term guarantee that Germany would never become a hegemon again.

For the member states of the EEC, already shaken by these dramatic developments, Germany's demand for reunification was both unexpected and a tall order. At the beginning of the negotiations in November 1989, only French president François Mitterrand was won over to the novel idea of German reunification and its dizzying array of consequences for the European order. Support, however, began to grow; at the meeting of the European Council in Strasbourg on December 8–9, 1989, the heads of state and government of the twelve member-states agreed to enlarge the community. In London, Prime Minister Margaret Thatcher mounted a bitter resistance against this step because of her fear of German revanchism. She remained firmly entrenched in her position, which may have been motivated by the considerable degree of personal antipathy between Kohl and her; yet other

British political leaders began to express their willingness to yield. Her position on unification was undermined when her key cabinet ally Nicholas Ridley was forced to resign in July 1990 after he accused Germany of staging "a racket to take-over the whole of Europe" and the French of behaving like poodles to the Germans.[79] Thatcher finally acquiesced to German reunification, acknowledging that it was "an important step in overcoming the division of our continent."[80] Meanwhile, the Iron Lady's star was waning on the domestic front: a coup within the Tory Party forced her to resign in November 1990, a few days before she was to attend a meeting of the European Council.

A roadblock had been removed, but the European Council now faced a worrisome issue. The Enlarged European Spirit, feeding on energies accumulated during fifty years of totalitarian occupation, was taking on a life of its own. In contrast to the Spirits of Vienna and Geneva and the Postwar European Spirit that had initially been initiatives controlled by particular political classes or cultural elites, this was a grassroots movement—"Autumn of Nations" or "Peaceful Revolution" were not idle names—that was dragging the political leaders of Western Europe to places they had never dared imagine, straight into the heart of the former Eastern bloc. Helmut Kohl had, needless to say, taken quite a risk with his demand for German reunification. Yet the current was also sweeping away any political leader who dared to stand in its path, from the Polish president Wojciech Jaruzelski to the East German Egon Krenz. The wisest course, it seemed, was to go with the current, rather than against it.[81]

On September 12, 1990, forty-five years after the unconditional surrender of all German forces to the Allies, the Treaty of the Final Settlement with Respect to Germany was signed in Moscow. Nicknamed the "Two-Plus-Four Treaty," it was signed by the two German states and the four Allies of World War II: the United States, the Soviet Union, France, and Britain. Never in European memory had such a major settlement treaty been signed so long after the end of a large continental war; never was one subscribed to under such exceptional conditions. After referring to the postwar responsibility of the Four Allies, as well as to the Helsinki Accords and their contribution to a peaceful order in Europe, the treaty welcomed the fact "that the German people, freely exercising their right of self-determination, have expressed their will to bring about the unity of Germany as a state so that they will be able to serve the peace of the world as an equal and sovereign partner in a united Europe."[82]

This treaty was also a "confirmation that the definitive nature of the borders of the united Germany is an essential element of the peaceful order in Europe."[83] Reunification came, indeed, at the cost to Germany of the historical concessions demanded by Poland and Czechoslovakia. Germany would forever renounce irredentism and expansionism; it would maintain "no territorial claims whatsoever against other states and [would] not assert any in the future."[84] In particular, it gave up unconditionally the eastern territories annexed to Poland under the Versailles Treaty in 1919 *and* those summarily snatched for Poland by Stalin in 1945, as well as the Russian enclave of Kaliningrad (the northern half of East Prussia). Nor would Germany ever again claim the Sudetenland as Hitler had done in 1938.[85]

Quite significantly, the treaty declared that "only peace will emanate from the German soil," promising a reduction in size of the German Army and its armaments. The Soviet Army would withdraw its forces from East Germany, those institutions that had put Germany under Soviet tutelage after World War II would be dissolved, and Germany would have full sovereignty over its internal and external affairs. Never before had a European country signed such a commitment to perpetual peace in a multilateral treaty. Clearly, West Germany had gone a long way to redeem itself both politically and morally after the crimes of World War II: it had established a democratic civil society and foregone the essential attribute of an empire, the projection of military power.

It is easy to underestimate the momentous import of the resolution of the German Question in 1991. The Two-Plus-Four Treaty also resolved one of the most curious anomalies in European diplomatic history: World War II, concluded without a peace treaty, had seamlessly merged into another conflict, the Cold War, without any formal declaration of war. This new settlement treaty ended the litigation between the United States and the Soviet Union over the enforcement of the 1945 Potsdam Agreement. Yet it did far more than that—it was, to all intents and purposes, the peace treaty that resolved Germany's territorial quarrels with its neighboring countries stemming from World War II. It settled border issues that arose even before the Fifty Years' War began on September 1, 1939; it also solved the dispute that started on October 1, 1938, after the infamous Munich Conference and the annexation of Czechoslovakia's Sudeten-land. For Central Europe, ending such a long, dark conflict brought enormous relief.

The "Autumn of Nations," which involved Poland, Hungary, Czechoslo-vakia, Bulgaria, Romania, and East Germany—it was also called the "Peaceful Revolution" in Germany—was stunning for its minimal violence (with the notable exception of Romania), especially considering the earlier experience of the twentieth century with devastation, deportations, and mass slaughters.[86] Much of the credit for the absence of bloodshed must go to Mikhail Gorbachev—which was all the more paradoxical because he was the supreme leader of the Soviet Union, at the helm of the same totalitarian power that had maintained a military hegemony over half of Europe for the past five decades.

Although Gorbachev was a sincere supporter of the Soviet system, his support for a new unified peace system on the continent—the "common European home," as he called it—was instrumental in fostering the geo-political revolution of those years. As was the case with Alexander I in 1815 and Woodrow Wilson in 1919, one of the most influential actors in European peacemaking and unification hailed from the periphery of Europe; once again, this actor spurred innovation by turning his back on conservatives—in Gorbachev's case, the traditionalists of the Politburo. One could imagine how bloody the situation might have been had the standard Soviet operating procedure—sending armored divisions into cities—been applied. Even though the foundations of the European communist regimes were unsound and their collapse appeared inevitable, the unexpected forbearance of the Soviet Union in the face of popular resistance in the early 1990s should not be ascribed to chance: it was the result of Gorbachev's deliberate decision to rein in the Soviet military establishment.

The implosion of the Warsaw Pact released an enormous reservoir of compressed energies. Seen through another metaphor, Enlarged Euro-pean Spirit resembled an asteroid belt, formed of separate and diverse bodies drawn into the orbit of the Western European bloc. The two

Germanies fused into one, igniting a new star in the sky of Europe. Although West Germany was already part of the European Communities, other new players were drawn into the European bloc. Catalyzed by the sudden release of the Soviets' iron grip, the Spirit of an Enlarged Europe coalesced energetically.

The Collapse of the Soviet Edifice

The long flood wave also traveled east and southeast, from the Baltic Sea to the Balkan peninsula. It then lost momentum, and sapped of its energy, it stopped at the third geopolitical area of Europe: the "hard" borders of the former Soviet Union. The European "lake" now started lapping at the foothills of the Soviet Union, where the greatest challenge for Gorbachev lay. In the late summer of 1989, a cataclysm occurred in the three small Baltic Republics—Estonia, Lithuania, and Latvia—whose very existence had been all but forgotten in Western Europe, except in "once-upon-a-time" stories of a fabled Courland or a medieval Grand Duchy of Lithuania. These states secured their independence and membership in the League of Nations in the early 1920s, but Stalin then brutally annexed them in 1940. Since then, popular resentment against the Soviet Union in the Baltic Republics had continued unabated.

Their frustration erupted into one of the most extraordinary peaceful protests in recorded history when, on August 23, 1989, two million citizens, each holding hands with the next, many openly crying, formed a chain spanning the 600 kilometers between the three capitals. This peaceful human chain, over fields and city streets, was a spectacular sight; indeed, television coverage often cut the sound, lest any comment or music detract from the powerful images. The fall of the Berlin Wall had clearly been a blockbuster, but this was on quite another level. [87]

This event, known as the "Baltic Way" or the "Way of Freedom," took place on a highly charged anniversary: it was fifty years to the day, on August 23, 1939, on which the Third Reich and the Soviet Union had signed the Molotov-Ribbentrop Pact. This agreement, which had effectively started the Fifty Years' War, included an infamous secret appendix: in exchange for the USSR's recognition of Germany's occupation of western Poland, Ger-

FIG. 5.1 The Baltic Way on the Riga (Latvia)–Pskov (Russia) Highway, August 23, 1989. © Gunārs Janaitis.

many declared its "non-interest" in eastern Poland, as well as in the territories that had been lost by the Russian Empire after World War I, effectively placing them in the Soviet "sphere of influence."[88]

The Baltic Way had an enormous emotional impact in the Soviet Union and sent shockwaves through the highest political levels. An act of defiance of this magnitude had never been seen before. At Gorbachev's request, a commission was set up in Moscow in 1989 to confirm or dismiss the existence of the infamous secret clauses of the Molotov-Ribbentrop Pact. What followed was more than a recognition by the Congress of People's Deputies of the Soviet Union that the protocol "was in fact signed and existed"; it was a strong, unambiguous ideological condemnation:

> The August 23rd, 1939 Protocol and other secret protocols that were signed with Germany in 1939–1941 were deviations from the Leninist principles of Soviet foreign policy. From the standpoint of law, territorial division into Soviet and German spheres of interest and other actions were in conflict with the sovereignty and independence of several third countries.

The Congress notes that during this period the relations of the USSR with Latvia, Lithuania and Estonia were regulated by a system of treaties. Pursuant to the 1920 Peace Treaties and 1926–1933 Non-Aggression Treaties, the signatories were obliged to honor each other's sovereignty, territorial integrity, and inviolability under any circumstances. The Soviet Union had assumed similar obligations to Poland and Finland.[89]

The Congress of People's Deputies, however, needed to save face. It maintained that the secret protocol had been signed without the knowledge of the Soviet government, the Communist Party, or the Soviet people; it was therefore "an act of personal power and in no way reflected the will of the Soviet people, who bear no responsibility for this treacherous collusion."[90] In addition, this condemnation applied only to the Molotov-Ribbentrop Pact, which party leaders considered as nullified once Germany attacked the Soviet Union in 1941. The disavowal did not apply to the later agreement that Stalin reached with the Allied Powers in February 1945 at the Yalta Conference—which had the same effect on the territorial integrity of Poland and Romania and the sovereignty of the Baltic Republics.[91]

Meanwhile, perestroika continued to run its course. On Gorbachev's recommendation, the Communist Party of the Soviet Union agreed to relinquish its monopoly on power within the USSR. Throughout 1990, competitive elections took place in all fifteen republics.[92] In July, Gorbachev proposed to transform the USSR, created by treaty in 1922, into a Union of Sovereign States, handing over many powers to the Soviet republics themselves. His project gained traction, and an agreement was signed with nine of the fifteen republics on April 23, 1991.[93]

Gorbachev was, however, engaged in a very difficult balancing act as he tried to restructure the Soviet Union (*perestroika* literally means "restructuring"). This difficulty was, in fact, more or less the same as that faced by reformist tsars before him, but it was even more complex, with at least four unknowns operating at the same time. The first two were the well-known unknowns of Russian history: on one flank, the diehard conservatives (in this case, members of the communist nomenklatura), who persisted with a sullen resistance that threatened to degenerate into a coup d'état, and, on

the other extreme, the aggressive factions that sought a change of pace un-
attainable by the state—like the misguided Decembrists who plotted against
Alexander I in 1825 or the murderous anarchists of later decades who risked
plunging Russia into disorder. Third, one could, of course, never exclude an
unknown unknown, posed by some outsider group bidding its time in the
shadows, as the Bolsheviks did in October 1917. But the fourth and most
consequential unknown was how ethnic separatisms, which had already
caused the disintegration of tsarist Russia and the Civil War (1917–1922),
would play out again if things went wrong. The unifying ideology of communism had, with conviction or terror, managed to cement the outer rims
of the empire back into place in the 1920s, which fully restored the USSR's
integrity. (Stalin completed the edifice in 1945.) Those lateral forces, nevertheless, had never been eliminated; they were only being kept in check. In
sum, Gorbachev realized that the cement made up of ideological certainties
had weakened over the decades and that his necessary questioning of their
continued relevance had weakened it further. One shock too much before
the restructuration work was completed, and the whole edifice could come
crashing down—or, perhaps, it would suddenly give way on its own. No
one could know for sure.

A singular chain of events, in which successive groups attempted to grab
power only to be outflanked by others, led to that collapse. It started in August 1991, when hardline members of the Communist Party, led by Gennady Ivanovich Yanayev, staged a military putsch in Moscow in the time-
honored soviet manner—with tank battalions invading the capital. The
military placed Gorbachev, who was spending his summer holidays in
Crimea, under house arrest. In reaction, Muscovites confronted the rebels'
tanks. In the midst of this turmoil, the ambitious president of the Soviet Russian Republic, Boris Yeltsin, saw an opportunity and climbed onto a halted
tank to harangue the population.[94] Yeltsin, who had a personal grudge
against Gorbachev for opposing his election, hoped to replace him at the
head of the Soviet Union. Yeltsin did not account for secessionist pressures,
however. The leaders of Ukraine and Belarus realized that this power vacuum
represented a now-or-never opportunity for independence: they stepped in
and demanded the dissolution of the USSR. On December 8, 1991, Yeltsin
met with their leaders and signed an agreement that denounced the Treaty

on the Creation of the Soviet Union (1922) and established a new Common-wealth of Independent States (CIS).[95] Without realizing it, Yeltsin thus found the most radical means to oust his rival from power: knocking down the Soviet Union, leaving him as the de facto leader of Russia. He could have claimed for himself the maxim coined by Madame de Pompadour and later taken up by the Russian nihilists, *après moi, le déluge* ("after me, the flood").[96]

The preamble to the Agreement establishing the CIS described "attach-ment to the aims and principles of the Charter of the United Nations, the Final Act of Helsinki and other documents of the OSCE" and their com-mitment "to respect international treaties on human rights and the rights of the peoples," by asserting independence instead of sovereignty, and com-munity instead of union. By mid-December 1991, all the former republics of the Soviet Union had declared independence.

This creation of the CIS had the character of a revolution, rather than a peace process. The CIS was a severe blow to Gorbachev's own project for a Union of Sovereign States. This new "Commonwealth," a vague notion that existed mostly on paper, was not going to replace the ancient Soviet order with a new consensual one that would settle national and territorial issues. With the exception of the Federation of Russia (which inherited the Soviet nuclear arsenal), several of the new republics from the outset were crippled states and de facto vassals, unable to steer their development independently from Moscow. From that point on, the move to the CIS was hardly a peaceful change. As soon as free elections were allowed to take place, the Communist Party lost in six republics. Nationalist clashes broke out in the territories located on the southern and central Asian fringes of the former USSR—Georgia, Tajikistan, Uzbekistan, Azerbaijan, and Moldova—where the risk of balkanization had always been high.

On December 26, Gorbachev stepped down, giving a fateful speech ac-knowledging the fait accompli. He referred to the age-old political problem of Russia—the fierce struggle against opponents of change—which he cor-rectly described as "reactionary forces," a term hitherto reserved in the So-viet Union for those who had *opposed* the orthodoxy of the Communist Party. "The change ran up against our intolerance, a low level of political culture and fear of change. That is why we have wasted so much time. The old system fell apart even before the new system began to work. As a result, the societal crisis worsened."[97]

The fatal blow had come, however, from those who were impatient for change, expecting it to occur very quickly, and who advocated radical action—even if that meant a headlong rush forward: "I'm aware that there is popular resentment as a result of today's grave situation. I note that authority at all levels, [including] myself, are being subject to harsh criticisms. I would like to stress once again, though, that cardinal change in so vast a country, given its heritage, could not have been carried out without difficulties, shock, and pain."[98]

Gorbachev's speech, acknowledging the dissolution of the Soviet Empire, evoked earlier abdications by Francis II of the Holy Roman Empire in 1806 and Charles I of Austria-Hungary in 1918, which were similar in breadth and consequences. As mentioned, the new Commonwealth of Independent States was a loose association that had little in common with the former superpower. The Russian Federation was able to emerge from the rubble in triumph, taking the seat of the former Soviet Union at the UN Security Council. The CIS and the Russian "sphere of influence" then became, for all intents and purposes, the same thing. After the collapse, the foundations of a new, smaller, and more concentrated Russian state were laid—one that might someday still grow in size.

Gorbachev remains a controversial figure. He might have decided to relinquish Soviet control over its Eastern European satellites not because of noble sentiments, but from a determination to salvage the core territorial assets of the Soviet Union—all fifteen Soviet republics, including those forcibly acquired by Stalin between 1939 and 1945. After the three Baltic Republics declared independence in the spring of 1990, Gorbachev in the following January issued an ultimatum urging Lithuania to recognize Soviet rule. The Red Army intervened in Vilnius, leading to the death of 14 civilians and injuring 700 others.[99] That same month, he sent troops to Baku to restore Soviet rule, only three months after Azerbaijan declared independence on September 23, 1989: "Black January" resulted in more than a hundred civilian deaths. Gorbachev later called this latest incursion the "gravest mistake of [his] career."[100] Ukraine's population also protested during that same month. On January 22, 1990, its citizens created their own human chain nearly 500 kilometers long, which stretched across Kyiv, Lviv, and Ivano-Frankivsk. Finally, in August 1991, all three Baltic Republics joined Ukraine as member states of the United Nations General Assembly.

Clearly, Gorbachev's policies were dictated more by pragmatism than by emotion or dogmatic ideology. In his 1990 acceptance speech for the Nobel Peace Prize, he said it should be awarded to "*perestroika* and modern thinking."[101] This was his strongest statement that the principles governing both his foreign policy (making peace in the Cold War) and his domestic reforms were actually two sides of the same coin: one could simply not be understood without the other. His failure to create a union of sovereign states was a good illustration of the principle expressed by Tolstoy in *War and Peace*—events do not always follow the hopes of those trying to steer them.

Arguments whether the end of the Cold War should be considered a victory by the United States—either as a military power or as a torchbearer of American liberalism—or as due to Gorbachev's bold moves are moot because those two arguments operate on different planes: war and peace. If the strategic purpose of the economically superior United States in the Cold War had been to bring the Soviet Union's economy to its knees by fostering an arms race, then it had unequivocally scored a victory against its archenemy. Gorbachev had, however, already vowed to cease waging war and was in a spirit of peacemaking. The orderly withdrawal of the Red Army from Eastern Europe and the lifting of the Iron Curtain were the result of a deliberate order of retreat issued by the Soviet premier himself. The Warsaw Pact's armored divisions of 1989 still had an ample supply of tanks, men, and ammunition to implement a massive repression, and then another, more conservative Soviet leader might have succeeded in "restoring the peace," though not without a high human cost. Gorbachev clearly opted to exercise restraint.

That the collapse of the Soviet Union dovetailed with the US arms race strategy is thus logical within the cascading chain of events. After decades of Soviet economic mismanagement, the events initially triggered by the conservatives' 1991 coup precipitated the disaster. Reagan's attempt to weaken the Soviet Union through a renewed arms race in the early 1980s was no longer necessary; it was even counterproductive, because it pushed the Germans into the arms of Gorbachev and reinforced his commitment to perestroika. Reagan's inopportune rearmament policies against the Soviet Union drove a painful wedge between the United States and its European allies, which would later widen as years went on.[102]

Gorbachev's grandiose plan of a Union of Sovereign States envisioned it being part of the common European home, but that never came to pass. Whether this failure should be attributed to the various events that led to his ouster, which in turn freed the lateral separatist forces that finally brought the Soviet Union down, or whether the new edifice would have inevitably fallen apart even without these forces, we can never know. Certainly, US leaders were almost entirely blind to Gorbachev's program because of their Cold War tunnel vision. They thus did not take the pragmatic option that had dictated the policies of European great powers of the nineteenth century toward the Ottoman Empire, "the sick man of Europe": that a living Soviet Union in peace would have been a better bargain than the chaos of a vanquished and dismembered Soviet bloc. In addition, Western European states were too focused on their own problems to give political support to the embattled Soviet leader. From the perspective of the engineering of peace, we are left in awe at the daring spirit of perestroika that attempted to build this new structure but also in dismay at its ultimate wreckage.

For Russia itself, the post-1990 period under Boris Yeltsin is remembered as an era of economic chaos, political turmoil, corruption, and national humiliation—perhaps similar to the feelings of the German populace in the aftermath of the Versailles Treaty.[103] The decision to expand NATO across Central and Eastern Europe may not have been intended to impugn Russian national honor or to arouse revanchism, but those were its unintended consequences. In the US government's conduct of its relations with Russia in the post–Cold War period, there was a lack of compassion of a kind that both Roosevelt and Eisenhower had carefully guarded against in their dealings with Germany after World War II.

In fact, if any country deserves credit for "defeating" the Soviet Union in the Cold War, it was probably the Federal Republic of Germany—albeit in the most peaceful sense. The gleaming prosperity of this once-devastated country forced Soviet leaders to ask for financial help and drove the leaders of the Eastern bloc states to despair. It visibly demonstrated the failure of communist ideology, which may have hastened its end. The Paris Charter for a New Europe confirmed the victory of the peacemakers over the older "hard-nosed realists," Soviet and American alike, who had strived for decades to maintain the balance of power and could not break out of that mindset.

The unexpected collapse of Gorbachev's Soviet Union while in the last stages of transforming itself into a new "Union of Sovereign States" was not good news for the cause of peace. A permanent reconciliation of Russia with Europe and the United States would have provided an opportunity to secure lasting peace in the post–Cold War era—albeit without reference to the rising Chinese superpower—but it failed to take place. The authoritarian order of the Soviet Union was replaced by an anarchy of mutually hostile successor states.

In the absence of settlement treaties, civil wars and border clashes inevitably occurred, conveniently masking Russian "occupation without occupation" in the former republics of Moldova, Georgia, and Ukraine, all in the "interest of peace" and a "responsibility to protect."[104] The disproportionality of the Russian Federation forces compared to those of its neighbors was obvious and all too reminiscent of Prussia vis-à-vis its neighbors after its victory against Austria in 1866. The low standards of living in Belarus made for a sharp contrast to the economic renaissance in the neighboring Baltic Republics; similarly, the wealth differential between the richer villages on the Romanian and Moldovan sides of the Prut River was signaled by the large number of abandoned homes and the absence of lighting and paved streets in Moldova. Three decades after the end of communism, belonging to the Russian sphere of influence has not brought the same economic prosperity enjoyed by the rest of Europe.[105]

Thus, the founding treaty of the CIS, which was neither a peace treaty nor a territorial settlement, was the precursor to frozen conflicts that precluded economic development. Since its inception, this political sphere has become—in Saint-Pierre's terms—a system of war, albeit a defective one, in which no regional alliance has been able to restore a balance of power with Russia. The successor states to the Soviet Union, irresistibly attracted by the promise of immediate independence, were invited to a political game that only the Russian Federation could win in the long run. In the former Soviet republics, the Spirit of an Enlarged Europe under Gorbachev was thus as short as the bloom of an arctic summer. One can only speculate what kind of a system of peace might have emerged if those states had instead joined an orderly Union of Sovereign States under his guiding hand.

Maastricht and the Last Glimmers of the Postwar European Spirit

Turning to the western core of the European Communities, it seemed that the Abbé de Saint-Pierre's dream of a European Union was about to materialize, made possible by German reunification. Intensive negotiations opened in Rome in December 1990, two months after the ink was dry on the Final Settlement Treaty with Respect to Germany. The frail and incomplete institutions of the EEC would never have been able to withstand the strain of the enlargement that Poland and Czechoslovakia demanded in exchange for German reunification. Even though the Autumn of Nations was the trigger, the project of a continent-wide union had been in the works in Western Europe for decades: it was the result of the gestation of the Postwar European Spirit, conceived in the 1950s.

The first official joining together of the two words "European" and "Union" was in the declaration of the heads of state at the Paris Summit of the EEC in October 1972, which included the three newcomers at the time: Britain, Ireland, and Denmark. The participants announced their plan "to transform before the end of the present decade the whole complex of their relations into a European Union," a new entity endowed with sufficient personality to matter in world affairs:

> The construction of Europe will allow it, in conformity with its ultimate political objectives, to affirm its personality while remaining faithful to its traditional friendships and to the alliances of the Member States, and to establish its position in world affairs as a distinct entity determined to promote a better international equilibrium, respecting the principles of the Charter of the United Nations.[106]

The signatories reasserted their determination to achieve "economic and monetary union" by the end of the 1970s. The years came and went, but on June 19, 1983—still in the Cold War era—the ten heads of state, joined by Greece, finally signed a Solemn Declaration on European Union in Stuttgart, Germany. Based on a plan drafted by the foreign ministers of West Germany and Italy, Hans-Dietrich Genscher and Emilio Colombo respectively, and anchored in "an awareness of a common destiny and the wish to affirm European identity," the declaration committed to progress toward a "closer union among the peoples and member states of the European Community."[107] The two words "European" and "Union" appeared together only in the title of this declaration, however; in truth, they still referred to the *process* of uniting Europe, not to a hypothetical political institution called the "European Union." Indeed, the opening sentences of the preamble declared that pursuing the European construction to create a "united Europe" was "more than ever necessary in order to meet the dangers of the world situation."[108] The rest of the text was programmatic and conceptual, referring to the institutions of the European Community—the European Council, the Parliament, the Commission, and the Court of Justice—in highly technical language focused on economic issues.

Significantly, however, the preamble expressed the conviction that "by speaking with a single voice in foreign policy, including political aspects of security, Europe can contribute to the preservation of peace."[109] This was in the context of an intensified arms race prompted by President Reagan, the deployment of US and Soviet nuclear missiles in Europe, the escalation of conflicts around the world and, in response, a surge in antiwar movements. The previous year, 1982, Britain—an EEC member state—had engaged in the Falklands War (the Malvinas War) in the South Atlantic against Argentina. That year also saw massive pacifist demonstrations against nuclear weapons, both in Europe and the United States (one million people demonstrated in New York City on June 12). In the early 1980s, there was also increasing frustration in several Western European countries, where many felt as if they were being treated as pawns in the geostrategic game between the two superpowers.[110] They sought to reassert their sovereignty, no longer as strictly independent nations—because that would have been futile—but rather as interdependent parts of a European collective. Political loyalty was slowly shifting, at least among European elites, from the nation-state toward a supranational entity. The declaration was not yet a treaty, however, and the legislative bodies of the respective countries were not called to ratify it.

There was, however, little the EEC and its members could do about the US-Soviet confrontation. The only sensible course of action was to accept their helplessness as a fait accompli and to work on a long-term plan for a European Union, through which the member states would be in a position, one day, to defend their interests more effectively. As a sign of the times, the declaration's language made an unqualified reference to Europe, not as a "Community" or "Union" but as the subject of a sentence: "*Europe* can contribute to the preservation of peace."[111] This was one of the first manifestations of the major semantic shift that would occur over the next decade: from "Europe" referring only to a geographical or a cultural entity to designating it a political body and a social entity. This was a bold prospect, considering that the EEC was still confined to representing Western Europe and that it would not have been able to stand up militarily to the Soviet Union had it not been under the US umbrella. For better or worse, the EEC seemed to be sentenced to being a Western European system of peace encased in a global system of war.

Nevertheless, the Solemn Declaration on European Union was followed by action. Altiero Spinelli, an elected member of the European Parliament, was assigned the task of preparing a Draft Treaty Establishing the European Union. Spinelli had already made his name in June 1941 while imprisoned in an Italian Fascist jail, where he had co-authored the *Ventotene Manifesto* in favor of a United Europe; shortly after the war, he was one of the founding members of the federalist movement. His wartime manifesto argued that political union and direct elections for a European parliament should *precede* economic union. This approach had run contrary to precepts of the ECSC in 1950 and was sidelined. Now, Spinelli felt, he could bring his original idea back.[112]

On February 14, 1984, the European Parliament adopted a Draft Treaty Establishing the European Union (also known as the Spinelli Draft or Spinelli Plan), with a view to bringing about a redefinition of European institutions. The text established the concept of the "European Union," a union provided with legal personality and one that introduced the concept of union citizenship and the principle of subsidiarity. Its preamble retained the idea of a "European identity," democracy, and the rule of law from the earlier Solemn Declaration. It also acknowledged "the need to enable local and regional authorities to participate by appropriate methods in the unification of Europe."[113]

Unfortunately, the European construction's method had not been dictated by opinion but by necessity. Spinelli's plan met the same fate as the campaigners for a Federal Europe had with the Council of Europe in 1948: the member states of the EEC were not ready for this step, and the draft treaty was withdrawn by the governments of the member states. Back at the negotiating table, the member states of the EEC returned to the tried-and-true Schuman method of examining whatever worked and letting the form emerge as an afterthought. In February 1986, they signed a more conservative treaty, the Single European Act, which amended the Treaty of Rome; all twelve members ratified it, including two newcomers, Spain and Portugal. Referring to the Solemn Declaration signed in Stuttgart, the new preamble resolved to implement the European Union and promote its values, notably "freedom, equality and social justice."[114] Signaling the ambient frustration with the Cold War, it expressed the states' desire to speak "with one voice" so as to "contribute to the preservation of international peace and security." It also restated the members' aim to create a monetary union, which would facilitate the emergence of a single market.[115]

The Single European Act merged several preexisting treaties into one document; in particular, it gave an institutional basis to the European Council (composed of the heads of state or government of member states), to which it introduced the principle of majority rule. This was a crucial change, since the European Community's existing "unanimity rule" had meant that any member state could veto any decision—a policy that, as demonstrated by the Security Council of the UN, could result in institutional paralysis. The new treaty also proposed concrete measures for establishing a "European Single Market" of twelve countries by 1993.[116]

The Autumn of Nations accelerated movement toward the European Union. On December 14–15, 1990, two weeks after Helmut Kohl's electrifying speech on German reunification, a special European Council meeting was held in Rome.[117] The German government eagerly pushed for monetary union and an internal market, while the British were more reluctant. What was emerging was an "expansion project" of the European construction: a second and bigger edifice taking shape beside the existing one of the EEC. The new Treaty on the European Union (TEU), aka the Treaty of Maastricht, was signed on February 7, 1992, in that town in the Netherlands; it would come into effect on November 1 the following year. The original Treaty of Rome of 1957 remained in force and was relabeled Treaty on the Functioning of the European Union (TFEU). Maastricht, a quaint dormant Catholic town in an otherwise Protestant Netherlands, was selected for its location in the "European strip" between Germany and France. [118]

The word "peace" appeared only twice in the Maastricht Treaty (the famous statement "the Union's aim is to promote peace . . ." appeared as an amendment, with the Treaty of Lisbon in 2007). Nevertheless, the preamble referred to its opposite, the Cold War, by stressing "the historic importance of the ending of the division of the European continent and the need to create firm bases for the construction of the future Europe."[119] The intention of incorporating East Germany and other countries of the former communist bloc into a new European peace system could not have been clearer. One of the treaty's innovations was that "every person holding the nationality of a Member State shall be a citizen of the Union."[120] Through this provision, the new EU was establishing a direct connection to individuals themselves, over the heads of government. Importantly, Title V, "Common Foreign and Security Policy," resolved "to implement a common foreign and security policy including the eventual framing of a common defense policy, which might in time lead to a common defense, thereby reinforcing the European identity and its independence in order to promote peace, security and progress in Europe and in the world."[121] Simply put, the creation of a unified military force was envisioned as a necessary step to defend this peace system; the Cold War was over, yet the signatories admitted that their attempt to establish perpetual peace in Europe was not a sufficient guarantee by itself against future intimidation or aggression by a foreign power.

Yet the development of a common foreign and security policy remained at an embryonic stage; debate centered on whether Europe could do without NATO and its US commander-in-chief. Title V, however, did include a commitment "to safeguard the common values, fundamental interests and independence of the Union," as well as "to preserve peace and strengthen international security."[122] Even though the signatories realized that the balance of power was still the predominant political doctrine outside Europe, the language of the treaty framed its objective of peace and security "in accordance with the principles of the United Nations Charter, the Helsinki Final Act and the objectives of the Paris Charter."[123] Clearly, the leaders of the newly founded EU still saw themselves in the same world order that was forged after World War II, but as amended by the end of the Cold War and by the drive of the former Eastern bloc countries toward democracy.

Popular culture reflected the sense of living in historic times. In 1990, the winning song of the 35th Eurovision Song Contest was *Insieme: 1992* (Together: 1992) by the popular Italian singer, Totò Cutugno: "With you, so far and different / With you, friend I thought lost / You and I, under the same dream / Together, *unite, unite Europe*" (the italicized words were sung in English).[124] Music fans did not take Cutugno's lyrics as a political slogan but understood his message as an emotional need for solidarity between diverse peoples, especially of the younger generation. Since 1987 the popular Erasmus program—which enabled students to pursue part of their studies at a university in a different European Community state—had reflected this desire for cross-border collaboration and cooperation. Meanwhile, the cheerful opening fanfare of the European Broadcasting Union—first used in 1953 (copied from the *Te Deum* by French Marc-Antoine Charpentier, which he composed for the peace treaty of Turin of 1696) and always played at the Eurovision song contests—remained a household tune across the continent, a symbol of "peaceful togetherness" in popular culture.[125]

It was no coincidence that, in 1992, the English classical composer Tony Britten wrote a new anthem for the Champions League of the Union of European Football Associations (UEFA), complete with a choir, inspired by Georg Friedrich Handel's "Coronation Anthem" of *Zadok the Priest*. The multilingual lyrics ("*Ce sont les meilleures équipes / Es sind die allerbesten Mannschaften / The main event*") are best described as "macaronic," but they perfectly captured the delight of young Europeans in their rediscovery of expanded cultural diversity on the Continent. The anthem was an instant hit and maintains cult status even to this day. It spawned countless remakes, a sociologically significant fact given that football has long had an element of public ritual in Europe.[126] In the 1990s, as in the early hours of the Postwar Spirit in the 1950s, and as at the Peace of Utrecht in 1713, the majestic tones of Baroque music continued to provide a surefire recipe for "communion music" endowed with gravitas and a sense of the occasion, thanks to their ability to transport the imaginations of young Europeans from every corner of the continent.[127]

A Striking Difference of Spirits

For those still entertaining doubts that the Iron Curtain had been the dam blocking the eastward expansion of the European construction, evidence confirming this premise soon came pouring in. Austria, Finland, and Sweden, which had hitherto served as buffer states between the Western and Soviet blocs, all applied for membership in the EU between 1989 and 1991 and became full members on January 1, 1995. All three were members of EFTA but wanted to increase their economic integration with the European bloc. Too close to the Eastern bloc for their own comfort, they had stayed out of the European integration process to avoid angering the Soviet Union. They were more or less forced to maintain neutrality during the Cold War and thus had not sought membership in NATO.

In addition to its "enlargement" to the east, the European Union also sought a "deepening," a closer integration of the member states. One of its ambitions was to create a single space for the free circulation of people, capital, goods, and services. The solution came from outside the European framework: the Schengen Agreement between France, Germany, and the Benelux countries, signed in 1985, aimed to create a "Schengen Area" for the borderless movement of peoples. Yet again, it was signed on the same "European peace strip" that had been the hallmark of the Postwar European Spirit: this time, on a boat in the Moselle River—at the meeting point of France, Luxemburg, and Germany—close to the village of Schengen in Luxembourg. The implementation process dragged on for five years, but it received a welcome impetus from the Autumn of Nations. In 1990, the same

ATLANTIC
OCEAN

*North
Sea*

50°

ICELAND
1949
Reykyavik

IRELAND
Dublin

Edinburgh

UNITED
KINGDOM
1949
Left the EU in 2020
London

The Hague
NETHERLANDS
1949

Brussels
BELGIUM
1949

Paris

FRANCE
1949

NORWAY
1949
Oslo

SWEDE

DENMARK
1949
Copenhag

Berlin
GERMANY
United 1990
1955

L.
1949

LIECHTENSTEIN

Bern
SWITZ.

1999
Pra
CZECH R

Vien
AUSTR

SLOVEN
Ljubljana
2004
Zagr

ITALY
1949

MONACO

SAN
MARINO

2009
CROAT

PORTUGAL
Lisbon
1949

SPAIN
Madrid
1982

ANDORRA

Corsica

Sardinia

BOSI
HERZEGOVI
Rome

MONTENEC

Mediterranean Sea

Sicily

MALT

MOROCCO

ALGERIA

TUNISIA

40°
10°

30°

0   500 km

0   500 miles

0°

10°

Europe after the Maastricht Treaty, 1992

Founding members of the European Union (EU)

Members of the EU, 2020

○ Members of the European Free Trade Agreement (EFTA)

— Former western border of USSR

Members of the Commonwealth of Independent States (CIS)

☆ Former members of the Warsaw Pact

◇ Date of NATO accession

FINLAND
Helsinki
St Petersburg
Stockholm
Tallinn
ESTONIA ◇
2004
LATVIA
Riga ◇
◇ 2004   2004
LITHUANIA
Vilnius
R.F.
◇
1999
LAND
☆ Warsaw
Minsk
BELARUS
Moscow
Kiev
UKRAINE
RUSSIAN FEDERATION
Donbass
OVAKIA 2004
ava
◇ 1999
Budapest
NGARY
☆
MOLDOVA
Transnistria
◇
2004
ROMANIA
☆
Crimea
Belgrade
ajevo
Bucharest
SERBIA
Black Sea
Abkhazia
S. Ossetia
GEORGIA
ARMENIA
◇ 2017
☆
BULGARIA
Sofia ◇
2004
◇ 2009
ALBANIA   REP. OF MACEDONIA
Skopje
Istanbul
Ankara
GREECE
◇
1952
Athens
T U R K E Y
◇
1952
SYRIA
Nicosia
CYPRUS   LEBANON
IRAQ
ISRAEL
JORDAN
SAUDI ARABIA

countries undersigned a "Convention Implementing the Schengen Agreement," a technical document that outlined the responsibilities of the member states. It abolished checks on persons at the borders between these countries while reinforcing controls on the outer borders.[128] It was a big step forward in the creation of a borderless space, which started with the relinquishing of border controls and continued with the disappearance of the checkpoints themselves, which were replaced by simple road signs. Driving from Berlin to Paris became no more difficult than a trip from Philadelphia to New York.

To realize the aim of establishing a monetary union as agreed in the Treaty of Maastricht, the European Council met in December 1995 in Madrid and hammered out a two-phase plan. On January 1, 1999, there was the "changeover" to the European Currency Unit, which remained a pure accounting currency, while national currencies were still in circulation.[129] By January 1, 2002, when private bank accounts were officially expressed in Euros and banknotes and coins were issued, citizens had already had three years to get used to the idea, and the common currency was a fait accompli. The seat of the new European Central Bank (ECB) was set, quite symbolically, in Frankfurt, the financial capital of Germany and the seat of the German Federal Bank. Unfortunately, its implementation was punctuated by some characteristic horse-trading. When a majority of states put forward a Dutch central banker to head the ECB, the French government retorted that, because Germany had been selected as the seat of the institution, it was only fair to France that the head of the new bank should be a French individual. In the end it was agreed the Dutch candidate would stand down after five years, to be replaced by a French banker. The European Spirit notwithstanding, France and Germany were still more equal than other nations in the Eurozone.[130]

The name "Euro" was chosen for the new currency, because it was spelled and read almost the same way in the languages of all the EU member states, even in Greek script. The new currency immediately became a colossus on the world financial scene, just behind the US dollar, as if to prove the point that Europe now earned and controlled its own "pocket money."[131] The monetary union, however, had a rather unorthodox mode of governance. The Eurozone, as a supranational aggregate, was not the EU, much less a centralized state. Its member states retained full control of their own budgets, which did not bode well for the whole system if one of them failed to respect the standards of financial discipline. The United Kingdom, which held to its pound sterling, remained conspicuously absent from this process.[132]

The populations of Western Europe were not always enthusiastic about the European construction process of the 1990s, perhaps because some of their greatest ills had already been cured; they enjoyed relatively high living conditions and rarely heard about European-wide institutions except during important events or when something went wrong. One such case was the collapse of the Northwest Atlantic cod populations in 1992, an ecological disaster in Newfoundland that started a disastrous chain reaction for European fisheries. In February 1994, in the French city of Rennes, a violent street battle took place between 5,000 angry fishermen and riot police, causing a disastrous fire at one of the region's most important architectural landmarks, the Parliament of Brittany. This episode resulted in a great deal of negative press that was very critical of the EU administration in Brussels.[133] But for all the failings attributed to it, including the aloofness and impersonality of its bureaucracy, the EU remained, on the whole, a benevolent force: in 1999, a European Charter of Human Rights was passed, which was included in the EU's legal and institutional framework.

By the early twenty-first century, the Postwar European Spirit was breathing its last. The Schengen Agreements were a success—after Switzerland joined in 2005, one could drive from Copenhagen to Rome through the Gotthard Pass without showing a passport—and the Euro was a staple of the world's money markets. Yet public enthusiasm for the EU was no longer there. In Italy, for instance, trust in it was compromised by massive price increases occurring after introduction of the Euro, while the media became obsessed with a new national bogeyman, "the Spread": a percentage that showed how much higher was the interest rate that the Italian government paid on bonds than that paid by Germany.[134] There was a good reason why this episode in the European pursuit of peace seemed slightly less exalted than others—it was lacking zest. There was much lamenting about a "democratic deficit," a feeling of alienation from the bureaucratic elites in Brussels and even from the elected European Parliament.[135] Yet the root cause of the ill was located elsewhere: just one decade after Maastricht, the West was suffering from a chronic deficit of peace spirit. Were the buildings in the European district of Brussels becoming empty shells, holding a political body without a soul?

The contrast with the still energetic Spirit of Enlarged Europe was all the more striking. On the first day of January 2004, fifteen years after the Autumn of Nations, the fifth and largest enlargement in the history of the European Union took place. This moment, when the European construction finally moved beyond the former Iron Curtain, was the highwater mark of the Enlarged European Spirit. The preparatory work had started a decade earlier, with all the countries involved submitting their applications for accession between 1994 and 1996. The ten newcomers formed three groups. The Central European countries included the Czech Republic and Slovakia, the successor states to Czechoslovakia, Hungary, and Poland. The second group consisted of the Baltic Republics, which had left the Soviet bloc and resolutely turned to the West. The final group comprised countries farther south: Slovenia, Malta, and Cyprus. The rates of approval in the referenda were stunning: they ranged from two-thirds in Latvia to more than 90 percent in Slovakia and Lithuania. Television footage of the popular celebrations showed the relief, pride, and hopes of officials and citizens in the new member countries.[136]

In comparison to those explosions of joy, both the media and public opinion in the existing member countries appeared rather dispassionate. A cultural gap made it difficult for most Western Europeans to put themselves in the shoes of newcomers who had lived under political and economic duress for decades behind the Iron Curtain.[137] "Enlargement" was not a very accurate description of the rise of the European Spirit as it evolved in the 1990s. This expansion was accepted with some reluctance because it evolved organically, rather than from any conscious plan. It looked as if the countries of Central and Eastern Europe had seized the European peace spirit, uprooting it and planting it farther east. In any case, the idea that the European Union was built in the East without popular backing is incorrect: given voters' overwhelming support for joining, the EU arguably possessed greater democratic legitimacy than any previous continental formation on the planet. But it was one thing to liberate the ex-members of the Warsaw Pact; it was quite another to integrate them fully into a *Pax Europeana*.

In particular, reuniting the economically successful West Germany with its poorer communist counterpart was not an easy task. Tearing down the Berlin Wall was not enough to enable Germany to become a single space with free circulation; much additional work was needed to erase the Cold War's "Inner Border" from the minds of the population.[138] As noted earlier, the Christian Democrat Party emerged as the dominant political formation in East Germany, just as had been the case in West Germany after 1945. The economic reforms did not, however, satisfy everyone. In 1998, after the Social Democratic Party emerged victorious, Gerhard Schröder replaced Helmut Kohl as chancellor. (Kohl's fall was hastened by financial scandals that rocked the Christian Democratic Party.) After more than forty years of separation, profound differences persisted in the economic, social, and political structures of the two sides. The most consequential was that the eastern part had lower standards of living, obsolete infrastructure, high unemployment, a failed pension system, and widespread corruption. Its factories, unable to compete with their Western counterparts, often went bankrupt and were abandoned.[139] Few images illustrate this contrast better than the archaic Trabant cars, once the pride of the communist regime, lumbering in 1989 on the Western German autobahns and trying to get out of the way of Audis, BMWs, and Mercedes. Well into the first decade of the twenty-first century, citizens in East Germany had less disposable income and higher unemployment rates than their Western counterparts. The reconstruction of Berlin, once again the capital, was particularly significant in both a practical and a symbolic sense, yet the gap between the two parts of the city are still visible from outer space by the difference in the color and intensity of street lighting.[140]

More broadly, the four decades of political and economic alignment with the two superpowers help explain why the nations of both Eastern and Western Europe took the step of reasserting their sovereignty through merging into a single bloc. After the collapse of the Eastern bloc, movement toward European unification for once ran ahead of what most of the actors had envisioned; the trajectory from the Europe of twelve member states in the late 1980s to the Europe of the twenty-eight states of 2013 was dictated more by sheer momentum than by premeditation.[141] The Spirit of Enlarged Europe had sprung from the grassroots, not from any "grand plan," and was thus more emotional than intellectual. Its greatest legacy was in the newly admitted states of the EU: their increased political independence and freedom to circulate and to establish new lives in another country helped defuse irredentist claims based on ethnicity.[142] Yet sadly, the Spirit of Enlarged Europe was never able to revive the Postwar European Spirit.

Shockwaves in Southeastern Europe

Southeastern Europe had been involved in the Fifty Years' War along with the rest of the Continent, though in its own fashion. After the defeat of the Third Reich in 1945, these lands drifted into the Soviet Union's sphere of influence. Historically, the region had belonged to the cultural basin of Constantinople and the Eastern Roman Empire in the Middle Ages; they were called Rumelia ("Land of the Romans") under Ottoman rule. In the eighteenth and nineteenth centuries, many Slavs, Romanians, and Greeks turned to either Russia or Austria in an effort to achieve greater political autonomy and improved material conditions. Their lands became notorious as the Balkans, so famous for fragmentation and division—and later the flashpoint of the Great War of 1914—that the word "balkanization" still conjures up images of ancient hatreds and conflict. As early as the first decades of the twentieth century—before Soviet domination—local elites began considering southeastern Europe's "lag with the West," which was most apparent in its lack of economic development, especially in the countryside.[143]

An angry "Spirit of the Balkans," however, was also living in the rugged mountains of this region, and the birth of new states was accompanied by the aptly named "Balkan Wars" (1912–1913) that devastated the region. This spirit could be metaphorically connected to the Greek goddess Lyssa (Latin, Ira), the daughter of the night, who liked to seep into the dreams of political rulers and whisper guileful ideas that led them down the paths of tyranny and doom.[144] To complicate matters further, the Treaty of Trianon, a product of the Paris Conference of 1919, abruptly reassigned some of the territories of *Mitteleuropa* (Central Europe) to the southeast: Slovenia, wedged between Italy and Austria, was united with the kingdom of Yugoslavia, and Transylvania was made part of Romania and henceforth shared its destiny. Both Slovenia and Transylvania, even though their populations shared the same language as their neighbors, were molded by a different history and suffered from a love–hate relationship with their new host states.[145]

On the eve of the great turning point of 1989, southeastern Europe comprised six states: Yugoslavia, Albania, Romania, Bulgaria, Greece, and Turkey (but only East Thrace, on the left side of the Straits). All but Greece and European Turkey were communist led. Their outlier status had everything to do with their location on the Bosphorus: Britain and the United States had determined, as a result of the Yalta Agreements, to anchor those two countries in the "Western Bloc" to prevent the Soviet Union from gaining access to the Mediterranean Sea.[146]

The four southeastern communist countries fundamentally differed in one way from their Central and Eastern European cousins: not all their political leaders were the products of the kind of nomenklatura that could be found in Poland or Czechoslovakia. They were undisputed autocrats with long political careers, a modern version of warrior chieftains from the Balkan Wars. In this part of Europe, therefore, the fall of communism was as much a relief as elsewhere, but it was not synonymous with a return to peace.[147] On the contrary, it rekindled the strife of interminable nationalistic rifts reaching back to the Yalta Conference, the Treaty of Trianon, and even to the Balkan Wars. The 1989 revolutionary wave and its immediate aftermath seemed to repeat the horrific scenes of exodus, murder, and violence that the region had experienced in the past.

Bulgaria's leader Todor Hristov Zhivkov, in power since 1954, had been steadfast in his allegiance to Moscow and refused to support Gorbachev's perestroika. Since 1984, Zhivkov had pursued a policy of forced ethnic assimilation, cynically called the "Process of Rebirth," which forbade the Turkish minority in Bulgaria from practicing their customs, religions, and language.[148] In May 1989, responding to the freedom movements of that year, Zhivkov "granted permission" to the Turks to leave the country. This act led to a forceful expulsion of 360,000 Turks and other Muslims from Bulgaria—a disgraceful spectacle that even ardent communists hoped never to see again after Stalin's death.[149] However, it was not the expulsion of this minority that caused the demise of the country's regime, but its ill treatment of those progressives who pressed for reform. On November 10, Zhivkov was quietly ousted in a palace coup that brought in a more liberal regime and free elections. It was not, however, a clean break from the country's communist past: the nomenklatura remained in power for several more years.

In Romania, the word "revolution" took on a literal and brutal meaning. The leader Nicolae Ceauşescu had solidified his power through a cult of personality in a quasi-Stalinist regime but one not directly controlled by Moscow. In December 1989, protests against Ceauşescu by the Hungarian minority in Timişoara spiraled into a citywide revolt that transcended ethnicity. On December 21, Ceauşescu was delivering a public speech from a balcony overlooking a large square in Bucharest, when the crowd suddenly turned against the old dictator, who was left befuddled and petrified. The next day, the regime's security service responded with vigor—soldiers shot at a crowd of protesters, and a street battle ensued. Events then moved at lightning speed. His regime collapsed, and Ceauşescu was executed on December 25 after a short trial that was really a settling of scores. Meanwhile fierce infighting between forces loyal to the regime and insurgents continued, producing thousands of casualties.[150]

The more isolated communist regime of Albania avoided the wave of protests in 1989, but anticommunist revolts started early in the following year. After the seemingly indestructible Enver Hoxha died in 1985 after forty years in power, communist leader Ramiz Alia replaced him and started introducing reforms that actually helped the local Communist Party win elections in 1989. Albania signed the Helsinki Final Act agreement in September 1991. Despite doing so, strikes and protests led to the regime's collapse in 1992.[151]

All three of these countries—Bulgaria, Romania, and Albania—made the transition to multiparty politics, free elections, and a market economy. A particularly visible effect of that evolution was the explosion in the number of private cars, which rapidly choked cities that had never been designed for that mode of transportation. This dramatic increase in the number of private automobiles necessitated massive road renovations and other measures to alleviate urban congestion. Yet, these countries' lack of infrastructure, endemic corruption, and the shock of liberalization were obstacles to economic improvement. Most importantly, the people of these countries were not primarily motivated by a "return to Europe" but by the need to rebuild the state (starting by having free elections and reforms) and heal their own wounds. Continental unification was not their immediate concern. All three showed, however, the desire to raise their standards of living and to consolidate the rule of law, which the European Union was both willing and able to satisfy. It was no surprise when Romania and Bulgaria submitted their official applications for EU membership in 1995. In southeastern Europe, the Enlarged European Spirit blossomed, even if belatedly.[152]

About this same time, the shockwave of revolution reached Yugoslavia, giving new life to the angry Spirit of the Balkans. Josip Broz Tito, the charismatic founder of the Yugoslav postwar state, had died on May 8, 1980. Although communism still survived, his successors kept a mosaic of peoples together in a federal state—and in relative peace—while developing closer relations with the European Community. This was a mixed blessing: it provided increased opportunities for trade, but the collision between the inefficiencies of a Marxist system based on full employment with the market practices of Western Europe led to an increase in domestic prices. More seriously, the embers of nationalism were beginning to smolder again. As had been the case in the region since Ottoman rule, Yugoslavia's cultural landscape was fragmented, this time into four main groups: the Serbs, Croats, and Montenegrins; Slovenes; Macedonian Slavs; and Albanians, who had been established in the area since Antiquity. Layered on top of these ethnic divides were religious divisions: Catholic, Orthodox, and Muslim. After World War I, there was the hope that those populations, having escaped Austro-Hungarian and Ottoman domination, would finally experience peace and prosperity under the newly created Kingdom of Serbs, Croates, and Slovenes.[153] This hope proved overly optimistic. Resentments between the Serbs and Croats, in particular, started to flare up soon after the state's formation. During World War II, the rift increased when Nazi Germany set up an "independent" Croatia (1941–1945) as a puppet state, and the Ustaše official party engaged in the persecution and massacre of Serbs. During the postwar era, many Albanians from Kosovo moved to Albania and resented Tito's attempts to annex it.

In such a tense multiethnic, multireligious, and multistate environment— with the small state of Bosnia-Herzegovina being a microcosm of these differences—a strong will and an iron fist were indispensable to keeping the various centrifugal forces in check. Tito held sway with the aid of the National Liberation Army (the Yugoslav Partisans) and then, during the Cold War, with the Yugoslav Communist Party. The federal constitution of 1974 was an attempt to give more power to the Yugoslav republics and more institutional recognition to the two autonomous provinces of Serbia: Kosovo (with an Albanian majority) and Vojvodina (with a strong Hungarian minority). Communist Yugoslavia thus sought to embody the ideal of a hegemonic peace under an outwardly benevolent ruler, who had even handed over some of his central power to the regional states.[154]

Unfortunately, the decentralization along ethnic lines still drew inspiration from the surgery authorized by the Treaty of Trianon. Nationalistic aspirations among the Croat and the Slovene populations were particularly strong, while Serbs were frustrated by the decentralization process, finding themselves dispersed across several locations (including Kosovo or Bosnia) as "minorities within minorities." Serbian nationalism was therefore focused on maintaining the unity of large swathes of Yugoslavia under Serbian control.

The same causes led to the same effects. A key trigger for the violence was the release of the infamous "Memorandum" of the Serbian Academy of Sciences and Arts. Written in 1986 by the heads of the academy, this document expressed concern over Yugoslavia's "stagnating social development, economic difficulties, growing social tensions, and open inter-ethnic clashes," as well as its degradation of moral values and the invasiveness of its bureaucracy. Arguing that "no form of political oppression and discrimination on the basis of nationality is properly acceptable in modern society," it insisted not only that Serbs were being discriminated against but also that the Serbian nation had suffered a "historic defeat" in the "physical, political, legal and cultural genocide perpetrated against the Serbian population of Kosovo and Metohija." The document further asserted that "with the exception of the Independent State of Croatia from 1941–1945, Serbs in Croatia have never been as persecuted in the past as they are now." This memorandum, presented in inflammatory but vague terms, blamed these wrongs on the "nationalities policy" of the Communist Party of Yugoslavia (that is, decentralization), as well as on "the exorbitant ideological and political delusion, ignorance, immaturity, and chronic opportunism of an entire generation of post-war Serbian politicians."[155]

Leaked to the public in 1986, the memorandum and its account of the "Serbian Question" created considerable turmoil in Yugoslavia. "Rallies of Truth" were conducted throughout Serbian districts in Croatia, Bosnia-Herzegovina, and Kosovo, led by supporters of Serbian leader Slobodan Milošević and supported by extremist nationalist groups within the Serbian Orthodox Church. These rallies catalyzed Serbian putsches, called "anti-bureaucratic revolutions," in the Serbian semi-autonomous provinces of Vojvodina and Kosovo, as well as in Croatia and Bosnia-Herzegovina. Simultaneously, seeds of hatred were also being sown among Croatians and Albanians. Rarely had a text better expressed the convulsed and bilious Spirit of the Balkans.[156]

In November 1990, the Yugoslav delegation to the OSCE summit did sign the Charter of Paris for a New Europe, which came to symbolize the end of the Cold War, but this, unfortunately, was one of the Yugoslav Federation's last acts. In the confined and highly pressurized political environment of Yugoslavia, highly combustible nationalist hatreds ignited the conflagration. Slovenian independence was approved in a referendum on December 23, 1990, but only made official the next year, on June 25, 1991. The declaration of independence was followed by a brief conflict, called the Ten-Day War that lasted from June 27 to July 7, 1991 between the Slovenian Territorial Defense and the Yugoslav People's Army. The war was settled by a declaration (not a treaty) signed on the Brijuni Islands in Croatia, sponsored by the European Community on July 7, 1991. It is often remembered that, on that day, Luxemburg politician Jacques Poos optimistically declared "the hour of Europe had dawned."[157] Unfortunately, it was only a zodiacal light. Croatia declared its independence on June 25, 1991, followed by Bosnia on March 3, 1992. Predictably, each new republic immediately adopted policies that privileged its governing ethnic group, ushering in an era of discrimination, recrimination, and retaliation. Bosnia, for example, came under the control of its majority Muslim Slavs, because Bosnian Serbs had boycotted the vote for independence.[158]

The Paris Charter of 1990 had optimistically stated that "the era of confrontation and division of Europe has ended."[159] This announcement was regrettably premature and was immediately disproven by the dissolution of Yugoslavia. The successor states were swiftly swept up in violent warfare. Only Slovenia was somewhat spared because it lacked a Serbian minority and thus was of less interest to the Serbian government. After the skirmishes of the Ten-Day War, the fighting appeared to be more or less over. This was, however, only the prelude to a vast tragedy. Although Serbian animosity against other ethnicities was particularly fierce, the Serbian state was not the only instigator; the Catholic Croatians also engaged in a cruel fight against the Bosnian Muslim minority. The term "ethnic cleansing" entered common parlance as a euphemism that allowed discussions about "forcible mass deportations" and "genocide" without raised eyebrows or pinched noses. A contagion of abuses against populations spread over the land.[160]

Eventually, the tide turned against the Serbian leaders. A series of massacres committed by Serbian militias in Bosnia-Herzegovina prompted airstrikes from NATO, which effectively destroyed their resistance. By 1995, Serbian rebellions had been quelled in Croatia. In November of that year, an agreement between Croatia, the Federal Republic of Yugoslavia (Serbia), and Bosnia-Herzegovina was negotiated in Dayton, Ohio. Signed in Paris on December 14, the final agreement created a "comprehensive settlement" to "promote an enduring peace and stability." The three states promised to "conduct their relations in accordance with . . . the United Nations Charter, as well as the Helsinki Final Act."[161] The settlement agreed to peace and to a single sovereign state known as Bosnia and Herzegovina composed of two entities: a Bosniak-Croat federation and the Bosnian Serb Republic, with Sarajevo remaining as the undivided capital city. Yet another act of territorial surgery in the spirit of the Treaty of Trianon, the division was far from perfect and tensions remained, but at least the three sovereign states of Serbia, Croatia, and Bosnia-Herzegovina were barred from using military means to resolve their differences. In that sense, "pacification" was achieved under the banner of the OSCE, with the United States, the EU, and the Federation of Russia acting as brokers. The principle of "Europe's indivisible security" seemed to have scored a point.

The disputes of the embattled Serbian state with its neighbors was thus settled, yet this was not the end of its road to perdition. An armed militia called the Kosovo Liberation Army (KLA) seized Kosovo from the Serbian government in 1998, prompting yet another act of military repression from Belgrade, accompanied by atrocities against local populations. This, in turn, prompted renewed intervention by NATO in March 1999. Once again, events took on apocalyptic proportions. Serbian military forces caused the expulsion of half the ethnic Albanians in Kosovo (roughly 800,000) to neighboring Albania, Macedonia, and Bosnia-Herzegovina. Another round of NATO air strikes against the Serbian capital of Belgrade finally led to the fall of Milošević, and elections supervised by the OSCE took place.[162]

The Yugoslav Federation, while outwardly peaceful, had embodied the most critical flaw of hegemonic peace during the Cold War. Acting as a barrier like the steel outer layer of a steam cooker, it had kept the pressure of strife between peoples contained for decades. The decentralization policy started to let some of that pressure out. Yet, reconciliation after World War II between the former allies and enemies of Nazi Germany in the region had failed to occur. The belligerent states, with their focus on "ethnically pure nations," repeated two evils that had been prevalent in Europe in the interwar period: revanchism and irredentism. When the dust settled at the turn of the twenty-first century, Serbia's diminutive size sharply contrasted with Milošević's dream of a "Greater Serbia" that would include Kosovo, Montenegro, Bosnia-Herzegovina, and part of Croatia. Once again, a hegemonic power that arose against the social order of Europe was struck down without mercy by an international coalition. The course of events—similar to the misfortunes of post-Napoleonic France, postwar Germany, and the post-Soviet countries—seemed to confirm an implicit rule of thumb for European geopolitical conflicts: the most self-aggrandizing state in any war is likely to be the one that will suffer the most territorial losses in the end. Indeed, such states may even have to endure decades of a broken national heart, until they finally let go of Lyssa's spirit and find the spirit of inner peace.

Although nationalist divisions made the divorce from communism more painful in the former Yugoslavia than anywhere else, the attraction of the EU—with its promises of higher living standards and prospects for peace and democracy—provided an effective counterweight. The first southeastern state to join the *Pax Europeana* was the one least affected by civil war: Slovenia formally applied for EU membership in 1996 and joined the bloc on January 1, 2004, thirteen years after declaring its independence. On January 1, 2007, it adopted the Euro as legal tender and became part of the Schengen Agreements. The other successor states of Yugoslavia—Croatia, Serbia, Bosnia-Herzegovina, the North Macedonia ("Republic of Macedonia" until February 2019), Montenegro (which separated from a federation with Serbia in 2008), and Kosovo (which declared its independence from Serbia in 2008)—had to wait longer.

The fifth enlargement of the European Union occurred in 2007 with the accession of Bulgaria and Romania, both of which had needed time to meet the famous *acquis* of the European communities. The Enlarged European Spirit was living on, and political support was once again overwhelming: there were no public referenda, but the Romanian parliament adopted the treaty unanimously and Bulgaria registered only one vote against it, while relieved populations celebrated the end of more than a century of strife. Croatia joined in 2013; a referendum there had resulted in a majority of two-thirds in favor. At the time of this writing, all the states of southeastern Europe including Serbia have applied to join the EU and obtained candidate status, with only Bosnia-Herzegovina and Kosovo waiting to receive candidacy. With the Balkan Spirit largely defeated, the Spirit of Enlarged Europe stayed strong in the southeast, well into the present.

United Europe or Jumbled Europe?

The emergence of the Enlarged European Spirit was the driving force behind the fall of the Iron Curtain and the end of the Cold War in Europe. The Settlement Treaty of Germany marked the start of a new peace era for the whole continent. Meanwhile, in the western part, the last manifestations of the Postwar European Spirit were the founding of the European Union and its enlargement to include the bulwark states in 1995. That spirit was, however, already dying of weariness and old age. By contrast, its younger eastern counterpart still had a lot of energy in reserve, culminating in the European Union enlargement of 2004. The southeastern versions were slower to emerge, leading to additional enlargements between 2007 and 2013. Even though the European Union had been in the works since the early

1980s, one cannot underestimate the providential "help from above" that it received from a political figure hailing from the periphery of Europe.

Mikhail Gorbachev played the role of a tutelary figure for the continent in 1989, not unlike Alexander I in 1815 and Woodrow Wilson in 1919. In his effort to ensure the long-term survival of the Soviet Union, he released its iron grip on the eastern half of the European subcontinent and promoted the doctrine of a common European home: perestroika and Gorbachev's pursuit of lasting peace in Europe were always two sides of the same coin. His decision to rein in the Red Army combined with the relative calm of the Autumn of Nations showed that, on the path to a peaceful European order, pitched battles and bloody revolutions were not indispensable steps for bringing down an imperial tyranny. If left to their traditional course, events might have turned ugly indeed; in view of the spread of revolution to several countries, the tanks' rampage in city streets could have been on an entirely more violent level from the Prague Spring. Instead, a peaceful transformation occurred, which also struck a *coup de grâce* in Eastern Europe to the myth of "hegemonic peace": that the bayonets of a "Chosen Nation" led by an emperor or great leader—whether Austria, France, Germany, or Russia—could force Europeans to live together in peace. That is perhaps the most profound sense of the "crisis of empires" as applied to Europe: the ancient Roman myth of the conquering emperor marching through a triumphal arch in a foreign city, preceded by his eagle bearers and followed by his legions, suffered a more definitive defeat than even that of the fall of the Third Reich. The divorce between peace and empire, the seeds of which had been sown at Westphalia and confirmed by the Versailles Treaties, now appeared complete.[163]

Undoubtedly, the signing of the Settlement Treaty of Germany was the high watermark of the Enlarged European Spirit. In Eastern and Central Europe, euphoria at communism's collapse created the expectation of an "existential revolution," as Václav Havel called it in 1978.[164] When rapid westernization did not magically happen, the new spirit was condemned to become superficial. After the Treaty of Maastricht, the quick accession of Austria, Finland, and Sweden to the EU left little time for discussion of broad principles, with attention fixed on the practicalities of an untried institution and its new members. Indeed, there was no turning back after the fall of the Iron Curtain. The Enlarged European Spirit plunged head-long, with the member states of the European Union maneuvering as best they could through the breakneck pace of the expansion. It met its natural barriers at the foothills of the ex-Soviet republics, but by then the Euro-pean spirit of peace had achieved its largest territorial extent in a long time. It perhaps did not rival the shining glory of the Spirit of Vienna, which extended from French Brittany all the way to Alaska, and even to *Krepost' Ross,* a humble Russian outpost in northern California. Yet it was surely very large, and to its breadth it added unprecedented levels of popular solidarity and political stability. After the EU enlargement of 2004, the Russian oblast of Kaliningrad (Königsberg) in former East Prussia stood as a lone island in the middle of the larger European zone of the *Pax Europeana.*

Yet, contrary to official narratives, the EU did not really "enlarge" to the east. It instead became the center of attraction for countries that, released from outside control by a sudden vacuum of power, fervently desired to join it. In this sense, the Enlarged European Spirit was different from the Spirit of Vienna in 1815, the Spirit of Geneva in the 1920s, or the Postwar European Spirit after 1945. In all those earlier cases, the allied states had to work to-gether against the odds to create a new political order after the destruction of a continental war. By contrast, the protagonists of the Enlarged European Spirit were acting on the spur of the moment, by "instinct" rather than reason, without always considering the long-term consequences of the on-going transformations on the continent. The architects of the European Union did not have a chance to consider fully where they were coming from and where they were going. The bureaucracy in Brussels forged ahead like a spiritless automaton, producing multilingual paperwork at dizzying speeds. By the time they could collect themselves, the Postwar European Spirit was already buried.

In 2012, the Norwegian Nobel Committee granted the Peace Prize to the European Union for having "over six decades contributed to the advance-ment of peace and reconciliation, democracy and human rights in Eu-rope."[165] Symbolically, the prize was awarded to recognize the accession of Croatia to the EU the following year, in July 2013. The prize came, however, after popular enthusiasm in Europe had already been waning for several years and when international attention was focused on the profound debt crisis in several European states, especially Greece. Still, the Nobel Committee certainly wanted to make a strong statement that might help revive the European spirit of peace.

Although it did not succeed in this aim, the committee unwittingly touched on one of the most important themes of this book by giving strong symbolic tribute to the remarkable continuity of the tradition of perpetual peace in European history. In his speech, the Prize Committee chair Thorbjørn Jagland explicitly connected the creators of the EU to old acquaintances: the authors of the Locarno Treaties (Chamberlain and Dawes in 1925, and Briand and Stresemann in 1926), as well as Gorbachev, all of whom had also received Nobel Peace Prizes. He also referred to the Coal and Steel Community of 1951 as marking "the start of a process of reconciliation which has continued right to the present day. Beginning in Western Europe, the process continued across the east-west divide when the Berlin Wall fell, and has currently reached the Balkans, where there were bloody wars less than 15 to 20 years ago."[166] In the same vein, Chairman Jagland framed the rapprochement between France and Germany after World War II as "the most dramatic example in history to show that war and conflict can be turned so rapidly into peace and cooperation." He also acknowledged that the ongoing reconciliation effort in the former Yugoslavia had brought some successes and emphasized that the European Union was supporting a new paradigm of coexistence between states, while changing the way they conceived of the identity of their citizens:

> The paramount solution is to extend the process of integration that has applied in the rest of Europe. Borders become less absolute; which population group one belongs to no longer determines one's security. The EU must accordingly play a main part here, too, to bring about not only an armistice but real peace.[167]

Jagland correctly emphasized the process of reconciliation between states that had been enemies and the replacement of strongly stereotypical "national identities" with state citizenship that admitted regional nuances. Reconciliation was, all in all, a major contribution of the European construction to the conquest of peace, second only to Schuman's superglue of de facto solidarity. This applied particularly to southeastern Europe, which had experienced some periods of freedom and peace in the past; unfortunately, the two had generally been mutually exclusive in a region that oscillated wildly between imposed, hegemonic peace and violent wars between neighboring nation-states. In the countries of ex-Yugoslavia, "reconciliation" could be interpreted in two ways: as the resolution of differences between two peoples, with the dissolution of old fears, jealousies, and hatreds; and as the reconciliation of initially divergent political aims within a supranational entity, achieving a balance between freedom and peace.

As the Yugoslav Wars demonstrated, the angry dogma of purity (whether ethnonational, religious, or the like)—the Spirit of the Balkans—was a villain in the tragedy, the cause of much bloodshed in modern Europe between and within states. The International Criminal Tribunal for the Former Yugoslavia—established in May 1993 in The Hague under the aegis of the UN Security Council—sentenced ninety ethnonationalists as war criminals, pointedly without regard to their professed "ethnicity." The accession of Slovenia and Croatia to the EU was a decisive, though not definitive, success in the engineering of peace over the destructive forces of ethnonationalism.

From Gorbachev's Peace Prize in 1990 to the EU's Peace Prize in 2012, the Spirit of Enlarged Europe thus came full circle. At the same time, the Nobel Committee's attempt to support the EU in the face of negative press demonstrates that the "three worlds" of contemporary Europe—the Western core (to which Greece has been attached since the 1970s), Eastern Europe, and the southeastern sector—had not yet fully blended. Each possessed a slightly different spirit, with a very different outlook and set of expectations: the Western bourgeois nation-states still trudging along their dreary route to European unity, mostly concentrated on deepening their own *acquis;* the popular Eastern spirit still expecting prosperity and freedom and sometimes venting its frustration that the expected utopian state was not yet a reality in Europe; and an extenuated southeast hoping that the EU would be able to bring them a breath of relief from one and a half-century of political torments. A united Europe or a jumbled Europe? Paradoxically, each EU member state has also maintained its own unilateral and often idiosyncratic definition of what this "United Europe" means. The lesson is that the birth of the European Union in 1992, the Holy Grail of political philosophers since the Enlightenment, has been but a stage on the road to peace—still far from the destination itself. The movement of the Enlarged European Spirit, played as *allegro con fuoco,* was like the combined performances of thousands of players, impossible to be carried out perfectly in tune and rhythm. Once the festive music subsided, the states of Europe were still left to face the challenges and frictions of life in common.

Conclusion

QUO VADIS, EUROPE?

We have now followed, over the course of three centuries, the conquest of peace—a clearly discernible thread of efforts by philosophers, political leaders, diplomats, and others to establish lasting peace in Europe. These figures with different origins, backgrounds, and ideological orientations joined hands repeatedly, after great wars, in what I referred to as a succession of "spirits." The Vienna Order of the post-Napoleonic era, the League of Nations that followed World War I, the foundation of the European Communities in the 1950s, and the expansion of the European Union after the fall of the Iron Curtain were all attempts to forge greater "togetherness." Importantly, those who participated in these endeavors, though they came from different backgrounds, had different viewpoints, and faced different circumstances, all drew inspiration from a common lore. They explicitly referred to the treatises and treaties, the experiments and experiences of their predecessors. Each group added its own ideas to that tradition, atop the deep thinking of those who came before them. Each new generation of writers or actors felt as if it were part of a secular cohort, engaged in a long-term, larger-than-life adventure in beating the odds of war.

The "Spirit of Lasting Peace" is the sum total of all conscious attempts to achieve peace, transcending national, cultural, and religious differences, as well as time. This thread was made by twisting and turning many variegated fibers into a single strand, from early English works on the balance of power and those of the Abbé de Saint-Pierre to the efforts of our day. The craftspeople unspooling this thread sometimes hesitated and sometimes took unexpected turns, borrowing from other influences; they experienced

348

successes, regressions, and failures, often even snapping the thread, which they repeatedly repaired.

Tracing this thread of interconnected experiences has enabled us to witness the Spirit of Lasting Peace through its successive avatars: the Spirit of the Enlightenment, the Spirit of Vienna, the Spirit of Geneva, and finally, the two European Spirits born out of the tragedy of World War II, which led to the European Communities and the European Union. Each of these successive spirits matured and progressed in its own way. No single avatar was ever the "spirit of all Europeans," because each spirit was the sum of efforts by specific individuals and groups; moreover, they were not the exclusive preserve of Europe. Each spirit was made up of ideas and hopes adopted by specific communities in different places; they were grafts of varietals that often did not even have their origins in local soils. It was natural for those who perceived a cosmopolitan spirit in Vienna, Geneva, Strasbourg, or Brussels to take pride in their locale and to embrace it. But the moment they tried to chain this spirit to their front porch, they lost it. Each of these spirits was a fleeting group experience, intense and deeply human—each finding its own particular place to flourish because it was at the right place at the right time.

This survey of three centuries of peacemaking showed that these spirits were the engine driving each of the fundamental shifts of the European system toward lasting peace. There was, of course, a mutual influence between spirits and their practical applications, in a dialectic of change. A spirit would lead to changes in political strategies, to the negotiation of new treaties, to shifts in norms, to the foundation of new institutions; later, after those structures had collapsed yet again due to the chaos of a continental war, a new spirit rose again to restart the cycle, which built on the productions and experiences of the earlier generation. When a unification of a large part of Europe was finally achieved in the late twentieth century, it did not arise from a continental empire—much less a "big bang" treaty as the Abbé de Saint-Pierre and Kant had fervently hoped—but was the result of a slow and iterative process, piloted by successive spirits. Situations, structures, and demands profoundly differed from one era to the other, and events often took erratic turns. The only tenuous "constant" and the occasional sense of direction has been the relentless drive toward lasting peace.

I used the term "engineering of peace" to describe the practical application of the knowledge accumulated by the Spirit of Lasting Peace. The engineering of peace encompasses both theories of the balance of power and of perpetual peace, which complement each other. It does not aim at eradicating war itself (a common misconception), because there were cases in which war was self-evidently the proper course of action to secure peace; it was the last resort of European states against the threat of conquest. Since the War of Spanish Succession, five military alliances arose to *restore* the balance of power against an equal number of attempts to forge a continental empire. Each time, a coalition of allied states fought wholeheartedly until victory: in the War of Spanish Succession, the Napoleonic wars, World War I, World War II, and the Cold War. If European states—or any other states—ever find themselves in this situation again, facing a potential hegemon, they will doubtless do the same. Simply stated: the balance of power—in its strictest sense—remains as applicable today as it has ever been.

In the engineering of peace, the first step to building any new and durable status quo has always been to raze the hostile empire threatening the pre-existing political edifice of Europe. These defensive wars were evidently necessary preliminary steps. Considering that they were an extreme remedy that was applied against a rising empire after all else had failed, Isaac Asimov's quip that "violence is the last refuge of the incompetent" is perhaps ungracious but nevertheless quite literally correct (from the Latin *in* "not" and *competens* "adequate").[1] One of the purposes of an adequate peace alliance is to deny threatening empires the opportunity to arise; in case of failure, the same powers must assemble a military alliance to fight the next great war. The observation that a coalition war is both the penalty for the failure of a peace system and the remedy against an imperial threat was confirmed so often it almost seems to be a natural law, as seen with the allies of the Napoleonic era and those of World War I, World War II, and the foundation of NATO in 1949 (the fact that NATO still exists today despite the ending of the Cold War is revealing in this regard).

Tolstoy noted that wars set in motion a "sea of events" with consequences that are, by their very nature, highly unpredictable.[2] Such violent and chaotic clashes have destroyed states and forged new ones from the rubble. Given that Europe is a continent, the Earth's mantle and crust may provide the best metaphor for understanding war and its effects. States and empires are mere structures on the surface. Seen from the perspective of the *longue durée,* they are the visible part of a deep metamorphic process in which the new constantly replaces the old. Napoleon's empire was erased, as was the earlier Holy Roman Empire. In 1919, four major European empires suddenly liquefied. Later, both the Third Reich and the Soviet Union crumbled into debris. Great actors also suddenly fell by the wayside. Popes played a major role in European affairs for nearly a millennium; the political power of the papacy is now a distant memory.

With advance warning, we may sometimes detect these tremors that bring about major changes and destruction. Yet, whatever a government tries to do, nothing can prevent these seismic waves from breaking through the crust of political reality. They start moving when there are widespread pressures for change, such as demands for greater social justice or for expanded political representation. During the Revolutionary and Napoleonic eras, loyalties to local patrimonial dynasties were transferred to national or imperial dynasties. Later, during the Reaction, the unsatisfied demands of bourgeois elites led to revolutions. As industrialization spread, so did the demand for increased political representation and better conditions for workers, accompanied by the rise of ethnic loyalties. These forces eventually led to the collapse of several monarchies and the rise of new democratic nation-states. And today we witness a shift in the concerns of the youngest generation, from demands for greater social equity to a focus on the preservation of the planet, and, for some, a transition from national loyalties to a sense of belonging to an international community with a shared fate. This is the seismic part of the equation. Unfortunately, leaders of most great powers have tended to respond to such challenges by clinging fiercely to their prerogatives and angrily refusing to yield, until they eventually collapse. But, as Metternich himself admitted in 1848, no one can stand forever in the way of these massive movements.[3]

What our survey tells us is that the most positive and effective approach that rulers and political leaders can take in response to these pressures is to keep their instincts in check and to channel these energetic surges from below toward constructive change. This is a central tenet of the modern engineering of peace in a democracy: "surfing the seismic waves" by standing at the crest of popular demands for change and riding the wave. Some of these attempts at restructuring will inevitably fail, as did Gorbachev's perestroika. Nevertheless, the slim chance offered by responding positively is always better than the certainty of failure and collapse (Soviet Marxism was doomed anyway): it was largely thanks to Gorbachev's foresight that the Autumn of Nations in 1989 was far more successful and less bloody than the Spring of Nations in 1848. The basic idea behind the engineering of peace, then, is to maintain a European system with anti-seismic properties and to continuously restructure this edifice in the hope it will survive the next earthquake or, failing this, to rebuild it from the rubble.

In engineering peace, it is important to distinguish between those atmospheric spirits that constitute the Spirit of Peace and other deep and often unpredictable subterranean movements.[4] Each of these deeper movements was unique to its time and place; each was an individual manifestation of the same metamorphic process, which kept resurging from the depths. These deep underground movements provided impressive reservoirs of energy for change. Rather than ignoring them, advocating for them passionately, or rejecting them without discussion, engineers of peace should consider this option: channeling these energies in constructive directions. If they do not, the pressures will release themselves through revolutions and wars.

Of course, many would be reassured if the existing nation-states on the Continent became permanent fixtures that continue forever, suspended in time. Yet today, states like France and the United Kingdom occupy the same political niche that a city-state like Venice did in the eighteenth century. The Republic of Venice was finally pronounced dead in 1814—becoming a mere paragraph in the secret appendix to the Treaty of Paris. Geneva, in contrast, weathered the storm and preserved its political identity by joining the Swiss Confederation. It was smaller than Venice, but what it lacked in prestige and glitz, it amply made up for in its realism and acute sense of how to conduct negotiations with the great powers. The same treaty that secretly struck Venice off from the map not only officially confirmed the status of Geneva but also expanded its territory. The cruel lesson of Venice's demise is that staying aloof does not always pay off in international diplomacy: keeping friendly ties with the powers that be usually does.

The European nation-states of our times exhibit similar weaknesses—insufficient population, internal markets, or resources to survive on their own or even to defend themselves against continental states. Some live as Vivaldi's Venice, dizzying themselves with costly reenactments of their past glories and deliberately ignoring their loss of political influence. Nation-states, just as city-states before them, are frail and impermanent entities, struggling unless they are constantly propped up or sheltered by some continental formation. As Czechoslovakia, Poland, Greece, and other countries well know, nation-states are often at the mercy of the random occurrence of highly chaotic events in the form of wars and revolutions, migration waves, economic crises, natural disasters, and epidemics. Even Russia suffers from the precariousness of its international role and a general angst about the steadfastness of its political regime. And Switzerland may be forced to hold onto its precious neutrality acquired in 1815, for as long as the last two great outliers, Russia and Britain, remain out of the European bloc.

The question remains: What power or force should dominate Europe after the twilight of its own nation-states? It was agreed as early as 1648 that a pan-continental *empire* (by which was meant a military power establishing its hegemony by conquest) was not desirable. The current European Union, which slowly evolved out of the European Communities, was but one among many alternative scenarios; it was not even the most plausible one. Indeed, the pursuit of lasting peace in Europe was not an abstract march toward today's European Union: the EU was never seen as the "manifest destiny" of the European Continent. Nevertheless, it is constructed and has provided a framework for lasting peace in Europe over the past decades.

My term "engineering of peace" is an indirect reference to those military engineers who rebuild bridges destroyed by conflict, build shelters and airline strips, and perform feats that also serve civilians in times of distress.[5] The metaphysical grounds for pursuing lasting peace are, however, best left to anyone's beliefs. Kant considered the pursuit of peace to be a categorical imperative; that is, if one adheres to the maxim that peace is morally good, one should pursue it without fail.[6] Some based the imperatives of peace and war on religious affiliation and ideas. As we saw, the zeitgeist of the first half of the nineteenth century was often as intensely religious as the prior Enlightenment era had been rational. Seekers of lasting peace such as Alexander I, Giuseppe Mazzini, and Victor Hugo found it necessary to make such canonical statements as "the law of the world is not and cannot be distinct from the law of God. And the law of God is not war, it is peace."[7] This religious imperative receded in the twentieth century. Even though Woodrow Wilson's personal motivations to pursue peace were intensely religious, the Covenant of the League of Nations was secular—with the possible exception of the term "covenant" itself. Similarly, there was no metaphysical disquisition in either the Charter of the United Nations or the Treaty of the European Union as to why these two institutions should strive for peace— except to avoid the horrors of war. In a modern secular society, the benefits of a lasting peace are simply taken as axiomatic.

Yet war and peace do not exist in separate realms; they are part of the same reality. The inner strength required of a soldier to fight a military engagement despite the fear of getting shot is in some ways comparable to the staying power required of a diplomat at a conference to obtain some kind of peace agreement. In both cases, the stakes are high: if the diplomat fails, whole nations and peoples may suffer for extended periods of time, as events in Central and Eastern Europe after 1918 and again after 1945 plainly show.

War and peace are both part of the same continuum of human interaction—they are two extremes of a single spectrum, not unlike health and disease. That said, we can evaluate relative success in the engineering of peace, as conditions ascend from a state of war to one of lasting peace:

	Lasting Peace	
	Solidarity	State of Peace
	Reconciliation	
↑	*Making Peace*	
	Peacekeeping	
	Ceasefire	State of War
	War	

The political situation in Europe after each of the continental wars described here can be placed somewhere on this scale: it is a useful yardstick for measuring the progress of and departures from the engineering of peace. The stages on this scale are based on observable behavior (what people do), rather than on the terminology they choose to characterize their behavior (the formulas found in treaties, agreements, and rules). Thus, conduct at each step on the scale is more important than the terms the actors use. A "ceasefire," for example, is any action in which belligerents stop firing on one another, whichever form their written agreement may take—whether capitulation, armistice, or "Christmas truce."

What defines the "state of peace" and the "state of war" is actually a question of mindset. The mindset of war uses force and deception to compel another party to do one's bidding. The mindset of peace uses dialogue and mutual trust to convince the other party of the legitimacy of one's policies and goals. The action of "making peace" symbolically draws a clear-cut line: it signifies the creation of a relationship of trust between parties that ushers in a state of peace. As a corollary, the use of intimidation, force, and deception is as legitimate in pursuing war as it is illegitimate in maintaining peace. The continuity between war and peace is best illustrated by the fact that the foundations of peace must be laid in time of war. Failing to do so may result in the kind of disaster that took place at the Paris Peace Conference after World War I. When victory is in sight, co-belligerents must transform themselves into solidly united allies. "Chaumont clauses" (in reference to the Treaty of Chaumont of 1814) are indispensable to committing allies to fight together until the enemy is defeated and not to negotiate separate ceasefires. The allies must continue to work together as one body, even after victory, toward a mutually agreed-on postwar order.

Here, one must keep in mind a corollary of Clausewitz's definition of war as "the pursuit of politics by other means"; namely, that coalition wars are fought to compel a would-be continental hegemon to abandon its threatening ways. Failing to emphasize publicly the achievement of victory over a hegemonic empire, as the Allies did by accepting Germany's armistice of 1918 instead of insisting on surrender, may be tantamount to throwing away the sacrifices of the war. Certainly, it compromises the work of peace diplomats after the war. In Europe, a bloodless but highly symbolic military parade in the capital city of a defeated empire has been a traditional preliminary to the peace process. The cases we examined seem to show the wisdom of a humane military occupation of the defeated power, both to give much-needed guidance and assistance to the civilian population and to prevent the risk of military resurgence, as occurred in 1815 during Napoleon's Hundred Days. These were also the objectives of the Allied Control Council that successfully supervised the occupation of Germany after 1945.[8] For obvious reasons—not least the burden to the victors—military occupation should be kept as brief as possible. As a rule of thumb, an occupation that lasts longer than five years is a clear indication that the peace process is failing.

As a "mindset," peace is clearly something that a document alone cannot encompass. Even though the words "peace" and "treaty" have long been used interchangeably, as in the Peace of Utrecht and the Treaty of Utrecht, they do not mean the same thing. This confusion has occurred because the legalist view, inspired by Roman law, emphasizes the document known as the peace treaty.[9] But, in fact, Europeans' mental representations of war and peace have been largely shaped by the oral traditions of Germanic and Slavic cultures. In these societies, peace after a feud was a homecoming, a solemn restoration of amity in the family: respectful social intercourse was restored by an honorary ritual performed in unison. Failing this, one would walk out *Fried-los* ("without peace"), which led to the dishonorable discharge of family members who had been denied every right to reparation.[10] It is this homecoming tradition that is the foundation of specifically European diplomatic practices. And it is this conception of "peace as a homecoming" that best explains the Holy Alliance's metaphor of a piously united family. Today, the state of peace is sealed with a solemn rite of honor ending with a signature, which symbolically represents the reunion of the family of states.

The source of lasting peace is indeed found in a spirit, a sense of togetherness. The desire to make others experience this spirit may well explain Tsar Alexander's and Giuseppe Mazzini's mystical journey to advocate for the Holy Alliance or Woodrow Wilson's biblical reference to Jewish tribes forging unity by striking a covenant with God. It is no longer necessary today to have recourse to mystical or biblical references.

It follows that the function of the written "peace treaty" is derived from the peace ceremony: it serves both as the authentic acknowledgment that the rite truly took place and as a record of the agreement's details.[11] Yet what constitutes the Peace of Utrecht or the Peace of Vienna is not only the seal-peppered documents we find in archives. The establishment of peace in these cases was derived from the social communion represented in countless paintings depicting groups of people together, in allegories, and in uplifting musical pieces such as those written by George Frederic Handel. "Peace" thus popularly refers to the deeply etched memory of the moment when former belligerents convened and, with the signature rite, gave birth to a new social bond. It is that bond, not the legal document itself, that we consider the spirit of peace.

The clauses in written agreements are, of course, of utmost importance; for example, this was the case for the Vienna Final Act of 1815. But even what is written down may not be sufficient to hold the peace. Experience with European treaties since World War II shows that governments often do not feel bound by the commitments undertaken by their predecessors at an earlier intergovernmental conference; sometimes they even campaign to reverse them. Similarly, the head of an autocratic country might reverse its policy without prior notice, as Stalin did by flouting Soviet pledges to respect international treaties after World War II. This is why it is necessary to conduct a second ceremony of honor: the exchange of ratification instruments. Such formal ratifications can increase the chances that a postwar agreement will be respected and actually usher in peace. In this respect, Kant was right that "true politics can never take a step without rendering homage to morality."[12] The formal process of ratification is thus a vital step for any peace treaty; once effected, it formally and publicly binds participating states by honor to respect it. Not even Nazi Germany and the Soviet Union could afford to disdain the mantle of honorability.[13]

The rites of the Peace of Utrecht of 1713 were concluded with particular grace and dignity because there were neither winners nor losers, and bonds between the diplomats had already grown during the course of negotiations. Similar bonds developed in Vienna in 1814–1815. Unfortunately, for the treaties after World War I, the proceedings of the Paris Conference were not performed according to the time-honored rites of Utrecht and Vienna. The treaties were drafted without the defeated parties being present, which precluded their participation or negotiation. Terms were offered to the defeated on a take-it-or-leave-it basis. At the signature ceremonies, which were orchestrated as capitulations, the defeated parties were not even permitted to sit at the same table as the victors, and they did not leave "in peace." The conventional term "Peace of Versailles" is a misnomer, because honor was not restored. Regardless of the rhetoric of diplomatic envoys, all steps short of the conclusion of the solemn ritual of making peace (both with full intent and commitment) leave in practice the belligerents in a state of war.

The League of Nations made commendable efforts later to establish a state of peace between France and Germany, and the Pact of Locarno (1925) nearly succeeded in that effort. There was, however, precious little time between the ceasefire in November 1918 and the breakout of hostilities in Central and Eastern Europe in September 1939 for that peace to take hold. After World War II, formal peace treaties in Western Europe were subordinated to the making of peace, and the role of peace institutions was redefined. Centuries earlier, the Abbé de Saint-Pierre had imagined a grand treaty; Immanuel Kant had declared that perpetual peace must be formally instituted by a multilateral treaty founding an alliance of peace.[14] It is easy to understand their logic—at that time, treaties were used everywhere to conclude wars and to reestablish peace between states, so a perfect treaty would be necessary to make peace perpetual. This reasoning was, however, backward because no spirit of peace can emerge, like a fully armed Athena from the head of Zeus, from the lifeless paper of a grand peace treaty. Both Saint-Pierre's and Kant's assumption—that a grand treaty was required— posed insurmountable practical problems whenever the international community tried to fashion and implement it. Such attempts fell victim to the clash of two demands. If the planned peace organization was too perfect (especially if it was egalitarian), it would be too restrictive, and the great powers would never agree to it—a case in point being the US Senate's rejection of the League of Nations' Covenant in 1919. The standards of such peace machinery would have to be relaxed, and "safeties," such as a "security council," would have to be introduced to preserve the prerogatives of the great powers. But, conversely, would these artificial tweaks really allow a grand peace institution to fulfill its purpose? Or, worse, would such concessions turn it into an instrument of oppression?

Considering that the League of Nations failed after twenty years, and the United Nations' engine, the General Assembly, has been forced to run in idle most of the time since 1945 because of the veto power of the Security Council, we now know that both Wilson and Roosevelt were pursuing an engineering solution to a problem that may not have any practical solution in the physical world. Pre-planned machineries of peace such as the League of Nations and the United Nations are simply too delicate; they are either too difficult to assemble, or they are destined to prove inadequate once they are in place.

The development of the European Communities took another, far more practical route based on the organic conception of multicellular organisms. An essential intellectual breakthrough of the last three centuries in the engineering of peace was Robert Schuman's realization in 1950 that if Europe as a political body were to emerge, it would have to proceed through the steps of natural development, from embryo to mature adult.[15] Overnight, the organic method (often called, as we saw, "functional") thus threw two centuries of mechanistic thinking out the window: Louis Pasteur triumphed over Isaac Newton. One can therefore amend the Schuman Declaration slightly, because its principle is still in force: *lasting peace* "will not be made all at once, or according to a single plan. It will be built through concrete achievements that first create a de facto solidarity."

If states are willing to wait sufficiently long to formalize aspects of their spirit of peace until after it has truly crystallized, as the European Communities did with the foundation of the European Union in 1992, the problem of engineering peace becomes more likely to be soluble. In other words, the problem of lasting peace is able to be resolved only if function is allowed to materialize before the legal form. The realization of the Abbé de Saint-Pierre's hope expressed in the early eighteenth century, the Maastricht Treaty, was anticlimactic for good reason: it was a formalization of practices and ideas that had already long been discussed. The Maastricht Treaty was not "perfect," but it had the advantage of being perfectible, as subsequent updates have shown. Yet even this evolutionary process has been fraught with difficulties and false starts. The later collapse of the over-ambitious Treaty establishing a Constitution for Europe (2004) shows that the EU political classes sometimes need to be reminded of the nimble and pragmatic policy that had originally made the efforts successful.[16] Whether the bureaucrats of the European Commission like it or not, functionalism is what has best worked to buttress the cause of lasting peace in Europe since the 1950s.

The complaints of legalists about the "gap" between an everyday practice that is ahead of the treaties may thus be safely ignored, as long as reasonable allowance is made for lawmakers to catch up with the peace process (and they are never allowed to move ahead of it). The safest road to lasting peace in Europe is for the spirit of peace to stay well ahead of treaties and for the letter of the treaties to remain subordinate to that spirit. In a system aiming to create a de facto solidarity, the lawyers' work in drafting treaty terms is bound to be more descriptive than prescriptive. This principle can be compared usefully to the German functionalist school of industrial design of the postwar era, which relentlessly sought formal perfection by improving the mundane function of a consumer product: "Good design is as little design as possible. Less is more, because it concentrates on the essential aspects, and products are not burdened with non-essentials."[17] This pragmatic, minimalistic approach is arguably at odds with the current sprawling, overregulated bureaucracy of the European Union, which churns out official documents in twenty-four official languages when even the global United Nations is able to function with only six.

A crucial obstacle to the engineering of peace needs to be addressed: the abuse to which the concept of "peace" has been continually subjected since 1945, which has given birth to a "newspeak" of international relations. The continual peddling of the state of war as "peace" has created an intellectual edifice that must be shattered. The state of peace is not the ersatz condition of ceasefire that defined the Cold War, with its military stalemate in Europe and its various proxy wars in Asia, Latin America, and Africa.[18] The Cold War was, as the term itself unambiguously indicates, a state of war— an armed truce between two blocs perpetually in the field—with not one day of actual peace. The Iron Curtain was not a peripheral issue but a central one: it was in reality a fortified no-man's land cutting the European continent in two from the Baltic Sea to the Adriatic. The myth of a "Long Peace" after World War II, which may make some sense to some readers today, would have sounded laughable to Europeans of the 1980s who lived with tank divisions of the Red Army stationed within a few hours' drive; Germans whose families had been divided for decades on both sides of the Inner Wall would have found the notion nonsensical.[19] New York City, seat of the meetings of the UN Security Council, was itself a battlefield. What were called "peace talks" between the two superpowers were, quite often, a cruel and sophisticated form of warfare better described as palace intrigues.[20]

To justify this devaluation of "peace," many historians have offered the following explanation: the decline in the number of peace treaties signed after World War II created a "new condition" in the postwar era, in which intergovernmental conferences took their place.[21] True, the number of peace treaties did decline, but that does not mean that this development was desirable, because it led to frozen conflict that was nothing more than a degraded form of ceasefire. Furthermore, it was a transient state of affairs. The experience of the twentieth century has shown that frozen conflicts are impermanent deadlocks with only two roads out: either the parties agree to go forward toward a peace agreement, or they slide backward toward open conflict. To counterbalance the disingenuous notion of the "Long Peace" since 1945, I introduced the term "Fifty Years' War" (1939–1989).[22] No peace was possible between the Soviet Union and the United States during the Cold War, because any such peace would have required them to settle their ideological differences and dismantle the Iron Curtain. In the early twenty-first century, a new balance of power emerged between the NATO alliance and Russia, which continues to be a system of war. Similarly, there is no state of peace between Cyprus and Turkey, any more than there is between Russia and its southern European neighbors, Ukraine, Moldova and Georgia.

Attributing the successful escape of Europe from the Fifty Years' War to the intercession of some abstract "better angels of our nature" (as Abraham Lincoln famously called them) also devalues the concept of peace.

In Western Europe, a small group of European leaders obtained a measure of peace in the 1950s by taking their own future in their hands. Similarly, steps toward peacemaking regarding Germany after 1945 were taken very slowly: the formal settlement of differences was only reached after 1991—forty-six years after the capitulation of the Third Reich. Significantly, the negotiation process that led to this settlement was neither started by nor conducted by the United Nations.

The emphasis on the UN's "peacekeeping" mission, a euphemism for the deployment of troops to maintain order in areas torn by regional wars, reflects the fact that this organization is denied the means to address its greatest concern with peace: reestablishing concord between mutually estranged great powers in its Security Council by providing arbitration services between them. As with the earlier systems (balance of power of the eighteenth century, the Concert System, and the League of Nations) the core function of any peace system should be to prevent the great powers at the top of the pyramid from declaring war on each other, through economic or military means.

The fact that during the Hungarian Revolution of 1956 and the Prague Spring in 1968 both the United States and the Soviet Union claimed at the Security Council that they were acting for the preservation of peace was also indicative of a dangerous inflation of the term "peace."[23] All this semantic abuse is to be contrasted with the declaration of President Truman in his inaugural address of 1949 that "above all else, our people desire, and are determined to work for, peace on earth—a just and lasting peace—based on genuine agreement freely arrived at by equals." In terms of the framework of the engineering of peace, this remains one of the most complete definitions of lasting peace in its highest sense, because it includes the mandatory rituals of peace ("agreement freely arrived at"). Truman's original aim was largely achieved in 2004 when the European Union accepted Hungary, the Czech Republic, and Slovakia as members—fifteen years after the Red Army's withdrawal from Eastern Europe.

*Y*et what happened to the Enlarged European Spirit of peace, from the Autumn of Nations in 1989 to the early 2000s? After the long euphoric

wave of growing democracy ebbed, political Europe entered into a new period of political and financial turmoil. With barely enough time to cele-
brate the accession of Romania and Bulgaria to the EU in 2007, events
started to take a turn for the worse. One year later, the bursting of the sub-
prime mortgage bubble in the United States launched a long wave of economic misfortune in Europe. Southern Europe suffered the most. The already unsustainable public deficits of Italy and Spain emerged as a threat to
the whole Eurozone. Greece, whose government and banks neared disaster
in 2009, was thrown into social and political chaos, followed by a crisis of
Cypriot banks in 2012–2013.

This turmoil came at a moment of self-doubt for the political classes of
Europe, which were in search of new guidelines and policies. With the enlargement of the EU completed and the ex-Soviet countries as the new
eastern frontier, what was to come next? The destabilizing effects of the financial and migrant crises were obvious, with countries and political parties taking divergent stances in response. Concern for the integration of Europe suddenly gave way to a renewed fear of external threats and fantasies
of a national past that predated the European construction. Antimigrant
and ethnonationalist factions in various countries started to capitalize on
the fear of "invasion" from the Middle East and North Africa, blaming the
crisis on the demise of fully independent nation-states and thus on the
shared powers of the EU. They were intent on re-creating autarkic models
from the interwar period that had led to authoritarian governments.

In reality, the immense disruptive force of the Enlarged European Spirit
had been concentrated at its inception. Well channeled first by Gorbachev
and then by the European Union, it was pushed along by inertial momentum—not by thoughtful, long-term vision. The sudden materializa-
tion of the century-old dream of European unification in 1992, against all
odds, was a destabilizing event by itself. It was, on the one hand, a victory
that confounded believers in the postwar myth of Westphalia, who had argued the very impossibility of such an entity as a united Europe in the mistaken belief that the preservation of complete national sovereignty was the
very essence of every nation-state. On the other hand, the sudden emergence
of the EU juggernaut stunned and disoriented the pro-European political
classes, after decades of painstakingly campaigning for unification. It

seemed that those who had pursued perpetual peace in Europe had prepared for every scenario save their own swift and decisive victory. Their seeming success, however, was dealt a serious blow. The Enlarged European Spirit quietly died on June 23, 2016, when a narrow majority in the United Kingdom voted, in a popular referendum, for withdrawal from the European Union. On January 31, 2020, Britain left the EU.

This new manifestation of the British Question did not, of course, kill the EU, but it left a spiritual wound. With the notable (and complicated) exception of Greenland, it was the first time a sovereign nation had sought to detach itself from the European Union. This exacerbated the moral and existential crisis in Western Europe, dredging up debates and disagreements from the early European construction. Although demands to leave the bloc subsided elsewhere, many countries' hearts were no longer in it. Without any shiny new goal to pursue, the Fifth European Commission (2014–2019) turned away from the forward-looking attitude that had characterized its predecessors. The European conscience—the desire to unify Europe—gave way to its opposite: a paralyzing fear of disaggregation and a desire to protect and defend the newly found *acquis* at all costs.[24] The political classes of Europe turned, almost overnight, from freethinkers into reactionaries. Indeed, as one historian pointedly put it,

> There is no dream any longer, and that is in some ways the biggest problem of all. Today's politicians are in thrall to a conception of themselves as short-term managers of events rather than as strategists governing for the long term. Crisis mode has become the norm, and events have emerged to fit that model. Stepping back and thinking about the EU's long-term evolution is now almost impossible. Yet never has it been more needed. If 200 years ago, for the architects of the post-Napoleonic peace, Europe was a slogan, a set of principles in search of institutional form, today it is a set of organizations in search of guiding principles.[25]

With the loss of the secular grand aim of the Europeanists, an "amnesia of peace" started to set in. Beset by armed conflicts in their own neighborhood and hit by acts of terrorism within, European political leaders started wondering whether a renunciation of the values of the Charter of Fundamental

Rights and a recourse to wars (economic or military) would again become options.[26] The "aim of peace," inscribed in Article 3 of the Treaty of the European Union, lost its appeal in favor of "securitarianism," the pursuit of security. This evoked the precedent of the Troppau Congress of 1820, when the great powers feared that their precious new order would be undermined by Carbonari and other revolutionaries.[27] As earlier, this is how peace can slide into an ersatz "keeping of the peace" with recourse to surveillance and repression and how tyranny begets more disorders, and disorders beget more tyranny, in a spiral of fear and anger.

Europe's devaluation of the goal of lasting peace in the early twenty-first century may explain why scholars once again are investigating the concept of a "security culture."[28] They are, however, aware, that it raises tough issues in the political context of Europe. If "security" were allowed, for example, to become the main goal of German foreign policy today, then the corollary would be that the European Union's aim of peace and even of Franco–German reconciliation could be sacrificed in the interests of German security. Would that not legitimize Germany to become a military power again, capable of projection into Eastern Europe or onto other continents? And—not to fall into the trap of double standards—would that not legitimize Russia's response of participating in an arms race?

There is a good argument for why the "realist" doctrine has caused the demise of so many great powers in the long term: political entities that aggressively pursue the aim of "security" on a continental scale do not afford peace to their populations. If not already steamrolled by a "Grand Alliance" (like Germany in 1945) or ruined by a lengthy war (Britain at the same time), then overextension and the exorbitant financial strain of a large standing army could eventually leave them bankrupt (the Soviet Union in 1991). It is unclear how a securitarian European bloc could hope to catch peace by fishing in such troubled waters. It is quite clear, however, that it could fall apart by following the road to perdition already traveled by past European empires.

Mixing the terms "security" and "peace" thus is a semantic contradiction. Those times when political leaders felt the urge to deploy military or police forces to ensure their internal security were also those times when they did not feel themselves to be in a state of peace. George Orwell's totalitarian slogan—"War is peace, freedom is slavery, ignorance is strength," from his 1949 dystopian novel *Nineteen Eighty-Four*—is a fitting representation of a semantic labyrinth from which there is no escape. For all we know, this theoretical alloy of security and peace is a political *unobtainium* that cannot be found in nature and also cannot be manufactured.

A typical example of the rhetoric of the state of war was the declaration by French president Emmanuel Macron to France's assembled ambassadors on August 29, 2017: "ensuring the security of our citizens makes the fight against Islamist terrorism the priority of our foreign policy."[29] This announcement was made despite the EU's stated goal of peace. To this declaration, Macron added in Orwellian doublespeak: "peace is built with military forces, dissuasion forces and intelligence services," and "who[ever] knows where peace is built knows where the [nuclear] missiles are."[30] On close examination, these two sentences are on the same logical plane as "war is declared with trust, negotiations and agreements" and "whoever knows where war is declared, also knows where the peace treaties are." This is a good reminder of why it is fundamentally important to keep the vocabulary of war and peace apart: to prevent spurious cross-references from corrupting our historical memory and halting our thought processes. In sum, it would be best to refrain from treating peace as "an old idol worshipped out of habit."[31] One should either pursue peace in its proper sense and with peaceful means, or else do as the United States does: openly commit to a military agenda in preparation for a possible war.

Similarly, the issue with declaring "war" on terror is that it blurs the semantic distinction between domestic and foreign policy, because a terrorist group is not a state. "Terror" being merely a tactic, the term is a sweeping generalization and there is *no one* in particular to declare war to, or else *anyone* could potentially be an enemy (particularly immigrants or minorities)—which could make it easy for users of that concept to drift into paranoia or even ethnic discrimination. Even supposing such a "war" could be waged against some state, winning it would entail ceasefires and subsequent "peacekeeping" in war-torn regions of the Black Sea, the Middle East, or Africa. As our peace scale illustrates, such ceasefires and peacekeeping still belong to a state of war. Military operations might be necessary, but achieving lasting peace for the citizens of Europe would require repairing the devastation caused by military strikes against other peoples.

In Europe itself, domestic "peace" has slowly transformed, under the impact of terrorism, into displays of heavily armed soldiers patrolling airports (while intelligence officers monitor cyberspace), and where blanket laws can accuse citizens of sedition, sabotage, or assassination—subjecting them to police surveillance without warning or recourse. Today, as at the time of the Reaction, even the European Commission seems to have drifted into a "siege mentality," seeing enemies lurking among the general citizenry itself, especially in social groups deemed to be "at risk." The political horizon has greatly shortened from the long-term future to a short-term "prevention of the threat." There is a dark side to the celebrated Schengen Agreements: electronic detection systems for airport controls, databases of suspect individuals, the construction of new walls along the fortified borders of Bulgaria and Greece with Turkey, and patrols across the Mediterranean Sea.

In 2020, several political leaders in Europe, Macron among them, resorted to "declarations of war" in their initial responses to the novel coronavirus pandemic.[32] It is worth questioning the rationality of using such a metaphor, because the preparation of a country for war requires spreading negative emotions such as hatred for enemies or at least creating a dispassionate willingness to destroy human life, whereas levelheadedness and compassion are better suited to efforts to heal sick people and present disease. The intention behind such a communication strategy was no doubt to arouse the same nationalistic fervor and unity as past mobilizations, while muting critics. Unfortunately, as we have seen, it raised much skepticism and even backlash. The martial metaphor could not help but awaken unfortunate memories of chaos, strings of defeats endured in World War II and subsequent conflicts, and generally the aversion for war that European public opinion has developed in consequence—which was already visible in the widespread grassroots opposition against the US-led invasion of Iraq in 2003.

While the idea that containing a viral pandemic should be a "war" remains controversial in Europe, there is a general consensus among most

Europeans that militarism and securitarianism are contagious political diseases. Media and political parties already started between 1985 and 1989 to criticize the raising of "Fortress Europe," a term disparagingly used for a continental system in which external border controls regulate the flow of people, goods, services, and ideas into and out of the European Communities.[33] The idea of creating a strong division between "inside" and "outside" was not new, but initially it seemed benign. It resurfaced when discussions took place to create the European Union: it seemed a more-than-reasonable consequence of the free circulation inside the internal borders of Europe and a prerequisite for member states to vote in favor of this free internal circulation.[34]

It had, unfortunately, a powerful side effect: it was as if, once the Iron Curtain had been dismantled, the EU decided to build its own wall farther east, from Narva on the Baltic Sea all the way to Edirne and the Aegean Sea.[35] The question is not whether Russia or Turkey should join the European bloc or not in some future scenario, because that is ultimately a decision only the Russians or Turks can make. But the new fence, which cuts Europe in two just as the previous one did, is a clear sign that the EU now defines itself by exclusion, rather than inclusion.[36] The demand for stronger external borders is also a violation of the inclusive principle Schuman formulated in 1949: "But Europe cannot possibly wait for definition, for the end of that controversy; she does, in fact, define her own bounds by the will of her peoples."[37] He meant that "Europe" could never limit itself to the borders of the European construction: if other states wanted to join the EU but were kept forcibly out by a hard border, what would this supranational entity be doing other than confiscating the Idea of Europe for its own profit? The term "Fortress Europe," in German *Festung Europa,* was an invention of the Third Reich's propaganda machine to describe the Atlantic Wall, fortifications built to prevent an Anglo-American landing. It was exhumed intentionally, around the 1980s, by critics of restrictive immigration policies of the European Communities, because it reminded Europeans of the unhappy times of tyranny.

The EU's eastern fortification system against migrants is paradoxical, because the concept of a "fortress" under siege obviously belongs to a state of war and suggests that the European Union is engaging in passive means of preparation against an invasion. It is obviously contradictory for an entity whose final aim is lasting peace, unless that term has been so debased by fear of the "Other" that it has been emptied of its meaning. This concept might promote a "European identity" built against "invaders" and disparaged minorities.[38] The consolidation of immigration policy at the level of the EU risks fostering an ethnic definition of "European" citizenship versus "non-European," which would be an extension of the ethnonationalism of the twentieth century at a continental level. In a worst-case scenario, Euro-ethnicism could represent a risk for world peace should it turn again into supremacism.[39] In any case, the migration movements belong to the class of metamorphic movements against which resistance is futile and with which only constructive channeling can achieve effects. One of the World War II Allied propaganda mottoes, *Die Festung Europa hat kein Dach,* "Fortress Europe has no ceiling," might be metaphorically applied to the EU of the early twenty-first century to illustrate the frailty of these fortification lines.[40]

To paraphrase a Latin adage, *si vis incolumitatem, para pacem* ("if you want safety, prepare peace"). Supporters of securitarian policies should reflect on the fact that a focus on the pursuit of security was the direct cause of past arms races, which in a vicious circle brought the countries involved closer to war. The European social upheavals of the 1820s, 1848, and 1968, as well as recent protests, suggest that the more a state slips from cultivating domestic political peace to "keeping the peace," the higher popular frustration and domestic disorders grow, with violence tending to spiral out of control.[41] Similarly, the eradication of terrorist cells may achieve a temporary capitulation but will not, by itself, bring a country closer to peace. The flaw in that reasoning is the reversal of cause and effect: only lasting peace has brought security in Europe, whereas there is little material evidence to argue that the opposite has ever been true.

Similarly, defining "peace" as the eradication of one's enemies—the peace of graveyards—would also be an abandonment of the Idea of Europe. If peace is still the goal of the EU, then something must be done about the undeclared states of war that surround its fortified borders. It is unclear how any citizen of the European continent could ever feel secure unless every country in Europe's neighborhood—notably Ukraine, Turkey, Syria, Israel,

Palestine, and Libya—was in a state of peace with their neighbors, with peace treaties duly signed, and already proceeding together up the path toward reconciliation and solidarity. The belt of battlefields and frozen conflicts that surround the eastern and southern borders of the European Union shows that the task of bringing lasting peace to Europe is still a colossal one.

As if this implicit rhetoric of war was not sufficient, the EU has faced, during the second decade of the twenty-first century, the resurgence of an antagonistic form of ethnonationalism whose general purpose is to replace the European construction with a new version of "Westphalian States." The rhetoric of these movements makes use of metaphors that belong to the state of war, reminiscent of their twentieth-century predecessors. Thus, Hungarian prime minister Viktor Orbán declared, "We've lived through the last nine or ten years with a bricklayer's trowel in one hand and a sword in another. We needed to build while at the same time continuously fight. . . . We've had to repel attacks."[42] This is not merely an abstraction; other leaders have called for revanchism against real or imagined affronts to the nation and for irredentism to reclaim territories. In Central Europe, old wounds caused by the Treaties of Versailles and Trianon have been reopened by present-day feuds.[43]

That these border conflicts threaten to compromise the rule of law and jeopardize economic prosperity poses no problem for these ethnonationalist movements, which find justification in a desire to unleash suppressed violence. The wars of the former Yugoslavia in the early 1990s are just the most recent reminder of how murderous ethnopolitical conflicts can be. When two irredentist states clash over territory, the most likely consequence will be civil war, frozen war, or interstate war.[44] In the same way Rousseau and Kant saw the cause of war in the greed of patrimonial monarchs, today we might consider the greed of ethnonationalist ideologies a social contagion, their spread as a direct threat to the long-term peace of the continent. It is fortunate this strain still does not seem to be as virulent as the movements of the interwar period and that modern German society still carries immunity defenses against the "brown plague" of Nazism.

The twenty-first-century strain of securitarian and militaristic ideologies, if not curbed, could bring down the European construction, replacing the *Pax Europeana* with a new balkanization. In the concluding words of his *Pan-Europe,* Coudenhove-Kalergi warned in the 1920s of the dire consequences for Europe if countries did not work together to create a common market and, in particular, if France and Germany failed to reconcile.[45] His warning could still be relevant if the European Union were to fall prey to national state-of-war ideologies.

*I*t might thus be useful to conceive, as "Yet Another Peace Plan," what a continental Grand Alliance of Europe should become in the ideal. It should obviously be peace-sustaining: internally by avoiding social, ethnic, or economic conflicts and externally by keeping peaceful and legal relations with its neighbors and promoting reconciliation and solidarity. It would be reassuring, for the rest of the international community, if the EU adopted a clause forbidding wars of aggression, reminiscent of the French Declaration of Peace to the World of 1790 or Article 2 of the 1990 Settlement Treaty of Germany, such as the following: "The Governments of the Federal Republic of Germany and the German Democratic Republic reaffirm their declarations that only peace will emanate from German soil."[46]

Domestically, a European Society of States would have to be able to assert the sovereignty of its member-states. As a condition for territorial sovereignty, it should have the means to deny any external military intervention or any undue influence from outside powers, whether the United States, Russia, China, or any other. A standing army might be necessary, though it would need to be defensive in nature. It would have to be a stable actor, using open and respectful negotiation to reach its goals. It might use its positive influence to bring peace, stability, and prosperity to its "neighborhood"— the Balkans, the Black Sea, the Caucasus, the Middle East, and North Africa—but it should not use aggressive force, military or economic, on its neighbors, allies, or adversaries to make them align with its policies or coerce them in any way into submission.

In any case, the very existence of the European Union is no longer in question. The crucial questions are whether the EU will remain faithful to the goal of lasting peace in the long term and whether it will continue to safeguard peace, the equality of states before the law, and the freedoms of its citizens. The challenge for the future will be how to keep a politically united continent on track with the Idea of Europe. It is more essential than ever to distinguish this Idea of Europe from the European Union, which is only its latest institutional incarnation. Brexit demonstrated to member states that the national mandate conferred by referendum on a pan-European institution is revocable and might need to be reconfirmed again and again by its member states.[47] To achieve a more permanent legacy, the EU must not only demonstrate its unwavering commitment to peace but also its effectiveness in delivering it.

Let us return to Shakespeare: "A peace is of the nature of a conquest; for then both parties nobly are subdued, and neither party loser." The quest of peace in Europe since the Treaty of Utrecht has indeed been a noble conquest; more accurately, it has been an effort to overcome the tendency of European states to behave as frightened horses in times of crisis and to run amok, as they spectacularly did in 1856 with the Crimean War or in the summer of 1914. A vivid proof of this statement is that, on the day in May 1950 when Germany and France turned around and saw each other for what they really were—partners in solidarity—their mutual fears started to vanish, and the ECSC was born.

At the outset of this book, I posed a profound and difficult question: How is it possible to ensure lasting peace while guaranteeing the liberties of all states? In investigating the answer, I focused on the European experience. In the two and a half centuries between 1713 and 1945, the great powers of Europe held a commanding global lead in military power, technological expertise, and economic resources; yet their internecine quarrels became the sources of the world's greatest and most far-flung conflagrations. Against this background, many of the world's greatest thinkers on questions of peace and war were also Europeans. Even more importantly, the continent of Europe became an experimental laboratory for trying out several theories of peace.

I intended to "provincialize Europe" by refraining from presenting European mores and habits as a yardstick for all humanity.[48] There is a cognitive bias in the demand that any survey of events in Europe must always cover the rest of the world. I wished to avoid the illusion of thinking that the European experience can be automatically transposed elsewhere—a failing of so many European and American studies, even in our era. Every people or culture may have its own deep cultural interpretation of what the ceremony of "making peace" means, be it an individual becoming whole again, a family reunited, a group of nations coming together as one, humanity at peace, the flourishing of an ecosystem that includes all plants and animals, or harmony of the cosmos. By emphasizing the struggles against attempts to establish continental hegemony in Europe, I was able to focus on Europeans' reflections on the destructive consequences of military violence: how it feels to have one's life and possessions threatened, to lose one's statehood, or even to be actually enslaved and what could—and did—change in the way in which the European colonial powers treated peoples on other continents. For the French, Dutch, Belgians, or Germans who suffered brutal foreign occupations or state violence, their experiences also became an opportunity to reflect on the virtues of compassion and respect for peoples elsewhere in the world.

Of course, as Immanuel Kant noted more than two centuries ago, peace in Europe could only last and flourish if the world as a whole also moved toward peace. So, could our exploration of the European experience in the conquest of lasting peace nevertheless provide a few lessons for the rest of the globe? That question is not for this book to answer. There is, however, one ready field of application. The United Nations was the brainchild of a US president in 1945; for better or worse, it was essentially a European artifact, born directly out of the perpetual peace tradition described here. Its current limitations are the product of the fears of great powers rooted in the European tradition and their refusal to surrender their sovereignty; these restrictions have maintained the great powers in its Security Council in a perpetual state of frozen war against each other. The functional approach of the European construction may offer a positive contrast, because it inspires teamwork.

Meanwhile, Americans today are living in an atmosphere of frustration and self-doubt of the kind that necessarily accompanies a world power's loss of influence and relative decline. The intense reflection in North America on the implications of the rise of a multipolar world closely mirrors European concerns after World War I on the "decline of Europe." This observation could provide an opportunity for US strategists and political thinkers to examine and determine what they may be able to apply from the European experience of political decline to their present situation, in the hope that they can do better than the European powers did.

European history, strewn with the cadavers of past continental empires, has made it clear that the paradigm of the balance of power worked best when it was confined to a defensive war against a would-be empire that threatened the sovereignty of a majority of states. It did not perform as well as ideological legitimization for punitive operations conducted by one major power against minor powers beyond the seas; rather, it always legitimized the entry of another major power into the fray to restore said balance of power.

The most important lesson may be this: it would be a sign of weakness for the leaders of any modern nation to place their faith in an offensive army or the "peacemaking" virtues of nuclear warheads as the chief guarantor of their national security. Modern European history shows that all the states—none excepted—that have followed this path of "grandeur" with militaristic ideologies and offensive armies have ended their course in the land of decadence, whether through military defeat or economic failure. In contrast, political greatness has repeatedly been found in the social bonds of togetherness and economic prosperity that only lasting peace can afford.

States that realize their momentary weakness are forced to coalesce into military alliances to restore the balance of power against a hostile empire. Only the strong—or those that wish to become strong—establish lasting alliances of peace. And the condition to remaining strong is to forge ahead relentlessly toward the goal of "a just and lasting peace, based on genuine agreement freely arrived at by equals"—without being seduced by the two selfish sirens of war: militarism and securitarianism. Peace is for the strong; war is for the weak.

Abbreviations and Note on Proper Names

ACV	Archives Cantonales Vaudoises, Lausanne
AFJME	Archives Fondation Jean Monnet pour l'Europe, Lausanne
AMAE	Archives du Ministère des Affaires Étrangères, La Courneuve
Angeberg, Congrès	Comte d'Angeberg [pseud. J. L. Chodźko], ed., *Le Congrès de Vienne et les traités de 1815, précédé et suivi des actes diplomatiques qui s'y rattachent.* 4 vols. Paris: Aymot, 1864.
CIS	Commonwealth of Independent States
Comecon	Council for Mutual Economic Assistance
CSCE	Conference on Security and Co-operation in Europe
CVCE	Centre virtuel de la connaissance sur l'Europe, Luxembourg
EC	European Community
ECB	European Central Bank
ECSC	European Coal and Steel Community
EDC	European Defense Community
EEC	European Economic Community
EFTA	European Free Trade Association
EPU	European Parliamentary Union
Erasmus	European Community Action Scheme for the Mobility of University Students
EU	European Union
Euratom	European Atomic Energy Community
FO	Foreign Office
FRUS	Joseph V. Fuller, ed., Tyler Dennett, gen. ed. *Papers Relating to the Foreign Relations of the United States: The Paris Peace Conference, 1919.* 13 vols. Washington, DC: United States Government Printing Office, 1942–1947.
FTA	Free Trade Area
GDR	German Democratic Republic
GNP	Gross National Product

HAEU	Historical Archives of the European Union, Florence
ICMEU	International Committee of the Movements for European Unity
ICRC	International Committee of the Red Cross
IPCH	Charles Seymour, ed. *The Intimate Papers of Colonel House*. 4 vols. Boston: Houghton Mifflin, 1926–1928.
KLA	Kosovo Liberation Army
LNA	League of Nations Archives, Geneva
NATO	North Atlantic Treaty Organization
NSDAP	National Socialist German Workers' Party
OECD	Organization for Economic Co-operation and Development
OEEC	Organization for European Economic Co-operation
OSCE	Organization for Security and Co-operation in Europe
PWW	Arthur S. Link, ed. *The Papers of Woodrow Wilson*. 69 vols. Princeton: Princeton University Press, 1966–1994.
PZPR	Polish United Workers' Party
Recueil des traités et conventions	*Recueil des traités et conventions entre la France et les puissances alliées, en 1814 et 1815, suivi de l'Acte du Congrès de Vienne*. Paris: Rondonneau et Decle, 1815.
RO IRLI	Department of Manuscripts, Pushkin House, St. Petersburg
SDI	Strategic Defense Initiative
TEU	Treaty on European Union
TIAS	Charles I. Bevans, ed. *Treaties and Other International Agreements of the United States of America, 1776–1949*, 13 vols. Washington, DC: U.S. Government Printing Office, 1968–1976.
TNA	The National Archives of the United Kingdom, Kew
UEFA	Union of European Football Association
UN	United Nations
UNGA	United Nations General Assembly
US	United States
USSR	Union of Soviet Socialist Republics
WEU	Western European Union

NOTE ON PROPER NAMES

Russian names are spelled in this book according to the standard (Library of Congress) system of transliteration, but common English spellings of well-known Russian names (Tsar Alexander, for example) are retained.

Notes

INTRODUCTION

1. Cesare Ripa, *Iconologia: Overo descrittione di diverse imagini cavate dall'antichità, e di propria invenzione,* introduction by Erna Mandowsky (Hildesheim: Georg Olms, 1970), 332–334; Peter Meurer, "Europa Regina: 16th Century Maps of Europe in the Form of a Queen," *Belgeo* 3–4 (2008): 355–370.

2. The Greek historian Herodotus had already observed in the fifth century BCE that the only connection between this Asian princess and the continent of Europe was a similarity of names; yet so many artists agreed to suspend their disbelief that, in a cultural sense, they have become one and the same. Herodotus, *The Histories,* ed. Walter Blanco and Jennifer Tolbert Roberts, trans. Walter Blanco (New York: W. W. Norton, 1992), 4 (1.1-2).

3. Luis Díez del Corral, *The Rape of Europe,* trans. H. V. Livermore (New York: Macmillan Company, 1959); Luisa Prandi, "Europa e i Cadmei: La 'versione beotica' del mito," *Contributi dell'Instituto di Storia antica dell'Università del Sacro Cuore (CISA)* 12 (1986): 37–48; Dario M. Cosi, "Dietro al fantasma di Europa: Sposa, madre, regina," *Contributi dell'Instituto di Storia antica,* 27–36.

4. Svetlana Alpers and Michael Baxandall, *Tiepolo and the Pictorial Intelligence* (New Haven: Yale University Press, 1994), 154.

5. There was a precedent in the association between two representations of *Europa Regina* and the bull, in the so-called Eitzing Atlas: Michael von Eitzing, *De Europae virginis, tauro insidentis, topographica atque historica descriptione liber* (Cologne: Gottfried van Kempen, 1588). It followed, however, that the traditional canon of the leaping bull did not attempt to create a tension between the two characters. On the representations of Europa/Europe in art and myth, see Michael J. Wintle, *The Image of Europe: Visualizing Europe in Iconography and Cartography throughout the Ages* (Cambridge: Cambridge University Press, 2009), 128–150.

6. Ernst's chaotic landscape is reminiscent of the color and consistency of the spectacular—and poisonous—chemical reaction known as the *pharaoh's snake* (mercury thiocyanate), which causes the growth of grotesque forms that seem to be alive. Pascal Dethurens, "Europe, lieu fantasme: Le mythe d'Europe dans l'histoire de l'art," in *Lieux d'Europe: Mythes et limites,* ed. Stella Ghervas and François Rosset (Paris: Éditions de la Maison des sciences de l'homme, 2008), 19.

7. On this "utopian" aspect see Jay Winter, *Dreams of Peace and Freedom: Utopian Moments in the Twentieth Century* (New Haven: Yale University Press, 2006), 48–74; Bo Stråth, *Europe's Utopias of Peace: 1815, 1919, 1951* (London: Bloomsbury Academic, 2016), 1–22.

8. Flavius Vegetius Renatus, *Epitoma Rei Militaris,* ed. and trans. Leo Stelten (New York: Peter Lang, 1990), 122–123 (III).

9. Ronald Reagan, "Address before a Joint Session of the Congress on the State of the Union" (February 6, 1985), Ronald Reagan Presidential Library, https://www.reaganlibrary.gov/research/speeches/20685e.

10. Both metaphors are borrowed from Lao Tzu, *The Tao Te Ching,* trans. Gia-Fu Feng and Jane English (New York: Vintage Book, 1989), strophes 6 and 66.

11. For a psychological study of these characters, see Leo Damrosch, *Jean-Jacques Rousseau: Restless Genius* (Boston: Houghton Mifflin, 2007); Beverley Clack, "Immanuel Kant 1724–1804," in *Misogyny in the Western Philosophical Tradition: A Reader,* ed. Beverly Clack (Basingstoke: Palgrave Macmillan, 1999), 144–160; Aleksandr Arkhangel'skiĭ, *Aleksandr I* (Moscow: Vagrius, 2000), 108-115; Patricia O'Toole, *The Moralist: Woodrow Wilson and the World He Made* (New York: Simon & Schuster, 2018).

12. *Churchill by Himself: The Definitive Collection of Quotations,* ed. Richard M. Langworth (New York: Public Affairs, 2008), 570–581.

13. Leo Tolstoy, *War and Peace* (1869), trans. Anthony Briggs (London: Penguin Classics, 2007), 1259.

14. This is the classic definition by Emer de Vattel, *The Law of Nations,* ed. Béla Kapossy and Richard Whatmore (Indianapolis: Liberty Fund, 2012), 67–70, originally published in 1758.

15. For the classic and narrow definition of diplomacy, perceived through a "Westphalian" lens as a system of international relations between states, see

Harold Nicolson, *Diplomacy,* 2nd ed. (Washington DC: Institute for the Study of Diplomacy, 1988), 3–5; Hans J. Morgenthau, *Politics among Nations: The Struggle for Power and Peace* (New York: Knopf, 1966), 139.

16. "Repos, estat d'un peuple qui n'est point en guerre." *Le Dictionnaire de l'Académie française,* 1st ed., 2 vols. (Paris, 1694), 2: "paix."

17. In the first edition (1694), second (1718), third (1745), fourth (1762), and fifth (1798).

18. "On appelle ainsi, certains Traitez de Paix plus fameux. La paix de Vestphalie." *Le Dictionnaire de l'Académie française,* 1st ed. (1694), 2: "paix."

19. Treaty of Osnabrück, [Münster] (October 24, 1648), Art. 1: "Instrumentum Pacis Osnabrugensis (IPO)," in *Die Friedensverträge mit Frankreich und Schweden,* ed. Antje Oschmann (*Acta Pacis Westphalicae,* ed. Konrad Repgen, Series III.B, vol. I), 3 vols. (Münster: Aschendorff, 1998–2007), 1: 98 (no. 18).

20. Emer de Vattel, *Law of Nations,* 663 (IV.ii.19); Richard Whatmore, "Vattel, Britain and Peace in Europe," *Grotiana* 31 (2010): 85–107.

21. Oona A. Hathaway and Scott J. Shapiro, *The Internationalists: How a Radical Plan to Outlaw War Remade the World* (New York: Simon & Schuster, 2017), 199–214.

22. Immanuel Kant, *Perpetual Peace: A Philosophical Sketch,* in *Kant: Political Writings,* ed. Hans Reiss, trans. H. B. Nisbet (Cambridge: Cambridge University Press, 1991), 93.

23. Jean-François Klein, "'Pacification,' an Imperial Process," *Encyclopédie pour une histoire nouvelle de l'Europe,* 2016, http://ehne.fr/en/node/1150.

24. According to *American Heritage Dictionary.*

25. Hugo Grotius, *On the Law of War and Peace* (1625), ed. Stephen C. Neff (Cambridge: Cambridge University Press, 2012), 23 (I.i.2); Richard Tuck, *The Rights of War and Peace: Political Thought and the International Order from Grotius to Kant* (Oxford: Oxford University Press, 2001), 78–108.

26. "Querelle entre deux Princes, entre deux Estats souverains, qui se poursuit par la voye des armes." *Le Dictionnaire de l'Académie française,* 1st ed. (1694), 1: "guerre" (war). The same definition was still present in the eighth edition (1932–1935) of the *Dictionnaire.*

27. Vattel, *Law of Nations,* 469 (III.i.1).

28. James Q. Whitman, *The Verdict of Battle: The Law of Victory and the Making of Modern War* (Cambridge, MA: Harvard University Press, 2012), 25–49; Hathaway and Shapiro, *The Internationalists*, 31–81.

29. John Locke called this the "appeal to Heaven"; see Matthew Grimley, "The Religion of Englishness: Puritanism, Providentialism, and 'National Character,' 1918–1945," *Journal of British Studies* 46, no. 4 (2007): 884–906.

30. Vattel, *Law of Nations*, 503 (III.iv.57).

31. "Guerre & pitié, ne s'accordent point ensemble." *Dictionnaire de l'Académie française*, 1st ed.

32. This phrase is borrowed from George Orwell, "As I Please," *Tribune*, February 4, 1944.

33. Jonathan Swift, *The Conduct of the Allies and of the Late Ministry, in Beginning and Carrying on the Present War* (London: Printed for John Morphew, 1711), 3.

34. Matthew C. Waxman, "Siegecraft and Surrender: The Law and Strategy of City as Targets," *Virginia Journal of International Law* 39, no. 2 (1999): 353–423.

35. Patryk I. Labuda, "Lieber Code," in *Max Planck Encyclopedia of Public International Law*, September 2014, http://opil.ouplaw.com; David Armitage, *Civil Wars: A History in Ideas* (New York: Knopf, 2017), 162–166, 183–193.

36. "Convention (IV) Relative to the Protection of Civilian Persons in Time of War," *The Geneva Conventions of August 12, 1949* (Geneva: International Committee of the Red Cross, 1949), 153–221.

37. Christopher Clark, *The Sleepwalkers: How Europe Went to War in 1914* (New York: Penguin Books, 2012), particularly 451–470.

38. Kant, *Perpetual Peace*, Appendix I, 116–117.

39. Paul Kennedy, *The Rise and Fall of the Great Powers: Economic Change and Military Conflict from 1500 to 2000* (London: Unwin Hyman, 1988), 365–372, 488–513.

40. Conrad Malte-Brun, *Précis de la géographie universelle ou Description de toutes les parties du monde sur un plan nouveau d'après les grandes divisions du globe*, 8 vols. (Paris: Buisson, 1812–1829), 2: 392–394; Elisée Reclus, *Nouvelle géographie universelle. La terre et les hommes* (Paris: Hachette, 1876), 33. Climate change has not yet had a measurable impact on that aspect.

41. Herodotus, *Histories*, 126 (4.45).

42. Denis Hay, *Europe: The Emergence of an Idea* (Edinburgh: Edinburgh University Press, 1957), 1–15; Anthony Pagden, "Europe: Conceptualizing a Continent," in *The Idea of Europe: From Antiquity to the European Union,* ed. Anthony Pagden (Cambridge: Cambridge University Press, 2002), 33–54.

43. On the same subject, Paul Valéry wrote that Rome bequeathed to posterity "the eternal paragon of stable and organized power." Valéry, *Oeuvres* (Paris: Gallimard, 1957), 1: 1008.

44. Bruno Arcidiacono, *Cinq types de paix: Une histoire des plans de pacification perpétuelle, XVIIe–XXe siècles* (Paris: Presses universitaires de France, 2011), 5.

45. On the concept of "universal monarchy," see Franz Bosbach, *Monarchia Universalis: Ein politischer Leitbegriff der frühen Neuzeit* (Göttingen: Vandenhoeck & Ruprecht, 1988); Steven Pincus, "The English Debate over Universal Monarchy," in *A Union for Empire: Political Thought and the Union of 1707,* ed. John Robertson (Cambridge: Cambridge University Press, 1995), 37–62; Klaus Malettke, "L'équilibre européen' face à la *monarchia universalis:* les reactions européennes aux ambitions hégémoniques à l'époque moderne," in *L'invention de la diplomatie. Moyen Age—Temps modernes,* ed. Lucien Bély (Paris: Presses universitaires de France, 1998), 47–57.

46. Federico Chabod, *Storia dell'idea d'Europa* (Bari: Editori Laterza, 1967), 48.

47. Niccolò Machiavelli, *Dell'arte della guerra,* in *Opere complete, Vol. 2: Arte della guerra e scritti politici minori,* ed. Sergio Bertelli, 7 vols. (Milan: Feltrinelli, 1960–1964), 2: 393; Quentin Skinner, *The Foundations of Modern Political Thought,* 2 vols. (Cambridge: Cambridge University Press, 1978), 1: 173–175; Michael Mallett, "The Theory and Practice of Warfare in Machiavelli's Republic," *in Machiavelli and Republicanism,* ed. Gisela Bock et al. (Cambridge: Cambridge University Press, 1991), 173–180.

48. The notion of universal monarchy thus became an alternative or (in Koselleck's terms) a counter-concept to Europe as the home of peace. Reinhart Koselleck, "Demokratie IV.1," in *Geschichtliche Grundbegriffe: historisches Lexikon zur politisch-sozialen Sprache in Deutschland,* ed. Otto Brunner et al., 8 vols. (Stuttgart: E. Klett, 1972–1997), 1: 849.

49. The Peace of Westphalia (1648) comprised in fact four items: (1) the Peace of Münster, between the Dutch Republic and the Kingdom of Spain; (2) the Treaty of Münster between the Holy Roman Empire, France, and their respective allies; (3) the Treaty of Osnabrück between the Holy Roman Empire, Sweden, and their respective allies; and (4) two conventions in Nuremberg (one

signed by the Holy Roman Empire and France, and the other signed by the Holy Roman Empire and Sweden) on the execution of the peace. See Fritz Dickmann, *Der Westfälische Friede,* 2nd ed. (Münster: Aschendorff, 1998); Klaus Bussmann and Heinz Schilling, *1648: Krieg und Frieden in Europa,* 3 vols. (Munchen: Bruckmann, 1998); Lucien Bély, ed., *L'Europe des traités de Westphalie: Esprit de la diplomatie et diplomatie de l'esprit* (Paris: Presses universitaires de France, 2000); Arnaud Blin, *1648: La Paix de Westphalie ou la naissance de l'Europe politique moderne* (Paris: Complexe, 2006).

50. Derek Croxton, "The Peace of Westphalia of 1648 and the Origins of Sovereignty," *International History Review* 21, no. 3 (1999): 569–591; Stella Ghervas and David Armitage, "From Westphalia to Enlightened Peace, 1648–1815," in *A Cultural History of Peace in the Age of Enlightenment,* ed. Stella Ghervas and David Armitage (London: Bloomsbury Academic, 2020), 7–10.

51. More accurately, the Swiss delegation to Münster and Osnabrück obtained confirmation of the "full freedom and exemption from the Empire." See Peter Stadler, "Der Westfälische Friede und die Eidgenossenschaft," in *1648: Die Schweiz und Europa. Aussenpolitik zur Zeit des Westfälischen Friedens,* ed. Marco Jorio (Zürich: Chronos-Verlag, 1999), 57–77.

52. Robert von Friedeburg, "*Cuius regio, eius religio:* The Ambivalent Meanings of State Building in Protestant Germany, 1555–1655," in *Diversity and Dissent: Negotiating Religious Difference in Central Europe, 1500–1800,* ed. Howard Louthan et al. (New York: Berghahn Books, 2011), 73–90.

53. Edward Keene, *Beyond the Anarchical Society: Grotius, Colonialism and Order in World Politics* (Cambridge: Cambridge University Press, 2002), 97–101.

54. Lucien Bély, "Le 'paradigme westphalien' au miroir de l'histoire: L'Europe des traités de Westphalie," *Annuaire Français de Relations Internationales* 10 (2009): 1–14; Blin, *1648: La Paix de Westphalie,* 165–210; Marc Belissa, *Repenser l'ordre européen (1795–1802): De la société des rois aux droits des nations* (Paris: Editions Kimé, 2006), 12–18.

55. Randall Lesaffer, *European Legal History: A Cultural and Political Perspective,* trans. Jan Arriens (Cambridge: Cambridge University Press, 2009), 308; Lesaffer, "The Westphalian Peace Treaties and the Development of the Tradition of Great European Peace Settlements prior to 1648," *Grotiana* 18, no. 1 (1997): 71–95.

56. These are not exactly the same reasons generally invoked by the literature criticizing the "Westphalian myth," notably Andreas Osiander, *The States*

System of Europe, 1640–1990: Peacemaking and the Conditions of International Stability (New York: Oxford University Press, 1994), 78–79; Benno Teschke, *The Myth of 1648: Class, Geopolitics and the Making of Modern International Relations* (London: Verso, 2003); Stephane Beaulac, *Power of Language in the Making of International Law: The Word "Sovereignty" in Bodin and Vattel and the Myth of Westphalia* (Leiden: Brill, 2004), 67–71; Pärtel Piirimäe, "The Westphalian Myth and the Idea of External Sovereignty," in *Sovereignty in Fragments: The Past, Present and Future of a Contested Concept,* ed. Hent Kalmo and Quentin Skinner (Cambridge: Cambridge University Press, 2011), 64–80.

57. Ghervas and Armitage, "From Westphalia to Enlightened Peace," 7–10.

58. Job 41: 12–34.

59. Thomas Hobbes, *Leviathan,* ed. Noel Malcolm, 3 vols. (Oxford: Oxford University Press, 2012), 3: 960 (ch. 44).

60. Hobbes, *Leviathan,* 2: 224 (ch. 15).

61. Maximilien de Béthune, Duc de Sully (1559–1641), *Mémoires, ou Oeconomies Royales d'Etat, Domestiques, Politiques & Militaires de Henri le Grand,* 12 vols. (Amsterdam: Aux dépens de la Compagnie, 1725), 2: 25.

62. For a map of Sully's Europe, see "La forteresse Europe: le projet politique du duc de Sully," in *Fragments d'Europe: Atlas de l'Europe médiane et orientale,* ed. Michel Foucher (Paris: Fayard, 1993), 21.

63. Voltaire, *La Henriade* (1723) (Amsterdam: François L'Honoré, 1775), 1–2 (canto 1, ll. 1-5).

1. THE ENLIGHTENED SPIRIT OF PEACE

1. "Congrès," in *Dictionnaire de l'Académie française,* 4th ed., 2 vols. (Paris: Veuve B. Brunet, 1762), 1: 367.

2. Hamish Scott, "The Second 'Hundred Years War,'" *Historical Journal* 35, no. 2 (1992): 443–469; François Crouzet, "The Second Hundred Years War: Some Reflections," *French History* 10, no. 4 (1996): 432–450.

3. Larry Wolff, *Inventing Eastern Europe: The Map of Civilization on the Mind of the Enlightenment* (Stanford: Stanford University Press, 1994), 144–194.

4. Vasily N. Tatishchev (1686–1750) is credited for the novel idea that the Ural Mountains would be more appropriate than a river as a border for Europe. That

choice followed an ideological agenda. See Tatishchev, *Obshchee geograficheskoe opisanie vseĭa Sibiri* (1736), in Tatishchev, *Izbrannye trudy po geografii Rossii* (Moscow: Gossudarstvennoe izdatel'stvo geograficheskoĭ literatury, 1950), 48–51; Mark Bassin, "Russia between Europe and Asia: The Ideological Construction of Geographical Space," *Slavic Review* 50, no. 1 (1991): 6.

5. Lucien Bély, *L'art de la paix en Europe: Naissance de la diplomatie moderne XVIe– XVIIIe siècle* (Paris: Presses universitaires de France, 2007), 103–130.

6. John B. Hattendorf, *England in the War of the Spanish Succession* (New York: Garland, 1987), 53–75; Kalevi J. Holsti, *Peace and War: Armed Conflicts and International Order, 1648–1989* (Cambridge: Cambridge University Press, 1991), 73–82; Lucien Bély, *La société des princes, XVIe–XVIIIe siècle* (Paris: Fayard, 1999), 307–332; Andrew C. Thompson, "Balancing Europe: Ideas and Interests in British Foreign Policy (c. 1700–c. 1720)," in *Ideology and Foreign Policy in Early Modern Europe (1650–1750),* ed. David Onnekink and Gijs Rommelse (Aldershot: Ashgate, 2011), 267–282.

7. John Robertson, ed., *A Union for Empire: Political Thought and the Union of 1707* (Cambridge: Cambridge University Press, 1995); Jeremy Black, *Britain as a Military Power, 1688–1815* (London: UCL Press, 1999), 45–78; Allan I. Macinnes, *Union and Empire: The Making of the United Kingdom in 1707* (Cambridge: Cambridge University Press, 2009).

8. Arie Th. van Deursen, "De Republiek der Zeven Verenigde Nederlanden (1588–1780)," in *Geschiedenis van de Nederlanden,* ed. J. C. H. Blom and E. Lamberts (Baarn: Hbuitgevers, 2005), 163; David Onnekink, *Reinterpreting the Dutch Forty Years War, 1672–1713* (London: Palgrave Macmillan, 2016).

9. Hamish Scott, *The Birth of a Great Power System 1740–1815* (Harlow: Pearson / Longman, 2006), 139.

10. David Hume, "Of the Balance of Power," in Hume, *Essays, Moral, Political, and Literary,* ed. Eugene Miller (Indianapolis: Liberty Fund, 1985), 332–341; Frederick G. Whelan, "Robertson, Hume, and the Balance of Power," *Hume Studies* 21, no. 2 (1995): 315–332.

11. It is also remembered in a version revised in the aftermath of the Seven Years' War. John Robertson, "Universal Monarchy and the Liberties of Europe: David Hume's Critique of an English Whig Doctrine," in *Union for Empire,* ed. Robertson, 349–374. Edward Keene makes the point that it would have been more relevant,

rather than always referring to Hume's essay, to consider the first edition of John Campbell's book, *The Present State of Europe: Explaining the Interests, Connections, Political and Commercial Views of its Several Powers* (London: Thomas Longman and C. Hitch, 1750). Edward Keene, "International Intellectual History and International Relations: Contexts, Canons and Mediocrities," *International Relations* 31, no. 3 (2017): 341–356.

12. Edward Vose Gulick, *Europe's Classical Balance of Power* (New York: W. W. Norton, 1955); Georges Livet, *L'équilibre européen de la fin du XVe siècle à la fin du XVIIIe siècle* (Paris: Presses universitaires de France, 1976); Michael Sheehan, *The Balance of Power: History and Theory* (London: Routledge, 1996); Klaus Malettke, "L'équilibre européen' face à la 'monarchia universalis': les réactions européennes aux ambitions hégémoniques," in *Imaginer l'Europe,* ed. Klaus Malettke (Paris: Belin & De Boeck, 2000), 117–124; Bruno Bernardi, "L'idée d'équilibre européen dans le *jus gentium* des modernes: esquisse d'histoire conceptuelle," in *Penser l'Europe au XVIIIe siècle: Commerce, Civilisation, Empire,* ed. Antoine Lilti and Céline Spector (Oxford: Voltaire Foundation, 2014), 19–46.

13. *Thirty-Six Stratagems: Secret Art of War,* trans. Liu Yi (Singapore: Asiapac, 1993), no. 3, 20.

14. In 1579, the first translation of Guicciardini's *History* introduced Italian balance-of-power thinking to a wider English audience. *The History of Guicciardini Conteining the Vvarres of Italie and other Partes, Reduced into English by Geffray Fenton* (London: Thomas Vautroullier, 1579); Alfred Vagts, "The Balance of Power: Growth of an Idea," *World Politics* 1, no. 1 (1948–1949): 82–101; Herbert Butterfield, "The Balance of Power," in *Diplomatic Investigations. Essays in the Theory of International Politics,* ed. Herbert Butterfield and Martin Wight (London: G. Allen & Unwin, 1966), 132–148; Moorhead Wright, ed., "The Italian Origins," in *Theory and Practice of the Balance of Power, 1486–1914: Selected European Writings* (London: J. M. Dent, 1975), 1–23.

15. Michael Sheehan, "The Development of British Theory and Practice of the Balance of Power before 1714," *History* 73, no. 237 (1988): 24–37; Jeremy Black, *A System of Ambition? British Foreign Policy 1660–1793* (Stroud: Sutton, 2000), 137–174.

16. A patrimonial state is any form of state considered as a patrimony ("a right or estate inherited from one's ancestors") that a monarch could obtain by inheritance, marriage, or bequest. "Patrimony," in Noah Webster, *An American*

Dictionary of the English Language, 2 vols. (New York: S. Converse, 1828), 2: [253].

17. "English Bill of Rights, 1689," in *The Essential Bill of Rights: Original Arguments and Fundamental Documents,* ed. Gordon Lloyd and Margie Lloyd (Lanham, MD: University Press of America, 1998), 57–60.

18. Charles Davenant, "An Essay upon the Balance of Power," in *The Political and Commercial Works of Charles Davenant LL.D.,* ed. Charles Whitworth, 5 vols. (London: R. Horsfield, 1771), 3: 299–430. For other significant texts on the balance of power at that time, see John Toland, *Anglia Libera, or The Limitation and Succession of the Crown of England* (London: Bernard Lintott, [1701]), 140–169 (sect. 17–18); Jonathan Swift, *A Discourse of the Contests and Dissensions between the Nobles and the Commons in Athens and Rome,* 1st ed. 1701, ed. F. H. Ellis (Oxford: Clarendon Press, 1967), 83–91.

19. Kustaa Multamäki, *Towards Great Britain: Commerce & Conquest in the Thought of Algernon Sidney and Charles Davenant* (Tuusula: Finnish Academy of Science and Letters, 1999), 149–185.

20. Davenant, "Essay upon the Balance of Power," 302–305.

21. The *Philosophiæ Naturalis Principia Mathematica* of Isaac Newton was published in London in 1687. See "Organic and Mechanical Metaphors in Late Eighteenth-Century American Political Thought," *Harvard Law Review* 110, no. 8 (1997): 1832–1849.

22. Davenant, "Essay upon the Balance of Power," 301. See also Istvan Hont, "Free Trade and the Economic Limits to National Politics: Neo-Machiavellian Political Economy Reconsidered," in *The Economic Limits to Modern Politics,* ed. John Dunn (Cambridge: Cambridge University Press, 1990), 41–120; David Armitage, *The Ideological Origins of the British Empire* (Cambridge: Cambridge University Press, 2000), 141–144.

23. On the quarrel between the Ancients and the Moderns in England, see Joseph M. Levine, *The Battle of the Books: History and Literature in the Augustan Age* (Ithaca: Cornell University Press, 1994).

24. Michael Sheehan, "The Sincerity of the British Commitment to the Maintenance of the Balance of Power 1714–1763," *Diplomacy & Statecraft* 15, no. 3 (2004): 489–506.

25. Davenant, "Essay upon the Balance of Power," 351–352.

26. Davenant, "Essay upon the Balance of Power," 359.

27. "Besides maintaining the *Balance of Europe,* it has been likewise another maxim of England since the Reformation *to keep itself the Head of the Protestant Religion all over the World.*": Toland, *Anglia Libera,* 148 (sect. 18).

28. Swift, *The Conduct of the Allies,* 27, 39–40, 71; Swift, *Some Remarks on the Barrier Treaty, between her Majesty and the States-General* (London: Printed for John Morphew, 1712), 21; Swift, *A Discourse of the Contests and Dissentions,* 5. See also Daniel Defoe, *The Balance of Europe; or, an Enquiry into the Respective Dangers of Giving the Spanish Monarchy to the Emperor as well as to King Philip* (London: John Baker, 1711).

29. *Les grands traités du règne de Louis XIV,* ed. Henri Vast, 3 vols. (Paris: A. Picard, 1899), vol. 3; *A Collection of Treaties between Great Britain and Other Powers,* ed. George Chalmers, 2 vols. (London: J. Stockdale, 1790), vols. 1–2; *The Treaties of the War of the Spanish Succession. A Historical and Critical Dictionary,* ed. Linda Frey and Marsha Frey (Westport, CT: Greenwood Press, 1995).

30. Paul Meerts and Peter Beeuwkes, "The Utrecht Negotiations in Perspective: The Hope of Happiness for the World," *International Negotiation* 13, no. 2 (2008): 159.

31. "Traité de paix et d'amitié conclu à Utrecht, le 13 mars–11 avril 1713, entre la France et la Grande-Bretagne," in *Recueil des traités de la France,* ed. M. de Clercq, 23 vols. (Paris: Amyot, 1880–1917), 1: 4 (Art. 6).

32. "Traité de paix et d'amitié conclu à Utrecht," 1: 4 (Arts. 4 and 5).

33. Not without a failed attempt to reinstate the Stuarts on the British throne in the Jacobite rebellion of 1715.

34. "Treaty of Peace and Friendship: The King" (November 5, 1712), in *A Collection of Treaties between Great Britain and Other Powers French translation of the time,* ed. Chalmers, 2: 14. For the Spanish and French versions, see "Renonciations du Roy d'Espagne à la Couronne de France, de Monseigneur le Duc de Berry, & de Monseigneur le Duc d'Orleans à la Couronne d'Espagne aves les Lettres Patentes . . ." in *Suite des actes, mémoires et autres pieces autentiques concernant la paix d'Utrecht,* ed. [Casimir Freschot?], 6 vols. (Utrecht: Guillaume vande Water and Jaques van Poolsum, 1713–1715), 2: 329–398.

35. The Latin *Equilibrium Potentiae* was also used in the Treaty of Utrecht, part II.

36. Frederik Dhondt, *Balance of Power and Norm Hierarchy: Franco-British Diplomacy after the Peace of Utrecht* (Leiden: Brill Nijhoff, 2015), 7–12; Stella Ghervas, "Balance of Power vs. Perpetual Peace: Paradigms of European Order from Utrecht to Vienna, 1713–1815," *International History Review* 39, no. 3 (2017): 404–425.

37. For the three possible uses of the balance of power (ensure security, prevent hegemony, and pacify), see Bruno Arcidiacono, "De la balance politique et de ses rapports avec le droit des gens: Vattel, la 'guerre pour l'équilibre' et le système européen," in *Vattel's International Law from a XXIst Century Perspective—Le droit international de Vattel vu du XXIe siècle,* ed. Vincent Chetail and Peter Haggenmacher (Leiden: Martinus Nijhoff, 2011), 77–100; Richard Little, *The Balance of Power in International Relations: Metaphors, Myths, and Models* (Cambridge: Cambridge University Press, 2007), 50–87.

38. "Traité de la barrière, entre l'Autriche, la Grande-Bretagne et les Etats-généraux des Provinces-Unies, signé à Anvers, le 15 novembre 1715" (Treaty of Antwerp, November 15, 1715), in C. G. de Koch, *Histoire abrégée des traités de paix entre les puissances de l'Europe depuis la paix de Westphalie,* ed. F. Schoell, 4 vols. (Brussels: Meline, Gans et Compagnie, 1837), 1: 226–228.

39. Ottokar Weber, *Der Friede von Utrecht, 1710–1713* (Gotha: F. A. Perthes, 1891), 334–411; Jonathan Israel, *The Dutch Republic: Its Rise, Greatness and Fall, 1477–1806* (Oxford: Clarendon Press, 1995), 968–985.

40. Ivan I. Rostunov, *Istoriia Severnoĭ Voĭny 1700–1721 gg.* (Moscow: Nauka, 1987), ch. 2; Bély, *La société des princes,* 363–368.

41. J. G. A. Pocock, *Barbarism and Religion,* Vol. 2: *Narratives of Civil Government* (Cambridge: Cambridge University Press, 1999), 137–152, 170–172.

42. Stella Ghervas, "In the Shadow of Utrecht: Perpetual Peace and International Order, 1713–1815," in *The 1713 Peace of Utrecht and Its Enduring Effects,* ed. Alfred H. A. Soons (Leiden: Brill, 2019), 192–224.

43. Campbell, *Present State of Europe,* 504.

44. J. Ewing Ritchie, *The Life and Times of Viscount Palmerston,* 2 vols. (London: London Printing and Publishing Company, 1866–1867), 2: 767.

45. The last invasion was the landing of a large Dutch naval force during the Glorious Revolution in November 1688. See Israel, *The Dutch Republic,* 807–862.

46. H. D. Schmidt, "The Idea and Slogan of 'Perfidious Albion,'" *Journal of the History of Ideas,* 14, no. 4 (1953): 604–616.

47. Campbell, *Present State of Europe,* 130.

48. F. H. Hinsley, *Power and the Pursuit of Peace: Theory and Practice in the History of Relations between State*s (Cambridge: Cambridge University Press, 1963), 33–91; Arcidiacono, *Cinq types de paix,* vii–xx; Stella Ghervas, "Peace Perpetually Reconsidered," in *Books & Ideas,* November 12, 2012, http://www.booksandideas .net/Peace-perpetually-reconsidered.html.

49. Abbé de Saint-Pierre, *Projet pour rendre la paix perpétuelle en Europe,* 2 vols. (Utrecht: A. Schouten, 1713). All subsequent references are to Saint-Pierre, *Projet pour rendre la paix perpétuelle en Europe,* ed. Simone Goyard-Fabre ([Paris]: Fayard, 1986). The word *projet,* as Saint-Pierre and Rousseau understood it, is a "false friend" that cannot be translated into English as *project.* According to *Dictionnaire de l'Académie française* (1st ed. 1694), *projet* is "the intention that has been conceived to do something in future (which also includes the arrangement of the means)." From the Latin *projectus,* it meant literally "throwing oneself forward into the future." It was also a keyword in eighteenth-century English ("a design, purposes, contrivance," according to Bailey's *An Universal Etymological Dictionary* of 1726). The word "project" is generally understood today to include doing practical steps to achieve stated aims in a finite amount of time. This explains why modern translations prefer the term "plan" of perpetual peace.

50. *Abbé* was a generic clerical title, not related to a specific abbey. On Saint-Pierre's life and work, see Jean-Pierre Bois, *L'abbé de Saint-Pierre: entre clacissicisme et Lumières* (Ceyzérieu: Champ Vallon, 2017).

51. The Houghton Library at Harvard University contains some well-formed drafts of the first printed version of Saint-Pierre's *Projet,* dating from 1711. See also Maria Grazia Bottaro Palumbo, "La Genesi dei 'Mémoires pour rendre la paix perpétuelle en Europe' dell'abate di Saint-Pierre," in *Studi politici in onore di Luigi Firpo,* ed. Silvia Rota Chibaudi and Franco Barcia, 4 vols. (Milan: Franco Angeli, 1990), 2: 561–588; Antonella Alimento and Koen Stapelbroek, "Trade and Treaties: Balancing the Interstate System," in *The Politics of Commercial Treaties in the Eighteenth Century: Balance of Power, Balance of Trade,* ed. Antonella Alimento and Koen Stapelbroek (London: Palgrave Macmillan, 2017), 15–24.

52. "Malheur des Souverains de ne pouvoir faire de véritable Paix": Abbé de Saint-Pierre, *Projet de paix perpétuelle,* Seconde ébauche (Paris?: s.n., 1711?), Houghton Library, Harvard University, Houghton | f | *FC7.Sa282.711, f. 1.

53. Abbé de Saint-Pierre, *Projet pour rendre la paix perpétuelle* (Paris?: s.n., September 1712), 22, 63 ("Quatrième avantage: A l'égard de la continuation du commerce").

54. This conception precedes Montesquieu's idea of commerce as an alternative to war by forty years. See Catherine Larrère, "Montesquieu et le 'doux commerce': un paradigm du libéralisme," *Cahiers d'histoire: Revue d'histoire critique* 123 (2014): 21–38.

55. Saint-Pierre, *Projet pour rendre la paix perpétuelle,* 24 ("Première proposition à démontrer").

56. Saint-Pierre, *Projet pour rendre la paix perpétuelle,* 49.

57. Saint-Pierre, *Projet de paix perpétuelle,* Seconde ébauche (Houghton Library), 1.

58. Duc de Sully, *Mémoires, ou Oeconomies Royales d'Etat,* 12 vols. (Amsterdam: Aux dépens de la Compagnie, 1725), originally published in 1638 (Part 1) and 1662 (Part 2). For more on Sully and the *Grand Dessein d'Henri IV,* see David Buisseret, "The Legend of Sully," *Historical Journal* 5, no. 2 (1962): 181–188; Jean-Raymond Fanlo, "Les fictions du 'Grand Dessein' d'Henri IV chez Sully et chez Agrippa d'Aubigné," *Albineana: Cahiers d'Aubigné* 26 (2014): 181–192; German A. de la Reza, "Las Memorias del duque de Sully (o los avatares del primer proyecto de unión europea)," *Revista Brasileira de Política Internacional* 52, no. 2 (2009): 102–114.

59. Hardouin de Péréfixe, *Histoire de Henri-le-Grand, roi de France et de Navarre: suivie d'un recueil de quelques belles actions et paroles mémorables de ce prince* (Amsterdam: s.n., 1661), 462–471. Though Péréfixe relied on Sully's *Memoirs,* this unfortunately does not eliminate the doubts about the historical existence of Henri IV's Grand Design. See Camille Seroux d'Agincourt, "Exposé des projets de paix perpétuelle de l'abbé de Saint-Pierre (et de Henri IV), de Bentham et de Kant" (PhD diss. University of Paris, 1905); André Piharré, *L'Europe vue par Henri IV et Sully: D'après le "Grand Dessein" des Economies royales: Avec de larges extraits des Mémoires de Sully* (Oloron-Sainte-Marie: Monhélios, 2002).

60. Saint-Pierre, *Projet pour rendre la paix perpétuelle.*

61. William Penn, *An Essay towards the Present and Future Peace of Europe, by the Establishment of an European Diet, Parliament, or Estates* (1693), in *The Political Writings of William Penn,* ed. A. R. Murphy (Indianapolis: Liberty Fund, 2002), sect. 4, 406.

62. Penn, *An Essay,* section 9, 411–412; sect. 10, 413–417. See also Peter van den Dungen, "The Abbe de Saint-Pierre and the English 'Irenists' of the 18th Century

(Penn, Bellers, and Bentham)," *International Journal of World Peace* 17, no. 2 (2000): 5–31.

63. The *Dictionnaire de l'Académie française* gave, in its first edition (1694), *dessein* and *projet* as close synonyms. See also Daniel Sabbagh, "William Penn et l'Abbé de Saint-Pierre: Le chaînon manquant," *Revue de synthèse* 118, no. 1 (1997): 90.

64. Saint-Pierre, *Projet pour rendre la paix perpétuelle*, "Premier discours," 22, 37.

65. Maria-Grazia Bottaro-Palumbo, *Ch.-I. Castel de Saint-Pierre e la monarchia di Luigi XIV* (Genoa: Ecig, 1983); Thomas E. Kaiser, "The Abbé de Saint-Pierre, Public Opinion, and the Reconstitution of the French Monarchy," *Journal of Modern History* 55, no. 4 (1983): 618–643; Simone Goyard-Fabre, *La construction de la paix ou le Travail de Sisyphe* (Paris: Vrin, 1994), 121–129.

66. Abbé de Saint-Pierre, *Abrégé du Projet de paix perpétuelle* [1728] (Rotterdam: Jean-Daniel Beman, 1729), 12–13. See Simone Goyard-Fabre, "'Je ne suis que l'apothicaire de l'Europe,'" in *Les projets de l'abbé Castel de Saint-Pierre (1658–1743)*, ed. Carole Dornier and Claudine Poulouin (Caen: Presses universitaires de Caen, 2011), 19–37.

67. Martti Koskenniemi, "The Public Law of Europe: Reflections on a French 18th Century Debate," in *Erzählungen vom Konstitutionalismus*, ed. Helena Lindemann et al. (Baden-Baden: Nomos, 2012), 43–73.

68. The number of member states varies according to chapters and editions of Saint-Pierre's work.

69. Saint-Pierre, *Projet pour rendre la paix perpétuelle*, Eclaircissement de l'article 9, 191. See Céline Spector, "L'Europe de l'abbé de Saint-Pierre," in *Les Projets de l'abbé Castel de Saint-Pierre*, 39–49; Jean-Pierre Bois, *La paix: Histoire politique et militaire, 1435–1878* (Paris: Perrin, 2012), 333–336.

70. Leibniz to Saint-Pierre, Hanover, February 7, 1715, in *Œuvres de Leibniz*, ed. A. Foucher de Careil, 7 vols. (Paris: Firmin Didot, 1859–1875), 4: 325–327; Leibniz, *Observations sur le projet d'une paix perpétuelle de M. L'Abbé de Saint-Pierre*, in *Œuvres de Leibniz*, 4: 328–336.

71. Stella Ghervas, "La paix par le droit, ciment de la civilisation en Europe? La perspective du siècle des Lumières," in *Penser l'Europe au XVIIIe siècle*, ed. Lilti and Spector, 47–69; Ghervas, "Balance of Power vs. Perpetual Peace," 404–425.

72. Holsti, *Peace and War*, 46–70, 83–113.

73. John G. Reid, "Political Definitions: Creating Maine and Acadia," in *American Beginnings: Exploration, Culture, and Cartography in the Land of Norumbega,* ed. Emerson W. Baker et al. (Lincoln: University of Nebraska Press, 1994), 173–190.

74. Jan Květina, "The Polish Question as a Political Issue within Philosophical Dispute: Leszczyński versus Rousseau," *Oriens Aliter: Journal for Culture and History of the Central and Eastern Europe* 2 (2014): 22–43.

75. *The Definitive Treaty of Peace and Friendship between His Britannick Majesty, the Most Christian King, and the States General of the United Province,* concluded at Aix-la-Chapelle, October 18, 1748 (London: Edward Owen, 1749), 8–9 (Arts. I and II).

76. Heinz Duchhardt, "Peace Treaties from Westphalia to the Revolutionary Era," in *Peace Treaties and International Law in European History,* ed. Randall Lesaffer (Cambridge: Cambridge University Press, 2004), 45–58.

77. Randall Lesaffer, "The Peace of Aachen (1748) and the Rise of Multilateral Treaties," *Oxford Public International Law* (2017), http://opil.ouplaw.com/page/Peace-Aachen.

78. Jeremy Black, "Essay and Reflection: On the 'Old System' and the 'Diplomatic Revolution' of the Eighteenth Century," *International History Review* 12, no. 2 (1990): 301–323; Charles W. Ingrao, *The Habsburg Monarchy* (Cambridge: Cambridge University Press, 2000), 157–177.

79. "Traité définitif de paix et d'amitié entre Sa Majesté Britannique, le Roi T. Chrétien et le Roi d'Espagne, signé à Paris le 10 Févr[ier] 1763," in *Recueil de Traités d'Alliance, de Paix, de Trève, de Neutralité . . . des Puissances et États de l'Europe,* ed. Geo[rg] Fréd. de Martens, 2nd ed., 8 vols. (Göttingen: Dieterich, 1817–1835), 1: 104–131.

80. Montesquieu, *Réflexions sur la monarchie universelle en Europe,* ed. Michel Porret (Geneva: Droz, 2000), 76.

81. Montesquieu, *Réflexions sur la monarchie universelle,* 108.

82. Montesquieu, *L'Esprit des lois,* ed. Robert Derathé, 2 vols. (Paris: Classiques Garnier, 2011), 1: 22 (II.iv).

83. Montesquieu, *L'Esprit des lois,* 2: 3 (XX.ii).

84. Treaty of Commerce and Navigation between France and Great Britain, signed at Utrecht, April 11, 1713 (28 CTS 1); Treaty of Navigation and Commerce between France and the Netherlands, signed at Utrecht, April 11, 1713 (28 CTS 83),

in *Oxford Public International Law,* 2015, http://opil.ouplaw.com. The question of how to keep the mutual "jealousy of trade" in check among states and to restore trade to its original peaceful function was a key theme of eighteenth-century European political thought. See Istvan Hont, "Needs and Justice in the *Wealth of Nations,*" in Hont, *Jealousy of Trade: International Competition and the Nation-State in Historical Perspective* (Cambridge, MA: Belknap Press, 2005), 389–397; Béla Kapossy et al., eds., *Commerce and Peace in the Enlightenment* (Cambridge: Cambridge University Press, 2017).

85. On Montesquieu's attitude about the moral aspect of slave trade, see Bruno Guigue, "Montesquieu ou les paradoxes du relativisme," *Études* 401, no. 9 (2004): 193–204.

86. "Paix," in *Encyclopédie, ou Dictionnaire raisonné des sciences, des arts et des métiers,* ed. Denis Diderot and Jean le Rond d'Alembert, 17 vols. (Paris: Briasson, 1751–1765), 11: 768.

87. "Paix," 768.

88. "Paix," 768.

89. [Saint-Pierre], *Mémoires pour rendre la paix perpétuelle en Europe* (Cologne: Chez Jacques le Pacifique, 1712), Preface, 3.

90. Abbé de Saint-Pierre to the Cardinal André Hercule de Fleury, prime minister of King Louis XV, 1740: "Je ne suis que l'apothicaire de l'Europe; vous en êtes le médecin. N'est-ce pas au médecin à ordonner et à appliquer le remède?"; quoted in Goyard-Fabre, "Je ne suis que l'apothicaire de l'Europe," 19.

91. Vattel, *Law of Nations,* 497 (III.iii).

92. Vattel, *Law of Nations,* 500 (III.iii).

93. Vattel, *Law of Nations,* 251 (III.i).

94. Vattel, *Law of Nations,* 252 (III.i).

95. Vattel, *Law of Nations,* 258 (III.i).

96. Sven Stelling-Michaud, "Ce que Rousseau doit à l'abbé de Saint-Pierre," in *Etudes sur le Contrat social de J.-J. Rousseau* (Paris: Les Belles Lettres, 1964), 35–45; Céline Spector, "Le *Projet de paix perpétuelle:* de Saint-Pierre à Rousseau," in Jean-Jacques Rousseau, *Principes du droit de la guerre: Ecrits sur la paix perpétuelle,* ed. Blaise Bachofen et al. (Paris: Vrin, 2008), 230–232. It is easy to misattribute Rousseau's text to Saint-Pierre, especially because Saint-Pierre himself had published a

Summary of his Plan in 1729: [Abbé de Saint-Pierre], *Abrégé du projet de paix perpé-tuelle, inventé par le roi Henri le Grand, approuvé par la reine Élisabeth, par le roi Jacques son successeur, par les républiques et par divers autres potentats . . .* (Rotterdam: J. D. Beman, 1729).

97. Rousseau, *Extrait du Projet de Paix perpétuelle,* in Rousseau, *Principes du droit de la guerre,* 95.

98. Jean-Jacques Rousseau, *Du contrat social, ou principes du droit politique,* in *Œuvres completes,* 5 vols. (Paris: Gallimard, 1959–1995), 3: 349–470 (1964).

99. Rousseau, *Extrait du Projet de Paix perpétuelle,* 98.

100. On what Rousseau owed to Geneva, see Helena Rosenblatt, *Rousseau and Geneva: From the First Discourse to the Social Contract, 1749–1762* (Cambridge: Cambridge University Press, 1997).

101. Rousseau, *Extrait du Projet de Paix perpétuelle,* 89–90; Spector, "Le *Projet de paix perpétuelle:* de Saint-Pierre à Rousseau," 280.

102. Rousseau, *Extrait du Projet de Paix perpétuelle,* 89.

103. Rousseau, *Extrait du Projet de Paix perpétuelle,* 92.

104. Bruno Bernardi, "Rousseau et l'Europe: sur l'idée de société civile euro-péenne," in Rousseau, *Principes,* 295–330; Armitage, *Civil Wars,* 164–165.

105. Jean-Jacques Rousseau, *Jugement sur la Paix perpétuelle,* in Rousseau, *Principes,* 117–120; Céline Spector, "Who is the Author of the *Abstract of Monsieur l'Abbé de Saint-Pierre's 'Plan for Perpetual Peace'?* From Saint-Pierre to Rousseau," *History of European Ideas* 39, no. 3 (2013): 371–393.

106. Rousseau, *Jugement sur la Paix perpétuelle,* 122–126; Stelling-Michaud, "Ce que Rousseau doit à l'abbé de Saint-Pierre," 35–45.

107. Spector, "L'Europe de l'Abbé de Saint-Pierre," 49.

108. Rousseau, *Jugement sur la Paix perpétuelle,* 103, 122–126; Ghervas, "La paix par le droit, ciment de la civilisation en Europe?" 55–57.

109. This *bon mot* is from Immanuel Kant, *An Answer to the Question: "What Is Enlightenment?"* (1784), in *Kant: Political Writings,* ed. Reiss, 58.

110. Voltaire, *Rescrit de l'Empereur de Chine à l'occasion du projet de paix perpétuelle* (1761), reproduced in *L'année 1796: Sur la paix perpétuelle, de Leibniz aux héritiers de Kant,* ed. Jean Ferrari and Simone Goyard-Fabre (Paris: Vrin, 1998), 200. See

also Patrick Riley, "The Abbé de St. Pierre and Voltaire on Perpetual Peace in Europe," *World Affairs* 137, no. 3 (1974–1975): 186–194.

111. Voltaire, *De la paix perpétuelle, par le docteur Goodheart* (1769), in *Œuvres complètes de Voltaire* (Paris: Garnier, 1877), 28: 103–128.

112. [Voltaire], *Traité sur la tolérance, A l'occasion de la mort de Jean Calas* ([Geneva: Cramer], 1763), 188.

113. [Voltaire], *Traité sur la Tolérance,* 196.

114. "Révolution," in *Dictionnaire de l'Académie française,* 4th ed., 2 vols. (Paris: Veuve Bernard Brunet, 1762), 2: 636; Keith Baker and Dan Edelstein, eds., *Scripting Revolution: A Historical Approach to the Comparative Study of Revolutions* (Stanford: Stanford University Press, 2015).

115. Steve Pincus, *1688: The First Modern Revolution* (New Haven: Yale University Press, 2011), 278–303.

116. "Texte du Décret adopté sur le droit de guerre et de paix, lors de la séance du 22 mai 1790," in *Archives Parlementaires de la Révolution Française* 15 (1883): 661–662.

117. Immanuel Kant, *Zum ewigen Frieden. Ein philosophischer Entwurf,* ed. Rudolf Malter (Stuttgart: Reclam, 2008). For the purpose of this work, I used both the German and the English translation: *Perpetual Peace: A Philosophical Sketch,* in *Kant: Political Writings,* ed. Reiss, 93–130. The more precise English translation of the title is "Toward Perpetual Peace".

118. Bruno Arcidiacono, "'Non par la guerre, à la manière des sauvages': Kant et l'avènement de l'état de droit entre les nations," *Journal of the History of International Law* 8 (2006): 39–89.

119. Emmanuel Kant, *Métaphysique des moeurs,* Part I: *Doctrine du droit,* trans. A. Philonenko (Paris: Vrin, 1971), 201. On this aspect, see also Jean Ferrari, "Kant, les Lumières et la Révolution française," *Mélanges de l'Ecole française de Rome* 104 (1992): 49–59; Thomas E. Hill, "A Kantian Perspective on Political Violence," *Journal of Ethics* 2 (1997): 105–140.

120. Kant, *Perpetual Peace,* 93.

121. Preliminary (*preliminär*) presumably in the Latin etymological meaning: "before reaching the threshold" (of perpetual peace).

122. Consider the successive bankruptcy of Emperor Charles V of Habsburg, the financial crisis following the Seven Years' War, and later the barely averted

bankruptcy of the United Kingdom and the very high taxation level in the United States after World War II.

123. Here is an insight that seems to have been little noted by later commentators. Napoleon went so far in waging all-out war that the Allied Powers committed, by the Treaty of Chaumont in 1814, not to sign any separate peace until complete victory. During World War II, Nazi atrocities made impossible any peace with the Allies, who agreed at the Yalta Conference of 1945 to refuse any armistice until the capitulation of Germany.

124. Kant, *Perpetual Peace,* 97. It is thus that the "Fourth Preliminary Article" should be applied so as to reduce those debts and finally cancel them: Kant, *Perpetual Peace,* 95. On the general articulation between theory and practice, as well as the conceptual frame and the "horizon of experiences," see the well-known dissertation by Jürgen Habermas, "Kant's Idea of Perpetual Peace, with the Benefit of Two Hundred Years' Hindsight," in *Perpetual Peace: Essays on Kant's Cosmopolitan Ideal,* ed. James Bohman and Matthias Lutz-Bachmann (Cambridge, MA: MIT Press, 1997), 113–153.

125. Kant, *Perpetual Peace,* 98.

126. Kant, *Perpetual Peace,* 99–100. He called democracy, in a pejorative sense, a system where the power was in the hands of the populace (mob rule).

127. Kant, *Perpetual Peace,* "First Definitive Article," 100; *L'année 1795: Kant, Essai sur la paix,* ed. Pierre Laberge et al. (Paris: Vrin, 1997), chapters by Jean Ferrari (25–40) and Simone Goyard-Fabre (41–59).

128. The terms "federalism" *(Föderalism)* and "League of Peoples" *(Völkerbund)* were used by Kant in the sense of a league—a confederation—that would leave full sovereignty to the states. He did not intend these terms to be interpreted in the modern sense of creating a supranational entity. See Marc Belissa, "Les projets de paix perpétuelle: une "utopie" fédéraliste au siècle des Lumières," *Nuevo Mundo Mundos Nuevos,* Coloquios, 2008, http://nuevomundo.revues.org/35192.

129. Lawrence Pasternack and Philip Rossi, "Kant's Philosophy of Religion," *The Stanford Encyclopedia of Philosophy* (Fall 2014), ed. Edward N. Zalta, https://plato.stanford.edu/archives/fall2014/entries/kant-religion/. On pietism, see Roger E. Olson, *Reclaiming Pietism: Retrieving an Evangelical Tradition* (Grand Rapids, MI: William B. Eerdmans, 2015), particularly 81–107.

130. In German, *Weltbürgerrecht,* in Latin, *ius cosmopoliticum:* Kant, *Perpetual Peace,* 105.

131. Kant, *Perpetual Peace*, 106–107; William Ossipow, "Kant's Perpetual Peace and Its Hidden Sources," *Swiss Political Science Review* 14, no. 2 (2008): 357–389; Daniel Weinstock, "Vers une théorie kantienne du droit de migration," in *L'année 1795*, 238–254.

132. Kant, *Perpetual Peace*, 107–108.

133. James Tully, "The Kantian Idea of Europe: Critical and Cosmopolitan Perspectives," in *The Idea of Europe*, 331–357.

134. Arcidiacono, "'Non par la guerre, à la manière des sauvages,'" 61.

135. *Prudence* [*Klugheit*] (see Latin *providentia*, foresight) is a concept from the Old Testament (Proverbs 8:12), best defined as "skillful conduct, when it concerns itself only with matters of this world and bears no relation with those of the Heaven" (*Dictionnaire de l'Académie française*, 4th ed., 1762). As an understatement, it could be translated (albeit approximately) into modern English as pragmatism, *Realpolitik*, or even shrewdness or Machiavellism.

136. In the sense of a Law of Nations.

137. Kant, *Perpetual Peace*, Appendix I, 121.

138. Getting rid of despots was arguably a step forward, but was far from sufficient, as Habermas remarked in "Kant's Idea of Perpetual Peace," 113–153.

139. Richard Whatmore, "'Neither Masters nor Slaves': Small States and Empire in the Long Eighteenth Century," in *Lineages of Empire: The Historical Roots of Imperial British Thought*, ed. Donald Kelly (Oxford: Oxford University Press, 2009), 53–81; Doohwan Ahn and Richard Whatmore, "Peace, Security, and Deterrence," in *A Cultural History of Peace in the Age of Enlightenment*, 117–132.

140. [Nicolas de Caritat, Marquis de Condorcet], "Notes sur Voltaire: Paix perpétuelle," in *Œuvres complètes de Condorcet*, 21 vols. (Paris: Henrichs, 1804), 7: 293.

141. [Condorcet], "Notes sur Voltaire: Paix perpétuelle," 294–295.

2. THE SPIRIT OF VIENNA

1. Aleksandr I. Mikhaïlovskiĭ-Danilevskiĭ, *Memuary, 1814–1815*, in *Rukopisnye Pamiātniki* (Saint Petersburg: RNB, 2001), 41–42; Charles Simond, *La vie parisienne à travers le XIXe siècle: Paris de 1800 à 1900, d'après les estampes et les mémoires du temps*, 3 vols. (Paris: Plon, 1900–1901), 1: 272; André Delrieu, *Testament d'un vieux diplomate*, 2 vols. (Paris: Baudry, 1846), 1: xvii–xix. See also Marie-Pierre Rey,

"Les Cossaques dans les yeux de Français, à l'heure de la campagne de 1814: Contribution à une histoire des images et des representations en temps de guerre," *Quaestio Rossica* 1 (2014): 55–68; Viktor Bezotosnyï and Elena Itkina, *Kazaki v Parizhe v 1814 godu* (Moscow: Kuchkovo Pole, 2015).

2. Nicolas Dalayrac, "Veillons au salut de l'Empire" (1791), in *Chansons populaires du pays de France: notice et accompagnement de piano,* ed. Jean-Baptiste Weckerlin, 2 vols. (Paris, 1903), 1: 147.

3. Hans Kohn, *Prelude to Nation-States: The French and German Experience, 1789–1815* (Princeton: Van Nostrand, 1967), 1–4, 168–179; Peter Brandt, "Die Befreiungskriege von 1813 bis 1815 in der deutschen Geschichte," in *Geschichte und Emanzipation,* ed. Michael Grüttner et al. (Frankfurt a. M.: Campus, 1999), 17–57; Philip Dwyer, "New Avenues for Research in Napoleonic Europe," *European History Quarterly* 33 (2003): 101–124; Katherine Aaslestad and Karen Hagemann, "1806 and Its Aftermath: Revisiting the Period of the Napoleonic Wars in German Central European Historiography," *Central European History* 39, no. 4 (2006): 547–579.

4. Henry A. Kissinger, *A World Restored: Metternich, Castlereagh and the Problems of Peace, 1812–22* (Boston: Houghton Mifflin, 1957). Historian Paul Schroeder was more circumspect with applying the notion of "balance of power" to the Vienna Order; he concluded it was a hybrid system, which he called a pentarchy: Paul W. Schroeder, *The Transformation of European Politics 1763–1848* (Oxford: Clarendon Press, 1994), 517–636; Schroeder, "Did the Vienna Settlement Rest on a Balance of Power?" *American Historical Review* 97, no. 3 (1992): 683–706.

5. Joanne Innes and Mark Philp, eds., *Re-Imagining Democracy in the Mediterranean, 1780–1860* (Oxford: Oxford University Press, 2018).

6. Morgenthau, *Politics among Nations;* George F. Kennan, *American Diplomacy, 1900–1950* (Chicago: University of Chicago, 1951). For later outlooks on this school of thought, see Richard Ned Lebow, *The Tragic Vision of Politics: Ethics, Interests and Orders* (Cambridge: Cambridge University Press, 2003); John Bew, *Realpolitik: A History* (Oxford: Oxford University Press, 2015).

7. Kissinger, *World Restored,* 1–6, 312–332.

8. The French word was borrowed from Italian *canaglia. Canaillocratie* was famously associated with the Savoyard conservative writer Joseph de Maistre, who declared: "I hope that one day . . . we will be able to talk about canaillocracy,

with our windows open!" Maistre, *Œuvres complètes,* 14 vols. (Lyon: Vitte et Per-russel, 1884–1886), 1: 54.

9. Maistre described democracy as a delusion. Joseph de Maistre, *Étude sur la souveraineté* ([Lyon]: s. n., 1884), 464.

10. Michael Broers makes an apt distinction between postrevolutionary "reaction" and "conservatism," in *Europe after Napoleon: Revolution, Reaction and Romanticism, 1814–1848* (Manchester: Manchester University Press, 1996). On the meaning of these two terms, see Markus J. Prutsch, *Making Sense of Constitutional Monarchism in Post-Napoleonic France and Germany* (Basingstoke: Palgrave Macmillan, 2013), 44–64; Brian Vick, *The Congress of Vienna: Power and Politics after Napoleon* (Cambridge, MA: Harvard University Press, 2014), 233–277; Ambrogio A. Caiani, "Re-Inventing the *Ancien Régime* in Post-Napoleonic Europe," *European History Quarterly* 47, no. 3 (2017): 437–460; Matthijs Lok, "The Congress of Vienna as a Missed Opportunity: Conservative Visions of a New European Order after Napoleon," in *Securing Europe after Napoleon: 1815 and the New European Security Culture,* ed. Beatrice de Graaf et al. (Cambridge: Cambridge University Press, 2019), 56–71.

11. On these revolutionary societies, see Alan B. Spitzer, *Old Hatreds and Young Hopes: The French Carbonari against the Bourbon Restoration* (Cambridge, MA: Harvard University Press, 1971); Maurizio Isabella, *Risorgimento in Exile: Italian Emigrés and the Liberal International in the Post-Napoleonic Era* (Oxford: Oxford University Press, 2009); Antonella Musitano, *Il Sud prima dell'Unità d'Italia tra storia e microstoria, 1848: Massoni e Carbonari a Santo Spirito* (Bari: Levante, 2011).

12. Paul Veyne, "Qu'était-ce qu'un empereur romain?" in Veyne, *L'Empire gréco-romain* (Paris: Seuil, 2005), 15–78; Valérie Huet, "Napoleon I: A New Augustus?," in *Roman Presences: Receptions of Rome in European Culture, 1789–1945,* ed. Catherine Edwards (Cambridge: Cambridge University Press, 1999), 53–69; Thierry Lentz, "Napoleon and Charlemagne," *Napoleonica. La Revue* 1, no. 1 (2008): 45–68; Andrew Roberts, *Napoleon: A Life* (New York: Viking, 2014), 347–355.

13. *Pax Romana* describes the state of relative tranquility from Augustus (27 BCE) to Marcus Aurelius (CE 180). During the Middle Ages, it became a paradigm for a peaceful order between peoples, enforced by a messianic leader (an emperor) through military force. See Adrian Goldsworthy, *Pax Romana: War, Peace and Conquest in the Roman World* (London: Weidenfeld & Nicolson, 2016), 15–18, 161–186; Ali Parchami, *Hegemonic Peace and Empire: The Pax Romana, Britannica and Americana* (New York: Routledge, 2009), 15–57.

14. David A. Bell, *The First Total War: Napoleon's Europe and the Birth of Warfare as We Know It* (Boston: Houghton Mifflin, 2007), 223–262.

15. See Caulaincourt's firsthand account, *Mémoire du général de Caulaincourt, duc de Vicence, grand écuyer de l'Empereur,* ed. Jean Hanoteau, 3 vols. (Paris: Plon, 1933), 1: 91–98; Herbert Butterfield, *The Peace Tactics of Napoleon, 1806–1808* (Cambridge: University Press, 1929); 202–278; Arkhangel'skiĭ, *Aleksandr I,* 160–165; Vladlen Sirotkin, *Napoleon I i Aleksandr I: Diplomatija i razvedka Napoleona i Aleksandra I v 1801–1812 gg* (Moscow: Ėksmo, 2003), 198–208.

16. Nathalie Petiteau, "Débats historiographiques autour de la politique européenne de Napoléon," in *Napoléon et l'Europe. Colloque de La Roche-sur-Yon,* ed. Jean-Clément Martin (Rennes: Presses universitaires de Rennes, 2002), 19–31.

17. *Pax Napoleonica* refers to the hegemonic peace system imposed by Napoleon's French Empire on Europe. In theory, states were to surrender their liberties in exchange for the gift of peace, which would bring them happiness and prosperity. It was a transposition of *Pax Romana* to the early nineteenth century. Stella Ghervas, "Definitions of Peace, 1815–1920," in *A Cultural History of Peace in the Age of Empire,* ed. Ingrid Sharp (London: Bloomsbury Academic, 2020), 24.

18. Kevin H. O'Rourke, "The Worldwide Economic Impact of the French Revolutionary and Napoleonic Wars, 1793–1815," *Journal of Global History* 1 (2006): 123–149.

19. Brendan Simms argues that geopolitical concerns were uppermost in the minds of the Prussian policy-making elite. Simms, *The Impact of Napoleon: Prussian High Politics, Foreign Policy and the Crisis of the Executive, 1797–1806* (Cambridge: Cambridge University Press, 1997).

20. Adam Zamoyski, *Rites of Peace: The Fall of Napoleon & the Congress of Vienna* (London: Harper Press, 2007), 15–63.

21. Karen Hagemann, "'Desperation to the Utmost': The Defeat of 1806 and the French Occupation in Prussian Experience and Perception," in *The Bee and the Eagle: Napoleonic France and the End of the Holy Roman Empire, 1806,* ed. Alan Forrest and Peter H. Wilson (London: Palgrave Macmillan, 2009), 191–213.

22. Katherine B. Aaslestad, "Introduction: Revisiting Napoleon's Continental System: Consequences of Economic Warfare," in *Revisiting Napoleon's Continental System: Local, Regional and European Experiences,* ed. Katherine B. Aaslestad and Johan Joor (New York: Palgrave Macmillan, 2014), 1–22; Alexander Mika-

beridze, *The Napoleonic Wars: A Global History* (Oxford: Oxford University Press, 2020), 228–241.

23. Dominic Lieven, *Russia against Napoleon: The Battle for Europe, 1807 to 1814* (London: Penguin, 2009), 250–284.

24. These peace efforts culminated in March 1814 in a peace conference held at Châtillon that French foreign minister Caulaincourt attended. The talks proved fruitless, and in the wake of Napoleon's uncompromising stance, the British government was able to unite the allies. See the firsthand account of Baron Agathon-Jean-François Fain, *The Manuscript of 1814: A History of Events which Led to the Abdication of Napoleon: Written at the Command of the Emperor, by Baron Fain* (London: Henry Colburn, 1834), 169–270. See also August Fournier, *Der Congress von Châtillon: Die Politik im Kriege von 1814* (Vienna: Tempsky, 1900), 178–183; Munro Price, *Napoleon: The End of Glory* (Oxford: Oxford University Press, 2014), 187–217.

25. "Traité d'alliance entre l'Autriche, la Russie, la Grande-Brétagne et la Prusse, conclu à Chaumont le 1 Mars 1814," in *Nouveau Recueil de Traités d'Alliance, de Paix, de Trève, de Neutralité . . . des Puissances et États de l'Europe*, ed. Geo[rg] Fréd. de Martens, 16 vols. (Göttingen: Dieterich, 1817–1841), 1: 684. On the Treaty of Chaumont, see Edward Vose Gulick, *Europe's Classical Balance of Power* (New York: W. W. Norton, 1955), 151–160, which includes the text of the treaty; Sir Charles Kingsley Webster, *The Foreign Policy of Lord Castlereagh, 1812–1815: Britain and the Reconstruction of Europe* (London: G. Bell and Sons, 1931), 211–232; Fournier, *Der Congress von Châtillon*, 178–183.

26. Napoleon, "Act of Abdication" (April 4, 1814), in *Cobbett's Political Register* 25 (January–June 1815), col. 493.

27. "Conventions Arrêtées entre S. A. R. Monsieur, Lieutenant général du Royaume, et les hautes Puissances alliées. Au château des Tuileries, le 23 Avril 1814," in *Recueil des traités et conventions*, 2.

28. "Sénat conservateur—Projet de Constitution. Extrait des registres du Sénat-conservateur, du mercredi 6 avril 1814," Art. 2, *Le Moniteur*, April 18, 1814.

29. "Traité de Paix entre le Roi et les Puissances alliées, conclu à Paris, le 30 mai 1814," in *Recueil des traités et conventions*, 6–26.

30. Baptiste Capefigue, *Le congrès de Vienne dans ses rapports avec la circonscription de l'Europe: Pologne, Cracovie, Allemagne, Saxe, Belgique, Italie, Suisse, 1814–1846* (Paris: Au comptoir des imprimeurs-unis, 1847), 25–28; Thierry Lentz, *Le Congrès de Vienne. Une refondation de l'Europe, 1814–1815* (Paris: Perrin, 2013), 77–100.

31. "Traité de Paix entre le Roi et les Puissances alliées," Art. 32, 19.

32. A complex affair but suffice it to say that many cities and states that had once been under the direct jurisdiction of the Holy Roman Emperor had been annexed by neighboring states; furthermore, the Holy Roman Empire ceased to exist in 1806. See Michael Rowe, "Political Culture of the Holy Roman Empire on the Eve of its Destruction," in *Bee and the Eagle,* 42–64; Barbara Stollberg-Rilinger, *Das Heilige Römische Reich Deutscher Nation: Vom Ende des Mittelalters bis 1806* (Munich: C. H. Beck, 2014), 110–115.

33. Josef Karl Mayr, "Aufbau und Arbeitsweise des Wiener Kongresses," *Archivalische Zeitschrift* 45 (1939): 64–127; Charles K. Webster, *The Congress of Vienna, 1814–1815* (London: Humphrey Milford, 1919), 73–97; Annie Jourdan, "Le Congrès de Vienne et les petites nations: quel rôle pour l'Angleterre?" *Napoleonica. La Revue* 24, no. 3 (2015): 110–125. For a comprehensive list of the participants see Karin Schneider and Eva Maria Werner, *Europa in Wien: Who Is Who beim Wiener Kongress 1814/15* (Vienna: Böhlau Verlag, 2015), 81–99.

34. These riparian states were Prussia, the Netherlands, France, Baden, Hessen-Darmstadt, Bavaria, and Nassau. The Treaty of Paris of May 30, 1814, laid down the principle of the freedom of navigation on the major international rivers of Europe: "Drafts of articles Paris Peace Treaty, mid-May 1814," TNA, FO 92/4, at Art. 11. The Central Commission for Navigation of the Rhine was formally constituted at the Congress of Vienna in 1815; see "Règlements concernant la libre navigation des rivières. Annexe n° 16 de l'Acte final du Congrès de Vienne du 9 juin 1815," in Angeberg, *Congrès,* 2: 957–969; Joep Schenk, "The Central Commission for the Navigation of the Rhine: A First Step towards European Economic Security?" in *Securing Europe after Napoleon,* 75–94.

35. Mayr, "Aufbau und Arbeitsweise des Wiener Kongresses," 95–119; Schneider and Werner, *Europa in Wien,* 18–26.

36. Henry Schnitzler, " 'Gay Vienna': Myth and Reality," *Journal of the History of Ideas* 15, no. 1 (1954): 103–105; Vick, *Congress of Vienna,* 112–152.

37. "Traité d'alliance entre l'Autriche, la Russie, la Grande-Brétagne et la Prusse, conclu à Chaumont le 1 Mars 1814," 683–688.

38. "Traité de Paix entre le Roi et les Puissances alliées," Secret Article 6, 12.

39. Vick, *Congress of Vienna,* 66–111.

40. In the preamble of the Final Act of the Congress of Vienna, the protocol order was alphabetic: Austria, Spain (*Espagne*), France, the United Kingdom (*Roy-*

aume-Uni), Portugal, Prussia, Russia, and Sweden. Of these Spain, Portugal, and Sweden were relegated to secondary roles, while France was working its way back to the inner circle. "Acte du Congrès de Vienne, du 9 juin 1815," in *Recueil des traités et conventions,* 100–105.

41. Schroeder, "Did the Vienna Settlement Rest on a Balance of Power?" 683–706. See also Matthew Rendall, "Defensive Realism and the Concert of Europe," *Review of International Studies* 32, no. 3 (2006): 523–540.

42. Lieven, *Russia against Napoleon,* 329–355.

43. Mark Jarrett, *The Congress of Vienna and Its Legacy: War and Great Power Diplomacy after Napoleon* (London: I. B. Tauris, 2013), 111–130.

44. Analyzing Metternich's views, Wolfram Siemann emphasizes the threat to Austrian security represented by repeated French occupations of Vienna. At the same time, Metternich hoped to increase Austria's relative power by opposing Russia in Poland, France in Italy, and Prussia in Saxony and Mainz. Siemann, *Metternich: Staatsmann zwischen Restauration und Moderne* (Munich: C. H. Beck, 2010), 52–59; Siemann, *Metternich: Strategist and Visionary,* trans. Daniel Steuer (Cambridge, MA: Harvard University Press, 2019), 422–448; also Alan Sked, *Metternich and Austria: An Evaluation* (Basingstoke: Palgrave Macmillan, 2008), 64–65.

45. Stella Ghervas, "Das Erbe des Wiener Kongresses und der Wert von Friedensstiftern," *Aus Politik und Zeitgeschichte (APuZ),* 22–24 (2015): 15–20.

46. Stella Ghervas, "From the Balance of Power to a Balance of Diplomacy? Peace and Security in the Vienna Settlement," in *Securing Europe after Napoleon,* 100–102.

47. On the episode of the Hundred Days, see Emmanuel de Waresquiel, *Cents Jours. La tentation de l'impossible, mars-juillet 1815* (Paris: Fayard, 2008); Jacques-Olivier Boudon, "Les Cents-Jours: un second Empire?" *Histoire, économie & société* 36, no. 3 (2017): 7–17; Katherine Astbury and Mark Philp, eds., *Napoleon's Hundred Days and the Politics of Legitimacy: War, Culture and Society, 1750–1850* (Cham: Palgrave Macmillan, 2018).

48. "Declaration des Plénipotentiaires des 8 Puissances sur l'evasion de Napoléon Bonaparte" (March 13, 1815), in *British and Foreign State Papers 1814–1815* (London: Ridgway, 1839), 665–667.

49. "Traité d'alliance entre l'Autriche, la Russie, la Grande-Brétagne et la Prusse, conclu à Chaumont le 1 Mars 1814," 687.

50. "Acte du Congrès de Vienne, du 9 juin 1815," 100–168.

51. Victor Hugo, "L'expiation," in *Les châtiments,* 1853.

52. "Le Traité de Paris du 20 novembre 1815," in Angeberg, *Congrès,* 4: 1599; Albert Sorel, *Le Traité de Paris du 20 novembre 1815* (Paris: G. Baillière, 1872), 9–67.

53. A specific clause of Article III provided guarantees for Switzerland's safety against France by durably removing the military threat against Basel (through the destruction of Huningen's fortress) and by extending Swiss neutrality around Geneva to include most of Savoy (as a bulwark against France). "Le Traité de Paris du 20 novembre 1815," 1598–1599. On France's occupation by the Allies, see Jacques Hantraye, *Les Cosaques aux Champs-Elysées: les occupations étrangères en France après la chute de Napoléon* (Paris: Belin, 2005); Christine Haynes, *Our Friends the Enemies: The Occupation of France after Napoleon* (Cambridge, MA: Harvard University Press, 2018).

54. Stella Ghervas, *Alexandre Stourdza (1791–1854): Un intellectual orthodoxe face à l'Occident* (Geneva: Suzanne Hurter, 1999), 28–29; John Bew, *Castlereagh: A Life* (Oxford: Oxford University Press, 2012), 407–409; Jarrett, *Congress of Vienna,* 171–172; Rory Muir, *Wellington: Waterloo and the Fortunes of Peace, 1814–1852* (New Haven: Yale University Press, 2015), 94–95.

55. Webster, *Foreign Policy of Lord Castlereagh,* 545–548; Andrew Roberts, *Napoleon and Wellington* (London: Weidenfeld & Nicolson, 2001), 187–198; Mark Jarrett, "Castlereagh, Ireland and the French Restoration of 1814–1815" (PhD diss., Stanford University, 2006), 526–606.

56. By the time of the Vienna Congress, the Allied powers had concluded that Murat, as a remnant of the Napoleonic Empire, had to be replaced. Jean-Claude Gillet, *Murat: 1767–1815* (Paris: Bernard Giovanangeli, 2008), 343–371; Renata De Lorenzo, *Murat* (Rome: Salerno, 2011), 321–333.

57. "Traité de la sainte Alliance entre les empereurs de Russie et d'Autriche et le roi de Prusse, signé à Paris le 14/26 septembre 1815," in Angeberg, *Congrès,* 4: 1547–1549; Andreï Zorin, *Kormīa dvuglavogo orla . . . Russkaīa literatura i gosudarstvennaīa ideologiīa v posledneĭ treti XVIII—pervoĭ treti XIX veka* (Moscow: Novoe literaturnoe obozrenie, 2001), 297–335.

58. Stella Ghervas, "Antidotes to Empire: From the Congress System to the European Union," in *EUtROPEs. The Paradox of European Empire,* ed. John W. Boyer and Berthold Molden (Chicago: University of Chicago Press, 2014), 49–81.

59. Quoted in Webster, *Foreign Policy of Lord Castlereagh,* 482.

60. Jarrett, *Congress of Vienna,* 176–178; Bew, *Castlereagh,* 410–411.

61. In Metternich's words: "From a union of religious and political-liberal ideas the 'Holy Alliance' was developed under the influence of Frau von Krüdener and Monsieur Bergasse. No one is so well acquainted as I am with the circumstances of this 'loud-sounding nothing.'" *Memoirs of Prince Metternich,* ed. Prince Richard Metternich, 5 vols. (New York: C. Scribner's Sons, 1880–1882), 1: 261–262; Metternich, *Aus Metternich's Nachgelassemen Papieren,* ed. Richard von Metternich, 8 vols. (Vienna: 1880–1884), 1: 216. See also Vasiliĭ K. Nadler, *Imperator Aleksandr I i ideǐa Svĭashchennogo soǐuza,* 5 vols. (Riga: N. Kimmel', 1886–1892), 5: 251–356; Francis Ley, *Madame de Krüdener, 1764–1824: Romantisme et Sainte-Alliance* (Paris: Honoré Champion, 1994), 281–322.

62. Roughly at the time of the Treaty of Verona and the French military intervention in Spain (1822) the idea emerged, in public opinion, that the Holy Alliance was one of "Northern Powers" intent on suppressing political representation and national aspirations, and eager to intervene militarily to break popular movements. See, for example, Edgard Quinet, *La France de la Sainte-Alliance en Portugal* (Paris: Joubert, 1847). For more on this point, see Guillaume de Bertier de Sauvigny, ed., *La Sainte-Alliance* (Paris: Armand Colin, 1972), 322–323.

63. Stella Ghervas, "A 'Goodwill Ambassador' in the Post-Napoleonic Era: Roxandra Edling-Sturdza on the European Scene," in *Women, Diplomacy, and International Politics since 1500,* ed. Glenda Sluga and Carolyn James (London: Routledge, 2015), 151–166.

64. Alexandre Stourdza, "Considérations sur l'acte d'alliance fraternelle et chrétienne du 14/26 septembre 1815," RO IRLI, 288/1, no. 21, f. 1–5.

65. Stourdza, "Considérations sur l'acte d'alliance," f. 1.

66. Stella Ghervas, *Réinventer la tradition: Alexandre Stourdza et l'Europe de la Sainte-Alliance* (Paris: Honoré Champion, 2008), 430–431.

67. V. V. Degoev, "Aleksandr I i problema evropeĭskogo soglasiĭa posle Venskogo kongressa," *Voprosy Istorii* 2 (2002): 119–132.

68. *Memoirs of Prince Metternich,* 1: 260–261; Siemann, *Metternich: Strategist and Visionary,* 442.

69. "Les *sujets des trois parties contractantes* demeureront unis par les liens d'une fraternité véritable" into "les *trois monarques* demeureront unis . . ." See Francis

Ley, *Alexandre Ier et sa Sainte-Alliance* (Paris: Fischbacher, 1975), 149–153; emphasis added. See also Werner Näf, *Zur Geschichte der Heiligen Allianz* (Bern: Paul Haupt, 1928), 34–37; H. G. Schenk, *The Aftermath of the Napoleonic Wars: The Concert of Europe—An Experiment* (Oxford: Oxford University Press, 1947), 31–43.

70. Ol'ga V. Orlik, *Rossiīa v mezhdunarodnykh otnosheniīakh, 1815–1829: Ot Venskogo kongressa do Adrianopol'skogo mira* (Moscow: Nauka, 1998), 16–24.

71. Guillaume de Bertier de Sauvigny, "Sainte-Alliance et alliance dans les conceptions de Metternich," *Revue Historique* 223, no. 2 (1960): 249–274. On the idea of the Holy Alliance as a precursor of the League of Nations of 1920 and of the foundation of the United Nations in 1945, see Reinhart Koselleck, "Die Restauration und ihre Ereigniszusammenhänge 1815–1830," in Louis Bergeron, François Furet, and Reinhart Koselleck, *Das Zeitalter der europäischen Revolution 1780–1848* (Frankfurt am Main: Fischer Bücherei, 1973), 218–220.

72. Roxandre Edling-Stourdza, *Mémoires de la comtesse Edling, née Stourdza* (Moscow: Imprimérie du St-Synode, 1888), 242.

73. Vasiliĭ F. Malinovskiĭ, "Rassuzhdenie o mire i voĭne," manuscript in three parts, 1790–1798, RO IRLI, 1261, no. 2825. First published in Saint Petersburg in 1803, Malinovlski updated the essay in 1812. For other Russian plans of perpetual peace, see Maria Mayofis, "After the Napoleonic Wars: Reading *Perpetual Peace* in the Russian Empire," in *Cosmopolitanism in Conflict: Imperial Encounters from the Seven Year's War to the Cold War,* ed. Dina Gusejnova (London: Palgrave Macmillan, 2018), 85–110.

74. Novosiltsev's report summarizing his discussions in London with the British Prime Minister William Pitt can be found in *Mémoires du prince Adam Czartoryski et correspondance avec l'Empereur Alexandre Ier,* ed. Ch. de Mazade, 2 vols. (Paris: Plon, 1887), 2: 45–56. ("Instructions secrètes à M. de Novosiltzow allant en Angleterre, le 11 Septembre 1804" and "Papiers relatifs à la mission de M. de Novosiltzow à Londres"); Lord Harrowby to Count [Vorontsov], Downing Street, June 26, 1804, printed in John Holland Rose, *Select Despatches from the British Foreign Office Archives Relating to the Formation of the Third Coalition against France, 1804–1805* (London: Royal Historical Society, 1904), 14–19.

75. The text of the *Instructions secrètes* is reproduced in *Vneshniāīa Politika Rossii XIX i načala XX veka,* ed. A. L. Narochnitskiĭ (Moscow: Gosudarstvennoe izdatel'stvo politicheskoĭ literatury, 1961), Series I, 2: 138–151. See also the firsthand account of Adam Czartoryski, *Essai sur la diplomatie, ou manuscrit d'un Philhellène,* ed. N. Toulouzan (Paris: Firmin-Didot, 1830); Constantin de Grunwald, *Trois siècles de diplomatie russe* (Paris: Calmann-Lévy, 1945), 146–159; W. H. Zavadzki, *A*

Man of Honour: Adam Czartoryski as a Statesman of Russia and Poland 1795–1831 (Oxford: Clarendon, 1993), 106–110; Zorin, *Kormi͡a dvuglavogo orla*, 305–315; Marie-Pierre Rey, *Alexandre Ier* (Paris: Flammarion, 2009), 131–170.

76. "Diplomatic note of Tsar Alexander I to the Plenipotentiaries of Austria, Great Britain, and Prussia," "Venskiĭ kongress," RO IRLI, 288/2, no. 6, ff. 35–41. See Maurice Bourquin, *Histoire de la Sainte Alliance* (Geneva: Georg, 1954),134; Ghervas, *Réinventer la tradition*, 72–73; Jarrett, *Congress of Vienna*, 174.

77. Nikolaĭ K. Shil'der, *Imperator Aleksandr I: Ego zhizn' i ͡tsarstvovanie*, 2nd ed., 4 vols. (St. Petersburg: A. S. Suvorin, 1904–1905), 3: 542–547; Ghervas, *Réinventer la tradition*, 264–265. From 1700 to 1918, Russia followed the Julian calendar, which ran thirteen days behind the Gregorian calendar in use in Western Europe.

78. *Memoirs of Prince Metternich*, 1: 262.

79. Stourdza, "Considérations sur l'acte d'alliance," f. 2. See Stella Ghervas, "La Sainte-Alliance: un pacte pacifique européen comme antidote à l'Empire," in *Europe de papier. Projets européens au XIXe siècle*, ed. Sylvie Aprile et al. (Lille: Presses Universitaires du Septentrion, 2015), 50–52.

80. Franz Baader, *Ueber das durch die französische Revolution herbeigeführte Bedürfnis einer neuen und innigern Verbindung der Religion mit Politik* (Nuremberg: Friedrich Campe, 1815).

81. Ghervas, *Réinventer la tradition*, 233–296.

82. Pope Clement XII, *In Eminenti* (on the condemnation of Freemasonry), Rome, Saint Mary Mayor (April 28, 1738); Pope Benedict XIV, *Providas Romanorum* (condemning Freemasonry), Rome, Saint Mary Mayor (May 18, 1751).

83. The tsar ordered the text of the Holy Alliance to be posted in St. Petersburg on Christmas Day, and as of March 1816 to be read in all churches of his empire. Näf, *Zur Geschichte der Heiligen Allianz*, 34–37.

84. Caused by the abdication of Emperor Francis II on August 6, 1806.

85. *La correspondance des papes et des empereurs de Russie (1814–1878)*, ed. Sophie Olszamowska-Skowronska (Rome: Pontificia Universita Gregoriana, 1970), 14–15.

86. A witness to the clash between Catholic and Orthodox visions of the social and political role of the church was the polemic pamphlet, *Considérations sur la doctrine et l'esprit de l'Eglise orthodoxe* (Stuttgart: J. G. Cotta, 1816), written by Alexander Stourdza, to which Joseph de Maistre angrily responded with his

famous *Du Pape,* 2 vols. (Lyons: Rusand, 1819). Stourdza's book introduced the French term *orthodoxe* to refer to the Eastern Christian rite, and from there into all Western languages. Ghervas, *Réinventer la tradition,* 313–334.

87. He had been ambassador of the king of Piedmont-Sardinia from 1803 to 1817. See Robert Triomphe, *Joseph de Maistre. Étude sur la vie et sur la doctrine d'un maté-rialiste mystique* (Geneva: Droz, 1968), 210–224.

88. Joseph de Maistre to Count Vallaise, October 1815, in Joseph de Maistre, *Œuvres complètes,* 14 vols. (Geneva: Slatkine Reprints, 1979), 13: 163–164. See also Triomphe, *Joseph de Maistre,* 309–310.

89. Ghervas, "Antidotes to Empire," 66–67.

90. It would be reductive, however, to limit this encyclical to being a response to the original Spirit of Vienna or even Metternich's Reaction. On the contrary, it was as much an assertion of authority toward the believers as an act of defiance against the great powers; in other words, a manifesto that the church was still a power to reckon with.

91. Pope Gregory XVI, "Mirari Vos" (August 15, 1832), in *The Papal Encyclicals,* ed. Claudia Carlen, 5 vols. (Wilmington, NC: McGrath, 1981), 1: 235–241.

92. "Traité entre l'Autriche, la Grande-Bretagne, la Prusse et la Russie, conclu à Paris le 20 novembre 1815," in *Traités et conventions conclus à Paris le 20 novembre 1815, suivis du Traité de 1814* (Paris: Galland, 1816), 105–106; Mark Jarrett, "The Quadruple Alliance of November 1815: To Secure the Blessings of Peace or to Combat the Threat of Revolution?" in *Der Wiener Kongress 1814/15,* ed. Brigitte Mazohl, 2 vols. (Vienna: Austrian Academy of Sciences, 2019), 1: 145–156.

93. On the Congress System, see Jarrett, *Congress of Vienna,* 158–205.

94. Brian Vick, "The London Ambassador's Conferences and Beyond: Aboli-tion, Barbary Corsairs and Multilateral Security in the Congress of Vienna System," in *Securing Europe after Napoleon,* 114–129.

95. James R. Sofka, "Agenda for 'Perpetual Peace,'" *Review of Politics* 60, no. 1 (1998): 115–149; Siemann, *Metternich,* 45–66; Alan J. Reinerman, "Metternich and Reform: The Case of the Papal State, 1814–1848," *Journal of Modern History* 42, no. 4 (1970): 524–548; Reinerman, "Metternich, Pope Gregory XVI, and Revolu-tionary Poland, 1831–1842," *Catholic Historical Review* 86, no. 4 (2000): 603–619.

96. James Sofka, "Metternich's Theory of European Order: A Plan for 'Perpetual Peace,'" *Post-Soviet Affairs* 14, no. 2 (1998): 115–164.

97. Kant, *Perpetual Peace,* "First Supplement," 114.

98. Kant, *Perpetual Peace,* "First Supplement," 114.

99. *Memoirs of Prince Metternich,* 1: 36–38; Hans Rieben, *Prinzipiengrundlage und Diplomatie in Metternichs Europapolitik, 1814–1848* (Aarau: Sauerlander, 1942), 14–18; Heinrich von Srbik, "Metternich's Plan der Neuordnung Europas, 1814–1815," *Mitteilungen des Institutsfür isterreichischen Geschichtsforshung* 50 (1936): 109–126.

100. For an explanation of the difference between Metternich's concept of equilibrium and balance of power, see Sofka, "Metternich's Theory of European Order," 125.

101. Kissinger, *World Restored,* 41–61; Schroeder, "Did the Vienna Settlement Rest on a Balance of Power?" 701–703; Enno Kraehe, "A Bipolar Balance of Power," *American Historical Review* 97, no. 3 (1992): 707–715. On this debate, see also Harold Nicolson, *The Congress of Vienna* (New York: Harcourt, Brace and Co., 1946), 38–41; Gulick, *Europe's Classical Balance of Power,* 121; Sked, *Metternich and Austria,* 53–63; G. John Ikenberry, *After Victory: Institutions, Strategic Restraint, and the Rebuilding of Order after Major Wars* (Princeton: Princeton University Press, 2001), 80–93.

102. Friedrich Gentz, "Consideration on the Political System in Europe" (1818), in *Metternich's Europe,* ed. Mack Walker (New York: Walker, 1968), 73.

103. Friedrich von Gentz, "Über den ewigen Frieden" (1800), in Gentz, *Gesammelte Schriften,* 12 vols. (Hildesheim: Olms-Weidmann, 1997–), 5: 603–682; Kurt von Raumer, *Ewiger Friede: Friedensrufe und Friedenspläne seit der Renaissance* (Freiburg: K. Alber, 1953), 174–207; Raphaël Cahen, *Friedrich Gentz, 1764–1832: Penseur post-Lumières et acteur du nouvel ordre européen* (Berlin: De Gruyter Oldenbourg, 2017), 160–164.

104. [Friedrich Gentz], *Fragmente aus der neusten Geschichte des politischen Gleichgewichts in Europa* (St. Petersburg [Leipzig]: [J. F. Hartknoch], 1806).

105. *Constitution de la République française: proposée au peuple français* (August 22, 1795) (Paris: Imprimérie de la République, [1795]), Part VI, Art. 132–134 et seq.; Arcidiacono, *Cinq types de paix,* 397–406.

106. Tsar Alexander I appointed the Duc de Richelieu governor of Novorossiya ("New Russia," an area including Odessa and Crimea) from 1803 to 1814. Richelieu was assigned in particular the mission of turning Odessa into an ideal port city, complete with all the urban and civic refinements; he made himself

popular in this role. Emmanuel de Waresquiel, *Le duc de Richelieu, 1766–1822: Un sentimental en politique* (Paris: Perrin, 1990), 136–73.

107. Zamoyski, *Rites of Peace*, 35–48; Jarrett, *Congress of Vienna*, 72–84.

108. Jean-Daniel Candaux, *Histoire de la famille Pictet, 1474–1974*, 2 vols. (Geneva: Braillard, 1974), 2: 287–310.

109. Although history all but forgot the legacy of this monumental collection (more than thirty-five thousand pages), it played a crucial role during the Napoleonic era in connecting the intellectual elite of Europe, not unlike that of the *Encyclopédie* of the previous era of the Enlightenment. See David M. Bickerton, *Marc-Auguste and Charles Pictet, the Bibliothèque britannique (1796–1815) and the Dissemination of British Literature and Science on the Continent* (Geneva: Slatkine Reprints, 1986).

110. Madame de Staël, *De l'Allemagne* (Paris: G. Dufour, 1814), 261; Glenda Sluga, "Madame de Staël and the Transformation of European Politics, 1812–1817," *International History Review* 37 (2015): 142–166.

111. Michal Chvojka, *Josef Graf Sedlnitzky als Präsident der Polizei- und Zensurhofstelle in Wien (1817–1848): Ein Beitrag zur Geschichte der Staatspolizei in der Habsburgermonarchie* (Frankfurt a.M.: Peter Lang, 2010), 36–40, 147–208.

112. Ido de Haan and Jeroen van Zanten, "Constructing an International Conspiracy: Revolutionary Concertation and Police Networks in the European Restoration," in *Securing Europe after Napoleon*, 171–192; Karl Gärter, "Security and Transnational Policing of Political Subversion and International Crime in the German Confederation after 1815," in *Securing Europe after Napoleon*, 193–213.

113. Manfred Brümmer, *Staat kontra Universität. Die Universität Halle-Wittenberg und die Karlsbader Beschlüsse 1819–1848* (Weimar: Böhlau, 1991), 36–51; Ghervas, *Réinventer la tradition*, 204–217.

114. R. John Rath, "The Carbonari: Their Origins, Initiation Rites, and Aims," *American Historical Review* 69, no. 2 (1964): 353–370.

115. On the motives of Kotzebue's assassination, see George S. Williamson, "What Killed August von Kotzebue? The Temptations of Virtue and the Political Theology of German Nationalism, 1789–1819," *Journal of Modern History* 72, no. 4 (2000): 890–943; Pierre Mattern, *"Kotzebue's Allgewalt": literarische Fehde und politisches Attentat* (Würzburg: Königshausen & Neumann, 2011); Siemann, *Metternich: Strategist and Visionary*, 574–592.

116. "Preliminary Protocol of Troppau, presented by Metternich to the Congress of the Powers at Troppau" (November 15, 1820), in *Metternich's Europe,* 127; Paul W. Schroeder, *Metternich's Diplomacy at its Zenith, 1820–1823* (Austin: University of Texas Press, 1962), 60–103.

117. "Circular Despatch of the Courts of Austria, Russia, and Prussia, to their Ambassadors and Agents at the German and Northern Courts, Troppau, December 8, 1820," in *Metternich's Europe,* 128.

118. See, for example, Louis-Pierre-Edouard Bignon, *Du congrès de Troppau* (Paris: Firmin Didot, 1821), 186–218.

119. "Circular Dispatch of the Courts of Austria, Russia, and Prussia," 128; "Report by Prince Lieven, Russian Ambassador in London, of an interview with Foreign Minister Castlereagh, concerning the Troppau Protocol, December 8, 1820," in *Metternich's Europe,* 130, 135; Webster, *Foreign Policy of Castlereagh,* 320–328; Bew, *Castlereagh,* 503–509; Jarrett, *Congress of Vienna,* 260–263, 277–280.

120. From Vulgar Latin *concertare,* "to settle by argument." To the best of our knowledge, the term "concert" (in a political sense) has been in use at least since 1806, as found in Gentz, "The Dangers and Advantages of the Present State of Europe, Impartially Considered," *The Times,* no. 6678 (March 8, 1806): 21; Gentz, "Sur les moyens de mettre un terme aux malheurs et aux dangers de l'Europe et sur les principes d'une pacification Générale" (1806), in *Aus dem nachlasse des grafen Prokesch-Osten . . . Briefwechsel mit herrn von Gentz und fürsten Metternich,* ed. Anton von Prokesch von Osten, 2 vols. (Vienna: C. Gerold's sohn, 1881), 2: 1–99. The first official use is in Article 1 of the Treaty of Chaumont (1814), which contains the phrase *dans un parfait concert* (in perfect accordance). Other examples from the time of the Vienna Congress show a number of variations ("general concert," "perpetual concert," "happy concert," "concert between allies"), but not yet "concert of Europe."

121. Giuseppe Mazzini, "Manifesto of Young Italy" (1831), in *A Cosmopolitanism of Nations. Giuseppe Mazzini's Writings on Democracy, Nation Building, and International Relations,* ed. Stefano Recchia and Nadia Urbinati (Princeton: Princeton University Press, 2009), 33–38.

122. Hans Gustav Keller, *Das "Junge Europa," 1834–1836* (Zürich: Max Niehaus, [1938]). On the principle of neutrality in Switzerland and broadly in Europe, see Maartje Maria Abbenhuis, "A Most Useful Tool for Diplomacy and Statecraft: Neutrality and Europe in the 'Long' Nineteenth Century, 1815–1914," *International History Review* 35, no. 1 (2013): 1–22.

123. Charles Forbes Montalembert, *Pius IX and France in 1849 and 1859* (Boston: Patrick Donahoe, 1861).

124. Giuseppe Mazzini, "Toward a Holy Alliance of the Peoples" (1849), in *Cosmopolitanism of Nations,* 117–131.

125. Mazzini, "Toward a Holy Alliance of the Peoples," 119.

126. Kant, *Perpetual Peace,* "First Definitive Article," 114–116; Pierre Rosanvallon, *La légitimité démocratique. Impartialité, réflexivité Proximité* (Paris: Éditions du Seuil, 2008); see also Rosanvallon course at Collège de France "Qu'est-ce qu'une société démocratique?" in January–February 2010. On the progressive rehabilitation of the notion of democracy in the nineteenth century, see Russell L. Hanson, "Democracy," in *Political Innovation and Conceptual Change,* ed. Terence Ball et al. (Cambridge: Cambridge University Press, 1989), 68–89; Paul Cartledge, Democracy: A Life (Oxford: Oxford University Press, 2016), 293–298.

127. The US Democratic-Republican Party was founded in 1792, four years after the US Constitution entered into force. On the notion of democracy in US politics, see, for example, James T. Kloppenberg, *Toward Democracy: The Struggle for the Self-Rule in European and American Thought* (Oxford: Oxford University Press, 2016), 314–407.

128. Richard J. Evans, *The Pursuit of Power: Europe 1815–1914* (New York: Viking, 2016), ch. 3.

129. "Congrès à Paris des amis de la paix universelle. Première séance. Mercredi 22 août 1849.—Présidence de M. Victor Hugo," in *Congrès des amis de la paix universelle réuni à Paris en* 1849, ed. Joseph Garnier (Paris: Guillaumin, 1850), 3–4; Thomas Hippler, "From Nationalist Peace to Democratic War: The Peace Congresses in Paris (1849) and Geneva (1867)," in *Paradoxes of Peace in Nineteenth Century Europe,* ed. Thomas Hippler and Miloš Vec (Oxford: Oxford University Press, 2015), 174–182.

130. Joseph Garnier, "Note sur le movement en faveur de la paix," in *Congrès des amis de la paix universelle, réuni à Paris en 1849* (Paris: Guillaumin, 1850), iii.

131. Victor Hugo, "Discours d'ouverture [Congrès de la paix, Paris]" (August 21, 1849), in Hugo, *Actes et paroles: Avant l'exil, 1841–1851* (Paris: Lévy Frères, 1876), 383.

132. Hugo, "Discours d'ouverture," 383.

133. Hugo, "Discours d'ouverture," 380; A key critic of Hugo at the time was Louis Veuillot, the editor of the Catholic newspaper *L'Univers*. On this polemic, see Jean-Claude Fizaine, "Journalisme et polémique religieuse: *L'Univers* et *L'Evénement*," in *Presse et Plumes: Journalisme et littérature au XIXe siècle*, ed. Marie-Eve Thérenty and Alain Vaillant (Paris: Nouveau Monde Éditions, 2004), 241–259.

134. J. A. R. Marriott, *The Eastern Question: An Historical Study of European Diplomacy* (Oxford: Clarendon Press, 1917); M. S. Anderson, *The Eastern Question, 1774–1923* (London: Macmillan, 1966); and for a discussion of the recent historiography, see Lucien Frary and Mara Kozelsky, eds., *Russian-Ottoman Borderlands: The Eastern Question Reconsidered* (Madison: University of Wisconsin Press, 2014), 3–34.

135. The eighth Russo-Turkish War (1806–1812), concluded by the Treaty of Bucharest in 1812. See Orlik, *Rossiīa v mezhdunarodnykh otnosheniīakh*, 76–77.

136. Claude-Henri de Saint-Simon and A[uguste] Thierry, *De la réorganisation de la société européenne ou De la nécessité et des moyens* (1814), in *Œuvres de Claude-Henri de Saint-Simon,* 6 vols. (Paris: Editions Anthropos, [1966]), 1: 204.

137. Saint-Simon considered that Europe being the site of civilization, the inequality of the "races" or "varieties of man" was self-evident: Saint-Simon, *Introduction aux travaux scientifiques du XIXe siècle* (1807), in *Œuvres de Claude-Henri de Saint-Simon,* 6: 129.

138. Will Smiley, *From Slaves to Prisoners of War: The Ottoman Empire, Russia, and International Law* (Oxford: Oxford University Press, 2018).

139. Alexander Sturdza, "Mémoire sur la question que présente l'Orient au mois de janvier 1825" (1825), RO IRLI, 288/1, no. 6; Alexander Sturdza, "Mémoire sur les relations à établir entre la Russie et la Grèce" (1830), RO IRLI, 288/1, no. 20.

140. See, for example, Lord Byron's poem "The Isles of Greece" (1819); Paschalis M. Kitromilides, *Enlightenment and Revolution: The Making of Modern Greece* (Cambridge, MA: Harvard University Press, 2013), 292–315.

141. Miroslav Šedivý, *Metternich, the Great Powers and the Eastern Question* (Pilsen: University of West Bohemia, 2013), 39–44.

142. Šedivý, *Metternich, the Great Powers and the Eastern Question,* 54–55.

143. Metternich to Lützow, Vienna, November 17, 1821, quoted in Bertier de Sauvigny, "Sainte-Alliance et alliance dans les conceptions de Metternich," 254.

144. Jennifer Pitts, *Boundaries of the International: Law and Empire* (Cambridge, MA: Harvard University Press, 2018), 28–67.

145. For a documentary account of the events, including by the British ambassador in Constantinople, Viscount Strangford, see *The Massacres of Chios Described in Contemporary Diplomatic Reports,* ed. Philip P. Argenti (London: John Lane, 1932), 3–50. See also David Brewer, *The Greek War of Independence: The Struggle for Freedom from Ottoman Oppression and the Birth of the Modern Greek Nation* (New York: Overlook Press, 2001), 154–167; Theophilus C. Prousis, "'Dreadful Scenes of Carnage on Both Sides': The Strangford Files and the Eastern Crisis of 1821–1830," in *Russian-Ottoman Borderlands,* 73–100.

146. On the philhellenic movement in general and the controversy around the Greek insurrection in Europe in particular, see Michel Espagne and Gilles Pécout, eds., *Philhellénismes et transferts culturels dans l'Europe du XIXe siècle,* special issue of *Revue germanique internationale* 1–2 (2005); Kōnstantinos Ap. Vakalopoulos, *Eurōpaioi philellēnes, paratērētes kai technokrates stēn epanastatēmenē Hellada kai sto Helladiko Vasileio, 1821–1843* (Thessaloniki: Ekdotikos Oikos Ant. Stamoulē, 2008); Denis Barau, *La cause des Grecs: Une histoire du mouvement philhellène (1821–1829)* (Paris: Honoré Champion, 2009).

147. See Gary J. Bass, *Freedom's Battle: The Origins of Humanitarian Intervention* (New York: Alfred A. Knopf, 2008), 45–152; Davide Rodogno, *Against Massacre: Humanitarian Interventions in the Ottoman Empire, 1815–1914* (Princeton: Princeton University Press, 2011), 63–90. On the specific traits of the Russian philhellenism, see Stella Ghervas, "Le philhellénisme d'inspiration conservatrice en Europe et en Russie," in *Peuples, Etats et nations dans le Sud-Est de l'Europe* (Bucharest: Anima, 2004), 98–110.

148. On the Russian-Turkish War of 1828–1829, see Helmuth von Moltke, *Der russisch-türkische Feldzug in der europäischen Türkei 1828–1829* (Berlin: Reimer, 1845); Colonel [Francis Rawdon] Chesney, *The Russo-Turkish Campaigns of 1828 and 1829* (New York: Redfield, 1854); Victor Taki, *Tsar and Sultan: Russian Encounters with the Ottoman Empire* (London: I. B. Tauris, 2016), 45–50.

149. Edouard Engelhardt, *La Turquie et le Tanzimât, ou Histoire des réformes dans l'Empire ottoman depuis 1826 jusqu'à nos jours,* 2 vols. (Paris: A. Cotillon, 1882–1884); Halil İnalcık and Mehmet Seyitdanlıoğlu, *Tanzimat: Değişim Sürecinde Osmanlı İmparatorluğu* (Ankara: Phoenix Yayınevi, 2006); Tunay Sürek, *Die Verfassungsbestrebungen der Tanzimât-Periode: Das "Kanun-i Esasî"—Die osmanische Verfassung von 1876* (Frankfurt a.M.: Peter Lang, 2015), 13–20, 45–60.

150. On differences of diplomatic strategy between Capodistrias and Nesselrode, see Patricia Kennedy Grimsted, *The Foreign Ministers of Alexander I: Political Attitudes and the Conduct of Russian Diplomacy, 1801–1825* (Berkeley: University of California Press, 1969), 226–287.

151. *A. S. Men'shikov v Krymskoĭ voĭne: Dnevniki, Pis'ma, Vospominanija,* ed. A. V. Efimof, Part I (Simferopol: Antikva, 2018), 74–211; *A. S. Men'shikov v Krymskoĭ voĭne: Prikazy 1853–1855,* ed. A. V. Efimov, Part II (Simferopol: Antikva, 2019), 10–125.

152. On the origins of the Crimean War, see Edmond Bapst, *Les origines de la guerre en Crimée: la France et la Russie de 1848 à 1851* (Paris: C. Delagrave, 1912), 155–244, 472–487; David M. Goldfrank, *The Origins of the Crimean War* (London: Longman, 1994); Orlando Figes, *The Crimean War: A History* (New York: Metropolitan Books, 2011), 23–98.

153. Louis Antoine Debrauz de Saldapenna, *Le traité de Paris du 30 mars, étudié dans ses causes et ses effets* (Paris: Amyot, 1856), Annexe A, Art. 7, 416. Emphasis added.

154. Winfried Baumgart, *The Peace of Paris 1856: Studies in War, Diplomacy and Peacemaking,* trans. Ann Pottinger Saab (Oxford: Clio Press, 1981), 158–164; Roderic H. Davison, *Reform in the Ottoman Empire, 1856–1876* (Princeton: Princeton University Press, 1963), 52–80; Roderic H. Davison, *Nineteenth Century Ottoman Diplomacy and Reforms* (Istanbul: The Isis Press, 1999), 169–174.

155. Miroslav Šedivý, *Crisis among the Great powers: The Concert of Europe and the Eastern Question* (London: I. B. Tauris, 2017), 49–113.

156. Benjamin Claude Brower, *A Desert Named Peace: The Violence of France's Empire in the Algerian Sahara, 1844–1902* (New York: Columbia University Press, 2009), 27–90; Alain Tirefor, "La 'pacification' du Madagascar: septembre 1896—mai 1905," in *Guerres et paix en Afrique noire et à Madagascar: XIXe et XXe siècles,* ed. Alain Tirefort (Rennes: Presses universitaires de Rennes, 2016), 187–203; Oliver Eberl, "The Paradox of Peace with 'Savage' and 'Barbarian' Peoples," in *Paradoxes of Peace in Nineteenth Century Europe,* 219–237; Ghervas, "Definitions of Peace," 23–41.

157. Gautam Chakravarty, *The Indian Mutiny and the British Imagination* (Cambridge: Cambridge University Press, 2005), 72–104.

158. Jürgen Osterhammel, *The Transformation of the World: A Global History of the Nineteenth Century,* trans. Patrick Camiller (Princeton: Princeton University Press, 2014), paticularly 392–403, 483–493.

159. "General Act of the Berlin Conference on West Africa" (February 26, 1885), Arts. 6 and 34–35.

160. Martti Koskenniemi, *The Gentle Civilizer of Nations: The Rise and Fall of International Law, 1870–1960* (Cambridge: Cambridge University Press, 2001), 116–131; Matthew Craven, "Between Law and History: The Berlin Conference of 1884–1885 and the Logic of the Free Trade," *London Review of International Law* 3, no. 1 (2015): 31–59.

161. Philippa Levine, "Anthropology, Colonialism and Eugenics," in *The Oxford Handbook of the History of Eugenics,* ed. Alison Bashford and Philippa Levine (Oxford: Oxford University Press, 2010), 45.

3. THE SPIRIT OF GENEVA

1. Margaret MacMillan, *Peacemakers: The Paris Conference of 1919 and Its Attempt to End War* (London: John Murray, 2001), 485–489.

2. Harold Nicolson, "Diary: June 28, 1919," in Nicolson, *Peacemaking, 1919* (London: Constable, 1933), 368.

3. Nicolson, *Peacemaking,* 369.

4. [Robert Lansing], "Memorandum by the Secretary of State. The Signing of the Treaty of Peace with Germany at Versailles on June 28, 1919," in *Foreign Relations of the United States: The Paris Peace Conference, 1919,* 13 vols. (Washington, DC: Government Printing Office, 1942–1947), 11: 600.

5. Howard Elcock, *Portrait of a Decision: The Council of Four and the Treaty of Versailles* (London: Eyre Methuen, 1972), 290–292; George Goldberg, *The Peace to End Peace: The Paris Peace Conference of 1919* (New York: Harcourt, 1969), 184–186.

6. On the structural roots of the instability that emerged from the Treaties of Paris, see Charles S. Maier, *Recasting Bourgeois Europe: Stabilization in France, Germany, and Italy in the Decade after World War I,* 2nd ed. (Princeton: Princeton University Press, 2015), 579.

7. [Raymond Poincaré], "The Opening Session of the Peace Conference. President Poincaré's Inaugural Speech" (January 18, 1919), in *Source Records of the Great War,* ed.-in chief Charles F. Horne, directing ed. Walter F. Austin, 7 vols. ([New York]: National Alumni, 1923), 7: 43.

8. Friedrich Wilhelm III, "An Mein Volk," Breslau (March 17, 1813).

9. In French, those treaties are collectively called "Suburban Treaties" (*Traités de la Banlieue*).

10. Sally Marks, "Mistakes and Myths: The Allies, Germany and the Versailles Treaties, 1918–1921," *Journal of Modern History* 85, no. 3 (2013): 632–659.

11. Lord Robert Cecil to Colonel House, London, September 3, 1917, in *IPCH*, 4: 6. See also W. Evans Darby, *The Political Machinery of Peace, during the Last Year* (London: Peace Society, 1908), 3–20.

12. Robert de Traz, *De l'Alliance des rois à la Ligue des peuples: Sainte-Alliance et S.D.N.* (Paris: Grasset, 1936).

13. Philip Henry Kerr Lothian, lord of, *The Ending of Armageddon* ([Oxford: Aldon Press, 1939]), 3.

14. Brian Morton, *Woodrow Wilson: United States* (London: Haus, 2008), 196. See also MacMillan, *Peacemakers,* 92.

15. See, for example, Gabriel Gorodetsky, "The Formulation of Soviet Foreign Policy—Ideology and *Realpolitik,*" in *Soviet Foreign Policy, 1917–1991: A Retrospective* (London: Frank Cass, 1994), 30–44.

16. See Zara Steiner, *The Lights that Failed: European International History, 1919–1933* (Oxford: Oxford University Press, 2005), 20–46; Susan Pedersen, "Review Essay: Back to the League of Nations," *American Historical Review* 112, no. 4 (2007): 1091–1117; Ruth Henig, "The League of Nations: An Idea before Its Time?" in *The Origins of the Second World War: An International Perspective,* ed. Frank McDonough (New York: Continuum, 2011), 34–49.

17. Most notably, Webster, *The Congress of Vienna;* Guglielmo Ferrero, *Problems of Peace: From the Holy Alliance to the League of Nations: A Message from a European Writer to Americans* (New York: Putnam, 1919), 29–64.

18. Mark Mazower, *Governing the World: The History of an Idea, 1815 to the Present* (New York: Penguin Books, 2012), 137–141.

19. The myth that everyone in August 1914 believed "it would all be over by Christmas" has been decisively overturned by recent scholarship. See, for example, Stuart Hallifax, "'Over by Christmas': British Popular Opinion and the Short War in 1914," *First World War Studies* 1, no. 2 (2010): 103–121.

20. Carl von Clausewitz, *On War* (1832), ed. and trans. Michael Howard and Peter Paret (Princeton: Princeton University Press, 1989), 75 (I.1.ii).

21. Clausewitz, *On War,* 76 (I.1.iii). On the principle of moderation, see Aurelian Craiutu, *A Virtue for Courageous Minds: Moderation in French Political Thought, 1748–1830* (Princeton: Princeton University Press, 2012).

22. Evidently, insufficient attention had been paid to the lessons of the eleven-month siege of Sevastopol in the Crimean War, as well as to battles of the US Civil War.

23. Clausewitz, *On War,* 76 (I.1.iii).

24. Romain Rolland, *Au-dessus de la mêlée* (Paris: Ollendorff, 1915), 34–35.

25. On the Christmas truce, see Malcolm Brown and Shirley Seaton, *The Christmas Truce* (Basingstoke: Papermac, 1994); Stanley Weintraub, *Silent Night: The Remarkable 1914 Christmas Truce* (New York: Free Press, 2001).

26. Benedict XV, "Al tremendo conflitto," in *Tutte le encicliche e i principali documenti pontifici emanate dal 1740,* ed. Ugo Bellocchi, 12 vols. (Vatican City: Libreria Editrice Vaticana, 1993-2004), 8: 94-96. See also John Pollard, "Papal Diplomacy and The Great War," *New Blackfriars* 96, no. 1062 (2015): 147–157; William Mulligan, *The Great War for Peace* (New Haven: Yale University Press, 2014), 133–222.

27. See Larry Zuckerman, *The Rape of Belgium: The Untold Story of World War I* (New York: New York University Press, 2004), 22–37; Thomas Weber, *Hitler's First War: Adolph Hitler, the Men of the List Regiment, and the First World War* (Oxford: Oxford University Press, 2010), 27–31, 329–330.

28. See Jerry White, *Zeppelin Nights: London in the First World War* (London: Bodley Head, 2004).

29. Bell, *The First Total War,* 223–262.

30. Anatole France, "On croit mourir pour la patrie, on meurt pour les industriels," *L'Humanité,* July 18, 1922, 1.

31. "Ministers in this country, where every part of the World affects us, in some way or another, should consider the whole Globe," wrote the Duke of Newcastle in 1758; see Richard Middleton, *The Bells of Victory* (Cambridge: Cambridge University Press, 1985), 77; Daniel Baugh, *The Global Seven Years War, 1754–1763: Britain and France in a Great Power Contest* (New York: Longman, 2011), 8–13.

32. Woodrow Wilson, "An Address to a Joint Session of Congress" (April 2, 1917), in *PWW,* 41: 520.

33. Robert Gerwarth and Erez Manela, eds., *Empires at War: 1911–1923* (Oxford: Oxford University Press, 2014), "Introduction," 1–16.

34. Woodrow Wilson, "Address to the Representatives of All the Allied and Associated Nations at the Paris Peace Conference" (January 25, 1919); "Protocol of a Plenary Session of the Inter-Allied Conference for the Preliminaries of Peace," in *PWW,* 54: 266.

35. "Armistice with Germany" (November 11, 1918), in *TIAS,* 2: 9.

36. *Agreement between France, Russia, Great Britain and Italy,* signed in London (April 26, 1915), Art. 9, in Great Britain, *Parliamentary Papers, Miscellaneous,* no. 7 (1920): 5.

37. The first Anglo-Japanese Alliance was signed on January 30, 1902. It bound the two countries to assist one another in safeguarding their respective interests in China and Korea.

38. *FRUS*, Vol. 3: *Paris Peace Conference,* 182/70; *FRUS*, Vol. 5: *Note Concerning the Minutes of the Meeting of the Council of Four,* series IC, particularly Documents 9–22; Paul Mantoux, *Les délibérations du Conseil des Quatre (24 mars–28 juin 1919): Notes de l'officier interprète,* 2 vols. (Paris: Centre national de la recherche scientifique, 1955); William Laird Kleine-Ahlbrandt, *The Burden of Victory: France, Britain and the Enforcement of the Versailles Peace, 1919–1925* (Lanham, MD: University Press of America, 1995), 21–94.

39. David Lloyd George, *British War Aims, January 5, 1918* (New York: George H. Doran, 1918), 3.

40. "Treaty of Peace with Germany (Treaty of Versailles)," in *TIAS,* 2: 136, 137–138.

41. "The Swiss Minister (Sulzer) to the Secretary of State Washington" (December 2, 1918), in *FRUS,* no. 763.72 / 12485, 2: 71–72; Sally Marks, "The Myths of Reparations," *Central European History* 11, no. 3 (1978): 231–255.

42. "By Count von Brockdorff-Rantzau. Letter to M. Clemenceau as President of Peace Conference . . . " (November 11, 1918), in *Source Records of the Great War,* 7: 159; "Armistice with Germany: Declaration by German Plenipotentiaries" (November 11, 1918), clause 26, in *TIAS,* 2: 19.

43. Seth P. Tillman, *Anglo-American Relations at the Paris Peace Conference of 1919* (Princeton: Princeton University Press, 1961), 266–267.

44. "Armistice with Germany," 2: 14.

45. "Armistice with Germany," 2: 18–19; N. P. Howard, "The Social and Political Consequences of the Allied Food Blockade of Germany, 1918–19," *German History* 11, no. 2 (1993): 161–188.

46. "Formal Swiss Protest," *New York Times,* June 1, 1919, 7; "Sweden and Denmark Won't Join Blockade; Will Stay Neutral if Germany Refuses to Sign the Peace Treaty," *New York Times,* June 4, 1919, 4.

47. On the opposition of the German delegation to the blockade, see "By Georges Clemenceau. Letter to the President of the German Delegation covering the Reply of the Allied and Associated Powers," in *Source Records of the Great War,* 7: 176–177; C. Paul Vincent, *The Politics of Hunger: Allied Blockade of Germany, 1915–1919* (Athens: Ohio University Press, 1985), 50.

48. Kaiser Karl I, *Seit meiner Thronbesteigung war ich unablässig bemüht, MeineVölker aus den Schrecknissen des Krieges herauszuführen, an dessen Ausbruch ich keinerlei Schuld trage . . .* (November 11, 1918) (Vienna: Staatsdruckerei, 1918).

49. *Traité de paix entre les puissances alliées et associées et l'Autriche. Protocole et declarations, signés à Saint-Germain-en-Laye, le 10 septembre 1919* ([Paris]: [1919]), Art. 177, 75.

50. Magda Ádám, *The Little Entente and Europe (1920–1929)* (Budapest: Akadémiai Kiadó, 1993), 111–192.

51. Istvan Polgar, "Perceptions on Trianon during the Interwar Period," *Analele Universității din Oradea: Relații Internaționale și Studii Europene* 3 (2011): 7–20; Andrzej Sadecki, "The Long Shadow of the Treaty of Trianon: Hungary's Struggles with the Past," *OSW Point of View* 80 (2020): 26–31.

52. Robert Gerwarth, *The Vanquished: Why the First World War Failed to End, 1917–1923* (London: Allen Lane, 2016), 187–198.

53. Leonard V. Smith, *Sovereignty at the Paris Peace Conference in 1919* (Oxford: Oxford University Press, 2018), 143–179; S. B. Vardy, "The Impact of Trianon upon Hungary and the Hungarian Mind: The Nature of Interwar Hungarian Irredentism," *Hungarian Studies Review* 10, no. 1 (1983): 21–42.

54. "Traité de paix entre les puissances alliées et associées et l'Autriche," Art. 89, 49.

55. J. Kim Munholland, "The French Army and Intervention in Southern Russia, 1918–1919," *Cahiers du Monde Russe* 22, no. 1 (1981): 43–66.

56. "Treaty of Sèvres" (August 10, 1920), in *The Treaties of Peace 1919–1923*, ed. Lawrence Martin, 2 vols. (New York: Carnegie Endowment for International Peace, 1924), 2: 789–941.

57. On British perceptions of the Treaty of Lausanne, see David Lloyd George, "The Treaty of Lausanne," in *Is It Peace?* (London: Hodder, [1923]), 254–266.

58. Florence Wilson, *The Origins of the League Covenant: Documentary History of Its Drafting* (London: Hogarth Press, 1928), xi–xiii; John Milton Cooper, *Woodrow Wilson: A Biography* (New York: Alfred A. Knopf, 2009), 454–475.

59. "Interventions de M. Léon Bourgeois à la Commission de la SDN du 3 février 1919," AMAE, Papiers Léon Bourgeois, PA-AP 029, vol. 18; "Exposé des motifs des amendements français au projet du Pacte" (n.d.), AMAE PA-AP 029, vol. 18; Bourgeois to Clemenceau, February 7, 1919, AMAE PA-AP 029, vol. 18; "Notes et propositions remises à la Séance du 11 février par M. Léon Bourgeois," AMAE, PA-AP 029, vol. 18. See also Scott Blair, "La France et le Pacte de la Société des Nations: le rôle du gouvernement français dans l'élaboration du Pacte de la Société des Nations" (PhD diss., University of Paris I–Sorbonne, 1991), 418–431.

60. "[Proposals of the German Government for the establishment of a League of Nations]" (undated), Foundation principles I.1, in *FRUS*, 6: 765; "German Note" by Brockdorff-Rantzau, Deutsche Friedensdelegation, Versailles, May 9, 1919, in *FRUS*, 5: 563.

61. Paul Gordon Lauren, "Human Rights in History: Diplomacy and Racial Equality at the Paris Peace Conference," *Diplomatic History* 2, no. 3 (1978): 257–278.

62. On this point, see Edward Howland Tatum, *The United States and Europe, 1815–1823: A Study in the Background of the Monroe Doctrine*, 2nd ed. (New York: Russell & Russell, 1967).

63. *IPCH*, 1: 209–210. See also Article X of "The Covenant of the League of Nations": "The members of the League undertake to respect and preserve as against external aggression the territorial integrity and existing political independence of all Members of the League. In case of any such aggression the Council shall advise upon the means by which this obligation shall be fulfilled."

64. Hamilton Foley, *Woodrow Wilson's Case for the League of Nations* (Princeton: Princeton University Press, 1923), 90–92; Kirby Page, *The Monroe Doctrine and World Peace* (New York: Doubleday, Doran & Company, 1928), 3–22.

65. *IPCH*, 4: 3.

66. Woodrow Wilson, "An Address in Washington to the League to Enforce Peace" (May 27, 1916), in *PWW*, 37: 113–116. On the importance of this speech, see Woodrow Wilson to Colonel House, May 18, 1916, in *PWW*, 37: 68–69.

67. Foley, *Woodrow Wilson's Case*, 149–210; John Morton Blum, *Woodrow Wilson and the Politics of Morality* (Boston: Little, Brown, 1956), 181–199; Richard M. Gamble, "Savior Nation: Woodrow Wilson and the Gospel of Service," *Humanitas* 14, no. 1 (2001): 4–22.

68. The "Zimmermann Telegram," issued from the German Foreign Office in January 1917, proposed a military alliance between Germany and Mexico. Thomas Boghardt, *The Zimmermann Telegram: Intelligence, Diplomacy, and America's Entry into World War I* (Annapolis, MD: Naval Institute Press, 2012), 59–79.

69. The "Ems Telegram," in Lawrence D. Steefel, *Bismarck, the Hohenzollern Candidacy, and the Origins of the Franco-German War of 1870* (Cambridge, MA: Harvard University Press, 2014), 257–258.

70. Woodrow Wilson, "An Address to the Senate" (January 22, 1917), in *PWW*, 40: 535.

71. Wilson to House (August 23, 1917) and Robert Lansing to Pope Benedict XV (August 27, 1917), in *PWW*, 42: 34 (draft), 58.

72. "In the meantime, the British draft was completed and sent to Colonel House, who on January 19 forwarded a copy to the President [Wilson]." In *Papers of Colonel House*, 4: 287. On this American-British collaboration in drafting the Covenant of the League, see David Hunter Miller, *The Drafting of the Covenant*, 2 vols. (New York: Putnam, 1928), 1: 3–75.

73. Miller, *Drafting of the Covenant*, 1: 65–71. See also *Papers of Colonel House*, 4: 279–320; Erez Manela, "Woodrow Wilson and Colonel House," *Diplomatic History* 31, no. 2 (2007): 341–345.

74. Woodrow Wilson, "An Address to a Joint Session of Congress" (January 8, 1918), in *PWW*, 45: 538. See also Lloyd E. Ambrosius, *Woodrow Wilson and the American Diplomatic Tradition: The Treaty Fight in Perspective* (Cambridge: Cambridge University Press, 1987), 35–37.

75. Wilson, "An Address to a Joint Session of Congress," 538. "In fact, they pinned their hopes for a just and lasting peace upon a Fifteenth point, the character of Woodrow Wilson"; David Loth, *Woodrow Wilson: The Fifteenth Point* (Philadelphia: J. B. Lippincott, 1941), 191.

76. Woodrow Wilson, "Address to the Representatives of all the Allied and Associated Nations at the Paris Peace Conference" (January 25, 1919), in *PWW*, 54: 266.

77. See, in particular, the preamble of the Treaty of Paris of 1815.

78. Wilson, "Address to the Representatives of all the Allied and Associated Nations," 265–266.

79. Erez Manela, *The Wilsonian Moment: Self-Determination and the International Origins of Anticolonial Nationalism* (Oxford: Oxford University Press, 2007), 3–7.

80. Wilson, "Address to the Representatives of all the Allied and Associated Nations," 267–268.

81. Wilson, "An Address to the Senate," 535.

82. Arno Mayer, *Wilson vs. Lenin: Political Origins of the New Diplomacy, 1917–1918* (Cleveland: World Publishing Company, 1964); Derek Benjamin Heater, *National Self-Determination, Woodrow Wilson and His Legacy* (London: Macmillan, 1994); David Raic, *Statehood and the Law of Self-Determination* (The Hague: Kluwer Law International, 2002), 177–188; Klaus Schwabe, "Woodrow Wilson and Germany's Membership in the League of Nations, 1918–1919," *Central European History* 8, no. 1 (1975): 3–22.

83. Ikenberry, *After Victory*, 148–155.

84. Woodrow Wilson, "The Ideals of America. A Commemorative Address" (December 26, 1901), in *PWW*, 12: 222. See also Evan Thomas, *The War Lovers: Roosevelt, Lodge, Hearst, and the Rush to Empire, 1898* (New York: Little, Brown, 2017).

85. "America Isolated without Treaty: Its Defeat, Washington Feels, Will Add to Our Unpopularity Abroad," *New York Times*, March 20, 1920, 1.

86. Henry Cabot Lodge, *Treaty of Peace with Germany, Speech . . . in the Senate of the United States* (August 12, 1919) (Washington, DC: US Government Printing Office, 1919), 16.

87. "The Covenant of the League of Nations," Avalon Project, http://avalon.law.yale.edu/20th_century/leagcov.asp.

88. Luke 22:20, Matthew 26:28. In the King James Bible, the word was "testament," which, at the time, could be used interchangeably with covenant.

89. See John A. Thompson, *Woodrow Wilson* (London: Longman, 2002), 65–95; Niels Thorsen, *The Political Thought of Woodrow Wilson, 1875–1910* (Princeton: Princeton University Press, 1988), 18–31. For a summary of this historico-biographical debate, see Malcolm D. Magee, "Wilson's Religious, Historical, and Political Thought," in *A Companion to Woodrow Wilson,* ed. Ross A. Kennedy (Malden, MA: Willey-Blackwell, 2013), 238–254.

90. John Mulder, *Woodrow Wilson: The Years of Preparation* (Princeton: Princeton University Press, 1978), 269–277.

91. Woodrow Wilson, "Remarks about Giuseppe Mazzini" (January 5, 1919) and "Further Remarks in Genoa" (January 5, 1919), in *PWW,* 52: 614; Mazzini, "Toward a Holy Alliance of the Peoples," 117–131. See also Stefano Recchia and Nadia Urbinati, "Introduction: Giuseppe Mazzini's International Political Thought," in *Cosmopolitanism of Nations,* 3; Denis Mack Smith, *Mazzini* (New Haven: Yale University Press, 1994), 221.

92. Cooper, *Woodrow Wilson,* 454–464. More generally on US foreign policy and religion, see Andrew Preston, *Sword of the Spirit, Shield of Faith: Religion in American War and Diplomacy* (New York: Knopf, 2012), 233–290.

93. French versions of the Bible used the word *alliance* for God's covenant with Israel, the usual term used in diplomacy.

94. "Loi concernant la Séparation des Eglises et l'Etat," December 9, 1905.

95. Discussions on the Covenant were based on the English text, and the French version was a direct translation from the original. On this, see Philip Baker, "The Making of the Covenant," in *Les Origines et l'œuvre de la Société des Nations,* ed. P. Munch, 2 vols. (Copenhagen: Rask-Ørstedfonden, 1923–1924), 2: 411–412; Charles Howard Ellis, *The Origin, Structure & Working of the League of Nations* (Boston: Houghton Mifflin, 1929), 89.

96. E. B. Copeland, *The Sole Condition of Permanent Peace* (Chico, CA: s.n., 1919), 8.

97. Paul Otlet, *Constitution mondiale de la Société des Nations: Le nouveau droit des gens* (Geneva: Atar, 1917), 85–98, 127–137. Otlet also included a remarkable bibliography on peace, 239–246.

98. Otlet, *Constitution mondiale,* 149.

99. Peace Plans, Woodrow Wilson Memorial Library Pamphlet Collection, LNA, Box 89. I considered only those peace plans that are closely connected to the drafting of the League's Covenant.

100. *Sir Edward Grey on Union for World Peace, from his Speech in the House of Commons, March 13, 1911* (Boston: World Peace Foundation, 1911).

101. Cecil to Colonel House, London, September 3, 1917, 4: 6; Viscount Cecil, *A Great Experiment: An Autobiography* (New York: Oxford University Press, 1941), 47, 60.

102. "Phillimore Committee 1917 and 1918: Lord Robert Cecil's Advisory Committee on the League of Nations" (March 20, 1918) [file created in 1938], FO 371 22559/802; "Interim Report" (aka "Phillimore Report") (March 20, 1918), in Florence Wilson, *The Origins of the League Covenant: Documentary History of its Drafting* (London: Hogarth Press, 1928), 114–172. Phillimore's league scheme is also reproduced in Miller, *Drafting of the Covenant*, 2: 3–6.

103. Walter Georg Frank Phillimore, *Three Centuries of Treaties of Peace and Their Teaching* (London: J. Murray, 1917); George W. Egerton, *Great Britain and the Creation of the League of Nations: Strategy, Politics, and International Organization, 1914-1919* (Chapel Hill: University of North Carolina Press, 1978), 65.

104. [Walter G. F.] Lord Phillimore, *Schemes for Maintaining General Peace* (London: HM Stationery Office, 1920), 1. Phillimore knew about Saint-Pierre's *Plan* through the works of the nineteenth-century American lawyer Henry Wheaton, who was an acknowledged expert on this subject. Henry Wheaton, *Histoire des progrès du droit des gens en Europe, depuis la paix de Westphalie jusqu'au Congrès de Vienne. Avec un Précis historique du droit des gens Européen avant la paix de Westphalie* (Leipzig: F. A. Brockhaus, 1841), 194–196.

105. Joseph H. Choate, *The Two Hague Conferences* (Princeton: Princeton University Press, 1913), 3–44; Arthur Eyffinger, *The 1899 Hague Peace Conference: "The Parliament of Man, the Federation of the World"* (The Hague: Martinus Nijhoff, 1999), 16–40; Antony Adolf, *Peace: A World History* (Cambridge: Polity, 2009), 178–181.

106. "Concerning the Pacific Settlement of International Disputes" (July 25, 1899), in *The Proceedings of the Hague Peace Conferences* (New York: Oxford University Press, 1920), 107–108.

107. "Pacific Settlement of International Disputes" (July 29, 1899), Part IV, in *The Proceedings of the Hague Peace Conferences,* 239; Francis Anthony Boyle, *Foundations of World Order: The Legalist Approach to International Relations, 1898–1922* (Durham, NC: Duke University Press, 1999), 25–36.

108. Phillimore, *Schemes for Maintaining General Peace,* 66–67.

109. "Interim Report," in Wilson, *The Origins of the League Covenant,* 119.

110. Martin Ceadel, *Semi-Detached Idealists: The British Peace Movement and International Relations, 1854-1945* (Oxford: Oxford University Press, 2000), 187–238.

111. Ferrero, *Problems of Peace,* 240; Gentz, "Considerations on the Political System Now Existing in Europe" (1818), in *Metternich's Europe,* 71–72.

112. Ferrero, *Problems of Peace,* 269.

113. De Traz, *De l'Alliance des rois à la Ligues des peoples,* 93–97.

114. Austin Harrison, "Kant on the League of Nations," *English Review* 29 (1919): 454–462; Karl Vorländer, *Kant und der Gedanke des Völkerbundes* (Leipzig: F. Meiner, 1919). For a closer examination of Kantian influence on Wilson's political thought, see Gerhard Beestermöller, Die *Völkerbundsidee: Leistungsfähigkeit und Grenzen der Kriegsächtung durch Staatensolidarität* (Stuttgart: Kohlhammer, 1995), 94–142.

115. Kant, *Perpetual Peace,* "Second Preliminary Article," 94.

116. If a member of the League resorted to war in disregard of its covenants, the Council could only "recommend to the several Governments concerned what effective military, naval or air force the Members of the League shall severally contribute to the armed forces to be used to protect the covenants of the League" (Art. 16 of the Covenant). See also Arcidiacono, *Cinq types de paix,* 377–388.

117. See the firsthand account of Lloyd George, *Is It Peace?* 40–48; Adam Tooze, *The Deluge: The Great War, America, and the Remaking of the Global Order, 1916–1931* (New York: Penguin Books, 2014), 288–304.

118. [William E. Rappard], "Le choix de Genève" (June 11, 1945), Archives de la RTS, http://www.rts.ch/archives/radio/divers/emission-sans-nom/4246279-le -choix-de-geneve.html.

119. "Seat of the League of Nations," LNA, 1919, R1568/40/2477/527; for the position of the Foreign Office in this negotiation, "Switzerland and the League of Nations," LNA, R1445/28/2266/44.

120. Paul Pictet, "Genève, siège de la Ligue des Nations," Speech by the President to the Grand Council of Geneva on the choice of Geneva as the seat of the League, May 7, 1919, LNA, R1568/40/1844/527; Professor Rappard, "Accession of Switzerland to the League," September 24, 1919, LNA, R1446/28/2337/44.

121. Not to be confused with the International Red Cross Movement (today, the International Red Cross and Red Crescent Movement), founded in 1919 by representatives of the victorious powers and of which ICRC became part.

122. François Bougnion, *Confronting the Hell of the Trenches—The ICRC and the First World War* (Geneva: ICRC, 2018). On Dunant, see Martin Gumpert, *Dunant: The Story of the Red Cross* (New York: Oxford University Press, 1938); Gabriel Mützenberg, *Henry Dunant, le prédestiné* (Geneva: Société Henry Dunant, 1984).

123. Robert de Traz, *L'Esprit de Genève* (Lausanne: L'Age d'Homme, 1995), 47. It was translated into English in 1935, with a foreword by the French writer André Maurois.

124. De Traz, *L'Esprit de Genève*, 46.

125. De Traz, *L'Esprit de Genève*, 46.

126. "Salle de la Reformation et hôtel Victoria," Geneva, January 1, 1920, LNA, https://notrehistoire.ch/entries/EdaWEG9kBzo; Luc Weibel, *Croire à Genève: La Salle de la Réformation (XIX–XXe siècle)* (Geneva: Labor et fides, 2006), 150–172.

127. According to Webster's Dictionary, s.v. "settlement," definition 10: "adjustment of differences; pacification; reconciliation."

128. Patrick O. Cohrs, "The First 'Real' Peace Settlements after the First World War: Britain, the United States and the Accords of London and Locarno, 1923–1925," *Contemporary European History* 12, no. 1 (2013): 1–31.

129. League of Nations, "Protocol for the Pacific Settlement of International Disputes" (October 2, 1924), in David Hunter Miller, *The Geneva Protocol* (New York: Macmillan, 1925), 133–135.

130. "Protocol for the Pacific Settlement of International Disputes," Art. 3, 135.

131. Miller, *Geneva Protocol*, 5.

132. F. P. Walters, *A History of the League of Nations*, 2 vols. (London: Oxford University Press, 1952), 1: 283–285. Britain's inconstant engagement in the cause of international peace does not diminish the Locarno Treaty's achievement of Europe's "relative stabilization." See an appraisal in Maier, *Recasting Bourgeois Europe*, 579–580.

133. "Treaty Relating to the Use of Submarines and Noxious Gases in Warfare," (Washington, February 6, 1922), in *The Laws of Armed Conflicts: A Collection of Conventions, Resolutions, and Other Documents*, ed. Dietrich Schindler and Jiří

Toman (Dordrecht: Nijhoff, 1988), 877–879. The Washington Naval Conference of 1922 on the Limitation of Armaments, in which five of the victorious Powers of World War I took part, drafted the present Treaty. However, due to the failure of France to ratify it, it did not enter into force.

134. Tooze, *The Deluge,* 453–461.

135. Rodolfo Huber, "Il Patto di Locarno nell'ottica del XXX Congresso universal della pace," in *La Conferenza di Locarno del 1925: "Locarno: c'est la necessité de discuter." Atti del Convegno in occasione del settantesimo anniversario,* ed. Laura Semprini et al. (Bellinzona: Archivio Storico Ticinese, 1997), 201–214; Patrick O. Cohrs, "The Quest for a New Concert of Europe: British Pursuits of German Rehabilitation and European Stability in the 1920s," in *Locarno Revisited: European Diplomacy 1920–1929,* ed. Gaynor Johnson (London: Taylor and Francis, 2004), 23–40.

136. Speech by Chamberlain, in "Notes of an International Conference held at the Foreign Office on December 1, 1925 . . . for the purpose of signing the Treaties of Locarno," British Foreign Office Documents, FO. 840/1, file 2, no. 4.

137. Speech by Chamberlain, British Foreign Office Documents, FO. 840/1, file 2, no. 3. See also Kleine-Ahlbrandt, *The Burden of Victory,* 224–225.

138. Austen Chamberlain to Sir Eric Drummond (Secretary-General of the League of Nations), British Delegation, Grand Hotel, Locarno, October 16, 1925, 1.

139. Gustav Stresemann, "The Treaty of Locarno," in *Essays and Speeches on Various Subjects,* trans. Christopher R. Turner (London: Butterworth, [1930]), 238–239; Jonathan Wright, "Stresemann and Locarno," *Contemporary European History* 4, no. 2 (1995), 109–131.

140. Georges Scelle, *Une crise de la Société des nations. La réforme du Conseil et l'entrée de l'Allemagne à Genève (Mars–Septembre 1926)* (Paris: Presses universitaires de France, 1927), 79–104; Jean-Michel Guieu, "Les Allemands et la Société des nations (1914–1926)," *Les cahiers Irice* 2, no. 8 (2011): 81–90.

141. Locarno Treaties, General Treaty, June 16, 1925, LON/CRID/AdmL /287/83/1-1; Copies of the Final Act of Locarno Conference, 1925, LON/CRID /AdmL/287/83/2-1. No official explanation has been offered for the presence of Kant's essay in these papers, yet we can surmise that this text seemed to be in accord with the aims of the delegates at the Locarno Conference.

142. William Martin, "La Séance," *Journal de Genève,* September 11, 1926; Pable de Azcárate, ed., *William Martin, un grand journaliste à Genève* (Geneva: European Center of the Carnegie Endowment for International Peace, 1970), 142–143.

143. The Nobel Peace Prize 1926, Presentation Speech by Fridtjof Nansen, Oslo, December 10, 1926.

144. Gaynor Johnson, "Austen Chamberlain and the Negotiation of the Kellogg-Briand Pact, 1928," in *Locarno Revisited,* 41–54.

145. Kellogg-Briand Treaty (also known as the Pact of Paris) (August 27, 1928), in US Department of State, *Treaty for the Renunciation of War: Text of the Treaty, Notes Exchanged, Instruments of Ratification and of Adherence, and Other Papers* (Washington, DC: US Government Printing Office, 1933), 1–6.

146. The Nobel Peace Prize 1930, Johan Ludwig Mowinckel, "Award Ceremony Speech," December 10, 1930, https://www.nobelprize.org/nobel_prizes/peace/laureates/1930/press.html. See also Hathaway and Shapiro, *The Internationalists,* 101–130.

147. Mowinckel, "Award Ceremony Speech," quoted after De Traz, *L'Esprit de Genève,* 144.

148. Winston Churchill, "The Tragedy of Europe," 7: 7380.

149. Richard N. Coudenhove-Kalergi, *Pan-Europe,* introd. Nicholas Murray Butler (New York: A. A. Knopf, 1926), xii.

150. Coudenhove-Kalergi, *Pan-Europe,* xiv.

151. Coudenhove-Kalergi, *Pan-Europe,* 4–7.

152. Coudehove-Kalergi, *Europe Must Unite* (Glarus: Pan-Europa, 1940), 100; Coudenhove-Kalergi, "Russisch-europäischer Friede" (1933?), ACV, Fonds Coudenhove-Kalergi, PP 1000 / 83, no. 6.

153. Coudenhove-Kalergi, *Pan-Europe,* 22–24, 60–64.

154. Coudenhove-Kalergi, "L'Europe et la Société des Nations" (c. 1933–1937), ACV, Fonds Coudenhove-Kalergi, PP 1000 / 83, no. 15.

155. Coudenhove-Kalergi, *Pan-Europe,* 81–87; Marco Duranti, *The Conservative Human Rights Revolution: European Identity, Transnational Politics, and the Origins of the European Convention* (Oxford: Oxford University Press, 2017), 74–75; Dina

Gusejnova, *European Elites and Ideas of Empire, 1917–1957* (Cambridge: Cambridge University Press, 2016), 80–84.

156. Richard N. Coudenhove-Kalergi, *Europa Erwacht!* 3rd ed. (Vienna: Pan-Europa, 1936), 67.

157. Richard Coudenhove-Kalergi, "The Pan-European Outlook: Address Given at Chatham House on June 4, 1931," *International Affairs (Royal Institute of International Affairs 1931–1939)* 10, no. 5 (1931): 638. See also Patricia Wiedemer, "The Idea behind Coudenhove-Kalergi's Pan-European Union," *History of European Ideas* 16, nos. 4–6 (1993), 827–833; Conan Fischer, *A Vision of Europe: Franco-German Relations during the Great Depression, 1929–1932* (Oxford: Oxford University Press, 2017), 56–122; Gaines Post Jr., *The Civil-Military Fabric of Weimar Foreign Policy* (Princeton: Princeton University Press, 1973), 142–143.

158. Coudenhove-Kalergi, *Europe Must Unite,* 89.

159. Coudenhove-Kalergi, *Europe Must Unite,* 81.

160. Coudenhove-Kalergi, *Europe Must Unite,* 84.

161. On the debate on the future of "mega-powers," after World War I, see Sönke Neitzel, *Weltmacht oder Untergang: Die Weltreichslehre im Zeitalter des Imperialismus* (Paderborn: Schöningh, 1999), 367–372.

162. Papiers de l'Union paneuropéenne internationale, ACV, Fonds Coudenhove-Kalergi, PP 1000/70–88; PP 1000/93. Coudenhove-Kalergi expressed strong opposition to Hitler's rise to power in "Antisemitismus" (1929) and an unpublished novel "Hitler contra Juda" (October 31, 1933), ACV, Fonds Coudenhove-Kalergi, PP 1000/121; PP 1000/131.

163. Aristide Briand, "Une sorte de lien federal," Speech to the League Assembly, September 5, 1929, in *Actes de la Dixième session ordinaire de l'Assemblée, Sixième séance plénière, jeudi 5 septembre 1929,* 51–52.

164. Gustav Stresemann, Speech to the League Assembly, September 9, 1929, in *Vermächtnis, der Nachlass . . . ,* ed. Henry Bernard, 3 vols. (Berlin: Ullstein, 1932–1933), 3: 577–579; Jonathan Wright, "Stresemann and Locarno," *Contemporary European History* 4, no. 2 (1995): 129–131.

165. [Aristide Briand], "Memorandum sur l'organisation d'un régime d'union fédérale européenne" (May 1, 1930), in *Documents relatifs à l'organisation d'un régime d'Union fédérale européenne* ([Paris]: [Impr. nationale], [1930]), 16–17.

166. [Aristide Briand], "Memorandum sur l'organisation," 21; Conan Fisher, *A Vision of Europe: Franco-German Relations during the Great Depression, 1929–1932* (Oxford: Oxford University Press, 2017), 56–73.

167. Tomoko Akami, "The Limits of Peace Propaganda: The Information Section of the League of Nations and its Tokyo Office," *Exorbitant Expectations: International Organizations and the Media in the Nineteenth and Twentieth Centuries,* ed. Jonas Brendebach et al. (New York: Routledge, 2018), 70–90.

168. Withdrawal of Germany from the League, Konstantin von Neurath to Joseph A. Avenol, Berlin, October 19, 1933, LNA, R3637/1/7475/7475.

169. "Address of Haile Selassie before Assembly" (June 30, 1936), in *From Collective Security to Preventive Diplomacy: Readings in International Organization and the Maintenance of Peace,* ed. Joel Larus (New York: John Wiley, 1965), 140.

170. Laval, who never admitted having made an error in this matter, was not to return to power until after the defeat of 1940. He famously declared on June 22, 1942, "I wish for the victory of Germany." He was executed on October 15, 1945, for having collaborated with the Nazis after a brief and botched trial.

171. Neville Chamberlain, "Speech to the 1900 Club" (June 10, 1936), *The Times,* June 11, 1936, 10.

172. Benjamin Madley, "From Africa to Auschwitz: How German South West Africa Incubated Ideas and Methods Adopted and Developed by the Nazis in Eastern Europe," *European History Quarterly* 35, no. 3 (2005): 429–464. For an alternative view, see Thomas Weber, *Becoming Hitler: The Making of a Nazi* (New York: Basic Books, 2017), 313–328; Brendan Simms, *Hitler: A Global Biography* (New York: Basic Books, 2019), 273–299.

173. Tim Bouverie, *Appeasing Hitler: Chamberlain, Churchill and the Road to War* (London: Bodley Head, 2019). On earlier practices of appeasement, see Edward N. Luttwak, *The Grand Strategy of the Byzantine Empire* (Cambridge, MA: Harvard University Press, 2008), 53–55.

174. Henri Noguères, *Munich: The Phoney Peace* (London: Weidenfeld and Nicolson, 1965)), 25–81; Susan Bindoff Butterworth, "Daladier and the Munich Crisis: A Reappraisal," *Journal of Contemporary History* 9, no. 3 (1974): 191–216. See also Daladier's reminiscence about the events: "Munich: vingt-trois ans après," *Le Nouveau Candide,* September 7, 1961.

175. Paul Robert Magocsi, *With Their Backs to the Mountains: A History of Carpathian Rus' and Carpatho-Rusyns* (Budapest: Central European University Press, 2015), 269–278.

176. "Ligi Natsiĭ. Soobshenie TASS ot 14 dekabrī̃a ob 'isklī̃uchenii' SSSR iz Ligi Natsiĭ," *Pravda,* December 16, 1939; Ivan M. Maĭskiĭ, *Vospominanii̇̃a sovetskogo posla: voĭna 1939–1943* (Moscow: Nauka, 1965), 41–48.

177. John Maynard Keynes, *The Economic Consequences of the Peace* (New York: Harcourt, Brace and Howe, 1920), 35.

178. Marks, "The Myths of Reparations," 231–255.

179. See Étienne Mantoux, *La paix calomniée, ou les consequences économiques de M. Keynes (1913–1945)* (Paris: Gallimard, 1946).

180. Daniel Guérin, *La peste brune a passé par là: À bicyclette à travers l'Allemagne hitlérienne* (Paris: Éditions L.D.T., 1933), 3–26.

181. By a vote of 237–138, with 5 abstentions (out of 421 delegates in total). See Christian Tomushat, "The 1871 Peace Treaty between France and Germany and the 1919 Peace Treaty of Versailles," in *Peace Treaties and International Law,* 383.

182. The minutes of this meeting are printed, in English translation, in *Papers and Documents Relating to the Foreign Relations of Hungary,* ed. Francis Deák and Dezsö Ujváry (1919–1920) (Budapest: The University Press, 1939), vol. I, appendix 3, no. 8. See also Francis Deák, *Hungary at the Paris Peace Conference: The Diplomatic History of the Treaty of Trianon* (New York: Columbia University Press, 1942), 337; C. A. Macartney, *Hungary and Her Successors: The Treaty of Trianon and its Consequences, 1919–1937* (London: Oxford University Press, 1937), 54–60; George W. White, *Nationalism and Territory: Constructing Group Identity in Southeastern Europe* (Lanham, MD: Rowman & Littlefield, 2000), 101.

183. Recent works have reappraised the structural obstacles to lasting peace after 1919. See Charles S. Maier, "The Two Postwar Eras and the Conditions for Stability in 20th-Century Western Europe," *American Historical Review* 86 (1981): 327–352; Patrick O. Cohrs, *The Unfinished Peace after World War I: America, Britain and the Stabilisation of Europe, 1919–1932* (Cambridge: Cambridge University Press, 2006), 46–67; James J. Sheehan, *Where Have All the Soldiers Gone? The Transformation of Modern Europe* (Boston: Mariner Books, 2008), 92–118.

184. Richard J. Connors, *The Road to the Armistice 1918* (Pittsburgh: Dorrance Publishing, 2018), chs. 6–8.

185. "Traité d'alliance entre l'Autriche, la Russie, la Grande-Brétagne et la Prusse, conclu à Chaumont le 1 Mars 1814," Art. 2, 684.

186. Marks, "Mistakes and Myths," 654.

187. "The League of Nations, 1920," Milestones: 1914–1920, https://history.state .gov/milestones/1914-1920/league.

188. Salvador de Madariaga, "The Difficulty of Disarming," in *Problems of Peace: Lectures Delivered at the Geneva Institute of International Relations,* 5th series (London: Oxford University Press, 1931), 296.

189. See on this point William E. Rappard, *The Geneva Experiment* (Oxford: Oxford University Press, 1931), particularly 87–111.

190. The term "meaculpism" (from Latin *mea culpa,* "my fault") was coined by Mantoux, *La paix calomniée,* 48–49.

191. Winston Churchill, "[Speech on] Sir Anthony Eden's Resignation," House of Commons (February 22, 1938), in *Winston S. Churchill: His Complete Speeches, 1897–1963,* ed. Robert Rhodes James, 8 vols. (New York: Chelsea House Publishers, 1974), 6: 5915–5917.

192. In July 1936, ten years before Churchill, the British journalist Henry N. Brailsford stated that the failure was not the fault of the League of Nations, but of the nations in the League: H. N. Brailsford, *Towards a New League* (London: New Statesman and Nation, 1936). For more on this position, see Victor-Yves Ghebali, "*Avaritia et ambitio* dans les relations internationales de l'entre-deux-guerres: la gestion des conflits internationaux par la Société des Nations," in *Guerres et paix,* ed. Michel Porret et al. (Geneva: Georg, 2000), 715; Arcidiacono, *Cinq types de paix,* 378–388.

193. Winston Churchill, "The Tragedy of Europe," Speech delivered at the University of Zurich (September 19, 1946), in *Churchill: His Complete Speeches,* 7: 7379.

194. André Maurois, "Foreword," in Robert de Traz, *The Spirit of Geneva* (London: Oxford University Press, 1935), xvii.

195. Keith Neilson, *Britain, Soviet Russia and the Collapse of the Versailles Order, 1919–1939* (Cambridge: Cambridge University Press, 2006), 318–333.

4. THE POSTWAR EUROPEAN SPIRIT

1. See Wolfgang Malanowski, "'Stunde Null' oder 'Pausenzeichen der Geschichte?'" in *1945: Deutschland in der Stunde Null,* ed. Wolfgang Malanowski (Hamburg: Rowohlt, 1985), 7–28; Richard Bessel, *Germany 1945: From War to Peace* (London: Harper Collins, 2009), 385–401; Ian Buruma, *Year Zero: A History of 1945* (New York: Penguin, 2013).

2. Mark Mazower, *Hitler's Empire: How the Nazis Ruled Europe* (New York: Penguin, 2008); Timothy Snyder, *Bloodlands: Europe between Hitler and Stalin* (New York: Basic Books, 2010); Vladimir Solonari, *A Satellite Empire: Romanian Rule in Southeastern Ukraine, 1941–1944* (Ithaca, NY: Cornell University Press, 2019).

3. Richard Overy, *The Bombing War: Europe 1939–1945* (London: Allen Lane, 2013), 185–196.

4. Both of the terms "European Communities" (in the plural) and "European Community" (in the singular) were used in official documents. It took over a decade before the several communities (ECSC established in 1951, the European Economic Community in 1957, and Euratom in 1957) merged into just one in common usage, even though they remained technically distinct. For the sake of precision, I have generally kept to the plural, though I use here and there the singular form as a more generic term. In 1992, the Treaty of Maastricht re-established the "European Economic Community" as the "European Community" tout court. On the distinction between "Atlanticist" and "Europeanist" institutions, see Raymond Aron, *Paix et guerre entre les nations* (Paris: Calmann-Lévy, [1962]), 436–447; Veronyka Heyde, *De l'esprit de la Résistance jusqu'à l'idée de l'Europe. Projets européens et américains pour l'Europe de l'après-guerre (1940–1950)* (Brussels: Peter Lang, 2010), 365–431; Jenny Raflik and Nicolas Vaicbourdt, "Européisme versus atlantisme, 1956–1973," *Relations internationales* 139, no. 3 (2009): 89–99.

5. Calling it "European" was, of course, somewhat arbitrary, because other spirits with a European scope had existed before it.

6. Luuk van Middelaar, *The Passage to Europe: How a Continent Became a Union,* trans. Liz Waters (New Haven: Yale University Press, 2013), 5.

7. "Statement by Robert Schuman" (London, May 5, 1949), AHCE, Conference for the Establishment of a Council of Europe, 0120, available at CVCE.

8. John Christopher and Campbell McCutcheon, *The Second World War in Photographs,* 7 vols. (Stroud: Amberley, 2015), 7, ch. 5: "May 1945."

9. Peter Clarke, *The Last Thousand Days of the British Empire: The Demise of a Superpower* (New York: Allen Lane, 2007), xviii.

10. Tony Judt, *Postwar: A History of Europe since 1945* (New York: Penguin, 2005), 21. See also Lizzie Collingham, *The Taste of War: World War II and the Battle for Food* (New York: Allen Lane, 2012), 467–475.

11. Churchill, "Tragedy of Europe," 7379.

12. Churchill, "Tragedy of Europe," 7379.

13. Winston Churchill, "The Sinews of Peace," Speech delivered at Westminster College, Fulton, Missouri, March 5, 1946, in *Churchill: His Complete Speeches,* 7: 7287. For more on Churchill's Europeanism, see Duranti, *Conservative Human Rights Revolution,* 96–122.

14. Churchill, "Sinews of Peace," 7290.

15. Michael Howard, *The Invention of Peace: Reflections on War and International Order* (London: Profile Books, 2000), 78–79; Patrick Wright, *Iron Curtain: From Stage to Cold War* (Oxford: Oxford University Press, 2007), 154–161.

16. Churchill, "Sinews of Peace," 7290.

17. See Roger Moorhouse, *The Devils' Alliance: Hitler's Pact with Stalin, 1939–1941* (New York: Basic Books, 2014), 19–41; Marek Kornat, *Polen zwischen Hitler und Stalin. Studien zur polnischen Außenpolitik in der Zwischenkriegszeit* (Berlin: be.bra. verlag, 2012); Thomas Lane, *Victims of Stalin and Hitler: The Exodus of Poles and Balts to Britain* (New York: Palgrave Macmillan, 2004).

18. "Declaration Made by President Roosevelt, Prime Minister Churchill, and Premier Stalin at Tehran Conference" (December 1, 1943, and released December 6, 1943), in *TIAS,* 3: 859.

19. Franklin D. Roosevelt, "Address to Congress, reporting on the Yalta Conference" (March 1, 1945), in Roosevelt, *The Public Papers and Addresses of Franklin D. Roosevelt,* 13 vols. (New York: Random House, 1938–1950), 13: 586.

20. Roosevelt, "Address to Congress," 586.

21. Franklin D. Roosevelt, "Draft of Undelivered Address Prepared for Jefferson Day," in *Public Papers and Addresses,* 13: 615.

22. Anne Applebaum, *Iron Curtain: The Crushing of Eastern Europe 1944–1956* (London: Allen Lane, 2012), 3–23; S. M. Plokhy, *Yalta: The Price of Peace* (New York: Viking, 2010), 139–182.

23. Stephen C. Schlesinger, *Act of Creation: The Founding of the United Nations. A Story of Superpowers, Secret Agents, Wartime Allies and Enemies, and Their Quest for a Peaceful World* (Boulder, CO: Westview Press, 2003), 93–110.

24. *The Charter of the United Nations: Commentary and Documents,* ed. Leland M. Goodrich and Edvard Hambro (Boston: World Peace Foundation, 1949), Art. 1.1, 60.

25. Gilbert Murray, *From the League to the U.N.* (London: Oxford University Press, 1948), 155–176; Mark Mazower, *No Enchanted Palace: The End of Empire and the Ideological Origins of the United Nations* (Princeton: Princeton University Press, 2009), 14–27; Mazower, *Governing the World,* 191–213.

26. *Charter of the United Nations,* Art. 27, 345–346. On the procedural framework of the Security Council, see Loraine Sievers and Sam Daws, *The Procedure of the UN Security Council* (Oxford: Oxford University Press, 2014), 1–15.

27. "Appeal by the Finnish Government" (Geneva, December 13, 1939), *Series of League of Nations Publications. Political* 7, no. A. 46 (1939): 1–2; Brendan Simms, *Europe: The Struggle for Supremacy from 1453 to the Present* (New York: Basic Books, 2013), 388–391.

28. On the origins of the veto power, see Mitchell Franklin, "The Roman Origin and the American Justification of the Tribunal or Veto Power in the Charter of the United Nations," *Tulane Law Review* 22, no. 1 (1947): 24–61. On the Russian interpretation of the veto power, see Lauri Mälksoo, *Russian Approaches to International Law* (Oxford: Oxford University Press, 2015), 37–39.

29. Plokhy, *Yalta,* 119. Roosevelt also considered that he might need a veto power as his discussion of US-Mexican relations can suggest.

30. Plokhy, *Yalta,* 122.

31. On Allies' negotiations on the Security Council and the veto power, see Edward C. Luck, "A Council for All Seasons: The Creation of the Security Council and Its Relevance Today," in *The United Nations Security Council and War: The Evolution of Thought and Practice since 1945,* ed. Vaughan Lowe et al. (Oxford: Oxford University Press, 2008), 61–85; Nico Krish, "The Security Council and the Great Powers," in *The United Nations Security Council and War,* 133–153.

32. Schlesinger, *Act of Creation,* 263–280; Ikenberry, *After Victory,* 191–203.

33. Hans Kelsen, "Recent Trends in the Law of the United Nations," *Social Research* 18, no. 2 (1951): 14–142.

34. "The Berlin (Potsdam) Conference. Protocol of Proceedings" (August 1, 1945), in *A Decade of American Foreign Policy: Basic Documents, 1941–1949* (Washington, DC: US Government Printing Office, 1950), 28–38; Michael Neiberg, *Potsdam: The End of World War II and the Remaking of Europe* (New York: Basic Books, 2015), 183–204.

35. *Berlinskaia (Potsdamskaia) konferentsiia rukovoditeleĭ trëkh soiuuznykh derzhav— SSSR, SShA i Velikobritanii* (Moscow: Politizdat, 1980), 131–134, 421–422; Geoffrey Roberts, "Stalin at the Tehran, Yalta, and Potsdam Conferences," *Journal of Cold War Studies* 9, no. 4 (2007): 28–38.

36. See C. G. Paikert, *The German Exodus: A Selective Study on the Post-World War II Expulsion of German Populations and Its Effects* (The Hague: Martin Nijhoff, 1962), particularly 8–33; Gerhard Ziemer, *Deutscher Exodus: Vertreibung und Eingliederung von 15 Millionen Ostdeutschen* (Stuttgart: Seewald, 1973), 69–104; Norman M. Naimark, *Fires of Hatred: Ethnic Cleansing in Twentieth-Century Europe* (Cambridge, MA: Harvard University Press, 2001), 108–138. This movement would lead to the "Fourth Geneva Convention" (1949), which forbade the forcible transfer or deportation of civilians (Art. 49). See Jean S. Pictet, *Geneva Convention for the Amelioration of the Condition of the Wounded and Sick in Armed Forces in the Field: Commentary* (Geneva: International Committee of the Red Cross, 1952), 277–283.

37. "Tripartite Dinner Meeting, February 4, 1945, 8:30 P.M., Livadia Palace," Conferences at Malta and Yalta, 1945, in *Foreign Relations of the United States. Diplomatic Papers* [hereafter *FRUS: Yalta*] (Washington, DC: US Government Printing Office, 1955), 589. See also Charles E. Bohlen, *Witness to History, 1929–1969* (New York: Norton, 1973), 181.

38. David Reynolds and Vladimir Pechatnov, *The Kremlin Letters: Stalin's Wartime Correspondence with Churchill and Roosevelt* (New Haven: Yale University Press, 2018), 528–531, 584–586.

39. Joseph E. Davies, "Memorandum" (September 29, 1945), in US Department of State, *Foreign Relations of the United States, Diplomatic Papers: The Conference of Berlin (The Potsdam Conference),* 2 vols. (Washington, DC: US Government Printing Office, 1945), 1: 210–220; Elizabeth Kimball MacLean, *Joseph E. Davies: Envoy to the Soviets* (Westport, CT: Praeger, 1992), 155–162.

40. Felix Wittmer, *The Yalta Betrayal: Data on the Decline and Fall of Franklin Delano Roosevelt* (Caldwell, ID: Caxton Printers, 1953), 96–98; Lonnie R. Johnson, *Central Europe: Enemies, Neighbors, Friends,* 3rd ed. (New York: Oxford University Press, 2011), 216–220.

41. "Coercive diplomacy" is the use of diplomatic means instead of the military to achieve foreign policy aims through a mix of threats (including ultimatums), retaliation, and promises. It thus follows the principles of war, particularly that "might makes right" and the legitimacy of deceit. See Paul Gordon Lauren, "Ultimata and Coercive Diplomacy," *International Studies Quarterly* 16, no. 2 (1972): 131–165; Alexander L. George, *Forceful Persuasion: Coercive Diplomacy as an Alternative to War* (Washington, DC: United States Institute of Peace Press, 1991), 3–14.

42. Andrei Gromyko, *Memories,* trans. Harold Shukman (London: Hutchinson, 1989), 115–134; Norman Stone, "Gromyko as Foreign Minister: The Problems of a Decaying Empire," in *The Diplomats, 1939–1979,* ed. Gordon Craig and Francis Loewenheim (Princeton: Princeton University Press, 1994), 593–608.

43. United Nations Security Council, *Resolutions and Decisions of the Security Council* (New York: United Nations, 1968–), particularly vol. 1 (10 January–14 February 1946), A / 64; vol. 2 (23 October–15 December 1946), A / 64 / Add.1.

44. Harry S. Truman, "Address to the US Congress" (March 12, 1947), in *Public Papers of the Presidents of the United States: Harry S. Truman; Containing the Public Messages, Speeches, and Statements of the President, January 1 to December 31, 1947* (Washington, DC: US Government Printing Office, 1963), 178.

45. Truman, "Address to the US Congress," 179.

46. Truman, "Address to the US Congress," 179.

47. Truman, "Address to the US Congress," 179. On the significance of the Truman Doctrine, see Denise M. Bostdorff, *Proclaiming the Truman Doctrine: The Cold War Call to Arms* (College Station: Texas A&M University Press, 2008), 91–133; John Lewis Gaddis, "Was the Truman Doctrine a Real Turning Point?" *Foreign Affairs* 52 (1974): 386–402.

48. "Britain Ends Rationing of All Food," *Washington Post and Times Herald,* July 4, 1954, 4.

49. Hildegard Marcusson, *Das Wachstum von Kindern und Jugendlichen in der Deutschen Demokratischen Republik: Grösse, Gewicht und Brustumfang nach Unter-*

suchungen in den Jahren 1956–1958 (Berlin: Akademie, 1961), 129; Alice Autumn Weinreb, *Modern Hungers: Food and Power in Twentieth Century Germany* (New York: Oxford University Press, 2017), 187; Antoni Czubiński, *Polska i Polacy po II wojnie światowej (1945–1989)* (Poznań: Wydawnictwo Naukowe UAM, 1998), 844–850.

50. [Henry Morgenthau], Memorandum "Suggested Post-Surrender Program for Germany" (Washington, D.C., September 1, 1944), in Franklin D. Roosevelt Presidential Library and Museum, Box 31, Folder Germany: Jan.–Sept. 1944 (i297); Simms, *Europe,* 383–384.

51. Forrest C. Pogue, *George S. Marshall,* Vol. 3: *Organizer of Victory, 1943–1945* (New York: Viking Press, 1973).

52. "The Marshall Plan Speech" (June 5, 1947), transcript in Benn Steil, *The Marshall Plan: Dawn of the Cold War* (New York: Simon & Schuster, 2018), 441–444.

53. "The Marshall Plan Speech," 442–443. See also Stanley Hoffmann and Charles Maier, eds., *The Marshall Plan: A Retrospective* (Boulder: Westview Press, 1984); Maier, "The Marshall Plan and the Division of Europe," *Journal of Cold War Studies* 7, no. 1 (2005): 168–174.

54. "The Marshall Plan Speech," 443.

55. "The Marshall Plan Speech," 443.

56. On these achievements, see Jean Monnet's witness account, *Mémoires* (Paris: Fayard, 1976), 313–328.

57. Bronislaw Geremek, "The Marshall Plan and the European Integration," in *The Marshall Plan: Lessons Learned for the 21st Century,* ed. OECD (Paris: OECD, 2008), 43–50.

58. Joseph Stalin, "Address to the People (Victory Speech)," May 9, 1945, in "Soviet Propaganda to and about Europe, 11–17 May 1945," TNA, PRO, FO 371 / 47893, no. 5940. See also Hermann Weber, *Von der SBZ zur DDR* (Hannover: Verlag für Literatur und Zeitgeschehen, 1966), 11; R. C. Raack, "Stalin Plans His Post-War Germany," *Journal of Contemporary History* 28, no. 1 (1993): 53–73.

59. "Possibility of a Three-Power Treaty on German Disarmament. Memorandum by the Secretary of State for Foreign Affairs" (December 10, 1947), in "Stalin and the Berlin Blockade Papers," TNA, CAB 129 / 22, CP (47) 326.

60. On the British position during the conference, see "Conclusions of a Meeting of the Cabinet Held at 10 Downing Street, on Thursday, June 24, 1948," TNA, CAB/128/13, CM (42) 48.

61. *Berlin Airlift* (1949), Central Office of Information, film directed by Agnew Fisher. See also Lowell H. Schwartz, *Political Warfare against the Kremlin: US and British Propaganda Policy at the Beginning of the Cold War* (New York: Palgrave Macmillan, 2009), 70–123. A major Hollywood film studio turned this subject into *The Big Lift* (1950), distributed by Twentieth Century-Fox Film Corporation.

62. Jann K. Kleffner, "Scope of Application of International Humanitarian Law," in *The Handbook of International Humanitarian Law,* ed. Dieter Fleck (Oxford: Oxford University Press, 2013), Art. 223, 62; Timothy Garton Ash, *In Europe's Name: Germany and the Divided Continent* (New York: Vintage, 1994), 51–57.

63. "Joint Resolution to Terminate the State of War between the United States and the Government of Germany" (October 19, 1951), House Joint Resolution 289, 82nd US Congress; "Proclamation 2950: Termination of the State of War with Germany" (October 25, 1951), in *Public Papers of the Presidents of the United States: Harry S. Truman; January 1 to December 31, 1951* (Washington, DC: US Government Printing Office, 1965), 598–599.

64. Lawrence S. Kaplan, *NATO Divided, NATO United: The Evolution of an Alliance* (Westport, CT: Praeger, 2004), 1–8.

65. "The North Atlantic Treaty," Washington, DC, April 4, 1949, in *Charter of the North Atlantic Treaty Organization: Together with Scholarly Commentaries and Essential Historical Documents*, ed. Ian Shapiro and Adam Tooze (New Haven: Yale University Press, 2018), Art. 1, 3.

66. Hathaway and Shapiro, *The Internationalists,* 309–351.

67. "The North Atlantic Treaty," Preamble, 3.

68. "Negative Votes of Permanent Members at Public Meetings of the Security Council," 1946–2004, in UN General Assembly, Official Records A/58/47, Annex III, 13–19.

69. See, for example, Michael Scheibach, *Atomic Narratives and American Youth: Coming of Age with the Atom, 1945–1955* (Jefferson, NC: McFarland, 2003), 72–103.

70. The phrase "balance of terror" is mostly used for rhetorical purposes. It was possibly coined by Lester Pearson in a speech at San Francisco on June 24, 1955, on the tenth anniversary of the signing of the Charter of the UN, in which he stated, "The balance of terror has succeeded the balance of power." A. J. C. Edwards, *Nuclear Weapons, the Balance of Terror, the Quest for Peace* (London: Palgrave Macmillan, 1986), 238n.

71. "Convention Regarding the Regime of the Straits" (Montreux, July 20, 1936), Art. 20.

72. Melvyn P. Leffler, "Strategy, Diplomacy, and the Cold War: The United States, Turkey, and NATO, 1945–1952," *Journal of American History* 71, no. 4 (1985): 807–825. On "closed" and "open" periods in the history of the Black Sea, see Stella Ghervas, "The Black Sea," in *Oceanic Histories,* ed. David Armitage et al. (Cambridge: Cambridge University Press, 2018), 234–266.

73. "Treaty of Friendship, Cooperation and Mutual Assistance (Warsaw Pact)," May 14, 1955, in United Nations, *Recueil des traités,* 219 (1955): 3–33.

74. Judt, *Postwar,* 129–164; Plokhy, *Yalta,* 341–352.

75. French historian Robert Frank calls this early manifestation of the European Spirit, from 1946 to 1949, the "second golden age of European commitment" to distinguish it from the first one of the 1920s spearheaded by Coudenhove-Kalergi and Briand, which ultimately belongs to the Spirit of Geneva (or the League of Nations era). Robert Frank, "Les contretemps de l'aventure européenne," *Vingtième Siècle. Revue d'histoire* 60 (1998): 82–101.

76. "Les 12 Points de la charte d'Hertenstein" (September 21, 1946), HAEU, Mouvement européen, ME 404.

77. Comité international de coordination des Mouvements pour l'unité européenne, ed., *Congrès de l'Europe, La Haye—Mai 1948: Resolutions* (Paris, 1948), 5–7; Patrick Pasture, *Imagining European Unite since 1000 AD* (London: Palgrave Macmillan, 2015), 179–181.

78. "Discours d'ouverture du congrès par Richard N. Coudenhove-Kalergi" (Gstaad, September 8, 1947), ACV, Fonds Coudenhove-Kalergi, PP 1000 / 100, no. 16; "Discours de fermeture du congrès par Richard N. Coudenhove-Kalergi," PP 1000 / 100, no. 11. For other papers of the conference, see "Ier Congrès parlamentaire européen" (Gstaad, September 8–10), ACV, Fonds Coudenhove-Kalergi, PP 1000 / 100.

79. "Congrès de l'Europe (La Haye, du 7 au 10 mai 1948)," ACV, Fonds Coudenhove-Kalergi, PP 1000/101. For Churchill's Opening Speech, see "The Congress of Europe" (May 7, 1948), in *Winston S. Churchill: His Complete Speeches,* 7: 7635–7637.

80. "Résolution politique," in *Congrés de l'Europe, La Haye—Mai 1948,* 5. For an overview, see Jean-Michel Guieu and Christophe Le Dréau, eds., *Le "Congrès de l'Europe" à La Haye (1948-2008)* (Brussels: Peter Lang, 2009).

81. Churchill, "The Congress of Europe," 7635.

82. Churchill, "The Congress of Europe," 7635; emphasis added.

83. [Denis de Rougemont], "Message aux Européens," in *Congrés de l'Europe, La Haye—Mai 1948,* 15.

84. [De Rougemont], "Message aux Européens," 15.

85. "Statute of the Council of Europe" (London, May 5, 1949), in United Nations, *Recueil des Traités,* 87 (1951): 104 (Art. 1a); 106 (Art. 1b).

86. Jacques Willequet, *Paul-Henri Spaak: Un homme, des combats* (Brussels: Renaissance du Livre, 1975), 131–170.

87. Robert Bichet, "Drapeau," in *Europes: De l'Antiquité au XXe siècle. Anthologie critique et commentée,* ed. Yves Hersant and Fabienne Durant-Bogaert (Paris: Robert Laffont, 2000), 807–811; Tobias Theiler, *Political Symbolism and European Integration* (Manchester: Manchester University Press, 2005), 1–2.

88. Yves Hersant, "Rally Round the European Flag?" *The Monist* 92, no. 2 *Europa!* (April 2009): 258–267.

89. "Statement by Robert Schuman."

90. Russia, a country overwhelmingly located in Asia, joined the Council of Europe in 1996. Armenia and Azerbaijan, two countries formally located in Asia, joined in 2001. Belarus remains the only country in greater Europe that is not a member of the Council of Europe.

91. Wilhelm Röpke, *Die deutsche Frage* (Erlenbach-Zürich: E. Rentsch,1945), 221–252; François Henry, "Réflexion sur le problème allemand," *Reconstruction* 4 (May 3, 1946).

92. Henry Rousso, "L'épuration en France: une histoire inachevée," *Vingtième Siècle. Revue d'histoire* 33, no. 1 (1992): 78–105.

93. Nathalie Carré de Malberg, "Les fonctionnaires (civils) sous Vichy: essai histo-riographique," *Histoire@Politique* 2, no. 2 (2007); René Sigrist and Stella Ghervas, "La mémoire européenne à l'heure du 'paradigme victimaire,'" in *Lieux d'Europe*, 225–226; Geneviève Maelstaf, *Que faire de l'Allemagne? Les responsables français, le statut international de l'Allemagne et le problème de l'unité allemande (1945–1955)* (Paris: Ministère des Affaires étrangères, 1999).

94. "Aide-mémoire sur le détachement des regions industrielles de l'Allemagne" (September 8, 1945), AFJME, Fonds AME, 58/1/10.

95. François Duchêne, *Jean Monnet: The First Statesman of Interdependence* (New York: Norton, 1994), 126–156.

96. Rainer Hudemann, "Die Saar zwischen Frankreich und Deutschland 1945-1947," in *Die Saar 1945–1955/La Sarre 1945–1955: Ein Problem der europäischen Geschichte/Un problème de l'histoire européenne*, ed. Rainer Hudemann and Raymond Poidevin (Berlin: De Gruyter, 1995), 13–34.

97. Daniel F. Harrington, *Berlin on the Brink: The Blockade, the Airlift, and the Early Cold War* (Lexington: University Press of Kentucky, 2012), 141–164.

98. William Henry Harbold, "The Monnet Plan: The French Experiment in Na-tional Economic Planning" (PhD diss., Harvard University, 1953); Philippe Mioche, *Le Plan Monnet: genèse et elaboration, 1941–1947* (Paris: Publications de la Sorbonne, 1987); Gérard Bossuat and Andreas Wilkens, eds., *Jean Monnet, l'Eu-rope et les chemins de la paix* (Paris: Publications de la Sorbonne, 1999).

99. Robert Schuman, "Déclaration du 9 mai 1950," AFJME, AMG 1/2. For the English version, "Declaration of 9 May 1950," see Pascal Fontaine, *A New Idea for Europe: The Schuman Declaration, 1950–2000* [hereafter: "Schuman Declaration"] (Luxembourg: Office for Official Publications of the European Communities, 2000), 36–37.

100. Fontaine, *A New Idea for Europe,* 10–12.

101. "Schuman Declaration." On the birth of the European Coal and Steel Community, see Robert Schuman, *For Europe,* 5th ed. (Paris: Éditions Nagel, 2010), 107–125; Monnet, *Mémoires,* 435–460.

102. Sylvain Schirmann, ed., *Quelles architectures pour quelle Europe? Des projets d'une Europe unie à l'Union européenne (1945–1992)* (Brussels: Peter Lang, 2012).

103. David Mitrany, *A Working Peace System: An Argument for the Functional Development of International Organization* (London: Oxford University Press, 1943), 42–45; Gerhard Michael Ambrosi, "David Mitranys Funktionalismus als analytische Grundlage wirtschaftlicher und politischer Neuordnungen in Europa," in *Zur deutschsprachigen wirtschaftswissenschaftlichen Emigration nach 1933,* ed. Harald Hagemann (Marburg: Metropolis, 1997), 549–575.

104. David Mitrany, "A War-Time Submission" (1941), in Mitrany, *The Functional Theory of Politics* (London: Martin Robertson, 1975), 141.

105. Mitrany, *Working Peace System,* 6.

106. One of the proponents of this principle of subsidiarity was Wilhelm Emmanuel von Ketteler, bishop of Mainz, a prominent opponent to the political doctrines on which the German Reich was founded after 1871—particularly the *Kulturkampf,* the anticlerical policy pursued by Chancellor Otto von Bismarck. For a selection of his writings, see *The Social Teachings of Wilhelm Emmanuel Ketteler: Bishop of Mainz (1811–1877),* trans. Rupert J. Ederer (Washington, DC: University Press of America, 1981). See also Martin J. O'Malley, "Currents in Nineteenth-Century German Law and Subsidiarity's Emergence as a Social Principle in the Writings of Wilhelm Ketteler," *Journal of Law, Philosophy and Culture* 2, no. 1 (2008): 23–53.

107. Jean Monnet is often presented as the inventor of the European unification project and the mind behind the Schuman Plan. See notably Alan S. Milward, *The Reconstruction of Western Europe 1945–1951* (London: Methuen, 1984): "The Schuman Plan was invented to safeguard the Monnet Plan" (395). Recent publications, relying on the opening of Schuman's archives in 2007, seem to corroborate that Schuman and his staff had indeed been behind this plan. David Heilbron Price makes clear in his *Schuman or Monnet? The Real Architect of Europe* (Brussels: Bron Communications, 2003), that Paul Reuter, Schuman's right-hand man, wrote the first draft of the Schuman proposal. On this debate, see also Margriet Krijtenburg, "Schuman's Europe: His Frame of Reference" (PhD diss., Leiden University, 2012), 155–163.

108. Gérard Bossuat, *Les fondateurs de l'Europe* (Paris: Belin, 1994), 147–168; Mauve Carbonell, *Des hommes à l'origine de l'Europe: Biographies des membres de la Haute Autorité de la CECA* (Aix-en-Provence: Presses universitaires de Provence, 2008), 15–34; Christine Cadot, *Mémoires collectives européennes* (Saint-Denis: Presses Universitaires de Vincennes, 2019), 49–65.

109. Jean-Dominique Durand, *L'Europe de la Démocratie chrétienne* (Brussels: Editions Complexe, 1995), 235–240; Carolyn M. Warner, "Strategies of an Interest Group: The Catholic Church and Christian Democracy in Postwar Europe, 1944–1958," in *European Christian Democracy: Historical Legacies and Comparative Perspectives*, ed. Thomas Kselman and Joseph A. Buttigieg (Notre Dame, IN: University of Notre Dame Press, 2003), 138–163.

110. Winfried Becker, *CDU und CSU, 1945–1950: Vorläufer, Gründung und regionale Entwicklung bis zum Entstehen der CDU-Bundespartei* (Mainz: Hasse & Koehler, 1987), 16–30; Thomas Mergel, *Progaganda nach Hitler: Eine Kulturgeschichte des Wahlkampfs in der Bundesrepublik, 1949–1990* (Göttingen: Walstein, 2010).

111. The Benelux Customs Union came into effect on January 1, 1948. The Treaty Establishing the Benelux Economic Union was signed on February 3, 1958, and entered into force in 1960. Unlike the European Communities, it was never a supranational organization, because the three members retained their full sovereignty in all areas of common policy. See Milward, *Reconstruction of Western Europe*, 233–255; Craig Parsons, "Showing Ideas as Causes: The Origins of the European Union," *International Organization* 56, no. 1 (2002): 47–84.

112. On the term *construction* as applied to the European process, see Jean Monnet, "Nous ne coalisons pas des Etats, nous unissons des hommes," in *Les Etats-Unis d'Europe ont commencé: La Communauté européenne du charbon et de l'acier. Discours et allocutions, 1952–1954* (Paris: Robert Laffont, 1955), 129–133.

113. Ernst B. Haas, *The Uniting of Europe: Political, Social, and Economical Forces, 1950–1957* (Stanford: Stanford University Press, 1958), xii.

114. Haas, *The Uniting of Europe*, 32–59.

115. "Complaint of Aggression upon the Republic of Korea," in UN Security Council Resolution 82 (June 25, 1950), in *Resolutions and Statements of the United Nations Security Council (1946–1989)*, ed. Karel C. Wellens (Dodrecht: Martinus Nijhoff, 1990), 252; Alexander Bevin, *Korea: First War We Lost* (New York: Hippocrene Books, 2004), 1–9.

116. On October 24, 1950. Monnet, *Mémoires*, 396–407.

117. Jan van der Harst, "The European Defence *Community* and NATO: A Classic Case of Franco-Dutch Controversy," in *NATO's Retirement? Essays in Honour of*

Peter Volten, ed. Margriet Drent et al. (Groningen: Centre for European Security Studies, 2011).

118. Raymond Aron, "Esquisse historique d'une grande querelle idéologique," in *La querelle de la CED: Essais d'analyse sociologique,* ed. Raymond Aron and Daniel Lerner (Paris: Armand Colin, 1956), 9.

119. "Communauté européenne de défense," Débat de l'Assemblée nationale (August 30, 1954), *Journal officiel de la République française,* August 31, 1954, A.N. 85 (Paris: Imprimérie nationale, 1954), 4455–4474; Jacques Fauvet, "Naissance et mort d'un traité," in *La querelle de la CED,* 23–58. On the proverbial weakness and instability of the executive power during the French Fourth Republic, see Daniel Gaxie, "Les structures politiques des institutions: L'exemple de la Quatrième République," *Politix: Revue des sciences sociales du politique* 20 (1992): 72–98.

120. Stanley Hoffmann, "Les oraisons funèbres," *La querelle de la CED,* 86–87.

121. Sally Rohan, *The Western European Union: International Politics between Alliance and Integration* (New York: Routledge, 2014), 20–40.

122. On this aspect, see Martin Thomas, L. J. Butler, and Bob Moore, *Crises of Empire: Decolonization and Europe's Imperial States* (London: Bloomsbury Academic, 2015).

123. See the firsthand account of the French minister of foreign affairs Christian Pineau, *1956, Suez* (Paris: Robert Laffont, 1976), 158–160.

124. Eisenhower to Eden, Washington, July 31, 1956, in *The Eden-Eisenhower Correspondence, 1955–1957,* ed. Peter G. Boyle (Chapel Hill: University of North Carolina Press, 2005), 156–157. See also Randall Fowler, "Lion's Last Roar, Eagle's First Flight: Eisenhower and the Suez Crisis of 1956," *Rhetoric and Public Affairs* 20, no. 1 (2017): 33–68.

125. Geoffrey Warner, "The United States and the Suez Crisis," *International Affairs* 67, no. 2 (1991): 303–317; James M. Boughton, "Northwest of Suez: The 1956 Crisis and the IMF," *IMF Staff Papers* 48, no. 3 (2001): 425–446.

126. See, for example, the Debate on the Commons (London, October 29, 1956), vol. 558, cc1068–1072; "Der Blutsonntag von Budapest," *Luxemburger Wort,* no. 310 (November 5, 1956), 1; Alfred Grosser, "Suez, Hungary and European Integration," *International Organization* 11, no. 3 (1957): 470–480.

127. "The Permanent Representatives of France, the United Kingdom, and the United States to the President of the Security Council concerning the Situa-

tion in Hungary" (October 27, 1956), in *Consideration of Questions under the Council's Responsibility for the Maintenance of International Peace and Security,* Repertoire of the Practice of the Security Council, Supplement Oct.–Dec. 1956, 8: 109–110.

128. Fisher, *A Vision of Europe,* 123–150.

129. Willequet, *Paul-Henri Spaak,* 205–230.

130. Britain, which had detonated its first nuclear bomb in 1952 and was already associated with nuclear research programs in the United States and Canada, did not wish to compromise them by associating itself with Euratom. See *Negotiations for a European Free Trade Area. Documents Relating to the Negotiations from July 1956, to December 1958,* Cmnd. 641 (London: HMSO, 1959); Martin Schaad, "Plan G—A 'Counterblast'? British Policy toward the Messina Countries, 1956," *Contemporary European History* 7, no. 1 (1998): 39–60.

131. "Treaty Establishing the European Economic Community" (Rome, March 25, 1957), in *Treaty Establishing the European Economic Community and Connected Documents* (Luxembourg: Publishing Services of the European Communities, [1957]), 5–6.

132. Christian Pineau, "Discours à l'occasion de la signature des traités de Rome" (Rome, March 25, 1957), HAEU, CM3/NEGO-098.

133. Pineau, "Discours à l'occasion de la signature des traités de Rome." See also Laurent Warlouzet, "Négocier au pied du mur: La France et le projet britannique de zone de libre-échange (1956–1958)," *Relations internationales* 136, no. 4 (2008): 33–50.

134. Laurent Warlouzet, "De Gaulle as a Father of Europe: The Unpredictability of the FTA's Failure and the EEC's Success (1956–58)," *Contemporary European History* 20, no. 4 (2011): 419–434.

135. "Convention Establishing the European Free Trade Association" (Stockholm, January 4, 1960) (Geneva: EFTA, December 1963), Art. 2, 8; Hugh Corbet, "Role of the Free Trade Area," in *Europe's Free Trade Area Experiment: EFTA and Economic Integration,* ed. Hugh Corbet and David Robertson (Oxford: Pergamon Press, 1970), 1–42.

136. Valérie Rosoux, "La réconciliation franco-allemande: crédibilité et exemplarité d'un 'couple à toute épreuve'?" *Cahiers d'histoire: Revue d'histoire critique* 100 (2007): 23–36.

137. Paul Legoll, *Charles de Gaulle et Konrad Adenauer: la cordiale entente* (Paris: L'Harmattan, 2004); Maurice Vaisse, "La reconciliation franco-allemande: Le dialogue de Gaulle-Adenauer," *Politique Etrangère* 58, no. 4 (1993): 963–972.

138. "Traité de l'Élysée" (January 22, 1963), in *Recueil des traités et accords de la France* (Paris: Impr. des journaux officiels, [1963]).

139. Roger Massip, "Britain and the Schuman Declaration," *European Community* 134 (May 1970): 6–8.

140. Curry, "Dommage, commençons sans lui!" *Le Franc-Tireur,* June 5, 1950; Woop, "Et bien! on va continuer le voyage sans lui," *L'Aurore* 1.789, June 14, 1950.

141. "Record of conversation between Ernest Bevin, Dean Acheson, and Robert Schuman" (London, May 11, 1950), Anglo-French Discussions Regarding French Proposals for the Western European Coal, Iron, and Steel Industries, "Schuman Plan," TNA, CAB 21/3235.

142. Telegram from René Massigli to Robert Schuman, June 27, 1950, quoted in Gérard Bossuat, *D'Alger à Rome (1943–1957): Histoire de la construction européenne, choix de documents* (Louvain-la-Neuve: Ciaco, 1989), 131–132.

143. "Manifesto by the National Executive Committee of the British Labour Party on European Unity" (May 1950) (London: Labour Party, 1950), 3–15.

144. Kristian Steinnes, "The European Challenge: Britain's EEC Application in 1961," *Contemporary European History* 7, no. 1 (1998): 61–79.

145. Steinnes, "The European Challenge," 65.

146. Léon Noël, "Le projet d'union franco-britannique de juin 1940," *Revue d'histoire de la Deuxième Guerre mondiale* 6, no. 21 (1956): 22–37; Robert and Isabelle Tombs, *That Sweet Enemy: Britain and France, the History of a Love–Hate Relationship* (London: Pimlico, 2007), 566–570.

147. Charles de Gaulle, "Conférence de presse du 14 janvier 1963" (January 14, 1963), INA.fr. video record, 01:22:42. In that same conference de Gaulle announced France's refusal to participate in a multinational nuclear force and its plan to keep sole control of its own nuclear forces.

148. Charles de Gaulle, *Discours et messages,* Vol. 4: *Pour l'effort (1962–1965)* (Paris: Plon, 1963), 66–71.

149. De Gaulle, "Conférence de presse du 14 janvier 1963."

150. De Gaulle, "Conférence de presse du 14 janvier 1963."

151. Charles de Gaulle, "Conférence de presse du 27 novembre 1967" (November 27, 1967), INA.fr. video record, 01:33:07.

152. For a description of these events, see the standard work of Zbigniew Brzezinski, *The Soviet Bloc: Unity and Conflict* (Cambridge, MA: Harvard University Press, 1967).

153. Marc Trachtenberg, *A Constructed Peace: The Making of the European Settlement, 1945–1963* (Princeton: Princeton University Press, 1999), 352–402. On the Norwegian question, see Ingrid Sogner and Clive Archer, "Norway and Europe: 1972 and Now," *Journal of Common Market Studies* 33, no. 3 (1995): 389–410.

154. Robert Schuman, "Address before the Franco-British Society London" (January 22, 1970), in *European Community,* 134 (May 1970): 8.

155. See Tim Oliver, "To Be or Not to Be in Europe: Is that the Question? Britain's European Question and an in/out Referendum," *International Affairs* 91, no. 1 (2015): 77–91; Shamil Shams, "Obama Celebrates Shakespeare as UK Debates—To Be or Not to Be in the EU," *Deutsche Welle,* April 23, 2016, https://p.dw.com/p/1IbU2.

156. *Charter of the United Nations,* Preamble.

157. "Character Sketches: Andrei Gromyko by Brian Urquhart," UN News, https://news.un.org/en/spotlight/character-sketches-andrei-gromyko-brian-urquhart.

158. This obligation to provide peacekeepers is mentioned in the *Charter of the United Nations*, Arts. 43–45. See United Nations, *The Blue Helmets: A Review of United Nations Peace-Keeping* (New York: United Nations Department of Public Information, 1996), 4–13. On the rationale behind Arts. 43–45, see Ruth B. Russell, *A History of the United Nations Charter: The Role of the United States, 1940–1945* (Washington, DC: Brookings Institution, 1958), 92–124, 227–229; James S. Sutterlin, *The United Nations and the Maintenance of International Security: A Challenge to Be Met* (Westport, CT: Praeger, 2003), 1–11.

159. Schuman, *For Europe,* 135.

160. Petra Goedde, *The Politics of Peace: A Global Cold War History* (Oxford: Oxford University Press, 2019), 19–31.

161. Churchill, "Tragedy of Europe," 7381.

162. Viktor J. Vanberg, "The Freiburg School: Walter Eucken and Ordoliberalism," *Freiburg Discussion Papers on Constitutional Economics* 4, no. 11 (2004): 1–21.

163. Herman Walker, "Dispute Settlement: The Chicken War," *American Journal of American Law* 58, no. 3 (1964): 671–685.

164. Quinn Slobodian, *Globalists: The End of Empire and the Birth of Neoliberalism* (Cambridge, MA: Harvard University Press, 2018), 91–120.

165. Víctor Fernández Soriano, "'Quel pays plus que la Grèce?' La place de la Grèce dans la construction de l'Europe: une mise en perspective historique," *Histoire@Politique* 2, no. 29 (2016): 141–157.

166. Olivier Deslondes, "L'évolution de la population grecque (1981–1991): vers le 'modèle européen'?" *Méditerranée* 1–2 (1995): 53–62.

5. THE SPIRIT OF ENLARGED EUROPE

1. Yuri V. Andropov to Samantha Smith, Moscow, April 19, 1983, Samantha Smith Foundation Archives, ff. 1–2.

2. Yuri V. Andropov to Samantha Smith, 2.

3. Andreï Kozovoï, "L'enfance au service de la guerre froide. Le voyage de Samantha Smith en URSS (juillet 1983)," *Vingtième Siècle: Revue d'Histoire* 96, no. 4 (2007): 195–207; Matthias Neumann, "Children Diplomacy During the Late Cold War: Samantha Smith's Visit of the 'Evil Empire'," *History* 104, no. 360, (2019): 275–308.

4. See Gábor Ágoston, "Defending and Administering the Frontier: The Case of Ottoman Hungary," *The Ottoman World,* ed. Christine Woodhead (New York: Routledge, 2012), 220–236; Géza Dávid, "The Origins and Development of the Border Defence System against the Ottoman Empire in Hungary (up to the Early Eighteenth Century)," in *Ottomans, Hungarians, and Habsburgs in Central Europe: The Military Confines in the Era of Ottoman Conquest,* ed. Géza Dávid and Pál Fodor (Leiden: Brill, 2000), 3–70.

5. Yu. V. Andropov, *Shest'desiat let SSSR: Doklad v Kremlëvskom Dvortse s"ezdov, 21 dekabria 1982 goda* (Moscow: Izdatel'stvo politicheskoĭ literatury, 1983); "Excerpts from Andropov's Speech on Reduction in Nuclear Missiles, 21 December 1982," in *The Cold War through Documents: A Global History,* ed. Edward H. Judge and John W. Langdon (Lanham, MD: Rowman & Littlefield,

2018), 309–310. See also G. Vasilyev, "'Do Everything Possible to Preserve Peace': Letters Sent by Americans to Yuri Andropov," *International Affairs* 29, no. 4 (1983): 60–64.

6. Peter Reddaway and Dmitri Glinski, *The Tragedy of Russia's Reforms: Market Bolshevism against Democracy* (Washington, DC: United States Institute of Peace, 2001), 17–38.

7. "With all the fuss and noise, not a single new idea has come out of Eastern Europe in 1989," François Furet, the great historian of the French Revolution, famously observed; quoted in Ralf Dahrendorf, *Reflections on the Revolution in Europe* (New Brunswick, NJ: Transaction, 2005), 27. Other observers from the West, including Timothy Garton Ash, Jürgen Habermas, and Stephen Holmes, expressed a similar view; see Barbara J. Falk, *The Dilemmas of Dissidence in East-Central Europe: Citizen Intellectuals and Philosopher Kings* (Budapest: Central European University Press, 2003), 335–337.

8. Maria Mälksoo, "The Memory Politics of Becoming European: The East European Subalterns and the Collective Memory of Europe," *European Journal of International Relations* 15, no. 4 (2009): 653–680.

9. Richard Black et al., eds., *A Continent Moving West? EU Enlargement and Labour Migration from Central and Eastern Europe* (Amsterdam: Amsterdam University Press, 2010), 7–22; Ali M. Mansoor and Bryce Quillin, eds., *Migration and Remittances: Eastern Europe and the Former Soviet Union* (Washington, DC: World Bank, 2006), 1–22; Charles Walker and Svetlana Stephenson, "Youth and Social Change in Eastern Europe and the Former Soviet Union," *Journal of Youth Studies* 13, no. 5 (2010): 521–532.

10. The Russian historian Yuri N. Afanasiev argued that the USSR entered the war in 1939 in collusion with Nazi Germany and remained on friendly terms with it until 1941. Iu. N. Afanas'ev, "Drugai͡a voĭna: istorii͡a i pami͡aat'," in *Drugai͡a voĭna: 1939–1945,* ed. Afanas'ev (Moscow: RGGU, 1996), 15–31. Timothy Snyder expanded on this argument in *Bloodlands,* 119–154.

11. For an overview of the popular movements of 1989, see Vladimir Tismaneanu, ed., *The Revolutions of 1989* (London: Routledge, 1999).

12. I use the expression "the West" metaphorically to denote the countries that were on the noncommunist side of the Iron Curtain. Stella Ghervas, "L'Europe élargie d'après 1989: comment se réorienter dans la pensée?" *Questions internationales* 68 (2014): 94–101.

13. Roger Cohen, "The Accommodations of Adam Michnik," *New York Times Magazine,* November 7, 1999.

14. Philip Rosin, *Die Schweiz im KSZE-Prozeß 1972–1983: Einfluß durch Neutralität* (Munich: Oldenbourg, 2014), 33–84.

15. David J. Galbreath, *The Organization for Security and Co-Operation in Europe* (London: Routledge, 2007).

16. "Final Act of the Conference for Security and Co-operation in Europe" (Helsinki, August 1, 1975), 14 ILM 1292, Preamble. On the political context of this conference, see Victor-Yves Ghebali, "L'Acte final de la Conférence sur la sécurité et la coopération en Europe et les Nations Unies," *Annuaire Français de Droit International* 21 (1975): 73–127; Max M. Kampelman, "The Helsinki Final Act: Peace through Diplomacy (Coping with Internal Conflicts: Dilemmas in International Law)," *Georgia Journal of International and Comparative Law* 13 (1983): 327–333.

17. Thomas Buergenthal, "International Human Rights Law and the Helsinki Final Act: Conclusions," in *Human Rights, International Law, and the Helsinki Accord* (Montclair, NJ: Allanheld, Osmun, 1977), 3–10; Samuel Moyn, *The Last Utopia: Human Rights in History* (Cambridge, MA: Belknap Press, 2010), 120–175; Steven L. R. Jensen, "The Politics of Meaning: The Helsinki Final Act and the Legacy of UN Human Rights Diplomacy, 1960–75," in *The "Long 1970s": Human Rights, East-West Détente and Transnational Relations,* ed. Poul Villaume et al. (Abingdon: Routledge, 2016), 33–50.

18. Pieter van Dijk, "The Final Act of Helsinki–Basis for a Pan-European System?" *Netherlands Yearbook of International Law* 11 (1980): 97–124.

19. "Conference on Security and Co-Operation in Europe: Final Act. Declaration of Principles Guiding Relations between Participating States," *American Journal of International Law* 70, no. 2 (1976): 417.

20. [Alexei N. Kosygin], "Press-Konferentsiia Predsedatelia Soveta Ministrov SSSR A. N. Kosygina, 13 iiulia v Stokgol'me," *Pravda,* no. 197, July 15, 1968, 4. See Boris Meissner, *The Brezhnev Doctrine* (Kansas City, MO: Park College, 1970); Dr. Eugene V. Rostow, "The Challenge of the Brezhnev Doctrine: Modus Vivendi or Peace?" in International Security Council, *International Security and the Brezhnev Doctrine* (New York: CAUSA Publications, 1985), 43–62; Vladislav M. Zubok, *A Failed Empire: The Soviet Union in the Cold War from Stalin to Gorbachev* (Chapel Hill: University of North Carolina Press, 2007), 192–226.

21. "Press-Konferent͡sii͡a Predsedateli͡a Soveta Ministrov," 4.

22. Leszek Kolakowski, "The Eurocommunist Schism," *Dissent Magazine* 25, no. 1 (Winter 2012): 33–37.

23. Zubok, *Failed Empire,* 207–217.

24. See Françoise Thom, *La langue de bois* (Paris: Julliard, 1987), 29–36; Gérard Lenclus, "Parler bois: À propos d'un ouvrage de Françoise Thom," *Études rurales* 107–108 (1987): 263.

25. Commission on Security and Cooperation in Europe, *The Helsinki Process and East West Relations: Progress in Perspective. A Report on the Positive Aspects of the Implementation of the Helsinki Final Act, 1975–1984* (Washington, DC: CSCE, 1985); John Fry, *The Helsinki Process: Negotiating Security and Cooperation in Europe* (Washington, DC: National Defense University Press, 1993), 47–60, 79–91.

26. Yuri V. Andropov, "Rech' na plenume T͡sK KPSS, 15 ii͡uni͡a 1983 goda" (June 15, 1983), in Andropov, *Izbrannye rechi i stat'i* (Moscow: Politizdat, 1983), 204–207.

27. Nikita S. Khrushchev, "Doklad na Moskovskoĭ konferent͡sii predstaviteleĭ 81 kommunisticheskikh i rabochikh partiĭ," speech delivered in November 1960, broadcast on Soviet Radio on January 6, 1961; published as *Za novye pobedy mirovogo kommunisticheskogo dvizheniiâ* (Moscow: Politizdat, 1961). For analysis, see Testimony of Dr. Stefan T. Possony, US Senate, 87th Congress, First Session, June 16, 1961 (Washington, DC: U.S. Government Printing Office, 1961), 19; Odd Arne Westad, *The Global Cold War: Third World Interventions and the Making of Our Times* (Cambridge: Cambridge University Press, 2007), 365.

28. Christian Philip Peterson, "'Confronting' Moscow: The Reagan Administration, Human Rights, and the Final Act," *Historian* 74, no. 1 (2012): 57–86; Barbara Farnham, "Reagan and the Gorbachev Revolution: Perceiving the End of Threat," *Political Science Quarterly* 116, no. 2 (2001): 225–252.

29. Taylor Downing, *1983: Reagan, Andropov and a World at the Brink* (New York: DaCapo, 2018), 222–233; Simon Miles, "The War Scare that Wasn't: Able Archer 83 and the Myths of the Second Cold War," *Journal of Cold War Studies* 22, no. 3 (2020): 86–118.

30. For an attempt to explain why the Soviet leadership failed to take account of the US position in that moment of the Cold War, see Lawrence T. Caldwell and

Robert Legvold, "Reagan through Soviet Eyes," *Foreign Policy* 52 (1983): 3–21; more generally, see Barbara Farnham, "Reagan and the Gorbachev Revolution: Perceiving the End of Threat," *Political Science Quarterly* 116, no. 2 (2001): 225–252; Westad, *Global Cold War,* 367–372.

31. Mikhail Gorbachev, "Nastoĭchivo dvigat′sia vperëd. Vystuplenie na sobranii aktiva Leningradskoĭ partiĭnoĭ organizatsii 17 maia 1985 goda," speech of May 17, 1985, in *Sobranie sochineniĭ M. S. Gorbachëva,* ed. V. T. Loginov et al., 28 vols. (Moscow: Ves′ mir, 2008–), 2: 262–263.

32. The Nobel Peace Prize 1990, Mikhail Gorbachev, "Acceptance," in *Nobel Lectures, Peace 1981–1990,* ed. Tore Frängsmyr and Editor Irwin Abrams (Singapore: World Scientific Publishing Co., Singapore, 1997), 281.

33. Gorbachev, "Acceptance," 281.

34. This is a thesis defended by Kennedy, *Rise and Fall of the Great Powers,* 488–513; and Niall Ferguson, *Empire: The Rise and Demise of the British World* (London: Allen Lane, 2002), 351. See also Martin Malia, *The Soviet Tragedy: A History of Socialism in Russia, 1917–1991* (New York: Free Press, 1994), 382–389.

35. Gorbachev, "Acceptance," 284.

36. Mikhail Gorbachev, "Vystuplenie na obede v posol′stve SSSR vo Frantsii 4 oktiabria 1985 goda" (October 4, 1985), in *Sobranie sochineniĭ M. S. Gorbachëva,* 3: 49–50; speech also reproduced in *Pravda,* no. 277, October 4, 1985.

37. Henry Kissinger, *Diplomacy* (New York: Simon & Schuster, 1994), 762–803.

38. Mikhail Gorbachev, "Speech Delivered at the 43rd General Assembly Session, United Nations" (New York, December 7, 1988), in *Mikhail Gorbachev: Prophet of Change. From the Cold War to a Sustainable World,* ed. Green Cross International (East Sussex: Clairview, 2011), 21.

39. Mikhail Gorbachev, "Address to the Council of Europe" (Strasbourg, July 6, 1989), in *Mikhail Gorbachev: Prophet of Change,* 26. On Victor Hugo's speech, see Chapter 2.

40. Gorbachev, "Address to the Council of Europe," 26.

41. Gorbachev, "Address to the Council of Europe," 29. According to Neil Malcolm, the term "common European home" has antecedents in the foreign policy of Brezhnev, who used the phrase—albeit for a different purpose—during a visit to Bonn in 1981. Malcolm, "The 'Common European Home' and

Soviet European Policy," *International Affairs* 65, no. 4 (1989): 662. For more on the genesis of the concept, see Mikhail Gorbachev, *Zhizn' i reformy,* 2 vols. (Moscow: Novosti, 1995), 2: 70–77; Gorbachev, *Memoirs* (London: Doubleday, 1996), 427–438.

42. Gorbachev, "Address to the Council of Europe," 29; Marie-Pierre Rey, "Europe Is Our Home: A Study of Gorbachev's Diplomatic Concept," *Cold War History Journal* 4, no. 2 (2004): 33–65.

43. Kant, *Perpetual Peace,* "First Supplement," 114.

44. On the "balance of interests" as a precept of foreign policy, see Ramesh Thakur, "A Balance of Interests," in *The Oxford Handbook of Modern Diplomacy,* ed. Andrew F. Cooper et al. (Oxford: Oxford University Press, 2013), 70–90.

45. Birte Wassenberg, *Histoire du Conseil de l'Europe (1949–2009)* (Brussels: Peter Lang, 2012), 380–383.

46. *Charter of Paris for a New Europe* (November 19-21, 1990) (Paris: Organization for Security and Co-operation in Europe, 1990), 3.

47. *Charter of Paris for a New Europe,* 5.

48. *Charter of Paris for a New Europe,* 11.

49. Eric Remacle, "La CSCE: Mutations et perspectives d'une institution paneuropéenne," *Courrier hebdomadaire* 1348–1349, no. 3 (1992): 32–38.

50. The Nobel Peace Prize 1990, "Announcement," in *Nobel Lectures,* 269.

51. The Nobel Peace Prize 1990, "Announcement," 269.

52. The Nobel Peace Prize 1990, Gidske Anderson, "Presentation," in *Nobel Lectures,* 271.

53. Gorbachev, "Acceptance," 278–279.

54. Gorbachev, "Acceptance," 279.

55. Robin Okey, "Echoes and Precedents: 1989 in Historical Perspective," in *The 1989 Revolutions in Central and Eastern Europe: From Communism to Pluralism,* ed. Kevin McDermott and Matthew Stibbe (Manchester: Manchester University Press, 2013), 33–54.

56. Adam Michnik, "Why You Are Not Signing . . . : A Letter from Białołęka Internment Camp 1982," and "Why You Are Not Emigrating . . . : A Letter from

Białołęka 1982," in Michnik, *Letters from Prison and Other Essays,* trans. Maya Latynski (Berkeley: University of California Press, 1985), 13–24.

57. Jürgen Habermas, "What Does Socialism Mean Today? The Rectifying Revolution and the Need for New Thinking on the Left," *New Left Review,* no. 183 (Sept.–Oct. 1990): 5, 7; Habermas, *Die Nachholende Revolution* (Frankfurt a.M.: Suhrkamp, 1990).

58. Milan Kundera, "The Tragedy of Central Europe," in *Re:Thinking Europe. Thoughts on Europe: Past, Present and Future,* ed. Mathieu Segers and Yoeri Albrecht (Amsterdam: Amsterdam University Press, 2017), 191–214; Ivan Krastev and Stephen Holmes, *The Light that Failed: Why the West Is Losing the Fight for Democracy* (New York: Pegasus Books, 2020).

59. On the Solidarność movement, see Alain Touraine, *Solidarité: analyse d'un movement social, Pologne 1980–1981* (Paris: Fayard, 1982); Jerzy Holzer, *"Solidarność" 1980–1981: geneza i historia* (Warsaw: Krag, 1984); Timothy Garton Ash, *The Polish Revolution: Solidarity* (New York: Vintage Books, 1985).

60. Jerzy Kłosiński, *Solidarność: kronika lat walki 1980–2015* (Kraków: Biały Kruk, 2015), 60–62.

61. Grzegorz Ekiert, "Peculiarities of Post-Communist Politics: The Case of Poland," *Studies in Comparative Communism* 25, no. 4 (1992): 341–361; Ekiert, *The State against Society: Political Crises and Their Aftermath in East Central Europe* (Princeton: Princeton University Press, 1996), 215–221.

62. László Nagy, "'Break It down and Bring It with You!' The Pan-European Picnic and the Opening of the Border on the 11th September 1989," *Deutschland Archiv* 34, no. 6 (2001): 943–955; András Oplatka, "The Pan-European Picnic— Well-known Facts and Blind Spots," in *Prelude to Demolishing the Iron Curtain: Pan-European Picnic, Sopron 19 August 1989,* ed. György Gyarmati (Sopron: L'Harmattan, 2012), 65–72.

63. Harold Gordon Skilling, "Czechoslovakia between East and West," in *Central and Eastern Europe: The Opening Curtain,* ed. William R. Griffith (Boulder: Westview Press, 1989), 241–262; Skilling, *Czechoslovakia's Interrupted Revolution* (Princeton: Princeton University Press, 2015), 803–804.

64. Terry Cox, "1989 and the Transformations in Eastern Europe," *Europe-Asia Studies* 63, no. 9 (2011): 1529–1534; Pierre Grosser, *1989: L'année où le monde a basculé* (Paris: Perrin, 2009), 260–317.

65. Jonathan Rynhold, "The German Question in Central and Eastern Europe and the Long Peace in Europe after 1945: An Integrated Theoretical Explanation," *Review of International Studies* 37 (2011): 250–251.

66. West Germany's GNP per capita was US $18,000 compared to the Soviet Union's US $8,700; see *1989 World Factbook* (St. Paul, MN: Quanta Press, 1989).

67. Michael Meyen, "The Viewers: Television and Everyday Life in East Germany," *Historical Journal of Film, Radio and Television* 24, no. 3 (2004): 355–364; Ferdinand Protzman, "East Germany Losing Its Edge," *New York Times,* May 15, 1989; Pierre Grosser, *1989, 1989,* 163–175; Mary Elise Sarotte, *1989: The Struggle to Create Post-Cold War Europe* (Princeton: Princeton University Press, 2009), 38–47.

68. Richard von Weizsäcker, "Was ist das eigentlich: deutsch?" in Weizsäcker, *Reden und Interviews,* 10 vols. (Bonn: Presse- und Informationsamt der Bundesregierung, 1986–), 2: 395–412; Tony Paterson, "Fall of the Berlin Wall: History Catches up with Erich Honecker—the East German leader Who Praised the Iron Curtain and Claimed It Prevented a Third World War," *The Independent,* October 29, 2014.

69. Ronald Reagan, "Mr. Gorbachev, Tear Down This Wall!" Speech delivered at the Brandenburg Gate (West Berlin, June 12, 1987), in *The Last Best Hope: The Greatest Speeches of Ronald Reagan,* ed. Michael Reagan (New York: Humanix Books, 2016), 214.

70. Reagan, "Mr. Gorbachev, Tear Down This Wall!" 215.

71. "Springsteen—Chimes of Freedom," East Berlin, 1988, https://www.youtube .com/watch?v=9_hQit-3Vho. For an assessment of the actual impact of Reagan's speech in Berlin, see Sarah Pruitt, "The Myth that Reagan Ended the Cold War with a Single Speech," *H—History,* May 1, 2018.

72. Michael Meyer, *The Year that Changed the World: The Untold Story behind the Fall of the Berlin Wall* (London: Pocket Books, 2009), 65–78.

73. Gorbachev, *Zhizn' i reformy,* 2: 411–412; see also Gorbachev, speech at the Palace of the Republic (Palast der Republik) in Berlin on October 6, 1989, "Rech' na torzhestvennom sobranii vo Dvortse Respubliki v Berline, posviashchënnom 40-letiiu GDR, 6 oktiabria 1989 goda," in *Sobranie sochineniĭ M. S. Gorbachëva,* 16: 223–233, in which he pleaded the need for reforms and modernization in socialist countries.

74. Charles Maier, *Dissolution: The Crisis of Communism and the End of East Germany* (Princeton: Princeton University Press, 1997), 108–167; Mary Elise Sarotte, *The Collapse: The Accidental Opening of the Berlin Wall* (New York: Basic Books, 2014), 105–124.

75. Helmut Kohl, "Ten-Point Plan for Overcoming the Division of Germany and Europe: Speech before the Bundestag" (November 28, 1989), in *German Unification and Its Discontent: Documents for the Peaceful Revolution,* ed. Richard T. Gray and Sabine Wilke (Seattle: University of Washington Press, 1995), 84.

76. Kohl, "Ten-Point Plan," 85.

77. "Treaty Establishing a Monetary, Economic, and Social Union" (Bonn, May 18, 1990), in *The Unification of Germany in 1990: A Documentation* (Bonn: Press and Information Office of the Federal Government, 1991), 11–30; Helmut Kohl, *Ich wollte Deutschlands Einheit,* ed. Dargestellt von Kai Diekmann and Ralf Georg Reuth (Berlin: Propyläen, 1996), 341–343; "Statement by Helmut Kohl, Chancellor of the Federal Republic of Germany, on the occasion of the signing of the Treaty" (Bonn, May 18, 1990), in *The Unification of Germany in 1990,* 31–33.

78. Alfred de Zayas, "The Legality of Mass Population Transfers: The German Experience 1945–48," *East European Quarterly* 12, no. 2 (1978): 143–160; Peter Polak-Springer, *Recovered Territory: A German-Polish Conflict over Land and Culture, 1919–89* (New York: Berghahn, 2015), 138–182.

79. Dominic Lawson, "Saying the Unsayable about the Germans: Dominic Lawson Meets Nicholas Ridley and Hears an Impassioned Denunciation of a Country He Accuses of Trying to Take over Europe," *The Spectator* 265, no. 8453 (July 14, 1990): 8–9; "'They Didn't Naturally Enjoy Each Other's Company,' Conversation with Sir Christopher Mallaby, Britain's Ambassador to Germany from 1988 to 1992," *Der Spiegel,* September 14, 2009.

80. Margaret Thatcher to Helmut Kohl, London, October 3, 1990, TNA, Prime Minister's office files, 1989–1990, PREM 19/3002; Carsten Volkery, "The Iron Lady's View on German Reunification: 'The Germans Are Back!'" *Der Spiegel,* September 11, 2009.

81. Adam Przeworski, "The 'East' Becomes the 'South'? The 'Autumn of the People' and the Future of Eastern Europe," *PS: Political Science and Politics* 24, no. 1 (1991): 20–24; Timur Kuran, "The East European Revolution of 1989: Is it Surprising that We Were Surprised?" *American Economic Review* 81, no. 2 (1991): 121–125.

82. Treaty of the Final Settlement with respect to Germany, (September 12, 1990), called also the Two-Plus-Four Treaty. See *Bundesgesetzblatt,* Part II, no. 38 (1990): 1318; Maier, *Dissolution,* 244–284.

83. Treaty of the Final Settlement, Art. 1, 1320.

84. Treaty of the Final Settlement, Art. 1, 1320.

85. According to polls in 2005, 61% of Poles and 38% of Czechs believed Germany would try to get back these territories and demand compensation. Timothy Burcher, *The Sudeten German Question and Czechoslovak-German Relations since 1989* (London: Royal United Service Institute, 2004), 17.

86. Such notions have extended histories given the pervasive view of the impact of the events of 1989 on Europe. See Pamela Ballinger, "Whatever Happened to Eastern Europe?: Revisiting Europe's Eastern Peripheries," *East European Politics and Societies* 31, no. 1 (2017): 44–67; Dirk Philipsen, *We Were the People: Voices from East Germany's Revolutionary Autumn of 1989* (Durham, NC: Duke University Press, 1993), particularly 292–328; Sarotte, *1989,* 81–87.

87. "The Baltic Way—Human Chain Linking Three States in Their Drive for Freedom," UNESCO, Memory of the World. Documentary heritage submitted by Estonia, Latvia, and Lithuania, and recommended for inclusion in the Memory of World Register in 2009, https://goo.gl/apqUkr, http://www .thebalticway.eu/en/history/. Kristīne Beķere, ed., *25 Years After. The Baltic Way and the Collapse of Totalitarian Communism: European Memory and Political Inspiration* (Riga: LZA Baltijas stratēģisko pētījumu centrs, 2015); Daina S. Eglitis and Laura Ardava, "The Politics of Memory: Remembering the Baltic Way 20 Years after 1989," *Europe-Asia Studies* 64, no. 6 (2012): 1033–1059.

88. "Treaty of Nonaggression between Germany and the Union of Soviet Socialist Republics," Secret Additional Protocol, Moscow, August 23, 1939, in *Nazi-Soviet Relations: Documents from the Archives of the German Foreign Office,* ed. Raymond James Sonntag and James Stuart Beddie (Washington, DC: Dept. of State, 1948), 78; Roger Moorhouse, *The Devils' Alliance: Hitler's Pact with Stalin, 1939–1941* (New York: Basic Books, 2014); Aline Sierp, "1939 versus 1989—A Missed Opportunity to Create a European Lieu de Mémoire?" *East European Politics and Societies* 31, no. 3 (2017): 439–455.

89. Mikhail S. Gorbachev, "O politicheskoĭ i pravovoĭ otsenke sovetsko-germanskogo dogovora o nenapadenii ot 1939 goda (Postanovlenie S"ezda narodnykh deputatov Soĭuza Sovetskikh Sotsialisticheskikh Respublik 24 dekabria 1989 g.)," *Pravda,* no. 362 (December 28, 1989): 3.

90. Gorbachev, "O politicheskoĭ i pravovoĭ otsenke sovetsko-germanskogo-dogovora," 3.

91. Alexander Jakowlew, "Die Ereignisse von 1939 aus heutiger Sicht," in *Der Hitler-Stalin-Pakt: Die sowjetische Debatte,* ed. Achim Bühl (Cologne: Pahl-Rugenstein, 1989), 173–189; Afanas'ev, "Drugaiᾱ voĭna: istoriiᾱ i pamiᾱat'," 15–31; Izidors Vizulis, *The Molotov-Ribbentrop Pact of 1939: The Baltic Case* (New York: Praeger, 1990), 117–130; Edward H. Judge and John W. Langdon, *A Hard and Bitter Peace: A Global History of the Cold War,* 3rd ed. (Lanham, MD: Rowman & Littlefield, 2018), 361–367.

92. "Soviet Union: Human Rights Developments," *Human Rights Watch World Report,* 1990, https://www.hrw.org/reports/1990/WR90/HELSINKI.BOU-03.htm.

93. Serhii Plokhy, *The Last Empire: The Final Days of the Soviet Union* (New York: Basic Books, 2014), xvii–xxii.

94. Boris Yeltsin, "The 'Tank' Speech," 1991, https://www.youtube.com/watch?v=-zXChf5tEMI.

95. "Soglashenie o sozdanii sodruzhestva nezavisimykh gosudarstv" (Minsk, December 8, 1991), in *Informatsionnyĭ Vestnik "Sodruzhestvo,"* no. 1 (s.l., Council of Heads of State: 1992); Plokhy, *Last Empire,* 295–316.

96. This phrase roughly meaning "I do not care what happens after my death" has special resonance in Russian political culture. It was used by the prosecutor at the trial of Dimitri Fyodorovich Karamazov to describe the nihilists (Fyodor Dostoevsky, *The Brothers Karamazov,* 1880). Boris Yeltsin and his political team often conjured the idea of *après moi le déluge* with explicit reference to Vladimir Zhirinovsky and other nationalist politicians—suggesting that if Yeltsin were swept from office, an authoritarian regime in Russia would be only a step away. See, for example, "Press Conference by Russia's Choice Leaders Yegor Gaidar and Sergei Kovalev," Official Kremlin International News Broadcasts, December 13, 1993; "Yeltsin Vows to Push ahead with Reforms as He Keeps an Eye on Right-Wing Leader," *Vancouver Sun,* December 23, 1993.

97. Mikhail Gorbachev, "Farewell Address" (December 26, 1991), published with the headline, "Living in a New World," *Los Angeles Time,* December 26, 1991.

98. Gorbachev, "Farewell Address"; Plokhy, *Last Empire,* 378–387.

99. "1991: Bloodshed at Lithuanian TV Station," BBC Home (January 13, 1991), http://news.bbc.co.uk/onthisday/hi/dates/stories/january/13/newsid_4059000/4059959.stm.

100. "Gorbachëv: Vvod voĭsk v Baku—moi͡a samai͡a bol'shai͡a oshibka," Minval. az, https://minval.az/news/123537763. "Black January," also known as "Black Saturday," was a violent crackdown on civilians in Baku on January 19–20, 1990, during a state of emergency declared after the dissolution of the Soviet Union. See *"Chërnyĭ i͡anvar'." Baku—1990: Dokumenty i materialy* (Baku: Azerneshr, 1990); and the testimonies of V. A. Guseĭnov, *Bol'she chem odna zhizn'* (Moscow: Krasnai͡a Zvezda, 2013).

101. Gorbachev, "Acceptance."

102. On two competing interpretations of the end of the Cold War—structural explanations versus individualistic accounts—see, respectively, Langdon and Judge, *Hard and Bitter Peace,* 371–394, and Archie Brown, *The Human Factor: Gorbachev, Reagan, and Thatcher, and the End of the Cold War* (Oxford: Oxford University Press, 2020), 386–389.

103. Niall Ferguson and Brigitte Granville, "'Weimar on the Volga': Causes and Consequences of Inflation in 1990s Russia Compared with 1920s Germany," *Journal of Economic History* 60, no. 4 (2000): 1061–1087.

104. On a recent interpretation of this aspect, see Elizabeth Cullen Dunn and Michael S. Bobick, "The Empire Strikes Back: War without War and Occupation without Occupation in the Russian Sphere of Influence," *American Ethnologist* 41, no. 3 (2014): 405–413.

105. Caroline Humphrey, *The Unmaking of Soviet Life: Everyday Economies after Socialism* (Ithaca, NY: Cornell University Press, 2002); Nancy Ries, "Potato Ontology: Surviving Postsocialist in Russia," *Cultural Anthropology* 24, no. 2 (2009): 181–212.

106. "Statement from the Paris Summit" (October 21, 1972), *Bulletin of the European Communities* 5, no. 10 (1972): 16.

107. "Solemn Declaration on European Union" (Stuttgart, June 19, 1983), *Bulletin of the European Communities* 18, no. 6 (1983): 25.

108. "Solemn Declaration on European Union," 24.

109. "Solemn Declaration on European Union," 24.

110. Sean N. Kalic, "Reagan SDI's Announcement and the European Reaction: Diplomacy in the Late Decade of the Cold War," in *The Crisis of Détente of Europe: From Helsinki to Gorbachev 1975–1985,* ed. Leopoldo Nuti (London: Routledge, 2009), 99–110.

111. "Solemn Declaration on European Union," 24.

112. Altiero Spinelli, *The Eurocrats: Conflict and Crisis in the European Community* (Baltimore: Johns Hopkins University Press, 1966), 11. On Spinelli's authorship and background, see Edmondo Polini, *Altiero Spinelli: appunti per una biografia* (Bologna: Il Mulino, 1988).

113. "Draft Treaty Establishing the European Union" (February 14, 1984), *Bulletin of the European Communities* 17, no. 2 (1984), 7–28.

114. "Single European Act (SEA)" (Luxembourg, February 17, 1986, and in The Hague, February 28, 1986), *Official Journal of the European Communities (OJEC)* 50, no. L 169 (June 29, 1987): 1.

115. "Single European Act," 1; Lord Cockfield, *The European Union: Creating the Single Market* (London: Wiley Chancery Law, 1994), 61–76.

116. Cockfield, *The European Union,* 77–94.

117. "Rome European Council" (December 14–15, 1990), *Bulletin of the European Communities* 23, no. 12 (1990): 7–18; "Press Conference by President Delors before the European Council" (Strasbourg, December 12, 1990), http://aei.pitt.edu /1406/.

118. On the main protagonists of the movement which lead to the Treaty of Maastricht, see Kenneth Dyson and Ivo Maes, eds., *Architects of the Euro: Intellectuals in the Making of European Monetary Union* (Oxford: Oxford University Press, 2016), 1–7; and more specifically on the role of Jacques Delors, see Dermot Hodson, "Jacques Delors," in this volume (212–232).

119. "Treaty on European Union," *Official Journal of the European Communities,* no. C 191 (July 29, 1992): 1.

120. "Treaty on European Union," 7.

121. "Treaty on European Union," 1.

122. "Treaty on European Union," 58.

123. "Treaty on European Union," 58.

124. Totò Cutugno, *Insieme* ("Together"), 1992 Eurovision, https://www.you tube.com/watch?v=ob5whZydVZc.

125. On Erasmus (European Community Action Scheme for the Mobility of University Students), see Fatma Mizikaci and Zülal Ugur Arlan, "A European Per-

spective in Academic Mobility: A Case of Erasmus Program," *Journal of International Studies* 9, no. 2 (2019): 705–726.

126. John Bale, "Identity, Identification and Image: Football and Place in the New Europe," in *Football and Regional Identity in Europe,* ed. Siegfried Gehrmann (Münster: Lit, [1997]), 279–294; Anthony King, "The New Symbols of European Football," *International Review for the Sociology of Sport* 39, no. 3 (2004): 323–336.

127. Thomas Betzwieser, "European Anthems—Musical Insignia of Understanding and Identity," in *The Role of Music in European Integration: Conciliating Eurocentrism and Multiculturalism,* ed. Albrecht Riethmüller (Berlin: De Gruyter, 2017), 148–169.

128. In particular, it created a common system of visas, introduced police and judicial cooperation, and established the principle of *ne bis in idem* (i.e., the same penalty could not be imposed in two different countries for the same offense). It also set out a common information system for sharing data among the member states. "The Schengen *acquis*—Convention Implementing the Schengen Agreement of 14 June 1985 between the Governments of States of the Benelux Economic Union, the Federal Republic of Germany and the French Republic on the Gradual Abolition of Checks at their Common Borders," *Official Journal of the European Communities* 43, no. L 239 (September 22, 2000): 19–59.

129. "Presidency Conclusions" (Madrid, December 15–16, 1995), Annex 1: The Scenario for Changeover to the Single Currency, DOC / 95 / 9.

130. David Marsh, *The Euro: The Policy of the New Global Currency* (New Haven: Yale University Press, 2009), 206–221; Kenneth Dyson and Ivo Maes, "Intellectuals as Policy-Makers," in *Architects of the Euro,* 1–7; Eelke de Jong and Femke van Esch, "Culture Matters: French-German Conflicts on European Central Bank Independence and Crisis Resolution," in *Financial Cultures and Crisis Dynamics,* ed. Bob Jessop et al. (London: Routledge: 2015), 253–277.

131. Marsh, *The Euro,* 177–179.

132. Marsh, *The Euro,* 196–200; Lionel Barbier, "Banque centrale européenne: l'histoire d'une nomination mouvementée," *Le Temps,* April 7, 1998.

133. David Bensoussan, "La manifestation des pêcheurs du 4 février 1994," *Place Publique. La revue urbaine Rennes—Saint Malo,* no. 29 (May–June 2014).

134. Paolo Del Giovane and Roberto Sabbatini, eds., *Perceived and Measured Inflation after the Launch of the Euro: Explaining the Gap in Italy* (Berlin: Springer,

2008), 13–49; Sergio Cesaratto, *Europe, German Mercantilism and the Current Crisis,* in *Working Paper* no. 595 ([Sienna]: University of Siena, 2010), 3–5, 10–13.

135. See, for example, Andrew Moravcsik, "In Defense of the 'Democratic Deficit': Reassessing the Legitimacy of the European Union," *Journal of Common Market Studies* 40, no. 4 (2002): 603–634.

136. John O'Brennan, *The Eastern Enlargement of the European Union* (New York: Routledge, 2006), 50–52; Wilfried Loth, *Building Europe: A History of European Unification* (Berlin: De Gruyter Oldenbourg, 2015), 372–383.

137. Jürgen Kocka, "Das östliche Mitteleuropa als Herausforderung für eine vergleichende Ge- schichte Europas," *Zeitschrift für Ostmitteleuropa-Forschung* 2 (2000): 159–162; Peter Haslinger, "Vor einem Paradigmenwechsel? Die Osteuropäische Geschichte und die EU-Osterweiterung," *Osteuropa* 54, no. 4 (2004): 40–46.

138. Astrid M. Eckert, *West Germany and the Iron Curtain: Environment, Economy, and Culture in the Borderlands* (Oxford: Oxford University Press, 2019), 1–12; on the cultural dimension of the Iron Curtain, see also Yuliya Komska, *The Icon Curtain: The Cold War's Quiet Border* (Chicago: University of Chicago Press, 2015), 9–19.

139. Maier, *Dissolution,* particularly 215–329.

140. Halle Institute for Economic Research, ed., *The Economic Integration of East Germany: 25 Years after the Fall of the Berlin Wall,* ed. (Halle: Halle Institute, 2014), 5–13.

141. The twelve members of the 1980s, called "Europe of the Twelve," were Belgium, Germany, France, Italy, Luxembourg, the Netherlands, Denmark, Ireland, the United Kingdom, Greece, Spain, and Portugal; by 2013, the sixteen additional members were Austria, Finland, Sweden, Czech Republic, Estonia, Cyprus, Latvia, Lithuania, Hungary, Malta, Poland, Slovakia, Slovenia, Bulgaria, Romania, and Croatia. See Frank Schimmelfennig, *The EU, NATO and the Integration of Europe: Rules and Rhetoric* (Cambridge: Cambridge University Press, 2003), particularly 194–228; Andreas Schneider, "The History of EU Enlargement," *Wirtschaftspolitische Blätter* 51, no. 1 (2004): 47–62.

142. Elie Barnavi and Krzysztof Pomian, *La révolution européenne: 1945–2007* (Paris: Perrin, 2008), 9–21, 248–257.

143. Stevan K. Pavlowitch, *A History of the Balkans, 1804–1945* (London: Longman, 1999), 95–114; Alexander Kiossev, "Legacy of Legacies: Competitions

and Conflicts," in *Europe and the Historical Legacies in the Balkans,* ed. Raymond Detrez and Barbara Segaert (Brussels: Peter Lang, 2008), 49–68.

144. Maria Todorova, *Imagining the Balkans* (Oxford: Oxford University Press, 2009), particularly 116–139. On the myths of Lyssa/Ira/Furor, see Michael Potegal and Raymond W. Novaco, "A Brief History of Anger," in *International Handbook of Anger: Constituent and Concomitant Biological, Psychological, and Social Processes,* ed. Michael Potegal et al. (New York: Springer, 2010), 9–24.

145. Pavlowitch, *History of the Balkans,* 249–265.

146. Charles King, *The Black Sea: A History* (Oxford: Oxford University Press, 2004), 229–233; Marie-Janine Calic, *The Great Cauldron: A History of Southeastern Europe,* trans. Elizabeth Janik (Cambridge, MA: Harvard University Press, 2019), 466–547.

147. Maria Todorova, "Introduction: Similar Trajectories, Different Memories," in *Remembering Communism: Private and Public Recollections of Lived Experience in Southeast Europe,* ed. Maria Todorova et al. (Budapest: Central European University Press, 2014), 1–28.

148. Called in Bulgarian "Văzroditelen protses." Evgenia Kalinova, "Remembering the 'Revival Process' in Post-1989 Bulgaria," in *Remembering Communism,* 567–594.

149. Tomasz Kamusella, *Ethnic Cleansing during the Cold War: The Forgotten 1989 Expulsion of Turks from Communist Bulgaria* (London: Routledge, 2019), ch. 5.

150. Alina Mungiu-Pippidi, *Românii după '89: istoria unei neînțelegeri* (Bucharest: Humanitas, 1995); Jean-Marie Le Breton, *La fin de Ceausescu: Histoire d'une revolution* (Paris: L'Harmattan, 1996); Pavel Câmpeanu, *Ceaușescu, anii numaratorii inverse* (Bucharest: Polirom, 2002).

151. Fred S. Abrahams, *Modern Albania: From Dictatorship to Democracy in Europe* (New York: New York Press, 2015), 84–110.

152. Christophe Solioz, "Rethinking South-Eastern Europe through a Pan-European Perspective," *SEER Journal for Labour and Social Affairs in Eastern Europe* 10, no. 2 (2007): 67–80; Alina Mungiu-Pippidi, "EU Accession Is No 'End of History,'" *Journal of Democracy* 18, no. 4 (2007): 8–16.

153. Ljubo Boban, "Kada je i kako nastala Država Slovenaca, Hrvata i Srba," *Radovi* 26, no. 1 (1993): 187–198.

154. Sergej Flere and Rudi Klanjšek, *The Rise and the Fall of Socialist Yugoslavia: Elite Nationalism and the Collapse of a Federation* (Lanham, MD Lexington Books, 2019), 115–136; Flere, "Autentičnost osnivanja Titove Jugoslavije kao federacije," *Sociološki pregled* 52, no. 4 (2018): 1115–1146.

155. "Serbian Academy of Arts and Sciences Memorandum, 1986," *Making the History of 1989,* no. 674, http://chnm.gmu.edu/1989/items/show/674; Audrey Helfant Budding, "Systemic Crisis and National Mobilization: The Case of the 'Memorandum of the Serbian Academy,'" *Harvard Ukrainian Studies* 22 (1998): 49–69.

156. Jasna Dragovi-soso, "Rethinking Yugoslavia: Serbian Intellectuals and the National Question in Historical Perspective," *Contemporary European History* 13, no. 2 (2004): 170–184.

157. Jacques Poos, May 1991, quoted in Alan Riding, "Conflict in Yugoslavia; Europeans Send High-Level Team," *New York Times,* June 29, 1991.

158. Reneo Lukic and Allen Lynch, *Europe from the Balkans to the Urals: The Disintegration of Yugoslavia and the Soviet Union* (Oxford: Oxford University Press, 1996), 144–173.

159. *Charter of Paris for a New Europe,* 3.

160. Catherine Baker, *The Yugoslav Wars of the 1990s* (New York: Palgrave, 2015), 62–65.

161. "The General Framework Agreement for Peace in Bosnia and Herzegovina" (Dayton Peace Agreement), initiated in Dayton on November 21, 1995, and signed in Paris on December 14, 1995. UN General Assembly, Security Council A/50/790, S/1995/999.

162. Tim Judah, *Kosovo: War and Revenge* (New Haven: Yale University Press, 2000), 197–226; Baker, *The Yugoslav Wars of the 1990s,* 78–88.

163. James Mark and Quinn Slobodian, "Eastern Europe in the Global History of Decolonization," in *The Oxford Handbook of the Ends of Empire,* ed. Martin Thomas and Andrew Thompson (Oxford: Oxford University Press, 2018), 1–28.

164. Václav Havel, "The Power of the Powerless" (1978), in *Václav Havel or Living in Truth,* ed. Jan Vladislav (London: Faber and Faber, 1987), 115–119.

165. The Nobel Peace Prize 2012, Press Release, Oslo, October 2012, https://www.nobelprize.org/prizes/peace/2012/press-release/.

166. The Nobel Peace Prize 2012, Presentation Speech by Thorbjørn Jagland, Chairman of the Norwegian Nobel Committee, Oslo, December 10, 2012. https://www.nobelprize.org/nobel_prizes/peace/laureates/2012/presentation -speech.html.

167. The Nobel Peace Prize 2012, Presentation Speech by Thorbjørn Jagland.

CONCLUSION

1. Isaac Asimov, *Foundation,* Part I: *The Psychohistorians,* 3 vols. (New York: Alfred A. Knopf, 2010), 1: 28.

2. Tolstoy, *War and Peace,* 1259.

3. Metternich to his Emperor, March 18, 1848: "Europe, Sire, is giving in to a crisis that is far worse than a political movement; this crisis is taking place in the body politic. . . . Stopping a flood is not in the power of men: the only thing they can do, is to dam it. My efforts were in vain, and . . . I bowed down from the scene." *Mémoires du Prince de Metternich,* ed. M. A. de Klinkowstroem (Paris: Plon, 1884), 7: 607–608.

4. Dipesh Chakrabarty, "The Planet: An Emergent Humanist Category," *Critical Inquiry* 46 (2019): 1–31.

5. See, for example, Colonel Garland H. Williams, *Engineering Peace: The Military Role in Postconflict Reconstruction* (Washington, DC: United States Institute of Peace Press, 2005).

6. On the morality of peace, see Habermas, "Kant's Idea of Perpetual Peace," 113–153.

7. Victor Hugo, "Discours d'ouverture," 379–389.

8. Anne Whyte, "Quadripartite Rule in Berlin: An Interim Record of the First Year of the Allied Control Authority," *International Affairs (Royal Institute of International Affairs 1944)* 23, no. 1 (1947): 30–41.

9. Boyle, *Foundations of World Order,* 71–85; Eric A. Posner, *The Perils of Global Legalism* (Chicago: Chicago University Press, 2009), 50–70.

10. Karol Modzelewski, *L'Europe des barbares: Germains et slaves face aux héritiers de Rome,* trans. Agata Kozak and Isabelle Macor-Filarska (Paris: Aubier, 2006), 99–128.

11. Tanisha M. Fazal, "The Demise of Peace Treaties in Interstate War," *International Organization* 67 (2013): 696.

12. Kant, *Perpetual Peace,* Appendix I, 116–125.

13. G. G. Fitzmaurice, "Do Treaties Need Ratification?" *British Year Book of International Law* 15 (1934): 113–137; Jana von Stein, "Making Promises, Keeping Promises: Democracy, Ratification and Compliance in International Human Rights Law," *British Journal of Political Science* 46, no. 3 (2016): 655–679; and for specifically US issues, see Michael G. Glennon, "The Senate Role in Treaty Ratification," *American Journal of International Law* 77, no. 2 (1983): 257–280.

14. Kant, *Perpetual Peace,* sect. II, 98.

15. "Schuman Declaration."

16. Marco Dani, "Constitutionalism and Dissonances: Has Europe Paid off Its Debt to Functionalism?" *European Law Journal* 15, no. 3 (2009): 324–350.

17. Dieter Rams, "Ten Principles for a Good Design," *Domus* 748 (1993): 27–28.

18. On the rhetoric of peace after 1945, see Goedde, *The Politics of Peace,* 12–38.

19. On the idea of the "Long Peace," see John Lewis Gaddis, *The Long Peace: Inquiries into the History of the Cold War* (New York: Oxford University Press, 1987), 215–246; Michael Mandelbaum, *The Dawn of Peace in Europe* (New York: Twentieth Century Fund Press, 1996); John E. Mueller, *Retreat from Doomsday: The Obsolescence of Major War* (New York: Basic Books, 1989); Howard, *The Invention of Peace;* Sheehan, *Where Have All the Soldiers Gone?;* Steven Pinker, *The Better Angels of Our Nature: Why Violence Has Declined* (New York: Viking, 2011).

20. See especially the "peace talks" between the United States and the Soviet Union during the Cuban Missile Crisis: William M. LeoGrande & Peter Kornbluh, *Back Channel to Cuba: The Hidden History of Negotiations between Washington and Havana* (Chapel Hill: University of North Carolina Press, 2015).

21. Tanisha M. Fazal evaluates their number as "less than a quarter of what it was during the nineteenth and early twentieth centuries." Fazal, *Wars of Law: Unintended Consequences in the Regulation of Armed Conflicts* (Princeton: Princeton University Press, 2018), 131–160.

22. For a rebuttal of the idea of "long peace," see Burned Bridge Sheffer, "How East and West Germans Made the Iron Curtain" (PhD diss., University of California, Berkeley, 2008), 8; Wilfried Loth, "The Cold War: What It Was about and

Why It Ended," in *Perforating the Iron Curtain: European Détente, Transatlantic Relations, and the Cold War, 1965–1985,* ed. Paul Villaume and Odd Arne Westad (Copenhagen: Museum Tusculanum Press, 2010), 20.

23. "The Situation in Hungary," in *Resolutions and Decisions of the Security Council 1956, Security Council Official Records: 11th Year,* 7–8; "Question concerning Czechoslovakia," in *United Nations Security Council, Resolutions and Decisions of the Security Council 1968,* Security Council Official Records: 23rd Year, 13–15.

24. Elie Barnavi, *L'Europe frigide: réflexions sur un projet inachevé* (Brussels: André Versaille, 2008).

25. Mark Mazower, "Lessons from the Past Are Key to Europe's Survival," *Financial Times,* January 22, 2019.

26. Ivan Krastev, *After Europe* (Philadelphia: University of Pennsylvania Press, 2017), 61–112.

27. Stella Ghervas, "Ten Lessons for Peace in Europe: From the Congress of Vienna and World War I, to the Failure of the G8," in *Multilateral Security Governance,* ed. Felix Dane and Gregory John Ryan (Rio de Janeiro: Konrad-Adenauer-Stiftung, 2014), 212–227.

28. Eckart Conze, "Sicherheit als Kultur: Überlegungen zu einer 'modernen Politikgeschichte' der Bundesrepublik Deutschland," *Vierteljahrshefte für Zeitgeschichte* 53 (2005): 357–380.

29. Emmanuel Macron, "Discours du Président de la République à l'ouverture de la conférence des Ambassadeurs" (August 29, 2017), https://www.elysee.fr /emmanuel-macron/2017/08/29/discours-du-president-de-la-republique-a-l -ouverture-de-la-conference-des-ambassadeurs.

30. "Politique de lute contre le terrorisme. Discours d'Emmanuel Macron" (April 19, 2017), GC de campagne (Paris 15), https://en-marche.fr/articles/discours /meeting-macron-politique-lutte-contre-le-terrorisme.

31. This phrase is borrowed from Montesquieu, who applied those words to the pope: *Lettres persannes* (1721), letter 29.

32. See, for example, Emmanuel Macron, "Adresse aux Français" (March 16, 2020), https://www.elysee.fr/emmanuel-macron/2020/03/16/adresse-aux-francais -covid19; the Cypriot EU Commissioner Stella Kyriakides, in Louise Miner, "We're all in a war against COVID-19 together," Euronews, April 7, 2020,

https://www.euronews.com/2020/04/07/we-re-all-in-a-war-against-covid-19 -together. Among recent analyses of this subject, see Nathaniel Popkin, "A Pandemic Is Not a War (and Other Consequences of Male Inferiority)," *Literary Hub,* April 6, 2020; David A. Bell, "'La guerre au virus,' le passé d'une métaphore," *Le Grand Continent,* April 7, 2020; Lawrence Freedman, "Coronavirus and the Language of War," *New Statesman,* April 11, 2020; Charles S. Maier and Ian Kumekawa, "Responding to COVID-19: Think through the Analogy of War," Edmond J. Safra Center for Ethics, *White Paper* 10 (April 21, 2020): 1–18.

33. To my knowledge, the first study on this principle dates from 1985. See Wolfgang Hager, "Fortress Europe: A Model?" in *Europe at the Crossroads: Agendas of the Crisis,* ed. Stefan A. Musto and Carl F. Pinkele (New York: Praeger, 1985), 65–76.

34. Andreas Weiss, "'Fortress Europe' or 'Europe as Empire': Conflicts between Different EU Long-Term Strategies and Its Effects on the Representation of Europe," *Zeitschrift für Globalgeschichte und vergleichende Gesellschaftsforschung* 22, no. 6 (2012): 61–79.

35. John Stone, "The EU Has Built 1,000km of Border Walls since Fall of Berlin Wall," *The Independent,* November 9, 2018.

36. Stella Ghervas, "Who Is in and Who Is Out? Inclusion and Exclusion in European Conference Diplomacy, 1815–2015," Speech delivered at international conference, "200 Years of Conference Diplomacy: From the Congress of Vienna to the G7," German Institute for International and Security Affairs, Berlin, June 8, 2015, https://gerda-henkel-stiftung.de/who_is_in_and_who_is_out_inclusion_ and_exclusion_in_european_conference_diplomacy_1815_2015?nav_id=5738.

37. "Schuman Declaration." See also Schuman, "France and Europe," *Foreign Affairs* 31, no. 3 (1953): 349–360.

38. Kenneth Keulman and Agnes Katalin Koós, *European Identity: Its Feasibility and Desirability* (Lanham, MD: Lexington Books, 2014).

39. Roxana Barbulescu, "Inside Fortress Europe: The Europeanisation of Immigrant Integration and Its Impact on Identity Boundaries," *Politique européenne* 47, 1 (2015): 24–44.

40. "Die Festung Europa hat kein Dach [aerial leaflet]" (1943), Imperial War Museum, LBY AERIAL 3/2237.

41. Yann Algan et al., "Qui sont les Gilets jaunes et leurs soutiens?" *Note de l'OBE,* Observatoire du Bien-être du CEPREMAP, no. 3 (2019): 1–13.

42. "Prime Minister Viktor Orbán's Speech at the 30th Bálványos Summer Open University and Student Camp," Tusnádfürdő (Băile Tuşnad) July 27, 2019.

43. In Transylvania (between Hungary and Romania), in South Tyrol (between Austria and Italy), in Silesia (between Germany and Poland), in Belarus (between Poland and Belarus itself), in the Baltic Republics (which the Federation of Russia still claims for itself), not to mention the Russian postwar enclave of Kaliningrad/Königsberg in Eastern Prussia, which would come under siege in the event of conflict between the NATO alliance and Russia.

44. For a discussion on "ethnic" conflicts or whether "ethnic" can ever be divorced from political motivations, see Armitage, *Civil Wars*, 196–230; Sean Byrne and Loraleigh Keashly, "Working with Ethno-Political Conflict: A Multi-Modal Approach," *International Peacekeeping* 7, no. 1 (2000): 97–120.

45. Coudenhove-Kalergi, *Pan-Europe*, 211–213.

46. "Treaty of the Final Settlement with Respect to Germany, September 12, 1990," in *Treaty Series,* no. 88 (London: HMSO, 1991), Art. 2, 4.

47. Beatrice Heuser, *Brexit in History: Sovereignty or a European Union?* (London: Hurst, 2019).

48. Dipesh Chakrabarty, *Provincializing Europe: Postcolonial Thought and Historical Difference* (Princeton: Princeton University Press, 2000).

Acknowledgments

Conquering Peace had a distinct beginning, a dozen years ago, on a rainy day in Paris. I was strolling along the famed book stalls by the Seine River, where my attention was caught by a yellowed French paperback book with an odd title, *From the Alliance of Kings to the League of Nations: The Holy Alliance and the League of Nations,* by Robert de Traz (1936). With a disarming mix of faith and realism, De Traz drew a bold parallel between Tsar Alexander I and President Woodrow Wilson, who had fathered the League of Nations after World War I. What on earth could relate two characters separated by a whole century, one an absolute Russian autocrat and the other an elected president of the great US democracy? These questions resonated strongly for me: first, because the Holy Alliance of 1815 (brainchild of Russia's Tsar Alexander) was the subject of my previous book; and second, because the author hailed from Geneva, the home of the League of Nations and a city that had adopted me twenty-five years ago.

This Genevan perspective inevitably drew me to the vexed questions of peace in Europe and of European identity by fruitfully broadening my own viewpoint. My own roots had been on the eastern frontier of Europe, in today's Moldova. As a child of perestroika, and later as a student at the University of St. Petersburg and at the Institute for South-East European Studies in Bucharest, I embraced early Mikhail Gorbachev's idea of a "common European home," and this left an indelible mark. Due to that, I later realized the thread that connected Alexander I to Woodrow Wilson had found its way back to St. Petersburg. Peaceful interconnections between my native land, placed between Russia and the Western world, thus had an uncanny tendency to crisscross, both in my personal life and my research. In Russian, there is a saying that *"perpetual peace* lasts until the next war." That one line, which might summarize this book, never left my mind. It might even be the seed from which *Conquering Peace* grew.

This research would never had seen the light of day without the faith that several institutions and individuals put in me, during the inordinate number of years that this project has taken. It was supported by fellowships and grants received from the Institut d'Etudes Avancées in Paris, the Fondation Maison des Sciences de l'Homme in Paris, the Maison des Sciences de l'Homme in Bordeaux, the Mellon Foundation and the University of Chicago, the Harvard Ukrainian Research Institute, the Foundation philantropique orthodoxe in Chambésy, and the European Research Council. Last but not the least are the Association des Amis de la Fondation pour Genève and the Fondation des Archives de la Famille Pictet, which represents a long Genevan tradition of patronage and humanism. I should also add other institutions where my research was pursued and developed, such as the Graduate Institute in Geneva (the former HEI), the Minda de Gunzburg Center for European Studies at Harvard, the Harvard History Department, the University of Alabama at Birmingham, Durham Law School, and Newcastle University.

I wish to thank particularly three of those institutions which provided the facilities where this research took shape. In Paris, where this project started, a fellowship at the Institut d'Etudes Avancées in 2008–2009 gave me the chance to organize and to lead a series of research seminars where I could test the very first ideas of my book project. More than thirty scholars and political leaders participated with papers and discussion in the seminar. I especially wish to thank Alain d'Iribarne, at the time director of the Fondation Maison des Sciences de l'Homme, who believed from the start in my project and has supported me to lay its first foundations; Jean-Luc Racine, director of the newly founded IEA; and Jean-Luc Lory, who with the assistance of Nadia Chenour and Marie-Thérèse Cerf, provided me with the ideal conditions and much hospitality at the Maison Suger, where I always felt welcome. I next pursued my project at the University of Chicago in the Department of Politics. I wish to thank Dan Bertsche, Bernard Harcourt, Jennifer Pitts, Paul Cheney, Robert Morrissey, Dustin Simpson, and the fellow members of the Mellon program at Chicago in 2011 who facilitated my entry into the Anglo-American world in the best possible way.

Most of the research for this book was conducted during my fellowship at the Minda de Gunzburg Center for European Studies at Harvard. I would like to thank the Center for its wonderful support, as well as the faculty, staff, and fellow members for an intellectually stimulating stay, among whom Grzegorz Ekiert, Elaine Papoulias, Elizabeth Johnson, Anna Popiel, Roumiana Theunissen, Laura Falloon, Filomena Cabral, Gila Naderi, Paul Dzus, and Peter Stevens stand out. They made my work at the Center for European Studies one of the most fruitful and rich periods of my academic life. It was there that I organized together with David Armitage a 2014 bicentenary conference, "The Power of Peace: New Perspectives on the Congress of Vienna." This conference started a series of international events around the bicentenary of the Congress of Vienna but, first and foremost, constituted the start of a fruitful collaboration and friendship with David. Thank you for having believed in my project from day one.

During the years of my research, I benefited from the expertise of librarians and archivists at many institutions, which are too numerous to list here. I would like to thank all of them, particularly the League of Nations Archives in Geneva, where I benefited so much from the assistance of Jacques Oberson, and Harvard's Houghton and Widener Libraries.

In both Europe and the United States, I appreciated opportunities to discuss my research with colleagues and students. For welcome invitations to speak on various pieces of my work, I must thank: Bruno Arcidiacono (HEI, Geneva), Rencontres du Lundi (Geneva), Igor Cașu (Chișinău), Marie-Elisabeth Ducreux (EHESS, Paris), Emmanuelle Boulineau (Collegium de Lyon), the Institute of Philosophy of Ukrainian Academy of Sciences (Kyiv), Entretiens autour de l'identité européenne and Institut européen (Nice), Corin Braga (Cluj), the Institute of History of the Academy of Sciences of Moldova (Chișinău), Georges-Henri Soutou (Paris Sorbonne), Centre français de coopération "Jean Monnet" (Skopje), Ivan Čolović (Belgrad), Maria Bucur and Aurelian Crăiuțu (Indiana University), the Interdisciplinary Workshop on France and the Francophone World (Chicago), the University of Chicago Center in Paris, Alfred H. A. Soons (Utrecht), René Leboutte and Sylvie Aprile (Luxembourg), David Armitage and Erez Manela (Harvard International and Global History Seminar), Glenda Sluga (Sydney), Felix Dane and Gregory John Ryan (Rio de Janeiro), Beatrice de Graaf (Amsterdam), Victoria de Grazia (Columbia University), Anna Plassart (Oxford), Robert Schütze (Durham), Richard Burke (Wissenschaftskolleg, Berlin), Stephen Taylor (Durham), Michael Broers and Ambrogio A. Caiani (University of Kent in Paris), the Graduate History Conference (Birmingham, Alabama), Yoeri Albrecht and Mathieu Segers (Forum of European Culture, Amsterdam), Christophe Daase and Wolfgang Seibel (German Institute for International and Security Affairs, Berlin), the Studium Generale Schuman Lecture 2017 (Maastricht), Raphaël Cahen (Brussels), Ulrich Schlie and Thomas Weber (Budapest), David Armitage (Wissenschaftskolleg, Berlin), and Brendan Simms (Cambridge). I would also like to thank my students who have awed and inspired me with their incredible minds at Harvard Summer School, where as a visiting professor I have taught since 2015 a course "What is Europe?" on the material and the main theses of this book.

Some ideas developed in chapters 1 and 2 were first presented in "Balance of Power vs. Perpetual Peace: Paradigms of European Order from Utrecht to Vienna, 1713–1815," *International History Review*, 39 (2017), and in "Antidotes to Empire: From the Congress System to the European Union," my contribution to *EUtROPEs: The Paradox of European Empire*, edited by John W. Boyer and Berthold Molden (University of Chicago Press, 2014).

Finally, my eternal gratitude goes to those indefatigable companions who supported me through hell and high water. David Armitage, Laurent Franceschetti, William A. Graham, Alain d'Iribarne, Mark Jarrett, Charles S. Maier, Ambassador François Pictet, Jean-Jacques Rey, and Thomas Weber all read the manuscript in its entirety and offered their advice and encouragement. I owe a special debt of gratitude to David, Laurent, and Mark, who have read my chapters so many times that I lost count. Thanks to them and the others mentioned, the project came into sharper focus.

While revising the original manuscript I also benefited from the questions, suggestions, and helpful comments provided on specific chapters by a number of other scholars and friends, among them Helen Berry, Raphaël Cahen, Dipesh Chakrabarty, Aurelian Crăiuțu, Rachel Hammersley, Violetta Hionidou, Akira Iriye, Erez Manela, Jennifer Pitts, Serhii Plokhii,

David Saunders, Robert Schütze, Daniel Siemens, and Brendan Simms. Finally, Harvard University Press's two anonymous readers provided invaluable feedback and immeasurably improved the book. The work's remaining flaws are solely my own responsibility.

I have also benefited from the encouragement, questions, and suggestions of other scholars and friends, among them the late Bruno Arcidiacono, Béatrice Demetriades, Isabelle Gilliéron, Lia Glovsky, Charles King, the late (and much missed) Patricia Herlihy, David Herlihy, Martti Koskenniemi, Terpsi Lambrinopoulou, George Liber, *mon cher ami* Carl M. F. (Fritz) Meyer, the late Gabriel Minder, Samuel Moyn, Dustin Simpson, Elena Siupiur, Céline Spector, and Ștefan Vianu.

For guiding my manuscript into print, I am indebted to my editor Kathleen McDermott; she helped me wrangle it into a manageable length and was always responsive and helpful. I also wish to thank Kenneth L. Chumbley for his assistance with the image permissions and Emily Silk and Julia Jarrett for having proofread one of the multiple versions of the manuscript. At the very end of the process, copyeditor Gail Naron Chalew and production editor Angela Piliouras provided excellent support, though I fear I greatly tried their patience.

The book could not have been completed without the friendship and hospitality of Albert and Clara Franceschetti, Lia Glovsky, Terpsi Lambrinopoulou, Gabriel and Perrine de Maistre, Mark and Malgorzata Jarrett, George and Deborah Liber, and Jean-Jacques and Marie-Jo Rey, who provided me safe harbors at their houses for working on the manuscript. I always felt at home with them, and this gave me peace.

Finally, I am so thankful to Laurent who bravely and enthusiastically accompanied me from my very first thoughts on this journey with his support, patience, and kindness. And for everything else, my parents Petru and Vera Ghervas, and my family, particularly Rodica and Mirela. They have been my rock. My father suddenly passed away while this book was in completion, but his unwavering dignity, inspiration and generosity continue to sustain me. I dedicate this book to him.

Index

Page number in *italics* refer to illustrations.

and, 279; peace process and, 226; responsibility for World War II and, 217; Stalin and, 234; tragedy of Europe, 224–225; United Nations and, 229

citizenship, 77

civil commissions, 217

civilians: bombings of, 155; death of refugees, 231; the murder of, 155, 168, 221. *See also* atrocities

civilizing mission, of colonialism, 133, 145

Clarke, Peter, 223

class interests, 123. *See also* elites

Clausewitz, Carl von, 154, 355

Clemenceau, Georges, 162, 166

Club of Rome, 270

coalition wars, 350, 355

Colbert de Torcy, Jean-Baptiste, 50

Cold War: arms race, 244, 278, 318–319, 322; Berlin Wall, 304, 305, 306–307; duration of, 285; economic cost of, 297; ending of, 295–298, 307, 318; era of, 119; European Defense Community (EDC) and, 260; European Economic Community (EEC) and, 324; Europe's peace problem and, 279; Helsinki Accords and, 292; nuclear threat, 244, 322; Security Council and, 237, 361; Soviet occupation of half of Europe, 16; as a state of war, 360–361; Strategic Defense Initiative (SDI) and, 293; United Nations and, 278; United States and, 84, 222, 261, 282, 319; World War II and, 245, 302, 310

collaboration, with the Nazis, 251

Colombo, Emilio, 322

colonialism: Africa, 146; Anglo-French competition for colonial empires, 57; anticolonial insurrection, 263; of

Britain, 121, 173, 271, 272, 273; civilizing mission of, 133, 145; colonial empires, 3–4, 5, 57; colonial trade, 44, 146; crises of empire, 263–264; decolonization, 263; of France, 59–60, 173; League of Nations and, 173–174, 271; moral justification of, 133; the Ottoman Empire and, 138–139; pacification operations, 12; peace and, 7; trade and, 44, 46, 63. *See also* empires; imperialism

Comecon, 280, 290

commerce, spirit of, 119

commerce, war and, 62

Commission on the League of Nations, 168

Committee of the Eight, 93

"Common European Home," 307, 311, 319, 343

Common Market. *See* European Economic Community (EEC)

Common Power, 186

Commonwealth of Independent States (CIS), 316, 317, 320

Commonwealth of Nations, 271, 273, 274

communications, advances in, 100–101

communism: Central Europe, 240; collapse of, 343; Eurocommunism, 291; fall of in the German Democratic Republic, 303–312; Soviet Union, 294, 300

Communist Party, East Germany and, 240

Communist Party of the Soviet Union, 314, 316

community, international, 351

Concert of Europe, 126, 141–142, 413n120

Condorcet, Nicolas de, 80–81

German reconciliation and, 279; Gorbachev and, 296–297; Holy Alliance and, 200; political discourse of, 287; Schuman and, 255; scuttling of the EDC and, 263; Suez crisis and, 265

European Union: borders of, 368; Britain leaving, 364, 372; bureaucracy of the, 360; closer integration of the states, 327; Draft Treaty Establishing the European Union, 323–324; EEC and, 321–322, 323; enlargement of, 327, 332, 342, 344, 362; ethnonationalism, 369; Europa and, 6; formation of the, 323–325; future of, 371–372; granted the Nobel Peace Prize, 344, 346; League of Nations and, 202; migration and, 369; peace and, 253; public enthusiasm for, 331; small-steps approach, 254; Treaty of the, 354. *See also* Maastricht, Treaty of

European Union of Federalists, 245–246
Eurovision Song Contest, 326
Eurozone, 330–331
Expiation, 103

Falklands War (1982), 322
Farnese, Elisabeth, 56
Farouk of Egypt, 264
federalism, 248, 255, 257, 398n128
federation, 68, 111, 112, 114, 118, 120, 181, 182, 183, 245, 247–248, 255, 260, 267, 283
Ferdinand I of the Two Sicilies, 125, 126
Ferrero, Guglielmo, 184
feudal system, 60
Fifth European Commission (2014–2019), 364

Fifty Years' War (1939–1989), 288, 301, 334, 361
Finland, 208, 288, 327
fisheries, European, 331
Five Powers, 121–122, 126, 137, 139, 141, 146, 159
Flag of Europe, 249–250
Flanders, 33, 34
Florence, 21–22
Florida, 60
Fontainebleau, Treaty of (1814), 91
food shortages, 224, 238, 301
foreign policy: of England / Britain, 37, 38, 43, 48; France, 269; United States, 4, 175, 236, 261; Vattel and, 66
foreign relations, 65
Fortress Europe, 368, 369
Forty Years' War (1672–1712), 33
Founding Fathers of Europe, 258
Four Powers, 212, 213, 217
Fourteen Points, 171, 175, 184
Fragments of the New History of the Political Equilibrium in Europe, 120
France: Algerian liberation war, 264; Austria and, 57, 59; balance of power and, 42–43; Britain and, 141; censorship and persecutions in, 61, 63; collaboration with the Nazis, 251; colonialism of, 59–60, 173; "Crime of August 30," 262; declaring war on Germany, 208; England and, 37–38, 43, 48; Estates General, 67; expansionism of, 43–44, 145; Fifth Republic, 264, 269; foreign policy, 269; Franco-British reconciliation, 274; Franco-German reconciliation (*see* Franco-German reconciliation); Free France movement, 252; French Antiwar Spirit of the

France (continued)
Enlightenment, 61–67; French Army, mutinies, 156; French Empire, 6, 18, 90; French Republican constitution, 120; French Revolution, 67, 72, 80; geographic contours of, 44; *Grande Armée*, 82; Hundred Days, 100–103, 106, 112, 121; Indochina and, 263; invasion of Russia, 113; League of Nations and, 173–174, 216; Marshall Plan and, 240; NATO and, 275; occupation of the Ruhr region, 193; Peace of Utrecht and, 42, 44; post-Napoleonic era, 83–84, 91–93, 121–122; rationing, 238; reintegration into the European system of peace, 121; religion and, 62, 131; restoration of the Bourbon monarchy, 92, 100, 101, 106, 142; Second French Empire, 132; settlement following the Hundred Days, 103–104; social protests, 275–276; Spain and, 32–34, 57, 89; the Terror, 72, 85; Vichy regime, 251; West Germany and, 252–253
France, Anatole, 148, 156
Francis I of Austria, 106, 110
Francis Joseph I of Austria, 129
Franco-German reconciliation: Britain and, 273, 274–275; Congress of Europe and, 247; Council of Europe and, 249; de Gaulle / Adenauer and, 270–271; de Gaulle and, 274–275; EDC and, 262; peace and, 279, 282, 345; Schuman / steel industry and, 251–253; Soviet threat and, 252–253; success of, 282
Franco-Spanish Alliance, 33–34
Frederick II of Prussia, 57, 59
Frederick III of Prussia, 82
Frederick William I of Prussia, 40, 49

Frederick William III of Prussia, 106
freedom: of conscience, 116; political, 301; of the press, 124, 125; to publish, 116
Free France movement, 252
Freemasonry, 114
free movement of peoples, 327, 330
Free Trade Area (FTA), 269
French Empire (1799–1815), 6, 18
French Revolution (1789), 67, 72, 80
Friedland, battle of, 88
From the Alliance of Kings to the League of Nations, 151, 184
frozen conflicts, 361, 370
functionalism, 255, 256–257, 260, 280, 360

Galicia, 99
General Assembly, United Nations, 228, 235, 359
Geneva, 187–190, 352
Geneva Agreements (1954), 263
Geneva Convention IV (1949), 16, 439n36
Geneva Protocol (1925), 192, 197, 204
Geneva, Spirit of, 151, 188–190, 197
Genoa, 97, 102
genocide, 340
Genscher, Hans-Dietrich, 322
Gentz, Friedrich von, 120, 184
Georgia, 320
German People's Party, 194
German populations, expulsion of, 231
German Question, 303, 304, 307, 310
Germans, deportations of, 277–278
Germany: annexation of Austria, 205; assassination of von Kotzebue, 124–125; Berlin (*see* Berlin); Christian Democrats, 307, 333; conditions imposed on at Versailles, 7, 163–164; Congress of Vienna and, 94, 96, 97;

Council of Europe and, 249; defeat of the Soviet Union and, 319–320; East Germany, 238, 240, 286, 289, 304; economy of, 193, 238, 240, 304; fall of the Berlin Wall, 306–307; Federal Republic of, 241–242; final peace settlement for, 286, 343; food shortages, 238; Franco-German reconciliation (*see* Franco-German reconciliation); German confederation, 25; German Empire, 6, 210, 211–212; joint military occupation of, 220, 231; the *Konzerne*, 251–252, 254; League of Nations and, 174, 195, 201, 203–204; living standards, 286, 333; Marshall Plan and, 242; mystical movement in, 113, 114; Nazi regime, 2, 201, 203–204, 205, 209, 288; postwar settlement of, 308, 309; rearmament of, 205, 252, 261, 262; reparations, 163, 193; reunification of, 298, 303–312, 333; Ruhr region, 193, 251–252, 253; Settlement Treaty and, 343–344; sovereignty of, 310; Soviet Union and, 240–241; taking Poland, 208; territorial demands of, 193; Third Reich, 16, 23, 164; unification of, 127; United States and, 170–171, 172, 308. *See also* East Germany; West Germany

Gibraltar, 44
Giovine Europa, 127
Giovine Italia, 127
glasnost, 286
globalization, 77
Glorious Revolution (1688–1689), 34, 36, 72
Gorbachev, Mikhail: Autumn of Nations and, 311; Baltic Way and, 313–314; Berlin Wall and, 305; Cold War and, 293–300; dissolution of the Soviet

Empire, 316–319; foresight of, 352; Germany and, 286, 306, 308; *glasnost / perestroika*, 286; Molotov-Ribbentrop Pact and, 313–314; Reagan and, 7, 293, 305; role of a tutelary figure, 342; Second European Spirit and, 287, 321

governance, monetary union, 330
Grand Alliance, 31, 86, 91, 117, 371
Grand Dessein d'Henri IV, 51
Grande Armée, 82
Great Depression, 202
Great Discoveries, age of, 21
Great Game, 146
Great Northern War (1700–1721), 44
great powers: accountability of, 219, 229; allied powers of 1814–1815, aims of, 84; allies in War / partners in peace, 99–106; the Congress System as a Council of the, 116–122; diplomacy and, 100; dynastic issues, 32, 38; falling into political insignificance, 279; five, 121–122, 126, 137, 139, 141, 146, 159; Great War and, 154; military power and, 98; peace systems and, 362; predatory appetites of, 146; the Reaction, 87; United Nations and, 373

Great War. *See* World War I
Greece: Anatolia and, 167; EEC and, 282–283; as European, 134, 145; financial distress of, 345, 363; the Great Catastrophe, 168; Greek peninsula, 137; the Hellenic Republic, 137; joining NATO, 244; Philiki Etairia, 136; Russia and, 135; Yalta Agreements and, 335

Greek Orthodox Church, 140
Gregory XVI, Pope, 115–116
Grey, Edward, 169, 180

173–174, 204, 205; Japan and, 203;
Kantian model and, 185–186; lack of
military force / World War II, 215;
moral punishment by, 218–219; Pact
of Locarno and, 195; Paris Conference
and, 151, 173; peace and, 7, 172–173,
255, 358; peace betrayed, 203–208;
Protocol in the Pacific Settlement
of Disputes, 190–191; Soviet Union
and, 152, 208; spirit of the, 173,
188; structural weakness of, 217;
supranational character of, 182;
Treaties of Paris and, 168, 173; Treaty
of Versailles and, 173, 176, 183, 255;
undermining of, 209; United Nations
and, 218, 228, 277; United States and,
152, 153, 175, 176, 190, 196, 214–215, 358;
war and, 11; Wilson and, 153, 168–169,
172, 187–188, 214–215; World War II and,
208–209, 215, 219. *See also* Covenant of
the League of Nations
League to Enforce Peace, 169
Léger, Alexis, 202
legitimacy: bottom-up, 129; divine, 144;
of monarchs, 68, 143; political, 113,
128
Leibniz, Gottfried Wilhelm, 30, 54–55,
69, 142, 254
Leipzig, battle of (1813), 90, 154
Lesaffer, Randall, 25
*Leviathan or The Matter, Forme and Power
of a Common-Wealth Ecclesiastical and
Civil*, 25–26
liberalism, 85, 86, 110, 281
Lieber Code (*General Orders No. 100*), 15
Lieber, Francis, 15
limited sovereignty doctrine, 291
linguistics: balance of power and, 42–43;
diplomacy and, 179

Lithuania, 312–313, 317, 332
living standards: Baltic Republics, 320;
Germany, 286, 333; Southeastern Europe,
337; Soviet Union, 286, 292, 294, 301
Lloyd George, David, 162, 166
Locarno Agreements. *See* Locarno,
Pact of
Locarno Conference (1925), 194–197
Locarno, Pact of (1925), 152, 153, 194, 195,
201, 358
Locarno, Spirit of, 190–197
Lodge, Henry Cabot, 175, 176
London Protocol (1828), 137
London, Treaty of (1915), 159, 173
London, Treaty of (1949), 248
Long Peace, the, 361. *See also* peace
longue durée, 80
Lorraine, Duchy of, 57
Louis XIV of France, 5–6, 7, 32, 33, 51,
61–62
Louis XV of France, 59
Louis XVI of France, 60, 72
Louis XVIII of France, 92, 100, 101,
106, 121
Luxembourg, 259, 266

Maastricht, Treaty of (1992), 325–327,
343, 359–360
Macedonia, 341
Machiavelli, Niccolò, 21–22, 37
machinery(ies) of peace, 4, 8, 151, 152,
217, 256, 280, 358, 359
Macmillan, Harold, 269, 273–274
Macron, Emmanuel, 366, 367
Madariaga, Salvador de, 215
Mahmud II, Sultan of the Ottoman
Empire, 135
Maistre, Joseph de, 115, 401n9
Malaya, 273

Monroe Doctrine, 169, 170, 176, 183; European, 201
Montesquieu, Charles-Louis Secondat, Baron de, 62
morality: politics and, 357; war and, 15, 38
Morgenthau, Hans, 260
Morgenthau, Henry Jr., 238
Mountbatten, Louis 1st Earl Mountbatten of Burma, 272
Mowinckel, Johan Ludwig, 197
Mulder, John, 178
Munich Agreement (1938), 12, 216
Munich Conference (1938), 206, 231, 311
Munich, Spirit of, 216
Münster, Treaty of. *See* Westphalia, Peace of
Murat, Joachim, 92, 106
Muscovy, 32
music, popular culture and, 326–327
Muslim League, 272
Mussolini, Benito, 204, 206, 216
mutinies, French Army, 156
mysticism, the Holy Alliance and, 108, 112–113

Nansen, Fridtjof, 196
Nantes, Edict of (1598), 62
Naples, 57
Napoleonic Spirit, 99
Napoleonic wars, 16, 30, 114, 123, 124
Napoleon I, Emperor of France: defeat of, 91–92; enthusiasm for, 83; European unification and, 200; exiled to Saint Helena, 106; hegemonic peace of, 89–90; Hundred Days, 100–103, 106, 112, 121; *Pax Napoleonica*, 87–91; rapid ascent of, 81; as villain of the peace, 7

Napoleon, Louis III, Emperor of France, 132, 139, 141, 145
narratives, historical, 84
Nasser, Gamal Abdel, 264
nationalism: ethnonationalism, 200, 272, 346, 363, 369, 370; European, 89, 200; Yugoslavia, 337, 338
nationality, principle of, 127
national question, 210
National Socialist German Workers' Party (NSDAP). *See* Nazi regime
nation-building, 83
Native Americans, 56
natural law, 10, 31, 66
Navarino, battle of (1827), 137
navy(ies), of Britain, 48, 137, 186, 191, 212, 223; of France, 137; of the U.S., 35, 186, 191, 223
Nazi regime, 2, 201, 203–204, 205, 209, 288
ne bis in idem, principle, 465n128
neo-functionalism, 260
Nesselrode, Count Karl von, 112, 139–140
Netherlands: Bilderberg Club, 281; Congress of Vienna and, 97; decline of, 33; European Coal and Steel Community, 259; Indonesia and, 263; League of Nations and, 187; postwar, 224. *See also* Dutch Republic
Neurath, Konstantin von, 203–204
neutral states, 290
Newfoundland, 44
Nice, Treaty of (1748–1749), 58
Nicholas I of Russia, 129, 137, 139, 140, 141
Nicholas II of Russia, 181
Nicolson, Harold, 148
Nine Years' War (1688–1697), 36

omissions of, 217; League of Nations and, 168, 173; reparations, territorial losses and, 190, 213; repression of prewar disputes, 190; revanchism / irredentism and, 151; struggle to correct failures of, 152; US Senate's refusal to ratify, 174. *See also* Saint-Germain, Treaty of; Sèvres, Treaty of; Trianon, Treaty of; Versailles, Treaty of

Paris, Treaty of (1763), 59–60

Paris, Treaty of (1814), 92–94, 116–117, 121, 177, 199, 352

Paris, Treaty of (1856), 140, 145

Paris Peace Conference (1919–1920): chaos and precipitation, 157–168; exclusion of the defeated powers, 149, 357–358; Four Powers and, 213; intentions of the victorious powers, 208; Italy and, 210; League of Nations and, 151, 173; revanchism / irredentism and, 151; Treaties of Paris and, 151; Treaty of Versailles and, 211; Wilson and, 175. *See also* Paris, Treaties of (1919–1920)

parliaments, role as instruments of peace, 144

paternalism, the Holy Alliance and, 110

Pax Europeana, 308, 332, 341, 344, 371

Pax Napoleonica, 87–91, 402n17

pax perpetua, 5. *See also* perpetual peace

Pax Romana, 20, 25, 88, 401n13

peace: abstract ideal of, 6; amnesia of, 364; definitions of, 50, 63; hegemonic peace of Napoleon, 89–90; the institution of, 75; lasting, 96, 348–349, 359–360, 365, 373; the Long Peace, 361; machinery(ies) of, 4, 8, 151, 152, 217, 256, 280, 358, 359; the meaning of, 10; politics and, 10; prosperity and, 305;

republicanism and, 69; system of, 53; term, 12; trade and, 62–63; true peace, 9; war and, 4, 5, 354–355, 366. *See also* perpetual peace

peace alliances, 76, 77–79, 215, 350

peaceful change, 256

Peaceful Revolution, the (1989), 309, 311

peace institutions, 8, 358–359

peacekeeping, 122–127, 278, 361, 365, 366, 369

peacemaking, 355, 373

peace plans, the ideal, 371–374

peace process, 349

peace settlements, the drafting of, 100

Peace Society, 183

peace systems, 8

peace treaties. *See* treaties

Penn, William, 51–52, 53, 130

pentarchy, 121, 400n4

people, as property, 185

Péréfixe de Beaumont, Hardouin de, 51

perestroika, 286, 288, 297, 314, 318, 319

Permanent Court of Arbitration, The Hague, 177, 181

Permanent Court of International Justice, The Hague, 177, 181, 182, 191, 243

perpetual peace: conception of, 30; Covenant of the League of Nations and, 177; following World War II, 226–227; the Holy Alliance and, 111; intellectual tradition of, 17; Kant and, 12, 17, 30, 73–79, 118–119; League of Nations and, 169; literary genre, 49, 74; models of international order, 31; philosophical plans of, 80–81; plans, 49–61; political tradition of, 11–12; quest for, 8–9; Saint-Pierre and, 30, 50–61; Soviet Union and, 299–300;

perpetual peace *(continued)*
spirits and, 6; toolkit of, 290; the
tradition of, in European history, 345;
unification plans and, 200
Perse, Saint-John, 202
persecutions: by the Catholic Church,
22; France, 61; Serbs in Croatia, 338
Petersberg Agreement (1949), 241
Peter the Great of Russia, 32
philhellenism, 134, 145
Philiki Etairia, 136
Philippines, 175
Philip V of Spain, 32, 39, 42, 56
Phillimore, Walter 1st Baron, 180–181,
183
Phillimore Report, 182
Picasso, Pablo, 2
Pictet de Rochemont, Charles, 122
Piedmont-Sardinia, 97
Pietism, 76, 108
Pineau, Christian, 267, 268
Pius VII, Pope, 115
Pius IX, Pope, 128, 132
Plan of Perpetual Peace (Saint-Pierre), 50,
86, 118
Pleven, René, 261
Poincaré, Raymond, 149, 193
Poland: Alexander I of Russia and, 99;
Congress of Vienna and, 97; Czecho-
slovakia and, 206; EU membership,
332; food shortages, 238; German
reunification and, 308, 310; Germany /
Soviet Union's attack on, 208; invasion
of, 209, 226; living standards, 286;
partitioning of, 94, 99, 102; political
change in, 301–302; proposal to
restore sovereignty to, 171; Prussia
invading Silesia, 57, 58; repression in,
125; risk of a German-Soviet pact,

201; Soviet Union and, 167, 208, 242;
territorial settlement of western
border, 287; Treaty of Versailles and,
167; uprisings, 129, 276; War of Polish
Succession, 57; World War II, 288
policy(ies): common defense, 325;
détente policy, 293; domestic and
foreign, 366; foreign and economic,
279; foreign policy (*see* foreign policy);
immigration, 368–369; international,
170; peace, 196; securitarian, 369
Polish Communist Party (PZPR),
301–302
Polish-Lithuanian Commonwealth,
31–32, 57
Polish Question, 167
Polish-Saxon crisis (1814–1815), 142
Political Equilibrium, 118
politics: balance of power and, 38;
Christian Democrat, 258; divine rights
of monarchs and, 108; international,
178; morality and, 357; the papacy and,
115–116; peace and, 5, 10; political
alliances, 36; political change, 300;
political discourse, 287; political
disenfranchisement, 125; political
engineering, 96; political freedom,
301; political greatness, 374; political
legitimacy, 113, 128; political liberalism,
110; political power, 85; political
realism, 17; political representation,
113, 127, 128–129, 143, 210, 351; political
repression, 132; political rights, 85;
political union, 130–131; public
opinion and, 124, 137; public relations
and, 98; reactionary, 85; religion
and, 107, 115–116; representation of
ethnic groups, 210; secret political
associations, 85; secularized European

political system, 116; theory of political
order, 68
Pomerania, 193, 231
Poos, Jacques, 339
popular movements (1989), 288–289
population increases, 154
population transfers, 231
populism, 132
Portugal, 93, 125, 269, 283
Posen (Poznań), Grand Duchy of, 99
Postwar European Spirit, 222, 226, 228,
258, 277, 278, 321, 331, 342
Potsdam Agreement (1945), 231, 234–235
Potsdam Conference (1945), 220
power: balance of military power, 58–59;
balance of power (*see* balance of power);
Common Power, 186; devolution of,
130; feudal system and, 60; great
powers (*see* great powers); military
power of Russia, 98; naval power of
England, 35; political, 85
Prague, 242
Prague Spring (1968), 291, 362
Pravda, 295
press: freedom of the, 124, 125; role as
instruments of peace, 144
Principal Allied and Associated Powers,
159, 166, 167, 212
*Problems of Peace: From the Holy Alliance to
the League of Nations,* 184
Process of Rebirth, 335
prohibiting clauses, of Kant, 74
projet, 391n49
"Projet d'instruction générale pour les
missions de Sa Majesté Impériale," 112
*Projet pour rendre la paix perpétuelle en Eu-
rope (Plan for Perpetual Peace)*, 50, 86, 118
propaganda, 85, 284–286
property: landed, 53; people as, 185

protectorates, 146
Protestantism, 22
protest movements, 127
protests, against Great War in Russia, 156
Protocol in the Pacific Settlement of
Disputes (1924), 190–191
Prussia: Austria and, 99; Britain and,
99; Carlsbad Decrees (1819), 124;
Congress of Vienna and, 98, 102;
defeat of by Napoleon, 88, 89; dislike
of disorder, 121; Duchy of Posen
(Poznań), 99; East Prussia, 167, 231;
the Holy Alliance and, 110; invading
Silesia, 57–58, 59; Saxony and, 102
public deficits, 363
public disorder, 124
public opinion, 124, 137
public relations, 98
public support, against colonial wars, 5
Puerto Rico, 175

Quadruple Alliance (1815), 117, 141
Quadruple Alliance, War of the
(1718–1720), 56
Quakers, 51, 52, 53, 130
Quintuple Alliance (1818), 121, 126, 137,
139, 141, 146

racial biases, of the Nazis, 205
racial equality, 6–7, 146, 169
racialism, triumph of, 146–147
racism, non-Europeans and, 133–134
Rape of Belgium, 155
Rape of Europa, 1, 2
Rappard, William E., 186, 187
ratifications of peace treaties, 357
rationing, 224, 238
Reaction, the, 87, 122–127, 143, 144, 145,
351

Reagan, Ronald, 4, 7, 293–294, 304–305, 318–319, 322
realism, political, 17
Realist school of thought, 84
realist theory, international relations, 260
Realpolitik, 79, 230
rearmament: of Germany, 205, 252, 261, 262; Second Hague Conference and, 182
reason of state, 79
reconciliation: Franco-British, 274; Franco-German (*see* Franco-German reconciliation); functionalism and, 280; of historical differences, 8–9; postwar, 121; process of, 345–346; Treaties of Paris and, 190
reconstruction, postwar, 222
Red Army, 241, 247, 252, 286, 292, 317, 318
Red Cross, 187
Reflections on Peace and War, 111
Reformed religion, 22
reforms, Soviet Union, 286
refugees, 231, 265. *See also* migration
religion: Catholicism (*see* Catholicism); Christianity, 68, 110, 131, 197; Congress of Vienna and, 107; France and, 62, 131; freedom to exercise, 23; Greek Orthodox Church, 140; Holy Alliance and, 107, 108, 110, 112, 113, 114–115; peace and, 354; Pietism, 76, 108; politics and, 107, 115–116; Protestantism, 22; Quakers, 51, 52, 53, 130; religious intolerance, 70–71; religious relativism, 114; Serbian Orthodox Church, 339; treaties and, 107; war and, 13; Wilson and, 178–179, 354; Yugoslavia, 337
renunciation clause, Treaty of Utrecht, 46
reparations: Germany and, 163, 193; Treaties of Paris and, 190, 213

representation: political, 113, 127, 128–129, 143, 351; popular, 124, 126, 143
repression: by Alexander I of Russia, 125; Metternich and, 124–125; by the Nazis, 205; by the Ottoman Empire, 136–137; in Poland, 125; political, 132
republicanism, 69, 76, 77, 80
Republic of States, 102
Rescript [Reply] *of the Emperor of China*, 70
resources, the pooling of, 280
restructuring attempts, 352
revanchism, 151, 341, 370
revolution(s): Age of Revolutions, 126–127, 143; against communist regimes, 288, 300–301; elites and, 351; meaning of the term, 71–72
Reynaud, Paul, 262
Rhineland, 251
Rhineland Pact, 194–195
Rhine (river), 96, 102, 259
Richelieu, Armand-Emmanuel du Plessis, Duc de, 121, 411n106
Ridley, Nicholas, 309
rights: Convention for the Protection of Human Rights and Fundamental Freedoms, 248–249; cosmopolitan rights, 77; and duties, of the individual, 61; dynastic rights, 39, 46, 108; hereditary rights of royal dynasties, 108; human rights (*see* human rights); inheritance rights, 35–36, 143; political, 85; right of succession, 42; to self-determination, 174; sovereign, 246; states and, 77; of states, nationalities, human beings, 180
rivers, great international, 102
Rolland, Romain, 154–155
Roman Empire, political frontier of, 20
Romania: Ceaușescu regime, 336; EU membership, 337, 342; Hungary and,

Second Punic War (201 BCE), 209
Secret du Roi, 59
secret societies, 136
securitarianism, 365, 368, 369, 370, 374
Security Council: as a battlefield, 361;
    Cold War and, 237, 361; Germany and,
    195; International Criminal Tribunal
    for the Former Yugoslavia, 346; peace
    and, 277; Soviet Union and, 230, 235;
    in a state of frozen war, 373; United
    Nations and, 228, 230. *See also* United
    Nations
security culture, 365–366
security, system of collective, 119
security, the indivisibility of, 290
self-determination, 165, 174
self-justification, 14–15
"Separate and Secret Articles," 97
Serbia, 340–341
Serbian Orthodox Church, 339
Serbian Question, 339
Serbs, 337, 338, 340
settlement process, postwar Europe, 214
settlement treaties, 14, 24, 103, 190
Sevastopol, 140, 141
Seventh Coalition (1815), 102
Seven Years' War (1756–1763), 2, 59
Sèvres, Treaty of (1920), 167
Sicily, 57
*Signing of Peace in the Hall of Mirrors,
    Versailles, The, 150*
Silesia, 57, 58, 59, 193, 231, 252, 473n43
Silistra, 140
Single European Act (1986), 324
Sinope, 140
slave trade, 44, 63, 118
Slovakia, 165, 332
Slovenia, 165, 332, 334, 335, 339, 340, 342,
    346
Slovenian Territorial Defense, 339

Smith, Samantha, 284–285
smuggling, 89
social and economic change, 144
social bonds, 357
social contract, 26, 61, 67–70, 75, 129, 253
Social Contract, The, 67
social democracy, 281
Social Democratic Party, 333
socialism, 245, 291
Socialist Movement for the United
    States of Europe, 245–246
social movements, Central and Eastern
    Europe, 300–303
social peace, 130
social protests, 275–276
social question, 210
social upheavals, 369
societal changes, 275
Society of Friends. *See* Quakers
Söderblom, Nathan, 197
Solemn Declaration on European Union
    (1983), 322, 323, 324
solidarity, the fostering of, 9, 360
Solidarity Citizens' Committee
    (Solidarność), 301
Southeastern Europe, 289, 334–342, 346
Southern Europe: car ownership 336;
    economic crisis and, 363
South Korea, 260–261
sovereignty: of Baltic Republics, 314;
    Congress of Europe and, 246, 248;
    of Germany, 310; great powers and,
    373; military autonomy and, 262; of
    peoples, 170, 174; relinquishing of, 256;
    sovereign rights, 246; Soviet Union
    and, 291, 292, 296; of states, 126, 182, 371;
    superioritas and, 22–23; a supranational
    army and, 261
Soviet Union: Afghanistan and, 293;
    collapse of, 18, 289, 312–321;

communism, 294, 300, 314, 316; Czechoslovakia and, 215, 242, 291; disarmament and, 297; dominance over half of Europe, 6; economic development, 292–293; elections, 314, 316; expansionism of, 224, 231, 242; financial distress of, 292, 294–295, 303–304; Germany and, 240–241; hegemony, 16; Helsinki Accords and, 291–292; Hungary and, 215, 242; League of Nations and, 152, 208; living standards, 286, 292, 294, 301; Marshall Plan and, 239–240; nuclear capacity of, 244; opening up of, 293, 294, 299; Poland and, 167, 208, 242; Red Army, 241, 247, 252, 286, 292, 317, 318; reforms, 286; Security Council and, 230, 235; social and economic degeneration of, 286; South Korea and, 260–261; sovereignty and, 291, 292, 296; as a superpower, 223, 263; as a threat, 279; as a totalitarian state, 288; Union of Sovereign States, 314, 316, 318, 319, 320, 321; United Nations and, 244; United States and, 293, 310; uprisings, 276; Warsaw Pact, 245, 296, 311, 318; and the Western Allies, 227. *See also* Russia

Spaak Committee, 266–267

Spaak, Paul-Henri, 246, 248, 258, 266, 281

Spain: Bourbon kingdom of, 57, 106; ceding Florida to Britain, 60; Congress of Vienna and, 97; EEC and, 283; financial distress of, 363; France and, 32–33, 57, 89; Habsburgs of Spain, 56; restoration of the monarchy, 97; revolution in, 125; Spanish empire, 21; Treaty of Paris (1814), 93

Spanish-American War (1898), 175

Spanish Netherlands, 43

Spinelli, Altiero, 323

Spinelli Draft, 323–324

spirit of commerce, 119

Spirit of Geneva, The, 188, 218

Spirit of the Laws, The, 62

spirit(s): change and, 349; leading to lasting peace, 349, 356; of the League of Nations, 173, 188; Napoleonic Spirit, 99; spirit of commerce, 119; Spirit of Europe, 250; Spirit of Lasting Peace, 348, 349, 350; Spirit of Locarno, 190–197; Spirit of Munich, 216; Spirit of the Balkans, 334, 337, 339, 342, 346; Spirit of Troppau, 126; Spirit of Yalta, 226–237, 278; Spirits of Peace, 8, 9; term, 6. *See also* Enlarged Europe, Spirit of; Geneva, Spirit of; Postwar European Spirit; Utrecht, Spirit of; Vienna, Spirit of

spirituality, Christian, 110

Spring of Nations (1848), 129–130, 133, 352

Staël, Germaine de, 122

Stalin, Joseph: agenda of, 227; Churchill and, 234; Germany and, 240–241; League of Nations and, 208; peace process and, 226; postwar victory of, 231, 233–235; the Security Council and, 230; United Nations and, 229; as a villain of peace, 7

Stanislas I Leszczyński, 57

state of nature, 75

state of peace, 9, 13, 14, 177, 354–355, 358, 360

state of society, 75

state of war, 8, 13, 14, 354–355, 366

state(s): attributes of, 24; based on ethno-nationalism, 166; changing nature of, 352; church and, 179; city-states, 252, 253; compared to private citizens, 67–68; dynastic issues of, 32;

state(s) *(continued)*
European nation-states, 265, 352–353; new replacing old, 351; non-action of, 74; notion of statehood, 182–183; patrimonial, 67, 387n16; Peace of Utrecht and, 46; peace / war and, 62; Republic of States, 102; rights and, 77; single society of European states, 111; sovereignty of, 126, 182, 371; state-sponsored peace plans, 50; totalitarian, 288; a union of sovereign European states, 51, 53–54; Union of Sovereign States, 314, 316, 318, 319, 320, 321
status quo ante bellum, 58, 60
Strasbourg, 249, 259
Strategic Defense Initiative (SDI), 293
Stresemann, Gustav, 193, 194, 195–196, 201, 202, 266
strikes, Poland, 301
Stuart dynasty, 33, 38, 40, 45, 389n33
Stuart, James Francis Edward, 45
student movements, 303
Stunde Null, 221. *See also* Zero Hour
Sturdza, Alexander, 109, 110, 113
Sturdza, Roxandra, 109, 111, 122
Sublime Porte, 135–136, 137, 139, 140.
    See also Ottoman Empire
submarine warfare, 156, 169, 170–171
subsidiarity, 24, 257, 446n106
subversion, the principle of, 109
succession, right of, 42
succession feuds, 57, 60
Sudetenland, 205–206, 209, 310, 311
Suez crisis, 264–265
suffrage, 85, 129, 131, 132, 209, 302
Sully, Duc de, 26, 27, 51, 392n59
Summary of Military Science, A, 4
superioritas, notion of, 22

superpowers, 223, 263, 278, 281, 284–285, 293, 322
supremacism, 369
surveillance, 124, 367
Sweden, 31, 44, 93, 269, 327
Swift, Jonathan, 15, 38–39, 44
Swiss Confederation, 22, 23, 97
Switzerland: Davos Forum, 281; European Free Trade Association, 269; League of Nations and, 187; mystique of, 246; neutrality of, 117, 127–128, 253, 406n53; Peace of Westphalia and, 24. *See also* Swiss Confederation
Sykes-Picot Agreement (1916), 173
system of peace, 53, 61, 69, 71, 142, 143, 300, 321; European system of peace, 71, 121, 133, 134, 297, 323; lasting system of peace, 142; new, 171; Western, 277, 323
system of war, 52–53, 56, 86, 239, 245, 277, 297, 320, 361; global, 323

Taft, William Howard, 180
Talleyrand Périgord, Prince Charles-Maurice de, 93, 106, 121
Tanzimat, 138
Tatishchev, Vasily, 32, 385n4
technical commissions, 96
technological advances, 147, 153, 157, 158
Ten-Day War (1991), 339, 340
Ten-Point Plan for German Unity (1989), 307
territorial consolidation, 55
territorial integrity: of Germany, 254; of Poland and Romania, 314; of small states, 170
territorial issues, postwar Europe, 214
terrorism, 364, 366–367, 369
Terror, the, 72, 85
Thatcher, Margaret, 308–309

War of Austrian Succession (1740–1748), 2, 35

War of Spanish Succession (1701–1714), 15, 34, 38–39

war(s): anti-independence wars, 5; the balance of power and, 61; coalition wars, 350, 355; commerce and, 62; declaration of, 13; defensive wars, 350; defined, 12–13, 355; as a disease of the body politic, 65; dispute resolution and, 48–49, 52–53; Europe and it's, 31–34; financial implications of, 17–18; the French republic and, 72–73, 80; function of in European history, 13; just and unjust, 15; law/morality and, 15, 38, 197; League of Nations and, 11; legitimacy of, 48–49; metaphor of, 367; mitigating the effects of, 192; peace and, 4, 5, 354–355, 366; preventive war, 36; as product of the sickness of humanity, 64; religion and, 13; state of war, 8, 13, 14, 354–355, 366; system of war, 53, 56; unacceptable behavior during, 15; unavoidability of, 5; warfare, 13. See also *individual wars*

Warsaw, 99, 224

Warsaw Pact, 245, 290, 296, 311, 318

Waterloo, battle of, 102–103

weapons, 192, 204. *See also* nuclear threat

Weizsäcker, Richard von, 304

Wellington, Arthur Wellesley, 1st Duke of, 106

Western European Union (WEU), 262–263

Western Front, 154

westernization, Ottoman Empire, 138

West Germany: economy of, 238, 304; Federal Republic of, 241–242; France and, 252–253; joining NATO, 245; Marshall Plan and, 240; rearmament of, 205, 252, 261, 262. *See also* Germany

Westphalia, Peace of (1648), 10, 22, 23–25, 26, 27–28, 29, 383n49

Westphalian states, 22–23

What Is Enlightenment?, 73

William of Orange, William III of England, 33–34, 72

Wilson, Harold, 275

Wilsonian moment, 170, 173

Wilson, Woodrow: Alexander I of Russia and, 184; Council of Four and, 162; Covenant of the League of Nations and, 255; death of, 177; defeat of, 175; failure to represent mainstream US opinion, 174–175, 214; flaws of, 6; Fourteen Points of, 171, 175, 184; Great War and, 156–157, 170–171; League of Nations and, 153, 168–169, 172, 187–188, 214–215; Paris Peace Conference and, 158, 159, 162, 166; religion and, 178–179, 354; self-determination and, 165, 174

women, diplomacy and, 122–123

Working Peace System, A, 256

World Council of Churches, 197

world peace, League of Nations and, 172–173

World War I: armistice, 158; arms race leading to, 147, 177; atrocities of, 155–156; casualties of, 154; causes of, 174, 177; Christmas truce, 155; as civilization's suicide, 153–157; defeat of the four empires in, 210; Habsburgs of Austria and, 164; impact of, 156; Italy and, 156, 159; massacres, 155–156; Paris Peace Conference (*see* Paris Peace Conference); peace efforts, 155; peace treaty closing, 148–150;

settlement process following, 214; starting of, 16; total war, 7; United States and, 158, 170–171; unresolved territorial issues, 167; US-German Peace Treaty, 177

World War II: anti-Versailles propaganda and, 209; capitulation of the German Reich, 220; Cold War and, 245, 302, 310; and the collapse of its great powers, 84; Eastern European perceptions of, 288; Ernst's portrayal of, 2–3; Geneva Protocol and, 192; lack of a peace treaty ending, 242, 310; League of Nations and, 208–209, 215, 219; military standoff after, 226; settlement of, 310; shift in US foreign policy following, 236; starting of, 16; twin tragedies of Europe and, 223–226

Würzburg, 1, 3

Yalta Agreements (1945), 334, 335; Europe after the, *232–233*

Yalta Conference (1945), 227, 314

Yalta, Spirit of, 226–237, 278

Yanayev, Gennady Ivanovich, 315

Yeltsin, Boris, 315–316, 319

Young Europe, 200

young people: cultural diversity and, 326–327; migrating to the West, 287–288

youth education programs, 271

Ypsilantis, Alexander, 136

Yugoslavia, 164, 165, 334, 337–342, 345–346, 370

Yugoslav People's Army, 339

Yugoslav Wars, 346

Zero Hour, 221

Zhivkov, Todor Hristov, 335–336